In the World of Stalinist Crimes:

Ukraine in the Years of the Purges and Terror (1934–1938)
from the Polish Perspective

The Peter Jacyk Centre
for
Ukrainian Historical Research

Monograph Series
Number ten

In the World of Stalinist Crimes:

Ukraine in the Years of the Purges and Terror (1934–1938) from the Polish Perspective

Robert Kuśnierz

Translated from Polish by
Tomasz Krzysztof Blusiewicz

Canadian Institute of Ukrainian Studies Press
Edmonton • 2020 • Toronto

Canadian Institute of Ukrainian Studies Press

University of Alberta
Edmonton, Alberta
Canada T6G 2H8

University of Toronto
Toronto, Ontario
Canada M5T 1W5

Copyright © 2020 Canadian Institute of Ukrainian Studies
Copyright © 2020 Robert Kuśnierz
ISBN 978-1-894865-57-9 (paper)

Library and Archives Canada Cataloguing in Publication
Title: In the world of Stalinist crimes: Ukraine in the years of the purges and terror (1934-1938) from the Polish perspective / Robert Kuśnierz; translated from Polish by Tomasz Krzysztof Blusiewicz.
Other titles: W świecie stalinowskich zbrodni. English | Ukraine in the years of the purges and terror (1934-1938) from the Polish perspective
Names: Kuśnierz, Robert, 1977- author.
Description: Translation of: W świecie stalinowskich zbrodni: Ukraina w latach czystek i terroru (1934-1938) w obserwacjach i analizach MSZ oraz wywiadu wojskowego Drugiej Rzeczypospolitej. |
Includes bibliographical references and index.
Identifiers: Canadiana 20190224045 | ISBN 9781894865579 (softcover)
Subjects: LCSH: Political purges—Ukraine—History—20th century. | LCSH: Political persecution—Ukraine—History—20th century. | LCSH: Ukraine—History—1921-1944. | LCSH: Ukraine—Politics and government—1917-1945. | LCSH: Poland. Ministerstwo Spraw Zagranicznych.
Classification: LCC DK508.833.K8713 2020 | DDC 947.7/10842—dc23

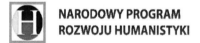

NARODOWY PROGRAM ROZWOJU HUMANISTYKI

From 2015 to 2019 this scholarly work was the recipient of financial aid from the "National Program for the Development of the Humanities" of the Minister of Science and Higher Education of the Republic of Poland.

(*Praca naukowa finansowana w ramach programu Ministra Nauki i Szkolnictwa Wyższego pod nazwą „Narodowy Program Rozwoju Humanistyki" w latach 2015–2019.*)

The publication of this book has been funded by a generous grant from the Cosbild Endowment Fund at the Canadian Institute of Ukrainian Studies (University of Alberta). A publication grant for this publication has also been provided by the Canadian Foundation for Ukrainian Studies.

Printed in Canada

Table of Contents

Introduction

Soviet Ukraine was one of the most important republics of the USSR. Its significance was based chiefly on the fact that it was one of the main breadbaskets of the Soviet Union, and at the time grain was the main export product of the Soviet state. Furthermore, Ukraine shared a land border with the Second Polish Republic, a state that the Bolsheviks considered—especially in the second half of the 1930s—one of their main enemies (alongside Germany and Japan) in a future war. The Treaty of Riga (1921) had decided the fate of Central Ukraine (the area around the Dnipro River), which became part of the newly formed Bolshevik state. The conclusion of military hostilities was succeeded by another, "cold" war between the Bolsheviks and the Second Polish Republic.[1] The Polish Ministry of Foreign Affairs (henceforth MFA) and the Second Department of the Main Staff of the Polish Army—the so-called *Dwójka* (charged with military intelligence)—were very interested in the transformations taking place in Soviet Ukraine throughout the entire interwar period.

Publication of the Second Republic's MFA and military intelligence papers pertaining to the Great Famine (Holodomor) in the Ukraine in 1932 and 1933[2] has demonstrated that the Polish archives are an immeasurably

---

[1] Jan Jacek Bruski covered this topic extensively in his book *Między prometeizmem a Realpolitik: II Rzeczpospolita wobec Ukrainy Sowieckiej 1921–1926* (Kraków: Historia Iagiellonica, 2010).

[2] The following edited volumes on this topic have appeared: R. Kuśnierz, ed., *Pomór w "raju bolszewickim": Głód na Ukrainie w latach 1932–1933 w świetle polskich dokumentów dyplomatycznych i dokumentów wywiadu* (Toruń: Wydawnictwo Adam Marszałek, 2008); J. J. Bruski, ed., *Hołodomor 1932–1933: Wielki Głód na Ukrainie w dokumentacji polskiej dyplomacji i wywiadu* (Warsaw: PISM, 2008); *Hołodomor 1932–1933 w Ukrajini/Wielki Głód na Ukrainie 1932–1933* (edited vol.; Warsaw-Kyiv, 2008); this publication has also appeared in English: *Holodomor: The Great Famine in Ukraine 1932–1933* (Warsaw and Kyiv: Institute of National Remembrance, 2009). See also R. Kuśnierz, "Głód na Ukrainie w latach 1932–1933 w świetle zbiorów Archiwum Akt Nowych oraz Centralnego Archiwum Wojskowego w Warszawie," *Dzieje Najnowsze* 2007, no. 2: 129–59. The following articles also cover this topic: R. Kuśnierz, "Głód potępienia," *Wprost* 10 (March 11, 2007); idem, "Obraz głodującej wsi ukraińskiej w latach trzydziestych XX w. w dokumentach polskich przedstawicielstw dyplomatycznych w ZSRR i polskiego wywiadu," *Polska i Jej Wschodni Sąsiedzi*, 2009, 64–75; idem, "Dokumenty pol's'koï dyplomatiï pro holodomor," *Ukraïns'kyi istorychnyi zhurnal*, 2008, no. 6: 196–211; idem, "Holod w Ukraïni 1932–1933 rr. (za dokumentamy pol's'kykh dyplomativ)," *Arkhivy*

valuable source for studying Soviet history, including that of Ukraine, and constitute a major contribution to the global field of Soviet studies. Moreover, they help to understand better the criminal system that developed just over the Polish eastern border. Therefore I decided, using the Polish archives, to trace and present another phase in the development of the Stalinist regime—the phase of purges and terror. That phase began with the murder of the Leningrad dignitary Sergei Kirov in that city on December 1, 1934, and culminated in the Great Terror of 1937 and 1938.

During that period, two Polish consulates operated in Ukraine. One was located in Kharkiv, the capital of the Ukrainian Soviet Socialist Republic, where, until mid-1934, the consulate general was based, and another was in Kyiv. After the capital was moved to Kyiv, the Kharkiv post lost its status as a consulate general, which was taken over by the one in Kyiv. The Polish embassy in Moscow was, of course, also an important source of information about Ukraine.

During the period under investigation here, the Polish post in Kharkiv was first headed by Jan Karszo-Siedlewski,[3] from July 1, 1932, until 1,

---

Ukraïny, 2008, no 3–4: 46–52; idem, "The Question of the Holodomor in Ukraine of 1932–1933 in the Polish Diplomatic and Intelligence Reports," Holodomor Studies 1, no. 1 (Winter–Spring 2009): 77–90; idem, "Dokumenty pol's'koï dyplomatiï ta rozvidky pro holodomor," in Holod 1932–1933 rokiv v Ukraïni: Prychyny, demohrafichni naslidky, pravova otsinka. Materialy naukovoï konferentsiï, Kyiv 25–26 veresnia 2008 roku, ed. I. Iukhnovs'kyi (Kyiv: Vydavnychyi dim "Kyievo-Mohylians'ka akademiia," 2009), 144–68; idem, "Unknown Polish Photographs of the Holodomor," Holodomor Studies 2, no. 2 (Summer–Autumn 2010): 249–55; J. J. Bruski, "Polska wobec Wielkiego Głodu na Ukrainie 1932–1933," in Polska-Ukraina-Osadczuk: Księga jubileuszowa ofiarowana Profesorowi Bohdanowi Osadczukowi w 85. rocznicę urodzin (Lublin: Wydawnictwo UMCS, 2007), 213–46; idem, "Bolshoi golod na Ukraine v svete dokumentov polskoi diplomatii i razvedki," Evropa, 2006, no. 6: 97–152; idem, "Nieznane polskie dokumenty na temat Hołodomoru: Efekty rekonesansu archiwalnego w Moskwie," Nowa Ukraina, 2008, no. 1–2.

3 Jan Karszo-Siedlewski (1891–1955) was a diplomat who worked in the Soviet Union beginning in 1931. Initially he worked at the Polish legation in Moscow, then in Ukraine. He was head of the Kharkiv consulate (1932–34) and then head in Kyiv, until October 1937. On October 1, 1937, Karszo-Siedlewski returned to the MFA in Warsaw. While he worked in Soviet Ukraine, he also cooperated with the Dwójka. He headed the post "Karsz" between 1932 and 1937. At the end of 1938, he became the Polish envoy to Afghanistan, Iraq, and Iran. Karszo-Siedlewski headed that mission until mid-1942, when he was moved to a post in Beirut. Between August 1943 and July 1945, he worked for the MFA-in-exile in London. After the war, he remained an émigré; he was active in the Free Europe Committee (initially, the National Committee for a Free Europe) and was an assistant editor at the Library of Congress in Washington, DC. He died there in 1955. See Library of Congress Information Bulletin 10, no. 33 (August 13, 1951) and 13, no.

August 1934, and then by Stanisław Sośnicki,[4] from August 4, 1934, until November 1, 1936. After Sośnicki's recall to Poland, Tadeusz Błaszkiewicz (the head of the consular department at the Polish embassy in Moscow) served for a brief period as acting head of the consulate in Kharkiv. He was succeeded by Tadeusz Brzeziński[5] (November 1, 1936–mid-December 1937), who was the last Polish consul in Kharkiv before World War II.[6]

After the capital of Soviet Ukraine was moved from Kharkiv to Kyiv in mid-1934, Jan Karszo-Siedlewski became the head of the Polish consulate in Kyiv. He replaced Stanisław Sośnicki, who was transferred to Kharkiv. Karszo-Siedlewski remained in Kyiv until September 1937, when he was recalled to the MFA in Warsaw for a brief time before being appointed the Polish ambassador in Tehran. After Karszo-Siedlewski's departure from Kyiv to Warsaw, Jerzy Matusiński took over his post. It should be noted that both Karszo-Siedlewski and Matusiński were

---

51 (December 20, 1954). Marcin Kruszyński has written about his cooperation with military intelligence; see M. Kruszyński, "Przyczynek do badań nad powiązaniami wywiadu ze służbą dyplomatyczną," *Przegląd Historyczno-Wojskowy*, 2009, no. 4: 169–78.

4 Stanisław Sośnicki (1896–1962) was a lieutenant colonel, an MFA official, and an Olympic athlete. He moved to the MFA from the Ministry of Military Affairs in 1931. In 1933, Sośnicki became the Polish consul in Kyiv, and between August 4, 1934, and November 1, 1936, he was the consul in Kharkiv. He was recalled after a conflict with the post's employees and because of some mistakes he had made in managing the consulate's casino (for more information on this, see below, chap. 1, sec. 3). After returning from Kharkiv, he retired. Sośnicki participated in the Paris Olympics in 1924, competing in the 100-meter dash and in the long jump. He fought in the 1939 September Campaign, and he was interned in the Woldenburg Oflag II-C. After World War II, he was appointed Poland's ambassador to Turkey. He served for many years in the Polish Athletics Federation; see Z. Głuszek, *Polscy Olimpijczycy, 1924–1984* (Warsaw: Sport i Turystyka, 1988), 381.

5 Tadeusz Brzeziński (1896–1990) worked at the MFA starting in 1921. Before becoming head of the Kharkiv post on December 1, 1936, he was the consul in Essen (1921–22), Lille (1928–31), and Leipzig (1931–35). After the consulate in Kharkiv was closed down at the end of 1937, Brzeziński returned to Warsaw, where he was appointed Polish consul in Montreal, Canada. He retained that post until July 1945, when Canadian authorities officially revoked their recognition of the Polish government-in-exile in London. He decided to remain in Canada permanently. He was active in the Polish-Canadian diaspora, e.g., as director of the Canadian Polish Congress. See P. Vaughan, *Zbigniew Brzeziński* (Warsaw: Świat Książki, 2010), 7–19; and A. Ziółkowska, *Kanada, Kanada...* (Warsaw: Wydawnictwo Polonia, 1986), 94–118.

6 In 1937, under pressure from the Soviet authorities, the Polish consulates in Kharkiv and Tbilisi were closed (which also happened to the consulates of numerous other countries with diplomatic presence in the USSR). The Polish consulate in Kharkiv was reopened in 1994.

members of the diplomatic corps (they served as counselors to the Moscow legation—later, from 1934, embassy).[7] Matusiński was the last prewar head of the Polish consulate in the capital of Ukraine. On the night of October 1–2, 1939, thirteen days after the Soviet invasion of Poland, functionaries of the People's Commissariat for Internal Affairs (the NKVD) kidnapped him and two other employees of the Polish consulate general in Kyiv, Andrzej Orszyński and Józef Łyczek. Matusiński was treacherously lured out of the post's building and disappeared without a trace. The Soviet authorities officially declared that they knew nothing about the consul's whereabouts.[8]

During this same period, the Polish embassy in Moscow was headed by Juliusz Łukaszewicz (February 1, 1933–June 20, 1936[9]),[10] who was succeeded by Wacław Grzybowski (July 4, 1936–September 17, 1939).[11] Władysław Harland served as the (acting) military attaché between February 1933 (when Lieutenant Colonel Jan Kowalewski[12] was recalled)

---

[7] This was a consequence of the Polish-Soviet agreement of 1923, confirmed in the Polish-Soviet consular convention of July 18, 1923. It warranted that the heads of the Polish consulates in Kharkiv and Minsk were formally recognized as belonging to the diplomatic corps. See W. Materski, "Polsko-radziecka konwencja konsularna z 18 lipca 1924 roku," *Dzieje Najnowsze*, 1973, no 4: 67–68; and W. Skóra, "Organizacja i działalność służby konsularnej II Rzeczypospolitej na terenach Rosji, Ukrainy i ZSSR w dwudziestoleciu międzywojennym (1918–1939)," in *Stosunki polityczne, wojskowe i gospodarcze Rzeczypospolitej Polskie i Związku Radzieckiego w okresie międzywojennym*, ed. J. Gmitruk and W. Włodarkiewicz (Warsaw: Muzeum Historii Polskiego Ruchu Ludowego; Siedlce: Uniwersitet Przyrodniczo-Humanistyczny, 2012), 265.

[8] For more information about Jerzy Matusiński's kidnapping, see W. Skóra, "Porwanie kierownika polskiej placówki konsularnej w Kijowie Jerzego Matusińskiego przez władze radzieckie w 1939 r.," in *Polska dyplomacja na Wschodzie w XX–początkach XXI wieku*, ed. H. Stroński and G. Seroczyński (Olsztyn and Kharkiv: Wydawnictwo LITTERA, 2010), 414–37; and M. Słowikowski, *W tajnej służbie: Jak polski wywiad dał aliantom zwycięstwo w Afryce Północnej* (Poznań: Dom Wydawniczy REBIS, 2011), 17.

[9] Until April 12, 1934, Łukaszewicz headed the Polish legation to Moscow as an envoy. On that day the legation's status as an embassy was officially recognized and Łukaszewicz was recognized as ambassador.

[10] For more information about Łukasiewicz's stint in Moscow, see M. Kornat, "Posłowie i ambasadorzy Polscy w Związku Sowieckim (1921–1939 i 1941–1943), *Polski Przegląd Dyplomatyczny*, 2004, no. 5: 157–67. After his recall from Moscow, he became ambassador in Paris.

[11] M. Kornat, "Ambasador Wacław Grzybowski i jego misja w Związku Sowieckim (1936–1939)," *Zeszyty Historyczne* 142 (2002): 5–80.

[12] Kowalewski was the military attaché to the Polish legation in Moscow between 1929 and 1933. He proved himself as a competent expert on the Soviet regime. He was one of the

and December 1935, when Lieutenant Colonel Konstanty Zaborowski arrived. Zaborowski served until May 1939; he was succeeded by Stefan Brzeszczyński.[13]

It needs to be stressed that a considerable fraction of the consular corps also co-operated with military intelligence, that is, with the Second Department of the Main Staff of the Polish Army, the *Dwójka*.[14] This was a consequence of the specific nature of the field of Soviet affairs, where any intelligence activity was much more difficult in comparison with the other main state hostile to Poland—the Third Reich.[15] Polish intelligence had to base its operations at consular posts, because the intelligence network outside of them was an easy target for surveillance. Consequently, Marshal Józef Piłsudski drew lessons from the Trust affair,[16] and in 1927

first foreign observers who noticed and analyzed the Soviet turn to rearmament in 1930. Unsurprisingly, the Soviets did not feel comfortable about Kowalewski's operations on their territory. He eventually became a persona non grata. See J. J. Bruski, "Sowieckie przygotowania wojenne w 1930 r. w ocenie attaché wojskowego RP w Moskwie," *Arcana* 2006, no. 2(68): 140–55; P. Kołakowski, *Czas próby: Polski wywiad wojskowy wobec groźby wybuchu wojny w 1939 r.* (Warsaw: Demart, 2012), 26. For more information about the circumstances of Kowalski's explusion, see Archiwum Akt Nowych w Warszawie, zespół: Sztab Główny (AAN, SG), sygn. IV/5. See also M. Kruszyński, *Ambasada RP w Moskwie, 1921–1939* (Warsaw: Instytut Pamięci Narodowej, 2010), 223–25; and M. Kruszyński, "Inwigilacja polskich placówek dyplomatycznych w ZSRR w okresie międzywojennym," in *Między I a IV Rzeczpospolitą: Z dziejów lustracji na ziemiach polskich w XIX i XX wieku*, ed. M. Korybut-Marciniak and P. Majer (Olsztyn: WUWM, 2009), 79–80.

[13] Robert Majzner wrote a brief survey of the operations of the Polish attaché post, with an emphasis on the 1920s; see R. Majzner, "Wpływ stosunków polsko-radzieckich na organizację i funkcjonowanie Attachatu Wojskowego przy Poselstwie/Ambasadzie RP w Moskwie (1921–1939): Zarys problematyki," in *Stosunki polityczne, wojskowe i gospodarcze Rzeczypospolitej Polskiej i Związku Radzieckiego w okresie międzywojennym*, ed. J. Gmitruk and W. Włodarkiewicz (Warsaw: Muzeum Historii Polskiego Ruchu Ludowego; Siedlce: Uniwersytet Przyrodniczo-Humanistyczny, 2012), 241–57.

[14] After the May Coup of 1926, Marshal Józef Piłsudski delegated some of his most trusted officers to the MFA, where they were appointed to high offices in the Soviet Union (for example, consuls Adam Stebłowski and Stanisław Sośnicki). See W. Skóra, *Służba konsularna II Rzeczypospolitej: Organizacja, kadry i działalność* (Toruń: Wydawnictwo Adam Marszałek, 2006), 355–66.

[15] A. Pepłoński, *Wywiad a dyplomacja II Rzeczypospolitej* (Toruń: Wydawnictwo Adam Marszałek, 2005), 66; Kołakowski, *Czas próby*, 193; and A. Misiuk, *Służby specjalne II Rzeczpospolitej* (Warsaw: Bellona, 1998), 51.

[16] The Monarchist Union of Central Russia, usually called "Trust," was a fictitious anticommunist monarchical organization, fabricated by the State Political Directorate (GPU), whose goal was, on paper, to overthrow Soviet power. The operation was conducted by the Soviet security organs between 1921 and 1927. Thanks to this sham

he ordered his subordinates to focus more of their intelligence activity on observation and press analysis, significantly limiting so-called offensive intelligence (recruiting informants).[17] The placement of intelligence posts (usually limited to one officer) at the consulates had its pluses and minuses. One advantage, certainly, was the permanent inflow of information, which could be obtained more easily under cover of a consular officer, since consular work was associated with frequent trips into the field: visits to industrial factories and to the *novostroiki* (newly built residential projects) and contacts with various Soviet officials, fellow foreign representatives, members of the local Polish diaspora, and even casual Soviet citizen acquaintances. Information obtained in this way could be passed on to Warsaw through the relatively safe diplomatic postal service. The comfortable working conditions offered by the exterritorial status of consular and diplomatic posts were of no small significance. Moreover, such an intelligence unit was easier to install, and the costs of its operation were much lower compared with other structures outside of the MFA. The disadvantage, no doubt, was the correlation between the performance of the posts and the political situation in the country of operations. In the event of a military conflict, both diplomats and the consular service (and, thus, the officials co-operating with the *Dwójka* on a regular basis) would have to abandon their field of operations. The government tried to guard against this scenario by creating more deeply covered posts (so-called mobs), which would begin their activities in the event of war. Furthermore, the possibility of exposure (e.g., the

---

organization, Soviet intelligence was able to establish contacts not only within the Russian émigré communities, but also within foreign intelligence services, including the Polish one. As a result, many intelligence networks operating in the USSR were uncovered. For more on this topic, see, e.g., R. Wraga, " 'Trust,' " *Kultura*, 1949, no. 4/21–5/22: 156–77; and W. Michniewicz, *Wielki bluff sowiecki* (Chicago: Publishing Wici, 1991). See also H. Kuromiya and A. Pepłoński, *Między Warszawą a Tokio: Polsko-japońska współpraca wywiadowcza, 1904–1944* (Toruń: Wydawnictwo Adam Marszałek, 2009), 113–14; and A. Krzak, *Czerwoni Azefowie: Afera "MOCR-TRUST," 1922–1927* (Warsaw: WCEO, 2010).

[17] See Michniewicz, *Wielki bluff sowiecki*, 268; A. Grzywacz, ed., *Oddział II Sztabu Głównego: Raport ppłk. Józefa Englichta, Arcana*, 1999, no. 2: 145; A. Pepłoński, *Wywiad polski na ZSRR, 1921–1939* (Warsaw: Bellona, 1996), 102–5; W. Włodarkiewicz, *Przed 17 września 1939 roku: Radzieckie zagrożenie Rzeczypospolitej w ocenach polskich naczelnych władz wojskowych 1921–1939* (Warsaw: Neriton, 2002), 62–64; and M. Kruszyński, "Z działalności konsulatu polskiego w Charkowie do początku lat 30. XX wieku," in *Stosunki polsko-ukraińskie: Historia i pamięć*, ed. J. Marszałek-Kawa and Z. Karpus (Toruń: Wydawnictwo Adam Marszałek, 2008), 244–46.

Albert Ran Affair in 1936) would obviously throw a negative light on the entire consular post.[18]

Despite these disadvantages, however, because of the particularity of the Stalinist regime, in practice there was virtually no way to conduct intelligence other than through units affiliated with the consular posts. The main task of intelligence units in the field of Soviet affairs was to collect all information pertaining to the Red Army and other military issues (mobilization, demobilization, operational plans for a future war, and the like).[19] Nonetheless the reports delivered from military intelligence to the *Dwójka* did contain considerable relevant information about the not strictly military Soviet reality of those days, including political campaigns, terror, the consequences of Soviet policy, societal attitudes toward repression, and all kinds of propaganda campaigns.

A letter from the chief of the "East" Section (Referat "Wschód") of the Second Department, Captain Jerzy Niezbrzycki,[20] addressed to *Dwójka* head Tadeusz Pełczyński (on October 15, 1931), is evidence that not many volunteers were willing to serve in Soviet territory: "There is widespread disillusionment about intelligence service within the officer corps: no one wants to apply himself to this work, and one has to search hard for those who would like to sacrifice their future, and this is getting increasingly difficult because our people have gotten smarter."[21]

---

[18] Kołakowski, *Czas próby*, 75; Skóra, *Służba konsularna*, 775–77.

[19] T. Kmiecik, *Sztab Generalny (Główny) Wojska Polskiego w latach 1918–1939* (Słupsk: Wydawnictwo Pomorskiej Akademii Pedagogicznej, 2005), 107.

[20] Jerzy Antoni Niezbrzycki (1901–68) was the head of the "East" Section between 1931 and 1939. Earlier, he headed intelligence post O.2 in Kyiv (1928–30). During the Second World War and afterwards, he stayed out of Poland. He died in the United States. He was a renowned Sovietologist and a public intellectual (his pen names: Ryszard Wraga, Wincenty Maliniak). For more information about his life, see A. Krzak, "Kapitan Jerzy Antoni Niezbrzycki," *Rocznik Archiwalno-Historyczny Centralnego Archiwum Wojskowego*, 2009, no. 2/31, 300–310; M. Ławrynowicz, "Jerzy Antoni Niezbrzycki (1901–1968): Przyczynek do działalności dyplomatycznej, wywiadowczej i publicystycznej, in *Polska dyplomacja na Wschodzie w XX–początkach XXI wieku*, ed. H. Stroński and G. Seroczyński (Olsztyn and Kharkiv: Wydawnictwo LITTERA, 2010), 327–32. See also T. Wolsza, *Za żelazną kurtyną: Europa Środkowo-Wschodnia, Związek Sowiecki i Józef Stalin w opiniach polskiej emigracji politycznej w Wielkiej Brytanii 1944/1945–1953* (Warsaw: Instytut Historii PAN, 2005), passim; and the papers of Jerzy Niezbrzycki at Centralne Archiwum Wojskowe w Warszawie (CAW), Akta personalne oficerów, sygn. 1769/89/3673. The materials pertaining to his émigré activity are held in the Ryszard Wraga archival fond located at the Józef Piłsudski Institute in New York.

[21] AAN, SG, sygn. IV/5, n.p., doc. 8.

Consequently, the likelihood of installing successful intelligence posts in the USSR and in Ukraine varied greatly, as did the quality of the work. For example, post Z.12 (Zofia Więckowska) produced no significant results. Instead it delivered reports about internal relations within the consulate and some complaints about its head, Stanisław Sośnicki. The head of post H.5, Lieutenant Stefan Kasperski (Albert Ran), was arrested in Moscow while he was receiving intelligence materials. He displayed considerable amateurishness: when he was arrested, a calendar notebook that included telephone numbers to the main office of the *Dwójka* and the last names of its officers, Jerzy Niezbrzycki and Jan Urjasz, among others, was found on him. On the other hand, Major Ludwik Michałowski (Leon Michałowski, code name Zygmunt Schmidt), was highly praised by his senior colleagues. Jan Karszo-Siedlewski, counselor to the legation/ embassy in Moscow and head of the consulate in Kharkiv and later in Kyiv, gathered much rich (if not, strictly speaking, intelligence-related) material that captured the socioeconomic reality prevailing at the time in the Soviet Union. Stanisław Suchecki and Zdzisław Miłoszewski also enjoyed the respect of their superiors, even if their personal reputations were not impeccable.

Based on material available from the period under investigation here (that is, from December 1934 until 1939), eighteen intelligence posts were active in Soviet Ukraine—in Kharkiv and in Kyiv (see tables 1 and 2).

Table 1. Intelligence units active in Kyiv from 1934 to 1939

Code name	Head	Period
Kh	Henryk Jankowski[22] (consul) Władysław Michniewicz[23] Stanisław Sośnicki (consul, code name Norman Nagel)[24]	1932–36

---

[22] After Jankowski was recalled from Kyiv in December 1932, the *Dwójka* advised Branch (*Ekspozytura*) no. 5 in Lviv to begin surveillance of Jankowski and his wife. The couple stayed in Rivne. Surveillance lasted from January 3 until January 7 with negative results, for unknown reasons. See Rossiiskii gosudarstvennyi voennyi arkhiv v Moskve (Russian State Military Archive, RGVA), fond 453k, op. 1, d. 6, l. 64–66 v.; CAW, Oddz. II SG, sygn. I.303.4.1982, n.p., doc. 26.

[23] Michniewicz was recalled to Poland on June 14, 1933, after which he returned under another surname—Mitkiewicz—and headed post B.18.

[24] After he took over the consular post in Kharkiv, Stanisław Sośnicki led intelligence post Kh in that city.

Ku	Piotr Kurnicki (vice-consul, code name Napoleon Nalewajko)	1932–36
Z.12	Zofia Więckowska (later Kurnicka)[25]	1931–32 and 1933–36
B.18	Władysław Michniewicz (Mitkiewicz)	1933–36
B.41	Wiktor Zaleski (code name Nal Niger)	1933–36
Z.14	Maria Połońska (code name Nina Nowicka)	1932–35
F.8	Aleksander Stpiczyński (worked as Albert Stpiczyński)	1934–36
Karsz	Jan Karszo-Siedlewski (counselor to the Moscow legation/embassy, head of the consulate)	1934–37[26]
G.27	Ludwik Michałowski[27] (code name Zygmunt Schmidt; worked as Leon Michałowski)	1936–39
H.5	Stefan Kasperski (worked as Albert Ran)	1936
E.15	Stanisław Nawrocki (code name Narcyz Napiórkowski)	1936–37
No data	Mieczysław Słowikowski (worked as Edward Zarębski)	1937–39
No data	Antoni Minkiewicz (worked as Antoni Majewski)[28]	1938

Sources: RGVA, f. 453k, op. 1, d. 6, l. 59–97; Pepłoński, *Wywiad polski na ZSSR*, 126–27; S. M. Nowinowski, "Specyfika funkcjonowania polskich placówek dyplomatycznych i konsularnych w Związku Sowieckim (1936–

---

[25] Between 1932 and 1933, Więckowska worked in Moscow for a few months.

[26] Earlier Counselor Karszo-Siedlewski headed a post under the same code name when he was head of the Polish consulate general in Kharkiv.

[27] Previously Michałowski headed a post in Kharkiv; after an incident involving Consul Sośnicki, however, he was moved to Kyiv (for more about this incident, see chap. 1, sec. 3).

[28] Antoni Minkiewicz is present, between 1936 and 1939, in the personnel records of the consular department of the embassy, as well as those of the consulates in Kharkiv and Kyiv, and then in the embassy records; see Nowinowski, *Specyfika funkcjonowania polskich placówek*, 126.

1939)," in *Z dziejów polskiej służby dyplomatycznej i konsularnej: Książka upamiętniająca życie i dzieło Jana Nowaka-Jeziorańskiego (1914–2005)*, ed. J. Faryś and M. Szczerbiński (Gorzów Wielkopolski: Wydawnictwo Sonar, 2005), 121; and Kołakowski, *Czas próby*, 214.

Table 2. Intelligence posts active in Kharkiv from 1934 to 1939

Code name	Head	Years
Karsz	Jan Karszo-Siedlewski (counselor to the Moscow legation/embassy, head of the consulate)	1932–34
G.27	Ludwik Michałowski[29] (code name Zygmunt Schmidt, worked as Leon Michałowski)	1934–36
E.10	Stanisław Suchecki[30] (Jan Konopka)	1936
M.13	Zdzisław Miłoszewski (code name Oleg Ostrowski)	1932–35[31]
H.23	Zofia Miłoszewska (code name Olga Oberman)	1932–35
X.37	Jerzy Kamiński[32] (code name P. Nowicki; served as Michał Kamiński)	1937
Unidentified	Antoni Minkiewicz (worked under the name of Antoni Majewski)	1937

Sources: RGWA, f. 453, op. 1, d. 6, l. 59–97, and f. 308k, op. 19, d. 63, passim; Pepłoński, *Wywiad polski na ZSRR*, 126–27; Nowinowski, *Specyfika funkcjonowania polskich placówek*, 125; and Kołakowski, *Czas próby*, 214.

It should be noted that relations between the purely professional diplomats or consular officials and those who were simultaneously co-operating with the *Dwójka* also varied considerably.[33] Karszo-Siedlewski

---

[29] After the incident involving Consul Sośnicki, Michałowski was transferred to Kyiv.

[30] Previously Suchecki led an intelligence post in Moscow (in November and December 1935); see RGVA, f. 453k, op. 1, d. 6, l. 42.

[31] In October 1935 Miłoszewski arrived in Moscow. On October 12, 1935, after being caught with a prostitute, he was sent back to Poland.

[32] Kamiński led the Kharkiv post until the consulate was closed, and later he was moved to Moscow, where he headed another post under the same code name until December 1, 1938; see CAW, Kolekcja Akt Rosyjskich, sygn. VIII.800.71.4.

[33] For more information about relations between the two groups—diplomatic/consular

was known for his exceptionally welcoming attitude toward the *Dwójka*.
He was its co-worker and directed—as noted—the "Karsz" post from 1932
to 1937, first in Kharkiv, then in Kyiv. Stanisław Sośnicki, too, was a
Dwójka co-worker and led the Kharkiv post from 1933 to 1936,[34] but he was
known for his difficult manner, which was a source of conflict with his
staff.[35] Though not close associates of the *Dwójka*, other heads of consulates
(Jerzy Matusiński, Tadeusz Brzeziński) did not create any difficulties for
the intelligence officers operating in Kyiv and Kharkiv, even if some
tension was unavoidable.[36]

The Second Department's main office considered the intelligence
competence of some officials to be low. For example, in the *Dwójka*'s
opinion, Vice-consul Adam Koch, who worked in Kyiv, not only did not
know the Russian language and local conditions but was reluctant to cooperate with the Second Department and wasted his time plotting
intrigues.[37] With respect to his "knowledge of local conditions," this
evaluation seems too harsh if one examines, for instance, his reports to
Ambassador Grzybowski. Koch was not as knowledgeable about the
Stalinist regime as Jan Karszo-Siedlewski, for instance, and at times his
analyses were of questionable value, but nonetheless he was right about
much of what was occurring in the USSR.

Intelligence gathering on the USSR was conducted by the "East"
Section (Referat "Wschód") of the Second Department (Oddział II). For
many years, from 1931 to 1939, Captain Jerzy Antoni Niezbrzycki headed
the section. There was also an Independent "Russia" Section
(Samodzielny Referat "Rosja"), which was charged with gathering
intelligence materials and their evaluation and analysis. Major Wincenty
Bąkiewicz headed that section until February 1939.

***

Stalin announced that 1929 was the "Year of the Great Breakthrough,"
and, indeed, at the end of that year a chain of events had been initiated
that eventually led to the calamities of the 1930s, when millions of people

---

officials, on the one hand, and *Dwójka* agents on the other, see Pepłoński, *Wywiad a
dyplomacja*, 129–58; and Skóra, *Służba konsularna*, 798–816.

[34] CAW, Oddz. II SG, sygn. I.303.4.1982, passim; Kruszyński, *Ambasada RP w Moskwie*, 258.

[35] For more information on this issue, see chap. 1, sec. 3.

[36] See chap. 1, sec. 3.

[37] Pepłoński, *Wywiad a dyplomacja*, 139.

lost their lives. The situation in Ukraine, as in the entire USSR, began to escalate at the end of 1929. It was then that Stalin defeated his last real political opponents still in the field—Nikolai Bukharin, Aleksei Rykov, and Mikhail Tomsky—after which he initiated the agricultural collectivization campaign. The purpose of collectivization was to guarantee a permanent grain supply for the Bolshevik state, necessary not only for the domestic market, but also for export purposes. At the time grain was the main Soviet export product. By selling grain the Bolshevik government could receive the hard currency necessary for another great campaign—industrialization and the expansion of the military complex.[38]

The ruthless collectivization campaign, with its liquidation of the so-called kulaks in combination with the very high compulsory delivery quotas imposed on the villages (Rus. *khlebozagotovki*; Ukr. *khlibozahotivli*), was the underlying cause of the Great Famine of 1932 and 1933. The grimmest harvest was reaped in the breadbasket of the USSR—Ukraine.[39]

---

[38] See B. Musiał, *Na Zachód po trupie Polski* (Warsaw: Prószyński i S-ka, 2009), 171 et seq.; and B. Musiał, "Geneza paktu Hitler Stalin," in B. Musiał and J. Szumski, eds., *Geneza paktu Hitler-Stalin: Fakty i propaganda* (Warsaw: Instytut Pamięci Narodowej, 2011), 39.

[39] There is already a large volume of work on the Great Famine. In a survey issued by the Odesa Regional Library in 2001, more than 6,300 publications were noted; see L. Burian and I. Rykun, eds., *Holodomor v Ukraïni 1932–1933 rokiv: Bibliohrafichnyi pokazchchyk* (Odesa and Lviv: Vyd-vo M. P. Kots', 2001). For publications that appeared in Poland (not including those already listed in note 2 above, which were based on Polish archival materials), see, e.g., R. Kuśnierz, *Ukraina w latach kolektywizacji i Wielkiego Głodu (1929–1933)* (Toruń: Wydawnictwo GRADO, 2005; 2nd ed., 2008; 3rd ed., 2012); idem, "Propaganda radziecka w okresie Wielkiego Głodu na Ukrainie (1932–1933)," *Dzieje Najnowsze*, 2004, no. 4: 29–36; idem, "Głód na Ukrainie w roku 1933 na łamach prasy," *Res Historica* 21 (2005): 79–90; idem, "Problematyka głodu w "raju bolszewickim" na łamach lwowskiego "Diła," in *Ukraińcy w najnowszych dziejach Polski 1918–1989*, vol. 3, ed. R. Drozd (Słupsk: Wydawnictwo Akademii Pomorskiej, 2007), 7–24; idem, "Kwestia Wielkiego Głodu w prezydenturze Wiktora Juszczenki," *Rocznik Instytutu Europy Środkowo-Wschodniej* 5 (2007): 75–79; idem, "Komunistyczna zbrodnia Wielkiego Głodu w życiu społeczno-politycznym Ukrainy," in J. Sadowska, ed., *Dziedzictwo komunizmu w Europie Środkowo-Wschodniej* (Białystok: Wydawnictwo Uniwersytetu w Białymstoku, 2008), 65–80; idem, "Obchody rocznic Wielkiego Głodu w niepodległej Ukrainie," in *Historia, mentalność, tożsamość: Miejsce i rola historii oraz historyków w życiu narodu polskiego i ukraińskiego w XIX i XX wieku*, ed. J. Pisulińska, P. Sierżęga, and L. Zaszkilniak (Rzeszów: Wydawnictwo Uniwersytetu Rzeszowskiego, 2008), 690–703; R. Dzwonkoski, SAC, ed., *Głód i represje wobec ludności polskiej na Ukrainie 1932–1947: Relacje* (Lublin: Towarzystwo Naukowe KUL, 2005); C. Rajca, *Głód na Ukrainie* (Lublin: Wyd-wo Werset; Toronto: Polski Fundusz Wydawniczy w Kanadzie, 2005); S. Kulczycki, *Hołodomor: Wielki Głod na Ukrainie w latach 1932–1933 jako ludobójstwo. Problem świadomości* (Wrocław:

Waves of repression ensued. After the Kirov murder on December 1, 1934, a period of purges and terror began. Initially repressions targeted figures associated with the Party and the state apparatus, but over time they were aimed at common citizens, especially national minorities, including Poles, immigrants, remaining kulaks, or anyone who had any connection with the *ancien régime* (i.e., the wrong kind of social background, a history of service in tsarist institutions, and so on). The apogee of this period of repression arrived in 1937–38, that is, during the Great Terror.

As stated, Polish diplomats, consular officials, and intelligence agents had a difficult job conducting intelligence and observation operations because of the specific conditions on Soviet territory. The source of any knowledge was, first and foremost, observation of the areas surrounding their workplaces, as well as surveys done during trips in the field. They also held conversations with visitors[40] (to their diplomatic or consular posts), Soviet officials, and diplomats from other countries. Other activities included analysis of the Soviet press and professional journals. Some information was derived from letters sent by Soviet citizens. Despite the obstacles, it was possible to obtain some data that threw realistic light on the situation in the USSR. It was more difficult, however, to collect information about military issues—the Red Army, troop movements, or operational war plans.[41]

Kolegium Europy Wschodniej im. Jana Nowaka-Jeziorańskiego, 2008); S. Kulchytsky, *The Famine of 1932–1933 in Ukraine: An Anatomy of the Holodomor* (Edmonton and Toronto: CIUS Press, 2018); and R. Wysocki, "Postawa społeczności ukraińskiej w Drugiej Rzeczypospolitej wobec 'wielkiego głodu' na Ukrainie w latach 1932–1933," *Annales Universitas Mariae Curie-Skłodowska, Sectio F* 60 (2005): 451–64; P. Eberhardt, "Klęski głodu na Ukrainie w pierwszej połowie XX wieku na podstawi literatury ukraińskiej," *Studia z Dziejów Rosji i Europy Środkowo-Wschodniej*, 40 (2005): 271–83.

[40] Soviet repression (detainment, arrest, or espionage charges) against people who visited foreign diplomatic and consular posts led to a gradual decrease in the number of visitors, and during the "Yezhovshchina" this led to their reduction to an absolute minimum. During the Great Terror (1937–38), it was impossible to conduct normal trips in the field because of very direct and unceremonious surveillance and because of the many obstacles created for Polish and other foreign diplomats and officials, which made their daily existence very difficult. For more information on this topic, see R. Kuśnierz, "Funkcjonowanie polskich placówek dyplomatycznych w ZSRS w warunkach Wielkiego Terroru (1937–1938)," in *Polska dyplomacja na Wschodzie w XX–początkach XXI wieku*, ed. H. Stroński and G. Seroczyński (Olsztyn and Kharkiv: Wydawnictwo LITTERA, 2010), 374–403.

[41] See Kołakowski, *Czas próby*, 195. While an emigrant, and a month after the German invasion of the Soviet Union, Jerzy Niezbrzycki prepared, on July 21, 1941, a report about

The officers of the intelligence posts did have their permanent informants. In the USSR, however, the NKVD had eyes and ears virtually everywhere and knew almost everything about those who could in theory co-operate with a foreign intelligence service. The NKVD paid special attention to personnel at foreign diplomatic and consular posts. Therefore the likelihood that a supposed informant could in fact be an NKVD agent was fairly high. Even if an informant was not an agent, it could be assumed, again with high probability, that the NKVD would become interested in that individual sooner or later. A student named Buchak, who for a long time shared information with Vice-consul Kurnicki, was one such example of a "suspect" informant.[42] The commanding officer of post X.37, Jerzy Kamiński, had informants who also reported to the NKVD.[43]

Despite these uneasy working conditions, the Polish observers were usually correct in evaluating conditions prevailing in the USSR, the intentions of the regime, which was engaged in an all-inclusive purge, and the consequences of those actions, both for the citizens of "the Soviet paradise" and for capitalist countries, particularly Poland.

---

the informational state of readiness of German (military and political) intelligence for war with the Soviet Union. In the document, which was based on his knowledge and experience in the intelligence profession, he compared the quality of Polish and German intelligence services. The latter, according to Niezbrzycki, was equipped with excellent expertise in Soviet affairs, as long as it could rely on the German-speaking diaspora. This ended after the effective dekulakization of that group. Afterwards the Germans were forced to obtain information the way their Polish colleagues did: "the volume of information about the German farmers and social atmosphere in the villages, due to the resettlement of the Germans, fell to a very low level. When I came to the USSR [in 1928], the Germans had excellent knowledge about the mood in the villages, about the process of collectivization, about the harvests and food reserves; when I was leaving [in 1930], the German consuls roamed alone in the field, just the way we did, trying to collect random information, creating evaluations based solely on their own observations and on press reviews, which, due to the organizational specificity of intelligence in the USSR, began to play an increasing role." (Józef Piłsudski Institute of America in New York, Archiwum Ryszarda Wragi [Antoniego Jerzego Niezbrzyckiego], sygn. 1, n.p.)

[42] Buchak supplied much information to Kurnicki, particularly about the devastating famine in Soviet Ukraine in 1932 and 1933. The authenticity of his information cannot be questioned, particularly because the content was confirmed by numerous other sources of different provenance. At the end of 1934, however, Kurnicki decided to abruptly end his contact with the informant, suspecting him of exaggerating the facts and even of co-operating with the NKVD. See CAW, Oddz. II SG, sygn. I.303.4.1993, b.p., doc. 22 (1934) and doc. 3 (1935).

[43] Archiwum Instytutu Pamięci Narodowej w Warszawie: zespół: Ministerstwo Bezpieczeństwa Publicznego w Warszawie, sygn. IPN BU 1572/1169, n.p.

Still, the quality of the Polish reports sent back to the MFA or the *Dwójka* was uneven and depended upon the author's competence. After analyzing Polish archival records, and based on the knowledge of the course and consequences of the Stalinist terror of the 1930s, it is fair to conclude that the most highly professional Polish official serving in Ukraine—and certainly one of the best overall in the field of Soviet affairs—was Jan Karszo-Siedlewski.[44] He did not hide his contempt for the political system that had been built in the USSR and influenced his own sense of superiority, which he occasionally betrayed in front of local Communist authorities. But his reports were marked by a high level of quality that stemmed from his in-depth familiarity with the Soviet system. As early as 1933, he mentioned on multiple occasions that the Soviet regime posed an enormous threat to Poland and the entire civilized world, and that this would become evident sooner or later. It was precisely his knowledge of the system, and of its repressiveness and ruthless brutality, that influenced Karszo-Siedlewski's attitude toward the Bolshevik state.

***

The attitude of the Polish MFA and the Second Department (the *Dwójka*) toward the purges and the terror of the second half of the 1930s remains an unexplored topic, although a few publications about the Polish consular posts in the Soviet Union have recently appeared. These studies concern different aspects—from an overview of the posts' activities to a closer look at particular periods, structural analysis, operational directions, and contacts with the *Dwójka*.[45] Publications about the political

---

[44] This judgment is based not only on the quality of his reports, but also on the opinion of other foreign consuls. The German consul in Kyiv, Andor Hencke, considered Karszo-Siedlewski well versed in political affairs. In his memoirs, written years after the fact, he still remembered that it was always worthwhile talking with Karszo-Siedlewski. Taken from H. Kuromiya, *Głosy straconych* (Warsaw: Wydawnictwo AMBER, 2008), 38.

[45] The works by Marcin Kruszyński cited earlier need to be brought to the reader's attention again. Other important publications on this topic include: J. Książek, "Powstanie i działalność Poselstwa i Konsulatu Generalnego RP w Charkowie w okresie międzywojennym," *Polski Przegląd Dyplomatyczny*, 2006, no. 2 (30): 131–54; I. Urbańska, "Ambasada Rzeczypospolitej Polskiej w Moskwie w latach 1936–1939: Warunki pracy w rzeczywistości stalinowskiej," *Dzieje Najnowsze*, 2006, no. 4: 95–107; A. Wasilewski, "Gry dyplomatyczne," *Nowa Europa Wschodnia*, 2009, no. 5: 84–95; A. Wasilewski, *Polskie Konsulaty na Wschodzie 1918–1939* (Warsaw: MSW, 2010); Nowinowski, "Specyfika

and intelligence activity of the heads of the Polish consulates in Soviet Ukraine have come out.[46] Individual contributions pertaining to how the *Dwójka* perceived the social, economic, and military situation of Soviet Ukraine and the USSR have also appeared.[47] The attitude of Polish diplomats to the Soviet campaign of repression against the Poles during the period under investigation is a topic that is poorly covered in the publications dedicated to the Polish diaspora in the USSR.[48] There does

---

funkcjonowania"; and S. M. Nowinowski, "Zakończenie działalności ambasady i konsulatów RP w Związku Sowieckim jesienią 1939 r.," *Zeszyty Historyczne* 164 (2008): 3–60. On June 4–6, 2010, several studies were presented at a conference in Kharkiv titled "Polish Diplomacy in the East in the Twentieth and the Beginning of the Twenty-first Century," organized on the 85th anniversary of the creation of the Polish interwar consulate in Kharkiv and the fifteenth anniversary of the current one. See J. Książek, "Historia Konsulatu Generalnego RP w Charkowie—fakty, refleksje, skojarzenia," in *Polska dyplomacja na Wschodzie w XX–początkach XXI wieku*, ed. H. Stroński and G. Seroczyński (Olsztyn and Kharkiv: Wydawnictwo LITTERA, 2010), 197–212; T. Grajżul, "Poselstwo i Konsulat Rzeczypospolitej Polskiej w Charkowie w latach 1921–1937," in ibid., 213–25; and A. Michalski, "Z działalności wywiadowczej konsulatu RP w Charkowie w latach dwudziestych i trzydziestych XX w.," in ibid., 226–39. See also Kuśnierz, "Funkcjonowanie polskich placówek," 374–403.

[46] M. Kruszyński, "O współpracy konsula Jana Karszo-Siedlewskiego z Oddziałem II w latach 1932–1936: Przyczynek do badań nad powiązaniami wywiadu ze służbą dyplomatyczną," *Przegląd Historyczno-Wojskowy*, 2009: no. 4; and Skóra, "Porwanie kierownika polskiej placówki."

[47] See A. Smoliński, "Sytuacja wojskowa, ekonomiczna i społeczna na Sowieckiej Ukrainie w latach 1921–1939 w ocenach Oddziału II polskiego Sztabu Głównego," *Pivdennyi arkhiv: Istorychni nauky*, 2004, no. 16: 239–50; idem, "Oddział II Sztabu Głównego Naczelnego Dowództwa Wojska Polskiego," *Wschodni Rocznik Humanistyczny* 3 (2006): 269–87 (in vol. 5 [2008] of that journal, Smoliński submitted a correction of the title: "Rola Oddziału II Sztabu Głównego Wojska Polskiego w rozpoznaniu sytuacji wojskowej, ekonomicznej i społecznej ZSRS w latach 1921–1939 oraz próba oceny wartości poznawczej akt pozostałych po tej instytucji"); and idem, "Robotniczo-Chłopska Armia Czerwona jako obiekt rozpoznania polskiego wywiadu wojskowego: Próba oceny efektywności," in *Stosunki polityczne, wojskowe i gospodarcze Rzeczypospolitej Polskiej i Związku Radzieckiego w okresie międzywojennym*, ed. J. Gmitruk and W. Włodarkiewicz (Warsaw: Muzeum Historii Polskiego Ruchu Ludowego; Siedlce: Uniwersytet Przyrodniczo-Humanistyczny, 2012), 207–40.

[48] See M. Iwanow, *Polacy w Związku Radzieckim w latach 1921–1939* (Wrocław: Wydawnictwo Uniwersytetu Wrocławskiego, 1990 (in 2014 Iwanow published his last monograph on the topic: *Zapomniane ludobójstwo: Polacy w państwie Stalina „Operacja polska" 1937-1938* [Kraków: Wydawnictwo Znak, 2014]); idem, *Pierwszy naród ukarany: Stalinizm wobec polskiej ludności kresowej (1921–1938)* (Warsaw: PWN, 1991); H. Stroński, *Represje stalinizmu wobec ludności polskiej na Ukrainie w latach 1929–1939* (Warsaw: Stowarzyszenie Wspólnota Polska, 1998); idem, "Losy ludności polskiej na Ukrainie Sowieckiej a

exist a historiography that covers relations between the Soviet state and the Catholic Church, also in Ukraine.[49] Other publications that should be mentioned here are those that deal with the way that the Polish press covered the Stalinist repressions in the "Bolshevik paradise."[50] And some parts of this book have previously been published.[51]

For this work, I have relied primarily on three archives: two are in Warsaw—Archiwum Akt Nowych (Archive of Modern Records, AAN) and Centralne Archiwum Wojskowe (Central Military Archive, CAW)—

---

dyplomacja II RP w latach 1921-1939," in *Polska dyplomacja na Wschodzie w XX–początkach XXI wieku*, ed. H. Stroński and G. Seroczyński (Olsztyn and Kharkiv: Wydawnictwo LITTERA, 2010), 248–73; J. Kupczak, *Polacy na Ukrainie w latach 1921–1939* (Wrocław: Wydawnictwo Uniwersytetu Wrocławskiego, 1994). In 2018 appeared a book with Polish MFA and military intelligence documents on the repressions against the Poles in the USSR in the second half of the 1930s: R. Kuśnierz, ed. „*Nas, Polaków, nie ma kto bronić ...*" *Represje wobec Polaków w Związku Sowieckim w latach 1935–1938 w materiałach MSZ i wywiadu wojskowego Drugiej Rzeczypospolitej*", (Łomianki: Wydawnictwo LTW 2018).

[49] This issue is also addressed in the works devoted to the Soviet Polish diaspora listed in the previous footnote. See also R. Dzwonkowski, SAC, *Kościół katolicki w ZSSR, 1917–1939: Zarys historii* (Lublin: Towarzystwo Naukowe KUL, 1997), 301–34; R. Dzwonkowski, SAC, "Władze II RP a Kościół katolicki w ZSRR," *Więź*, 1996, no. 5, 137–58; and W. Rosowski, "Polska dyplomacja w obronie Kościoła rzymskokatolickiego na Ukrainie Radzieckiej w latach 1921–1939," in Stroński and Seroczyński, *Polska dyplomacja na Wschodzie*, 274–89.

[50] See J. Romanek, *Totalitaryzm sowiecki w ocenie polskiej prasy wojskowej lat 1921–1939* (Toruń: Wydawnictwo Adam Marszałek, 2009); T. Tokarz, "Interpretacje genezy 'Wielkiej Czystki' w ZSRR w prasie polskiej (1936–1938)," *Dzieje Najnowsze*, 2004, no. 4, 47–57; and idem, "Architekt terroru: Józef Stalin w oczach prasy polskiej w okresie Wielkiej Czystki (1936-1939)," *Glaukopis*, 2007, no. 7-8: 144–54.

[51] In addition to the article in the collective volume about Polish diplomacy in the East, I have written the following texts: "Afera Rana—wpadka polskiego wywiadu w ZSRS w 1936 r.," *Studia z Dziejów Rosji i Europy Środkowo-Wschodniej* 46 (2011): 159–79; "Pogłodowa wieś ukraińska w polskich raportach wywiadowczych i konsularnych (1934–1937)," in *Studia nad wywiadem i kontrwywiadem Polski w XX wieku*, ed. W. Skóra and P. Skubisz, vol. 1 (Szczecin: Wydawnictwo IPN, 2012), 251–66; "Próby skompromitowania oraz werbunku przez sowieckie służby specjalne pracowników polskich placówek dyplomatycznych w ZSRS w latach 30. XX w.," in *Służby specjalne w systemie bezpieczeństwa państwa: Przeszłość—Teraźniejszość—Przyszłość. Materiały i Studia*, vol. 1, ed. A. Krzak and D. Gibas-Krzak (Szczecin and Warsaw: Wojskowe Centrum Edukacji Obywatelskiej, 2012), 135–48; "Próby interwencji dyplomacji polskiej w obronie prześladowanej Polonii na Ukrainie Sowieckiej w latach trzydziestych XX wieku," *Studia Polonijne* 32 (2011): 143–68; and "Represje wobec Polaków na Ukrainie podczas Wielkiej Czystki: Wiedza i reakcja polskiej dyplomacji," in *Polska-Ukraina: Dziedzictwo i współczesność*, ed. R. Drozd and T. Sucharski (Słupsk: Wydawnictwo Akademii Pomorskiej, 2012), 67–79.

and one is in Moscow—Rossiiskii gosudarstvennyi voennyi arkhiv (Russian State Military Archive, RGVA).

The most valuable materials in the Archiwum Akt Nowych are located in the MFA (Ministerstwo Spraw Zagranicznych) and Main Staff (Sztab Główny) collections. I have used, to a lesser extent, the records of the Polish embassy in Moscow (Ambasada RP w Moskwie). I researched some other AAN records but found no valuable materials there.

The most valuable material I found in the CAW (for the purposes of this book) was in the Second Department of the Main (General) Staff (Oddział II Sztabu Głównego [Generalnego]) collection. I also made use of the following groups of records: the personal papers of officers; the Samodzielne Referaty Informacyjne [Autonomous Informational Units] DOK; the Samodzielne Referaty Informacyjne of the Navy Command of 1919–39; Samodzielny Referat Informacyjny DOK nr IX Brześć nad Bugiem; and Kolekcja Akt Rosyjskich (The Russian Files Group).

In the RGVA, the most valuable material was in *fond* 308k: Vtoroi otdel General'nogo shtaba Pol'shi, g. Varshava (Department II of the General Staff, Warsaw). I also made use of other *fonds* from this archive, e.g.: *fond* 453k: Dokumentalnye materialy o deiatel'nosti razvedki burzhuaznoi Pol'shi protiv SSSR (kollektsiia) (Documents pertaining to the intelligence operations of bourgeois Poland against the USSR); *fond* 462k: Ekspozitura nomer 5 otdela General'nogo shtaba, g. Lvov (Branch no. 5 of the Department of the Main of Staff, Lviv); and *fond* 464k: Biuro inspektsii pri General'nom inspektore Vooruzhonnykh sil Pol'shi, g. Varshava (Bureau of Investigation at the General Inspectorate of the Armed Forces, Warsaw).

I also used collections from the following eight archives whose materials were of an auxiliary nature:

- Archiwum Instytutu Pamięci Narodowej w Warszawie (Archive of the Institute of National Remembrance in Warsaw);

- Archiwum Straży Granicznej w Szczecinie (Archive of the Border Patrol Troops in Szczecin);

- Gosudarstvennyi arkhiv Rossiiskoi Federatsii, GARF (State Archive of the Russian Federation);

- Rossiiskii gosudarstvennyi arkhiv noveishei istorii, RGANI (Russian State Archive of Contemporary History);

- Rossiiskii gosudarstvennyi arkhiv sotsialno-politicheskoi istorii, RGASPI (Russian State Archive of Sociopolitical History);

- Tsentralnyi dezhavnyi arkhiv hromads'kykh obiednan' Ukraïny, TsDAHOU (Central State Archive of Social Organizations of Ukraine);

- Haluzevyi derzhavnyi arkhiv Sluzhby bezpeky Ukraïny, HDASBU (Branch State Archive of the Security Service of Ukraine in Kyiv);
- Józef Piłsudski Institute of America in New York (JPIA).

In addition, I consulted two more archives to obtain photographs: the National Digital Archive in Warsaw (Narodowe Archiwum Cyfrowe) and the Security Service of Ukraine Archive in Mykolaiv Oblast (Arkhiv upravlinnia Sluzhby bezpeky Ukraïny v Mykolaïvs'kii oblasti).

On March 3, 1936, the head of the Soviet Department of the MFA, Stanisław Zabiełło, gave a talk to the officers of the foreign service. He made the following apt remarks: "Our task, the task of MFA officials, is a sober, objective, and careful examination of the transformations taking place in the USSR in order to make a veritable assessment of our Eastern neighbour's strong and weak sides, since only such an assessment of the situation can help us to weigh the issue's true significance, as well as to suggest some options and methods of counteracting them, especially considering the potential threat that it poses."[52]

The purpose of this book is to present the extent of knowledge that the MFA and military intelligence of the Second Republic possessed about the events taking place east of the Zbruch River and to examine the way this knowledge has been used. This study has both a thematic and a chronological structure. It focuses on the period of 1934–38. If one examines Soviet policy with respect to the peasants, 1934 was the first post-famine year, when the countryside began slowly to recover from the enormous damage inflicted by the Holodomor. If one is looking at the political situation, the Kirov murder at the end of 1934 must again be noted: after that event, the wave of massive purges and increasing terror began. It peaked in 1937–38 and began to subside after the dismissal of the chief of the NKVD, Nikolai Yezhov, in November 1938. I have tried to stay within this temporal framework. Occasionally, however, when attempting to show the full historical picture, I have needed to trace events back to the earlier period, as was the case with my analysis of the situation in the countryside after the Great Famine, the Soviet nationalities and religious policy, and comparative aspects of some issues, such as the evolution of the position of the Polish consular posts throughout the 1930s.

---

[52] Biblioteka Narodowa w Warszawie, opracowanie: *Rosja Sowiecka: Wykład wygłoszony w dn. 3 marca 1936 r. na Kursie Naukowym dla urzędników służby zagranicznej przez p. Stanisława Zabiełłę, kierownika referatu w MSZ* (n.p., n.d.), 42.

This study is focused on Soviet Ukraine. Occasionally, however, my analysis has been extended to cover some events taking place in Russia, especially if the event initiated some new form of repressive campaign, like the Kirov murder, the Moscow show trials, or the Tukhachevsky trial. When analyzing propaganda mechanisms, I have at times described a few characteristic phenomena typical of the entire Soviet state. In a few places, in order to demonstrate how the Ukrainian situation compared with the rest of the country, I have extended the geographical framework, e.g., when comparing the Russian and Ukrainian villages, road infrastructure, or living conditions of the countryfolk.

This monograph has six chapters. The first one focuses on the operational conditions and functioning of the Polish consular posts in Ukraine in the 1930s. The conditions endured by Polish consular personnel in the Soviet Union were never easy, but as the Stalinist repressions increased, so did invigilation of the foreign posts. The most tragic period coincided with the Yezhovshchina years. At that time, the operational conditions of the Polish posts resembled a prison-like situation. This first chapter also sheds light on prevailing relations between the chiefs of the posts and their personnel, as well as on the situation of other foreign consulates in Ukraine, using information gathered by the Polish foreign service.

The second chapter describes the post-Holodomor situation of the Ukrainian village. After the immense trauma of the Great Famine, the countryside slowly began to recover. Of course, just after the famine, especially in 1934, conditions were still very difficult. Many places reported that the famine continued, but, as time passed, the situation seemed to return to "stability." However, even if the peasants were no longer hungry, they were gradually being transformed into automatized cogs in the Soviet agricultural output machine.

The third chapter discusses everyday life in Soviet Ukrainian cities, including their external appearance. In addition, the chapter includes Polish analyses of the living conditions of the population (perpetual queues, residential shortages, incomes and prices, "social nourishment"). The chapter ends with some evaluations of the Stakhanovite movement written by Polish diplomatic, consular, and intelligence officials.

The fourth chapter contains analyses and observations of the political repression that followed after December 1, 1934, and lasted until the end of 1938. Ukraine was not spared during the wave of repression that followed after the Kirov murder. These repressions chiefly targeted

Ukrainian émigrés from the Second Polish Republic. The case of the Krushelnytsky family, who had come to Soviet Ukraine from Lviv a few months before being sentenced to Gulag camps and death, came to symbolize the entire ordeal. Such massive repressions lasted until Nikolai Yezhov was dismissed from his position as head of the NKVD. This chapter also includes Polish analyses of the anti-Trotskyite campaign and social attitudes toward state-driven repressions. It presents the level of Polish knowledge about the all-embracing Yezhovshchina terror and the attitudes and actions of the Polish consular posts, as well as those of the authorities of the Second Polish Republic with respect to the repressions targeting the Polish community in Ukraine.

The fifth chapter covers the anti-religion campaign, and the sixth deals with propaganda.

***

Two documents used in the book I received from Professors Hiroaki Kuromiya and Piotr Kołakowski. I would like to thank them both for their help.

I would also like to express my gratitude to the institutions that supported my research in libraries and archives: the Lackoroński Foundation (Fundacja Lanckorońskich) and the Foundation for Polish Science (Fundacja na Rzecz Nauki Polskiej). Thanks to these two institutions, I was able to travel to the Ukrainian and Russian archives on several occasions. My stay at Harvard University was of invaluable importance. My study there was made possible by the Harvard Ukrainian Research Institute, which invited me to participate as the Eugene and Daymel Shklar Fellow. I would like to express my gratitude to the directors of the institute.

I would like to thank the journal *Polityka* for granting me the "Zostańcie z nami" (Stay with us) stipend and Poland's Ministry of Science and Higher Education for granting me the "Exceptional young scientists" stipend, both of which helped considerably in covering expenses associated with my research. I would also like to thank the Ministry of Science and Higher Education for granting me the "Mobilność plus" (Mobility Plus, first edition) stipend that covered expenses associated with my year at the Davis Center for Russian and Eurasian

Studies at Harvard University in 2013–14, which enabled me to finish this book and another monograph.[53]

I thank the Ministry of Science and Higher Education of the Republic of Poland for awarding me grants in 2015 through 2019 from the Narodowy Program Rozwoju Humanistyki (National Program for the Development of the Humanities) covering the translation and publication cost of the English edition of my monograph. I am grateful to Dr. Tomasz Blusiewicz for undertaking the translation.

I would also like to express my gratitude to the Canadian Institute of Ukrainian Studies Press for undertaking the publication of this book. In particular, I am grateful to the press's executive director, Dr. Marko Robert Stech, and to the book's editors Kathryn Dodgson and Roman Senkus, all of whom prepared the final version of the English text. I would also like to thank the Peter Jacyk Centre for Ukrainian Historical Research at the Canadian Institute of Ukrainian Studies, University of Alberta, for including my book in its monograph series. And finally, I would like to thank the Canadian Foundation for Ukrainian Studies and the Cosbild Investment Club Endowment Fund at the CIUS for their generous financial support for the publication of this monograph.

[53] The Polish edition of this work was published in 2013. The second book was published in 2016: *Czystki i terror na Ukrainie (1934–1938)* (Toruń: Wydawnictwo Adam Marszałek).

Chapter One

The Operational Conditions and Functioning of the Polish Consulates in Soviet Ukraine in the 1930s

1.1. The Position of Polish Consular Posts until 1936

The USSR was a peculiar country, to put it euphemistically. It was the first state to attempt to create "the most just" system of all, the communist system. The Soviet people saw through the façade, however, and quickly realized what Bolshevism really meant. That state, throughout its entire existence, functioned solely on the ubiquitous application of terror against its own citizens. The state made sure that society—particularly its youth, who had no recollection of prerevolutionary times—had as little contact with foreigners as possible. On the one hand, the people were told they had the privilege of living under the best system of governance in the world—communism—and that their situation contrasted with the allegedly horrible life in capitalist countries. On the other hand, the residents of the USSR were kept as far as possible from anything capitalist. As the terror intensified, the Soviet authorities limited the possibility of travel abroad for their own citizens and reduced the (already low) number of foreign tourists visiting the USSR. In the eyes of Commissar for Foreign Affairs Maxim Litvinov, the radical restrictions on foreign arrivals to the USSR stained the country's international reputation. He shared his thoughts on this issue with Stalin, Molotov, and Yezhov on April 27, 1937.[1] Judging from the continuing, unchanged Soviet policy of insulating the country from the world, Litvinov's appeals fell on deaf ears.

As the terror intensified, foreign diplomats and consular workers were increasingly fenced off from Soviet citizens. Each applicant to a foreign diplomatic and consular post was considered a potential "spy" or "enemy of the people." The obstacles in reaching Soviet citizens rendered the daily operations of foreign posts extremely difficult. But this was merely where their troubles began.

In examining the content of the Polish archives, one stumbles upon innumerable confirmations of just how badly the NKVD wanted to make

---

[1] S. Dullin, *Stalin i ego diplomaty: Sovetskii Soiuz i Evropa, 1930-1939 gg.* (Moscow: ROSSPEN, 2009), 207.

the lives of foreign representatives miserable. More or less vulgar provocations were devised to intimidate them, prevent them from touring the countryside, or even to recruit them. It should be noted that occasionally the Polish officials had only themselves to blame. This observation applies particularly to their social life.[2] A good example is Zdzisław Miłoszewski, an official in the Polish consulate in Kharkiv between 1932 and 1935 (and later in Moscow), who was caught in a prostitute's apartment on October 12, 1935.[3] Despite the backing he received from the Second Department, ultimately he was be sent back to Poland.[4]

Incidents of violence against Polish diplomatic and consular officials, and burglaries of Polish establishments, did occasionally take place. It needs to be kept in mind that most Soviet people had to struggle with issues of survival on a daily basis. Some of these issues, such as the constant deficit of food and fuel and unreliable transportation and

---

[2] See Kruszyński, "Inwigilacja polskich placówek dyplomatycznych," 78; and Kuśnierz, "Próby skompromitowania oraz werbunku," 147.

[3] As the Soviet terror and the surveillance of foreigners grew, it was increasingly difficult for foreigners to maintain relations with local women without markedly increasing their risk of a slip-up. In this context, the letter written by the head of intelligence post N.38 in Moscow (his identity remains unknown) about "women's services" appears particularly interesting. His first letter to the main office of the Second Department was written on January 10, 1939. It reads: "Diplomats and the higher-ranking echelons, well-supplied with wives and skivvies of all sorts, have excluded all the other clerks from sexual opportunities. It creates yet another unnecessary daily nuisance for our existence here, and it leads to a harmful softness vis-à-vis the subordinates, who do it [sexual services] as if it was a great favor." Next N.38 wrote that he told a clerk named Tadeusz Parczewski, who was then embarking on a short-term trip to Warsaw, to find the right kind of maid to "take care" of four or five loners for 200 zlotys per month plus full monthly upkeep. Such a woman could be employed in the intelligence sector in the future. On January 17, 1939, the head of post N.38 wrote to the main office again about "the urgent need to dispatch a maid." On January 20, 1939, the main office forwarded copies of letters written by Maksymilian Kurnatowski (intelligence post Z.15), mentioning that they had nothing against supplying such a maid in principle, but she could not be a courtesan at the same time, and her intelligence deployment "was completely out of the question." Z.15 was advised to speak about this matter to N.38 and "bring him down a peg or two." N.38 received a reply from the main office to his letter of January 10, 1939, that the plan he suggested was unacceptable: "We are aware of the sexual issues, but they cannot be approached so liberally as you, sir, imagine. The maid cannot be a courtesan simultaneously, and your office cannot be a brothel. This matter will be further addressed by the post's director" (CAW, Oddz. II SG, sygn. I.303.4.2097, n.p., doc. 2.)

[4] Note that the Second Department believed that Miłoszewski was the victim of a provocation, while the embassy thought that he had only himself to blame, because he picked the woman up in the restaurant himself. See RGVA, f. 308, op. 19, d. 58, l. 250–52.

communications, were also bound to impact the lives of foreigners negatively. On May 5, 1934, in a typical case representative of the Soviet system as a whole and of the travails awaiting the Polish officials in that country, the Polish consulate general ordered a phone call with the consulate in Kyiv. It was scheduled for 11:00 a.m. Despite several reminders from the Polish side, their Soviet hosts did not establish the connection until late evening. It was the second such delay in a row. The transmitting station explained that the orders from the Polish consulate general were dealt with "seventh in the rank of priority," after all orders from the Soviet institutions had been fulfilled, even if these were placed later.[5]

Adam Stebłowski shed some light on the functioning of Polish (and other foreign) diplomatic and consular posts in the USSR,[6] especially after the controversial case of the Soviet diplomat Grigorii Besedovsky, who had fled from the Soviet embassy in Paris in 1929.[7] Besedovsky provided much valuable information detailing the activities of Soviet diplomats, both official and unofficial.[8] Inspired by Besedovsky's revelations, Stebłowski wrote a 27-page report based on the experiences of Polish and other diplomats in the USSR, titled *Life and Work of Foreign Representatives in Soviet Russia*, in which he depicted the proverbial other side of the coin, i.e., the operations of foreign posts within the Soviet Union.[9] For foreign diplomats, their problems began even before their deployment to "the Soviet paradise." They had to wait up to two months to receive an entry visa—a delay necessary to give the GPU's foreign section time to screen the diplomats meticulously enough.[10] After they received their visas, they

---

[5] RGVA, f. 308k, op. 4, d. 24, l. 74

[6] Adam Stebłowski (1896–1941) was an employee of the Ministry of Foreign Affairs and a secret associate at the Second Department. He was the head of, among others, the Polish consulate in Kharkiv (1928–32) and Tbilisi (1932–33). See CAW, sygn. 1769/89/4857, Akta personalne Adama Stebłowskiego.

[7] For more details about the escape and its consequences, see, e.g., V. Genis, "Grigorii Zinovevich Besedovskii," *Voprosy istorii*, 2006, no. 7: 37–58.

[8] His memoirs have also been published in Poland; see G. Z. Biesiedowskij, *Pamiętniki dyplomaty sowieckiego* (Katowice: Polski Instytut Wydawniczy, n.d.).

[9] CAW, Oddz. II SG, sygn. I.303.4.3014, k. 1–27.

[10] Until 1936, visa acceptance/rejection decisions were issued by individual Soviet posts abroad. On February 28, 1936, the Central Committee of the All-Union Communist Party (Bolsheviks) issued a decree "On measures protecting the USSR against infiltration by intelligence, terrorist, and subversive elements," which prohibited individual foreign Soviet posts from issuing visas to foreigners wishing to visit the USSR without first

would experience that moment of being transferred to an entirely different world just on the other side of the border. Stebłowski remarked: "It's a border between two worlds, not two countries, beyond doubt; this can be felt from the very first step one takes on Soviet soil. The first official seen upon entry, and the last upon departure, is a uniformed functionary of the GPU, which is an integral part of the border-protection service."[11]

After an official's arrival at his post, wrote Stebłowski, the GPU did all they could to get to know him as thoroughly as possible. They examined his lifestyle, habits, character, every single detail, including the intimate sphere, as all information "could become valuable at the right time." Consequently, each foreign diplomat had to be constantly on alert, since such information could be turned against him. This threat did not exclude his liquidation "if he turns out to be a bold and active individual, uncompromising with respect to the USSR—all in all, an undesirable individual for the Soviets"; to compromise him on moral (e.g., by dispatching women to "distract" him) or political grounds would lead to his dismissal. This type of information could be useful to "buy," persuade, or blackmail him to betray his country to the USSR's benefit, in exchange for leaving him uncompromised or simply for cash.

Another kind of danger could come from the visitors to one of the consulates. Many of them were sent by the GPU/NKVD with fake offers of co-operation. Some of them applied for a visit to a consulate merely to eavesdrop in the waiting room, hoping that its extraterritorial status would loosen tongues. Stebłowski remembered a few cases of visitors who, when their turn to see the consul came, refused and walked out. Furthermore, strange technical surveys of the diplomatic establishments took place quite frequently, during which, as it turned out later, the interiors were tapped. The consular buildings remained under a permanent watch. As a rule, a post's location had to be easy to monitor (the Soviets did not allow entire buildings or squares to be purchased), in a blind alley, for example, or at an intersection with low traffic intensity.

---

consulting Moscow. Commissar for Foreign Affairs Maxim Litvinov (rightly) remarked that such a practice was not present anywhere else in the world, and that it was in conflict with "international standards and courtesy." He was especially concerned about visas issued for high foreign officials, diplomats, couriers, etc., who visited the USSR as part of their professional duty. After Litvinov's interventions, the types of persons he mentioned were excluded from the new regulations that required Moscow's prior agreement. See Dullin, *Stalin i ego diplomaty*, 206–7.

[11] CAW, Oddz. II SG, sygn. I.303.4.3014, k. 8–9.

Soviet agents photographed, more or less subtly, persons and vehicles seen near the foreign posts.

In the conclusion of his report, Stebłowski somberly sketched the big picture: "Spying, provocations, and all kinds of hindrances thrown at the foreign diplomatic posts, including the personal lives of the officials, are deployed by the GPU deliberately and are calculated, in the long run, to undermine the work of the targeted foreign authorities psychologically; it is a well-tried and effective method, aimed at constantly irritating and disturbing the peace of mind of the targeted individuals, and, as a result, at disorganizing the operations of foreign posts in general, making them less effective, preoccupied primarily with all kinds of daily inconveniences and petty incidents, all in unlimited numbers. It is well known that the GPU deploys such 'tools' extraordinarily fruitfully and succeeds in disturbing, to a large extent, the process of capturing the sad and ominous Soviet reality by foreign representatives."[12]

It was in such an atmosphere that the Polish diplomatic and consular officials had to work. Their situation turned increasingly worse as the USSR entered upon "the path of socialist reconstruction." The operational conditions of the Polish officials employed at the consulates in Kyiv and Kharkiv were the same as those of other representatives of the Second Polish Republic in the Soviet Union. In 1929, after eliminating his few remaining real political contenders, Stalin effectively became the country's dictator and started to implement his ideas. First and foremost he initiated the agricultural collectivization and industrialization campaigns. Collectivization, with unreal grain quotas imposed on the village, not only ruined the peasants, but also, in the longer term, led to the horrible famine of 1932–33. During the Holodomor the Soviets attempted to discourage locals from visiting the Polish consular posts, primarily relying on arrests, long interrogations and other repressive methods. In April 1933, at the height of the famine, the Polish vice-consul in Kyiv, Piotr Kurnicki, recorded the facts of arrests of Poles and Ukrainians who visited the Polish post. In his report, he mentioned that the Polish staff was under "intensifying watch and supervision": "The correspondence mailed to the consulate is being intercepted, [and] even the postage stamps are not spared; they check if there is something hidden underneath."[13]

---

[12] Ibid., k. 26.
[13] Ibid., sygn. I.303.4.1867, k. 42–43.

On January 20, 1934, Jan Karszo-Siedlewski, the head of the Polish consulate general in Kharkiv at the time, observed that the consulate was becoming increasingly isolated from the surrounding world. People were not only afraid to stop by, but even to talk to Poles they randomly encountered in the city.[14] On February 14, 1934, he remarked: "my situation, both professional and personal, as well as the situation of my co-workers, is becoming increasingly difficult."[15] When Piotr Kurnicki, Jan Karszo-Siedlewski, and other representatives of the Second Polish Republic wrote such words in 1933 and 1934, they could not have realized that it was all mere child's play compared to what was soon to unfold. After the Kirov murder, the USSR set upon a course of purges and terror. It was that event that marked a significant change in the position of foreign diplomatic and consular representatives, who were now subject to very thorough surveillance.[16] Kurnicki noticed that after the death of the prominent Leningrad dignitary, their post was constantly guarded by unshakable "rascals"[17] (łapsy), who openly followed the consulate's employees, three steps behind them.[18]

After a few weeks, the level of surveillance decreased slightly. In a letter to the Second Department written on January 27, 1935, Jan Karszo-Siedlewski observed that the Poles were no longer so closely followed when in town. It was not uncommon that they seemed to be

---

[14] Ibid., sygn. I.303.4.1985, n.p., doc. 7 (1934).

[15] Ibid., doc. 3 (1934).

[16] Even before the Kirov murder, the attitude of the local authorities toward Polish consular officials had changed dramatically. On October 4, 1934, Karszo-Siedlewski wrote to the Second Department: "It is truly astounding how the attitude of the local administration toward Poland has changed for the worse just over the past two weeks, and how fundamentally their behavior toward me and other employees of the Polish consulate general has been transformed." The diplomat identified the cause of such a state of affairs as a directive that came from Moscow; see ibid., doc. 39. In a similar report to the ambassador, written on October 3 and 5, he emphasized: "All members of the consular corps are now under a scrupulous, if still discreet, watch, and an aura of suspicion has been created around us so that people are not only afraid to visit us, but also to talk or even nod their head in our direction on the streets. The local GPU has contributed to this new reality boldly. They are apparently highly satisfied by the green light given for instigating all kinds of incidents targeting Poland" (ibid., n.p., no doc. no).

[17] Łapsy was the term used by the employees of the Polish embassy and the consulates to describe the NKVD agents who surveilled them. According to a letter written by Władysław Michniewicz, the head of post B.18, at least until the mid-1930s some Polish officials used to bribe those "rascals," likely to make sure they did not do their job so zealously. See RGVA, f. 453k, op. 1, d. 2, l. 141.

[18] CAW, Oddz. II SG, sygn. I. 303.4.1993, n.p., doc. 22.

unaccompanied at all, even at night, which made it easier for observation and to initiate casual conversations with locals they encountered. However, the isolation of the post increased.[19] Not only were visitors who wished to enter the building harassed, but it was also increasingly difficult for representatives of the Second Polish Republic to get in touch with Ukrainian authorities. One example of this type of intimidation was the absence of an invitation to Polish representatives to attend the commemorative events of March 10, the anniversary of the death of the Ukrainian poet Taras Shevchenko.[20]

Polish-German negotiations, finalized in the Non-Aggression Pact signed on January 26, 1934, influenced the Soviet attitude toward Poland. Piotr Kurnicki saw a clear connection between the two. In one of his reports to the Second Department, he emphasized that the negative shift in attitude toward the Polish consular posts dated roughly to the moment of the first conciliatory Polish-German talks. To some extent, but only temporarily, Foreign Minister Józef Beck's visit to Moscow in February 1934, and the prolongation of the Polish-Soviet Non-Aggression Pact on May 5, 1934, reversed the otherwise negative trend.[21] The most noticeable

---

[19] Ibid., Sygn. I.303.4.1985, n.p., doc. 1 (1935).

[20] Ibid., doc. 4.

[21] In the same report, Kurnicki emphasized that the signing of the pact had improved the situation of the Polish consular corps in the USSR and had changed the attitude of the official Soviet authorities toward his post. The number of arrests among Soviet Poles, applicants to the consulate, and those who maintained contact with it via mail correspondence decreased. Soviet policy toward the churches and priests also visibly softened. The Soviet press almost completely stopped releasing materials hostile to Poland; see ibid., sygn. I.303.4.1993, b.p., doc. 1 (1935). For more details about the Polish-Soviet Non-Aggression Pact, see M. J. Zacharias, *Polska wobec zmian w układzie sił politycznych w Europie w latach 1932–1936* (Wrocław: Zakład Narodowy im. Ossolińskich, 1981), 34–50, 107–28; S. Gregorowicz and M. J. Zacharias, *Polska-Związek Sowiecki: Stosunki polityczne, 1925–1939* (Warsaw: Instytut Historii PAN, 1995), 43–54; M. Gmurczyk-Wrońska, "Negocjacje polsko-sowieckie o pakt o nieagresji w roku 1927 i w latach 1931–1932," *Dzieje Najnowsze*, 2012, no. 3: 21–51; S. Patek, *Raporty i korespondencja z Moskwy (1927–1932)*, ed. M. Gmurczyk-Wrońska (Warsaw: Wydawnictwo Neriton, Instytut Historii PAN, 2010); W. Rezmer, "Polsko-radziecki pakt o nieagresji z 1932 roku: Aspekty polityczne i militarne," in *Stosunki polityczne, wojskowe i gospodarcze Rzeczypospolitej Polskiej i Związku Radzieckiego w okresie międzywojennym*, ed. J. Gmitruk and W. Włodarkiewicz (Warsaw: Muzeum Historii Polskiego Ruchu Ludowego; Siedlce: Uniwersytet Przyrodniczo-Humanistyczny, 2012), 149–56; and W. Materski, "Polska i ZSRR na przełomie lat dwudziestych i trzydziestych XX wieku," in *Białe plamy—czarne plamy: Spawy trudne w polsko-rosyjskich stosunkach 1918–2008*, ed. A. D. Rotfeld and A. Torkunow (Warsaw: PISM, 2010), 89–94.

changes, however, took place during the negotiations of the Treaty of Good Understanding and Co-operation[22] (signed by the Baltic states) and the so-called Eastern Pact. During this period, hostile relations with the Polish Republic, and consequently with the Polish consulates, began to trickle down to the broader Soviet society. As a result, the number of visitors decreased, surveillance began, and some visitors to the consulate were arrested shortly after their visits.[23]

Adolf Petrovsky, a representative of the People's Commissariat for Foreign Affairs (PCfFA), held a conversation with Karszo-Siedlewski on February 22, 1935, during which he emphasized the significance of the Eastern Pact and Soviet anxieties about progress in Polish-Japanese relations. In a note based on that conversation for the *Dwójka*, the Polish counselor admitted that he was pessimistic about the future trajectory of Polish-Soviet relations. He underscored that the Soviets were afraid of the Japanese and certain ideas promoted by the German press. They also accused the Poles of plotting with the Japanese. It was precisely this international entanglement that generated the pressure on Poland to join the Eastern Pact.[24]

As is commonly known, Poland rejected the idea of the pact. Formally the Eastern Pact guaranteed help for Poland from all of the region's countries in the event of an external threat. In practice it opened the door for foreign meddling in Polish domestic affairs. Particularly ominous, from the Polish point of view, was the scenario in which the Red Army, while "rushing to help" another nation in danger, would pass through Polish territory. Warsaw believed, presciently it turned out, that the neighbouring armies would likely stay in Poland for longer.[25]

The Bolsheviks were very dissatisfied with the Poles' unwillingness to sign the Eastern Pact. Moscow took it as a sign that Poland was likely to oppose the USSR in any future military clash.[26] High diplomacy had a

---

[22] An Estonian-Latvian-Lithuanian agreement, based primarily on the Baltic Pact signed in Geneva on September 12, 1934.

[23] CAW. Oddz. II SG, sygn. I.303.4.1993, b.p. doc. 1 (1935).

[24] Ibid., sygn. I.303.4.1985, doc. 3 (1935), n.p.

[25] W. Materski, *Tarcza Europy: Stosunki polsko-sowieckie, 1918–1939* (Warsaw: Książka i Wiedza, 1994), 287.

[26] See ibid., 288. For more details about the Eastern Pact, see S. Gregorowicz, "Koncepcja paktu wschodniego na tle stosunków polsko-sowieckich," in A. Ajnenkiel et al., eds., *Międzymorze: Polska i kraje Europy Środkowo-Wschodniej, XIX–XX wiek. Studia ofiarowane Piotrowi Łossowskiemu w siedemdziesiątą rocznicę urodzin* (Warsaw: Instytut Historii PAN, 1995), 321–31; Gregorowicz and Zacharias, *Polska-Związek Sowiecki*, 125–30; and Zacharias, *Polska wobec zmian*, 129–80.

real impact on the operations of the Polish diplomatic and consular corps on the ground. Over time Soviet harassment increased, which was reflected in the daily work of the consulates and, especially, intelligence agents. In September 1935, Władysław Michniewicz[27] informed Jerzy Niezbrzycki that the conditions prevailing at the time did not allow for frequent meetings with the agents, and, when they did occur, such meetings had to be safeguarded with all kinds of precautions. The number of legitimate visitors to the Polish consulates fell, while the number of provocateurs grew: "We do what we can," concluded the head of post B.18, "but our work conditions have deteriorated enormously. We are now blatantly followed, by car and on foot."[28]

On April 20, 1936, Jan Karszo-Siedlewski wrote about "the growing insolence of our supervisors," both with respect to the Polish staff and with respect to visitors. All of them would eventually be arrested and searched by the police, while packages with food or clothing received at the consulate would be confiscated. The diplomat wrote that the NKVD followed his subordinates' every step, even entering bookstores the Poles visited to check which books they had been browsing moments earlier.

According to the report's author, the only effective countermeasure against this type of "work" conducted by the NKVD was to retaliate accordingly against Soviet diplomats, consular workers, and applicants in Poland. Karszo-Siedlewski requested that this information be passed on to the head of the Second Department, Colonel Tadeusz Pełczyński, and to tell the colonel that he would be personally much obliged for an immediate deployment of similar methods against the Soviet consulate in Lviv: "It would be healthy also for our domestic atmosphere. Enough of being gentle with these boors, who care nothing for us and do not understand what decent manners mean, who respect only unwavering will and the fist."[29] Such a measure was not taken by the Polish side at that time, but it was taken later, in 1938. By then the Polish consulates in the Soviet Union were functioning in a prison-like environment. Their dramatic position will be described in detail later in this chapter.

---

[27] Władysław Michniewicz (1900–95) was an intelligence officer and the head of intelligence posts Kh and B.18 in Soviet Ukraine. In his book *Wielki bluff sowiecki* (Chicago: Publishing WICI, 1991), which dealt with the Trust affair, he accused, without grounds, the chief of the East Section of the Second Department, Jerzy Niezbrzycki, of being a Soviet agent.

[28] RGVA, f. 453k, op. 1, d. 2, l. 141.

[29] CAW, Oddz. II SG, doc. 14 (1936).

Meanwhile, all kinds of unpleasant incidents began to happen at the Polish consulates across the entire USSR. During Christmas 1935, two windows were broken in the consulate general in Kyiv. The offender was arrested and the official explanation given to the Polish officials was that the perpetrator was intoxicated. There were no apologies from the Soviet side, however.[30] In mid-May 1936, while the Polish consul in Kharkiv, Stanisław Sośnicki, was on leave (between May 15 and May 18 he was on a field trip in the provinces, passing through Zaporizhia, Nikopol, Kryvyi Rih, Dnipropetrovsk [now Dnipro] and Kamianske), windows at the front of the Polish consulate building were broken (in the office of the consul and in Ludwik Michałowski's apartment). Sośnicki's windows were broken by a stone, and Michałowski's by a shot from a small-caliber rifle. After his return, Sośnicki immediately intervened and sent a written note to the People's Commissariat for Foreign Affairs. On May 21, a representative of the PCfFA named Mikhailov phoned to express his regret and asked for permission to initiate an investigation. On May 22, after receiving approval from the Polish authorities, the oblast vice-prosecutor, named Lipsky, appeared, accompanied by an expert who evaluated the damage and took photographs. It should be noted that both windows at the front of the building faced Olminsky Street, which was an area constantly patrolled by police on duty. Given the harsh realities of the Stalinist police state, it was hard to imagine this to be a spontaneous act of sabotage.[31]

Other more or less serious incidents were also reported, such as the attempted arrest of embassy and consular workers on March 7, 1936. At 5:45 p.m., the courier for the Polish embassy, Jan Łagoda, arrived at the Southern Railway Station in Kharkiv after a four-hour delay, on a train traveling from Tbilisi to Moscow. The consul, Stanisław Sośnicki, and the consulate's secretary, Ludwik Michałowski (unofficially the head of intelligence post G.27), together with his wife, went to the station to give him their mail. Once the mail had been handed over, Sośnicki started heading toward the station exit. At that same moment, Michałowski, who was still standing by the train, was approached by a railway policeman, who asked him to go to the commanding officer's office. Seeing this, Sośnicki said that Michałowski was the secretary of the Polish consulate, and that he was the consul. The policeman then asked Sośnicki to go to

---

[30] Ibid. sygn. I.303.4.1867, k. 354.
[31] Ibid., k. 210.

the commanding officer's office with Michałowski. Sośnicki pointed out that it was not within the police's purview to detain him and that he did not feel obliged to comply. Sośnicki's reminder to the policeman that he was talking to the consul of a foreign power was met with the following words: "We know that you are the Polish consul" (*Eto my znaem, chto Vy polskii konsul*). Sośnicki then tried showing the policeman his consular ID, which said that he could only be stopped under a judiciary act and under special circumstances. The policeman's reply was that he did not wish to read it (*Etovo ia ne zhelaiu chitat'*). Upon hearing this, Sośnicki started heading toward the exit but was intercepted by the policeman and ordered to stop. Sośnicki's answer was that they were not going to see any commander, and in general, if they had any issues with them, they should contact them through Mikhailov, the representative of the People's Commissariat for Foreign Affairs. The policeman then left, saying that he was going to make a phone call.

The Poles, surrounded by undercover civilian agents, waited for about eight minutes for the gendarme to return. As soon as Michałowski's wife started toward the railway car in which Łagoda was seated, another gendarme summoned one of the civilian agents, pointed toward the woman, and said, "Watch this citizen, she is suspect." In the meantime, the gendarme who had gone to make a phone call returned and told the Poles they were free to go.[32] The next day Sośnicki went to Mikhailov, the PCfFA representative, to lodge a complaint about the events at the train station.[33] On March 9, 1936, he submitted a written note of protest,[34] a copy of which he forwarded to the Polish ambassador in Moscow on March 14, 1936.[35] The Polish consul was backed by the German consul in Kharkiv, named Walther, who, on March 10, 1936, personally expressed his solidarity with the Polish consulate to Mikhailov. Mikhailov's answer to both voices of protest was that there must have been a misunderstanding, that an investigation was going to be carried out, and that the perpetrators would be penalized. His answer was only verbal and not in writing, however.[36]

Several days later, on March 20, 1936, at noon, Mikhailov came to the Polish consulate with the deputy chief of Kharkiv's city council, whose

---

[32] Ibid. k. 158–61.
[33] Ibid., k. 160.
[34] Ibid., k. 159–61.
[35] Ibid., k. 158.
[36] Ibid.

name was Hekker, to express his apologies for the incident at the train station. He claimed that the leadership of the railway police was also oblivious to what had gone on and that the gendarmes had acted independently and had already been penalized. Sośnicki would not be fooled so easily. He knew that the NKVD must have orchestrated the entire incident: "As could have been predicted, the railway police and the local NKVD excused themselves by putting all the blame on the ignorance of ordinary functionaries," he wrote to the ambassador.[37]

Sośnicki's two Soviet guests assured him that such incidents would not happen again. However, one did not have to wait long for another event to occur. On March 26, 1936, another railway policeman, assisted by an undercover NKVD agent, detained Jan Kazimierczak, the consulate's chauffeur, at the Southern Railway Station in Kharkiv at 11 p.m. and told him to visit the commanding officer's office. Secretary Michałowski intervened, saying that Kazimierczak was not going anywhere because he was a member of the consular staff. Furthermore, Michałowski added, Kazimierczak was at the station on duty (they had both come to meet the acting military attaché, Major Władysław Harland, who had just arrived from Rostov). Hearing this, the functionary left the scene for a moment, and Michałowski told the chauffeur to get in the vehicle. When the gendarme came back, he asked about Kazimierczak's whereabouts, and Michałowski replied that Kazimierczak was under no circumstances going to leave the vehicle, which belonged to the consulate. Both functionaries then left the scene.[38]

Similar, more or less successful, provocations began happening on a regular basis. They were aimed at compromising the Polish personnel, "proving" that they were engaged in espionage operations and supporting their home-based subversive organizations, especially the Polish Military Organization (*Polska Organizacja Wojskowa*, POW).[39] Systematic harassment of Poles living in the USSR had already begun in 1933. Polish Communists fell victim to the first wave of purges, and subsequent waves spared no one who was of Polish nationality. The zenith of the repression came in 1937, when the NKVD implemented order no. 00485, also known as the Polish Operation.[40] Most of the sentenced

---

[37] Ibid. k. 183–84.

[38] Ibid., k. 185–86.

[39] For more details on this topic, see Kuśnierz, "Próby skompromitowania oraz werbunku," 135–48.

[40] Further discussion of this subject is in chap. 4.

Poles were charged with covert membership in the POW. Because the Soviets considered the POW a branch of the Polish Second Department, employees of Polish posts in the USSR were, by definition, suspect. Attempts were made to implicate them in various scandals. Zdzisław Miłoszewski, a clerk in the Polish consulate in Kharkiv and head of intelligence post M.13 (code name Oleg Ostrowski), reported on one such attempt. At midnight between January 1 and 2, 1935, a woman phoned the consulate asking to speak to Consul Stanisław Sośnicki. Since he was on vacation and his deputy Miłoszewski was already asleep, Miłoszewski's wife, Zofia (code name Olga Oberman, of post H.23), answered the phone. A female voice, speaking in Russian, asked whether she could come to the consulate. Miłoszewska replied that it would be possible to do so between 10 a.m. and noon the following day. Then the woman asked whether the building was surrounded by police and whether there was any security screening at the entrance door. This questioning irritated Miłoszewska, who urged the caller to cut to the chase and state her business, which was apparently so important that it justified calling in the middle of the night, adding that she considered the conversation over. Upon hearing this, the caller clearly hesitated and, after a long pause, said: "I'm not calling because of my personal business, but for political reasons. I am a member of the Polish organization. Are you in touch with them?" (*Ia, vidite, ne po lichnomu, a po politicheskomu delu, ia ot imeni polskoi organizatsii. Imeete li Vy s nei sviaz'?*) Miłoszewska then replied in Russian: "Are you crazy? Do you know who you are talking to? You are talking to an official representative of Poland. This conversation is over." (*Vy s uma spiatili, Vy znaete z kem Vy razgovarivaete? Vy govorite z ofitsialnym predstavitelem Pol'shschi. Razgovor okonchen.*) Miłoszewska hung up without waiting for a reply.

The caller was not to be intimidated so easily. She called again on January 4, insisting that she wanted to talk to the head of the post. Zdzisław Miłoszewski reported the incident to the Second Department, as follows: "Can you imagine that that woman (Pol.: *owa baba*) would not be persuaded to give it up? She called again this afternoon and again asked the operator whether the consul was back and whether our building was surrounded by police."

"It was certainly a provocation, for two reasons," concluded Miłoszewski after the event. "According to Olga [i.e., Zofia Miłoszewska], the clear hesitation of the caller was not an indication of her unwillingness to speak openly on the phone, but rather of the fact that she did not know what to say, and it was clear that she spoke only after she had received instructions from someone standing next to her. Second, it is logical that 'the Polish organization' should have known beforehand whether we had any contacts with them or not. Why would they call to ask us about it? Last but not least, this self-proclaimed Polish conspirator spoke Russian the whole time."[41]

Needless to say, the POW did not exist; it was merely a fiction spun by the Bolsheviks to help them in their persecution of the Polish people. However, this does not mean, of course, that the Polish consulates did not host any intelligence officers. The possibility of their exposure entailed serious consequences. The Albert Ran Affair was the greatest blunder to compromise Polish intelligence in the USSR in the 1930s. The aftershock had an extremely negative effect on the Polish diplomatic and consular corps. Albert Ran was a fictional name that served as a cover for Lieutenant Stefan Kasperski, who officially worked as a clerk in the Kyiv consulate. Unofficially, he was the head of intelligence post H.5. Kasperski described the exact circumstances of his exposure, his imprisonment in Moscow, and the interrogations he was subjected to in writing after he was released and returned to Poland. On August 12, 1936, in Warsaw, he wrote a 164-page report. In it he described his interrogation and detention in two Moscow jails—in a special NKVD prison and in the Butyrka prison.[42] Ran's blown cover and arrest were the perfect excuse the Bolsheviks needed to justify their long-perfected practice of surveillance of foreign diplomatic posts, which were seen as "a breeding ground for spies." The fact that an intelligence officer was hiding behind an official consular cover cast a long shadow on the operations of the Polish consulates in the USSR.

Stefan Kasperski's involvement in this scandal began quite accidentally. He was assigned to a routine duty that normally would have been carried

---

[41] CAW, Oddz. II SG, sygn. I.303.4.2012, doc. 6, n.p.; Kuśnierz, "Próby skompromitowania oraz werbunku," 138–39.

[42] CAW, Oddz. II SG, sygn., I.303.4.1974, k. 1–164. For more information about this case, see. Kuśnierz, "Afera Rana," 159–79 [I published Kasperski's report together with Piotr Kołakowski: *Afera Rana: Zatrzymanie przez sowiecki kontrwywiad por. Stefa Kasperskiego w świetle jego sprawozdania z 12 sierpnia 1936 r.* (Kraków: Avalon 2014). The official Soviet protocols of Lieutenant Stefan Kasperski's interrogations were published in J. Bednarek et al., eds., *Polska i Ukraina w latach trzydziestych–czterdziestych XX wieku: Nieznane dokumenty z archiwów służb specjalnych*, vol. 8, *Wielki Terror: operacja polska 1937–1938*, part 1 (Warsaw and Kyiv: Instytut Pamięci Narodowej, 2010), 710–83.

out by Aleksander Stpiczyński, the head of intelligence post F.8.[43] It involved nothing but picking up some intelligence materials from an agent, which Stpiczyński was unable to do because he had broken his leg after falling, intoxicated, from the consulate's window in Kyiv at 3:00 a.m. on the night of May 15–16, 1936. After receiving instructions from Michniewicz and Stpiczyński, Kasperski went to Moscow, where he met with the agent on May 28, 1936. The transfer of intelligence materials took place in the agent's apartment. After the meeting, Kasperski was arrested by the NKVD: the Moscow agent turned out to be a Soviet-provided imposter.

After Kasperski's arrest, on May 30, 1936, the Second Department ceased all operations in the USSR, until further notice.[44] This decision was revoked on September 8, 1936. The East Section justified the September decision in the following way: "We should continue our operations per usual. We should be extra careful though, because of possible provocation. Consequently, I cancel the ban on leaving your base [of operations], while maintaining the order to keep the Center posted about every single outing."[45]

Lieutenant Kasperski was a prisoner in Moscow for two months altogether. After a few days of interrogations, he admitted that he was an intelligence officer working under a false name in the consulate, but he did not betray his network. Following the nearly two months of interrogations, and after feeding the Soviets with all kinds of fabricated stories about the circumstances of his supposedly singular escapade as an intelligence liaison, Moscow decided to let Ran return home. This generosity was brought about by the fact that a Soviet spy named Sokolin had been intercepted under similar circumstances in Warsaw.[46]

---

[43] Aleksander Stpiczyński (1898–1987) was an intelligence officer. Between 1934 and 1936, he served as the head of intelligence post F.8 in Kyiv. After the Ran Affair, he was sent back to Warsaw. Later he directed some other intelligence units, e.g., in Bratislava. During the Second World War, he served as an envoy between the Home Army and the Polish government-in-exile in London. He was parachuted into Poland in 1944 and later detained in a Nazi camp in 1944 and 1945. He emigrated to Ecuador in 1945, where he stayed until 1974, when he returned to Poland. Stpiczyński wrote of his wartime experiences in his book *Wbrew wyrokowi losu* (Warsaw: Pax 1981).

[44] RGVA, f. 308k, op. 19, d. 63, l. 23.

[45] Ibid., l. 24.

[46] In a letter from the Second Department to Jan Karszo-Siedlewski on July 4, 1936, it was mentioned that an official from the Soviet consulate had been detained by Polish security forces a few days earlier. He was detained in circumstances similar to Kasperski's arrest—while picking up some intelligence materials from his informant. "This investigation is underway," wrote the author of the letter, "and we will not hesitate to

Independently of Warsaw's actions, both the embassy and the consulate general in Kyiv tried to help the detained officer. Jan Karszo-Siedlewski left for Moscow immediately once he learned about the arrest. The Soviets, still hoping to benefit from Kasperski's capture, did not allow anyone to see him. The counselor's endeavors were futile. On June 17 he wrote a report from Moscow in which he expressed his concerns about the state of Kasperski's psychological endurance and advised the center to do all it could to help by pulling some strings in Warsaw and Lviv.

Back at home, Polish intelligence upped the ante, which led to Sokolin's arrest. At the same time, the Second Department insisted that the military attaché, Lieutenant Colonel Konstanty Zaborowski, should put some pressure on Counselor Tadeusz Jankowski, and on the ambassador himself, to "strengthen their resolve to issue a calm but determined and measured statement."[47] During this time, the NKVD was well aware of the unambiguous success they had achieved thanks to Kasperski's arrest. They wanted to push the investigation in the direction of identifying as many of his colleagues as possible. When Karszo-Siedlewski was in Moscow trying to intervene to help Ran, Aleksander

---

make sure it wins a lot of publicity, which might hurt our friends [i.e., the Soviets], because the little tasks mentioned in the [intercepted] materials are not something to be proud of and, if published, could throw a lot of light on the activities of the so-called Soviet diplomats. We are inclined, nevertheless, to settle the issue. Negotiations are well underway." On the same day, the Second Department sent a letter to Tadeusz Jankowski, ambassadorial counselor, detailing the circumstances in which Sokolin was arrested: "Sokolin behaved extremely inappropriately and the security forces were not happy with it; they accused him of refusing to obey legitimate authority. According to the judge, the case is unambiguous. We conclude that the Soviet side feels awfully embarrassed due to the nature of the tasks [disclosed]. The Soviet embassy has intervened vigorously. Sokolin put forth outlandish demands. I am hereby attaching a copy of one of his letters (needless to say: undelivered) to the Soviet embassy for the counselor's and the ambassador's exclusive information." (The attachments could not be found in the archive.) According to Colonel Stefan Mayer, Polish counterintelligence had known about Sokolin for at least a year. They had made earlier plans to catch him red-handed and label him a persona non grata. Fortunately they decided to wait and then use Sokolin's exposure to the greatest possible benefit at the most desirable moment, which happened after Ran's arrest. See AAN, SG, sygn. IV, n.p. doc. 40; Kuśnierz, "Afera Rana," 173–74; M. Kwiecień and G. Mazur, "Wykłady pułkownika Stefana Mayera o wywiadzie polskim w okresie II RP," *Zeszyty Historyczne* 142 (2002): 127.

[47] It was also underscored that Zaborowski should not betray his interest in this case to outside observers, who could potentially blame him for it. It was particularly stressed that, during critical moments, the coded letters should not be mailed from the attaché's office, but from the Foreign Ministry. AAN, SG, sygn. IV/8, doc. 7, n. p.

Stpiczyński, who was hospitalized at the time, was visited by an NKVD officer. The unexpected visit took place on June 15, 1936. The officer, who claimed he knew Stpiczyński a long time ago, was trying to use this alleged old acquaintance to blackmail Stpiczyński with some compromising materials about his private life. Stpiczyński was not impressed. On his next visit, on June 18, the Soviet agent tried to make him believe that "an influential organization" had told the agent that Albert Ran had testified against Stpiczyński in Moscow and that this could lead to very unpleasant consequences, including the permanent detention of Stpiczyński in the USSR. The officer promised that as soon as Stpiczyński began co-operating, everything could be smoothed over, or even bring him some real gains. Before saying goodbye, the officer said he would let Stpiczyński consider things until 10:00 a.m. on June 20, the time of his next visit.

Karszo-Siedlewski returned from Moscow on June 18. Stpiczyński told him all about the hospital incident. The counselor wanted to meet the inquisitive NKVD agent himself and arrived at Stpiczyński's hospital bed half an hour before the officer's scheduled arrival on June 20. After waiting an hour by Stpiczyński's bed, Karszo-Siedlewski left the building. His final advice to his colleague was to inform the NKVD agent that the consul ordered him not to speak to strangers. Immediately after Karszo-Siedlewski's departure, the stranger showed up at the patient's bed and was told exactly what the consul recommended. He then left, saying that he saw unpleasant consequences awaiting Stpiczyński in the near future.

After his wife's return to Kyiv on June 21, Stpiczyński was transferred to the consulate building. One day later, Jan Karszo-Siedlewski went to see Adolf Petrovsky, the representative of the PCfFA. He expressed his outrage at the hospital incident and even compared it to the infamous practices of the tsarist police. The Polish diplomat was under the impression that Petrovsky must have been unaware of the incident. The Soviet official initially tried to play down the event's significance, but after more pressure from his Polish interlocutor, he promised to take care of it, adding that he considered such behavior toward an ill person "despicable." Karszo-Siedlewski concluded that, in his eyes, the matter was unambiguously condemnable and called for a strong reaction from the Soviet side. He was merely doing his duty by bringing this issue to the attention of the PCfFA's representative.

The hospital incident sharpened Karszo-Siedlewski's sense of urgency in trying to obtain access to the imprisoned Stefan Kasperski. The counselor suspected that Kasperski had already been blackmailed with news of Stpiczyński's alleged denunciation. In a letter to the ambassador on June 24, 1936, Karszo-Siedlewski suggested that if a meeting with Kasperski could somehow be secured, it would be necessary to ("casually") mention to him that Stpiczyński was still ill and had long been confined to his bed in his own room in the consulate. This information would presumably reassure Kasperski that his colleague could not have divulged any information to the NKVD.

As we know, no meeting with Kasperski was allowed. However, the reports of Kasperski's investigation do not indicate that he was blackmailed by Stpiczyński's fabricated confessions. Nonetheless the Second Department asked Karszo-Siedlewski (in a letter from July 4, 1936) to send Stpiczyński back to Warsaw as soon as possible. The version manufactured for public consumption had it that the quality of health care in the USSR was poor, making it necessary for Stpiczyński to return home for treatment. The center requested that someone from the consulate should assist Stpiczyński to get to the border and prevent a potential provocation.[48]

After the Polish officer made it back home, the Second Department built on the new lessons learned from the Ran Affair. On August 7, 1936, a detailed instruction was compiled that specified what sort of behavior was expected of Polish officers if they are detained abroad. The following points were included in the report:

1. It is prohibited to carry anything that could betray the true identity of the officer (anything with a signature, e.g., a book, a document, a letter, anything with a personal inscription). Failure to obey this order would amount to a betrayal of official secrecy and would be penalized with all severity. This clause extends to family members and anyone else who visited or was hosted by the officer.

2. It is prohibited to carry any photographs of family members or close friends, whose recognition could lead to exposure.

3. External layers of clothing should have as few pockets as possible. When leaving public or other unsecured establishments where the owner had to leave his garments out of sight, it is recommended to discreetly check all the pockets. If something unusual is found, the nearest cloakroom attendant or police officer should be informed. It is categorically prohibited to sign any external statements or check the contents of unidentified packages.

---

[48] Kuśnierz, "Afera Rana," 175–78.

4. When leaving the workplace, either alone or with family members, particularly if with women, all pockets should be checked before exiting. It is specifically prohibited to take any personal belongings (notebooks, correspondence, any notes regardless of their content) apart from absolutely necessary documents and cash.

5. When at an unsecured establishment, never accept any books, packages, or items that can be used as a cache for invisible and undesirable contents. Request their delivery to the workplace, or (if impossible) send a lower-ranking officer to pick them up, but only after a thorough examination.

6. Never sign any statements, even if only as a witness of some incident in town, or any other written reports requested by security functionaries after private apartment searches.

7. All written materials, books, or documents should be received only at one's workplace. Under special circumstances, if the source's content appears significant enough, pick-up locations should be chosen outside towns and residential spaces, but never in a dense forest, by a fence, a ditch, or an abandoned building. In case of such special pick-up arrangements, the highest level of caution must be observed. The meeting can only take place if the officer is absolutely convinced that he has not been followed. Under no circumstances can pick-up meetings take place in publicly accessible spaces, private apartments, or the street.

8. If stopped in the street, do not enter any gates, apartments, shops, or offices, even if requested politely. If an arrest is imminent, it would be better to take place in the street. Protest against an arrest should be vocal and resolute, but peaceful. High caution is advised against any attempt to slip something [into your clothing or belongings] during the arrest.

9. If caught red-handed, categorically refuse to give any verbal testimony. If requested to identify yourself, do nothing apart from showing ID.

10. Refuse to sign any statements, depositions, or receipts. Not one signature of the detainee should make it into the records of the local authorities. The only recommended strategy is to write administrative grievances, complaints, and other protests against poor treatment while demanding to be seen by a doctor and to be kept in better accommodations.

11. Answer all questions verbally only (refuse to submit any written accounts): for example, "I do not know anything," "no," "I will say nothing," "I don't remember."

12. Do not participate in any discussions, even if they might seem reasonable. Anyone who agrees to start a discussion is already half-ready to plead guilty, because no discussion can be beneficial for the detainee.

Under such circumstances, one should not be arrogant. Do not believe that the other side can be outsmarted. There are no known precedents.

13. When presented by the authorities with some unambiguously negative evidence or when confronted with a witness, moral blackmail, or torture, stick to the original position and do not change [your] testimony under the influence of new developments. It has to be kept in mind that the other side will attempt to surprise the detainee by claims or facts that are unverified and uncertain to the investigators themselves.

14. The will not to betray any secrets must be unshakeably watertight. No details or circumstances, however immaterial, can be shared or confirmed. [Maintain] silence, silence, and silence yet again.

15. It must be kept in mind that the other side will not refrain from anything in order to weaken the will to resist; to undermine trust in one's own strength, as well as trust in the homeland authorities and their ability to intervene; to break the ideological backbone; [and] to convince the accused of his own guilt and the overall hopelessness of his situation.

16. Verbal and psychological arguments interrogators use will be, in principle, false. Never trust a word from them. Do not betray, by words or behavior, any sign of interest in or awareness of anything presented by the authorities.

17. It must be kept in mind that the homeland authorities will do everything and will neglect no avenue to get the officer out of trouble, but this confidence should not be displayed in front of the other side. Do not set yourself any imaginary deadlines. Treat the entire detainment experience as if you were a prisoner of war indefinitely, meaning that no confessions whatsoever are allowed.

18. Stay calm and dignified, [and] do not become hysterical or provoke the other side by assuming an unnecessarily arrogant stance or with insults or threats. Use every opportunity to protest calmly and firmly against mistreatment, use of force, and bad accommodations or food, and to request medical help, walks, or books.

19. When experiencing a moral or psychological breakdown, watch carefully whether it is not caused by poor health, especially by digestive issues. Do not think about the future and your own fate. Refrain from negative thoughts about loved ones, remembering that all information from the other side is, in principle, false and provocative.

20. Make sure to fill every moment with meaningful activity. Do not refrain from even the most strenuous kind of physical work. Stay fit and

active. Memorize any books available, regardless of their content. Translate them into foreign languages. Solve some math problems.

21. Never try to foresee what might happen at the next interrogation. Do not try to conjure any defensive postures, especially of a theatrical kind. One can be assured that the proceedings will unfold in an absolutely unpredictable way.

22. Keep in mind that a "giveaway" or a "slip-up" is always a possibility, given the nature of our profession. It should be approached as an unpleasant but nonetheless natural and explicable by-product, just like a wound or being captured in battle. Accordingly, behavior during detention must not make things worse. If carried out well, it can in fact be life-saving. It should be based on the following principles:

- do not prattle; stay silent;
- take everything patiently and with dignity;
- do not lose faith in the possibility of a positive outcome.

23. When being released (whether as part of an exchange or not), do protest vehemently, mention all kinds of bad treatment, moral blackmail or torture, poor conditions, harassment, and complain about all possible ailments, etc.

The report concluded with a statement warning officers against any breach of these stipulations and other rules of secrecy; such a breach would be punished severely. It was emphasized that one always had to stay on the alert with respect to oneself and to family members. Stay natural and calm, the center advised, remembering who one is and that one does nothing beyond what is stated in the official documents, and that one stays on good terms with the local authorities. Keep in mind that one's fate is, in the final analysis, in the hands of the team leader—in this case, the consul. Only being an exemplary official can save one from troubles. Such an attitude was often lacking among the consular rank and file, complained the authors of the report: "No altercations or frictions are acceptable, neither are 'becoming independent,' childish ambitions, arrogant manners, and so on, because it is precisely the wrong kind of individualism on the part of an official that leads to his exposure. No 'sanctity' of private, independent life is acceptable; foreign service should be approached as a duty of war; and thus, any talk about a thick line separating 'work' and 'private' hours is a breach of honor and duty, as well as unpardonable childishness."[49]

---

[49] See CAW, Oddz. II SG, sygn. I.303.4.1956, n.p. doc. 1; and sygn. I.303.4.1989, b.p., doc. 123.

On August 21, 1936, the Center dispatched a message to its agents abroad that recapitulated "a few characteristic moments of Ran's case." The document listed the following points: (1) He was arrested on the street while carrying secret files. They were hidden under his clothes and so could not be thrown away just before the arrest. (2) The contact was an imposter, which was the cause for the slip-up. (3) The interrogations were normal, with no physical compulsion. The prison conditions, both in terms of cells and food, were very good. (4) He received food, money, and daily essentials via the Red Cross. (5) Ran did not betray our network. (6) He spent in all two months in prison.[50]

In the aftermath of the Ran Affair, Władysław Michniewicz lost his job. In a letter to the head of intelligence post B.18, written on July 24, 1936, Jerzy Niezbrzycki wrote that Michniewicz's dismissal was because of organizational and technical reasons. His duties were to be taken over by Stanisław Nawrocki from Minsk, who was scheduled to arrive in Kyiv on August 1, 1936.[51] Nawrocki actually began his service at post E.15 on August 15, 1936. He worked there until the end of April 1937. Lieutenant Kasperski retired in late March 1938.[52]

1.2. Under Yezhov's Bloody Reign[53]

Nikolai Yezhov's term at the helm of the NKVD coincided with the most violent phase of the purges. Any conceivable enemy of Communism could become a victim. Anyone who had something to do with the *ancien régime*, anyone who was a member of "the wrong" prerevolutionary social class, anyone who belonged to a national minority (considered "the fifth column" by the Bolsheviks) was under threat. This policy entailed that any

---

[50] Ibid., sygn. I. 303.4.1967, n.p., doc. 99. For an identical letter to the Kjd post, see ibid., sygn. I.303.4.1989, n.p., doc. 129.

[51] Ibid., sygn. I.303.4.1927, b.p. doc. 238.

[52] Ibid., sygn. 1769/89/2205, Akta personalne Stefana Kasperskiego, b.p.; and Pepłoński, *Wywiad polski na ZSSR*, 123. ," 117–51.

[53] Sizable portions of this section were published in a volume dealing with Polish diplomacy in the East: see Kuśnierz, "Funkcjonowanie polskich placówek," 374–403. Note that Iwona Urbańska and Sławomir Nowinowski have also (preliminarily) analyzed this topic: see Urbańska, "Ambasada Rzeczypospolitej Polskiej," 95–107; and Nowinowski, "Specyfika funkcjonowania polskich placówek," 121–39. Additional information can also be found in some publications detailing the operations of the Moscow embassy and Ambassador Wacław Grzybowski: Kruszyński, *Ambasada RP*, passim; Kornat, "Ambasador Wacław Grzybowski," 5–80; and Kornat, "Posłowie i ambasadorzy polscy," 117–51.

representatives of foreign powers—especially of those states thought to be potential opponents in a future war, such as Germany, Japan, Italy, or Poland—were by definition enemies, and their diplomatic posts in the USSR "a breeding ground for spies." On October 28, 1937, the NKVD issued order no. 00698, "On combating counterrevolutionary, terrorist, subversive activity of the personnel of the embassies and consulates of Germany, Japan, Italy, and Poland." It envisaged an intensified level of surveillance of the representatives of the four countries. All Soviet citizens who were in touch with foreign consulates and embassies (of all countries, not just those four) were to be arrested, and accessibility of other Soviet citizens to foreign institutions was to be reduced to the lowest possible level.[54]

Representatives of these four countries suffered the most, both before and after the decree,[55] but operational conditions for all other foreign representatives also left plenty to be desired. The Soviets aimed to limit their number to a bare minimum and to restrict their focus primarily to the embassies located in Moscow. Those few bold adventurers scattered around "the country of workers and peasants" were heavily monitored and practically isolated, which rendered anything resembling normal work impossible. On November 24, 1937, George F. Kennan, who worked at the European Desk of the US State Department at the time, put together a report titled *The Position of an American Ambassador in Moscow*, based on the experiences of two ambassadors, William Bullitt and Joseph Davis. In the report, Kennan wrote that it was (unspoken but clear) Soviet policy to make the life of foreign representatives as miserable as possible: "The Soviet leaders appear to welcome the presence of foreign envoys in Moscow as something contributory to Soviet prestige; but they make it very evident that, in their opinion, these envoys—like well-trained children—should be seen and not heard."[56]

---

[54] N. Petrov and M. Jansen, *"Stalinskii Pitomets"—Nikolai Yezhov* (Moscow: ROSSPEN, 2008), 109.

[55] See L. P. Belkovets, *"Bolshoi terror" i sud'by nemetskoi derevni v Sibiri (konets 1920tykh–1930tie gody)* (Moscow: IVKD, 1995), 236–70; and L. Belkovets and S. Belkovets, "Konsul'skie otnosheniia Germanii i Sibiri w 1920–1930-e gg.," in V. Molodin et al., eds., *Nemetskii etnos w Sibiri* (Novosibirsk: Izdatelstvo Novosibirskogo universiteta, 1999), 75–79.

[56] United States Department of State, *Foreign Relations of the United States: Diplomatic Papers; The Soviet Union 1933–1939*, ed. E. R. Perkins (Washington, DC: Government Printing Office, 1952), 446.

There were two ways of reducing the number of foreign posts in the USSR. The official channel was to formally request that the "surplus" number of consulates be eliminated.[57] The unofficial practice revolved around making everyday living conditions so impossibly difficult that any normal diplomatic work was out of the question. Needless to say, such conditions not only quickly demotivated the foreign representatives, but also made them actively seek a way out of the USSR.

The quality of life of foreign diplomats in the specific country called the USSR always differed from what they could expect in civilized countries. However, the kinds of "excesses" the Soviet security apparatus engaged in regularly during the Great Terror were not only far beyond any notion of diplomatic *savoir-vivre*, but could only be called sheer barbarism. Foreign posts, especially those of the countries considered hostile, were subject to all kinds of harassment. The more ordinary kinds of treatment included disturbances in food provisioning and newspaper delivery, or property damage (broken windows). The more serious ones went as far as physical violence, intimidation and threats, public insults, or brazen attempts at recruitment through blackmail or corruption. All posts, including even those of the more respected countries such as the United States, France, or Great Britain, operated in total isolation from local society and authorities. All of these measures, as has been emphasized, were aimed at eliminating the "surplus" number of foreign posts and at minimizing the operations of the surviving branches. On August 23, 1937, the head of the Polish consulate general in Kyiv, Jan Karszo-Siedlewski, remarked on what he saw around him: "My general impression is that the Soviet authorities have initiated a systematic campaign of provocation aimed at inciting conflict and eliminating foreign consulates in the USSR."[58]

How difficult the situation of Polish diplomats and consular officials in the Soviet Union was is reflected in an accurate observation by Stanisław Zabiełło, head of the Soviet section in the Polish Ministry of Foreign Affairs (MFA), who had earlier worked in Moscow: "The day is nigh when deploying an official or a clerk to the USSR will equal sending him to a penal colony in Siberia." Zabiełło had no doubt that using the

---

[57] Given these methods, the Polish side was forced to close down two consulates in 1937, in Kharkiv and Tbilisi.

[58] CAW, Oddz. II SG, sygn. I.303.4.1867, k. 613.

word "catastrophic" was not an exaggeration of what the Polish diplomats faced in the USSR.[59]

After the war, Colonel Stefan Mayer, a Polish intelligence chief in the 1930s, painted a similar picture of work in the East:[60] "The fate of the Foreign Ministry officials [deployed in the USSR] was not something to be envied; it would not be an exaggeration to say that they were sentenced to hard labor in 'a penal colony' that titled itself the Union of Soviet Socialist Republics. On the one hand, they were expected to deliver increasingly detailed information about the country of their 'exile,' and on the other hand they were greeted with increasingly malicious harassment, difficulties, and provocations by their hosts."[61] The German ambassador in Moscow, Hans von Herwarth, jotted down an interesting remark. In his memoirs, he quoted the newly arrived diplomat from Berlin, Herbert von Mumm, who, after familiarizing himself with the conditions prevailing in the USSR, exclaimed: "It is better to be a lavatory attendant on Unter der Linden street in Berlin, than a high counselor in the Moscow embassy!"[62]

In the second half of the 1930s, several distinct phases in the performance of Polish diplomatic and consular posts in the USSR can be identified: "the usual inconveniences" that were the reality for "state workers and peasants"; the intensification of Soviet harassment after late October 1937; a retaliatory period from July 18 to August 21, 1938; and then a return to the starting point, that is, to the pre-retaliatory period before July 1938.

1.2.1. The Dispute about the Provincial Press

The mildest form of harassment was the failure to deliver, often with ludicrous excuses, the usual batch of local newspapers to foreign

---

[59] AAN, MSZ, sygn. 6755 A, k. 109.

[60] Stefan Antoni Mayer (1895–1981) was an officer in the Second Department for many years. Between 1923 and 1924 and between 1926 and 1928, he headed Branch no. 1 of the Second Department in Vilnius. For the next two years, he worked as head of Second Department "B" (Counterintelligence), and between 1930 and 1939 he headed Second Department "A" (Intelligence). During the Second World War, Mayer also served as commander of an intelligence school in Glasgow, UK. He remained an émigré after the war. See Kwiecień and Mazur, "Wykłady pułkownika," 81–83; and T. Gajownik, "Pierwsze lata kariery Stefana Antoniego Mayera jako oficera polskiego wywiadu: Przyczynek do biografii," *Echa Przeszłości*, 2009, no. 10: 277–86.

[61] Kwiecień and Mazur, "Wykłady pułkownika," 119–20.

[62] H. von Herwarth, *Miedzy Hitlerem a Stalinem. Wspomnienia dyplomaty i oficera niemieckiego 1931–1945* (Warsaw: Bellona, 1992), 101–2.

representatives. On July 31, 1937, for example, the Chernihiv branch of Soiuzpechat' informed the Polish consulate general in Kyiv that, due to an "enormous increase in demand" for the local press among the citizenry of Chernihiv oblast (a sudden spike in subscriptions), they were compelled, beginning on August 1, to stop delivering their publications beyond the boundaries of the oblast. A return of 12,50 rubles for "*nevypolnennyi zakaz*," failure to deliver on the subscription order, came with the message.[63] Jan Karszo-Siedlewski wrote a note protesting the decision to the representative of the PCfFA, requesting he intervene.[64]

In early September 1937 the Kyiv branch of Soiuzpechat' refused to deliver many of the provincial newspapers to the Polish consulate, arguing that the Poles were late with their payments by a few days. Until that point there had never been any problems with similar delayed payments. The head of the consulate general notified the deputy representative of the PCfFA, Vladimir Neverovich, who replied after a few days that it was acceptable to renew the subscription of the oblast press, but it was impossible with respect to the raion press (raion being the administrative subunit within an oblast). To justify his decision, Neverovich referred to a recent decree that specified that the raion press could only be delivered to those subscribers who lived within the boundaries of their raion. The Polish consulate could not be exempted from this rule. In response, Karszo-Siedlewski asked the Polish ambassador to intervene with the Moscow PCfFA or through the Polish MFA, which was in a position to threaten the Soviet embassy in Warsaw and the consulate in Lviv with similar sanctions: "I fear that if we give way now, then our posts in the USSR will be deprived of the oblast press in the near future. Perhaps they will eventually stop delivering even the Moscow press, for which a suitable excuse can easily be found."[65]

Other forms of "benign" harassment were the sorts of "episodic" incidents that were more common especially in the preceding period. They usually included property damage—typically a window broken with a stone thrown by "an unidentified perpetrator."

---

[63] CAW. Oddz. II SG, sygn. I. 303.4.1867, k. 622–23.
[64] Ibid., k. 619–20.
[65] Ibid. k. 640–41.

1.2.2. The Consulates in Isolation: Potential Applicants Discouraged from Visiting

Another way of making functioning more difficult for the Polish (and just about all other foreign)[66] posts was to reduce the number of visitors to a bare minimum. The Soviet authorities always looked with suspicion at those of their citizens who were interested in staying in touch with the "capitalists." Consequently the number of such contacts was effectively reduced through all forms of harassment, from interrogations to arrests to prison sentences for espionage. As noted in the first part of this chapter, as the Stalinist purges and terror grew in intensity, regular Soviet citizens became increasingly hesitant about contacting foreign diplomatic posts, fearing arrest. During the Yezhovshchina period the situation further deteriorated. In late October 1937 the consulate general in Kyiv informed Warsaw that virtually no Poles were visiting the post on personal business. All who had continued any form of contact with foreign consulates had either been either arrested or deported.[67]

In the late 1930s the number of Soviet citizens visiting a foreign post fell dramatically. Those who did come often turned out to be provocateurs offering espionage services. The Soviet authorities attempted to blemish the reputation of the Polish posts by trying to implicate them in espionage scandals. In March 1937 the consulate general in Kyiv received a letter

---

[66] On September 20, 1937, the American chargé d'affaires, Loy Henderson, wrote to the secretary of state about the anti-foreigners campaign: "Although the American Embassy is probably permitted to have more contacts with Soviet citizens that any other diplomatic mission, with the exception of the Spanish Embassy and perhaps the Lithuanian Legation, nevertheless during the last few months one by one most of the few Soviet citizens who from time to time have been willing to see members of the Embassy staff have either pointedly avoided continuing their relationships or have reluctantly stated that because of certain developments they must sever all relations with foreigners. Several of them have frankly stated that they have been questioned by the police with regard to their motives for having anything to do with foreigners. The Soviet employees of this Mission state in confidence that their position is gradually becoming worse. Their former friends avoid seeing them for fear that they themselves may be charged with engaging indirectly in espionage. Although only two of them have been arrested during the last year, a number of them to the knowledge of the Mission are summoned to the police from time to time for questioning. The husbands of two Soviet employees of the Mission have been arrested as well as relatives of others. In each case it is emphasized by the Soviet authorities that the arrests have nothing to do with the American Embassy. … Soviet language teachers, hairdressers, and athletic instructors who have had contacts with foreigners have also been arrested" (United States Department of State, *Foreign Relations*, 392).

[67] CAW, Oddz. II SG, sygn. I.303.4.1867, k. 676.

from one Petr Savich Brin.[68] The young man introduced himself as an
enemy of the Soviet state and a resident of Kyiv who worked in a local
military factory. He offered to share some valuable information about his
factory with the Polish authorities. In the letter Brin claimed that he was
not a provocateur, that everything he wrote was the result of his own
initiative, and that he was well aware of what awaited him if he was
discovered. He proposed that if the consul was interested in learning more
about him, he should send a reply within three days, no later than on
March 16. The consul's reply should indicate where the meeting was going
to take place, Brin wrote, whether at the consulate or elsewhere. Stanisław
Nawrocki, the head of intelligence post E.15 (code name Narcyz
Napiórkowski), had no doubt that Brin's letter was a provocation. He sent
a copy of Brin's letter to the Second Department, with the comment that
"this letter seems to be exemplary of the tools of trade deployed by the
local GPU [sic]. This letter, as well as the recently very frequent attempts
at provocation performed by some applicants in person, might indicate a
very strong interest in compromising our local office."[69]

Returning to the methods Soviet authorities employed to isolate
foreign posts: On August 5, 1937, the head of the Polish consulate general
in Kyiv wrote a report titled "On Isolating Foreign Posts in Soviet
Ukraine."[70] In it he indicated that the process of isolating Soviet citizens
from foreigners "has progressed disturbingly quickly" over the previous
two months, even when considering the fact that the Bolsheviks had
always sought to make it difficult for Soviet citizens to get in touch with
foreigners. The arrests of Tukhachevsky, Yakir, Postyshev, Balytsky, and
others who pleaded guilty of plotting with foreign intelligence services
had a direct influence on this policy, according to the author. In the end,
it resulted in a state of near panic among both Soviet citizens and officials,
who did all they could to avoid being in contact with foreign "strangers."[71]
Karszo-Siedlewski wrote about his own post in Kyiv in the following way:
"All of us, without exception, are considered to be thinly disguised spies,
any contact with whom is not merely undesirable, but simply dangerous.
It was never exactly safe in the past, but at least those persons who had a
legitimate reason to reach out to us—due to their representative,

---

[68] The last name Brin is mentioned twice in the letter's copy; once the last name used instead
is Brenk.

[69] CAW, Oddz. II SG, sygn. I.303.4.1956, n.p., doc. 87.

[70] Ibid., sygn. I.303.4.1867, k. 700–706.

[71] Ibid., k. 701.

bureaucratic, or artistic background—could do so relatively freely. After the recent [show] trials, those reasons are no longer sufficient. No one is free from suspicion. The local people prefer to stay on the safe side and avoid us as if we were plague-stricken. They will not even nod slightly to greet us in the streets, [for] nothing should betray that they know us. Even our old acquaintances among the barbers, manicurists, shop attendants, booksellers, or waiters prefer not to talk to us at all."[72]

The position of the Polish consulate, as well as the German one, was made worse by Soviet propaganda, which claimed that Poland and Germany were both readying themselves to attack the USSR. The press constantly advised the public to be on the alert against foreign spies.[73] Jan Karszo-Siedlewski also noticed the increasingly discernible tendency of the authorities not only to make it more difficult for him and his professional colleagues to get by, but also to bar them from any sources of information, which the ban on free circulation of the press exemplified.[74]

Another problem for his consulate, wrote Karszo-Siedlewski, was the illness of Petrovsky, the representative of the PCfFA, who at least understood, to some extent, the specifics of consular work. He also enjoyed some respect from the Kyiv authorities. "His successor, Neverovich, comes from Moscow. He is inexperienced, unacquainted with the highly specific Ukrainian environment, [and] without any friendships or clout among the local politicians. His one answer to all of our complaints is that he will have to ask Moscow,"[75] concluded the head of the Polish consulate general.

The situation for other Polish posts was also deplorable.[76] How grave this was is clear from the fact that members of the Moscow diplomatic

---

[72] Ibid., k. 702.

[73] Ibid. The subject of propaganda is discussed in chap. 6.

[74] Ibid., sygn. I.303.4.1867, k. 703.

[75] Ibid. k. 706.

[76] Witold Okoński, head of the Polish consulate general in Minsk, informed Ambassador Grzybowski that the very existence of his post was now threatened. His post no longer received the local newspapers. During the previous six weeks not a single applicant had come to visit, not even any of those who used to visit the consulate regularly to ask for support. Okoński also complained of the intolerable level of surveillance (on foot, through eavesdropping, by car, etc.). The diplomat's requests to obtain a pass to visit Poland were only processed after one to two weeks, and other (related to living conditions) requests, only after serious delays. One of the doctors who served at the consulate on a regular basis suddenly announced that from that point on he would come in only after receiving

corps considered issuing a joint communiqué addressed to the Soviet authorities. Jan Szembek, the undersecretary of state in the MFA between 1933 and 1939, wrote the following in his notes after a conversation with Ambassador Wacław Grzybowski which took place in late December 1937: "This measure could turn out to be of some impact, especially since it is precisely joint statements that the *Narkomindel* [the Soviet Foreign Ministry] does not want to see. Thus far, however, there is no unanimity on this issue within the international diplomatic corps; particularly problematic is the soft line taken by the French ambassador, Mr. Coulondre."[77]

Under such circumstances, consular trips within the region became much more strenuous. The NKVD followed the Polish consular personnel at every step. On August 5, 1937, Karszo-Siedlewski complained that their business trips did not lead to the results they expected. In the past, an NKVD vehicle had followed the consular vehicle at a certain distance; now it stayed directly behind it. Anyone they approached during the trip, even if merely to ask for directions, was immediately questioned by the NKVD. The NKVD began following not only the higher-ranking officers, but even the janitors and chauffeurs. "When in a theater or a cinema, we usually have a few guardians surrounding us on all sides, the better to hear our conversations."[78]

Tadeusz Brzeziński, the Polish consul in Kharkiv, also wrote to the ambassador complaining about the growing isolation of his post. The Soviet authorities made it very difficult, he wrote, for Polish observers to leave their office and visit the outside world—a factory, for example. In practice, such visits were virtually impossible. It was similarly difficult to organize a field trip: "the local authorities met on the way are either dead scared when they meet a foreigner, or so suspicious that their help on the spot is normally reduced to buying us a ticket ... outbound."[79]

According to Adam Koch, the Polish vice-consul in Kyiv, the period between November 4 and 10, 1937 (the twentieth anniversary of the

---

permission from a representative of the PCfFA. In stores clerks refused to sell items to consulate workers, claiming that they had already been sold. Okoński asked the embassy to intervene, because, he stressed, if similar harassments were to continue, the operations of the posts would be futile. Ibid., k. 1060–1062.

[77] Jan Szembek, *Diariusz i teki Jana Szembeka (1935–1945)*, vol. 3 *(1937)*, ed. T. Komarnicki (London: Polish Research Center, 1969), 233.

[78] CAW, Oddz. II SG, sygn. I.303.4.1867, k. 703.

[79] Ibid., k. 276.

October Revolution), was one of the worst times in terms of the Soviet policy of isolation. NKVD vehicles kept on driving by day and night and followed behind Polish personnel by just a few meters. When one of the Poles directly asked why the NKVD was incessantly following him, he received the reply, "we cannot vouch for the mood of the masses." The same applied to the practice of "snooping on foot." Vice-consul Koch went for a walk through a local market, only to find himself surrounded by three NKVD agents, two on each side and one right behind him. Soviet "supervision" became physically invasive in a literal sense: the agents followed hard on the heels of the Polish employees. The vice-consul complained that all protest was in vain. After November 11 the surveillance level returned to "normal." The consulate's doorman was forbidden to enter the consulate's building, which meant that his wages had to be paid on the spot—right at the gate.[80]

1.2.3. Violence and Provocations

In addition to the more mundane inconveniences described above—which, after all, characterized the entire Soviet world of that period—more serious incidents took place as well. On May 24, 1937, Feliks Tadeusz Haczyński, a correspondent for the Polish Telegraph Agency (PTA) in Moscow, and Jan Łagoda, the deputy economic counselor of the Polish embassy in Moscow, together with their chauffeur, Edward Brabec, a citizen of Czechoslovakia, were physically assaulted on their return journey from Kyiv to Moscow.

After hearing of the incident, Karszo-Siedlewski, together with Ludwik Michałowski, headed immediately to Chernihiv. During his absence, on May 25, the deputy representative of the PCfFA (Adolf Petrovsky was ill) visited the consulate to express his regrets about the incident. According to Karszo-Siedlewski, it made no sense to discuss this issue with the Ukrainian authorities, since it was certainly "Moscow's doing," as he put it in a letter to the ambassador. This was why he merely informed the representative of the PCfFA of the incident and, while there, also announced that he was leaving immediately for Chernihiv to see his injured colleagues. "I am absolutely certain that the assault must have been designed and prepared at Moscow's instigation. I do not think that the local authorities in Kyiv would dare to do something that serious on their own. The execution was extremely primitive and unprofessional,

---

[80] Ibid., k. 655–56.

which goes against the hypothesis of a robbery-motivated assault. Based on the event's details, it is possible to assume that the assault was an attempt at intimidation, both with respect to Editor Haczyński, whom the Soviet authorities wanted to see finished in Moscow, and with respect to Counselor Łagoda, whom they wanted to dissuade from traveling through the Soviet Union once and for all. Furthermore I perceive this incident as another manifestation of the Soviet desire to isolate foreigners from [Soviet] society and to prevent [these] foreigners—but particularly foreign representatives—from familiarizing themselves with the quality of life prevailing in the USSR, particularly in the countryside and the borderlands."[81]

The details of the incident were first reported by Haczyński in a statement typed in the presence of Karszo-Siedlewski,[82] and then by Łagoda in his letter to the Eastern Department of the Polish MFA.[83] The two Poles and the Czechoslovak citizen reported seeing a GAZ truck parked sideways across the street, with twelve to fourteen people inside, around 8:00 p.m. ninety-nine kilometers from Kyiv and forty-four kilometers from Chernihiv. Haczyński, who was driving, had to stop their car, because the truck made it impossible to continue on. The passengers in the Polish car did not expect anything bad to happen because they were used to seeing roadwork and similar trucks filled with workers on the Kyiv-Chernihiv and Moscow-Kyiv highways. Earlier some road workers had even helped the Poles pull their vehicle out of the mud. However, when the people whom Haczyński and Łagoda initially considered to be workers started running toward their car, they realized that both the attire and the overall appearance of those men did not resemble those of a worker. The men opened all of the car's doors and demanded that an allegedly ill companion be taken to a hospital in Chernihiv. Haczyński explained that there was no room in the car because it was already overloaded, and he advised the men to use the NKVD vehicle following his car, but to no avail. Initially both the Poles and the Czechoslovak citizen were called names. When Brabec stepped out to explain once again that the car was overloaded, the assailants began beating and strangling him. Seeing this, Haczyński also stepped out of the car to allow the men to use it, only to be assaulted and beaten as well. Haczyński and Łagoda,

[81] Ibid., k. 671-672.

[82] Ibid., k. 673-678.

[83] AAN, SG, sygn. IV/8, doc. 10, n.p.

who meanwhile had been dragged out of the car, wanted to call out for help, but then he noticed that the NKVD car that normally followed fifty or sixty meters behind them had suddenly disappeared.

The victims' ordeal lasted for about fifteen minutes. They were beaten with clubs and other heavy objects. Their car was heavily damaged. Łagoda wrote about what happened to him: "I was assaulted by four bandits. Two of them attempted to twist my arms, but I resisted. At the same time, all kinds of blows fell upon me. They targeted my head, face, and diaphragm. Suddenly, one of them yelled, 'strangle him' [*dushi ego*].[84] Someone assaulted me from behind and grabbed my throat. I must have resisted enough that he let go of my throat and I found myself on the ground. They punched me all over my body. I could barely breathe, since my throat hurt terribly after they tried to strangle me. I tried to stand up but was pulled to the ground again and again. When I was already severely weakened, I noticed that another bandit was running toward me with a wooden club. He hit me on my legs and back. I was convinced at that time that they were going to kill me, because all that it would have taken then was one more hit to my head. Apparently, it must have been difficult for them to make that move, because I fought back with all my strength and kept on moving my head. During my ordeal, the bandits pulled off my shoes and hit me on my face with them, trying—I am fully convinced—to damage my eyesight. I did not lose consciousness, but I was beaten horribly and was bleeding profusely from my head, forehead, lips, and nose. My eyes were flooded with blood; I could barely see. Eventually they stopped the beating. With effort I rose to my feet, feeling horrible pain all over my body, particularly around my diaphragm."[85]

Łagoda was beaten most severely; Haczyński was also bleeding. Brabec was the least injured of the three. Fortunately a truck with five collective-farm workers from the Seventeenth of October Collective Farm near Chemer village in the vicinity of Olshivka in Chernihiv oblast, eventually drove by.[86] As the truck approached, the assailants fled the scene, heading for Chernihiv. Mykola Pozniak, the highway patrolman of that section of the highway (km. no. 1,100, nine kilometers from Kyiv),

---

[84] "*Dushi ego*" [lit.] appears in the original.

[85] Ibid.

[86] Łagoda recorded the identities of the five collective-farm workers (Stepan Tarashchuk, Iakiv Chyhunets, Fedir Taran, Anastasiia Cherviak, and Oleksander Shuha) and the other witnesses, who, besides the highway patrolman Mykola Pozniak, included Ivan Khomenko and Fedir Bezludny, drivers of the TsUDOR trucks.

informed the victims that the car with the assailants had been parked at that spot since 4:00 a.m. They had come to him to get some water and to talk. Their car's license plates had been covered with bags, but, as they were arriving, one of the bags became a little displaced, exposing the last two digits of the license plate number—85—which the collective-farm worker Stepan Tarashchuk noted.

With the collective-farm workers' assistance, the assaulted foreigners cleaned their wounds a bit, replaced the car's right-rear tire, and then drove away, despite the fact that their car was still partially out of order (the lights were out).[87] Fearing another assault, Łagoda persuaded the collective-farm workers, who did not know that it was NKVD agents who were behind the attack, to escort them to Chernihiv. They agreed, asking for reimbursement for the cost of fuel, which Łagoda was happy to agree to. One of the collective-farm workers rode in the Polish car; the others remained in their own vehicle.

Earlier, while the tires were being replaced, two TsUDOR (Central Highway Administration) trucks arrived. Their drivers confirmed that they also had seen the assailants waiting in a truck when they were transporting their cargo (paving stones and bricks) earlier in the day. Neither they nor the collective-farm workers who spoke to the victims, realized that they were dealing with foreigners. They assumed that they were talking to Soviet citizens who had fallen victim to assault.

Before driving on toward Chernihiv, Haczyński and Łagoda saw two military men riding a motorcycle. When the men came within ten or fifteen meters from the scene of the assault, bloodied Haczyński ran toward them, calling for help. Not only did the soldiers pay no attention to him, however, but they immediately turned around and headed back in the direction of Chernihiv.[88] After driving a dozen or so kilometers, the assaulted foreigners caught up with the soldiers, resting on a bench by the roadside. They stopped and asked for assistance.

The two soldiers refused to help. While they were talking, the NKVD escort vehicle (which had disappeared immediately before the assault) arrived. The NKVD agents rebuked the soldiers for not chasing after the criminals. One of the soldiers (a captain) made the excuse that his

---

[87] The assailants destroyed not only the windows of the car, but also the electric system and the speedometer. They also punctured the tires.

[88] Łagoda was certain that they were also NKVD agents and had approached the victims only to check on their condition.

motorcycle's tire had a damaged inner tube. The NKVD agents, in turn, said their absence was due to the need to repair the line to their gas tank. Haczyński pointed out that even "the least skilled chauffeur would normally be able to fix such a nuisance as a broken gas tank line in fifteen to twenty minutes," yet the NKVD agents had been gone for about an hour and a half.

During this exchange, it turned out that both rear tires of the Poles' car were flat. Someone had damaged them and the spare tire. Since a nearby village was within a reachable distance, the Poles headed there and began repairs. A private car with a medical aide soon reached the village, and he provisionally dressed their wounds. He did not have enough bandages to stop all the bleeding, however. While the tires' inner tubes were being repaired, a GAZ truck drove by. Łagoda recognized the driver as one of the assailants. He stopped the vehicle and informed the NKVD agents of his suspicions. The agents checked the driver's documents but allowed him to continue on his way.

Robbery was certainly not the motivation behind the assault, as no money or valuables were stolen. The assailants did take Łagoda's Browning revolver, however, and a Leica camera and some color film. The light meter for Łagoda's camera was destroyed, as were his pen, watch, shirt, and suit. Haczyński's Rodenstock camera had been taken out of the suitcase, smashed, and the pieces scattered on the road. The pockets of the two Poles and the Czech driver were not searched, nor was their money stolen.

After reaching Chernihiv, Haczyński went to the local NKVD office because he wanted to dispatch a message to Kyiv and Moscow. Despite a delay and various other obstacles put forward by the local staff, he finally managed to send his message. Haczyński encountered similar problems at the telegraph office, where he attempted to establish a connection with the Polish consulate general in Kyiv.

An ambulance arrived at the NKVD's headquarters. The medics dressed the victims' wounds and took them to the hospital. While there, the victims submitted their depositions but did not sign them because the NKVD agents asked them to sign just one copy, blaming the lack of paper and promising to send another copy to Kyiv later. Considering this, the Poles decided they would sign their depositions at the consulate. While they were submitting their depositions, the NKVD agents tried to convince them that the aggressors must have been intoxicated.

All of the assailants were well built and well dressed. Haczyński had the impression that they had been hand-picked specifically for this kind of operation. Furthermore, the editor noticed one more telling detail. During their trip from Moscow to Kyiv they were accompanied by a car with two NKVD agents and two chauffeurs. During their return from Kyiv to Moscow they were also accompanied by two NKVD agents, but by only one driver, "a clear indication that the agents did not really intend to travel to Moscow but expected to remain in Chernihiv instead."

The victims reached Kyiv on May 25 between 5:00 and 6:00 pm. Their injuries were not life threatening, and the doctors did not detect any major internal injuries. Nevertheless they had been severely beaten, particularly Łagoda. After a few days of recuperation in Kyiv, Łagoda and Haczyński reached Moscow on May 31.

A car crash took place a few months later, the circumstances of which suggest it was not accidental. On October 22, 1937, twenty-three kilometers from Kyiv in the direction of Odesa, a car carrying Jan Jerzy Jackowski, the agricultural counselor to the embassy, and Ludwik Michałowski, an official from the Polish consulate general in Kyiv, was hit by a truck. In the report Feliks Tadeusz Haczyński[89] sent to the Polish Telegraph Agency in Warsaw that same day, he wrote: "The accident's circumstances are very strange. The chauffeur noticed the oncoming five-tonne truck driving on the wrong side of the road, and because the truck did not give way, he wanted to pass it from the left, but while the two vehicles were about to pass each other, the truck suddenly veered back to its proper lane and hit the consulate's car, destroying it completely with minor damage to the truck. Luck had it that all the passengers came out of it unscathed." Haczyński asked that this information be shared with Editor in Chief of the PTA Mieczysław Obarski, indicating that the people involved requested that it not be published.[90]

Just how serious the situation had become is confirmed by the fact that Ambassador Grzybowski, expecting the level of harassment to rise,

---

[89] In a document Major Jan Gurbski, acting head of the KOP (Korpus Ochrony Pogranicza; Border Protection Corps) intelligence agency, prepared on October 27, 1937, for the head of Section IIa of the Second Department of the Main Staff, he misspelled Haczyński's name as Kaczyński.

[90] Archiwum Straży Granicznej w Szczecinie, Dowództwo KOP, sygn. 541/566, k. 68. See also P. Kołakowski, *Pretorianie Stalina: Sowieckie służby bezpieczeństwa i wywiadu na ziemiach polskich, 1939–1945* (Warsaw: Bellona, 2010), 74.

considered requesting the provision of a life-insurance policy for all Polish officials in the USSR.[91]

This period also witnessed Soviet provocations aimed at compromising Polish consular officials. In this regard, it is worth mentioning that the secretary of the consulate (and a functionary of the *Dwójka*), Ludwik Michałowski, was, informally and ridiculously at the same time, accused of setting a Soviet train car on fire. On December 18, 1937, Soviet Chargé d'affaires Vinogradov, while in conversation with Jan Szembek in the presence of Tadeusz Kobylański,[92] submitted a note of protest about the act of arson of a Soviet train that took place on December 14, 1937 near Zdolbuniv. The document blamed Michałowski for the incident. Vinogradov added that if the Soviet side did not receive redress for these repeated incidents (a similar fire had happened in late November 1937),[93] they would be compelled to cease all train traffic between

---

[91] Jan Szembek, *Diariusz i teki Jana Szembeka (1935–1945)*, vol. 4 (1938–1939), ed. J. Zarański (London: Polish Research Center, 1972), 44.

[92] Tadeusz Kobylański (1895–1967) was an officer of the Polish General Staff who worked for the MFA from 1929. Between 1929 and 1935, he was a counselor to the Polish legation in Bucharest; between 1935 and 1939, he was the vice-head of the Political Department of the MFA and the head of the East Section (P III).

[93] On December 3, 1937, the Soviet newspaper *Pravda* published that, on November 29, at the Polish train station of Zdolbuniv, Soviet train no. 34/2591, which was returning to the USSR from Poland, was suddenly stopped. According to *Pravda*, the Poles subjected the Soviet crew to a humiliating search procedure. Those who resisted were threatened at gunpoint, and engine operator Khilchuk was beaten because he resisted. Later the Soviet newspaper published materials that accused the Polish side of setting a train car on fire. At the last station (Mohyliany) before the train reached the Soviet border, the Soviet conductor, Saviuk, allegedly saw a Polish soldier quickly approach the car and put in some kind of container with liquid just before the train was scheduled to leave. The fire broke out just before the train reached the Soviet border, in car no. 201. Saviuk raised the alarm while he tried to extinguish the fire. The Polish officials and military men, who jumped off the train, allegedly threatened Saviuk not to leave the train until it crossed the border. Saviuk, disregarding the threats, decided to separate the burning car from the rest of the train. On the day after the event, two representatives of the Southwestern Railway came to Mohyliany. One of them was Chernii, head of the Shepetivka section railway administration, and the other Voronin, the head of the train carriages administration. The Poles, according to *Pravda*, were particularly unpleasant and unkind to them and forced them to return to the USSR on foot at 4:00 a.m. on December 1. The newspaper reported that the Polish side attempted to blame the train's crew for the fire. Finally, they quoted the TASS agency, which reported that the Soviet mission in Warsaw received an order to present a strong protest to the Polish MFA and request that an investigation be launched that would find and punish the guilty and provide the

Shepetivka and Zdolbuniv. In reply, Szembek said that he had immediately ordered an investigation after reading the TASS report on the November fire. As a matter of fact, the report indicated that quite the opposite had happened: the fire had already started in Soviet territory, in Slavuta. Witnesses had smelled smoke coming from the train's ticket collector's compartment. "The fire was certainly caused by the Soviet railway administration's negligence, for which the Polish government can bear no responsibility. Furthermore, we are inclined to believe that, considering how high the penalties levied on Soviet functionaries are, they are willing to blame the Polish side instead of acknowledging their fault." Vinogradov replied that there were Soviet witnesses, whose testimonies suggested something quite different. He said that he also had a statement from an Austrian citizen, who said that the fire was set by a Polish citizen. Hearing this, Szembek asked whether the Austrian citizen was able to verify the alleged Polish citizen's identity. The response was that rumors were floating about that the fire had been started by Michałowski, an official from the consulate general in Kyiv.[94]

1.2.4. Polish Countermeasures

Until mid-1938, the performance of Polish posts in the USSR (as well as those of the other four countries mentioned earlier) and their situation continued to change for the worse. On April 2, 1938, the political department of the Polish MFA asked the embassy in Moscow and other Polish posts in the USSR to provide some information about "the living conditions of the posts and their employees."[95] Three days later, on April 5, 1938, Wacław Grzybowski wrote in his reply about the kinds of harassment practiced by the Soviets: sporadic reliance on provocations; delays in issuing entry visas or refusing to issue reentry visas to the embassy's officials; difficulties in shipping personal belongings from abroad; frequent requests to expel Polish officials from the USSR without providing any justification; arrests of Soviet citizens who had visited the embassy, including ordinary technicians; making professional trips difficult; constant and insolent surveillance of (all) the embassy's workers;

---

appropriate indemnity to the Soviet side. See "Provokatsionnaia vykhodka polskoi voenshchiny," *Pravda*, December 3, 1937; "Nota protesta poverennogo v delakh SSSR v Pol'she (TASS)," *Pravda*, December 7, 1937; "Nota NKID pol'skomu posol'stvu," *Pravda*, January 4, 1938.

[94] *Diariusz i teki Jana Szembeka*, 3:216–17. See also RGVA, f. 464k, op. 1, d. 2424, l. 74.

[95] AAN, MSZ, sygn. 6755 B, k. 2.

the prohibition against parking and walking on public roads in the vicinity of Moscow that happened to be occasionally frequented by Soviet officials; and banning Polish officials from renting dachas during the summer in the more upscale suburbs of Moscow (the claim being that they were closed zones.)[96]

Tadeusz Błaszkiewicz, head of the consular section of the Polish embassy in Moscow, reported that, beginning in mid-November 1937, the NKVD was closely following all the employees from his office: the agents followed them to offices and hairdressers and eavesdropped on their conversations with shop attendants. A small number of embassy visitors were stopped and asked for their IDs after leaving the building. Workers were afraid to work for the embassy, fearing arrest. The situation was so bad that some personal belongings (e.g., shoes) had to be shipped back to Poland for repairs, because the local cobblers were afraid to visit the Polish post. The rest of his report mentioned other typical modes of harassment.[97] Similar reports were received from other Polish consulates in the USSR.[98]

---

[96] Ibid., k. 4–5.

[97] Ibid., k. 6–7.

[98] On April 7, 1938, Witold Okoński, the head of the Polish mission in Minsk, issued a reply to a letter from the Political Department of the MFA. In it he mentioned a conversation he had overheard between two railway men talking about a special meeting at which railway employees received detailed instructions on how to approach foreigners. Their attitude had changed completely, from the earlier display of courtesy toward Polish officials to a stance of confrontation and constant trouble-making, e.g., a ban on entering the platform without a ticket in hand. Similar attitudes were held by workers in other public institutions Polish staff visited. "In such conditions, life in Minsk," complained Okoński, "is particularly displeasing to the entire staff and is reflected in the poor psychological health of those who stay here longer, even more so because Minsk, unlike other cities, offers no proper opportunities to relax, e.g., by enjoying the city's beauty, visiting a good theater, a decent restaurant, or any place of entertainment. All non-work activities necessarily focus around home and household issues.... Such a state of affairs compels me to grant employees holidays more frequently than elsewhere, so as to maintain at least some degree of mental health." Eugeniusz Weese, the Polish consul in Leningrad, wrote a similar report to the Eastern Department of the MFA regarding the harassments experienced by the employees of his post. As in other cities, the intensity of such harrasments grew in November 1937. Weese mentioned the following issues: nondelivery of the local papers, constant surveillance, interrogation of visitors (later, arrests and deportations). He remarked that even the British consul general, Giliath Smith, was stopped right outside the Polish consulate. The NKVD attempted to recruit the chauffeur Edward Suciński. The consul also wrote about a very interesting and telling conversation he had with a Polish citizen, Abram Brajterman, who, together with his wife, spent three and a half years in a Soviet prison. Brajterman reported to the consul

On May 30, 1938, Jerzy Matusiński, head of the Polish consulate general in Kyiv and a counselor to the embassy, sent a report to the MFA detailing the harassment his post suffered. He wrote that the Soviet authorities' actions focused on separating the post from the flow of information and contacts with the locals; creating an atmosphere of hostility around the post; and exerting an intimidating influence on the officials' mental state (which was effective in conjunction with the generally abysmal standard of living in the USSR). He listed the following NKVD techniques: personal surveillance—following a person directly, standing behind him or her in lines, listening to a conversation just behind one's back; interrogating visitors (even a doctor, who had been called to see an ill Polish official, asked that his help not be requested anymore, while postmen left mail out in the street, under the watch of agents who surrounded the consulate); lack of contact with local authorities, with the exception of the PCfFA representative; nondelivery of the local press; mail being screened; phones bugged (the consulate had no direct connection with Poland, while the telegraph office was unreliable and caused artificial delays); extremely rigorous screening of officials at the border crossing, in particular those without diplomatic passports (the vice-consul's wife, Mrs. Koch, was subjected to a detailed search).

Matusiński stressed that the Soviet authorities had increased the tariff on foodstuffs imported from Zdolbuniv (which had to be delivered from Poland, because there was no way to obtain supplies in Kyiv). The diplomat added, based on the reports of a few visitors, that when someone asked for directions to the Polish consulate, people ran away at the mere mention of the name, while policemen replied that they did not know or that it had

---

that the NKVD forced confessions from Poles that "confirmed" that the consulate was "a spy nest." Brajterman was also accused of spying for the consulate, but he refused to plead guilty. Apparently impressed by his fortitude, the judge said that "the Soviet authorities are in fact convinced that the accusation put forward against him is immaterial, but his confession is necessary to obtain some material incriminating the Polish consulate in Leningrad in order to close down this institution." Not even a month later, on May 10, 1938, Weese informed the Eastern Department about the intensifying NKVD provocations he had experienced personally. On May 7 and 8, NKVD agents followed him and his wife much more closely than usual, literally elbowing them and calling them names. They sat directly behind him and his wife in St. Catherine's Church. After Mass, they ridiculed their behavior. One of them insinuated that it would be good to sharpen their knives on Stanisław Ratomski's (an official in the consulate) neck. They were even coarser with lower-ranking personnel, e.g., the janitor Wacław Paprocki, at whom they yelled, "back to your kennel, you dog." Ibid., k. 8–13, 15–17, 21.

been closed.[99] The counselor made the picture even gloomier by mentioning that the office had insufficient space for all of its employees and the building was poorly heated in wintertime, while the electricity was so weak that one had to strain to see anything. What was missing especially was some sort of social life outside the confines of the post.

At the end of his report, Matusiński suggested some ways to remedy the situation. First of all, similar retaliatory measures should be applied to Soviet diplomats in Poland. Then, any candidates selected for work in the field of Soviet affairs needed to be appointed responsibly (with special consideration given to their health and psychological endurance). He also advised selecting, if possible, married men who had no children yet; not keeping people in one place for too long (two years maximum); allowing frequent home leaves, given the lack of appropriate Soviet employees, who were usually NKVD agents anyway; making a special selection from among the lower ranks; looking for bright, confident, disciplined workers who were fluent in Russian or Ukrainian and willing to engage in physical labor; and increasing salaries so that the consulate personnel could afford more frequent trips home.[100]

The worsening situation of the Polish posts induced the MFA and secret services to respond with retaliatory measures. On July 16, 1938, Tadeusz Kobylański, the deputy head of the Political Department of the MFA, informed the embassy in Moscow that the MFA, with the support of the security services, was going to launch a retaliatory campaign against Soviet diplomats and consular officials in Poland. This would include stopping, interrogating, and checking identities of all persons leaving the Soviet posts in Warsaw and Lviv, apart from members of the diplomatic corps; creating a brigade tasked with openly following Soviet officials, analogous to the practices of the NKVD with respect to Poles; discouraging Polish citizens from accepting any positions at Soviet posts; and screening the mail and nondelivery of newspapers, apart from local Warsaw and Lviv sources. The MFA pledged to ask the authorities of the Free City of Gdańsk to enforce a similar set of practices against the Soviet consulate there. All requests for intervention from the Soviet embassy were to be rejected, following the principle of reciprocity.[101] This campaign was launched without prior consultation with Ambassador Wacław

---

[99] Ibid., k. 26–29.
[100] Ibid., k. 25–34.
[101] Ibid., k. 40–41.

Grzybowski, who wrote (post factum) in one of his reports that, while he supported the reciprocity principle, he thought that the MFA had made a mistake by beginning the campaign on July 18 without consulting with him on either the start date or other details.[102]

The MFA, following up on their earlier announcement, launched its retaliatory campaign on July 18, 1938, at 1:00 p.m. Pavel Listopad, the Soviet chargé d'affaires in Warsaw, submitted a note of protest to the MFA (he was hosted by Jan Karszo-Siedlewski, who, for some time after returning from Kyiv and before being dispatched to Tehran in late 1938, worked temporarily in the main Warsaw office as vice-director of the Political Department) regarding the harassment of Soviet posts.[103] The Soviet chargé d'affaires received the reply that the security authorities had initiated certain measures that "had no connection whatsoever with Polish-Soviet relations." Next, Karszo-Siedlewski expressed his "diplomatic regret" about the identity verification process for Soviet officials that was taking place. He categorically rejected the suggestion that the work of Soviet posts had been rendered more difficult on purpose.

Given his several years of professional experience in the USSR, it appears he could not resist expressing his own view on the issue of the inadequate situation of the Soviet posts in Poland and the Polish ones in the USSR. Karszo-Siedlewski said that the Soviet embassy "had been spoiled by the hitherto prevailing courtesy of the Polish security services, and now, after they had begun to verify the identities of Polish citizens for security reasons, it [the embassy] began to protest that they could not live and function normally." "What are the Polish diplomats, who have been operating under such conditions for years, supposed to say?" Karszo-Siedlewski, the former head of the Polish consulate in Kharkiv and later in Kyiv, asked. Listopad interrupted him then, asking whether the practices of the Polish authorities that began on July 18 were to be considered a retaliatory measure. Not at all, said Karszo-Siedlewski. The situation of the Polish officials had remained unchanged for the past six years, a state of affairs that he had experienced himself, and nothing had

---

[102] Ibid., k. 202.

[103] The types of harassment Listopad mentioned were: controlling all visitors; forcing Andrzejewski (a mailman) and the wife of the Soviet courier, Mariia Sushchenko, to go to the police station; and identity verification of the embassy's first secretary, Chebyshev, second secretary Boris Lebezhikhin, and Major Aleksandr Zavialov.

happened recently that could incline the Polish authorities toward introducing such retaliatory measures.[104]

On July 20, Karszo-Siedlewski held another conversation with Listopad. The Pole expressed his regret that, among other things, not all policemen knew the employees of the Soviet embassy and thus had to verify their identities. This circumstance explained, in his view, the situation in which someone without appropriate ID had to be escorted to the nearest police station. Listopad was glad to hear such regrets, but he soon emphasized that embassy officials were nonetheless being escorted to police stations multiple times on the same day. Furthermore, he had ordered that employees were to wear their professional IDs. He complained that Polish agents continued to stand near the embassy building, clenching their fists in an aggressive manner, behaving rudely, and elbowing Soviet officials passing by. Similar occurrences were observed in Lviv as well. The Polish interlocutor expressed his usual regrets, promised to check on the situation, and repeated that the Polish security functionaries had received instructions not to cause any trouble for the employees of the Soviet embassy, and that they had been advised to treat embassy employees courteously. As for the accusation of coarse treatment by Polish secret agents (elbowing, threatening), he replied in the oh-so-familiar manner of his counterparts in Soviet Ukraine, namely, that he did not believe those individuals were security officials, that they must have been passers-by, and that he was going to inform the relevant security authorities, who, by the way, had already informed him that no agents were on duty in front of the embassy.

Listopad then responded that, if necessary, he could deliver photos of those persons taken by the embassy. Furthermore, he complained that the embassy had been receiving no mail and no newspapers, while a telegram from Moscow had been delivered with a ninety-minute delay. The mailman had explained that the police were not allowing him inside the embassy. A Polish female cook was stopped by the police in town a few times, making it impossible for Listopad to have his dinner, while the painters stopped their work, half-way completed, and would not finish. In view of all this, said the Soviet chargé d'affaires, he perceived these practices as a retaliatory measure. Karszo-Siedlewski replied that he could not add anything else to the official statement, nor could he pursue any further discussion. Privately, and with unconcealed satisfaction, he

---

[104] AAN, MSZ, sygn. 6755 B, k. 43, 45–61.

commented that, just as, for five years, he had had to engage in such futile talks with the PCfFA representatives on many occasions, now, on this day, a Soviet official was forced to complain in the same way.[105]

Three days later, on July 23, 1938, the head of the Soviet division of the MFA, Stanisław Zabiełło, held a similar conversation with the first secretary of the Soviet embassy, Chebyshev. Chebyshev essentially reiterated the previous complaints (e.g., that the agents stared straight at him and followed him everywhere), while Zabiełło—just as Karszo-Siedlewski had done earlier—expressed his regrets and repeated that it was not the intention of the Polish authorities to make the life of Soviet diplomats troublesome, adding, at the end, that the Polish posts in the USSR functioned under conditions that were considerably worse.[106]

The Soviets did not give up, however. The Polish embassy in Moscow informed the MFA that on July 24, 1938, on one of the streets, the military attaché Colonel Konstanty Zaborowski was asked to show his documents. "The incident can be characterized as harassment," the report concluded.[107]

The situation escalated in early August after the Soviet press published a TASS report on the harassment of Soviet diplomats in Poland.[108] In response, the situation at the Polish posts worsened dramatically. In Ukraine, the speech made by Representative Shcherbakov during a session of the Supreme Soviet was a grim foreshadowing of the troubles to come. On August 15, 1938, Counselor Jerzy Matusiński wrote, Shcherbakov "harshly criticized the behavior of the Polish authorities who blocked the Soviet posts in Poland," and, quoting Shcherbakov, "If you want the Polish posts to operate on the territory of the Soviet Union in a normal way, immediately cease your indecencies. We are not the sort of people who, when they are struck on their right cheek, turn the other cheek. We hold to another rule: 'return it, but a hundred times stronger.'"[109]

Matusiński reported on many daily problems encountered by the employees of his post. Apart from the typical nondelivery of mail and

---

[105] Ibid., k. 66–74. One day later, on July 20, 1938, Kobylański delivered Karszo-Siedlewski's note about his conversation with Listopad to Colonel Pełczyński.

[106] Ibid., k. 77–80.

[107] Ibid., k. 84.

[108] See "Naglye deistviia pol'skikh vlastei v otnoshenii sovetskikh predstavitel'stv v Pol'she: Informatsiia TASS ot 21 iiula 1938," *Pravda*, July 23, 1938.

[109] CAW, Oddz. II SG, sygn. I.303.4.1867, k. 761.

newspapers, he also mentioned that the "rascals" (*łapsy*) followed all employees of the Polish consulate, without exception: "Mrs. Koch and Mrs. Szyszkowska, who went out for a walk in the zoological garden, were harassed by agents by being elbowed or kneed, as well as by rude staring. At one point, one of the rats approached a worker and spoke with him for a while. The worker then approached Mrs. Koch and verbally abused her while vehemently performing hostile gestures. Mrs. Koch did not understand what he said to her because she does not speak Russian."[110] The NKVD agents parked their car in the entry gate of the Polish post, blocking egress for the consulate's car. The policeman who was asked by the head of the post to intervene did not do anything. The Polish car had to bypass the NKVD vehicle by driving on the sidewalk.

On August 7, a policeman stopped a cook's assistant named Cieślówna near the consulate as she was making her daily trek to the market. He wanted to see her passport, looked at it, and then left with it. Since Cieślówna did not speak Russian, she did not know whether she was free to go or arrested. She thought it must have been the former, but after a moment she decided to walk back to the consulate. After several steps, she heard the policeman's whistle and started running toward the gate of the Polish post.[111]

That afternoon, Matusiński went to see the PCfFA representative to protest all of the above-mentioned practices. The representative greeted him politely. He said that those practices were in response to the actions directed against the Soviet posts in Poland. He was certain, he said, that as soon as the Poles ceased their repressive measures, similar acts of repression would also cease for the Polish posts. He expressed his regret that bilateral relations, though not ideal to begin with, had deteriorated. In response, the Polish diplomat listed all the harassments he and his co-workers had experienced from the moment of their arrival in the USSR, i.e., long before the recent retaliations.[112]

In the afternoon of the same day, Matusiński again intervened with the PCfFA representative, because of the arrest of Vice-consul Koch in the afternoon of August 7. Koch had been stopped by the police, ostentatiously escorted through the center of the city, and released after

---

[110] Ibid., k. 762.
[111] Ibid.
[112] Ibid., k. 763–64.

one hour.[113] Initially the PCfFA representative refused to meet again, claiming he was busy with work. Matusiński had to voice his protest over the phone. After a while, however, the representative called Matusiński in and, in the presence of his secretary, protested in "a bombastic tone" the behavior of Cieślówna, a consulate employee, who allegedly threw her passport at the policeman and declined to take it back, thus offending the Soviet authorities. The PCfFA representative returned Cieślówna's passport, but his protest was rejected by the Polish diplomat as groundless. Matusiński reminded the representative about Koch's case. The Soviet official promised to investigate it.[114]

One day later, on August 8, the mail was finally delivered, and the "rats" no longer elbowed the passers-by. The cars blocking the post's entry gate were withdrawn. But other forms of harassment began, some more and some less severe. For example, during the night of August 7–8, 1938, between 3:30 and 6:00 a.m., someone phoned the consulate a few times and made ridiculous demands, such as to dispatch a car to pick up a dead body.[115] During the night of August 8–9, a dozen or so fragments of bricks were thrown onto the consulate's garden-facing porch.[116] The next night, between 1:15 and 5:00 a.m., a series of six incredibly loud sounds were heard, each several minutes long and occurring at regularly spaced intervals. They were produced by a car that was being shifted from the front of one building to another, right in front of the consulate. The sounds were so loud that the consulate's windows shook and objects inside could be seen vibrating.[117]

A few of the lower-ranking consulate employees, especially domestic service staff members, were arrested. Initially the length of their detainment was three hours, but then it increased to five and then to eight and even ten hours. That practice was more than a nuisance, because it made it impossible to get anything done in town—for instance, to send a message or to buy groceries or tickets. Matusiński was eventually forced to stop sending his janitors on shopping errands; he had to start making the trips himself.[118]

---

[113] AAN, MSZ, sygn. 7655 B, k. 92.
[114] CAW, Oddz. II SG, sygn. I.303.4.1867, k. 763–64.
[115] AAN, MSZ, sygn. 6755 B, k. 275.
[116] Ibid. k. 276.
[117] Ibid. k. 277.
[118] CAW, Oddz. II SG, sygn. I.303.4.1867, k. 764–65.

The Soviet authorities delayed the issuance of technical inspection certificates for vehicles owned by the Polish diplomatic corps, thus making it impossible for them to drive on public roads. Even if inspections had been conducted, Matusiński surmised, the vehicles probably would have failed to pass inspection because some of their parts were indeed out of order. Furthermore, the vehicles' license plates could not be updated, again because of delays caused by the Soviet side. Disturbing phone calls late at night and bricks thrown onto the garden porch were the kinds of incidents that continued to occur. The janitor who swept the pavement in front of the building was withdrawn, even though he was paid by the consulate. Eventually the PCfFA representative stopped responding to Polish official notes altogether. Someone in his office said that he had left for an unknown destination, and no one knew when he would return. He left no instructions, meaning that no one could answer the consul's notes.[119]

Ambassador Grzybowski wrote to the MFA that, on August 7, two embassy chauffeurs had been stopped and escorted to a police station because of an alleged traffic violation. A few housemaids and the janitor had been stopped as well. Editor Haczyński's driver's license had been confiscated, and he was unable to reach Warsaw by phone. The harassment of MFA employees was the subject of the ambassador's intervention with the deputy people's commissar for foreign affairs of the USSR, Vladimir Potemkin, on the previous day. Of course, his attempt to intervene was in vain. All that Potemkin would talk about was the harassment of Soviet diplomats in Poland.[120]

What was MFA's reaction to those events? They continued to examine the reports reaching them from the Soviet Union and maintained their course of retaliatory action, accompanied by careful observation of their opponent. On August 8, 1938, the MFA informed the Moscow embassy that the campaign would be continued without increasing in intensity, whereas the next steps vis-à-vis the Soviets were to be designed following "the delivery of a thorough evaluation of the campaign initiated by the Soviets." The MFA asked the ambassador to advise the consuls to stay calm, be careful, and record and inform the MFA about all incidents.[121]

---

[119] Ibid., k. 766–67.
[120] AAN, MSZ, sygn. 6755 B, k. 97–98.
[121] Ibid., k. 96.

On August 9, 1938, the MFA informed the embassy once again that the measures against the Soviet posts mentioned in the letter of July 16, 1938, were to be continued. In response to the Soviet blockage of the consulate vehicles in Kyiv and Minsk, an identical step was to be initiated in Lviv. The Lviv voivode received instructions to meet with the Soviet consul and tell him the same story that Pavel Listopad had heard from Karszo-Siedlewski earlier.[122] At the same time, the MFA advised the embassy in Moscow and the consulates in Leningrad, Kyiv, and Minsk to resist, if possible, all kinds of Soviet repressions; to conduct several interventions, if necessary, on a single case; to exercise extreme caution regarding being outside the post; to continue to encourage all personnel to endure the harassment; and to send reports to both the embassy and the MFA.[123]

Polish Deputy Foreign Minister Mirosław Arciszewski informed Grzybowski on August 11, 1938, that the information about the harassment of the Polish officials had been passed on to the security authorities, who were to initiate identical measures immediately. Arciszewski wrote that the Soviet chargé d'affaires had approached him to lodge a protest about the janitor of the Soviet consulate in Lviv, who had been detained by Polish authorities for eight hours and about Polish security agents bullying the children of Soviet officials. Arciszewski spoke of the treatment of the Polish posts in the USSR; he reminded his Soviet interlocutor that the Soviet posts could not complain about the treatment they were receiving from the Poles, since the Polish posts were in trouble all the time.[124]

Under these circumstances, instructions—or, to be more precise, words of encouragement—were sent from the central office of the Second Department to the employees of the "double shifts" (that is, those working undercover). On August 12, 1938, the central office wrote that the recent "rat-organized" campaign to make life miserable for all the Polish posts in the USSR was the result of the "nervousness and disorganization of the NKVD authorities, a consequence of the retaliatory action that we have applied toward the Soviet posts in Poland. The rats must have lost their minds and they are now lashing out without rhyme or reason." The central office next wrote that such a situation had to be considered

---

[122] Ibid., k. 104.
[123] Ibid., k. 117.
[124] Ibid., k. 124.

temporary and that a détente was soon to follow: "We never stop monitoring the situation, we have it under control, [and] we always have. You are on our minds. Do not lose your pluck, remain calm, and take all this ratty circus with a dose of humor."[125]

It was difficult, however, to brush away the Bolsheviks' behavior with humor alone. After several lower-ranking officials of the consulate were arrested, Counselor Matusiński stopped sending them to town altogether after August 14, 1938. For the next few days, he went out by himself to take care of daily business; after that, a few fellow officials accompanied him.[126] When, on August 19, Antoni Majewski[127] and Henryk Słowikowski went out without their boss's company, they were immediately detained by the police and held for seven hours. Consequently, from August 20 on, only the head of the conculate went into town, either alone or accompanied by Koch.[128]

On August 18, 1938, the following incidents took place in Kyiv. Jerzy Matusiński, accompanied by three consular officials, visited the telegraph office. Initially four, then later six, NKVD agents followed them, behaving in a provocative way, coming up very close to the Poles and uttering contemptuous remarks. One of them barred the exit as they tried to leave a store. The Poles used their arms to move by him, only to be met with name-calling. Later, when an NKVD agent tried to push between Matusiński and the colleague walking by his side, one of the Poles again put out an arm to stop him. After this, the agent yelled, on crowded Kirov Street: "Polish spies are walking in the streets and are pushing people aside" (*Polskiie shpiki khodiat po ulitsam i tolkaiut liudiei*).[129] on August 19, 1938, the consulate submitted protests against this kind of behavior and the earlier incident that happened to Mrs. Koch and Mrs. Szyszkowska in the park.[130]

---

[125] CAW, Oddz. II SG, sygn. I.303.4.1967, doc. 14.

[126] On August 20, 1938, Matusiński sent a message to the MFA: "I do not let the janitors and maids out because their arrest while in town is certain, the vehicles are still immobilized, all kinds of excursions, including shopping, are undertaken by officials only under my personal escort. Since August 18, the trend has been worsening in the direction of terrorizing and starving the consulate; the outbound journey of the diplomatic courier is also in question. The PCfFA does not want to see me, does not respond to my notes. The situation is difficult, prestige-wise. Please inform me about any prospect of this conflict coming to an end, or about other possible outcomes." AAN, MSZ, sygn. 6755 B, k. 175.

[127] The cover name of Major Antoni Minkiewicz.

[128] AAN, MSZ, sygn. 6755 B, k. 174.

[129] Ibid., k. 260.

[130] Ibid.

A few days earlier, on August 16, 1938, the Kyiv consulate submitted a note of protest to the Soviet PCfFA representative concerning the difficulties encountered when attempting to purchase a train ticket for a diplomatic courier. Two days earlier, the director of the railway station in Kyiv had received a written request to issue a ticket for a sleeping car on the train from Kyiv to Moscow on August 15. The director's bureau promised to make the ticket available the next day by noon. When Polish officials arrived at the agreed-upon time, they were told, after waiting an hour, that the ticket could not be issued. They were offered instead a ticket for a "regular" (second-class) car, which, of course, the Polish side would not accept. Finally, the Polish officials submitted another request for a seat reservation for the following day (August 16), or, in the event that was not possible, for the day after (August 17). The request was accepted, a favorable outcome was promised, and the applicants were told to wait for a phone call. When the consulate called on August 16 to check about the reservations, the reply was an arrogant "no, there is no such ticket available" and that the request could not be accepted. The Polish consulate's next step was to ask for a ticket at the Intourist agency. Initially, the agency said that the ticket was ready, but when the officials tried to pick it up, they were told that it was not available. Later, the agency again offered a "regular" car ticket. Ultimately the Polish post submitted a letter of protest about this behavior and included another request for a ticket for August 21, with a plea that the matter be decided favorably.[131]

1.2.4.1. Soviet Attempts to Recruit Polish Diplomatic and Consular Workers in the USSR

In addition to all these hindrances, this period also saw heightened NKVD activity aimed at recruiting employees of Polish posts. Most such attempts took place outside Ukraine. Nonetheless, arrests, recruitment attempts (often accompanied by threats), and even physical violence against the detainees had a depressing and negative effect on the behavior of the Polish staff working in Kyiv and Kharkiv. The arrest of Franciszek Szałapski, a janitor in the embassy, in April 1937, cast a long, horror-filled shadow within the Polish milieus.[132] During the night of

---

[131] Ibid., k. 770–71.

[132] In connection with this issue, the Main Intelligence Office sent a general letter to the Polish

April 9/10, 1937, Szałapski visited his friend Sakhina, who lived in
Moscow. A trap had been set in her apartment. The woman asked him
to send a letter (of no specific content) to Ambassador Juliusz
Łukaszewicz's butler, Henryk Matysiak, with whom she was in touch.
She gave as the explanation for her request that if such a letter were sent
from Moscow, it would take a lot of time to be delivered. Szałapski said
he would think about it. Then (around midnight) someone claiming to be
her husband started banging on the door, opened it, and tried to pick a
fight with Szałapski. Someone else soon appeared and announced he was
going to inform the police who arrived after a while and took both men to
the police station, where they were searched and the letter from Sakhina
was found. It turned out to be written in special security ink and included
some information about the Soviet motorization drive and a request for
money. Szałapski maintained that he had not taken the letter himself,
but that someone must have slipped it into his belongings. Of course, the
case was redirected to the NKVD. There Szałapski was presented with
two options: immediate arrest, or cooperation with the NKVD. The
NKVD investigator told him that Poland would be Communist in two
years, so the decision was a no-brainer. He was offered three thousand
rubles and told to sign a receipt. Szałapski initially declined, but then
two men came in and put their guns to his head. He signed what he was
told out of fear; he did not want to take the money. An NKVD officer
divided the pile of cash into two parts: Szałapski was told to take one of
them (1,260 rubles); the other, he was told, he would receive later. The
next meeting was set for April 12. Szałapski was then offered some
cognac and threatened that if he informed the embassy of this incident,
he would receive a bullet through his head. He returned to the embassy,
intoxicated, at 5:00 a.m. On April 11, 1937, Szałapski reported the
incident to the military attaché, Lieutenant Colonel Konstanty
Zaborowski. Zaborowski at first thought he should allow the janitor to
meet with the Soviets again, but he decided to send him back to Poland.
On April 16, 1937, Szałapski was sent back in the company of two
officers. Zaborowski advised him to tell everyone the reason for his
return was disciplinary, because of alcohol abuse.

At the Soviet border post in Negoreloe, Szałapski was summoned and
asked whether he had said anything to his superiors. No, he answered,

---

posts advising them "not to worry and to continue doing your job." Ibid., sygn.
I.303.4.1956, doc. 96; sygn. I.303.4.2101, doc. 22.

and was told he would be able to cooperate with Soviet authorities in Warsaw. He was told to write a letter to the following address: *Poczta Główna, Poste Restante, Moscow, Ivan Ivanovich Ivanov*. He did not have to sign it, because they already knew his handwriting. Furthermore, someone would contact him and hand over the money to him.[133]

After Szałapski's departure, and after the completion of an investigation by the Second Department, the foreign minister, Józef Beck, advised Ambassador Grzybowski to submit a protest against this provocation and to turn in the material evidence, that is, the money that Szałapski had been forced to accept.[134] Acting on this recommendation, the embassy issued a formal protest and returned the 1,260 rubles.[135] In their reply, dated May 5, 1937, the PCfFA maintained that their investigation had shown that Szałapski had never been arrested by the NKVD and that the embassy must have fallen victim to his subterfuge. The evidence—the money—was sent back with the note.[136] After reading this reply, Jan Szembek, under secretary of state in the MFA, advised the embassy to issue another note, in which the Soviet protest would be recognized as groundless, and to transfer the returned 1260 rubles to the International Red Cross before submitting the second note.[137]

Similar incidents followed, especially after tensions peaked in July and August 1938. In July, the NKVD attempted to recruit a female cook in the consulate general in Minsk, Anna Paczkowska. At the end of 1937, she was being treated in hospital for typhus. After her release, Witold Okoński, the head of the consulate general in Minsk, noticed that her behavior had begun to change. Although the cook admitted that she had been approached by the Soviet secret service with offers in exchange for her cooperation, Okoński still considered Paczkowska's loyalty to be

---

[133] AAN, MSZ, sygn. 6755, k. 5–6; k. 33–38. The Second Department issued the following opinion about Szałapski: "He worked for a long time in the personal guard of Marshal Piłsudski, [but] he was also his hairdresser. Very cunning and clever, a great informant, disliked by his peers due to his intrigues and arrogance. Prone to alcohol abuse, but not in a chronic way. Absolutely certain from a political point of view. A type of ruthless gendarme who loves to do his duty" (Ibid. k. 7).

[134] Ibid., k. 12.

[135] Ibid., k. 52–54.

[136] Ibid., k. 17–20; Ibid., sygn. 1472 C, k. 72–73.

[137] Ibid., sygn. 6755, k. 14. A delegate of the International Red Cross refused to accept the money, indicating that he could do so only from the Red Cross's main office or on its recommendation. The next day, Szembek advised Jankowski to submit a note immediately (on May 15) without waiting for the money issue to be resolved. Ibid., k. 49.

uncertain and wanted to see her deported back to Poland. Finally, despite the negative attitude of the relevant Soviet authorities, he managed to obtain a return visa for her. Quoting family issues as the reason for her departure, the consulate sent her back to Poland on July 20, 1938.[138] After her departure, on July 23, 1938, Okoński informed the embassy in Moscow about this incident. He asked that they intervene with the PCfFA and that Paczkowska's behavior be monitored for some time following her return to Poland.[139]

The written reports about Paczkowska's investigation are quite interesting, especially considering the lack of access to the same materials at the Lubianka. They reveal plenty of operational details about NKVD methods with respect to foreign cadres. On July 12, 1938, Paczkowska had her first deposition in front of Okoński. She said that on July 12, 1938, at 9:00 a.m., she had gone shopping and was approached by an NKVD agent, who asked to see her passport. She said that she did not have it, to which he replied that he had to arrest her, because it was illegal to move around without a passport. Then another agent came and forced her to go with him. They passed the government's building, moved into the old district with wooden houses, and entered one of them. There a different (senior) agent began to interrogate her. He asked: "Are you citizen Paczkowska?" "Yes," was her answer.

"You occupy yourself with espionage and smuggling, don't you?"

"Neither," said Paczkowska.

Next, the agent showed her some receipts from a pawn shop, asking whether they belonged to her. "Yes," she said. He asked her why she had to sell items to a pawn shop—whether it was due to her low pay—and whether she was aware of the fact that foreigners were prohibited from selling there. Paczkowska answered: "I did not know." The agent compiled the report, attached the pawn-shop receipts, and asked her to sign it. She declined, saying that she was illiterate, and, besides, the agent had not shared the statement with her. The agent replied that he knew that she was able to write because he had seen her signatures on the receipts, and that she had to sign the written statement because anyone who lived in the USSR had to submit to his will. "Even if Piłsudski himself rose from the dead and came here, he would have to submit to my will. We are strong, rich, and afraid of no one. If you do not sign, we will arrest you. If

---

[138] CAW, Oddz. II SG, sygn. I.303.4.1867, k. 315.
[139] Ibid., k. 328–36.

you sign, you will be released," said the NKVD agent. The woman signed the statement after hearing those guarantees.

Immediately after that the agent said that because she had signed the statement, it meant she had admitted she was a spy and a contrabandist, and so she was under arrest. Paczkowska said she had not confessed to spying, but merely admitted that she had sold some items to a pawn shop. The agent replied: "We know very well what goes on at your place. What we do not know is what all of you in the consulate are thinking."

The cook asked to be released and allowed to return home. The investigator agreed, but only under the condition that she not tell anyone what she was about to hear. He told her to visit office every third day and to bring information that the NKVD needed.

"I don't know," said Paczkowska.

The agent: "We will be asking some questions, and you will need to tell us the truth. If you bring information that is useful to us, we will give you so much money that you will not have to work anymore. You will be allowed to deal in contraband and smuggle whatever you wish across the border with no restrictions whatsoever."

Paczkowska: "Agreed."

The agent: "Are you a wise person?"

Paczkowska: "I do not know."

Then the cook was asked about the chauffeur, Osmólski, his relations with his wife, and whether he had a lover. She said that his relations with his wife were good and that she did not know whether he was seeing another woman. The agent replied that he knew that Osmólski was seeing another woman.

At the end of the meeting, the agent gave Paczkowska 100 zlotys, asked her to sign a receipt, and said that from now on she was to report under the code name "Jadwiga." Paczkowska asked why she would need Polish money in the Soviet Union. The NKVD agent replied that he could send the money to Poland and give her Soviet money instead. The woman agreed. One of the agents said: "You are free to go. Come again to this office on Thursday."[140]

The next interrogation report is dated July 15, 1938. Paczkowska reported that on July 14 she went to the same house, at Karl Liebknecht Street, 58. There, she was greeted by two NKVD men who shook her hand. She told them she had no time, because the consulate was expecting a

---

[140] Ibid., k. 317–19.

guest and she had to prepare the supper. They said that they would not keep her long.

Question: "What's going on in the consulate?"

Answer: "Nothing."

Next, they asked about specific people working at the post, among others, about Osmólski and his lover again; how often Paczkowska traveled to Warsaw; whether the consul strictly controlled the housekeeping personnel, etc. She was told to show up again on July 21.[141]

However, on July 16 she was stopped by NKVD agents when she was in town. They said they wanted to talk to her, took her to a school nearby, on Marx Street, and began questioning her.

The NKVD agents: "In the morning, you usually receive [espionage] orders and you act on them; who gives them to you, surely [Wacław] Krygier?"[142]

Paczkowska: "I deliver no information and receive no orders like that."

The NKVD: "We saw you receiving letters from the collective-farm workers when you were handing over change [coins]."

Paczkowska: "Nothing like that has ever happened."

The agents asked about the kinds of intelligence materials she brought from the church. She answered that she had visited the church only twice and did not bring any information from there.

The NKVD: "It is not true. If you are going to answer this way, we will stop working with you and this will end very badly for you."

Paczkowska: "What am I supposed to tell you if I have gathered no information whatsoever?"

The NKVD: "You're not the only spy from the consulate, another one [a female] works much better than you. She knows and tells us much more."

Paczkowska: "Who is it?"

The NKVD: "We will not tell you."

During the next part of the conversation, the agents asked about Okoński again, whether he had a wife and children, and how his office looked; they asked about other employees, too. Paczkowska's answers were evasive. She answered affirmatively to the question about whether her colleagues from the consulate knew that they were being followed by the NKVD. The agents asked how the Poles recognized them, to which she replied that it was easy, since the NKVD walked directly behind them.

---

[141] Ibid., k. 320–21.

[142] The code name of the head of intelligence post H.12, Gustaw Olszewski.

The agents were curious as to who was the greatest Polish patriot in the consulate, to which she replied: "All of us." They said: "We know certainly not all of you, because some inform on you."

One of the agents then started yelling at Paczkowska, demanding to know how he was supposed to talk with her if she said she knew nothing. The cook replied: "Do you really think that the Polish lords [*panowie*] are going to talk to their servants?" The agent laughed at her words and told her to sign a document stating the following (an approximation, according to Paczkowska's reporting): "Wolski [the consulate's secretary] is a spy; he collects all possible information about the USSR. In the winter of 1936/1937, together with Mrs. Piotrowska and Mr. Koch, he transported [by vehicle] a Soviet officer out of town and left him in a roadside ditch." Paczkowska replied that she knew nothing of this event and was not going to sign anything. She suggested that she could learn more about Wolski and would tell them and sign the document the next time. The functionaries agreed and told her to come on July 19. Finally, they asked whether she knew what happened to the secret files at the consulate. She said that it was likely that they were burned. They asked whether she could deliver some of those materials. She replied that she would try, at an opportune moment. At the end, the NKVD agent advised her to cooperate better instead of replying "I don't know," because "the other [female informer] is more pleasant to work with."[143] As mentioned earlier, the next meeting could not have taken place, because Paczkowska was already back in Poland on July 20.

The NKVD sometimes tried to persuade a person to cooperate using much more brutal methods. On August 8, 1938, a janitor at the Polish consulate in Leningrad, Władysław Matulko, was arrested and beaten at the NKVD office. Threatened with firearms, he was "encouraged" to sign a declaration of cooperation with the Soviet security services. He signed nothing and was released after eight hours.[144] The next day, Matulko related all he knew about this incident to the consul, Eugeniusz Weese. He was arrested, he said, and forced into a vehicle on Krasnaia Street. During his detainment, he was beaten and encouraged to betray state secrets.[145]

---

[143] CAW, Oddz. II SG, sygn. I.303.4.1867, k. 322–24.

[144] AAN, MSZ, sygn. 6755 B, k. 107.

[145] Malutko reported to the consul, inter alia, the following content: "I was tormented for a few hours, between 11:00 p.m. and 4:30 a.m. I was given money and asked to sign a declaration of intent to cooperate. One of them, threatening me with a revolver, said that

He came back all bruised and swollen, especially his elbow and right side. Weese forwarded the statement of Matulko's deposition to the embassy: "After all that he went through, Matulko is so scared that, I am afraid, he will no longer be capable of working for the consulate."[146]

Weese made the following suggestion to the ambassador: decorate the janitor with the silver Cross of Merit for his behavior during detainment and for his unbroken perseverance. Weese emphasized that the Matulko incident was not an isolated episode; on the contrary, it was another manifestation of a systematic campaign that had been waged against the consulate the past few days. In addition to Matulko, a female cook, a Soviet citizen, was also detained on August 8, and a day later, so was a Polish citizen, a cook's assistant, Tekla Iliszko. Both women were forbidden to go shopping for the consulate, which forced the consul and his wife to do it on August 9.[147]

1.2.4.2. The Illusion of Normalization

While the retaliatory campaign was underway, the Polish MFA also attempted to come to an agreement with the Soviet side and to de-escalate the conflict, if possible. On August 13, the MFA sanctioned the ambassador in Moscow to initiate negotiations and work out a modus vivendi with the Soviets regarding the recent events. The MFA instructions sanctioned Ambassador Grzybowski to submit a binding statement announcing that Poland was going to stop all measures targeting the Soviet posts in Poland and was going to treat them according to the most-favored nation clause, with the condition that the discriminatory measures against the Polish posts, which had already been in place for quite some time (and which had put them in a much worse

---

if I did not sign I would disappear without a trace. Finally, I was asked: if I did not wish to sign now, can I agree to sign a declaration on August 16? My appointment was scheduled for 8:00 p.m., near the circus. To this I replied that if I was able to do it, I would come. I was told that they would prepare a special party for me, with drinks and ladies, and I would learn everything else then. They wanted me to swear on my daughter's life that I was going to come. To this I replied that I would be happy if I could see my family. I was advised to come to the meeting. Then they told a policeman to walk me out into the street and explain how to get back to the consulate. I returned to the consulate and immediately reported everything to you, sir, Mr. Consul." CAW, Oddz. II SG, sygn. I.303.4.2084, doc. 17.

[146] Ibid.
[147] Ibid.

situation relative not only to the Soviet posts in Poland, but also to other most-favored foreign posts in the USSR), had to end.[148]

On August 16, 1938, after receiving the MFA's instructions, and also after a conversation with Jan Karszo-Siedlewski, who was in Moscow at the time, Grzybowski went to see Vladimir Potemkin, who asked that the MFA avoid provoking any serious incidents.[149] Complying with his request, the Polish side halted all retaliatory actions that same day, August 16, limiting themselves to measures aimed merely at isolation.[150]

When Grzybowski arrived to see Potemkin, he began by saying: "We wish to have normal and good relations with the Soviet Union, but not at the price of suffering insults and abuse. Such a price is too high for us." After a few polite remarks, Potemkin mentioned "the Polish incidents" and asked, "What do you propose, Mr. Ambassador?" Grzybowski made three proposals:

1. Cessation of all unwarranted arrests and detainments at police stations (he mentioned the numerous cases of provocation and the attempts to recruit Poles to work for the Soviet secret services).

2. Normalization of existing conditions within the area of customs, provision of labor, renovations, etc. Potemkin added postal, telegraph, and telephone services to the list.

3. Exterritoriality for the Polish drivers.[151]

Potemkin promised an answer after he had consulted with the relevant authorities. He remained silent for a few days. Finally, on August 21, 1938, he invited Grzybowski to see him and told him the first two suggestions made at the previous meeting had been accepted. Potemkin proposed that arrests, detainments at police posts, and demands for identity verification would cease on August 22; as for existing conditions, the form of operations normally applicable to diplomatic and consular corps would be in place, without any discrimination. However, the

---

[148] AAN, MSZ, sygn. 6755 B, k. 132.

[149] Ibid., k. 139.

[150] Ibid., k. 172. Despite these changes, on August 17, 1938, the Soviet embassy in Warsaw issued a vehement protest to the Polish MFA that included a description of all the Polish repressions that began on July 18, 1938: identity verification, detentions, provocative behavior, and nondelivery of mail. Ibid., 154–58; E. Basiński et al., eds., *Dokumenty i materiały do historii stosunków polsko-radzieckich*, vol. 6, *1933–1938* (Warsaw: Książka i Wiedza, 1967), 405–8. See also O. Rublov and N. Rubl'ova, eds., *Ukraïna-Pol'shcha 1920– 1939 rr.: Z istorii dyplomatychnykh vidnosyn URSR z Druhoiu Richchiu Pospolytoiu. Dokumenty i materialy* (Kyiv: Dukh i litera, 2012), 55.

[151] AAN, MSZ, sygn. 6755 B, k. 200–201.

condition of exterritoriality for chauffeurs was something he did not wish to accept, while at the same time indicating that he "was ready to look for a conciliatory way out in each single case."[152]

According to his encrypted telegram, sent immediately after the meeting to Warsaw, Grzybowski believed, perhaps overly optimistically, that the continuing incidents would now certainly come to an end. He asked for an immediate cessation of the overt surveillance and identity verification of the Soviet officials in Poland.[153] On the following day, Jan Karszo-Siedlewski left for Warsaw with a detailed report on the meeting with Potemkin.[154]

In fact, the intensified harassment did stop on August 21, or, to be more precise, conditions returned to the pre-retaliatory period. The Soviet authorities found a new middle ground between their behavior before and their behavior after the Polish retaliatory measures — that is, as the counselor Matusiński observed, the "rats" still followed the consulate's employees, but they no longer did it "so insolently as in the past: now they tried to put on a bit of a disguise." There were some manifestations of normalization. A janitor who had been employed to sweep the street in front of the Kyiv consulate returned to his workplace.[155] The NKVD car that had been parked directly in front of the Polish post was moved toward the police station located on the other corner of the street. During the afternoon of August 21, someone called Matusiński from the office of the PCfFA representative with the message that the courier's ticket was ready (several days after the aforementioned delay), and then another message came in saying that it would be possible to reregister the car the next day.[156]

---

[152] Ibid., k. 201.

[153] Ibid., k. 176.

[154] Ibid.

[155] Unofficially the man told a Polish janitor that "they fired me from work, and now they told me to return and to say that I was sick." CAW, Oddz. II, SG, sygn. I.303.4.1867, k. 780.

[156] Ibid., k. 777–781. Other officials also delivered similar news about "repressions slowing down." On September 23, Adam Koch wrote to the embassy that the Soviet attitude toward the post had returned to pre-August 6 levels: "spying on foot and in vehicles [continues], the same about following us into buildings." On October 15, 1938, Witold Okoński informed the embassy that the Minsk consulate essentially had experienced no harassment since August. What had not changed was the isolation and surveillance of the post, some difficulties with supplies, etc. Consul Eugeniusz Weese had similar impressions. On October 19, 1938, he reported that the Leningrad authorities applied the

In an after-action report written on September 1, 1938, the Political Department of the MFA submitted an application to the diplomatic protocol listing all the persons who, at the MFA's request, had been engaged in the retaliatory campaign against the Soviets.[157] Despite the agreement reached with Moscow, Warsaw knew full well that it could be temporary. On September 2, 1938, the main office of the *Dwójka* wrote a letter to its agents, thanking them for their perseverance but also warning them to remain cautious: "The two-week period that you have gone through recently, with the resulting increased harassment applied against you by our dear hosts, has demonstrated a high level of endurance in all our agents, which manifested itself in remaining calm and cold-blooded, and in the right kind of attitude toward the situation, for which, on our bosses' recommendation, we would like to express our deep satisfaction and recognition of merit. The games are not over yet; you need to approach the current state of affairs as an armistice. But as you can see, we have things under control and are systematically striving to re-establish relatively normal conditions for our life in the field."[158]

The near future would soon show that the armistice would not last long. The extensive and exhaustive report that Jerzy Matusiński sent to the MFA on October 13, 1938, offers a glimpse into the operational conditions of the Polish posts. He wrote that everything stayed more or less the same—surveillance, isolating the posts from both official and social contacts, nondelivery of the press, screening and interception of correspondence, problems with supplies, and difficulties with border crossings. Unsurprisingly, the number of visitors was extremely low. From the end of the period of increased harassments, i.e., August 21, 1938, until the submission of the report—that is fifty-four days later—the Polish consulate general in Kyiv had a total of fourteen visitors, not counting Intourist customers. Matusiński wrote that visitors were no longer interrogated immediately after leaving the consulate, as they had in the

---

same measures after the truce as in the pre-retaliatory period. Some visitors, in particular foreigners who applied for transit visas, were asked for their IDs; the agents followed two or three steps behind all of his posts' employees, entered into stores and theaters, and listened to conversation. Based on the materials delivered by the consulates on October 31, 1938, the Polish embassy in Moscow sent a report to the MFA that concluded that the Soviet attitude toward the Polish posts had returned to that held during the pre-retaliatory period. AAN, MSZ, 6755 B, k. 301–2, 308–11, 328–34.

[157] AAN, MSZ, 6755 B, k. 290.

[158] CAW, Oddz. II SG, sygn. I.303.4.1967, n.p., doc. 15.

past, but he suspected that this simply could have taken place elsewhere. To support this, he quoted the case of one visitor, a female Soviet citizen, who was asked to return to the consulate two hours after her initial visit. However, she did not return, which, as the diplomat suspected, could have been the result of NKVD persuasion.

Jerzy Matusiński focused on one more aspect during the post-retaliatory period, namely, the psychological depression Polish officials experienced working in the Soviet Union. This condition was caused by all the affronts they experienced, which resulted in a dramatic fall in the level of prestige a member of the consular corps normally enjoyed. Matusiński's report included the following: "From a moral point of view, it is good for us to know that analogous methods are currently applied to the Soviet officials in Poland. However, it is hard not be aware of the decline in prestige of our profession, and hence of our personal status. The insolent, sometimes even insulting, behavior of NKVD agents toward us, as well as the disregard for the gravitas of the office and the head of the consulate personally manifested by the representative of the PCfFA, which took place during the recent period of repressions, could not have left anything but a very sorry, not to say humiliating, atmosphere of permitted insolence on the Soviet side. We are still surrounded by and, it has to be added, dependent on the very same individuals who have already learned how to pester and humiliate us, and this circumstance must be recognized as immeasurably sad and harmful."[159]

On November 2, 1938, Matusiński's deputy, Vice-consul Koch, put together a report about the Soviet attitude toward his post. The report essentially included all the main points that his boss had already mentioned. Koch added the worsening state of relations with the PCfFA, which had ceased to respond altogether to the various grievances. In answer to all grievances, the representative of the PCfFA redirected the Polish side to the relevant local authorities, meaning he had effectively resigned as mediator between the Polish office and those same authorities. This, in Koch's words, was "a new line vis-à-vis the consulate." All attempts to change anything and all the claims filed with the local authorities were futile, however. Those institutions usually did not even bother to reply. When, for example, the consulate was able to hire some workers (to chop wood) directly from the labor pool, the

---

[159] AAN, MSZ, 6755 B, k. 312–19.

workers were likely either arrested or persuaded not to go back to work, because they failed to show up the second day and did not even bother to ask for their pay for the first day. Koch also mentioned the fact of putting up a four-meter-high wire fence around the Polish post on November 1, 1938. It separated the consulate from the tenement house across the yard.[160]

Unsurprisingly, the issue of the Polish posts in the USSR soon reappeared on the agenda, this time in talks between Ambassador Grzybowski and the head of the PCfFA, Maxim Litvinov. Of course, that was not the only topic that was discussed. It was just one issue among others in the overall problematic state of relations with the Soviet Union, especially in the context of the need to strengthen the Polish position vis-à-vis Germany. Poland tried this way to send the message to Berlin that it had other options than relying on German goodwill.[161]

On October 25, 1938, on the initiative of the people's commissar, a conversation took place on the issue of good, neighborly relations. Grzybowski mentioned the following basic premises: a return to the legitimate legal order by respecting the treaties that had already been signed (e.g., the change in the train schedule between Kyiv and Zdolbuniv, which meant that train journeys took place during the night; and the disappearance of Polish citizens in the USSR); cessation of propagandistic attacks in Soviet newspapers on Polish foreign policy; increase in the amount of trade; and better treatment of Polish diplomatic and consular posts. Litvinov answered that these proposals were not the foundation, but the roof. When a foundation is being laid, one has to keep in mind the design for the entire building. According to Litvinov, the foundation should be "a political conception aimed at preserving peace in our part of Europe, with a simultaneous determination of the measures that will help to reach that goal." He suggested the concept of "a mutual strengthening of our countries." When Grzybowski asked for more details, he replied that "it was merely an example."[162]

As a result of subsequent talks, the content of a communiqué was determined. It was published in the Soviet press on November 27, 1938, and in the Polish press one day later. It itemized the following: "First,

---

[160] CAW, Oddz. II SG, sygn. I.303.4.1867, k. 793–95.
[161] M. Kornat, *Polska 1939 roku wobec paktu Ribbentrop-Mołotow: Problem zbliżenia niemiecko-sowieckiego w polityce zagranicznej II Rzeczypospolitej* (Warsaw: PISM, 2002), 249–52.
[162] AAN, MSZ, sygn. 6755 A, k. 14–15; M. Kornat, ed., *Polskie Dokumenty Dyplomatyczne: 1938* (Warsaw: PISM, 2007), 732–33.

the many talks between Litvinov and Grzybowski led to a clarification that the Polish-Soviet Non-Aggression Pact of July 25, 1932 (extended on May 5, 1934, until the end of 1945) remains the foundation for mutual relations. Second, both governments look forward to increasing the volume of trade. Third, both governments agree on the necessity of resolving many ongoing issues originating in bilateral treaty relations, especially those outstanding, and on the elimination of the recently arisen border incidents." Finally, the communiqué declared that the Litvinov-Grzybowski talks, as well as the communiqué itself, were an expression of the permanent and unchangeable will of both governments to regulate bilateral relations through a faithful realization of those treaties. "This most recent inclination seems to provide a sufficient basis for the stabilization of relations in the Polish-Soviet borderlands."[163]

On November 29, 1938, Grzybowski informed Foreign Minister Beck about his last conversation with Litvinov. Among the few important issues, the situation of the Polish posts was also discussed. Litvinov's remark, when the interlocutors reached that point on the agenda, was highly characteristic and can partially be read as an explanation for the Bolsheviks' motives: "In the future, Mr. Ambassador, the relationship toward third countries will certainly be of significance. You, sir, and your colleagues guide your relations with Germany through the necessity of neighborly cooperation, but Japan is not your neighbor. We are certain, however, that all the information about the USSR obtained by Polish intelligence is communicated to Japanese intelligence, and vice versa. Please believe me that our public opinion is deeply hurt by all the favorable Polish gestures toward Japan."[164] Grzybowski answered that he

---

[163] See AAN, MSZ, sygn. 6755 A, k. 49; Ibid., k. 50; *Official Documents Concerning Polish-German and Polish-Soviet Relations, 1933–1939* (London and Melbourne: Ministerstwo Spraw Zagranicznych, 1940), 181–82; *Polish-Soviet Relations, 1918-1943: Documents* (New York: Polish Government Information Center, 1943), 21–22; *Dokumenty i materiały do historii*, 422; *Diariusz i teki Jana Szembeka*, 4: 450; R. Debicki, *Foreign Policy of Poland, 1919–39: From the Rebirth of the Polish Republic to World War II* (New York: Praeger, 1962), 122; I. Kostiushko, ed., *Materialy "osoboi papki" Politbiuro TsK RKP(b)-VKP(b) po voprosu sovetsko-polskikh otnoshenii 1923–1944 gg.: Sbornik dokumentov* (Moscow: Institut slavianovedeniia i balkanistiki RAN, 1997), 116–17; Kornat, *Polskie Dokumenty Dyplomatyczne*, 793–94; and A. Bondarenko et al., eds., *God krizisa, 1938–1939: Dokumenty i materialy*, vol. 1, *29 sentiabria 1938 g.–31 maia 1939 g.* (Moscow: Politizdat, 1990), 117.

[164] AAN, MSZ, sygn. 6755 A, k. 114–15, 118–19; Kornat, *Polskie Dokumenty Dyplomatyczne*, 802.

was not aware of any exchange of information and that there was no Polish-Japanese treaty directed against the Soviets.

How did the new declaration influence the process of improvement in the way the Polish posts functioned? It is not difficult to guess: almost nothing whatsoever changed. What can be mentioned as changing are the cessation of press attacks[165] and the resolution of some minor logistical problems the consulates experienced. Tadeusz Jankowski did inform the MFA, on December 10, 1938, that the NKVD's behavior in relation to the embassy was quite proper, but he also wrote that he saw no change for the better.[166]

Jerzy Matusiński in turn, on December 11, 1938, wrote in a report to the embassy that, after the Litvinov-Grzybowski agreement of November 27, 1938, a degree of improvement could be seen, especially with the anti-Polish campaign in the Ukrainian press ceasing. And, inter alia, the old train schedule on the Kyiv-Shepetivka-Zdolbuniv route had been reinstated, and subscriptions to all the requested journals had been renewed. There was no improvement in terms of isolation and surveillance, however. Furthermore, more Soviet agents appeared on duty before the consulate's entrance. And the behavior of agents did not change; they continued to walk right behind the consulate's employees. Both those visitors who entered and those who left the Polish consular building were interrogated. There was no improvement with respect to communications: the Soviet side continued screening the mail, and supply and technical issues remained unaddressed, e.g., the consular phone had already been out of commission for two months.[167]

The words of the Leningrad consul, Eugeniusz Weese, can serve as a summary of the sorts of conditions in which the Polish posts had to work. He wrote them on December 9. In his opinion, nothing had changed after the November 27, 1938 treaty. He emphasized: "The state of complete isolation, combined with the harassment by [Soviet] agents, creates conditions of existence for the officials that are so difficult that they can be compared with prison life."[168]

---

[165] Kornat, *Polska 1939 roku*, 249.

[166] AAN, MSZ, sygn. 6755 A, k. 130.

[167] Ibid., sygn. 6755 B, k. 354–55.

[168] Ibid., k. 356-357. As evidenced by the November 21, 1938 letter written by Pavel Listopad to the Soviet PCfFA in Moscow, the behavior of the Polish security forces was adequately proportional to the behavior of the Soviet NKVD with respect to the Poles. See Bondarenko et al, eds., *God krizisa*, 109.

1.3. Internal Relations in the Polish Consulates

Constant harassment, difficulties encountered when trying to solve even the most prosaic of issues, and detainment of and attempts to recruit members of the consular and auxiliary corps on the part of the Soviets all influenced the consulates' daily operations extremely negatively. The officials deployed in the field of Soviet affairs had to be well equipped to bear the psychological burdens of their work. In such uneasy surroundings as the Soviet Union, it was of the utmost importance to provide the workers, particularly for their superiors, with the best possible working conditions, at least within the posts themselves. This meant, more than anything else, avoiding unnecessary conflict situations.

Relations between the management and the personnel developed differently in the two consulates in Ukraine. Insofar as the posts that Jan Karszo-Siedlewski led are concerned (Kharkiv initially, then Kyiv from mid-1934), we can conclude that no major conflicts or tensions took place, judging from the available material.[169] The same cannot be said about the leadership of Stanisław Sośnicki (initially in Kyiv and later in Kharkiv.)[170]

Sośnicki had a difficult personality. Despite the fact that he was the head of intelligence post Kh, he was often in conflict with the other intelligence agents, who, since they worked in the consulate as officials, were technically his subordinates. Zofia Kurnicka (former last name, Więckowska), who led intelligence post Z.12, complained to Jerzy Niezbrzycki in March 1934 that cooperation with Sośnicki did not develop smoothly ("prejudices, constant distrust, and envy of everything"). The consul's behavior, according to Kurnicka, stemmed from rumors about the reasons he had had to abandon the Kyiv post and be replaced by Jan Karszo-Siedlewski, which made him "more irritable than ever before... He cannot bear the thought that Piotr [Kurnicki] could stay here for longer than he did." Kurnicka had her own reasons for writing about Sośnicki this way, which ultimately backfired against Piotr Kurnicki, for the consul was capable of talking to him while turned away from him, "projecting upon him all of his endless grievances, dissatisfaction, and bad blood."

---

[169] See also Kruszyński, *Ambasada RP*, 276.

[170] In the preceding period, some conflicts between the leaders of the posts, i.e., Konstanty Skrzyński and Adam Stebłowski, and their personnel did take place. Both were heads of the Polish consulates in Kharkiv, and Stebłowski later led the Tbilisi post. CAW, Oddz. II SG, sygn. 2095, n.p., doc. 23.

The situation was bad enough that Kurnicka and Sośnicki agreed to "mutually relieve themselves of the duty of accompanying each other at the dinner table."[171]

After Sośnicki took over the Kharkiv post, his relations with his subordinates there were also far from exemplary. Near the end of 1936, a rather serious conflict with Ludwik Michałowski unfolded, and also with Stanisław Suchecki, who backed Michałowski. The conflict ended with Sośnicki's dismissal from the Kharkiv post on November 1, 1936, after which, by order of the chief of the Main Staff, he was hurried into retirement on December 31, 1936.[172]

On October 4, 1936, around 1:00 p.m., Michałowski slapped Sośnicki in the face after a personal affront. Afterwards Michałowski, who was head of intelligence post G.27, immediately reported the incident to the ambassador and to Wiktor Tomir Drymmer.[173] He also informed the *Dwójka* that he was willing to accept a dismissal. In a letter to Jerzy Niezbrzycki he stressed that, in his opinion, the consul needed to be dismissed to protect the good name of the service.[174]

Michałowski was summoned to Warsaw. He left Kharkiv on October 10, 1936, together with his wife. After his departure, Stanisław Suchecki took over the consular affairs, apart from the lockbox, codes, and passport blanks, which Sośnicki still controlled.

Michałowski arrived in the capital on October 12, 1936. He immediately submitted a detailed verbal report of the incident. At the same time, he filed a claim with the Court of Honor. During the scuffle with Michałowski, Consul Sośnicki had sprained his arm and could not appear right away in Warsaw. Instead he arrived in early November.[175]

Stanisław Suchecki, an official in the consulate and head of intelligence post E.10, intervened in the Sośnicki-Michałowski conflict in

---

[171] Ibid., sygn. I. 303.4.2095, n.p., doc. 3.

[172] RGVA, f. 453 k, op. 1, d. 6, l. 64, v.-65.

[173] Wiktor Tomir Drymmer (1896–1975) was an officer who joined the MFA in 1929. Between 1931 and the war's outbreak, he was head of the HR department of the MFA and, from 1933, head of the consular department. He emigrated after the war. For more information about his career, see K. Paduszek, "Meandry kariery Wiktora Tomira Drymmera w wywiadzie II Rzeczypospolitej," *Przegląd Historyczno-Wojskowy*, 2008, no. 4: 47–64. See also his memoirs: W. T. Drymmer, "Wspomnienia," *Zeszyty Historyczne* 127 (1974): 172–94; 128 (1974): 173–218; 129 (1974): 157–86; 130 (1974): 196–227; 131 (1975): 53–121; and idem, *W służbie Polsce* (Warsaw: Warszawska Oficyna Wydawnicza "Gryf," 1998).

[174] CAW, Oddz. II SG, sygn. I.303.4.1967, n.p. doc. 136.

[175] Ibid. n.p., no doc. number.

a determined and radical way. He had witnessed, on October 1 and October 11, the consul talking on the phone with someone whom Sośnicki addressed as "Mr. Consul" (most likely, it was Consul Tadeusz Błaszkiewicz). Those conversations were handled in a particularly indiscreet way, especially considering that the Bolsheviks were likely eavesdropping. Sośnicki paid no attention to this, however, and openly discussed the entire incident with Michałowski, using the real names of those involved. Among other things, he said that "one of them has already left [Michałowski], while he would talk to the ambassador about the second one [Suchecki]." Given this, and the fact that Sośnicki promised to call again, Suchecki gave the order to cut the telephone lines, because, in his opinion, there was no other way to avoid the leaking of information to the outside world, since the phone was located in Sośnicki's apartment. Suchecki wrote a letter to the ambassador informing him of the decision to cut the phone cable. Wanda Czarnocka, an official in the consulate, who was also supposed to inform her superiors about the consulate's work in more detail, delivered the letter to Moscow.[176]

Suchecki wrote another letter to Sośnicki. In it he advised Sośnicki to reflect on his behavior, warning him that, if he did not, Suchecki would be forced to apply another set of measures against him:

"I have learned that you pay visits to a doctor. In this regard, I am obliged to communicate to you that I consider this to be inadvisable, or — I must underline — tactless, for you to see a doctor, because you need to be aware of the fact that it can lead to undesirable comments in the outside world, particularly after the phone calls to Moscow.

I hope that you will take the aforementioned advice seriously and that you will not compel me to apply more measures, which will have to be done if you, sir, do not, follow my advice.

At the same time, please allow me to tell you that I have ordered the phone cable cut due to your careless conversation with Moscow, which forced me, by the way, to deal with all the consequences. I will order the phone to be repaired if I am sure that it will not be used to hold indiscreet conversations.

Furthermore, I ask you, sir, for calm and tactful behavior, not only regarding the outside world but also inside your own institution, if you do not wish to force me to apply harsher measures. Please patiently wait

---

[176] RGVA, f. 308 k, op. 19, d. 63, l. 251.

for the relevant decision to arrive from the authorities, and do not cause unnecessary disruption in the normal flow of work and life."[177]

In the letter Wanda Czarnocka delivered to Ambassador Suchecki, he mentioned some other problematic issues for which, in his opinion, the consul was to blame. He accused Sośnicki of mismanagement and financial malversations. The mismanagement pertained to the way the casino was run. Until October 5, 1936, Sośnicki personally managed the casino; after that, Wanda Czarnocka did. Judging by the books and receipts, and by the opinions of the casino employees, Sośnicki had run it in a way that raised questions.[178]

The other charges were about some overdue financial obligations and about an act of appropriation that Sośnicki committed using wages due to auxiliary personnel. The Michałowski couple had not received a 200 zloty reimbursement they were owed for leaving the apartment they rented earlier. The housekeeping personnel did not receive their wages for the month of October. Furthermore, Sośnicki deducted forty zlotys from the September salary of a housemaid, Bronisława Ozimkowa, because she accidentally broke a few plates. However, that fact had not been registered anywhere. Yet Sośnicki's books stated that the entire monthly payment had been paid in full.[179]

Suchecki drew the ambassador's attention to the fact that the housekeeping personnel knew of the incident. In addition to Sośnicki's indiscretion, this could have caused additional complications, since, the behavior of the consulate's head was known not only to officials, but also to housekeeping personnel. Faced with these facts, the head of intelligence post E.10 wrote, the continuation of Sośnicki's service and his presence in the office was impossible, given the harm it caused to the reputation of the consular office. "If this consideration had been somehow removed, then

---

[177] Ibid., l. 250.

[178] Wanda Czarnocka ran the casino until October 27, 1936. On October 5, 1936, after the Michałowski incident, she received 100 rubles from Sośnicki with verbal instructions to run the casino. As she herself emphasized, because of some inaccuracies in the books, a deficit, and the inability to cover the casino's debts and dues (including the employees' payroll), she was not able to carry on managing the casino: she could not afford to carry both the moral and the material aspects of responsibility for it. Consequently, she handed over the accounting book (for the period from October 5 until October 27), together with the receipts and the cash lockbox (135,65 zlotys and 205,02 rubles), to Tadeusz Błaszkiewicz, the acting head of the consulate. Ibid., l. 265.

[179] Ibid., l. 251–52.

the continuation of Mr. Sośnicki's presence in the office would have been possible only if the entire staff had been replaced."[180]

Suchecki advised the authorities to form a special commission and send it to Kharkiv as soon as possible to investigate the consulate's operations and improve its internal situation. Until the arrival of such a commission, Suchecki told the ambassador, he would not let anyone near the post's papers and finances. He would cancel this policy only if the ambassador unambiguously requested it be lifted.[181]

A day after sending his letter to Ambassador Grzybowski, Suchecki composed another letter, this time to the East section of the Second Department. In it he wrote that one could cooperate with a person like Sośnicki for as long as he remained useful, but "as soon as he becomes harmful, there can be no talk of cooperation." Suchecki had mistrusted Sośnicki from the very beginning, but, because he wanted to leave in early November, he wanted to keep their working relationship proper until the end. The head of post E.10 underlined that he asked for a "commission" to be established not on a personal whim but for professional and formal reasons: "I have to stay fair to myself, especially because I cannot expect S. to deal with this matter the way it should be, especially because I have evidence of his disloyalty with respect to some of the previous employees."

Suchecki remarked that he was going to pursue this matter to the end: "Regardless, after this whole case is closed, I would like to ask for a holiday leave. I am a bit tired already."[182]

A few days letter, a reply from the East Section arrived. Captain Wacław Zalewski wrote back to Suchecki, saying that he should not have interfered in the conflict between "Mr. S and Mr. M."[183] As a result, Suchecki was called home on November 1, 1936. After his return, he received his November salary and a month-long leave. Before his departure from Kharkiv, on October 27, 1936, he married a Soviet citizen, Neonila Shyshkina.[184] In a note Zalewski wrote that dealt with the termination of Suchecki's intelligence post, he gives the following description of its head:

---

[180] Ibid., l. 253.
[181] Ibid., l. 253–54.
[182] Ibid. k. 90; ibid.d. 63, l. 249–249 v.
[183] Ibid., op. 19, d. 63, l. 236.
[184] Ibid., l. 292.

"Suchecki was unable to stay neutral with respect to the incident between Michałowski and Sośnicki. The whole range of his measures with respect to the consulate, Sośnicki, and the cadres was completely inappropriate. He exposed himself to criticism from the embassy and the MFA. He could not have been allowed to stay in the field any longer. The results of his work are essentially satisfactory. He displayed a lot of initiative and was a risk taker. He could not have remained in the field of Soviet affairs, however, due to the flaws of his character, which bordered on occasional unreliability and unpredictability."[185]

On October 24, 1936, a general meeting took place, attended by the officials of the Polish consulate in Kharkiv in the presence of Consul Błaszkiewicz (Czarnocka and Suchecki were also present). The casino issue was on the agenda. After the meeting, a plan of action to deal with the problems of Sośnicki's mismanagement and the underpayment of forty zlotys to Ozimkowa was put together.[186] Ludwik Michałowski was initially sent to Kyiv, but then, after the Second Department intervened, he was again sent to Kharkiv,[187] where he stayed until the end of March 1939.

After Sośnicki's dismissal, Tadeusz Błaszkiewicz took over his post until the arrival of the new consul, Tadeusz Brzeziński, on December 1, 1936. Brzeziński was the last Polish consul in Kharkiv, there until the post was closed at the end of 1937. Documents available indicate that the period of his leadership also suffered from some internal conflict. His relationship with Jerzy Kamiński, head of intelligence post X.37, was far from ideal. When the Polish consulate in Kharkiv was about to be closed down and its assets returned to the state, Kamiński accused Brzeziński's wife of appropriating a piece of silk for her personal use, i.e., as a lining for her capes, instead of letting it be used for its intended purpose, repairing the back of a sofa located in the consulate's guest chamber. Kamiński wrote a letter to the consular department of the MFA: "Mr. Brzeziński could not have been unaware of the fact that his wife appropriated a state-owned asset, because it seems unthinkable that Mrs. Brzezińska could have used the piece of silk, hidden in a drawer (alongside other government assets), without asking anyone about its provenance. Due to the fact that Mr. Brzeziński deserves no respect whatsoever regardless of this case (the evidence for which I can provide

---

[185] Ibid., l. 293.
[186] Ibid. l. 267–70.
[187] Ibid. f. 453 k, op. 1, d. 6, l. 86–86 v.

at request), I request to be withdrawn from the Kharkiv post as soon as possible."[188]

The later career of Consul Brzeziński leads us to conclude that this letter was probably not taken seriously. The consul was transferred to another post in Montreal.

1.4. The Position of Other Consular Posts

During the period under examination here, apart from the Polish consulates in Kyiv and Kharkiv, a few other countries also had consulates in Soviet Ukraine. Germany, Italy, and Czechoslovakia (1936–38) had their representatives in Kyiv. The Italian consulate was closed after the capital was moved from Kharkiv to Kyiv.[189] Germany, Italy, Japan, and Turkey had consulates in Odesa.

After pressure from the Bolsheviks in 1937 and 1938, not only the Polish consulate in Kharkiv but also all the German consulates in the USSR were closed (five of them by November 1937, and the two last posts, in Kyiv and Novosibirsk, in May 1938),[190] as were the Czechoslovak consulate in Kyiv (early 1938), the Japanese in Odesa (September 1937),[191] and the Turkish in Odesa (February 1938).[192] By the end of 1938, all of the existing Italian posts had been closed.[193] In the mid-1930s, the governments of France and the United States did consider establishing consulates in Kyiv, but they gave up on that idea, both because of the rather hostile attitude of the Soviets, who attempted to decrease rather than increase the density of the consular network in their country, and because of the uncertainty for any potential benefit in maintaining such a post in Kyiv.[194]

---

[188] CAW, Oddz. II SG, sygn. I.303.4.1867, k. 282-282 v.

[189] RGVA, f. 308 k, op. 19, d. 53, l. 117.

[190] AAN, MSZ, sygn. 1472 B, k. 13–14. As Hans von Herwarth noted following conversations with the German consuls who were returning to Germany through Moscow, the German Reich did not lose much from the closure of the posts, since the value of the information collected there was not proportional to the extraordinarily arduous work conditions for the German consuls in the field; see von Herwarth, *Między Hitlerem a Stalinem*, 127.

[191] "Zakrytie iaponskikh konsul'stv v Odesse i Novosibirske," *Pravda*, September 14, 1937.

[192] L. Belkovets, "Iz istorii konsulskogo prava: likvidatsiia inostrannykh konsul'skikh predstavitel'stv v SSSR w kontse 1930-kh godov," http://justicemaker.ru/viewarticle.php?id=11&art=680, accessed June 20, 2012; see also: http://www.turkey.mid.ru/20-30gg.html, accessed June 20, 2012.

[193] RGVA, f. 464 k, op. 1, d. 2424, l. 75; Skóra, "Porwanie kierownika," 418.

[194] RGVA, f. 308 k, op. 19, d. 53, l. 117, v.

Ultimately, the Polish consulate general in Kyiv was the only foreign post in Ukraine that survived until the end of the interwar period.[195] Needless to say, there were many other countries, in addition to these mentioned, whose posts were closed. The Bolsheviks wanted the countries that maintained diplomatic posts in the USSR to stick to the principle of equivalence, i.e., if a country had more posts in the USSR than the USSR had in that country, then the surplus number of the foreign posts in the USSR would be limited. It was in accordance with this principle that the consular posts of countries such as Denmark, Sweden, Afghanistan, Turkey, Finland, Great Britain, Estonia, and Latvia were closed down in the USSR.[196]

The relations between personnel of the Polish consulates and officials from other foreign posts were usually proper. The best relations were with the German and Italian representatives. Friendly relations were also maintained with the Japanese post in Odesa. The Poles stressed this fact in many of their reports. When Stanisław Sośnicki took over the Polish post in Kharkiv (on August 4, 1934), he immediately went on a courtesy tour of the posts occupied by his foreign colleagues. The German consulate was quick to offer close cooperation, particularly in the informational sphere.[197] Sośnicki reported that the information he received from the German consulate was subsequently verified by other sources, meaning that it was very likely authentic.[198] Earlier Jan Karszo-Siedlewski, Sośnicki's predecessor in Kharkiv, also enjoyed good relations with the Germans and the Italians.

Karszo-Siedlewski maintained friendly relations with the Italian consul, Sergi, and the German consul, Georg Grosskopf. The German official supported some of the initiatives that his Polish colleague launched. In October 1936, Karszo-Siedlewski and Grosskopf held a cordial conversation with the deputy representative of the PCfFA, Mikhail

---

[195] Moreover, the Polish consulates in Minsk and Leningrad also survived. The consular section of the Polish embassy in Moscow kept on operating as well, as did the military attaché. Indeed, as Sławomir Nowinowski noted, the number of consulates that Poland maintained in the Soviet Union was quite impressive compared with other countries; see Nowinowski, "Zakończenie działalności ambasady," 3.

[196] See AAN, MSZ, sygn. 1472 B, k. 1–15; and "The German Ambassador in the Soviet Union (Schulenburg) to the German Foreign Ministry": "Subject: The Closing of Foreign Consulates in the Soviet Union and the Abolition of Soviet Consulates," http://avalon.law.yale.edu/20th_century/nsa615.asp, accessed July 20, 2011.

[197] RGVA, f. 308 k, op. 4, d. 24, l. 184.

[198] Ibid., op. 19, d. 53, l. 132–34.

Yushkevich, in which they pointed out that the Soviet authorities should undertake some determined measures to put the Polish military cemetery on Baikova Hora in Kyiv back in order. Some cows and goats were grazing in it, damaging the crosses and tombs. Moreover, the dead from Kyiv infirmaries were being buried nearby. A few days after the conversation, this practice ceased. Earlier, as mentioned above, Walther, the German consul in Kharkiv, had supported Sośnicki's protest after the attempt at the Kharkiv railway station to detain Jan Łagoda and Ludwik Michałowski.[199]

The worst, at least in terms of personal affinities, were relations with the representatives of Czechoslovakia in Kyiv.[200] This was in part a consequence of the poor relations between Warsaw and Prague, and in part because of Czechoslovak admiration for the Soviets, which certainly irked the Polish side. Furthermore, the Czechoslovak consular personnel in Kyiv were completely oblivious to the particularity of the field of Soviet affairs.[201] The Polish records do not contain any traces of information about relations with the Turkish consulate in Odesa.

---

[199] CAW, Oddz. II SG, sygn. I.303.4.1867, k. 495-496, 499.

[200] As the Polish military attaché in Moscow, Lieutenant Colonel Konstanty Zaborowski, reported to Tadeusz Pełczyński, head of the *Dwójka*, on March 1, 1938, the first invitation to his Polish colleague from the Czechoslovak consul, Rudolf Brabec, came only in 1938, even though the Czechoslovak post had been in existence since 1936. This visit was not part of the standard courtesy or protocol meetings of the consular corps; rather, it was part of Czechoslovak attempts to improve their relations with Poland, as well as a continuation of the earlier contacts established in Moscow. In mid-February 1938, František Dastych, the Czechoslovak military attaché in Moscow, met with Zaborowski's assistant, Major Stanisław Maleciński. In addition, a representative of the Czechoslovak press met with Editor Feliks Tadeusz Haczyński. See P. Kołakowski, *Między Warszawą a Pragą: Polsko-czechosłowackie stosunki wojskowo-polityczne, 1918–1939* (Warsaw: Bellona, 2009), 459–61.

[201] Jan Karszo-Siedlewski characterized the newly appointed Czechoslovak consul in Kyiv, Rudolf Brabec, in the following way: "I heard he was a lawyer, but as a consul he does not display any initiative or perceptiveness. He is taciturn, awkward socially, makes an impression of a dull bureaucrat, has little knowledge about the foreign milieus, and does not seem to be interested in his surroundings. He is married [but] has no children. His attitude towards Poland is positive." On October 31, 1936, the Polish diplomat again restated his opinion about Brabec, emphasizing that he was not interested in anything and did not play any major role in consular life. His two secretaries, according to Karszo-Siedlewski, were Sovietophiles. They would call the Polish consulate to obtain information, as they lacked basic knowledge about the local environment. CAW, Oddz. II SG, sygn. I.303.4.1867, k. 470, 499.

The Polish reports also include some reflections on how the foreign posts of other countries operated in the second half of the 1930s. On February 23, 1935, Stanisław Sośnicki received a letter from Hirata, the Japanese consul in Odesa, who had also been the secretary of the Japanese mission in Warsaw for six years, in which he asked whether the consulates in Kharkiv were under heavy surveillance. Hirata wrote that the foreign posts in Odesa were being watched not only by Soviet agents in front of the consulate buildings, but also by agents who followed personnel when they were walking in the streets and going shopping. This form of surveillance was only abandoned after a joint protest of the Japanese, German, Italian, and Turkish consuls in Odesa.[202] At that time, the intensity of surveillance in Kharkiv was perhaps not as high, but the German consul, Walther, nonetheless complained to Sośnicki that all visitors to the consulate were being photographed. When one visitor to the German consulate was leaving Kharkiv, he was stopped at the railway station and asked about the purpose of his visit there. The man denied that he had been at the consulate, but he was shown a photograph. The same practice was inflicted upon visitors to the Polish consulate, who consequently avoided going there.[203]

On March 24, 1935, Jan Karszo-Siedlewski mentioned in a report to the Second Department that he had recently visited Odesa. While there, he met with Hirata, who could not have shared any valuable information with him, despite his genuine intention to do so, because "he was so isolated and guarded so carefully by the Soviet authorities that he could have neither moved nor communicated with anyone." No one was visiting the Japanese consulate, because everyone feared immediate arrest. Hirata himself had to limit his observations to the city of Odesa and its port. The Polish diplomat also held conversations in Odesa with the general consuls of Italy and Germany.[204]

---

[202] RGVA, f. 308 k, op. 19, d. 54, l. 56.

[203] Ibid., l. 76.

[204] The Polish report contained no details about the operations of those consulates in Odesa. It included only some brief notes about the conversations. The Italian consul said that the only kind of progress in the USSR that he noticed took place in military affairs, and that the West was blind to that threat. The conversation with the German consul, Friedrich Roth, revolved around the issue of anti-Semitism in Ukraine. According to Roth, the intensity of anti-Semitism was on the rise. Karszo-Siedlewski disagreed with him, even though he acknowledged the existence of anti-Jewish sentiment that could explode in the future; however, he did not expect it to happen in the near future, mostly

In the Polish documents, the greatest amount of attention dedicated to other foreign posts in the USSR appears in the years 1937–38, when NKVD activity was at its peak. This can be explained by the sheer number of hostile acts and operations targeting "representatives of the bourgeoisie" that the Soviet secret service performed. The Polish archival records indicate that the German consulates received the greatest share of attention. The situation for those posts was comparable to that suffered by the Polish posts—or even worse. Jan Karszo-Siedlewski described the situation of the German consulate in Kyiv in his report dated August 5, 1937. On July 11, 1937, Erna Gerndt, an official in the consulate, was arrested in Shepetivka while she was on her way to Berlin for vacation. Despite the fact that both Consul Georg Grosskopf and the German embassy in Moscow interceded, she was not released. Furthermore, not one German official was allowed to see her. No packages with supplies, clothing, or money were permitted. Grosskopf inquired at the PCfFA about the details of the espionage charge brought against Gerndt, but all he learned was that the investigation would last for two more months and that no information would be released until it was over. Grosskopf requested a meeting with Israil Leplevsky, the head of the Ukrainian NKVD, but he was told that Leplevsky had too many other duties to find the time for him.[205]

The German deputy consul, Walter Hagemeier, had asked to be recalled to his country and was scheduled to leave in a few days. Another clerk (Baum) "had run away" to Berlin earlier and showed no intention of returning, likely because, as Karszo-Siedlewski wrote, he must have been threatened with unpleasant consequences. Baum's wife arrived in Kyiv to move out of their apartment and to take their belongings back to Germany. Hermann Strecker, a long-time official in the German consulate in Kharkiv, who was married to a Russian woman, was appointed Baum's replacement. "Consul Grosskopf himself," wrote

---

because anti-Semitic behavior in the USSR was severely penalized. CAW, Oddz. II SG, sygn. I.303.4.3145, k. 625–26.

[205] Adam Koch informed the ambassador that, based on information from the German consulate, E. Gerndt was transported to the Polish-Soviet border (and handed over to the Polish side there) on October 21, 1937, in exchange for a Soviet official from the embassy in Berlin, who had been arrested there shortly before. The same source had informed Koch that Kremer, the secretary of the German consulate in Novosibirsk, was released after the German side threatened that if Kremer was not released within three days, the secretary of the Soviet embassy in Berlin would be arrested. Ibid., sygn. I.303.4.1867, k. 675.

Karszo-Siedlewski, "is in a state of deep mental depression, he does not go anywhere, [and] he does not even leave his house. He was summoned by his wife, who resides in Berlin, to pick her up in Warsaw, but he is afraid to leave the USSR, because he thinks that he might not be allowed back into Kyiv, despite the fact that he holds a return visa. In my opinion, the arrest of Mrs. Gerndt, who often typed the consul's reports and managed his personal archive, can be associated with the Bolsheviks' intent to implicate the consul in the espionage affair personally, thus forcing him, the most knowledgeable German expert on Soviet reality, to leave the USSR."[206]

In August 1937, Karszo-Siedlewski visited Japanese Consul Hirata in Odesa. His Japanese colleague told him that he had been appointed chargé d'affaires in Helsinki but was going to stay in Odesa because the Soviet authorities did not want to grant an *exequatur* to his successor, arguing that the Japanese did not really need a consulate in Odesa. "Hirata was furious [that he could not leave], because he hated the Soviets," wrote Karszo-Siedlewski. The diplomat characterized the position of the consular posts in Odesa as follows: "Hirata is completely isolated in Odesa, because not only have all the persons with whom he was in touch been arrested, but also, for instance, the two sons of the janitor in the Japanese post were arrested, even though they had never visited the consulate. The position the German consulate is in Odesa is even worse. For a considerable time already, the consulate has remained without a head, because after the departure of the last consul (Mr. Roth) the Soviets did not want to issue an *exequatur*, arguing that the Germans also did not need a consulate in Odesa. At the same time, mass arrests of Germans, both of Soviet and of German citizenship who still remained in southern Ukraine in significant numbers, were underway. Please allow me to mention here that a similar fate was being shared by the few remaining Poles who were Soviet citizens and lived predominantly in Right-Bank Ukraine. A few individuals who were in touch with our consulate in Kyiv at some point, such as, for instance, Aleksandra Skowrońska, who used to be a housemaid, have ended up arrested. It is only the Italian consul, Scarpa, who finds the local conditions quite agreeable, also because he remains in decent relations with the local authorities. He mentioned in

---

[206] Ibid., k. 705–6.

passing that the thirty-five hydroplanes based in the naval port of Sevastopol were of Italian origin."[207]

On October 30, Stanisław Nawrocki informed the Second Department about the harassment inflicted upon the German consulate in Kharkiv. The entire family of Strecker's Russian wife was arrested—her sister and brother-in-law—while her mother was forced to abandon her apartment and move down into the basement. On October 20, Erna Gerndt was released from prison and forced to leave the country. She left through Shepetivka, part of an exchange in which a member of the Soviet diplomatic corps was sent back to the USSR from Germany. During the investigation, she was blackmailed by the fact that the consulate had already been closed down; she was also offered Soviet citizenship.[208]

On November 13, 1937, Koch informed Ambassador Grzybowski that Consul Grosskopf and his wife had evidently become very nervous and hardly left the consulate building. All they could do was remain passive. The Polish vice-consul remarked that the Grosskopfs considered the behavior of the Japanese consul in Novosibirsk extraordinarily courageous: when the Soviet railway authorities refused to make a cargo train car available to ship the furniture from the consulate that was being closed down, he ordered the furniture cut into pieces and burned. Koch observed that Strecker, the secretary of the German consulate in Kyiv, behaved as though he believed he could also be arrested in the street at any time. Just as Nawrocki had done in one of the earlier reports, Koch mentioned that the Russian members of the Strecker family had been arrested. The Polish report also included a few words about the consulates of Czechoslovakia and Italy. The head of the former, Brabec, also found himself in a difficult position. "Snooping" on Brabec, according to Koch, did not differ greatly from the kind of "snooping" that the Poles had to endure. The Italian consul apparently was able to keep his nerve much better. Koch, perhaps a bit naively, concluded that he expected some of the abnormal behavior of the Soviet authorities and the PCfFA itself to end with the arrival of the new representative of the PCfFA, who used to be a consul in Japan, because "he is going to be able to approach our affairs more wisely than his two predecessors, who were dilettantes among the Soviet consular corps."[209]

---

[207] Ibid., k. 632-633.
[208] Ibid., sygn. I.303.4.1968, b.p., dok. 23.
[209] Ibid., sygn. I.303.4.1867, k. 656–57.

At the end of 1937, Ambassador Grzybowski shared with Jan Szembek his observations on the harassment diplomats had experienced. According to what he had learned, the entire interior of the Japanese consulate in Vladivostok was lit up by two giant searchlights. A similar practice was used against the Polish embassy as well. The Belgian representative had his diplomatic briefcase searched; there was a break-in at the German embassy and the encryption codes were stolen; a clerk from the Bulgarian mission was expelled under the charge of spying for the Polish embassy; and the Japanese diplomats who had been appointed to the Moscow embassy had their entry visas declined.[210]

On February 5, 1938, Grosskopf visited Adam Koch. The German consul told Koch that, on the previous day, three Soviet citizens working for the consulate (the cook, a watchman, and his son) had been arrested. As noted above, the wife of the German consulate's secretary, Strecker[211], who was a Soviet citizen, had been arrested, together with her family. The couple had gotten married a few months earlier, but, despite her efforts, Mrs. Strecker did not receive permission to renounce her Soviet citizenship. On February 2, the consulate's chauffer, also a Soviet citizen, was arrested. It did not help that he had to leave his job on February 1, by Soviet request. As a result, together with the five auxiliary personnel arrested on February 2 and February 4, the total number of arrests of employees of the German post during the previous seven months reached twelve persons. The seven earlier arrests included the legal counselor of the consulate, the chauffeur, four housekeeping personnel, and the clerk Erna Gerndt.[212]

Ultimately, by May 15, 1938, the German consulate had been shut down and its personnel evacuated. The consul employees, Grosskopf in particular, had been brutally harassed up to the very last day. By February 1938, the consulate had no auxiliary personnel, because all of them had been arrested. There was no one to chop wood, light the stove, and cook the meals.[213] The clerks who lived somewhere in the city often had their

---

[210] See *Diariusz i teki Jana Szembeka*, 3:233.

[211] Jerzy Matusiński reported that the Germans had received assurances from the Soviets that Mrs. Strecker would be released, together with her husband, as soon as the consulate was closed. The Bolsheviks did not keep their word, however, that she would be delivered to the border five days after the last German officials left the country. CAW, Oddz. II SG, sygn. I.303.4.1867, k. 737.

[212] AAN, MSZ, sygn. 6654, k. 212–13.

[213] Belkovets and Belkovets, "Konsulskie otnosheniia Germanii," 78.

water and electricity supplies cut off, while someone clogged the sewage pipes in such a way that waste would back up into their apartments. Of the personnel of the eliminated post, two returned to Germany: Grosskopf and the inspector Wilcke. Kremer was sent to Riga, Strecker to Toruń, and Krause to Katowice.[214]

---

[214] CAW, Oddz. II SG, sygn. I.303.4.1867, k. 737–38. In his memoirs, Hans von Herwarth dedicated a few paragraphs to the topic of German foreign posts in the sphere of Soviet affairs. Of the German consulate in Kyiv, he wrote: "In 1937, the German and the Polish consulates found themselves in the situation of a veritable siege. The authorities were highly creative in inventing all kinds of harassment: technical support staff members were arrested, the electricity was turned off, and the telephone lines cut off. Simply brilliant was the idea to clog the sewage pipes and pump some noxious liquid upwards at the same time, which led to flooding in the bathrooms. Some very loud sirens were installed near the building. They were operated at night, which turned them into nightmares. Of course, it affected the local Ukrainian residents who were unlucky enough to live nearby. Unsurprisingly, the consuls felt like soldiers at the frontlines, courageously battling the devil's encroaches. Ultimately both consulates were closed down upon the authorities' demand. I had an impression that this was an anti-Polish measure, which was applied to other countries as well merely to disguise the original intention. Historically the Poles have always enjoyed wide-ranging contacts in Ukraine, which brought them plenty of valuable information. We have not lost much due to the posts' closure—that was the conclusion I have reached after conversations with the German consuls who were returning to Germany via Moscow. The value of the information gathered there remained in no proportion whatsoever to the extraordinarily difficult conditions of consular work in the field" (von Herwarth, *Między Hitlerem a Stalinem*, 126–27). Jerzy Niezbrzycki had similar impressions with respect to the Soviets' "greater interest in the Poles." In 1941, he wrote: "I have always had an impression that the Bolsheviks were not afraid of German intelligence and paid much more careful attention to us, the Poles. This should not be explained merely by the differences in our positions and the friendly atmosphere for the Germans following the Rapallo Treaty. Despite that atmosphere, the Bolsheviks made sure they kept the German specialists and official German posts as isolated as possible, but they did it somewhat less diligently. One of my friends back in school, later a high Soviet economic official, told me at the time that Moscow had no need to be afraid of any German penetration in Russia, since the German Communists posed no threat, while the capitalists understood nothing anyway, because their mind was so pedantic and schematic that it was not capable of evaluating the global processes in light of the great experiment that was not always performed based on rigorous calculations or predictions. I thought that there was a lot of truth to his words" (JPIA, ARW [JAN], sygn. 1, n.p.).

Chapter Two

The Situation in the Countryside*

2.1. The Soviet Countryside after the Great Famine

The Great Famine (Holodomor, 1932–33) caused massive damage both to Soviet agriculture as a whole and to individual Ukrainian farmers. At least 3.5 million people died a horrible death.[1] The main result, from the regime's point of view, was that peasants were taught to fear the regime properly. After the Holodomor, the village was completely subjugated by the Bolsheviks, not only administratively but also psychologically. The famine not only made sure peasants forgot about the old, private way of working the land; it also convinced them they had no choice but to come to terms with the fact that they were now completely at the mercy of Soviet power, a power that did not hesitate to use the most horrible weapon—hunger—to enforce its will. The Bolshevik regime literally became the master of life and death for millions of peasants.

We have access to a vast array of sources of all kinds pertaining to the Holodomor. The post-Holodomor situation, however, has received little scholarly attention. Going forward, it is vital that light be shed both on the post-Holodomor situation and on the extent of knowledge the Polish MFA and military intelligence possessed about it.

After the Great Famine ended, the situation in the countryside began to stabilize. Massive mortality rates dropped, but reports on food shortages did not disappear completely. On January 4, 1934, the deputy

---

* I published some parts of this chapter in my article "Pogłodowa wieś ukraińska," 251–66, and I included some parts in my presentation "The Post-Holodomor Ukrainian Countryside Seen by Polish Diplomacy (1934–1939)," at the 44th Annual Convention of the Association for Slavic, East European, and Eurasian Studies, New Orleans, November 15–18, 2012.

[1] This figure is the most realistic approximation given by the team of Ukrainian demographers headed by Ella Libanova. See E. Libanova, "Otsinka demohrafichnykh vtrat Ukraïny vnaslidok holodomoru 1932–1933 rokiv," in *Holod 1932–1933 rokiv v Ukraïni: Prychyny, demohrafichni naslidky, pravova otsinka. Materialy naukovoï konferentsiï, Kyïv 25–25 veresnia 2008 roku,* ed. I. Iukhnovs'kyi (Kyiv: Vydavnychyi dim "Kyievo-Mohylians'ka akademiia," 2009), 266–77. This number has been persistently quoted by one of the foremost researchers on the Great Famine, Stanislav Kulchytsky, e.g., in Kulczycki, *Hołodomor: Wielki Głód,* 364.

chief of the GPU in Soviet Ukraine, Zinovii Katsnelson, wrote a letter to the republic's most important dignitaries, Stanislav Kosior, Pavel Postyshev, and Vlas Chubar, informing them that many regions of Ukraine continued to report food shortages. In Kyiv oblast, such deficits were reported in thirty-two villages of Olevsk, Malyn, Korosten, and Bohuslav raions. Hunger-related deaths from edema or starvation were still being registered at this point. In the eleven village communes (Rus. *selsovet*; Ukr. *silrada*) of Olevsk raion, forty-one collective and 101 individual households had no access to food. People tried to find all kinds of ersatz food. In Chernihiv oblast, starvation cases were registered in twelve villages in Ichnia, Bakhmach, Pryluky, Nedryhailiv, and Seredyna-Buda raions. In Kharkiv oblast, the same was true of Trostianets, Myrhorod, and Krasnokutsk raions. In fifty-two villages of Vinnytsia oblast, 750 families that remained outside of the collective system starved.[2]

On January 19, 1934, Katsnelson updated his letter of January 4. He reported that, according to GPU data from January 1, food supply issues afflicted 134 collective farms in 19 raions of Donetsk oblast. Among them were such units where up to half of their members had nothing to eat and sixty-seven people suffered from edema.[3] On February 15, 1934, Katsnelson wrote that, overall in Soviet Ukraine, food issues were reported in 349 villages in 74 raions. Some localities reported on the numbers of deceased and suffering from edema. In Kyiv oblast, 404 collective and 480 individual families suffered from famine and fifteen persons died.[4] In 112 villages and 17 raions along the Soviet-Ukrainian western border (with Poland and Romania), 6,621 families were starving (1,817 collectivized and 4,032 individual families).[5]

Table 3. Starvation figures in Ukraine, GPU data from February 15, 1934

Oblast	Number of villages starving	Number of raions afflicted by famine
Kyiv	58	16
Kharkiv	59	17
Chernihiv	59	15
Donetsk	29	1

[2] TsDAHOU, f. 1, op. 20, spr. 6571, ark. 5–12.

[3] Ibid., ark. 14–15.

[4] Ibid., ark. 21–22.

[5] Ibid., ark. 25.

Vinnytsia	24	4
Odesa	8	4
Along the western border	112	17

Source: TsDAHOU, f. 1, op. 20, spr. 6571, ark. 21.

A few days later, on February 19, 1934, the Ukrainian GPU informed the deputy chief of the OGPU, Iakov Agranov, that repeated instances of food shortages (*prodzatrudnenie*) affected 166 villages in 46 raions of Ukraine, in, among others: Kyiv oblast—58 villages in 16 raions; Kharkiv oblast—31 in 11; Donetsk oblast—29 in 1; Vinnytsia oblast—23 in 6; Chernihiv oblast—17 in 8; and Odesa oblast—8 in 4. In some villages, the shortages turned acute, and incidences of illness, edema, and death increased.[6] On October 27, 1934, Mendel Khataevich, the secretary of the Dnipropetrovsk Oblast Committee of the CP(B)U, asked Stalin, Kaganovich, and Molotov to supply the collective farms in his province with food aid. He described the situation in the countryside in his letter. In many raions, the population left their villages to search for a better life. In many villages, more than a third of households were abandoned.[7]

Throughout the entire year of 1934, as well as (sporadically) in 1935–37, many regions of Soviet Ukraine[8] still reported starvation cases, including some acts of cannibalism. Nonetheless, the very fact that there was no mass starvation of entire villages was "a great improvement" in peasant life. The Polish documents contain not only reports on the state of agriculture at the time but also more extensive analyses of the consequences of "Stalinist modernization"—not only for the residents of the Bolshevik state but also for foreign countries, including Poland.

The following phases can be distinguished in the period following the Great Famine in the second half of the 1930s: 1934 until mid-1936 were marked by relative improvement and stabilization; the second half of 1936 saw a deterioration due to a bad harvest caused by poor weather

---

[6] V. Danilov et al., eds., *Tragediia sovetskoi derevni: Kollektivizatsiia i raskulachivanie. Dokumenty i materialy v 5 tomakh, 1927–1939*, vol. 4, *1934–1936* (Moscow: ROSSPEN, 2002), 69–71.

[7] Ibid., 295.

[8] Ibid., 124–25, 302–3, 337–39, See also AAN, MSZ, sygn. 6938, k. 76; CAW, Oddz. II SG, sygn. I.303.4.1929, n.p. doc. 77; RGVA, f. 308 k, op. 19, d. 57, l. 281; CAW, Oddz. II SG, sygn. I.303.4.1985, n.p. doc. 8; and Kuśnierz, *Pomór w "raju bolszewickim,"* 145, 149, 152, 161–64, 171.

conditions (drought, rains); and after 1937 there was improvement brought about by a better harvest.

As already shown in Soviet documents, the first post-famine year, 1934, was still characterized by a great deal of tension and difficulty. Many regions of Right-Bank Ukraine experienced a typhoid epidemic.[9] In comparison with 1933, the situation was nonetheless much better.[10] Jan Karszo-Siedlewski wrote, on March 2, 1934, that Soviet reality was not as bad as it was "at the same time last year, when part of the population died due to starvation, but the reality of the situation nonetheless remained far from optimistic and completely detached from the picture painted at the official congresses."[11] The mass mortality rate had diminished, but the consequences of the so-called Bolshevik spring still remained tangible. Polish observers noticed depopulation, damage to households and agricultural facilities, the enormous poverty of rural residents, and the absence of farm animals. In April 1934, a clerk from the Polish consulate in Kyiv (and head of intelligence post B.41), Wiktor Zaleski (code name Nal Niger), visited villages near Kyiv. They made a very sorry impression on him. At least half of the houses were abandoned, their doors and windows boarded up, their fences damaged. There were no poultry or cattle to speak of in the yards, no tractors in the fields, and the fields were being plowed using horses and oxen. Zaleski was particularly struck by the completely abandoned villages of Velyki Dmytrovychi and Mali Dmytrovychi.[12]

Empty houses and completely abandoned villages continued to remind onlookers of the tragedy of the Holodomor and the lesson administered to "those unwilling to honestly till the socialist land." "The impression I had after seeing the Ukrainian countryside was that of

---

[9] RGVA, f. 308, op. 3, d. 314, l. 11 and 54; and Bruski, Holodomor 1932–1933, 687–88, 690.

[10] After "socialism's victory," universal poverty was widespread in the countryside in every part of the USSR, including the vicinity of Moscow. There, however, people had enough to eat and held some livestock. Captain Jan Szyndler traveled along the Moscow-Serpukhov-Kashina-Moscow route on August 1, 1934, and had the chance to see conditions near the capital. The fields were overgrown with weeds but the livestock looked good: cattle well fed, plenty of calves, a few horses. Structures were poor, and houses collapsing. Farming facilities—stables, barns, sheds—were made of brushwood and in a state of utter disrepair. The situation was similar in the state farms. Children were dirty, thin, and hungry. RGVA, f. 308 k, op. 6, d. 20, l. 218–19.

[11] AAN, MSZ, sygn. 6938, k. 75.

[12] Kuśnierz, Pomór w "raju bolszewickim," 165.

depopulation," wrote Jan Karszo-Siedlewski on October 25, 1935.[13] The head of intelligence post B.18, Władysław Michniewicz, wrote a travel log on August 31, 1935. He reported that in the southern parts of the republic, the villages were decimated, one-third of the houses were in ruin, their barely visible remains witnesses to the time of dekulakization and famine.[14] In an attachment to his log, Michniewicz added a few photographs capturing the reality of those days, a valuable source[15] reflecting the condition of the Soviet Ukrainian village after the famine. They show abandoned, damaged peasant abodes and farmsteads overgrown with weeds.

Earlier, on June 15–16, Piotr Kurnicki embarked on a field trip within his consular district (he visited, among other places, Bila Tserkva, Uman, Haisyn, Bratslav, Nemyriv, and Fastiv). He reported on his journey on June 20: "Usually the view of a village is a gloomy sight, due to the high number of abandoned abodes, damaged facilities, etc. This year, apparently due to a decision by the central authorities, a widespread campaign of disassembling and tearing down the abandoned houses was initiated, in consequence of which in many villages (mostly in Podilia) one can see relatively fresh foundations of ruins and chimneys sticking up from the ground. In other villages, one can only see empty sites left where houses stood, overgrown with weeds ... At various moments of the day, one can see very few people in the streets. Somewhere between Uman and Fastiv, I held a few conversations with the local folk, and I was repeatedly told that about half of the houses and one-third of the population remained in the villages (my interlocutors could not have known that they were talking to a representative of a foreign consulate)."[16]

The son of the famous writer Ivan Franko, Petro Franko,[17] originally from Lviv, worked in Kharkiv as a chemist during the years 1931–36. He

---

[13] CAW, Oddz. II SG, sygn. I.303.4.3144, k. 1358.

[14] Ibid., sygn. I.303.4.1926, n.p., doc. 154.

[15] I presented these photographs first publicly during the seminar "Ukraine during the Holodomor-Famine and Great Terror in Light of Polish Diplomatic and Intelligence Documents of the 1930s," held at Harvard University on February 22, 2010. Some of them were later published in the journal *Holodomor Studies*; see Kuśnierz, "Unknown Polish Photographs."

[16] CAW, Oddz. II SG, sygn. I.303.4.3144, k. 938–39.

[17] After his return to Lviv, Franko described in a letter to the MFA in Warsaw the kinds of scientific endeavors he pursued in Soviet Ukraine. The *Dwójka* investigated his case. They invited Franko to Warsaw and asked him to write about what was happening in

prepared a very interesting document for the *Dwójka* in which he wrote about the causes and consequences of the famine of 1932–1933.[18] He shared the opinion of the MFA and the intelligence circles about the post-famine picture of the Ukrainian village. He kept an eye on the so-called show (or "resort") villages near Kharkiv, Kamianets-Podilskyi, and Fastiv in 1932, 1934, and 1936. Although the situation in those villages began to change for the better after 1934, with the establishment of orchards and flowerbeds, planting of trees, or even the establishment of clubs and restaurants, the number of people he saw in 1934 and 1935 continued to be low. That low number was the result of the massive mortality rates prevalent in 1932 and in 1933. Franko wrote: "The village folk are usually good-natured, but suspicious. Children, when asked simple questions, usually do not answer or do so reluctantly." He also emphasized: "The structural outlook of the village has changed completely. The reluctant ones have died or moved out north."[19]

Ukraine. The letter was sent to Franko on December 1, 1936. In it, he was instructed to call 541-18 between 9:00 a.m. and 3:00 p.m. after arriving Warsaw and ask to speak to a Mr. Stankiewicz. If he was unable to come to Warsaw, he should write a few words and send them to Wanda Herc St, Warsaw 1, PO box 732. Franko arrived in Warsaw on December 11, 1936. There is no information about the course of the meeting, but from a letter later sent by the *Dwójka*, one can deduce that Franko was about to finish some parts of a manuscript (likely a book or a longer report—R.K.). He mentions titles of chapters: first impressions, daily life, residential issues, entertainment and relaxation, tourism, clothing, food, unemployment, work habits (*pracowitość*), scientific work, inventions and inventiveness, satire and humor, factories, schools, countryside, crime, Komsomol, Party, GPU (NKVD). Franko inquired about his employment prospects at the Instytut Badawczy. Attached to his letter was a handwritten 15-page chapter titled "The Village." From 1936 Franko worked as a teacher in gymnasiums in Lviv and Iavoriv. After the 1939 Soviet invasion, he became a dean at the Ukrainian State Soviet Trade Institute and a delegate to the Ukrainian Supreme Soviet. After the German invasion, he was arrested by the NKVD. There are various accounts of his death. One says that he was shot while attempting to escape from a train near Ternopil, that was carrying him east; another says that he was tortured to death in the NKVD prison in Lviv. See, e.g., I. Chornovol, "Syn Kameniara: Petro Franko," *L'vivs'ka hazeta*, September 8, 2006.

[18] There is a striking report about a case of cannibalism from schoolteacher N., the wife of an engineer in Kharkiv who was a friend of Petro Franko. The woman had not received any news from her parents, so she went to a village near Kharkiv to see them herself. The place looked abandoned; the houses were deserted. She entered her house. There appeared to be no one there. She looked at the stove, noticing someone. With difficulty, she recognized her brother, who looked at her, insanity in his eyes: "Ha," he whispered, "you look so nice, how round you are. I will eat you. I have eaten everyone." She ran away, fell ill shortly thereafter, went insane, and died.

[19] CAW, Oddz. II SG, sygn. I.303.4.3081, n.p., no doc. number.

Because of the disappearance of entire villages in Soviet Ukraine, the Bolsheviks initiated a resettlement campaign from central Russia and Soviet Belarus, as well as within Soviet Ukraine, in order to compensate for the loss of manpower.[20] The campaign failed. Most settlers, after discovering that the assurances of the authorities about the "brave new" conditions of the superb black earth region had nothing to do with reality, did what they could to return to their previous place of residence. Soviet data show that, by and large, settlers succeeded in returning to their original homes.[21] The Polish consular posts reported on the new settlers' difficult living conditions. On February 24, 1934, Piotr Kurnicki informed Jerzy Niezbrzycki: "'Emigrants were promised mountains of gold. They were settled in the empty places left by the deceased population and assured that they were going to receive help both with grain and with livestock. Reality, however, had no correspondence whatsoever with the prospects sketched out in front of them. The collective farms agreed to share some grain for sowing, but only from the current year's (1934) harvest. The livestock was so decimated that there was absolutely no chance of receiving a new cow or horse. The rare cases of greeting the new settlers with a cow unfolded as follows: the cows (as well as horses and pigs) were taken away from the individual farmers [edinolichniki] who had supposedly failed to satisfy the meat delivery [miasozagatovka] requirements, and were then sold at public auctions. The sole purchaser could, of course, only be the nearest collective farm, which acquired the auctioned stock for the base price. The money received for the sale was taken by the state as compensation for the insufficient miasozagotovka delivery.'"[22]

In August 1934, in another report Kurnicki prepared based on the Soviet press, he stressed the very negative feelings of the local population toward the new settlers.[23] This attitude, in combination with the poor prospects for "enrichment" at their new place of residence, led to a massive exodus of the non-Ukrainian population. Stanisław Sośnicki, who traveled from Kyiv to Podilia and Volhynia on June 16–18, emphasized that the peasants who came from other parts of Soviet Ukraine and the

---

[20] Kuśnierz, *Ukraina w latach kolektywizacji*, 198–202.
[21] I analyze this issue in my article "Przesiedlenia ludności na Ukrainie w latach 1933–1934," published in *Dzieje Najnowsze*, 2018, no. 1.
[22] Kuśnierz, *Pomór w "raju bolszewickim,"* 149 and 152–64.
[23] Ibid., 168–69.

USSR expected a poor harvest and hence left everything behind and returned to where they had come from.[24]

Jan Łagoda wrote an extensive report on the post-famine Ukrainian village. Between April 1 and 10, he made a journey that, in his words, targeted those parts of Ukraine[25] that were "affected the most by the famine, which, according to numerous and verified pieces of information we received about the winter of 1933/1934 and the preceding year, were those regions where the most significant damage was inflicted upon the people and livestock." After the journey, Łagoda concluded that the countryfolk still suffered from famine: "One can meet people who are clearly starving very frequently, [and] railway stations are full of parentless children who try to find food in whatever ways they can. Those who have something to eat are looked at enviously by the hungry children and adults. At the Uman railway station, I counted up to twenty-three abandoned children between five and twelve years of age."[26] He added: "Based on my observations, it is fair to conclude that famine in Right-Bank Ukraine exists as a widespread phenomenon. Its intensity increases just before the onset of the vegetation season, but it is already much less severe than last year, when the authorities were not able to keep up with proper burials. The physiological state of the population is severely compromised, which also helped in spreading a virulent flu epidemic that, similar to what happened in the West in 1918, is incredibly dangerous. It killed a lot of people. The experience of last year's famine is still fresh in popular memory; it is being talked about all the time, for example, in train cars. Women are more resistant than men, and a shortage of men is felt everywhere in consequence. One of the peddlers I met on the train boasted that he could bury up to fifty corpses per day during the famine."[27]

The amount of food supplies in towns, especially smaller ones, remained poor, but the countryside was most affected. Łagoda wrote: "Provisioning in the village is much worse, the people say that there is virtually no bread available: personal incomes at the collective farms were low, below an equivalent of 3 kg of grain per day. If one enjoyed good health, one could work up to 200 days and earn up to 600 kilograms of wheat on a collective farm. It was enough, with a large surplus, to feed the working person, but if we consider that he also had to provide for his

---

[24] Bruski, *Holodomor 1932–1933*, 699.

[25] His route was Moscow-Kyiv-Korosten-Zhytomyr-Bedychiv-Koziatyn-Uman.

[26] Kuśnierz, *Pomór w "raju bolszewickim,"* 163.

[27] Ibid., 164.

family, including very basic clothing, shoes, wood, kerosene, and a whole range of other necessary goods, it was understandable that the village folk were unable to escape starvation under such conditions. Especially the areas around sugar refineries suffered the most, because the locals were forced to grow beets to supply them, in return receiving a very low salary that often arrived with a delay. Consequently the people approach the refineries like a plague that deprived them of the best strips of land and forced them to engage in unprofitable labor."[28]

A few months later, between August 25 and 30, 1934, Piotr Kurnicki, the Polish vice-consul in Kyiv, also embarked on a field trip. After visiting the cities Bila Tserkva, Uman, Pervomaisk, Voznesensk, Balta, Bratslav, Nemyriv, Vinnytsia, Berdychiv, and Zhytomyr, he reported to the ambassador that "the entire area, especially south of Holovanivsk nearly all the way to Odesa, strikes one as permanently fallow. In Odesa oblast, the fields are already overgrown with grass up to two meters tall. Those uncultivated areas, stretching across thousands of hectares, look like a young forest from a distance."[29]

Kurnicki noticed that the fields in all of the areas he visited that suffered from negligence caused by "socialist transformations" were overgrown with weeds to such an extent that it could take up to a few years to restore their usual yields.[30] He saw only six teams with six to eight tractors each working together in the fields during his entire journey; in all other instances, he saw single vehicles. In the temporary garages set up in the fields, he frequently saw up to four or more parked, unused vehicles.[31]

As the evidence in the reports indicated, the situation in the countryside after the Great Famine was extremely difficult. Furthermore, the expectation of a poor harvest in 1934 further darkened the already gloomy mood in the villages. The heavy rains in the spring of 1934 increased everyone's fears of another famine.[32] Official data predicted poor harvests in the southern parts of the USSR, and this news alone diminished the level of provisioning in Kyiv and other Soviet Ukrainian

---

[28] Ibid., 162–63.
[29] AAN, MSZ, sygn. 6938, k. 129.
[30] Ibid.
[31] Ibid., k.130.
[32] CAW, Oddz. II SG, sygn. I.303.4.1985, n.p., doc. 22.

cities. In Kyiv, in both the non-state market and the *torgsin*[33] network, many stores had run out of basic goods, such as flour, and a number of bakeries were closed altogether. This led to enormous queues of as may as 800 or 1,000 people wherever bread could still be purchased.[34]

The Polish consulate in Kyiv reported on the recently observed increase in the free-market prices of foodstuffs following the distressing news of poor harvests (see table 4).

Table 4. Price increases of selected foodstuffs available on the free market in Kyiv between May 1 and June 1, 1934.

Product	Price as of May 1, 1934, in rubles	Prices as of June 1, 1934, rubles
Rye, one quintal	240	350
Wheat flour, one quintal	380	500
Rye flour, one quintal	570	1000
Potatoes, one quintal	190	300
Onions, one quintal	400	1000
Sugar, one kg	11–15	18
Wholewheat bread, one kg	2.5	3.5

Source: RGVA, f. 308 k, op. 3, d. 314, l. 116; Bruski, *Hołodomor 1932–1933*, 696.

The authorities were another cause for the pessimistic attitude of the countryfolk during the harvest, since they showed no intention of making life more bearable by decreasing the obligatory quotas following a poor harvest. This was particularly true for the remaining individual farmers. According to official data from September 11, 1934, the Ukrainian collective farms succeeded in meeting their obligations to the state at a rate of 86.8 percent, while the success rate for individual farmers was only 57.7

---

[33] The term *torgsin* comes from the abbreviation of two Russian words: *torg s inostrantsami* (trade with foreigners). *Torgsiny* appeared in July 1930. Initially, as their name suggested, they served exclusively foreigners who resided or worked in the Soviet Union or came as tourists. However, because of the low interest in items sold at the *torgsiny* among foreigners (in the spring of 1932, foreigners made up only two percent of the customers), the authorities gave the green light for their own citizens to shop there in the fall of 1931. *Torgsiny* were in operation until February 1936, losing their significance after the rationing system was abandoned. See E. Osokina, "Za zerkalnoi dveriu torgsina," *Otechestvennaia istoriia*, 1995, no. 2, 86–104; idem, "Sovetskaia zhizn': obidennost' ispytaniia (po primere istorii Torgsina i OGPU)," *Otechestvennaia istoriia*, 2004, no. 2, 113–24; and idem, *Zoloto dla industrializatsii: Torgsin* (Moscow: ROSSPEN, 2009).

[34] RGVA, f. 308, op. 3, d. 314, l. 115; and Bruski, *Hołodomor 1932–1933*, 695.

percent.[35] Piotr Kurnicki wrote the following words about the early moments of the harvest: "The worst factor is the mood of the population, who remember exactly how much and what kind of bread (for their personal use) they received last year when the crop yield was actually high; this year, they see the worst-case scenario approaching, the more so the more they hear about how rigorously '*khlebozdacha*' [grain requisitioning] is going to be enforced by the authorities."[36]

On October 3, 1934, Jan Karszo-Siedlewski wrote in a report to the Polish ambassador in Moscow: "The situation in the village is clearly developing in the wrong direction. The mood from a few years ago has returned, the state of physical and moral exhaustion is complete, people lack any hope for the future, they fear death due to starvation, [and] they feel apathetic and resigned to their fate, which sometimes assumes a form of passive resistance and sabotage."[37]

Such a passive attitude prevalent among the peasants could, of course, be dangerous for the regime. Therefore, the Bolsheviks decided to apply their usual problem-solving methods: to terrorize the peasants to work more effectively, and to organize a press campaign based on fabricated, outlandish reports of superb incomes earned by those who honestly toiled for the collective farms. Karszo-Siedlewski aptly captured the crux of the Bolshevik agricultural policy. He wrote that, in light of the authorities' continuing troubles with grain procurement, "there was no room for humanitarian feeling or for caring for human life, even if the number of new victims reaches millions." He called the relationship between the regime and the peasants a "quiet struggle for survival" (Pol. *cicha wojna o byt*), for the maintenance of the collective system, and for subduing the village. He had no doubt that the Bolsheviks were guided by a ruthless principle: "everything that is weak and unnecessary will have to perish."[38] Tax burdens were one example he quoted, alongside the witch hunt in the press against individual farmers, especially in Chernihiv oblast, where the number of individual households was the highest in Soviet Ukraine. Both of these actions were aimed at forcing the few remaining resisters to join the collective farms.[39]

---

[35] AAN, MSZ, sygn. 6728, k. 1.

[36] RGVA, f. 308 k, op. 4, d. 23, l. 292.

[37] AAN, MSZ, sygn. 6938, k. 143–44.

[38] Ibid., k. 144–45.

[39] Ibid., k. 145.

"The quiet war" between the peasants and the regime was uneven, and its outcome was predictable. The Bolsheviks managed to break the peasants' backbone and force them to perform slave labor. Stanisław Sośnicki accurately diagnosed the nature of that process: "Today the state forces its citizens to work literally day and night (I was able to confirm this myself many times during my field trips) pregnant women are not given as many days off as they need, forcing many of them to give birth in the fields (something that even the Soviet press began writing about, blaming individual brigade leaders); their work is not paid for and they receive no food; [and] in case of resistance, they are deported eastwards. Seeing this, the peasants say they would have no land to defend if a war came, while the press reports that acts of sabotage became more frequent and included setting the crops aflame and destroying threshing machines and grain silos. The losses caused by that activity were large. The press reported that in one of the Ukrainian oblasts, thirteen such machines and hundreds of quintals of grain were destroyed by sabotage in just one day."[40]

Poverty and shortages were common in the villages. A usual meal in a peasant household was a thin soup made of water, cabbage, and vetch, with no bread, let alone meat or fish. Władysław Harland had an opportunity to travel from Kyiv to Cherkasy in May 1935. He drove for forty kilometers, seeing a few roadside villages along the way. "The villages are extremely poor," he wrote in his travel log, "many facilities are missing, barns or stables are rarely to be seen. What one can see quite frequently are decent households with their windows boarded up (left behind by those who were de-kulakized)."[41]

The deputy economic counselor to the Polish embassy in Moscow, Jan Łagoda, had another chance to visit Ukraine on February 5–9, 1936, this time as a diplomatic courier. He noticed that the economic situation of the Ukrainian village was very difficult, a fact confirmed by the external appearance of farmsteads: the houses and farming facilities had virtually no fences around them. The houses had a shabby appearance, "in the past a situation uncommon in Ukraine, a country renowned for its neat white houses."[42]

The food supply continued to be insufficient. The selection of industrial and textile goods remained minimal. The situation in the cities

---

[40] RGVA, f. 308 k, op. 6, d. 21, l. 289–90.
[41] Ibid., d. 43, l. 19.
[42] AAN, MSZ, sygn. 9514, k. 125.

was slightly better in the sense that, if one stood in line long enough, one had a chance of obtaining something. Villagers frequently had no such opportunity, because, even if some goods were delivered to a store, they were immediately taken by the local administration. This was something Stanisław Nawrocki noticed. On December 23, 1936, he wrote that the village population was very poorly supplied with basic staples: stores remained empty, and even if something was eventually delivered, it was first snatched up by the raion and local officials, with nothing remaining for the ordinary peasants.[43]

Because of the food shortage, peasants often had to roam dozens of kilometers to find nourishment. Train cars overflowed with people carrying grain bags. As Jan Łagoda stressed in 1934, when he had an opportunity to travel on trains going to cities that had a (so-called) commercial store open had their third-class cars literally filled with people carrying grain bags.[44] Those who were too poor to buy a train ticket had to go to those cities on foot. And there was a shortage of horses. In May 1934, Wiktor Zalewski noticed large groups of peasants walking down the roads leading to Kyiv to bring back some bread for their families. Such pilgrimages were organized from villages that were as much as fifty to sixty kilometers from Kyiv, and occasionally even farther away. Between Bila Tserkva and Uman, Zaleski noticed some peasants carrying bags filled with press cake (*makukhy*)[45] from the refinery. After talking to them, he learned that they had purchased it for fifteen rubles per pood and then baked some pancakes to eat back home.[46]

Stanisław Sośnicki saw a similar picture in May 1934 when he went on two road trips (cited earlier). On the way to Kyiv, he saw a group of peasants from the village of Kryvets returning on foot from a nearby city, carrying bags filled with press cake on their backs. During their conversation, they told him that they purchased the cake in Uman, because there was no food to be found at their collective farm. The price of the cake was fifteen rubles per pood, while the price of grain was fifty rubles per pood. They had not seen grain for a long time. The previous

---

[43] CAW, Oddz. II SG, sygn. I.303.4.1956, n.p., doc. 97.

[44] Kuśnierz, *Pomór w "raju bolszewickim,"* 163.

[45] I.e., the remnants left after the act of pressing the oil out of certain oil-containing plants (e.g. sunflower, poppy seed, flax).

[46] Kuśnierz, *Pomór w "raju bolszewickim,"* 166.

year, they received a mere 830 grams of grain for a *trudoden'*[47] after the last harvest. No wonder they were forced to walk thirty to forty kilometers to obtain some press cake to eat. This example was not an isolated incident but common in the Soviet Ukrainian countryside at the time.[48]

A year later, in May 1935, while traveling from Kyiv to Cherkasy, Władysław Harland, also saw crowds of people walking back and forth between Kyiv and their villages. What made them do it? His answer: "Those walking to the city carry foodstuffs in their bags or baskets: bottled milk, eggs, occasionally a hen or some vegetables (e.g., onions). When they return from the city, their bottles are empty, but they carry a few loaves of bread on their backs. The traditional division of labor has been reversed. Now it is the city that supplies the nearby villages with bread, receiving dairy products and vegetables in return. The lack of horses forces those people to travel thirty to fifty kilometers on foot."[49]

Peasants also traveled to cities to find jobs.[50] Although the rate of exodus from the villages was not as high as in 1932 and 1933,[51] nonetheless the population shortage was evident to an outside observer. Władysław Harland was surprised to discover that there were virtually no middle-aged men left in Soviet Ukrainian villages. Most of them, after serving

---

[47] *Trudoden'* ("workday") was the basic unit of accounting between collective-farm workers and their employers, the collective farms. It did not mean that a collective-farm worker had to work one day to receive his payment for one *trudoden'*; sometimes he had to work up to several days to fulfill the norm.

[48] RGVA, f. 308 k, op. 4, d. 23, l. 188. After observing the peasants he met on his way, Sośnicki noted: "Resignation and exhaustion can be seen among the peasants. The hope among the poor masses for some helping hand from the outside is becoming widespread. On my way, there was not a single village where there were fewer than several or up to a dozen houses that were empty because their residents were dead. The peasants from the village of Kryvets, whom I mentioned earlier, told me that half of the farmers from their village had passed away. When I replied to their grievances by saying that it was still better this year, they said: "It is not better, because even if more food than last year can be obtained somewhere, it is because there are fewer people remaining. But one has to work more, because the amount of land left to be tilled is the same" (ibid., l. 189).

[49] Ibid., op. 6, d. 43, l. 19–20.

[50] Kuśnierz, *Pomór w "raju bolszewickim,"* 152. In May 1935, Piotr Kurnicki wrote that the Bolshevik policy with respect to the countryside, which was based on the greatest possible level of exploitation of and minimal benefits for the peasants, resulted in "everyone who can do it without punishment is escaping the village and looking for work elsewhere." CAW, Oddz. II SG, sygn. I.303.4.3145, k. 692.

[51] See Kuśnierz, *Ukraina w latach kolektywizacji,* 158–68.

their term in the army, sought jobs in the city to escape the poverty in the countryside.[52]

For those who had insufficient means to purchase food in the city, as during the Great Famine, the only way to obtain food was to steal it from a collective-farm field.[53] In July 1934, Piotr Kurnicki noticed that, in expectation of another round of grain shortage, already at the start of the harvest season "one can detect emptied grain ears, even if protective measures around the fields are better organized than last year. The previous year's experience with 'light cavalry' [*kawaleria lekka*, an ironic term for Soviet mounted activists] is now being deployed on a massive scale, but it does not lead to the expected results due to the popular expectation of another starvation."[54] Władysław Michniewicz demonstrated the extent to which the practice of theft had become widespread. He noticed a few watermelon fields near Kryve Ozero south of Uman, where the melons had numbers cut out with a knife, indicating that the fields where they grew were being patrolled by numerous guards."[55]

Peasants also had to take care of their livestock to make sure it was not stolen. In February 1936, when Jan Łagoda visited the collective farms near Kyiv, he noticed that farmstead facilities, e.g., barns or stables, stood empty because the members of the collective farm kept their animals in the vestibules of their houses instead.[56] The reasoning behind this practice was straightforward: they were afraid of thieves, for whom it was easier to steal farm animals from a barn than from a peasant's house.

2.2. Conditions in the Collective Farms

The creation of collective and state farms was one of the main goals of collectivization. The rationale behind the Stalinist plan was to gather all the peasants together in large agricultural units, where they had to work for very little pay and produce the grain the Soviet state so badly needed. Conditions in the collective farms were, of course, dependent on the general state of the countryside. Following the damage done by the Great

---

[52] RGVA, f. 308 k, op. 6, d. 43, l. 20.

[53] Due to widespread thievery, the law of "Five Ears of Grain" was issued on August 7, 1932. See Kuśnierz, *Ukraina w latach kolektywizacji*, 109–16; and I. Zelenin, " 'Zakon o piati koloskach': Razrabotka i osushchestvlenie," *Voprosy istorii*, 1998, no. 1, 114–23.

[54] RGVA, f. 308 k, op. 4, d. 23, l. 291.

[55] CAW, Oddz. II SG, sygn. I.303.4.1926, n.p., dok. 154.

[56] AAN, MSZ, sygn. 9514, k. 126.

Famine, those conditions slowly began to stabilize, which did not mean, as Soviet propaganda alleged, that collective-farm workers "achieved a state of enormous welfare" on their collective farms. The status of peasants on the collective farms did not differ greatly from their status during selfdom.[57]

Collective farms were "loaded" with cutting-edge technology: harvesters, tractors, trucks. This was supposed to highlight the progress of the Bolshevik peasant policy, especially to foreign delegations. As early as 1932, *Pravda* announced that the USSR was ahead of the United States in terms of tractor output.[58] However, the true state of the vast majority of collective farms had nothing to do with the picture drawn by Soviet propaganda. As reported by the Soviet press, tractors and other machinery used on the collectivized fields were usually of poor quality, broke down frequently,[59] and were in short supply. Hence most of the labor still had to be done by the most rudimentary means, usually manually. Harvested grain often remained in the field and rotted, because the right kind of machinery to gather it in was missing, there was no silo, or there was simply no manpower to attend to it. Observing the harvest season of 1935, Stanisław Sośnicki wrote that the lack of a labor force, combined with the poor quality of machinery, slowed harvesting significantly, which led to a large amount of waste: "Harvested grain continues lying in the field and rotting in the rain, while threshing wet grain, in order to provide as much of it to the state as quickly as possible, impacts its quality negatively."[60]

Officials of the Polish foreign service often noted the low level at which agricultural machinery was utilized. The Polish consulate in Kharkiv prepared an analysis, based on official data from Dnipropetrovsk oblast, which showed that, by July 10, 1935, harvesters were used to harvest a mere 76,376 hectares of a total of 1,452,900—that is just 5.3 percent. Consul Sośnicki explained this low figure as the result of a low number of qualified harvester operators, poor-quality machinery, field pollution, and frequent rain and strong winds in 1935, which, in many cases, caused the grain ears to collapse, making it impossible for the

---

[57] Ibid. sygn., I.303.4.1867, k. 542. See also Z. Miłoszewski, *Kolektywizacja wsi sowieckiej* (Jerusalem: printed by author, 1947), 113.

[58] *Pravda*, December 19, 1932.

[59] See, e. g., *Pravda*, June 2, 6, 11, 1937; and March 22, 31, 1938.

[60] RGVA, f. 308 k, op. 19, d. 57, l. 111.

harvesters to collect the grain.[61] Not only the harvesters were inefficient; so too were the reaping machines. In Petrove raion (Dnipropetrovsk oblast), only 486 out of 930 machines were in operation; the rest were out of order. And those in operation were inefficient. A large number of tractors were immobilized due to the lack of fuel.[62]

During the harvest campaign of 1935, Jan Karszo-Siedlewski completed a few field trips in Kyiv and Vinnytsia oblasts and in the northern fringes of Dnipropetrovsk and Odesa oblasts. During those trips, he failed to see a single harvester in many parts of those regions. All kinds of reaping machines were in operation, the most frequent type being the simplest, the so-called *lobogreika*. The diplomat made the ironic comment that the entire mechanization process facilitated by that machine was severely limited by the fact that the peasants still had to feed the harvested grain into it with pitchforks, in a quantity that had to be exactly enough to form a sheaf, but no more. Binder-reapers, or other forms of more advanced reapers, could only be used occasionally. Most reaping machines, or even the binder-reapers, needed to be run using a horse, an ox, or even a cow. The level of harvest mechanization was rudimentary, at least in those regions visited by the Polish official — contrary to an official declaration by the Soviet Ukrainian commissar of agriculture, Leonid Paperny, who said that the level of mechanization had reached 63 percent. In addition, the diplomat thought that the Soviet mechanization drive was going to lead to significant waste during the harvest, because "vast stretches of harvested grain will remain lying on the ground, not bound into sheaves."[63]

After the grain harvest, Karszo-Siedlewski repeated his comments about the effects of mechanization: "Mechanized work in Soviet agriculture is still underdeveloped, [and] basic manual labor still plays a leading role in all kinds of field work. The local population still has a hard time familiarizing itself with the complicated mechanism for servicing the harvesters. During our numerous travels across the Ukrainian countryside, we paid attention to the fact that we rarely saw harvesters in operation, and those that we did see were usually out of order."[64]

The subsequent years did not see significant improvement in this area. Officials from the Polish consulate general in Kyiv noticed that the sickle was the predominant tool during the 1937 harvest season in Vinnytsia

---

[61] Ibid., l. 39–40.
[62] Ibid., l. 40.
[63] Ibid., l. 82–83.
[64] Ibid., d. 58, l. 20.

oblast. The reasons for this were numerous: machinery not repaired on time, fuel shortages, and failure to pay the mechanics' wages.[65]

In an August 13, 1938, report that the Polish consulate general in Kyiv prepared for the MFA on the course of the harvest in Ukraine, several systemic problems negatively affecting Soviet agriculture were listed. Logistical problems—things that traditionally were repeated every year— were given as the number-one cause: poor quality of repairs, lack of fuel, frequent breakdowns, and so on. In Kamianets-Podilskyi oblast alone, 268 cars could not be dispatched to the field because they lacked some minor replacement parts or tires, which amounted to 25 percent of all vehicles in the oblast.[66] The mechanical condition of harvesters was also something that could have been improved. According to official statistics, there were 27,000 such machines in Ukraine at the time (per 27,300 collective farms). However, one did not see them in the fields very often because they broke down. In Kamianets-Podilskyi oblast, 637 harvesters were immobile during the harvest, and in Dnipropetrovsk oblast, 1,500. It should also be emphasized that those that did remain operational were of little use, for various reasons. "The attempt to raise up harvesters," the report stated, "as a symbol of the intensity and scale of socialist agriculture failed to yield positive results. Apart from the fact that the vehicle was designed in a shabby way and keeps on breaking down, it is well known that Soviet agriculture is equipped with a low number of operational harvesters, and it is doubtful that they are as widely distributed as the press boasts."[67] Another problem was the insufficient training given to the mechanics servicing them. This fact frequently led to accidents. In one of the collective farms of Donetsk oblast, the mechanic failed to fix the harvester's carburetor, which eventually led to a fuel leak. As a result, a fire broke out, consuming fifteen hectares of wheat and destroying two other harvesters.[68]

Nonetheless, model collective farms (and state farms) that served as exhibition showpieces for foreign visitors did exist. During the Great Famine, such places were shown—admittedly quite skillfully—to, for instance, the French politician Édouard Herriot. The Soviets managed to convince him that no one in the Soviet state was starving and that people did not lack a thing.[69] Representatives of the Second Polish Republic were

---

[65] AAN, MSZ, sygn. 6730, k. 3.

[66] Ibid., k. 22.

[67] Ibid., k. 23.

[68] Ibid., k. 23–24.

[69] See Kuśnierz, *Ukraina w latach kolektywizacji*, 183–88.

also shown model collective farms. On June 3, 1937, the Liubchenko state farm in Borky near Merefa was visited by Tadeusz Brzeziński, the Polish consul in Kharkiv, along with an official from the consulate, Jerzy Kamiński, and Piotr Żukowski, a clerk from the Polish embassy in Moscow. A representative of the PCfFA, Pavel Nekunde, accompanied the Poles. They saw what they were expected to see in a state farm—a model of a self-sufficient Soviet farmstead. The Poles were favorably impressed after seeing the farm, but they had no doubt that they had been shown a best-case scenario that was far from representative.[70]

On September 15–16, Brzeziński and a clerk from the consulate (who was also a *Dwójka* agent), Stanisław Rombejko, visited the capital of the Donbas, the city of Stalino (now Donetsk), and then the main port of the Sea of Azov, Mariupol. Along the way, they saw a collective farm named Shliakh Lenina (Lenin's Path), which specialized in grape vineyards. An unexpected scene unfolded while they were there, when one of the collective-farm workers mistook the Poles for local dignitaries. He "burst out in a discontented voice, complaining about his plight and inequalities." He was quickly moved out of sight of the foreign delegation.[71]

The Polish foreign-service dignitaries working in the field of Soviet affairs understood the situation of the collective farms very well, and no staged showings that the Soviets organized could alter their general image of collectivization. Piotr Kurnicki painted it in the following way in his report of his trip to Odesa on August 25–30, 1934: "In many collective farms, all the technical agricultural equipment is lying on the floor, scattered, out of order, and, with no fences in sight, the livestock has to remain in rudimentary sheds literally dug in the ground. Chaos, mismanagement, and carelessness were visible in the smallest of details in most collective farms in that part of Ukraine. The epitome of devastation and havoc can be seen between Odesa and Ananiv, where the so-called German colonies used to be located; now completely collectivized."[72] The former German settlements were, in general, in the most run-down condition.[73]

On the road between Kyiv and Cherkasy, the collective fields surrounding the road were extremely dusty, noticed Władysław Harland

---

[70] AAN, MSZ, sygn. 9515, k. 150–52.

[71] Ibid., k. 169.

[72] Ibid. sygn. 6938, k. 131.

[73] Ibid.

in 1935. Large groups of women and the elderly tried to reduce the amount of that dust using rakes.[74]

On August 8, 1935, Consul Sośnicki traveled to Bohodukhiv raion by car and visited two artels there: Chervonyi Promin (Red Beam) in Hubarivka, ninety kilometers from Kharkiv; and Peremoha (Victory) in Bohodukhiv. The trip had been organized, at the consul's request, by Mikhailov, a representative of the PCfCA. Both collective farms, even though one of them was located directly within sight of the local administration in Bohodukhiv, differed greatly from the other in their shortcomings. Here is Sośnicki's account: "The farming facilities are in a very bad condition, the yards are decrepit and dirty, [and] the agricultural tools, such as seeders and reapers, are rusty and remain outside with no roofing. The external appearance of the members of the collectives is very poor, their faces emaciated, [and] they certainly do not betray any signs of the well-being that is written and talked about so much."[75] Sośnicki added: "Both of the artels I visited give an impression of very neglected farms, the state of the livestock and the agricultural implements is poor, [and] the facilities in which they are stored are not something to be admired. This impression is not helped by the so-called electric threshing points, where threshing machines, fueled by electricity, can barely handle the workload, breaking down constantly due to their poor production quality. If these kinds of artels are shown to foreigners to convince them of the benefits brought about by collectivization, then it can hardly be imagined how other collective farms in the region, i.e., those not shown, must look.[76]"

While traveling to see the two collective farms, Consul Sośnicki had another opportunity to see the villages nearby. He reported: "the villages seen along the way make a poor, neglected impression, the population is deprived of clothing and hungry ...The roads and tracts in those regions are devastated."[77]

Sośnicki, who visited the area a few times, was able to compare the image sketched by Soviet propaganda of the "wealth of the collective farms" with the reality. On September 10, 1935, he commented on the official data about the average harvest per hectare and the alleged incomes of collective-farm workers. The official data for September 10, 1935 stated that the average yield per hectare in Soviet Ukraine was equal to 12–14

---

[74] RGVA, f. 308 k, op. 6, d. 43, l. 20.

[75] Ibid., op. 19, d. 57, l. 119.

[76] Ibid., l. 121.

[77] Ibid.

cwt. That data was undoubtedly exaggerated and not representative of most collective farms. The very same Communist press wrote that about 15 to 20 percent of the collective farms had an average yield rate of 5-6 cwt per hectare. Furthermore, German settlers held that the average yield was 8-9 cwt per hectare.[78]

Sośnicki correctly determined that the official data about grain yields pertained only to the first period of reaping, which did not account for the typically high amount of waste in the Soviet system, the amount of grain lost because of faulty storage (often, grain remained out in the open, completely uncovered), or theft. If the data about the real harvest rates was unreliable, the data about collective-farm incomes was even less reliable. The consul laughed at the official data about high incomes in the collective farms received in grain per *trudoden'*. He gave the official data from the collective farms in Molochansk raion in Dnipropetrovsk oblast as an example. In 1935, the wage for one *trudoden'* apparently equaled 13 kilograms of grain and 2 rubles. Each farm, in turn, supposedly received 1,800 rubles of income, compared to 800 rubles in 1934. Sośnicki wrote that even if one assumed that income in that region equaled the sums he had encountered earlier in the [model] "Bilshovyk" collective farm—that is, 7 kilograms per day—the figures quoted in the press remained impossible. If an artel in Molochansk raion was, on average, 1,800 hectares large and had 500 laborers, then collective-farm workers should have received 19,800 ctw of grain and 300,000 rubles for 300 *trudodni*. With an average yield of 10 ctw per hectare, if all the 1,800 hectares were used to plant grain, then the artel would have generated merely 18,000 cwt, most of which would have had to be given back to the state, to be used for sowing in the next season. Hence, as Sośnicki demonstrated, the statistics for Molochansk raion were absurd: "In light of all that, all the information about the alleged purchases of entire dozens of bicycles and cars to be used by the members of the collective to go into town and for other trips must be treated as unrealistic."[79]

According to the various data the Polish consulate in Kharkiv received on a regular basis, real compensation for one *trudoden'* was somewhere between 1.5 and 2 kilograms of grain and 10 to 20 kopecks in cash. Higher averages were rare, and, if they did exist, they were quoted so merely for propaganda purposes. Furthermore, according to information received by

---

[78] Ibid., l. 275.
[79] Ibid., l. 276–77.

the consulate, some collective farms did not pay for *trudodni* at all, giving their workers small prepayments instead. Consequently grain theft was a widespread phenomenon among the peasants.[80]

The Polish consulate general in Kyiv took a closer look at the real material situation of the members of collective farms. Taking into consideration the 1936 data about average incomes for a *trudoden'* in Kyiv and Chernihiv oblasts and in southern Ukraine, including all the taxes and commissions that collective-farm workers had to pay, the Polish officials Jan Karszo-Siedlewski and Adam Koch concluded that incomes the workers received must have been barely enough to cover their living expenses—meaning that they essentially worked for free. They were able to subsist only by growing vegetables on their own individual plots. Farmers who tilled higher-quality land were somewhat better off; those who had to till land of worse quality, especially considering that climate conditions in 1936 were poor (e.g., in Proskuriv [now Khmelnytskyi], Plyskiv, and Popilnia raions), found themselves in extreme poverty bordering on starvation.[81]

In the context of these facts, Polish officials formulated the following question: Would the collective-farm workers survive a few more years of deprivation and poverty until the agricultural economy could rise from the ashes? They gave the following answer: "Based on our knowledge of Russian folk mentality, on their inborn submissiveness and passivity, low moral values, and being accustomed to being flogged red and black, it can be concluded that the Russian peasant will endure all kinds of beatings administered by his overlords. As long as the issue is not about land ownership, the peasant will not rebel against the poverty caused by the experiments of those at the top, who are driven by the desire to increase yields with no concern for the well-being of the masses toiling in the fields. The discontent factor may form merely one among many elements, which, when all the other elements (e.g., revolution among factory workers, outbreak of war) also appear, could become significant and tip the scales. To confirm this conclusion, one can cite some peasants, who often say something like "let there be war, then another *derzhava* [power] will come and things will be different," or "when war comes, we will have access to weapons, and then we will show them [i.e., the current authorities]." These two most frequent comments from among the peasantry clearly

---

[80] Ibid., l. 280.
[81] CAW, Oddz. II SG, sygn. I.303.4.1867, k. 540–41; see also AAN, MSZ, sygn. 9515, k. 53.

demonstrate precisely this lack of active rebellious potential among the toiling masses with respect to the current authority."[82]

Jan Karszo-Siedlewski and Adam Koch emphasized that the Bolsheviks were well aware of the "psychic state of the Russian peasant" and thus were not expecting a threat from that direction during peacetime, especially when urban residents were terrorized. Nonetheless, they had to be careful not to allow a recurrence of the situation that took place in 1932–33, when "overwhelming apathy bordering on passive resistance" was widespread.[83]

When Jan Łagoda, the deputy economic counselor in the Moscow embassy traveled across Ukraine in February 1936, he went to one of the collective farms forty-five kilometers from Kyiv, in the direction of Zhytomyr. After familiarizing himself with the state of that farm, and after receiving information from three other nearby collective farms, he learned the collective-farm workers had been paid for a *trudoden'* that year only in kind, in grain and in potatoes. They had received no cash because there was a shortage in the collective-farm budget comparable to their needs. The members of the collective who had received no cash had no way of obtaining manufactured goods, in particular shoes, clothes, underwear, kerosene, and salt.

Łagoda gathered statistics on the incomes of these collective farms and translated them into payment-in-kind figures per collective-farm worker and per family. The average workload per family of two adults equaled 500 *trudodni* (see tables 5 and 6).

Table 5. Average norms of a collective-farm worker's income (in grain and potatoes) per one *trudoden* in the four collective farms Jan Łagoda visited near Kyiv

Collective farm's location	Grain earned per *trudoden'* (in kg)	Potatoes earned per *trudoden'* (in kg)
Kalynivka	3.0	4
Kvasivka	3.0	4
Kvasova	0.5	2
Kopyliv	1.7	3

Source: AAN, MSZ, sygn. 9514, 125.

---

[82] CAW, Oddz. II, sygn. I.303.4.1867, k. 544.
[83] Ibid., k. 544–45.

Table 6. Average norms of income per collective-farm worker's family in grain and potatoes in the four collective farms Jan Łagoda visited

Collective farm's location	Grain payment in the 1935/1936 agricultural season (in kg)	Potatoes payment in the 1935/1936 agricultural season (in kg)
Kalynivka	1,500	2,000
Kvasivka	1,500	2,000
Kvasova	250	1,000
Kopyliv	850	1,500

Source: AAN, MSZ, sygn. 9514, 125.

After examining this data, Łagoda wrote that this income was clearly insufficient: "In Kalynivka and Kvasivka, which received three kilograms of wheat each, the residents still could feed themselves somehow, but with great difficulty. In Kopyliv, however, and in particular in Kvasova, the issue of food shortage was a great problem throughout the year. The residents held that in some of the better collective farms there was enough income to feed small families with a small number of persons who had to be fed, while larger families, who had to maintain a few persons who were unable to work, were in extreme poverty."[84] Łagoda heard that nowhere in the region did anyone earn more than three kilograms of grain per *trudoden'*.[85] After seeing two collectives, he wrote that the private peasant yards housed up to one cow, heifer, or pig.[86]

Łagoda had a chance to see the private plots of the collective-farm workers up close. His impressions were as follows: "The residential houses were in an equally bad state of disrepair inside as they were on the outside. People were poorly clad and dirty. Their houses lacked soap, matches, [and] milk, [and] there was no allotted grain left because it had been consumed or sold. They eat mostly potatoes with garlic these days. The current peasant income is not enough to build a new house, which is not needed, by the way, because one can find unoccupied houses everywhere, [and] hence there is no need for investment in this domain."[87]

---

[84] AAN, MSZ, sygn. 9514, k. 125–26. That was why the collective farms were obliged to help these sorts of families.

[85] Ibid.

[86] Ibid., k. 126.

[87] Ibid. k, 126–27.

As mentioned earlier, conditions were similar in the Polish consular district around Kharkiv. Branch no. 5 of the *Dwójka* in Lviv received information that in a collective farm in the village of Fedorivka (Karlivka raion, Kharkiv oblast), merely 500 grams of grain, 1.5 kilograms of potatoes, and 5 kilograms of beets were paid per one *trudoden'*.[88] Based on his observations traveling along the Moscow-Kharkiv railway line, Captain Ludwik Michałowski, the head of intelligence post G.27, reported to the Second Department April 1, 1936 that "All the collective farms along the Moscow-Kharkiv line make a very sorry impression. Poverty is everywhere. The houses [are] miserable, unfenced. There are no gardens, no orchards. People [are] poorly dressed."[89] The head of another intelligence post (E.10) in Kharkiv, Stanisław Suchecki, registered a similar impression: "The collective farms that can be seen along the Moscow-Kharkiv railway line are a very sorry sight. The houses are small, [and] decrepit. Hens or pigs around them can be seen only rarely. No gardens [exist]. In general, the impression made by those collective farms is poor. Machine and tractor stations (MTS) are rare, [and] rudimentarily equipped. No paved roads [are] in sight. Passenger cars are [only] in some villages. People are dressed poorly, shabbily. Some female peasants sell baked poultry and fruit at railway stations. Their business is going poorly... What they sell looks so bad that one really has to be hungry to buy it. Finally, what needs to be added is that one does not see any communal farming facilities (barns, stables, sheds).... Amid the cultivated fields, one can see unplanted and uncultivated stretches of land. Horses and cattle cannot be seen."[90]

In comparison with the collective farms along the Moscow-Kharkiv railway line, the collective farms along the Kharkiv-Kyiv-Shepetivka line already looked much better. There one could see gardens around the houses and occasionally horses and cows, though the horses looked poorly fed, small, and neglected, and the cattle thin. People—similar to what Suchecki saw along the Moscow-Kharkiv line—were poorly and shabbily dressed.

Suchecki saw many collective-farm workers carrying bags to the railway station in Kharkiv, as he did at many other stations: they had come to pick up or deliver bread. In Kharkiv, the Polish intelligence officer met

---

[88] RGVA, f. 308, op. 19, d. 51, l. 289.
[89] CAW, Oddz. II, sygn. I.303.4.1967, n.p., 48.
[90] RGVA, f. 308 k, op. 19, d. 63, l. 52–53.

a dozen beggars—men and women—who said that they came to the village to get some bread to be able to carry on with their life, as there was nothing to eat in the collective farms. In response to his question about their quality of life, they threw up their arms and replied: "There is nothing to talk about, as you know" (*Net o chem govorit'*—*izvestno*). Suchecki added that he did see some posters around the city asking for workers to show up at bridge-construction or building-demolition sites. Nonetheless, information about poverty in the countryside came from various directions.[91]In the spring of 1936, Stanisław Sośnicki was able to observe conditions in the First of May collective farm in the village of Tarnivka, Zmiiv raion, Kharkiv oblast. There members of the collective farm received 500 grams of grain and 40 kopecks per *trudoden'*. One of them received 22 kilograms of wheat and two poods of rye grain, and, instead of the 40 rubles he was promised, received just 25. Furthermore, when he did not have to work for the collective farm, this person earned some extra money at the grain delivery depot [*ssypunkt*], where he received 2.75 rubles per day. The highest number of *trudodni* the collective farm reached was around 250 per annum.

Collective-farm workers who owned a cow were obliged to deliver 240 liters of milk to the state per annum. What they were left with was barely enough to feed their children. In addition to the milk, each of them had to pay a tax of 160 rubles and 22 kilograms of meat. To pay the tax in kind, ten members of the collective had to contribute some money toward buying a cow together. "Apart from the most repellent meals," noted the consul, "the collective-farm worker has to pay for everything himself. Most collective-farm workers in Tarnivka walk barefoot and without much clothing of quality. There is an enormous shortage of manufactured goods and shoes. This year, the local *univermag* [general store] received, for the first time, eight chests with forty pairs of shoes each, of poor quality with rubber soles, [costing] 40 rubles per pair, as well as seven kegs with eight poods of manufactured goods each and seventy-five pieces of clothing for 50 rubles. This quantity, divided per thirteen thousand residents, is, needless to say, scant. One liter of kerosene can be purchased only from workers servicing the railways, [and] it costs two rubles. Moreover, there is a shortage of foodstuffs."[92]

---

[91] Ibid., l. 53.
[92] CAW, Oddz. II SG, sygn. I.303.4.1867, k. 169–70.

A few months later, in September 1936, Sośnicki summarized the situation of the collective farms in the Kharkiv consular district and of their inhabitants. It was not the best, to put it mildly: "The population makes an impression of being tired, hungry, and poor. Official promises of constant improvement in the quality life no longer make any impact, [and] peasants are well aware that they are working for 'them,' and 'they,' as it is oftentimes said, will take everything away. 'They' is the Party, 'they' are some people in the cities, in Moscow, Leningrad, etc." Contrary to the empty slogans proclaiming wealth for all, almost all collective farms in Kharkiv oblast paid just 250–600 grams of grain and 50–100 kopecks per person per *trudoden'*. In his report, Sośnicki also cited a Ukrainian folk song sung by some children playing in the middle of the road in the Five-Year Plan collective farm near Poltava. This ditty conveyed the situation in the countryside well:

> Mother, father are in the collective farm
> While I am walking down the road (*po dorozi*)
> Hunger in my stomach, patches on my pants
> We are fulfilling the five-year plan.[93]

Many other, similarly poignant, ditties were sung in Soviet Ukraine at the time. A refugee from Volhynia, who came to Poland in the spring of 1934, told of some other songs hungry children sang in the schools:

> If Petliura was here
> Bread would be plentiful,
> Then the Communists came —
> There is nothing to eat.[94]

Disorder in the collective farms continued over the next few years. The Polish consulate general in Kyiv estimated that the amount of grain that was rotting and spoiled because of delayed delivery to the silos reached 20 percent during the harvest in 1937 and 1938, a figure lower than it was in 1936.[95] In a report by the consulate officials on August 13, 1938, it was reiterated that, based on their own observation along three routes (Kyiv-Bila Tserkva-Uman-Odesa-Crimea-Melitopol-Zaporizhia-Dnipropetrovsk-Kharkiv-Kyiv; Kyiv-Moscow; and Kyiv-Shepetivka), grain remained

---

[93] AAN, MSZ, sygn. 6720, k. 78–80.
[94] RGVA, f. 308 k., op. 19, d. 58, l. 123.
[95] AAN, MSZ, sygn. 6730, k. 3; Ibid., k. 20.

unharvested virtually everywhere. Heat waves and heavy rain had caused the spoilage of significant quantities of grain, whereas for the grain that had already been reaped there was often no place to store it, which led to further losses. The grain could be found everywhere, including in provisional heaps under the open sky. Storage room was lacking, and the silos that were available theoretically were not ready to receive grain: they had not been disinfected and were uncalcified and humid. Nonetheless, even unprepared silos were used to store the grain, which then, unsurprisingly, led to rotting. Ticks multiplied fast in the moldy, stale environment. To illustrate this conclusion, the consulate gave an example from Mykolaiv oblast, where out of 453 silos, only 89 were given a permit for operations by a special commission.[96]

The Bolshevik press paid a good deal of attention to this issue. Press communiqué no. 4, which the Second Department issued (February 1–March 15, 1939), dated February 4, reported on the very poor preparation for sowing in the Dimitrov collective farm in Kamianets-Podilskyi oblast. Not a single plow has been repaired, and the machinery was rusting and out of order, as it had been left outside for the entire duration of the winter. At least half of the horses were exhausted, the stable workers often forgot to feed and water them, and nearly all of the harnesses were torn (there was no spare halter on the entire farm). Hay, poorly gathered in loose heaps, got wet and had decomposed. In a report on March 9, 1939, the Voroshilov collective farm near Odesa was described. Sixteen horses had died there during the previous year from negligence and poor sanitary conditions. In the Kuibyshev collective farm, most of the twenty-three horses there were so exhausted that their potential use in working the fields was under question.[97]

2.3. "Improvement" in the Peasants' Situation

Despite repeated occurences of famine and a bad harvest because of unfavorable weather in 1936,[98] an "improvement" in the peasants' situation began in 1935 (relative to previous years).[99] In Władysław

---

[96] Ibid., k. 23–25.

[97] CAW, Oddz. II SG, sygn. I.303.4.5766, k. 17, 19.

[98] On October 26, 1936, the Polish embassy in Moscow informed Foreign Minister Józef Beck that, based on official Soviet data, the crop yield in the USSR was 20 percent lower in comparison with 1935 due to drought in the spring and summer of 1936. AAN, MSZ, sygn. 9514, k. 331.

[99] In 1937, each collective farm in the steppe regions of Ukraine received, on average, 149

Michniewicz's August 1935 report (cited earlier), in which he reported that a large part of the Soviet Ukrainian countryside was still depopulated due to collectivization and famine, he also mentioned that the extreme degree of deprivation experienced in 1933 was no longer seen. Based on his observations in stores and at outdoor markets, he concluded that the peasants had begun to enjoy some purchasing power.[100] Nearly a year later, on July 8, 1936, Michniewicz, the head of intelligence post B.18, submitted a report to the *Dwójka*, in which he said that the village now looked "quite affluent": "There are plenty of poultry, cows, and hogs. New houses can be seen, and the ruins left after 1933 are slowly disappearing. Large orchards are being planted. The people are dressed better than before."[101]

Jan Łagoda also noticed, when he was in Ukraine in February 1936, that in comparison with 1934, just after the Great Famine, the situation had improved, even if it still could not compare with prevailing conditions in the Polish countryside, even in the overpopulated eastern Polish voivodeships.[102]

Jan-Karszo Siedlewski wrote a few analytical reports about the situation in the countryside that he sent to the MFA and to the Second Department of the Main Staff. On July 24, 1935, he informed the *Dwójka*: "The situation in Ukraine last year has stabilized tremendously in the sense of a bourgeois normalization of relations in all aspects of economic life and the everyday needs of the average citizen. It does not mean, however, that it is good; on the contrary, most issues are still very bad, [and] the average living standard is very low, but in comparison with the situation two years ago, one can see significant and, what is important, constant improvement. This can be seen particularly in in the sphere of supplying food to the cities. This matter is still worse in the countryside, but there is marked improvement compared with the situation two years ago, or even last year;[103] we are particularly struck by the relatively large

---

poods of grain, which was a considerable addition for production purposes to the half-hectare private plots. During the years 1934–37, collective-farm workers purchased nearly a million and a half cows and heifers. There were, on average, 118 heads of large cattle per 100 collective farms. See S. Kulchyts'kyi, "Ukraïns'ke selo pislia Holodomoru," *Problemy istoriï Ukraïny: Fakty, sudzhennia, poshuky* 19, no. 2 (2010): 124.

[100] CAW, Oddz. II SG, sygn. I.303.4.1926, n. p., doc. 154.

[101] Ibid., sygn. I.303.4.1927, n.p., doc. 259.

[102] AAN, MSZ, sygn. 9514, k. 127.

[103] Other Polish reports also paid attention to the dramatic food-supply situation in the

number of pigs and hens, which could barely be seen last year. What is still lacking in the village is the availability of basic household durables."[104]

A month later, Karszo-Siedlewski told Niezbrzycki again that the situation in Ukraine was slowly but systematically improving. Undoubtedly it was far from ideal, since poverty still reigned in the countryside, and bread and other foodstuffs were completely lacking, as were essential textiles and industrial goods. The head of intelligence post "Karsz" wrote: "The countryside has gotten used to that state of affairs, it is staying at the subsistence level, but is not starving and slowly begining to recover, [and] hence things are begining to look better than two years ago, or last year. Individual peasants are begining to have more poultry and cows. The quality of horse upkeep has not improved, they look miserable, and their numbers have decreased. The worst situation is in southeastern Ukraine and the regions bordering Poland, where Soviet authorities are investing mainly in strategic highways and fortifications. They do not help the local population but try to make them leave those areas."[105]

A few days later, Karszo-Siedlewski traveled to Proskuriv, Kamianets-Podilskyi, and Dnipropetrovsk. This trip strengthened his earlier convictions, as he expressed in subsequent reports to the Second Department on September 7 and 29, 1935.[106] He wrote a similar report on October 25 and sent it to the Polish ambassador in Moscow.[107] As in his earlier reports to the *Dwójka*, he again emphasized the overall improvement in the countryside but immediately reiterated that this did not mean the situation was good; on the contrary, many localities still suffered from poverty: "Those who have seen the consequences of crash collectivization and of breaking the passive resistance of the village and who can compare it to the present state, they must recognize an enormous

---

countryside. In June 1935, Kurnicki reported that the situation was still dire: "Currently the people eat nothing but unripe vegetables, [and] weeds. They have not eaten their own bread in a long while; they acquire it in towns or at sugar refineries, often as advance payment for the beet cultivation they do" (Ibid., sygn. I.303.4.3144, k. 938–39). In another report, Jan-Karszo-Siedlewski wrote that, instead of sought-after industrial goods, peasants received goods that were completely superfluous, such as gramophones, hats, portraits of leaders, aluminum kitchenware, and books. Ibid., sygn. I.303.4.3145, k. 596.

[104] Ibid., sygn. I.303.4.1985, n.p., doc. 14.

[105] Kuśnierz, *Pomór w "raju bolszewickim,"* 177.

[106] Ibid., 178–79; and CAW, Oddz. II SG, sygn. I.303.4.1985, n.p., doc. 21.

[107] CAW, Oddz. II SG, sygn. I.303.4.3144, k. 1354–61.

and unexpected improvement." Next, Karszo-Siedlewski remarked that, after the harsh experiences of the previous past years, the village has understood that any resistance to the new collective order was futile and was in the process of getting used to it: "They do it without enthusiasm, but with a certain type of fatalism and inertia endemic to this region, which tells them to work just enough to survive, fulfill all the obligations toward the state, and obtain the most essential everyday goods. Faith in the goodwill of the Soviet authorities has been abused too severely due to pillage and excessive, unlawful requisitions practiced over many years. This people cannot be expected to believe that they are free to grow wealthy. The peasant is usually content if he can renovate his house, [and] raise one or two cows, a few pigs, and some poultry. He wants to acquire clothes and shoes, needs salt and household tools and supplies, and he then regulates his workload accordingly to make sure these primitive needs are satisfied, believing that any surpluses would be taken away by the state anyway, bringing him no benefit."

The Polish observer also paid attention to how the external appearance of the Ukrainian village changed after collectivization and the Holodomor. Not all traces of ruin had been eliminated, "but in many villages one can no longer find any traces of devastation, and only the knowledge of those villages from the old days allows one to spot the difference." Plenty of well-fed cattle, as well as pigs and poultry, could be seen everywhere; what was missing were horses.[108] That is why cows were frequently harnessed to work the fields instead. On May 16, 1935, the acting military attaché in Moscow, Władysław Harland, reported to the head of the Second Department that, based on his own observations, the Ukrainian countryside lacked horses, and that those few he had seen during his travels looked very emaciated. Harland remarked that horses in such bad condition could not be seen around Moscow.[109]

In 1936, the harvest in Ukraine ended up being a little worse than the year before because of the drought. In September 1936, Jan Karszo-

---

[108] The total number of horses in Ukraine had decreased by 3,185,400 in comparison with 1929. See Kuśnierz, *Ukraina w latach kolektywizacji*, 68.

[109] RGVA, f. 308 k, op. 6, d. 43, l. 20. Captain Jan Szyndler, who went on a road trip around Moscow (first he drove ninety kilometers along the Leningrad highway, and later he returned via minor country roads), also reported that horses and cattle in that area looked good, but the same could not be said about the general appearance of the villages. Structures were in a state of disrepair, and many houses were being supported by makeshift poles and "were so dilapidated that they would probably collapse if the wind was stronger" (Ibid., op. 9, d. 581, l. 168).

Siedlewski wrote that "things were going badly" for Ukrainian agriculture. The poor harvest caused by weather conditions led to a shortage of potatoes in the countryside. Karszo-Siedlewski estimated that the drought-afflicted harvest of 1936 was "worse than usual." The consequences of this were typically supposed to be borne by the peasants, since the Bolshevik state certainly did not intend to forgo their high delivery quotas and other fees.[110]

On August 21, 1937, Jan Karszo-Siedlewski wrote one of his last reports as head of the Polish consulate in Kyiv. He described that report addressed to the Polish ambassador in Moscow, and two days later to the Second Department, as the "quintessential summary of his views on the Soviet Union and the people in charge there" and "his last will and testament in the field of Soviet affairs." In it Karszo-Siedlewski again reported on the state of Soviet agriculture: "Now, it needs to be recognized that there is no famine in the countryside and that people, children in particular, look much better and the large natural population increase is noticeable. I have not seen enthusiasm for working for the Soviet regime anywhere, but the peasants have gotten used to the new collective order, which now tolerates some minimal level of private activity. Resistant elements and those living by the old rules have been completely eliminated, but one senses a clear reluctance and suspicion by the peasants toward the cities and all representatives of administration; they consider them to be the force that exploits the village's labor excessively, taking away the lion's share of the fruits of their labor."[111]

In his "last will and testament," the diplomat included fairly strong words that conveyed his attitude toward the country where he had worked for six years: "After taking a closer look at the Soviet regime, one cannot resist feeling growing repulsion, contempt, and hatred toward a bunch of people who, having put on the mask of Communism, which is supposed to make humanity happy, are able to wallow in human blood and misery, preying on the stupidity and helplessness of millions."[112]

On January 7, 1938, Karszo-Siedlewski's successor in Kyiv, Jerzy Matusiński, signed a report written by Henryk Słowikowski, who also emphasized that, despite all the typical problems in the field of Soviet affairs, the situation in the countryside had improved relative to preceding

---

[110] AAN, MSZ, sygn. 6669, k. 15–16.
[111] CAW, Oddz. II SG, sygn. I.303.4.1867, k. 628.
[112] Ibid., k. 631.

years. The harvest of 1937 was much better than the one in 1936, which was evidenced by "voices from the field reverberating with a more optimistic tone, reassuring that this year there will be no shortage of bread in the village, since it is already more plentiful than in 1936."[113] The more bountiful harvest helped to improve the peasants' income, a fact emphasized by all the consulate's informants; in 1937, the payment for one *trudoden'* was, on average, 4 kilograms of grain and 0.8 to 1.2 rubles, whereas in 1936 it had been 1.5 kilograms of grain and 40 kopecks[114] This "improvement" in the peasant's fate, however — as was rightly emphasized in the report — "can be reflected only in a certain stabilization of his living standard, but not in its expansion." The report continued: "It is likely that the peasant will no longer feel hungry, and the fear of not making it through the pre-harvest season, when [before] they had to walk to the cities to obtain bread, will diminish. For the Ukrainian peasant, in whose mind the memory of the 1933 famine is still fresh, this is the zenith of well-being. Apart from that, the village keeps on living in the same old primitive way, the peasant is still unable to obtain a whole range of essential products, whose supply continues to be low, and nothing promises that the situation is going to improve."[115]

The last paragraph of the report quoted above is especially significant. It demonstrates the lesson that the Bolsheviks were trying to teach the peasants: that they should be grateful to the authorities for the mere fact of having enough to eat. The famine policy was the method that the Bolsheviks used to subdue the village, and successfully so, as the Polish observers stressed.[116] In his report on September 14, 1936, Sośnicki wrote: "The apathy and passivity of the peasants is unique to this place and can be seen occuring in combination with fear of 'the powers that be,' which allows the authorities, at least at this stage, to do whatever they want....The peasants, in turn, are waiting patiently for the authorities to graciously grant them modest but more than hard-earned rations for their

---

[113] AAN, MSZ, sygn. 6730, k. 8–10.

[114] Ibid., k. 13. For more information about incomes in the earlier period, see the previous section.

[115] Ibid., k. 14–15.

[116] See, e.g., Kuśnierz, *Pomór w "raju bolszewickim,"* 148. This was something the engineer Petro Franko also noticed, as he wrote in his study (cited above): "A specter keeps on haunting the village even today, namely, that the Communists are going to replay their hard lesson of 'hammer and hunger'" (CAW, Oddz. II SG, sygn. I.303.4.3081, n.p., no doc. number).

trudodni, which they are then allowed to sell at the nearest co-op for a state-defined price."[117]

A year earlier, in 1935, the vice-consul in Kyiv, Piotr Kurnicki, painted a picture of the peasant's condition after "socialism's victory in the countryside." That condition was tragic. The peasant was reduced to being a fear-driven slave who produced grain for the authorities and expected the worst kind of punishment for the slightest offense, as happened in 1933. Kurnicki concluded: "In a society reduced to such a poor moral status, the issue of discontent and appeasement is regulated by very primitive means: the whip and bread. The smallest improvement in the economic conditions of life reduced grievances or even hatred toward the regime. The masses are convinced that the level of "wealth," exploitation, or abuse is modulated by the ruling powers regardless of all resistance or accompanying circumstances (such as crop failure, drought). Unsurprisingly, they believe that 'it is already good when it is not very bad.'…Since it is not as bad as it could be, one should already be thankful; and when a few pieces of leftovers are added on top of that, such as a food loan (with a 10-percent annual rate) and other measures mentioned above, 'the free and conscious' citizen of Soviet Ukraine, who already knows the power and wrath of the powers that be, is pretty much ready to accept the current state of affairs."[118]

According to Kurnicki, this fatalistic resignation to the rules of the game, or, to be more precise, to the fact that grain had to be given away to the state anyway, was what caused a successful fulfillment of requisition plans in Ukraine in 1935. This was the most important factor next to the more effective actions of the administrative and executive apparatus, which, in combination, led to the fulfillment of grain-delivery norms.[119]

Piotr Kurnicki paid attention to one more very important issue that was not only an intrinsic feature but also a precondition necessary to maintain the Communist system as such: the permanent poverty of the people. When a man is poor, all of his energy is expended on meeting his basic needs for existence, and he can hardly indulge in thinking about anything else.[120] Jan Karszo-Siedlewski mentioned the same fact, stressing that the Soviet authorities wanted to keep their society poor, because if affluence grew, new cultural or political aspirations could appear, and

---

[117] AAN, MSZ, sygn. 6720, k. 80.
[118] CAW, Oddz. II SG, sygn. I.303.4.1993, n.p., doc. 1 (1935).
[119] RGVA, f. 308 k, op. 19, d. 57, l. 252.
[120] CAW, Oddz. II SG, sygn. I.303.4.1993, n.p., doc. 1 (1935).

they would be too dangerous for the Bolshevik system. It was always easier to manage a population preoccupied with everyday struggles than a satiated one.[121]

An astute commentary appeared in an article titled "The USSR in Early 1938" ("ZSSR na przełomie 1937/1938"), which was published in a secret bulletin of the Polish MFA, *Polska a Zagranica* (Poland and Foreign Countries),[122] in March 1938: "The entire economic life of the Soviets is one giant deficit that has to be carried by the abused and exploited population, and the quantitative increase in the indicators of the country's might is directly proportional to the level of material exploitation and the decrease in the moral mettle of the society."[123]

The harvest of 1938 was slightly worse than that of 1937, but the peasant's situation remained relatively stable, i.e., he continued subsisting at a low level but did not starve. A report from the consulate general in Kyiv to the MFA, dated August 13, 1938, included the following remarks about the 1938 harvest in Ukraine: "The constant organizational chaos (which also exists outside of agriculture) makes it impossible, however, even when the harvest is good, to achieve some noticeable measure of progress in the economic life of the village. The organizational chaos and the state's still unsatisfied hunger for grain lead to a situation in which, even if the harvest is good, its fruit does not reach the peasant, whose existence still takes place at a miserably low level, even though it needs to be recognized that overall circumstances in the village have improved in 1937/1938 in comparison with what they were two years before."[124]

It can be seen that in the second half of the 1930s the situation in Soviet Ukraine, and in the entire USSR, "improved"—relative, of course, to the time of the famine of 1932–33. For some Polish diplomats who worked both in the USSR and in Warsaw, this permanent improvement, in combination with the campaign to glorify the "achievements" of Soviet Communism by some political sympathizers of the USSR abroad, posed a

---

[121] Ibid., sygn. I.303.4.314, k. 135; See also ibid., sygn. I.303.4.1867, k. 628.

[122] All issues of this journal were individually numbered and sent according to a state-established distribution list that included the most important persons and institutions in the country (the president, the prime minister, the general inspector of the armed forces, the chief of the main staff) and various officials in the MFA (the minister, the under-secretary of state, directors and vice-directors of departments and heads of sections, the Central Archive), as well as Polish foreign posts around the world. The issue quoted here was printed in 65 individual units.

[123] AAN, MSZ, sygn. 119, k. 75, *Polska a Zagranica*, no. 3 (March 9, 1938).

[124] Ibid. sygn., 6730, k. 20.

great threat, in the first order, to Poland, but then also to the rest of East-Central Europe. The head of the Soviet section of the MFA, Stanisław Zabiełło, analyzed the durability of the Soviet system in a lecture to foreign service officials. He said that he did not predict an imminent collapse of the USSR, despite numerous difficulties faced by that country; on the contrary, the status of its military and the economic position had improved, and the relationship of forces had changed unfavorably for Poland: "It is as dangerous a mistake to close your eyes to the growing power of Soviet Russia as it is to lower your hands in resignation in anticipation of the threat facing us."[125]

Jan Karszo-Siedlewski emphasized this threat on a few occasions. On May 18, 1936, when he described the Ukrainian situation for the Second Department, he stressed that stabilization and progress had occurred in all areas (even if the situation was still very difficult): "I am concerned not because of what is happening here, but mostly due to everything that is reaching me from the West, both from our own and other capitalist nations, in particular from France and Czechoslovakia, which are completely unaware of the slowly rising threat, not a Communist or a Bolshevik one but a Russian-Soviet one, which may become tangible earlier than we think."[126]

On August 21, 1937, in his "last will" report that Karszo-Sielewski sent to the ambassador in Moscow, he paid attention to the fact that the Bolshevik system, thanks "to its evolutionary tendencies, might become a real threat to the entire capitalist world in the near future, in particular to its direct neighbors."[127] The Polish diplomat's remark was not taken with due concern, however. Ambassador Wacław Grzybowski, in his report to the MFA on November 15, 1937, wrote: "a more serious military conflict probably exceeds Russia's capacity."[128]

---

[125] Biblioteka Narodowa w Warszawie (The National Library in Warsaw), *Rosja Sowiecka: Wykład wygłoszony w dn. 3 marca 1936 r. na Kursie Naukowym dla urzędników służby zagranicznej przez p. Stanisława Zabiełłę, kierownika referatu w MSZ* (n.p, n.d.), 42.

[126] CAW, sygn. I.303.4.1985, n.p., doc. 39.

[127] Ibid., sygn. I.303.4.1867, k. 627.

[128] AAN, MSZ, sygn. 6669, k. 34.

Chapter Three

Everyday Life in Soviet Ukraine's Cities

It is a truism to say that the situation of Soviet Ukraine's cities was much better than the one in which the countryside found itself during collectivization and the Holodomor. However, while it may have been better, this did not mean that the situation was satisfactory, at least for urban residents to feel comfortable enough. The average citizen faced the various challenges that Soviet reality posed—from matters of simple existence, reflected in the permanent shortage of essential products, to the ever-present threat of arrest or execution in one of the many operations the NKVD conducted during the Great Purge. Chapter Four will examine the issue of repressions. In this chapter, I will discuss the material that the Polish diplomats, consular officials, and military-intelligence officers produced on the prevailing general conditions of city life in "the Bolshevik paradise." While writing about Soviet reality, workers of the Polish MFA focused on certain aspects: the cities' external appearance, the level of food supply in the large urban agglomerations and in the provinces, the living conditions of the people, their attitude toward the authorities, and the like. The Polish observers also paid attention to Soviet propaganda and to how (in)accurately it portrayed the surrounding reality.

3.1. The External Appearance of the Cities

In 1929, the Stalinist leadership decided to prove that it was possible to build socialism in one country, and, in addition, in a predominantly agricultural one—the USSR. Industrialization was the goal. The process was eventually completed, but the price was millions of peasant lives. To obtain enough funds to finance the industrialization drive, the Bolsheviks had to find a product that they could sell abroad. This product could only be the grain that was taken away from peasants in a particularly brutal and ruthless way. Thanks to industrialization, the USSR would become an industrial country, a fully proletarian one, and, moreover, it would become independent of the capitalist world economy. The construction of a "new, industrialized country" was launched with much momentum. The First Five-Year Plan (which lasted for four years and three months) was implemented during the years 1929–33; the Second Five-Year Plan, during 1933–37; and the Third Five-Year Plan, during 1938–42.[1] Large industrial enterprises were erected at breakneck speed, something that the Soviet press boasted about constantly. Bolshevik agitators never failed to stress that the quality of life of the workers and peasants was positively affected by modernization. This was a particularly cynical statement, especially with respect to the peasants, whose farmsteads had been liquidated and devoured by the collective farms, while they themselves went through several waves of dekulakization, and many starved to death.

Regardless of the suffering and the enormous casualties, the USSR did change from an agricultural to an industrial country, even though, frequently, the quality of the products and the caliber of labor organization left much to be desired. The amount of waste was very high. Accidents, even catastrophes, happened quite frequently. In December 1934, an agent of branch no. 1 of the *Dwójka* in Vilnius wrote a report on the Dzerzhinsky metalworks factory in Kamianske near Dnipropetrovsk, an enterprise that hired more than 25,000 workers. In his estimation, the main product of the factory—rail tracks —manufactured in quantities of up to 500 tonnes per day, had only thirty percent of the quality content exhibited by its Western European counterparts. There were no catastrophes in that particular factory, but accidents, including fatal ones, happened nearly every day. They usually happened at the railway lines that crossed the area of the factory.[2]

Apart from the information the agencies delivered, employees of the Polish consular missions could see the Soviet industrial metamorphosis

---

[1] After World War II, the Bolsheviks returned to the five-year planning scheme. There were twelve such plans altogether, with the twelfth ending in 1990. The thirteenth one was scheduled for 1991–95 but it did not happen because of the collapse of the USSR.

[2] RGVA, f. 308 k, op. 6, d. 19, l. 240. While visiting Odesa in late March 1934, Stanisław Sośnicki learned on the spot that a recently finished, very large residential building for workers had collapsed just before the apartments were allotted to individual families. All the engineers involved in the construction were arrested. Ibid., op. 3, d. 314, l. 90. According to some incomplete official data from January 1, 1933, until May 1, 1937, there were 371 fatal accidents in the Donbas alone (1933: 33; 1934: 61; 1935: 79; 1936: 136; 1937: 62) and 141 breakdowns leading to permanent injuries (1933: 14; 1934: 18; 1935: 27; 1936: 56; 1937: 26). There were 672 other accidents (1933: 104; 1934: 217; 1935: 135; 1936: 152; 1937: 64). Altogether, according to this incomplete data, the number of accidents in the Donbas totaled 1,184. See V. Vasyliev, "Vplyv 'velykoho teroru' 1937–1938 rr. na ekonomichni protsesy v URSR," *Z arkhiviv VUChK-GPU-NKVD-KGB*, 2004, no. 1/2 (22/23): 49.

for themselves. From October 12 to 22, 1933, Jan Karszo-Siedlewski, accompanied by consular clerk Zdzisław Miłoszewski, toured the Donbas, visiting, among other places, Luhansk, Horlivka, Mariupol, and Makiivka. The metallurgical and machine-tool developments caught their attention. It was the opinion of the Polish observers that some plants, such as the October Revolution Train Factory in Luhansk, the Tomsky Metal Works in Makiivka, or the Azovstal Metallurgical Plant in Mariupol, could compete with the most modern Western European and American plants. Karszo-Siedlewski attributed the fact that their production failed to increase appropriately to the lack of experience among the engineering cadres and to organizational deficiencies.[3]

After visiting Zaporizhia and Nikopol between May 25 and June 5, Stanisław Sośnicki focused his attention on the development of the first of the two cities where industrialization led to the appearance of so-called New Zaporizhia. Two years earlier, the first streetcar in Zaporizhia had appeared, and when the Poles went there (Sośnicki was accompanied by the economic counselor at the embassy, Jan Łagoda), the streetcar network was already forty kilometers long. They had many reservations, however, about the residential-housing development. Sośnicki wrote that the houses constructed two years earlier, despite their modernist style, gave the impression that they had been erected "a few decades earlier." The sewage system did not function properly, the floors and doors were bent and damaged, plaster was falling off the walls, and roofs and walls were leaking.[4]

The changes taking place in the USSR had two basic purposes: to make the country self-sufficient and increase its military capacity. Already in 1933, Karszo-Siedlewski emphasized that the industrial development of the Soviet Union posed a giant threat not only to its neighbors, including Poland, but to Western civilization as a whole:[5] "From our point of view, one should only be glad that the pace of progress is so slow and that all their efforts have not led to the expected results ... that there are enough obstacles posed by the Communist system itself, both intrinsic and practical, that make fast progress impossible. If these obstacles were not there, and if Soviet industry, with its inexhaustible natural resources, could develop normally, then it would pose a threat to our entire capitalist

---

[3] AAN, SG, sygn. IV/5, k. 941.

[4] RGVA, f. 308, op. 19, d. 54, l. 105.

[5] The counselor expressed this same view in one of his last reports in the field of Soviet affairs as well, i.e., in his "last will and testament." See section 2.3 in the previous chapter.

world, not in the future but today—that is, in the next few years. Now we have the time to carefully and slowly look at the rising threat, which should neither be exaggerated nor underappreciated. One needs to study it very carefully and draw relevant conclusions from the actions of our eastern neighbors, who, disregarding the enormous difficulties and casualties, systematically and stubbornly continue, despite everything that is being written about them in the Western press, to develop their industrial might."[6]

The external appearance of Soviet cities changed as industrialization progressed. More and more people moved into the large industrial centers. Most of them came from the countryside, and they came for various reasons: some of them were running away from dekulakization, some from famine, and some just wanted to improve their standard of living. One who read the Soviet press or watched Soviet movies and documentary films could be inspired (as many leftist sympathizers in the West were) by the images disseminated by the modernizing Soviet state. This inspirational feeling quickly vanished as soon as one could independently juxtapose reality with the picture of "the Soviet paradise" painted in the press, literature, and cinematography. It was true that the cities grew as a consequence of the construction of many industrial plants and expansion of the urban infrastructure but the external appearance of the cities, as well as of numerous "cultural facilities" provided for the workers, left much be desired.

In this context, Polish reports containing descriptions of the external appearance of the Soviet cities, especially of the large industrial centers, are valuable and informative. In Soviet Ukraine, the Donbas was the hallmark Soviet industrial development project. The Stakhanovite movement[7] was born there in 1935, and it was also an area where very large mines and factories were located. Soviet propaganda painted the happy life of the worker, who enjoyed quality cultural entertainment after his well-paid workday ended in a modern Soviet city.[8] Reality, of course, diverged from that picture. During the October 1933 journey Karszo-Siedlewski and Miłoszewski made across the Donbas, the following details captured their attention. The expansion of Luhansk was striking (before World War I, the city had 52,000 inhabitants; by 1934, 150,000), and

---

[6] AAN, SG, sygn. IV/5, k. 942.

[7] See section 3.3.

[8] See, e.g., *Pravda*, March 9, 1937; July 12, 1937; August 26, 1937; October 4, 1937; October 11, 1937; and August 13, 1938.

large residential districts for workers were being erected. City sewer and streetcar networks were under construction. There was a new three-story hotel in the city, but it lacked running water, and its only toilet was located in the basement and lacked proper sewage lines. "Horrible amounts of dirt spoil even the main avenues of the city, [and] the quality of street lighting is poor," the Poles wrote in the conclusion of their report.[9]

The visitors were also unimpressed by the appearance of Horlivka, the would-be capital of the Donbas: "The streets are dirty, the lawns are completely downtrodden, fences are broken down, etc. It all gives the impression that some festivities took place here yesterday, for which the city had been prepared with makeshift decorations. The holiday is over now, and these decorations can be allowed to fall into disrepair; one can break, spoil, and step over them."[10]

The cities of the Donbas continued to fail to make a positive impression on the representatives of the Second Polish Republic. The Polish consul in Kharkiv, Stanisław Sośnicki, accompanied by Jan Łagoda and Zdzisław Miłoszewski, visited the Donbas from November 15 to 20, 1935. Based on his observations, Sośnicki wrote that the residential buildings completed the year before, e.g., in Kramatorsk, looked as if they had already been around for at least ten years: "the staircases were devastated, the doors and windows failed to shut, were dirty and neglected, [and] the sewage system barely functioned."[11]

The impressions Jan Łagoda registered were similar. He described the streets of the main city of the Donbas, Stalino (named after Stalin, of course) in the following words: "The external appearance of the streets is very poor, the people are dressed in some old, threadbare rags and tattered shoes. One could clearly spot a shortage of warm clothing not only in the stores, but also directly on people. The temperature outside was minus 12–15º Celsius. One does not even see the *valenki*, felt boots, that are so common in Moscow."[12]

The city had streetcars and one asphalt-paved street, both of which were new developments. But the side streets were paved with cobbles that were uneven, and most of them did not even have cobbles, including the main avenues leading to the large industrial plants. During heavy rains, most streets were flooded with mud. Only a few streets had sidewalks.

[9] AAN, SG, sygn. IV/5, k. 910.
[10] Ibid., k. 926.
[11] RGVA, f. 308 k, op. 19, d. 59, l. 36.
[12] Ibid., l. 128.

"The poor appearance of the city is in stark contrast with the one well-maintained street, which is, by the way, something typical of every provincial Soviet city."[13]

Stalino had only one small, shabby poorly designed hotel, built during the Second Five-Year Plan and opened to visitors in 1934. When the Polish delegation visited the hotel, the bathrooms were already out of order. There were no new buildings in the city apart from government buildings and academic districts. What was common were "shoddily constructed and badly functioning sewage installations."[14]

The Polish delegation also noted the fact that it was cold inside the government buildings: for example, the only heated room in the Oblast Executive Committee building was the chairman's office; his secretaries next door worked with their coats on. Due to the shortage of coal, circumstances were similar in other institutions, such as the post office, telegraph office, or city council. "If the Communist system was introduced in the Sahara Desert, then there would be a shortage of sand there," according to a popular Polish saying. This reflected the inefficiency of that system in terms of regulating resource supply and distribution. In the Donbas, one could see how close to reality that saying was. Despite the fact that the city of Stalino was surrounded by more than a dozen coal mines and several coke plants, the city lacked enough fuel to keep its residents warm.[15]

The capital of the Donbas also made a poor impression on Consul Tadeusz Brzeziński, who visited the city on September 15–16, 1937, and then traveled to Mariupol. According to Brzeziński, spatial urban planning in the city was poorly developed; apart from a few new streets, it was "a conglomerate of dirty alleyways and structures, and in the outskirts it resembled a village rather than a city." Next the consul went to see the factories along the Makiivka highway, where he was struck by the misery of the workers living in mud huts, "completely incomparable" with the miners' houses and districts he knew well in northern France and the Ruhr region in Germany.[16]

The impressions that the Polish officials had after seeing other Soviet Ukrainian cities were similar. During their November 1935 tour of the Donbas, the Polish delegation also visited the cities of Makiivka and

---

13 Ibid.
14 Ibid.
15 Ibid. l. 128–29.
16 AAN, MSZ, sygn. 9515, k. 168.

Horlivka. Jan Łagoda wrote, after seeing Makiivka: "It is very neglected and outrageously dirty. There are only a few stores, and the selection of goods is much poorer than in Stalino. Only a few streets are paved with cobblestones, [while] all the other streets are submerged in mud. There was no hotel or restaurant in the city. Only a few foul-smelling, repugnant eating-houses for the workers were open."[17]

Horlivka was divided into two parts: the new and the old. The old part, where the workers lived, was a depressing sight. In the new area, some new official buildings for the top cadres, as well as for the few more qualified workers, were being built. Order was maintained only along the main street, where a theater, stores, schools, and state institutions were located.

The city had one functioning and well-maintained hotel that was opened a week before the Polish delegation arrived. A plumbing system was under construction in the new district. The new structures were impressive on the outside, but they were in fact poorly finished; for example, the city council building, opened in 1934, had to be seriously renovated in November 1935. Particularly shoddily finished were the sewage, water, and electrical systems: "During my journey, I have not seen a single properly working installation: apparently the residents are used to a lower civilizational standard and do not miss them at all."[18]

In Horlivka, as well as in any other place in the USSR, the problems of daily existence described in this and other reports did not apply to top Party functionaries. Łagoda wrote: "In Horlivka, as everywhere else too, the thin top social layer enjoys a much better life than everyone else, for whom the commercial stores, theaters, restaurants, and clean hotels are something completely out of reach. In this respect, Horlivka is no different from other cities and industrial centers of the Soviet Union. The natural human tendency to indulge oneself is currently sanctioned both by the authorities and by the Party's ideology. Therefore in Horlivka's city restaurant music can be heard from 8:00 p.m. to 3:00 a.m., and the 'proletarians' who can afford to pay the high bill equivalent to a worker's monthly salary, dance to bourgeois tangos and fox-trots, the highest achievement of contemporary culture. In this respect, Horlivka is no worse than Moscow."[19]

---

[17] RGVA, f. 308 k., op. 19, d. 59., l. 140.
[18] Ibid., l. 141–42.
[19] Ibid., l. 143.

From March 25 to 28, 1936, Sośnicki visited Voroshylovhrad.[20] He was struck by the large structures he saw there. Next to the giant locomotive plant, a machine-tools college and a municipal health center were being erected. The city itself gave a general impression of negligence: the streets were very dirty and mostly unpaved, the houses very small, and three-fourths of the city had no connection to the plumbing system.[21] The only positive development in Voroshylovhrad that the consul noticed was the completion, during the previous two years, of forty kilometers of a streetcar line.[22]

From September 22 to 30, 1936, Sośnicki was on a tour of duty in Mariupol, Berdiansk, and Kerch. As before, he was struck by the high level of negligence around the houses and in the streets. The most common type of building under construction was a factory facility. The most favorable impression was made by the so-called *sotsgorodki*[23] (socialist districts), inhabited primarily by the technical-engineering cadres, while the worst impression was made by the workers' districts, which were dirty; the workers themselves frequently lived in mud huts, and there was no street lighting at all at night.[24]

---

[20] During the years 1935–58 and 1970–90, this was the name of the city of Luhansk. The consul's main aim was to see two factories there—the October Revolution Locomotive Factory and Threshing Machines Factory no. 60. He was able to see only the first of the two; he was prohibited from entering the second one because, as he was told, it had been out of commission for the previous several days. In reality, the factory worked nonstop, and the reason Sośnicki was not allowed in was that the factory also produced military gear, which was something Sośnicki knew from private conversations. The consul saw a few smaller factories in Voroshylovhrad, such as the Yakubovsky (industrial pipes), Artem (enameled tools), and Akulov (engine pistons) plants.

[21] AAN, MSZ, sygn. 9514, k. 491.

[22] Ibid., k. 492.

[23] *Sotsgorodki* was the name given to the cities built in the USSR in the late 1920s and early 1930s. They were constructed according to a uniform plan. For more information about their construction and history, see M. Meierovich, E. Konysheva, and D. Khmel'nitskii, *Kladbishche sotsgorodov: Gradostroitel'naia politika v SSSR, 1928–1932 gg.* (Moscow: ROSSPEN, 2011).

[24] CAW, Oddz. II SG, sygn. I.303.4.1867, k. 125. The Soviet press also wrote about similar conditions. Stanisław Sośnicki quoted an article titled "250 thousand tonnes of coal," published in the Kyiv newspaper *Komunist* on July 28, 1936. It mentioned that most buildings in the workers' districts in the Donbas were unlit. The workers and their families had to spend their evenings in darkness. Long lines gathered in front of the spots that sold bread. Other products, such as butter, sausage, and canned food, was in short supply. Ibid., k. 59.

In Kerch, Sośnicki viewed the panorama of the city from a hill in the evening. The only structure surrounded with street lighting was the Voikov plant in the city center; all the other streets remained in darkness. The situation was identical in Berdiansk. The existing electric-power plant was constantly out of order, while the new one was still being built. After talking to local authorities, Sośnicki grew convinced that electricity-saving measures, and the shortage of street lighting related to them, were the result of directives from Moscow. At the time, this area was affected by drought and the water level in the Dnipro River was low, making it possible for only two turbines of the Dnipro Hydroelectric Station (Dniprohes) to operate.[25]

Problems with street lighting were common. Almost every time the Polish consular or embassy officials had a chance to spend a night in some Ukrainian city, even if it was a very large industrial center, they experienced the absence of street or internal lighting. In March 1934, Sośnicki and Władysław Michniewicz visited the Japanese consul in Odesa. There the local electric plant broke down frequently, and the lights went off five times during their three-hour meeting. The Japanese consul told his Polish guests that "such a pleasure" was something he experienced every day.[26]

In August 1935, Sośnicki visited Poltava, where, on August 13–15, 1935, he toured the industrial enterprises. The local electric-power plant was not able to meet the needs of the city and the local factories, and therefore, because of the plant's overload, in the evening the street lamps barely produced any light.[27]

Little progress in electrification was made during the second half of the 1930s. On September 9, 1937, Jerzy Kamiński informed the main office of the *Dwójka* that there was no electricity for street lighting in Dnipropetrovsk; therefore, even the main street of the city, Karl Marx Avenue, was sunk in darkness in the evenings. Kamiński's informant told him that this was because of the drought and the low water level in the Dnipro, which disabled seven or eight of the nine turbines of the Dniprohes.[28] In Zaporizhia as well, all the streets were dark after dusk.

---

[25] Ibid., k. 126.
[26] RGVA, f. 308 k, op. 3, d. 314, l. 89–90.
[27] Ibid., op. 19, d. 57, l. 146–47.
[28] CAW, Oddz. II SG, sygn. 2101, b.p., doc. 94.

"Street lights are never on. The only lit places are factories and industrial and railway grounds. The lighting in the apartments is very weak."[29]

It was not only the lack of light that was a problem for residents of Soviet cities. The shortage of other goods, such as gasoline or water, significantly affected the everyday functioning of Soviet cities. In the report mentioned above, Jerzy Kamiński noticed that there were no shipping vessels or vehicles operating between Zaporizhia and Dnipropetrovsk because of shallow waters and because of the lack of gasoline and tires. In Kharkiv, in turn, public buses were out of service for a week because there was no fuel.[30]

In another report, on October 9, 1937, the chief of intelligence post X.37 noted: "The lack of water in the water-supply system can be felt more now than was the case in August. In the summer, this problem was explained by a higher than usual water demand due to hot weather. This shortage of fuel is so acute that even the Intourist [agency] keeps their vehicles parked. Automobile traffic is very low, as is air traffic. There is no coal for heating. It can be obtained only on the free market for a high price. Last year was much better. Power outages are quite common now."[31]

Jan Łagoda, who was on a tour of duty as a diplomatic courier in Ukraine from February 5 to 9, 1936, delivered much information about Kyiv, which became the capital of the Ukrainian Soviet Socialist Republic in 1934, replacing Kharkiv. With this change, a new wave of expansion and modernization began in that city. This did not save Kyiv, however, from typical Soviet mediocrity and disorder when it came to the aesthetics of urban planning. When Łagoda was in the city and its environs, he noticed that Kyiv's expansion was limited to refurbishing a few main streets in the city center; paving fifty kilometers of the Zhytomyr highway, as well as a few shorter sections in other directions, with asphalt; and erecting a few dozen large houses for the dignitaries and officials who were moving from Kharkiv. The city was still covered in enormous amounts of dirt, especially in the backyards and staircases of large houses, in the workers' lodgings, and even in the intelligentsia's apartments. It was difficult to keep the apartments and houses in order because of overcrowding and the unreliable water supply, which was common also on the lower floors.[32]

---

[29] Ibid.
[30] Ibid.
[31] Ibid., doc. 111.
[32] AAN, MSZ, sygn. 9514, k. 123–24.

Łagoda underlined that the transfer of the Ukrainian capital was not a positive change for the ordinary resident of Kyiv; quite the contrary. The standard apartment allotment per capita was lowered, as was the permitted consumption of water and electricity. The routes of several streetcar lines were changed due to the city's reconstruction.[33]

One of the few positive developments the Polish guest spotted was the quantity of supplies in the stores, both in the large city centers and in the provinces. They were well stocked with fruit, fish, meat, dairy products, and frozen foods, as well as with clothing and good-quality shoes. The prices were as high as in Moscow, but the actual price was given per 0.1 kilogram not per 1 kilogram, as in Moscow, because—as Łagoda was told—that was the usual amount that customers acquired.[34]

According to Consul Sośnicki, the transfer of the capital also had a negative influence on the level of security the residents of Kharkiv enjoyed, because of the lower number and quality of police there once the best units were transferred to the new capital. Therefore incidents of banditry increased. Assaults continued to be registered in the city center, sometimes accompanied by murders. The daughter of the director of the medical society and her fiancé were murdered in a city park. Elsewhere, an engineer was murdered and his gold teeth were extracted. In mid-August 1934, next to Iumovska Street (which ran parallel to Olminsky Street, where the Polish consulate was located), an entire family of seven— a mother and her six children—was murdered, also during a robbery. Theft and robbery were rife in the crowded commuter trains. At outdoor markets, money was regularly stolen, watches snatched from wrists, and earrings from ears. Residents were afraid to walk on the side streets in the evening.[35]

The port city of Odesa also did not make a good impression on foreign visitors. From March 25 to 28, 1934, Sośnicki and Michniewicz visited the city, which seemed to them neglected, with streets that were dirty and full of beggars who made it impossible for passers-by to pass by. The food supply left plenty to be desired. The Japanese consul told Sośnicki that matches were not to be found in Odesa because all of them had been purchased by profiteers, who sold them for ten times more than the original price. The same happened to kerosene. On the other hand, all the

---

[33] Ibid., k. 123.
[34] Ibid., k. 124.
[35] Ibid., sygn. 6710, k. 258–59.

stores were well supplied with vodka. The Japanese consul asked the Poles to help him get food from Poland.[36]

The examples given here apply mostly to the main industrial cities of Ukraine and to the capital. Circumstances were much worse in the provinces. In a report to the *Dwójka* on November 22, 1934, Wiktor Zaleski wrote that, one day earlier, Jan Karszo-Siedlewski and Piotr Kurnicki had traveled to Chernihiv: "The city itself is in a very neglected state and gives the impression of being half-dead." This was his summary of how the Polish delegation saw the city.[37]

Peasants were present in every larger city. They had come to purchase foodstuffs. Their numbers increased as the situation in the villages worsened, as was manifestly visible during the period of the Great Famine.[38] In 1936 a similar increase in the number of villagers coming to the city was also observed. As mentioned earlier, this was because of the poor harvest that year. In the situational report from October–December 1936 (cited above), Stanisław Nawrocki noted that Kyiv was also overrun by a large group of peasants from the Russian regions of Kursk, Voronezh, and Tambov: "From the many conversations with those peasants, it can be deduced that famine is currently being experienced in the area of former Kursk, Voronezh, and Tambov gubernias. Peasants are fleeing en masse from the collective farms, taking with them their cattle (private property), and in the cities (Kyiv, Kharkiv, Chernihiv) they sell them for next to nothing to the butcher and, in return, receive bread and flour. They say that in their region there is no grain even for sowing and that village stores have not had bread for a long time."[39]

3.1.1. Roads

Railways remained the most popular means of transportation in Soviet Ukraine, and in the entire Soviet Union, throughout the entire interwar period. Trains were full, they often arrived late, and accidents were not infrequent.[40] Automobile transportation was available only to a small degree. The road network was limited to urban and suburban areas, and only there could one see some private passenger cars. Highways between larger cities were usually in very poor condition in the early

---

[36] RGVA, f. 308 k, op. 3, d. 314, l. 89–90.

[37] CAW, Oddz. II SG, sygn. I.303.4.1929, doc. 198.

[38] See Kuśnierz, *Ukraina w latach kolektywizacji*, 158–62.

[39] CAW, Oddz. II SG, sygn. I.303.4.1956, n.p., doc. 97.

[40] The ubiquitous problem of train delays will be discussed in a later section of this chapter.

1930s, with uneven surfaces occasionally overgrown with weeds, with potholes, and no road signs. During his journey through Soviet Ukraine in May 1934,[41] Stanisław Sośnicki traveled on the roads between Kyiv and Zhytomyr and then on to Berdychiv and Troianiv, as well as from Kyiv to Uman, Vinnytsia, and Zhytomyr. He noticed that the roads and highways were poorly maintained, even if some parts were being repaired at the time (e.g., the Kyiv–Zhytomyr–Berdychiv highway). On the Vinnytsia–Berdychiv highway, a new section from Kalynivka to Makhnivka was under construction. Also under construction was the new highway between Bratslav and Nemyriv; under repair was the old section between Nemyriv and Vinnytsia.[42]

Two months later, Jan Karszo-Siedlewski had an opportunity to travel throughout almost all of Soviet Ukraine by car. On July 22, 1934, he got into a Buick (owned by the consulate) and traveled from Kharkiv to Warsaw. He drove through Poltava, Kyiv, Zhytomyr, and Novohrad-Volynskyi. Altogether, he covered 1,300 kilometers on Ukrainian roads. In his report on his journey (dated August 6, 1934), he reflected on the state of one of the main transportation arteries of the "most progressive country in the world." Between Kharkiv and Kyiv there was very little actual pavement to speak of, if one did not count the short sections near major cities. "The so-called main tract," the diplomat wrote, "is at times overgrown with weeds or so beaten down that one cannot find the road at all; between Poltava and Kyiv even the telegraph poles do not help one to find the direction. One can drive on these roads relatively comfortably, or even fast as long as it is dry; an average rain is enough, however, to render them impassable for a few hours."[43]

The next section, from Kyiv to the Polish border, did not look much better. "From Kyiv to Zhytomyr, and then on to Novohrad-Volynskyi, the highway is wide but badly maintained; in its better sections, it reminded me of our highway between Warsaw and Siedlce. On the way to Korets, more or less seven kilometers after passing Novohrad-Volynskyi, the highway (formally marked as a highway on all roadmaps) suddenly stops and nineteen kilometers of bumpy dirt road begin, which cannot be called a route or a highway at all. Those were some remnants of the prewar highway, where one proceeds from one large pothole to another risking

[41] See chapter 2.
[42] RGVA, f. 308 k, op. 4, d. 23, l. 190.
[43] AAN, MSZ, sygn. 6938, k. 124.

the destruction not only of the shocks, but of the entire vehicle as well.... Only the last two to three kilometers before reaching the Polish border are good. The pavement is mostly cobblestones overgrown with weeds because there is no car vehicle traffic along this highway, and my car was the first that drove on the section to Korets in the last few years."[44]

Such a state of affairs was typical not only in Soviet Ukraine. Road infrastructure was poor around Moscow, too. In the summer of 1935, Captain Jan Szyndler made two trips by car in the vicinity of Moscow. The first one was on July 18, 1935. He drove ninety kilometers on the Leningrad highway to the city of Klin, and then he returned to Moscow via side roads. The Leningrad highway was paved with asphalt within sixty-five kilometers of Moscow. The main highways were good, but the country roads were very badly maintained and lacked road signs. There were road signs indicating a locality's proper name, but only in the area near Moscow.[45]

On August 1, 1935, Szyndler went on a longer trip from Moscow and back, through Serpukhov and Kashino. His observations were as follows: "Highways are paved with asphalt and of very good quality within thirty to forty kilometers of Moscow. Farther away highways are poor, sometimes under repair. Country roads and routes are in very bad condition. There are no road signs to be seen. The roads marked as highways on the map are in fact dirt roads, badly damaged. Some roads considered as 'surely there' by the local population are no longer there because they have been ploughed through by tractors recently, with no rhyme or reason."[46]

As indicated by both Soviet data and Polish intelligence,[47] considerable investment was made to improve Soviet road infrastructure after 1934. Particular attention was paid to the roads of strategic significance along the Western European border of the USSR and in the Donbas, where many asphalt roads were under construction in the late 1930s. The paved width was eight meters. The roads were built to be tough, designed to carry vehicles exerting pressure up to fifteen kilos per square centimeter, which included tanks and armored vehicles with regular iron tracks. Road traffic was open to all vehicles. Gas stations were

---

[44] Ibid., k. 124–25.
[45] RGVA, f. 308 k, op. 9, d. 581, l. 168.
[46] Ibid., op. 6, d. 20, l. 218.
[47] See Ibid., f. 308 k, op. 6, d. 22, l. 166, 215–16; and op. 19, d. 51, l. 92. See also Smoliński, "Sytuacja wojskowa, ekonomiczna i społeczna," 249–50.

located at each tenth or twelfth kilometer, selling petrol for one ruble per kg [*sic*] and lubricants for 39–50 kopecks per liter. There were three such stations between Horlivka and Stalino (around forty kilometers). By the end of 1937, the following asphalt roads were open to traffic:

Leningrad–Moscow–Kharkiv–Stalino–Mariupol
Kharkiv–Mykytivka–Horlivka–Stalino
Kostiantynivka–Horlivka–Ienakiieve
Stalino–Ienakiieve [48]

Furthermore, the Kyiv–Zhytomyr highway (131 kilometers) was renovated at an expense of 16 million rubles. In general, according to official data, between 1934 and 1937, 4,585 kilometers of paved roads were built or renovated in Soviet Ukraine, which amounted to a total road infrastructure investment of 221,218 rubles. [49]

3.2. The Living Conditions of the Soviet People.
3.2.1. Queues

Polish observers were very interested in the living conditions that the Soviet people experienced. Multiple reports on this topic were sent to Warsaw. They included price lists for particular food items and industrial goods. As made evident in chapter two, bread and other daily essentials were scarcely available in 1934. [50] In order to receive rationed bread in Kyiv in early 1934, one had to join the line at 3:00 a.m. On February 13, 1934, at the bread ration sale point no. 39 at Shevchenko Boulevard 5 in Kyiv, the queue was about two thousand people long, according to data from the Polish consulate in Kyiv. People waited to pick up their ration of bread from 5:00 a.m. until noon — in vain, as it later turned out, because there was no bread in that store on that day. The crowd, made up chiefly of workers, was frustrated by the long wait. Eventually, they broke into the store, devastated the place, and injured a few attendants. The First Mounted Cavalry School troopers from the Baikova Hora area in Kyiv were called in, as was a squadron of mounted police from Saint Andrew's Descent. The crowd was surrounded and pushed back into the few nearby yards, where approximately two hundred people were arrested. [51]

---

[48] RGVA, f. 462 k, op. 1, d. 82, l. 35–36.

[49] A. Vadimov, "Dorogi Sovetskoi Ukrainy," *Pravda*, September 12, 1937.

[50] See chapter 2.

[51] RGVA, f. 308 k, op. 3, d. 314, l. 10–11; and Bruski, *Holodomor 1932–1933*, 689–90.

Long queues in front of the places where one could buy bread or other food items became a permanent part of the socialist landscape.[52] The Polish consul in Kyiv, Stanisław Sośnicki, took two business trips by car, on May 9–10 and 20–21, 1934. The first route went from Kyiv to Zhytomyr, Berdychiv, Raihorodok, Troianiv, and back; the second, from Kyiv to Uman, Haisyn, Bratslav, Nemyriv, Vinnytsia, Berdychiv, Zhytomyr, and back to Kyiv. In all of the towns he visited on the way, the consul saw enormous lines, counting up to a few hundred dirty and tattered individuals waiting for bread. Sośnicki arrived at both Uman and Berdychiv at 5:00 a.m.[53]

On June 16–18, 1934, Sośnicki travelled from Kyiv to Volhynia and Podilia. As on his trips a few weeks earlier, he frequently arrived at particular towns very early in the morning and witnessed enormous lines numbering thousands of impoverished people—particularly in Zhytomyr and in the northern towns.[54]

At the end of 1934, the Bolsheviks made the decision to shut down the rationing system starting from January 1, 1935. This was a measure calculated to be received as evidence of Soviet progress, but for many citizens, especially in urban areas, it meant additional difficulties, such as the need to wait in even longer lines because of the massive influx of the rural population into the cities.

Not long after the rationing system was abolished in January 1935, the free-market sale of bread proved unsatisfactory. The Party tried to spin it as a PR success, but the urban population was initially quite unhappy with this new development, especially the workers and the clerks, who had previously received ration cards and had been able to obtain the allotted amount of bread. After the rationing system was abolished, not only did prices go up, but, due to increased demand, a person who had been guaranteed to receive his or her normal amount earlier was now not so sure about it. Bakeries failed to keep up with the growing demand. In the Donbas, bread was sometimes only ready for sale in the evening instead of in the morning. The increased demand further diminished its already questionable quality. Furthermore, as mentioned, the shortages were exacerbated by the mass movement of the rural population into the cities. After rationing was abolished, bread did not become cheaper than what

---

[52] See Kuśnierz, *Pomór w "raju bolszewickim,"* 145, 163, 166, 167.
[53] RGVA, f. 308 k, op. 4, d. 23, l. 190.
[54] Bruski, *Holodomor 1932–1933*, 699–700; and RGVA, f. 308 k, op. 3, d. 314, l. 11.

previously could be purchased on the free market at "speculative prices." The cheaper kinds of bread disappeared quickly, and their shortage was felt permanently. More expensive baked goods, white buns for example, went bad due to the lack of demand.[55]

The early days of free-market bread were also difficult in Kharkiv. Speculation and corruption were rife. The municipal authorities tried to counteract this by imposing high penalties for purchasing or selling more than two kilograms of bread. The punishments ran from 100 rubles up to a month of compulsory labor. If someone was caught a second time, the regular criminal code was applied. Nonetheless, scandals that involved speculative turnover of bread abounded. Following the implementation of regulatory measures, the queues in the center of Kharkiv disappeared but continued to form in the outskirts, especially in the morning, when peasants arrived in town and formed lines in front of the stores. The cheapest black bread (90 kopecks per kilogram) sold out very quickly, but no one purchased buns because they were too expensive. Lines in front of bread stores also occurred in other cities—in Zaporizhia, Dnipropetrovsk, Stalino, and elsewhere.[56]

In the aftermath of the abolition of the rationing system, which led to a bread shortage in the countryside, many beggars appeared in Kharkiv. The police arrested them daily and transported them away by cars. Stanisław Sośnicki reported that groups of such "ragged beggars normally numbered around 150 people, who were surrounded by 20 to 40 policemen; these groups slowly marched through the city and became a permanent feature of the Kharkiv landscape."[57]

In smaller towns and in the countryside, the situation looked even worse. The smaller towns did not receive flour on time, and villages had no stores, which led to crowds of peasants flooding into the cities. Speculation was rampant. In Poltava, local speculators sold bread at outdoor markets for a price two times higher than in the stores. In the countryside in Kharkiv oblast, the shortage of bread was ubiquitous. According to the reports received by the Polish consulate in Kharkiv, collective-farm workers relied on a diet of beets and carrots. Peasants flocked to cities and towns, making the queues longer. Fights often

---

[55] RGVA, f. 308, op. 19, d. 53, l. 161–62.
[56] Ibid., d. 54, l. 32–35.
[57] Ibid., l. 78.

erupted among the frustrated crowds; a few persons were killed in Sakhanivka, for instance.[58]

In March 1935, Władysław Harland reported that the supply level of food provisions was not bad in Moscow, but the situation was worse in the provinces. In Odesa large quantities of stale bread were being sold, as they were in Zaporizhia. The stores were decrepit. Not enough black bread was being baked in Kharkiv, but there was a surplus of white buns, as elsewhere.

Harland saw long bread queues in many Soviet Ukrainian towns. He explained it as "excessive demand for bread exhibited by the members of the surrounding collective farms," who had a lot of time on their hands and formed lines early in the morning, preventing availability to the urban population, who had to start their workday around 7:00 a.m.[59]

In the second half of 1935, the various effects of the abolition of the rationing system lessened, but nonetheless continued until mid-1936. Stanisław Suchecki wrote in mid-1936 that the number of grocery stores in Kharkiv was satisfactory, and there were no lines to be seen in front of them. The shop attendants worked effectively. The quality of foodstuffs increased, lots of canned fish and fruit were available. The quality of other products, on the other hand, such as clothes or underwear, was poor or very poor.[60]

In the second half of 1936, the situation worsened again. As noted earlier, the harvest of 1936 was poor due to drought, and under Soviet conditions this was immediately reflected in the availability of food to urban and rural residents. In order to buy anything, one had to wait for up to a dozen or more hours in front of the stores. More than once one had to queue up in the middle of the night in order to have any chance of purchasing something in the morning. Queues again became an intrinsic feature of the Soviet landscape. On October 26, the Polish embassy in Moscow informed Foreign Minister Józef Beck that queues in front of stores and bazaars in Moscow had became an everyday occurrence.[61]

If one had to spend a substantial amount of time queuing up to buy the goods one needed in Moscow, this means the situation could not have been better elsewhere. The *Dwójka*'s main office and the MFA in Warsaw

---

[58] Ibid., l. 32–35.
[59] Ibid., op. 6, d. 20, l. 97–98.
[60] Ibid., op. 19, d. 63, l. 44.
[61] AAN, MSZ, sygn. 9514, k. 338.

received information, inter alia, about bread queues in Zhytomyr[62] and about the worsening food supply in Kharkiv. In early August 1936, the former capital of the Ukrainian SSR suffered from a worsening availability of vegetables, potatoes in particular, which resulted in huge crowds of people queueing up in front of stores or at vegetable stands in outdoor markets. Not infrequently, people stood in line in vain and left empty-handed. Consul Sośnicki remarked: "In large grocery stores, vegetables are not sold at all, and the shortage of sausages, dairy products, and meat is visible. Only dry sausage is sold, 27 rubles per kilo. Lines constantly form in front of stores to buy herring. Among meats, only pork can be purchased, [and] there is no beef whatsoever. Bread is plentiful at 1.50 rubles per kilogram. Even though it is summertime, very little fruit is being sold and it is frequently rotten and of inferior quality."[63]

Similar circumstances prevailed in the other cities of the Kharkiv consular district, including the cities of the Donbas.[64] Things were no better in the capital of Soviet Ukraine, Kyiv. On September 7, 1936, Stanisław Nawrocki reported to the headquarters of the Second Department that "it was not good" in Ukraine due to the food shortage. Nawrocki noticed very long lines in front of stores in the city, where one kilogram of potatoes cost fifty kopecks. One had to pay one ruble for ten average-sized potatoes at the local bazaars. This price set them out of reach for the majority of the population. Other types of goods that one had to stand in line for were textiles and shoes. If one had to spend a few hours waiting in lines, one did occasionally start a conversation about living conditions, which, in Soviet parlance, was considered grumbling, as the report emphasized. A popular saying in the city had it that the acronym SSSR (USSR) really meant *Smert' Stalina spaset Rossiiu* (Stalin's death will save Russia).[65] In July 1936, Władysław Michniewicz also recorded an interesting exchange of opinion among the locals standing in a huge line in the town of Pavoloch 120 km southwest of Kyiv. When he approached them and asked what they were waiting for, "bread" was their reply. After that, Michniewicz was surrounded by a crowd and heard loud complaints about the authorities, with some saying: "It is worse than in 1932–33—we are starving"; "This crook from the *raiispolkom*[66] does not care about a

---

[62] CAW, Oddz. II SG, sygn. I.303.4.1929, n.p. doc. 77.

[63] Ibid., sygn. I.303.4.1867, k. 52.

[64] Ibid., k. 53.

[65] Ibid., sygn. I.303.4.1956, n.p. doc. 21.

[66] The Raion Executive Committee.

thing"; "You drive around in cars while we are dying"; "Tell them everything over at the center." The crowd's rage grew so intense that Michniewicz had to escape as quickly as possible.[67]

The head of the consular post in Kyiv, Jan Karszo-Siedlewski, also noticed long lines there in the second half of 1936. On September 21, 1936, in a report to the ambassador in Moscow, he wrote that the level of food supply in 1936 was much worse than in the previous year. In Kyiv and other cities of central Ukraine, long lines formed in front of grocery stores. When he wrote the report, potatoes were the produce in shortest supply. After two to three hours of waiting in line, one received two to four kilograms of this vegetable. The worst availability of potatoes was in Odesa and other cities of southern Ukraine, where the most one could legally purchase was one kilogram. The price of potatoes in Kyiv was 50 kopecks, and in Odesa, 75 kopecks to one ruble. If someone had spare cash, he could purchase goods in the bazaars. In a Kyiv bazaar, potatoes cost from 90 kopecks to 1.15 ruble per kilogram. The availability of textiles or shoes was no better. Lines began forming at 2:00 or 3:00 a.m. in front of stores that sold those products.[68]

When scarce goods were delivered and the people waiting in line realized that there was not enough for everyone, riots broke out. On August 1, 1936, Sośnicki informed the ambassador about the situation in Kharkiv: "No clothing to be found. When a store receives a delivery of clothing, it is immediately besieged by crowds, triggering a military intervention. Recently, for example, in one of the stores at the 'horse bazaar,' the crowd grew so large that it had to be dispersed by mounted police, as the regular police alone was not able to win control of the situation. Due to the lack of clothing, textiles, and shoes, speculation and corruption are rife. The store clerks steal or resell their wares to speculators (for a surcharge, of course); thus, the population can only purchase some goods (fabric, shoes) at the bazaars from second-hand merchants.[69]

Based on his observations in Kyiv, Vinnytsia, Zhytomyr, Berdychiv, and Chernihiv, Stanisław Nawrocki also concluded that the residents there experienced an acute shortage of clothing, shoes, textiles, and rubber boots. "These items are nearly completely unavailable, e.g., rubber shoes

---

[67] CAW, Oddz. II SG, sygn. I.303.4.1927, n.p. 259.

[68] AAN, MSZ, sygn. 9514, k. 701–3.

[69] CAW, Oddz. II SG, sygn. I.303.4.1867, k. 244.

bought on the free market are 35 rubles per pair." Despite this, he reported that the countryfolk had it still much worse when it came to purchasing essential products.[70]

The queues could be observed not only in front of stores. People also had to wait for trains or other means of urban transport. Train delays happened on a daily basis, a result both of the poor condition of the railway infrastructure and the poor quality of the coal thrown into the locomotive engines.[71] In July 1935, Stanisław Sośnicki wrote in a report to Ambassador Łukasiewicz that train travel took place under "absolutely insane" conditions. Nearly all trains from Kharkiv arrived a few hours late. The train cars were so packed that in order to have any chance of getting on, one had to buy tickets a few days in advance. Long-distance trains passing through Kharkiv usually had no free seats, while the local trains had no "soft" cars.[72] Only on some lines, e.g., Tbilisi to Moscow, was there a sleeping car available. On the line from Baku to Shepetivka, a sleeping car was attached only twice a week, and it was fully booked by Intourist. On those two days, the car was already overloaded with foreign tourists at the departure station, i.e., either in Baku or Shepetivka.

Massive crowds always surrounded the train ticket sellers' booth in Kharkiv. Tickets were sold only from the moment the train arrived at the station. This led to various abnormalities. For a ticket that normally cost 50 rubles, passengers were ready to pay 100 rubles under the table. Such an occurrence took place when the German consul was scheduled to leave for holidays in Germany. His ticket had been sold at the last minute to someone else, and it was only after a major quarrel that it was given to him. It turned out that the clerk had received a 100-ruble bribe for the consul's reservation.[73]

With the urban reconstruction in Kyiv after the capital was moved there, some streetcar connections in the city were suspended. This fact, combined with other problems, such as the insufficient number of streetcars and blackouts because of electric power plants working at overcapacity, meant that a resident of Kyiv sometimes had to wait for hours for a streetcar to arrive. In early February 1936, Jan Łagoda saw a crowd of about a thousand people at a streetcar stop. The residents of Kyiv

---

[70] Ibid., sygn. I.303.4.1956, doc. 97.

[71] RGVA, f. 308 k, op. 6, d. 19, l. 217.

[72] That is, train cars with soft seats covered in fabric, versus those with rough, unprotected metal or wood benches.

[73] Ibid., op. 19, d. 57, l. 90–91.

had no other means of moving across the city, because the bus network was still in its infancy.[74]

Not much changed in the following period. The constant shortage of essential goods and long lines was a set part of life for a Soviet citizen. On October 18, 1938, the head of the Polish consulate general in Kyiv, Jerzy Matusiński, wrote a report for the MFA titled "The Goods Market and the Disorganization of Retail Trade." He concluded that the level of supply of industrial goods has further deteriorated from an already unsatisfactory situation. In front of all kinds of stores—food, clothing, shoes, etc.—the lines were even longer than usual. This state of affairs was a consequence of the smaller quantity of goods delivered to stores. Matusiński noticed that the stores in the capital of Soviet Ukraine had no butter and fruit. Even though only up to a liter of milk could be purchased, it was, nonetheless, still found lacking. Potatoes were essentially the only vegetable available, aside from the occasional onions, beets, and pumpkins. Some fruit, such as apples and pears, could only be acquired at the bazaar for one ruble per apple or two rubles per pear. In front of clothing stores, lines began forming the evening before. Long lines could be seen in front of shoe stores. It was no surprise that a customer who finally succeeded in making it through to the store attendant bought not what he initially intended to buy, but what was available at the time. Matusiński wrote: "One could witness such scenes: The happy face of a new owner of a pair of shoes turns into an irritated one as he inspects his new purchase more carefully on the street; he is joined by similarly 'satisfied' new owners, and they try to exchange the shoes. This is the only way of correcting the difference in size between the shoe and the foot!"[75]

In the Second Department's secret communiqué no. 19, "The Domestic Situation in the USSR," for the last quarter of 1938, printed in sixty copies and sent, inter alia, to the general inspector of the armed forces, the minister and vice-minister of military affairs, the chiefs of the Second and Third Departments, and the head of the Border Protection Corps, it was stated, based on data attached, that in the largest Soviet cities—e.g., in Moscow, Kyiv, Kharkiv, Leningrad—basic staples, such as vegetables (especially potatoes), milk, and meat were lacking. Consequently, long lines could be seen in front of stores in all those cities.

---

[74] AAN, MSZ, sygn. 9514, k. 123.
[75] Ibid., sygn. 6830, k. 29–30.

Largely, the lines were filled with peasants who were unable to buy the goods they needed locally and had to travel to the city.[76]

This same report, even if marked as secret, would not be particularly surprising to someone who followed the Soviet press at the time. Soviet newspapers, in October 1938, published many reports on the topic, explaining away the scarcity of potatoes and other vegetables as bureaucratic chaos among the organs responsible for delivering these products, as well as the actions of "the enemies of the people."[77] But, as Matusiński remarked, the "quantities of butter and shoes did not increase because of the efforts of Soviet propaganda."[78]

The Soviet people, who had been suffering from shortages of the most basic products for years, were very sensitive to any rumors, even the faintest, of new troubles in this area. When news of shortages or price hikes arrived, this immediately led to stores being stormed and whatever was still available being bought out. When, for example, someone spread a rumor that sugar prices were about to increase in Simferopol, people ran to the stores and bought out their entire stock. Those who had no time to stand in line remained without sugar. The same pattern held true for similar products: soap, salt, and matches.[79]

Polish intelligence was also interested in the quality of Soviet products—from food items to cleaning supplies, clothing, and metal products—and in the quality of steel produced in particular Soviet enterprises.[80] The East Section advised some of their informants to send back to Poland some everyday Soviet goods, such as

1. heavy industry: samples of materials, fabric, thread, leather, silk, tablecloths, linoleum, matches, soap, chemicals, etc.;

2. food: canned products, bread, chocolate;

3. optical instruments: binoculars, cameras, photographic film;

4. other products: jackknives, knives, pencils, pens, ink, paper, tobacco, cigarettes.

---

[76] CAW., Oddz. II SG, sygn. I.303.4.3228, k. 60–61.

[77] See "Neustanno zabotitsia o nuzhdakh naseleniia," *Pravda*, October 19, 1938; and "Torgovlia ovoshchami," *Pravda*, October 23, 1938.

[78] AAN, MSZ, sygn. 6830, k. 33.

[79] RGVA, f. 464 k, op. 1, d. 2996, l. 12 (this information was obtained via radio tapping on March 26, 1939).

[80] In July 1935, the East Section of the Second Department sent seven envelopes with samples of the Zaporizhia steel to the chief of the Independent Technical Bureau of the Second Department. Ibid., f. 308 k, op. 19, d. 57, l. 107.

The instruction was not to purchase those goods in large stores for "well-off" (*zazhitochnye*) individuals, but in the general (*shirpotreb*)[81] stores, especially those in villages and small towns.[82]

In Polish reports sent back to the MFA and the *Dwójka*'s main office, one finds a considerable amount of information about the quality of Soviet products. Usually the reports' evaluation was a negative one. After visiting the Hammer and Sickle factory in mid-1935, where he saw threshing machines being produced, Stanisław Sośnicki reported that the quality of production was not at a satisfactory level: "The threshing machines make a shabby impression; they leave the assembly line with bent, damaged parts, etc."[83]

After the Polish agents delivered Soviet products to Poland, their quality was examined in laboratories. Nothing surprising was usually discovered. Laboratory examinations confirmed the opinions of the Polish officials working in the field of Soviet affairs, who emphasized over and over again that the majority of goods available on the market was of very low quality. The exception to the rule was canned food. Of course, higher quality goods were available (e.g., in *torgsin* stores), but one condition had to be met. To purchase such a product one had to have cash, which was always in short supply for most citizens of "the Soviet paradise."

More detailed examination of particular Soviet products will be presented further on. In late December 1936, the Independent Technical Bureau of the Second Department analyzed the chemical composition of certain substances and made their evaluation. The quality of Soviet canned food (pork with beans, stewed meat, broad beans with lard, fish) was evaluated positively, even if similar Polish products were more nutritious. The evaluation of other products was much lower, including uncured tobacco, grains, and writing supplies. Wheat, for example, was judged to be heavily contaminated with weeds, the grains small, and the wheat itself damp.

---

[81] *Shirpotreb:* an abbreviation stemming from the Russian *shirokie potrebleniia*, i.e., mass consumer goods.

[82] RGVA, f. 308, op. 19, d. 63, l. 4. The same applied to the earlier period; e.g., the head of intelligence post X.22 in Kharkiv, Józefina Pisarczykówna, and the trade counselor of the embassy in Moscow, Antoni Żmigrodzki, sent back Soviet food samples: bread from the collective farms, cake, tea, etc. See Kuśnierz, *Pomór w "raju bolszewickim,"* 35 and 93.

[83] RGVA, f. 308 k, op. 19, d. 56, l. 100.

The assessment of other products was as follows:

1. Pencils: the graphite core was of the lowest quality, the wooden casing as well; such low-quality pencils could not even be found in Polish retail stores.

2. Ink: of the lowest quality. Clots began to form in the container soon after opening.

3. Letter paper: of a dirty-gray color, the lowest quality to be found on the market.

4. Paints for children's use: of a quality unseen on the Polish market. They were made from barely soluble glue, poured into cast containers, and fell apart when touched. They smelled horribly when in use.[84]

3.2.2. The Housing Problem

In addition to food shortages, the Soviet citizen had to face many other difficult problems. Housing was one of them. According to official data, the Second Five-Year Plan increased the amount of available housing space by three million square meters,[85] but most of that space was allotted to state and Party officials, military staff, the technical-engineering cadres, and so on. Ordinary working families could only dream about having their own place. Miners were in the worst position, and most of them lived in common mud huts.

Soviet reality meant that former multiroom apartments were now occupied by several families.[86] There were cases of up to forty (sic) families living in one apartment.[87] The situation was similar across the Soviet Union, from Moscow to small provincial cities. In March 1935, Władysław Harland prepared a report about the domestic situation in the USSR, in which he devoted a few paragraphs to the housing situation in Moscow. He began by remarking that the overall conditions were horrible. The official quota was six square meters of housing per person. This figure was not respected, because it was very difficult to do so in practice.[88] An

---

[84] Ibid., op. 6, d. 96, l. 3–6.

[85] W. A. Serczyk, *Historia Ukrainy* (Wrocław: Zakład Narodowy im. Ossolińskich, 2009), 314.

[86] This kind of apartment, the so-called *kommunalka*, was the most popular type of housing until the end of the Stalinist period: one family occupying one room, and a shared bathroom (if there was one at all), and kitchen, was a common situation. Three-fourths of the residents of Moscow and Leningrad lived this way in the mid-1930s. See O. Figes, *Szepty: Życie w stalinowskiej Rosji* (Warsaw: Wydawnictwo Magnum, 2008), 148.

[87] See *Pravda*, October 17, 1938.

[88] In 1940, there were only four square meters of housing space per one person in Moscow; see Figes, *Szepty*, 147.

ordinary apartment for a family of three to four included one room and shared (one-quarter, one-sixth) access to a communal kitchen. Kitchens were often divided into smaller sections. Deviations from this norm did occur, but usually in the unfavorable direction, e.g., one room shared by two families. "Her own room is a dream for an ordinary citizen in Moscow," Harland concluded.[89] Needless to say, persons in power were in a much better situation: for example, the head of the Internal Relations Department in the Defense Commissariat of the USSR, Anatolii Gekker, had two rooms (32 square meters) and a four-room apartment (116 square meters) at his disposal.[90]

The housing shortage obviously led to tensions and misunderstandings among the residents. Squeezed into one room, separated by cardboard or a makeshift screen, and sharing a bathroom and a kitchen (if they had the luxury of using them in their own apartment), people could only dream of privacy. Hence, not infrequently, if one looks just at what the Soviet press published, the main goal was to get rid of one's inconvenient roommate by any means. The most popular way to achieve this was to write a denunciation, dutifully informing the authorities that the neighbor was a quarrelsome drunkard or a shirker at work (*progul'shchik*). Or, much more seriously, a political accusation was put forward: that the neighbor was uncertain politically, that he met with suspect individuals, that he had the wrong kind of social background, or that he maintains or had maintained contact with "the enemies of the people" or with a foreigner. The Soviet press frequently reported on such conflicts between fellow residents.[91]

Reverberations of the housing shortage and the interpersonal conflicts arising from them reached the Polish consulates as well. In a general report for May 1935, Władysław Michniewicz wrote about those matters. He reported that, in consequence of the fact that six to seven families now lived in the old five- or six-room apartments, some rooms were divided by a cardboard screen. Next to the entrance door to each apartment, the following signs could be read: "Ring once for Apartment A, twice for Apartment B, six times for Apartment H." There were many court trials pertaining to the housing situation, and all kinds of denunciations were sent to the authorities.[92]

---

[89] RGVA, f. 308 k, op. 6, d. 20, l. 97.
[90] Ibid.
[91] See, e.g., *Pravda*, April 8, 1938.
[92] CAW, Oddz. II SG, sygn. I.303.4.1926, doc. 84, n.p.

Most people had no chance of finding their own apartment. The main obstacle was the lack of money. A very modest lifestyle in Kyiv, according to Michniewicz, cost up to 600 rubles per month, while the average salary rarely exceeded 300 rubles and retired citizens received 50–60 rubles as pensions per month, and widows, 20–50 rubles.[93] In 1936, in the capital of Ukraine, one had to first pay a deposit of 6,000 rubles to be able to rent a two-room apartment with a kitchen. Therefore the most popular option was to rent a section of a room for 30–40 rubles per month.[94]

Even if one occupied a small apartment, this did not guarantee any kind of stability. If rent was not paid on time, one could quickly be evicted. In a report on April 6, 1936, Stanisław Sośnicki informed Ambassador Łukasiewicz about the workers' situation. He emphasized that an acute housing shortage was endemic in Kharkiv, and one citizen could count, officially, on only thirteen square meters of housing: "Frequent evictions, forcible seizure of some of the larger apartments, and delays in rent payment occur on a daily basis; the courts are flooded with formal housing cases."[95] To illustrate this housing misery, Sośnicki gave an example of a Polish worker, Świątkowski-Lewandowski, who was employed as a highly qualified turner; unable to pay the rent, he attempted suicide. The man was already hanging when he was rescued by his family. He was arrested a few days later. In the month before his attempted suicide, the Polish worker earned 160 rubles per month working in his profession, after the norms had been increased.[96]

However, as noted above in the first section of this chapter, the worst situation was that of workers who lived in the workers' districts. They could only dream about living in a room divided by a cardboard screen, because usually they inhabited unlit mud huts or simply lived with no roof above their heads. To alleviate the situation, in 1935 a new district was opened near Nove Zaporizhia, where 4,500 families lived in mud huts—i.e., about 16,000 people, mostly workers, but also some families of Red Army soldiers. Some of those families had been living in mud huts since 1927.[97] This situation, regardless of what the propaganda said, did not change until the end of the interwar period. In a report by the Polish consulate general in Kyiv on March 29, 1939, its authors identified a new

---

[93] Ibid., doc. 77, n.p.
[94] Ibid., sygn. I.303.4.1956, n.p. doc. 97.
[95] CAW., Oddz. II SG, sygn. I.303.4.1867, k. 167.
[96] Ibid., k. 167, 208–9.
[97] RGVA, f. 464 k, op. 1, d. 954, l. 80–81.

type of nomadic, homeless miners. This was caused by the fact that the mines recruited collective-farm workers to come to the cities to work, but once they arrived, either they had no place to stay or managers refused to hire them.[98]

3.2.3. Prices and Wages

A worker's wages, regardless of his specialization, were barely enough to cover basic necessities. After the Stakhanovite movement was launched, the Soviet press came to be full of reports praising their enormous wages. It needs to be kept in mind, however, that the Stakhanovite-like records could obviously only be achieved in certain months, and thus, since those wages depended directly on one's labor output, they could not remain permanently high. Despite the unceasing efforts of Soviet propaganda, which advertised the constantly rising living standard of the working class, the situation did not look good. The head of intelligence post E.10, Stanisław Suchecki, aptly summed up the condition of the Soviet working class: "Due to the high prices and low wages (and, what also needs to be kept in mind, due to the lack of manufactured goods, clothing, and shoes), the living standard of the broad masses of Kharkiv is worse than miserable and can be characterized as well below the Western poverty line. In working-class families, meat is a luxury. One simply never consumes it. The people live mainly on poor-quality tea, herring, raw vegetables, and occasionally buckwheat, cabbage, and potatoes. In the milieus with which I am somewhat familiar, concepts such as breakfast, dinner, and supper do not exist. They usually eat once per day, whatever and however they can. Children of those people look undernourished." Better food and lifestyles were available only to the more important officials, senior military officers, higher technical cadres, and, of course, the NKVD.[99]

Based on his own observations and the data he received while touring many factories in Kharkiv, Dnipropetrovsk, Kryvyi Rih, Kamianske, Nikopol, and Poltava, Consul Stanisław Sośnicki concluded that the monthly salary of most workers fluctuated between 120 and 180 rubles, and about 15 percent of them earned between 180 and 300 rubles. Women in those same factories earned just 50 to 70 rubles per month.

---

[98] AAN, MSZ, sygn. 6731, k. 26.
[99] RGVA, f. 308 k, op. 19, d. 63, l. 45.

Next, to illustrate the living conditions of an average worker, Sośnicki cited the monthly budget of a worker from the Hammer and Sickle factory in Kharkiv, who earned about 130 rubles per month gross. Variouas taxes and fees were deducted before he even received his wages:

- income tax: 2.30 rubles
- cultural enterprises tax: 1.80 rubles
- social security: 2 rubles
- state bonds: 13 rubles
- newspaper subscription: 3.50 rubles
- airplane construction fee: 7 rubles
- extra charges for poor production quality: 4 rubles

Altogether, 33 rubles and 60 kopecks were charged, meaning that this worker received 96 rubles and 40 kopecks in hand. He had to pay his rent out of this amount. In July 1936, his total rent was 22 rubles and 50 kopecks (12 rubles for rent proper, 1.20 rubles for renovations, 4 rubles to repay a loan, 4 rubles for communal fees, 1.30 rubles miscellaneous).

After making those payments, the worker still had to pay for water and electricity (5 rubles); a trade-union membership fee (1.30 rubles); and the International Red Aid (MOPR) fee of 75 kopecks. These additional fees totalled 7 rubles and 5 kopecks.

His total disposable income, after all taxes, fees, and rents were subtracted, was 66 rubles and 55 kopecks. This man had a family — a wife and one child. Because of the scarcity of fats and meats (the family could hardly afford them anyway), the worker had to purchase two kilograms of bread daily to avoid starvation, which amounted to 60 rubles per month. For the remaining 6 rubles, one could purchase, for example, half a kilogram of meat.

In order to obtain other essential daily goods such as matches or soap, one had to cut the bread expenses. Furthermore, given how relatively expensive it was to purchase groceries, the daily meals of the workers were nearly always the same — soup and bread. Meat and butter were rarely seen. These difficulties were alleviated somewhat by the small individual plots factory workers were given, where they could grow vegetables. Once they had vegetables, the workers did not often buy meals in their factory dining halls, where the cheapest two-course dinner cost 65 kopecks.

The consul also reported on the incomes of qualified foreign workers. A foreigner working at the Kharkiv Tractor Plant earned 350 rubles gross, i.e., 250 rubles net. For the vouchers received from the plant, which could be exchanged for various kinds of goods, that individual received only 600 grams of butter and a piece of soap in July 1935. Unsurprisingly, a net outflow of foreign cadres from the Soviet enterprises was registered at that time.

Most workers were constantly sinking into debt. They usually had enormous rent-payment debts to cover. Inside the buildings, long "black" lists of debtors were hung on the bulletin board. Workers were told that if they did not repay their debts, their property would be confiscated and sold.[100]

Jan Łagoda, accompanied by consul Stanisław Sośnicki, gathered many important details about the workers' living conditions. Between May 25 and June 5, 1935, the two visited several industrial enterprises in Kharkiv, Zaporizhia, and Nikopol. They filed two special reports following their visit. Łagoda's report was particularly informative.[101] Even if some factories, such as the Kharkiv Tractor Plant, made a very positive impact on them ("the sight of the factory at work is quite impressive," wrote Łagoda[102]), the general outlook was negative; the weariness and penury of the workers in the giant Soviet factories was in plain sight essentially everywhere. Łagoda made note of the workers' exhaustion: "They are tired, apathetic, indifferent, physically and spiritually spent. Any kind of conversation with a janitor, a chauffeur, a railway conductor, an engineer, a doctor in his office, brings new evidence of just how difficult life is and how false is the propaganda distorting it. The narrow-mindedness, futile sophistry, and deep moral savagery of the masses have greatly progressed. The physical and moral endurance of the workers in Zaporizhia and Nikopol is very weak."[103]

The official from the Polish embassy in Moscow also noticed that the aggressiveness of the managerial cadres increased in parallel with the growing apathy of the working class: "Any conversation with representatives of the Soviet ruling circles betrays their aggressive moods. They do not hide their jealousy of the capitalist world, their desire to rob it, and to start a deadly struggle with it until a victorious end. Those circles are utterly convinced that an unavoidable war is already near, but that the Soviets are not sufficiently prepared for it yet, and that in a few years their

---

[100] Ibid., op. 6, d. 21, l. 284–86.
[101] RGVA, f. 308 k, op. 19, d. 54, l. 162–98.
[102] Ibid., l. 172.
[103] Ibid., l. 197–98.

strength will become visible and then the entire world will tremble (*ves' mir zadrozhit*), as expressed by my interlocutor."[104]

A few months later, Łagoda—again accompanied by Consul Sośnicki, as well as by Ludwik Michałowski, took a trip around Ukraine, this time focusing on the Donbas, from November 12 to 23, 1935.[105] Its purpose was to shed light on issues related to industrial production, the material conditions of the workers, the availability of housing, the Stakhanovite movement, and the railways and agriculture.

The deputy trade counselor carefully described all the factories visited. The workers appeared miserable in all of them. They lived in very bad conditions, sometimes in mud huts. All the directors claimed that the average wage was 250 rubles, which was not true. The workers at coke chemical plant no. 2 in Rutchenkove, working in the coal transportation section, received on average 150 rubles, while those handling the coke-processing apparatus received 200 rubles. Zamel, the deputy director of a factory in Kramatorsk reported that, thanks to the new Stakhanovite method, wages in his enterprise ranged from 320 to as high as 814 rubles. This data differed from what was reported by the workers themselves, who spoke of wages between 130 and 180 rubles, and up to 400 rubles for the most highly skilled. The engineers made (allegedly): the head of a department, 900 rubles (with a bonus of up to 1,400 rubles); an engineer without experience, 450 rubles; a general CEO, 2,000 rubles; a technical director, 3,000 rubles. Based on the clothing they wore, one could not tell an engineer from a worker, and their "thousand-ruble incomes" certainly did not show.[106]

The authors of that travel report emphasized the large turnover of cadres in the worst paid and heaviest branches of industry. Despite the hunger wages (100 rubles), there was no shortage of hands willing to work. This applied particularly to the country folk, who were ready to work anywhere after leaving their village.[107] One worker told Łagoda that a wage like that was not enough for him because he had a family to feed,

---

[104] Ibid., l. 198.

[105] These dates are of Jan Łagoda's trip. He began his round-trip journey in Moscow. Łagoda, together with Sośnicki and Michałowski, remained in the Donbas from November 15 to 20, 1935.

[106] RGVA, f. 308 k, op. 19, d. 59, l. 135, 149–50.

[107] Łagoda wrote that "thanks to the influence on the main reservoir of the labor force, i.e., the village, the Soviet government is capable, insofar as the village is fully subjugated, to exert the right kind of pressure on that reservoir and shape the labor supply according to the industry's needs" (CAW, Oddz. II SG, sygn. I.303.4.3144, k. 1535).

but his single colleagues often willingly agreed to work for such meager pay.

Comparing the existence of Soviet and for Polish workers, Łagoda wrote that, from the Polish perspective, the conditions the Soviet workers suffered were unbearable, "because our worker, due to the higher civilizational level and the higher standard of living, would experience the Soviet conditions as utter destitution. The Russian [i.e., Soviet] worker must not be experiencing this material deprivation this way or to such an extent because of his narrower spectrum of needs, and therefore he does not express his outrage openly. This state of affairs is to be explained by the low civilizational level, [and] secondly, by the hard lesson taught during the First Five-Year Plan, when, in most cases, the worker worked for one kilogram of bread per day mixed with hot water and some remnants of fat and potatoes. Consequently the resulting state of affairs might have been accepted as normal by many, or, in any case, much better than the one preceding it."[108]

The following case exemplifies the material condition of the Soviet workers. Jan Łagoda talked with an administrative director in one of the factories. The director had Polish origins and was a locksmith by training. He regretted that he had not gone back to his hometown near Hrodna, on the Polish side of the border, when he still could, because his directorial salary did not suffice to cover even a most modest lifestyle. He was very grateful to his relatives in Poland for sending an occasional package or two, but he regretted that he lacked the money to cover the very high custom fees imposed on those goods. Łagoda commented on that conversation thus: "I could not believe what I was hearing, especially because this conclusion came from an administrative director of a large, prosperous industrial enterprise."[109]

The management of these industrial enterprises did not care much for the housing needs of their labor force. There were very few new buildings in the Donbas, and those that had been constructed were used by the officials and institutions. The workers lived mostly on the outskirts, in little houses from the tsarist period or in the numerous new mud huts built during the interwar period. Łagoda wrote that "whatever the future was

---

[108] Ibid. k. 1534–35.
[109] Ibid. k. 1556.

going to bring, currently, eighteen years after the revolution, the workers live in conditions worse than before the revolution."[110]

The managers also did not care much about providing acceptable factory-floor conditions for the workers, especially during the heat waves of the summer. In the summer of 1936, the cities lacked sufficient quantities of water and cold beverages. According to information that Stanisław Suchecki received, Kharkiv's factories also lacked sufficient water. The workers drank whatever they could get ahold of, which obviously helped to spread diseases. The beverages available on the market were too expensive. A bottle of low-quality, bad-tasting fruit water or a bottle of beer, also of questionable quality, cost 65–75 kopecks. The places where one could buy cold beverages were too few, and those that there were did not pass any sanitary standards. Suchecki wrote that the sellers, most of them of Jewish background, looked shabby. On the outskirts and in the villages, one could not buy any cold beverages at all.[111]

The poor working and living conditions and low wages had a negative impact on the stability of the labor force. Soviet sources emphasized the volatility of labor cadres on many occasions. It was a permanent problem in many Soviet enterprises.[112] In a report from April 6, 1936, Stanisław Sośnicki paid attention to this problem as well. To give an example, he wrote about mine no. 3 in Krasnodon, where the daily fluctuation in personnel amounted to 75 workers.[113] In another report, on August 17, 1936, he quoted the figure of 100 workers who left the Krasnyi Oktiabr mine in July 1936.[114] The consul also emphasized that the turnover of working cadres in the Donbas sometimes reached 50 percent monthly. According to official data, in January 1936 the average number of days worked by a Donbas miner was 22.5 and in June of the same year, 21 —

[110] RGVA, f. 308, op. 19, d. 59, l. 132.

[111] Ibid., d. 63, l. 157.

[112] See, for example, D. Vadimov, "V Donbasse sabotiruiut' bor'bu s progulami," *Pravda*, May 23, 1937; and K. Zotin, "Tramvai v Gor'kom ne podgotovlen k zime," *Pravda*, October 17, 1938.

[113] CAW, Oddz. II SG, sygn. I.303.4.1867, k. 163. In the March 1938 informational bulletin issued by the MFA, *Polska a Zagranica*, the case of a cotton refinery was quoted as an example demonstrating the high labor turnover. In October 1936, 1,500 workers left their jobs (out of 21,000 employed) and 2,531 new workers were hired. In January 1937, 930 workers left and 1,083 were hired. At monthly turnover rates like that, it is not difficult to estimate that, within 9–10 months, all of the factory's workers would have been replaced. AAN, MSZ, sygn. 119, k. 110.

[114] CAW, Oddz. II SG, sygn. I.303.4.1867, k. 59.

below the official norm of 25 days.[115] In a survey prepared by the Polish MFA, *Poland and Abroad* (*Polska a Zagranica*), the official Soviet data from the Donbas region pertaining to this problem was quoted. In 1936 there were 432,606 cases of absenteeism, and in the first four months of 1937 there were 163,527 such cases.[116]

In the following years, despite repressive measures against the "workplace deserter" and some positive material incentives, the overall picture did not change much. In mid-August 1939, the Polish embassy in Moscow delivered a report to the MFA titled "A Survey of the Overall Situation in Soviet Industry in the Second Half [of 1939]." The authors of the survey emphasized that, based on official Soviet data, the high turnover of working cadres not only did not cease, but also failed to decrease. In the iron-ore mines in the Kryvyi Rih area, for instance, almost half of the labor force left in the first half of 1939. Not only the mining sector, but also other branches, such as the textile, iron, and construction industries, had similar problems with recruitment and high turnover rates, negatively impacting their ability to fulfill production plans. High labor turnover in one industry led to a similar problem in another. One of the causes behind the high rate of miners leaving their mines was the housing shortage; the construction industry administration cited the high labor turnover as a cause of the failure to fulfill the apartment-construction quotas.[117]

Mining jobs were abandoned not only by ordinary workers, but also by the Stakhanovites. On August 8, 1936, the newspaper *Za industrializatsiiu* (*For Industrialization*) included the story of Fedor Artiukhov, a Stakhanovite, to describe conditions in the life of the Donbas miners. A few months earlier, Artiukhov, like Stakhanov himself, was one of the Soviet heroes who broke a new mining-output record. However, because of the bad conditions (he lived with his wife and three children in

---

[115] Ibid., k. 60.

[116] AAN, MSZ, sygn. 119, k. 111. This data was also published by *Pravda*, among others; see Vadimov, "V Donbasse sabotiruiut bor'bu."

[117] AAN, MSZ, sygn. 6719, k. 31–33. The embassy also emphasized that the Bolsheviks made the high labor-turnover issue public enemy number one, replacing the previous enemy, industrial sabotage. This shift, according to the embassy, meant that the real negative impact of that turnover on production efficiency must have been low because "blaming the production process shortcomings" for the poor outcomes was a convenient way out for the factory management, since it diffused responsibility. Ibid., k. 33.

one room), he decided to leave the Krasnyi Oktiabr' mine and the Donbas. He got a job at the MTS near Armavir in the Kuban.[118]

Of course, in "the most just system in the world," the privileged Party members found themselves in a very different situation.[119] This was a taboo topic that could not be mentioned in public, and those who let it be known what they thought about the enormous inequity between the Party and the people were immediately arrested and severely punished as counterrevolutionaries. The following case serves as an example. In 1936, a Polish citizen was asked to give a speech at the Kharkiv Tractor Plant. He declined, citing his poor knowledge of Russian as the reason, but he also added as a reason his "views on the relations prevailing here, where only a few live well, and everyone else lives in poverty." Unsurprisingly, he was immediately arrested. Later he was sentenced to six years in prison for counterrevolutionary activity.[120]

In addition to better pay, privileged Party members also received vouchers that could be exchanged for various goods at so-called hard prices established by the state. Just how valuable those vouchers were is evidenced by the difference in price one paid for the same pair of leather shoes in 1935. If one used the voucher, the price was 25 rubles, whereas their free-market price reached 150 rubles. Unsurprisingly, this difference was significant enough to boost the free-market price of those vouchers to 1,500 rubles.[121]

Of course, it was not just Party activists who enjoyed a higher status in "the Soviet paradise." Other privileged professions included the military, the NKVD, the professoriat, and the bureaucracy. Estimates of income of some social groups were given in a few Polish reports, based on official data and some information provided by visitors. On February 10, 1936, Stanisław Nawrocki cited the following monthly incomes.

---

[118] CAW, Oddz. II SG, sygn. I.303.4.1867, k. 59.

[119] For more information about the social groups that enjoyed a privileged position in the USSR, see M. Matthews, *Privilege in the Soviet Union: A Study of Elite Life-Styles under Communism* (London and Boston: G. Allen & Unwin, 1978), passim; and E. Osokina, *Za fasadom "stalinskogo izobiliia": Raspredelenie i rynok v snabzhenii naseleniia v gody industrializatsii, 1927–1941* (Moscow: ROSSPEN, 2008), passim. It needs to be underlined that the number of privileged persons was relatively low and limited to the highest Party and state officials. Most regular functionaries, even if they were in a somewhat better situation than their fellow citizens, lived a modest life. What they received were additional food rations, coupons, clothes, and a larger apartment. See Figes, *Szepty*, 146.

[120] CAW, Oddz. II SG, sygn. I.303.4.1867, k. 80.

[121] Ibid., sygn. I.303.4.1926, doc. 84., n.p.

Stakhanovites received 400–1,000 rubles, and in the provinces, 60–120 rubles. Mid-level clerks received 200–300 rubles, and top-level, 500–600 rubles. Officers earned up to a thousand rubles per month; academic lecturers, between 205 and 570 rubles; and the free professions (doctors, artists, journalists, writers), between 300 and 1,500 rubles.[122]

According to the data Stanisław Sośnicki acquired (from late March 1936), members of the professoriat earned 700 rubles per month on average, with a workload of 440 hours. This amount did not include the remuneration received for laboratory or written work, which could result in about 300 rubles per month. Starting from April 1, 1936, the salaries of academicians were scheduled for a raise: a member of the Academy of Sciences was to be paid 2,200 rubles, a scholar with a doctorate,[123] 2,000, and other lecturers, 1,400, while the workload was to be reduced to 220 hours (from 440; the other 220 hours were to be devoted to research and experimental work).[124] According to the data Jan Karszo-Siedlewski gathered in 1936, clerks earned between 300 and 350 rubles, and head clerks, between 500 and 600 rubles.[125]

In addition to higher wages and vouchers, these privileged groups were surrounded by a social support network. Moreover, they could, for instance, spend holidays in special luxury spas or hotels. In the materials of Branch no. 1 of the Second Department in Vilnius, there is a description of a holiday hotel for officers in Amnishava, a village near Pleshchanitsy in the Belorussian SSR. Both the building's exterior and interior were, compared to the usual Soviet standards, impressive. It was very clean inside and boasted a reading room, a piano, a radio, and a billiards room. Next to the building, an artificial pool had been created by diverting the flow of the Omnishevka River, with additional structures such as a diving board and a dock.[126]

Ordinary citizens could only dream about such luxury. The Soviet press itself was full of reports of unsatisfactory conditions that awaited the working-class vanguard at holiday destinations. In July 1938, Moscow-

---

[122] Ibid., sygn. I.303.4.1956, n.p., doc. 32.

[123] In the Polish system, the equivalent position was called *doktor habilitowany* (advanced post-PhD degree). In the Soviet system, and in the system currently prevailing in the former Soviet republics, there was (is) one more degree before a scholar receives his doctor degree: *kandidat nauk* (candidate of sciences).

[124] AAN, MSZ, sygn. 9514, k. 423.

[125] Ibid., k. 701.

[126] RGVA, f. 308 k, op. 6, d. 19, l. 213–14.

based *Pravda* published the following description. Five teachers from the Volga region went to Yalta for the holidays. When they arrived, they were unable to find a hotel room. After searching in vain, they went to the Massandra Park, but at 2:00 a.m. they decided to return to the Central Hotel, where the director took mercy on them and allowed them to sleep on the floor. As the journalist reported, those teachers were lucky, because many other guests had to sleep outside on the beach or on roofless balconies, in hotel corridors, or simply in the streets of Yalta. Those travelers who were lucky enough to get a room still had no guarantee that they would be comfortable. The author cited the case of a Stakhanovite named Pozovsky, from a clothing factory in Smolensk, who, after arriving at the Central Hotel, found that his room was dark and damp and that there were four people in it instead of the two he had expected. Only two chairs were available for those four persons, and the dirty sheets and covers were disgusting. Pozovsky wrote to the director of this hotel: "It is a shame to rent out a room like that; holidays in such conditions bring torment instead of joy."[127]

The underprivileged residents of the "Soviet paradise," the vast majority of that society, had to struggle with everyday problems of existence and deal with prices that increase disproportionately to incomes. This was a universal problem across the entire USSR, including Moscow. A one-time informant of the *Dwójka*'s Branch no. 1 in Vilnius said that he witnessed a conversation between a secretary of a local Party cell and a railway worker, who said that he was not eating anything because he received only 2.4 kilos of bread daily, which he had to share with his wife and three children, and, because he lived at a distant railway switch post, he received no other products.[128]

In a report to the Polish ambassador in Moscow dated September 21, 1936, Jan Karszo-Siedlewski remarked that the situation of Soviet workers had deteriorated in practical terms because, even if their wages remained nominally the same, their workload had increased (in many sectors) and it now took more work to achieve a Stakhanovite bonus. The purchasing power of Soviet currency had decreased as well. The diplomat included the following data as an example of working-class incomes: in large cities, the workers earned between 120 and 250 rubles per month, and the

---

[127] I. Verkhovtsev, "V kurortnoi gostinitse: Ot korrespondenta 'Pravdy' po Krymskoi ASSS," *Pravda*, July 28, 1938.

[128] RGVA, f. 308 k., op. 6, d. 19, l. 217.

Stakhanovites, 300 rubles on average. Wages were lower outside the larger cities. It was possible for a Stakhanovite to earn more, but given the conditions of piecework employment, this happened rarely and was not representative of broader trends.[129]

Those who had money did not have much faith in Soviet currency anyway and attempted to convert it into goods. In a September 18, 1936 report titled "Current Conditions in Ukraine," Stanisław Nawrocki mentioned the inflating price indices in the stores, where it was difficult to buy something anyway because the cashiers dealt under the table.[130] He gave telling data about the incomes of particular social groups: unqualified workers received between 100 and 150 rubles; qualified workers, between 200 and 300; and the cost of living for a family of four in Kyiv, assuming that they ate meat twice a week and their children drank milk every second day, was between 400 and 500 rubles.[131]

The data quoted by various Polish sources differs slightly, but all the figures in the reports were real. The difference between them can be explained by whether the figures quoted were from official sources or whether they were obtained in private conversations with visitors (to the consulate) or Soviet officials. It is beyond doubt that the incomes of the unprivileged class were miserable and barely sufficed, if at all, to pay for essentials. For insight into the real purchasing power of the Soviet ruble, one needs to take a look at the prices of some everyday goods in various cities. Polish consular officials did this in reports to the embassy and the main office of the MFA in Warsaw on multiple occasions.[132] On February 10, 1936, Stanisław Nawrocki quoted the following prices in his report:

- leather shoes: from 120 rubles
- men's shirts: 27–54 rubles
- rubber boots: 25 rubles
- whole-wheat bread: 90 kopecks
- milk: 2 rubles per liter
- butter: 14–18 rubles per kilogram
- pork fatback: 12 rubles per kilogram

---

[129] AAN, MSZ, sygn. 9514, k. 699–700.
[130] Jan Karszo-Siedlewski informed the Polish ambassador in Moscow on September 21, 1936, that in Kyiv alone 600 persons were arrested and charged with speculation in July and August 1936.
[131] CAW, Oddz. II SG, sygn. I.303.4.1956, doc. 33, n.p.
[132] See table 4 in chapter 2.

- pork: 9.40 rubles per kilogram
- chicken: 7.50 rubles each.[133]

Stanisław Sośnicki gathered some data about price increases of produce as of July 1 and August 21, 1936 (see table 7).

Table 7. Prices of selected produce as of July 1 and August 21, 1936

	Price per kg, July 1, 1936 (in rubles)	Price per kg, August 21, 1936 (in rubles)
Cabbage	0.60	1.50
Carrots	0.40	1.50
Tomatoes	0.40	0.80–1
Potatoes	0.40	1–1.50

Source: CAW, Oddz. II SG, sygn. I.303.4.1867, k. 53.

The branches of the Second Department also collected similar information. Prices of goods in smaller cities and villages were frequently included in their reports. Informants of *Dwójka*'s Branch no. 5 in Lviv submitted the following representative prices:

Prices in the village of Slovechne, Ovruch raion, Zhytomyr oblast:
- one pood of rye flour: 35 rubles
- one pood of wheat: 32 rubles
- one pood of potatoes: 7 rubles
- one kilogram of whole-wheat bread: 1 ruble
- one kilogram of white bread: 3.50 rubles
- one kilogram of pork fatback: 20 rubles
- one kilogram of butter: 30 rubles
- one kilogram of sugar: 7.50 rubles
- one egg: 70 kopecks
- boots: 200–220 rubles

Prices in the town of Horodok, Vinnytsia oblast:
- one kilogram of whole-wheat bread: 90 kopecks
- one kilogram of white bread: 1.50 rubles

Prices in the village of Liskivtsi, Horodok raion, Vinnytsia oblast
- one kilogram of sugar: 7 rubles
- one kilogram of herring: 7 rubles
- one kilogram of pork fatback: 7 rubles
- one kilogram of sausage: 6 rubles

[133] CAW, Oddz. II SG, sygn. I.303.4.1956, doc. 22, n.p.

- one kilogram of whole-wheat bread: 90 kopecks
- one kilogram of white bread: 1.80 rubles.[134]

In a September 18, 1936 letter to the ambassador in Moscow, Jan Karszo-Siedlewski also underscored that food prices were constantly on the rise, as were prices for other essential goods, such as clothing, underwear, and shoes—all while nominal incomes for most citizens were stagnant. The diplomat predicted that the Soviet authorities would be obliged in the near future to find a solution to this problem, because he considered it impossible, in the long run, to keep the population passive solely through terror and the never-ending propaganda of class struggle and the fear of war.[135]

The Polish analyst was wrong in this respect, however. The situation did not change much until the end of the interwar period. Perusing the Soviet press is enough to create the gloomy impression of a reality in which everything, even nails, is unavailable.[136] It should come as no surprise, then, that in both the cities and the countryside, theft was a popular method of improving one's circumstances. Wladyslaw Michniewicz, writing in April 1935, aptly remarked: "Theft is such a ubiquitous phenomenon that it stopped being shameful in the eyes of witnesses. Nearly everyone who wants to eat moderately well must steal; therefore they steal wherever they can: in enterprises, in factories, in offices, on trains. These thefts are systematic; they constitute permanent auxiliary income; 90 percent of the perpetrators remain undetected, despite the widespread practice of neighbors denouncing neighbors, as their skill is ever-growing and former denouncers have already begun to steal for themselves too."[137]

Desperate workers sometimes tried organizing a strike, but this was a rare occurrence. The smallest measure of protest against the authorities brought very serious consequences. Those who decided to strike anyway must have known about the consequences beforehand, meaning that their behavior was further proof of just how miserable their situation was. On August 17, 1935, a strike of sweepers took place in Kharkiv. They did not sweep or wash the streets all day long, demanding a pay raise. Their wages were the lowest and amounted to 70–90 rubles. The workers from the Hammer and Sickle factory requested a raise, too. Of course, both

---

[134] RGVA, f. 308 k, op. 6, d. 22, l. 221–22.

[135] AAN, MSZ, sygn. 6669, k. 17.

[136] See, e.g., *Pravda*, September 2, 1938.

[137] CAW, Oddz. II SG, sygn. I.303.4.1926, doc. 84, n.p.

strikes ended the same way: their leaders were arrested, and the others were forced to continue working for the same wages.[138]

3.2.4. Restaurants and Dining Halls

The Polish diplomats and consular officials in the field of Soviet affairs suffered from a lack of those creature comforts that were normally taken for granted in advanced countries. In the USSR, many of these "bourgeois relics" of comfort had been eliminated. Higher-end restaurants were one of them. After the revolution, the Bolsheviks favored so-called collective consumption—that is, they attempted to create a dining hall next to every major work place so that the workers could dine there instead of wasting time eating at home.[139] As always, the reality was but a weak reflection of the plan. Dining-hall meals, apart from being expensive, were often tasteless. Some dining halls served only one type of food; for example, the dining hall at the agricultural equipment construction plant Krasnyi Oktiabr in Odesa oblast served nothing but cabbage in 1934.[140] The sanitary conditions in the dining halls were poor, even if some exceptions could be found. Jan Karszo-Siedlewski and Zdzisław Miłoszewski were positively impressed by the factory kitchen[141] near the Stalin Metal Works in Stalino. It served 18,000 meals daily. A two-course meal cost 66 kopecks, and a dessert was 25 kopecks. Reflecting on their impressions after a visit to the factory kitchen, the Poles wrote that the dining hall was relatively clean and very large, and the dinner itself looked fine.[142]

The dining halls considered good enough to host foreign visitors at were not, of course, representative of the overall state of "collective

---

[138] RGVA, f. 308, op. 6, d. 21, l. 287. Hiroaki Kuromiya gave me a part of Stanisław Sośnicki's report prior to my archival research in Moscow. See also H. Kuromiya, "Stalin's Great Terror and International Espionage," *The Journal of Slavic Military Studies* 24, no. 2 (2011): 241.

[139] For more information on this topic, see R. Kuśnierz, " 'Kolektywna konsumpcja' w okresie pierwszej radzieckiej pięciolatki: Propaganda a rzeczywistość (Mało znany absurd bolszewicki)," *Dzieje Najnowsze*, 2008, no. 2: 37–48; and O. Movchan, "Hromads'ke kharchuvannia robitnykiv URSR u 1930-ti roky," *Problemy istoriï Ukraïny: Fakty, sudzhennia, poshuky* 20 (2011): 211–38.

[140] W. Z. Goldman, *Terror and Democracy in the Age of Stalin: The Social Dynamics of Repression* (Cambridge: Cambridge University Press, 2007), 24.

[141] The factory kitchens were very large units serving food. For example, the factory kitchen in Cheliabinsk fed 100,000 people daily, and the factory kitchen near the Stalingrad Tractor Factory served 225,000 meals daily. Frequently they had their own security organs, including firemen, and horse stables (used for transportation); see Kuśnierz, "Kolektywna konsumpcja," 40–41.

[142] AAN, SG, sygn. IV/5, k. 920–21.

consumption." The other side of the coin can be seen in other reports. Those reports were not about the large factory kitchens but about regular restaurants and dining halls. These alternative spots of collective eating, also in the city of Stalino, were not awe-inspiring, to say the least. According to Jan Łagoda's report, the city boasted only two shabby restaurants and several poorly maintained dining halls for the workers, very much resembling bars, down in the mining shafts of the previous era. In this respect, Łagoda held that the direction of transformation was for the worse, despite the overall industrial progress and the construction of a few new mines and factories in the area.[143]

We have access to a few reports on the state of dining halls in Kharkiv. Stanisław Suchecki wrote, in an operational report for the period of March–May 1936, that these were accessible only to the better-paid workers. "Dirty. Food is bad," was his conclusion.[144]

On August 1, 1936, Sośnicki wrote to the ambassador: "Due to the high prices and low wages, the people eat poorly and irregularly. For the urban working class and in the countryside, concepts such as breakfast, dinner, and supper do not exist. People eat whatever they can in whatever ways they can. The kids are malnourished and look miserable. There are only three decent restaurants in Kharkiv—one at the Northern Railway Station, earmarked mostly for foreigners; the second, the so-called Krasnaia, downtown; and the third near the Dynamo stadium. Moreover, there are a few other mediocre restaurants and many so-called buffets built for the working class. Two 'obraztsovye stolovye' [model dining halls] exist besides the other dining halls. Except for the three restaurants mentioned first, unspeakable untidiness reigns everywhere. The meals are cooked without care and without taste. The prices are high. The attendants are numerous, but they are underpaid, dirty, and unskilled. Due to the high prices, all of the eateries mentioned above are basically inaccessible for most people. The usual guests are normally the NKVD agents, the military, the 'otvetstvennye rabotniki' [responsible workers], some youth, and Jews."[145]

During his September 1936 field trip to Mariupol, Berdiansk, and Kerch, Stanisław Sośnicki visited the factory dining hall at the Azovstal iron works. He saw workers there who, instead of a warm meal, ate

---

[143] RGVA, f. 308 k, op. 19, d. 59, l. 128.
[144] Ibid., d. 63, l. 45.
[145] CAW, Oddz. II SG, sygn. I.303.4. 1867, k. 243.

watermelon and bread, and the luckier ones could afford 100 grams of sausage. The consul asked one of them whether what he saw him eating was his dinner. The worker confirmed it was and named the price he had paid for his dinner: 2.75 rubles for a course of 100 grams of sausage, small watermelon, and half a kilogram of bread. The same price could be paid for a two-course dinner, but its quality was so bad that the worker preferred the watermelon, sausage, and bread.[146]

Based on his analysis of dining-hall prices and average wages, Sośnicki concluded that the situation for the workers in the "Soviet paradise" was miserable. Assuming that the worker he spoke to had to pay one ruble each for his breakfast and supper, in addition to the 2.75 rubles he paid for his dinner, he thus spent about 5 rubles daily for food, or 150 rubles per month. With a monthly wage of 200 rubles and a normal rent payment, the worker was left with nothing.[147] The Stakhanovites could receive 600 rubles or even more, but this was rare; furthermore, their work was piecework.

The same problem was highlighted by the other chief of the Polish consular mission in Ukraine, Jan Karszo-Siedlewski. On September 21, 1936, he wrote that the cheaper soup (without bread) in the factory dining hall cost 30 kopecks. It was so disgusting that very few were willing to buy it. The better soup cost 50 to 60 kopecks, a potato pancake was 90 kopecks, and a serving of meat, 1.60 rubles. The head of the consulate emphasized that, based on those prices, eating out was obviously too expensive for an average worker, and thus the number of collective dining points was declining.[148]

Stanisław Nawrocki also emphasized that, in many cases, the price of a dinner was de facto beyond reach of the average worker. In a report on September 18, 1936, he stressed that the dinners in workers' dining halls were very expensive. The price was 90 kopecks for the cheaper dinner and 2.20 rubles for the more expensive one. The latter was obviously unavailable to the Soviet worker because of the high price. "Under these conditions, the working class is never eating enough," he concluded.[149]

In addition to the cost of meals, the shortage of dining halls was also a problem. The Bolsheviks of course knew that this was the case and why, but they blamed the mythical enemies (Trotskyites, former kulaks,

---

[146] Ibid., k. 123.
[147] Ibid., k. 123–24.
[148] AAN, MSZ, sygn. 9514, k. 702.
[149] CAW, Oddz. II SG, sygn. I.303.4 1956, doc. 33, n.p.

followers of Bukharin), who "just waited for a chance to make the life of Soviet workers worse." It was never the system itself that was at fault. One of the Polish reports from early 1939 included the story of "the enemies of the people" in charge of the Kharkiv Dining Hall Trust. It was those people, the authorities said, who were responsible for closing down 120 eateries. They were exposed and eliminated, but, as the Soviet press reported, "cleaning up after their destructive activity took place too slowly. The dining halls are still messy, there are not enough plates, knives, and forks. Because the service is so slow, workers often cannot wait long enough for dinner and are forced to return to work hungry."[150]

3.3. The Stakhanovite Movement.
3.3.1. "Maximum Exploitation of the Worker"

On August 31, 1935, the worker Alexei Stakhanov broke a coal output record.[151] Using a jackhammer in the Central Irmino coal mine in the Donbas, he extracted 102 tonnes of coal instead of the plan's expected seven. In the minds of Communist propagandists, the example he set would inspire his fellow workers not only in the mining industry, but in many other fields as well, including intellectual work.

The press never ceased to report record after record being broken across the country. All kinds of conventions, conferences, councils, and radio broadcasts (*radiopereklichki*) focused on the movement, whose name was inspired by Stakhanov. Soviet propaganda used his feat to glorify "the enormous sacrifice and efficiency of the Soviet worker" who stretched the barriers of what was humanly possible. He did it, of course, for the Party, for the "beloved" leader, Stalin, and in order "to increase the well-being of the working class." Stakhanov himself was quickly promoted. He was told to come to Moscow, where he began studying at

---

[150] Ibid., sygn. I.303.4.5763, n.p.

[151] For more information about the Stakhanovite movement's birth and development, see O. V. Khlevniuk, *Udarniki pervoi piatiletki* (Moscow: "Znanie," 1989), 6; L. H. Siegelbaum, *Stakhanovism and the Politics of Productivity in the USSR, 1935–1941* (Cambridge: Cambridge University Press, 1988), passim; R. Thurston, "The Stakhanovite Movement: Background to the Great Terror in the Factories, 1935–1938," in J. A. Getty and R. T. Manning, eds., *Stalinist Terror: New Perspectives* (Cambridge: Cambridge University Press, 1993), 142–60; and S. R. Gershberg, *Stakhanov i stakhanovtsy* (Moscow: Izdatelstvo politliteratury, 1981). Among Polish historians, an informative survey on the movement (and the way it related to Poland) was written by Hubert Wilk; see H. Wilk, *Kto wyrąbie więcej ode mnie? Współzawodnictwo pracy robotników w Polsce w latach 1947–1955* (Warsaw: Trio, 2011), 19–46.

the Industrial Academy (*Promakademiia*). In 1937 he was elected a deputy to the Supreme Soviet from Voroshylovhrad raion, Donetsk oblast.[152] As a newly minted Soviet hero, he frequently wrote for newspapers, both about workers' output competitions and to glorify Stalin and the Communist Party.[153] He occupied high managerial positions both in mining enterprises and in the Coal Industry Commissariat, until his retirement in 1974.

Soviet propaganda of course held that the new initiative met with a lively response among the working masses, who were keen on joining the Stakhanovite movement. However, as Jan Karszo-Siedlewski rightly pointed out: "it was no longer really a privilege or a distinction to become a Stakhanovite. It is a burdensome duty that, to be sure, grants some higher income and better holidays from time to time, but the price that is paid in terms of enormous physical strain, bordering on the degradation of one's health, is so high that, in the eyes of the workers, it cannot be compensated with material advantages."[154]

Only a few, if any, of the myths Soviet propaganda created ever had any connection with reality, and the Stakhanovite campaign was no different. To begin with, what the Stakhanovite movement meant in practice was that output norms were increased overall, but wages remained stagnant. This was essentially because the workers received the same amount of money compared to what they would have been making before Stakhanov, when what they did was recognized as fulfilling the norm and they received extra compensation for exceeding the norm. If they did not reach the new norm, their salary decreased. For this reason alone, the new initiative of the Party could not have been very popular. It was not too difficult to see that what the Party wanted to achieve was to squeeze the maximum out of each worker and to keep on paying him as little as possible.

Officially the Stakhanovite movement was a bottom-up phenomenon. The petitions to increase production norms, or to initiate socialist output competitions, were allegedly made by the movement's individual pioneers or by entire working teams. One of Ludwik Michałowski's informants threw an interesting light on how those pioneers came to be. That particular informant read in a factory bulletin that one of the workers

---

[152] *Pravda*, December 15, 1937.

[153] A. Stakhanov, "Dva goda," *Pravda*, August 30, 1937; and idem, "My stalinskie ucheniki," *Pravda*, August 30, 1938.

[154] CAW, Oddz. II SG, sygn. I.303.4.3161, k. 27.

declared that he had decided to produce 150 percent of the current norm. As it later turned out, that particular worker was on holiday when this news was announced, and he knew nothing of his declaration.[155]

Members of the Polish foreign service working east of the Zbruch River had no doubts about the Bolsheviks' intentions. Information about the new campaign was compiled both from official data and their own research, and occasionally from news brought by those who visited the Polish consular agencies. Because of the make-up of his consular district (which included the Donbas), the Polish consul in Kharkiv, Stanisław Sośnicki, produced the greatest number of reports about the newly initiated Stakhanovite campaign. It is worth noting that more than half of the coal extracted in the Soviet Union came from Ukraine.[156]

Sośnicki wrote his first report on the new campaign in the Soviet Ukrainian industry on September 30, one month after Stakhanov set his record. He was certain of the authorities' true motives: "For the ordinary Donbas worker, this method will amount to nothing other than increasing the piecework output norm of labor, which he will now have to fulfill in order to receive the same renumeration that he received for hitherto prevailing norms of production."[157]

Sośnicki did write that some "achievements" were real thanks to the new campaign. However, he was quick to add: "The Stakhanovite method is turning into a magic wand whose wave is supposedly radically changing the economic landscape of the [Soviet] Union by means of reducing the number of workers required and disproportionately increasing the production totals." He cited the Makiivvuhillia mine as an example, where 159 brigades (1,259 workers in total) extracted 5,753 cartloads of coal during one shift. After switching to the Stakhanovite system, the number of workers in those brigades was reduced to 1,168, while the coal output grew to 6,973 cartloads, i.e., the growth in output was 21 percent and the reduction in the labor force, 9.8 percent.[158]

At the end of his report, the consul again stressed the fact that the new system essentially aimed at squeezing all that could be squeezed out of the workers: "It needs to be emphasized that the level of exploitation of the working masses in Ukrainian industry has crossed all reasonable bounds; one finds it hard to believe that one can force a worker to make

---

[155] Ibid., sygn. I.303.4.1967, n.p., doc. 33.
[156] Vasyliev, "Vplyv 'velykoho teroru,' " 37.
[157] CAW, Oddz. II SG, sygn. I.303.4.3144, k. 134.
[158] Ibid., k. 1342–43.

such a huge physical effort for so little in return. On the other hand, the passivity of the masses is remarkable. It is secured by means of propaganda that is extraordinarily mendacious, and by brute police force. This makes them unable to initiate any kind of protest. All traces of discontent after the Stakhanovite system was introduced in the Donbas mines are recognized as sabotage and eradicated most severely.

In order to make the mines and factories profitable, and in order to pay for the food subsidies (problematic in their own right), the working masses must deliver goods according to the Stakhanovite theory of labor, which, by introducing new and increased norms of output, increased worker exploitation to a level not seen in any capitalist country. The alleged record-breaking zeal of the workers, currently so skillfully deployed propagandistically in the Soviet press, is meant to provide justification for the new norms of output, which, if not introduced already, will be introduced in all the other industrial sectors in the near future—a measure that was, of course, made necessary because of the workers demanding it themselves."[159]

In another report about the Stakhanovite movement, dated October 25, 1935, Sośnicki wrote that the new system of labor was greeted with reluctance and, not infrequently, hostility.[160]

Polish military intelligence was also skeptical, especially with respect to the veracity of Soviet records. In their reports, agents of the *Dwójka* mentioned some blatant cases of exaggeration of the real results of the Stakhanovite record-breakers. Post no. E.10 reported on the Stakhanovite way of producing and selling kegged beer. The latter was prone to speculative corruption. The retailers added water to the beer, keeping the profits for themselves: "The people are furious, but nothing can be done, because the same kind of speculation is performed by breweries, which, unable to supply the people with beer, are helping themselves along the way in the same manner. This is an example of how a Stakhanovite 'production plan' is carried out in practice."[161]

In a secret Second Department brochure, titled "The Domestic Situation in the USSR" (communiqué no. 7, issued in December 1935), the authors admitted that it was too early for conclusions, but it was already

---

[159] Ibid., k. 1343–44.

[160] Ibid., k. 1464–66.

[161] RGVA, f. 308 k, op. 19, d. 63, l. 158. Major Wincenty Bąkiewicz, head of the Independent Bureau "Russia," estimated that the intelligence materials about malversations in beer production were useful. CAW, Oddz. II SG, sygn. I.303.4.1952, n.p., no document number.

highly probable that the numerical values of the Stakhanovite records were much inflated (e.g., 500 tonnes instead of seven). Furthermore, they wondered, even if the figures were taken at face value, how was it in fact possible to extract such an enormous amount of coal in one day? Such questions made the *Dwójka* highly skeptical of the Stakhanovite movement. In the brochure it was stressed that Soviet propaganda tried to paint the movement as "a spontaneous instinct of the worker who wants to build socialism," but the truth, the authors believed, lay elsewhere. There were instances when the initiators of the movement at a given workplace were beaten, and even killed.[162]

In another communiqué (no. 8), issued in March 1936 (for the first quarter of 1936), the authors again underscored that the Stakhanovite movement was not too popular among the broader working masses, who considered it yet another exploitation tool. Furthermore, the authors added that actual production output increases were insignificant.[163]

Initially the Polish embassy in Moscow evaluated the new campaign slightly differently, in a less negative light than in the estimation of the Polish consuls working in Ukraine. In a report to the MFA on 26 November 1935 (dealing with the first conference of Stakhanovite industrial and transportation workers that took place from November 14 to 17 with Stalin present), Henryk Sokolnicki, the embassy's chargé d'affaires, concluded that there was considerable genuine enthusiasm for the Stakhanovite movement among those who were its initiators and leaders, but not so much among the broader working masses, who sometimes responded with hostility and even open resistance. But Sokolnicki did not believe the movement was doomed to fail. He thought that time would show what its effects would be and that it certainly should not be neglected: "the material balance [of the Stakhanovite movement] will likely lead to an increase in output … If the work process becomes gradually better organized, incomes are going to increase and prices fall, and then tensions and discontent will eventually disappear, especially because the people will get used to it one way or another."[164]

To best demonstrate the full scope of knowledge and the assessment of the Stakhanovite movement in its early stages that the MFA and military intelligence officials made, one needs to cite Jan Karszo-

---

[162] CAW, Oddz. II SG, sygn. I.303.4.3149, k. 46–50.
[163] Ibid., sygn. I.303.4.3164, k. 107.
[164] Ibid., sygn. I.303.4.3144, k. 1485–89.

Siedlewski. The diplomat rarely made any errors of judgment about Soviet developments, but this time he put forward a rather speculative hypothesis. On December 2, 1935, in a letter to the Polish ambassador in Moscow, he wrote that the Stakhanovite movement was a "setback in the degree of influence the Party had on the state and on the economic life in the USSR." What he had in mind was: "Stalin decided to strengthen the state and no longer rely on demagoguery. He promoted the following strategy: 'The cadres, the people who manage the high-tech industry, they will decide all questions.'" According to Karszo-Siedlewski, the consequence of this policy was such that "the highly qualified engineers were gaining more importance, and those who were not skilled were gradually sidetracked, even if they were Party members."[165]

According to another hypothesis in the report, the Stakhanovite movement influenced the mood of young people, for whom it opened up new perspectives and possibilities, absorbing all of their attention and energy and diverting them away from the ideological impasse that the Kremlin had recently been struggling with: "Analogous to the declining influence of the Communist Party, we are noticing a similar decline in the Komsomol's influence (caused by the Stakhanovite movement), which was disarmed politically by recent restructuring that reduced it to an organ that monitored the youth's behavior"[166] — so Karszo-Siedlewski claimed.

A month and a half later, Karszo-Siedlewski changed his mind. On January 17, 1936, he wrote that the Stakhanovite movement was "an unprecedented feat of exploiting working-class labor." He expected that this movement, like any other similar utopian idea, was not going to last very long (the workers would give out physically, and so would the machines). To the end of 1936 was how long he thought it was going to survive, and then "it will die a natural death, sharing the fate of so many other slogans coined by the Bolsheviks; its place will be taken by Stalin's next 'brilliant idea.'"[167] The diplomat's prediction turned out to be wrong. He thought the Stakhanovite campaign was one of Moscow's temporary stratagems, since the Kremlin was interested in short-term objectives, i.e., to increase average labor efficiency and thus increase the national economic output for 1936: "a necessary condition to bring the budget back in line and strengthen the Soviet ruble, ultimately to stabilize it at the

---

[165] Ibid., k. 1529.
[166] Ibid., k. 1530.
[167] Ibid., sygn. I.303.4.3161, k. 27–28v.

established parity rate or facilitate another similar currency reform, which would make it possible for the USSR to make inroads into the international financial and trade markets."[168]

Jan Karszo-Siedlewski was mistaken in this case. The Stakhanovite movement was not a temporary stratagem designed to end one year after its creation. In various guises and forms, it functioned in the USSR until its demise (as well as in other so-called people's democracies). Of course, it was not kept alive through spontaneous social initiatives, but through central directives accompanied by all kinds of threats directed against its opponents or skeptics.

A few days later, Karszo-Siedlewski concluded that the Stakhanovite movement did not improve industrial labor efficiency but was instead a pure form of human exploitation. The main part of the document that the diplomat put together dealt with the threat originating with the Stakhanovite propaganda campaign and, in particular, with its reception abroad. The head of the consulate general in Kyiv advised that all manifestations of this campaign needed to be answered with a sufficiently determined reply. In fact, he thought it would be enough to cite official Soviet press articles or speeches by dignitaries in a skillful way.[169] He claimed that these measures would not violate the non-aggression pact, nor would they hurt the intention of maintaining neighborly relations with the Soviets, especially because the Bolsheviks, to support their theses about "hunger, poverty, unemployment, and terror in the capitalist countries," including Poland, selectively quoted excerpts from the press and political speeches of those countries. "It is not enough that those who are in the know, i.e., those who work in the USSR or who are familiar with its realities, can see clearly what is going on there and that they understand that the

---

[168] Ibid., sygn. I.303.4.1867, k. 29.

[169] In his report, Jan Karszo-Siedlewski quoted an excerpt from the speech by Stanislav Kosior at a Party meeting on January 2, 1936 (which was not published in the press until January 19, 1936). Kosior said: "Thanks to the Stakhanovite movement, we haved moved on to a new, higher level of technological mastery, something that is not yet understood by many economists, engineers, and technicians. They must be convinced, and those who cannot be convinced, particularly because we have so little time, will need to be removed from their managerial positions. Every new issue, every new movement initiative launched by our socialist state, is always met with fierce resistance from elements in the hostile classes, who once again are trying to pick a fight with us and, since they always fail, try to do anything to slow our progress. There are quite a few backward, uneducated workers who do not yet understand what kind of benefits the Stakhanovite movement is going to bring, and some are even afraid that it might do them some harm" (Ibid., sygn. I.303.4.1867, k. 373).

Stakhanovite movement is the unprecedented exploitation of the worker and the collective-farm worker. What is needed are unambiguous pictures and persuasion about the real dimension of that reality targeting our own society, and the working masses in particular, not only in Poland but in the entire civilized world in general. The world is bombarded with Bolshevik propaganda in ever new ways. It finds willing audiences in countries such as England, France, the United States, not to mention Czechoslovakia, etc. Stakhanovite propaganda is dangerous because, at first glance, many workers seem to benefit from it, an appearance skillfully used by Soviet authorities both domestically and abroad."[170]

Writing about the high labor turnover rates in Soviet mines, Karszo-Siedlewski highlighted that this was of special importance, given the news about Soviet deportations of the Polish population from the Soviet-Polish borderlands to the Donbas.[171] "The Soviets are trying to kill two birds with one stone this way. They are removing some uncertain elements from the border strip and delivering new manpower for the Donbas mines, a manpower that can be exploited easily and forced to perform slave labor."[172]

3.3.2. The Collapse of the Stakhanovite Idea

One did not have to wait long to see the tangible consequences of the Stakhanovite campaign. As early as March 9, 1936, Stanisław Sośnicki informed the Polish ambassador in Moscow, Juliusz Łukasiewicz, that the Stakhanovite movement in the Donbas was close to breaking down. The consul's thesis turned out to be very true: "The authorities did not realize that the miners' enthusiasm, especially if their norms of output were increased without an adequate material incentive in return, would be something problematic and unreliable."[173] He justified this claim as follows: "If the miner had to extract 3 or 5 cubic meters of coal and received a bonus payment for anything he managed to do extra, then today one cannot speak about growing incomes if the new norm is 5 or 9 cubic meters and only after exceeding them does the miner get extra

---

[170] Ibid., k. 372–374.

[171] Based on the decision of the Politburo of the CC CP(b)U on November 4, 1935 and the decision of the Council of People's Commissars on December 1935, 1,100 Polish families were deported from twelve raions of Vinnytsia oblast to Donetsk and Kharkiv oblasts in mid-January 1936. See chapter 4, section 7.

[172] CAW, Oddz. II SG, sygn. I.303.4.1867, k. 375.

[173] Ibid., k. 146.

payment. The miner today has to work extra hard to deliver the extra 2–3 cubic meters of coal just to fulfill the new norm now imposed on him — something he would have been paid extra for earlier."[174]

Jan Karszo-Siedlewski, head of the other Polish consular post in Soviet Ukraine, noticed the same thing. According to his revised assessment, most workers not only did not gain anything from the new policy, but, on the contrary, they lost: "The term 'shock worker' [*udarnik*] has been abolished, and it was something that all workers, at least for some time, could become. This status entailed some real privileges and gains. The Stakhanovite does not receive any privileges, and the higher wages he receives are not really something that makes his life easier but something that allows him to survive."[175]

The extreme exploitation of workers who were already overworked and paid as little as possible was essentially what the Stakhanovite movement was all about. It did not deliver the expected results in the Donbas. After the initial wave of excitement, boosted by new output records being established virtually every day, the time came to prepare a balance sheet. Even a perfunctory glance at the Soviet press gives one an idea of the real results of the Stakhanovite campaign.[176] Of course, the Bolsheviks were always capable of finding some excuse or explanation: the work of "enemies of the people"; an overly bureaucratic approach to the Stakhanovites; inadequate elimination of the losses inflicted by the alleged enemies of the people, and so on.

After the Stakhanovite campaign had been launched, Sośnicki wrote a detailed report about its course at the start of each month and submitted it to the ambassador. He stated that, based on the official data alone, the idea was not economically viable. In each report, he presented evidence demonstrating that the campaign did not improve the efficiency of coal extraction—or, that if it did, it did so only minimally. He wrote that eventually the output norms had to be lowered month after month, the plight of the miners got worse and worse, and their resistance to the idea increased. The average daily coal output in the Donbas region equaled 221.8 thousand tonnes in January 1936. After the new output norms were introduced, this figure declined. On March 6, the actual output equaled

---

[174] Ibid.

[175] Ibid, sygn. I.303.4.3161, k. 27 v.

[176] See, e.g., "Likvidirovat' pozornoe otstavanie Donbassa," *Pravda*, May 11, 1937; and D. Vadimov, "V Donbasse bez peremen," *Pravda*, May 14, 1937. See also *Pravda*, April 29 and May 10, 1937 and elsewhere.

200.1 thousand tonnes (94 percent), compared to the 212.8 thousand tonnes expected by the plan.[177] Of the thirty-seven mines in the Kadivvuhillia Trust, fifteen did not fulfill their minimum plan during the second Stakhanovite decade.[178]

In March 1936, the efficiency of coal extraction did not improve; on the contrary, compared with February it declined. The plan expected the average daily extraction figure to reach 229 thousand tonnes (t.), while the figure actually reached was 210 thousand t. (91 percent). There was not a single day in March when the plan was fulfilled. In the first five days of February, the average output was 236 thousand t., or 2.9 percent higher than the plan's predicted 230 thousand t. The month of March resulted in an overall shortfall of 600 thousand t. In general, in the first quarter of 1936, the Donbas succeeded in fulfilling 94.5 percent of the plan, producing 19.506 thousand t., with a shortfall of 836,219 t. Sośnicki calculated that, compared to April 1935, which predated the Stakhanovite movement, the total coal output grew by 10–12 percent, while the norms had been increased by 30–40 percent.[179]

In April 1936, the average daily coal output norm was increased in the Donbas to 231.3 thousand t. However, on no day during that month was the norm fulfilled. The closest it was ever reached was on April 7, when 221.9 thousand t. were extracted. The average daily extraction of coal that month equaled 205 thousand t. The monthly underperformance, compared to plan expectations, amounted to 700 thousand t.[180] In another report, from early June 1936, Sośnicki informed the ambassador that the situation had worsened again. The daily extraction norm had decreased, to 228.6 thousand t. from 231.3 thousand (in April). Then in May, compared to April, the actual average extraction rate decreased from 205 thousand to 196.8 thousand t. The underperformance in May was equal to 798 thousand t., which amounted to 2,335 thousand t. for the first months of 1936.[181]

In order to remedy the situation, the Bolshevik authorities applied a method by then very typical of them: appropriate scapegoats were found, blamed for this state of affairs, and then punished to set an example. On May 2, 1936, the Donetsk Oblast Party Committee ordered a purge to be

---

[177] CAW, Oddz. II SG, sygn. I.303.4.1867, k. 152.
[178] Ibid., k. 149.
[179] Ibid., k. 164–65.
[180] Ibid., k. 190–91.
[181] Ibid., k. 215.

conducted within the management of the oblast's industry. Many of the managers and leaders fell victim to that wave of repressions, which included expulsion from the Party, court trials, and exile from the Donbas. Their vacant positions were then taken by the brigade leaders and Stakhanovites.[182]

The Soviet leadership came to the conclusion that without offering proper rewards as an incentive to increase output, this outcome could not be achieved; and that workers would no longer perform merely because of empty propagandistic promises. In order to encourage *udarnichestvo* (shock work), two new working-class titles were introduced: a master of coal and a master of coal first-class. The first rank was to be awarded to a Stakhanovite who overfulfilled the monthly output norm twice, and the second, to one who did this three times. The bonuses for the masters of coal were expected to be between 50–150 rubles for the masters and 75–250 rubles for the first-class masters, depending on the kind of labor they performed.[183]

For most workers, these new measures were of little import. Their already unenviable situation was only worsened further by the new Stakhanovite labor methods. Already on January 17, 1936, Jan Karszo-Siedlewski wrote to the ambassador: "As the Stakhanovite movement progresses, it becomes more and more apparent that it is an attempt at exploitation of human labor that is unprecedented in the history of the working class. Just a glimpse of how Stakhanovites look after a few months of labor is enough to verify this thesis. Those people are so exhausted physically that they are literally running on empty and look like shadows. I talked with one of them, who said: 'You have no idea, sir, how hard it is. One no longer has the will to live. I am carrying on only in the hope that we will be taken to Moscow soon and shown to Stalin, after which I will be allowed to rest a bit. What can you do, there is no choice. If I was not a Stakhanovite, I would lose my job."[184]

In January 1936, Piotr Kurnicki, Karszo-Siedlewski's deputy, also noticed that the Stakhanovite movement had a negative influence on the workers' health. "We had the chance to observe many cases in which the Stakhanovites, after 7–10 weeks of their feats, had to apply for

---

[182] Ibid., k. 188.
[183] Ibid., k. 189.
[184] Ibid., k. 362.

rehabilitation holidays, the so-called *putievki*,[185] due to their enormous physical exhaustion."[186]

Kurnicki emphasized that the Bolshevik leadership attempted to impose Stakhanovite methods upon all areas of life (the theater, the circus, offices, stores, factories, collective farms, dining halls). In his opinion, the authorities were not interested in a real increase in productivity in these fields, but instead in making the movement universal, to generate popular enthusiasm, and force the heavy-industry and collective-farm workers to work harder: "The ability to use these statistical data to confirm the mass nature of the movement in retail trade and industry will become the moral justification for increasing the demands on the collective-farm workers, tractor and harvest drivers, etc."[187]

In his report March 9, 1936, Stanisław Sośnicki remarked: "The physical appearance of the workers is poor, their mortality is high. Those who arrive from the Donbas say that when the miners see a funeral taking place, they remark ironically that 'it must be a Stakhanovite who is being buried.'"[188]

In his next report, on April 6, 1936, he concluded that the situation had not changed. "Gloomy moods prevail among the workers. In addition to the usual food shortages, there are enormous insufficiencies of clothing and shoes. Their prices have increased recently: a regular, poor-quality shirt costs 46–50 rubles, a pair of shoes, 165–210 rubles. People gather in long lines in front of the few open stores, only to be dispersed by the police. This state of affairs in the villages and small towns is even worse; no clothing or shoes whatsoever are available."[189]

Based on official production data for 1935 and 1936, Sośnicki demonstrated that the Stakhanovite movement not only did not increase the coal extraction figures, but it actually contributed to their decrease. Sarkis Sarkisov, secretary of the Donetsk Oblast Party Committee, calculated that in order for the Donbas to fulfill the established production quotas, its coal mines would have to extract 214–215 thousand tonnes daily, but their production remained at the level of 170 thousand tonnes. Sośnicki underscored that instead of being a role model, the Donbas — the

---

[185] Vouchers designated to be spent in a particular hotel or sanatorium.
[186] CAW, Oddz. II SG, sygn. I.303.4.1927, doc. 38, n.p.
[187] Ibid.
[188] Ibid., sygn. I.303.4.1867, k. 154.
[189] Ibid., k. 167.

cradle of the Stakhanovite movement—"could be used for agitation in the opposite direction."[190]

On September 18, 1936, Jan Karszo-Siedlewski wrote that the Stakhanovite movement had gone completely bankrupt. It was enough to read the Soviet press, which wrote not about the first anniversary of the movement, but about the falling output figures in the Donbas. Thanks to the movement, there was a certain increase in those figures, but the price was very high. It was achieved, Karszo-Siedlewski held, at the expense "of human and industrial energy," which, in consequence, produced a negative outcome in the final analysis. The diplomat emphasized that a similar conclusion applied also to other branches of the economy, apart from the military-industrial complex, but nothing was written about it in public.[191]

A few months later, Karszo-Siedlewski repeated his opinion that the Stakhanovite movement had failed. It not only failed to deliver the goods, but it also disrupted factory-floor conditions. The quality of production decreased, while the factory equipment was dilapidated. The working masses were in an uncooperative, discontented mood. "Most workers earn less than they did, while prices are increasing. It is no better in the countryside, judging from the fact that the peasants come to the cities searching for bread."[192]

Despite all the propaganda surrounding it, the impact of the Stakhanovite movement on increasing the efficiency of the Soviet economy, on the work ethic, and labor conditions was slight. On May 29, 1939, the Polish consulate general in Kyiv sent a report to the embassy in Moscow dealing with production conditions in the Donbas in the spring of 1939, in particular with the two largest Ukrainian mining complexes— Stalino (eleven trusts) and Voroshylovhrad (nine trusts): "The general picture is negative. It is enough to mention the basic shortcomings—the neglected state of machinery and assembly lines, their poor repair, the lack of proper skills of servicing them (and their excessive exploitation), no servicing garages and equipment, a bureaucratic approach to production (*beschislennoye mnozhestvo prikazov*)—and this is not nearly an exhaustive list of all the shortcomings. Working schedules are not obeyed, [and] the instructions and orders of Commissar Kaganovich are ignored.

---

[190] CAW, Oddz. II SG, sygn. 6669, k. 16.
[191] AAN, MSZ, sygn. 6669, k. 16.
[192] CAW, Oddz. II SG, sygn. I.303.4.1985, n.p., doc. (3), 1937.

Frequently the quality of the coal extracted is very low (it is stony, contaminated, muddy), but the commanders of the shafts do not take any complaints from their clients into consideration."[193]

The following was reported about the workers' condition: "The cultural-existential environment of the workers is still primitive despite all the propagandistic claims and 'orders' we know so well from Kaganovich and other authorities. At the most basic, the catastrophic housing shortage is still a problem, as are a dearth of dining halls, buffets, various cultural and entertainment establishments, and produce, especially of berries and fruit."[194]

The Stakhanovite movement also did not lead to an increase in metal production. For example, in the Kryvyi Rih region, until July 1936, 51 tonnes of metal ore were produced daily, but then the amount dropped to 40–44 tonnes in July and August. Manganese production dropped to 75 percent of the former amount. Production quality in the steel plants decreased, as it also did in the coke-chemical plants and tractor, locomotive, and turbine factories.[195] Between January 1 and August 10, 1936, no industrial enterprise in the Donbas fulfilled the plan.[196]

Under the Soviet system, chasing a record was simply for its own sake. Some goods were produced in amounts exceeding the norm, and, as it later turned, these goods were of no use in other industrial enterprises. The economic counselor to the Moscow embassy, Antoni Żmigrodzki, prepared a report about the Stakhanovite movement that Tadeusz Jankowski sent on February 11, 1936 to Foreign Minister Beck. The report mentioned, for example, "completely pointless items" in the Soviet machine industry: an overproduction of some parts and the underproduction of others.[197] This uneven production was, of course, pointless from an economic point of view, but in the context of "fighting to overfulfill the norm," it conformed to its own kind of logic.

---

[193] AAN, MSZ, sygn. 6731, k. 25.
[194] Ibid., k. 26–27. As emphasized in the document, the two enterprises mentioned above, despite all their shortcomings, were able to deliver 180–190 thousand tonnes of coal daily, which amounted to 45–50 percent of the total amount extracted in the USSR.
[195] CAW, Oddz. II SG, sygn. I.303.4.1867, k. 55–56.
[196] Ibid., k. 64.
[197] AAN, MSZ, sygn. 9514, k. 119.

3.3.3. The Workers' Attitude toward the Output Competition

As noted earlier, the workers were not enthusiastic about the Stakhanovite movement, for reasons that were quite evident. It was futile to look for enthusiasts among other social groups. When members of the Polish foreign-service corps talked with ordinary Soviet citizens, or even with some Party members, they encountered neither genuine enthusiasm for nor joy in any improvement in one's living conditions thanks to the new campaign. Jan Łagoda met a person[198] in Moscow he used to meet in the northern Caucasus between 1916 and 1921. In the second half of the 1930s, that person lived in Moscow and was the director of a trade post. During the most recent wave of purges, because of a denunciation made against him, his activities prior to World War I were called into question, as was his early revolutionary past. Łagoda's Soviet interlocutor shared his feelings about the domestic situation. Primarily he emphasized the workers' situation, which, never the best, was not improved by the Stakhanovite movement: "empty promises that the campaign was going to improve the workers' standard of living significantly were no longer fooling anyone, because, for the great majority of people, that system of work was essentially all about decreasing wages and worsening the situation by means of the already nearly universal increase in the output quotas. Contrary to what the press claims, the society is not only not enthusiastic, but is not even calm anymore. Impatience and exhaustion brought about by the permanently extremely difficult conditions of life can be clearly seen."[199]

After a preliminary[200] observation in mid-1936 of some factories in his consular region (Dniprohes, Zaporizhstal), Stanisław Sośnicki, remarked: "The mood among the workers is certainly not as enthusiastic as the Soviet press reports. ... Electrifying the masses with the supposed benefits of the Stakhanovite movement is no longer effective, all the propaganda remains an abstraction, and in daily life the worker has understood that he is paying for all these new slogans through the doubling of his own efforts, while his wages remain the same. The worker's income is dependent on

---

[198] The name of this person is not disclosed.

[199] AAN, SG, sygn. IV/7, n.p., doc. 70.

[200] He could not visit the factories, because when he arrived (in Dnipropetrovsk and Zaporizhia), it turned out that the director of the City Soviet was not there, and no one had received any information from the PCoFA agent about the consul's arrival. Sośnicki had no doubt that the Soviet officials were instructed exactly how to make it difficult for the Polish consul to visit the factories.

constantly changing plans, new formulas, [and] their fulfillment in terms of percentages—all of which become a completely abstruse figure whose purposes and actual value remained a mystery to most workers; they learned what it really meant only when they were being paid."[201]

During his November 1936 Donbas visit, Jan Łagoda asked the administrative director of the Kirov steelworks in Makiivka in private whether the workers were expressing their discontent with the Stakhanovite movement, that is, with the exploitation and low wages they had to endure. The director's reply was that, yes, indeed, "they were outraged, but what can they do."[202]

Workers in the Communist system could not change much, but it did not mean that they always looked on passively at the Bolsheviks' new initiatives or merely grumbled about them in private. Often, due to their decreasing standard of life, people openly resisted the Stakhanovite movement. At various places (factories, offices, universities, dormitories) the NKVD located anti-Stakhanovite fliers, whose authors called for resistance to that system.[203] On February 21, 1936, in a secret report about the situation in Soviet Ukraine, Karszo-Siedlewski wrote to Ambassador Łukasiewicz that "despite the unceasing propaganda and pressure from the Party apparatus, the Stakhanovite movement is developing very slowly and encounters resistance in the form of sabotage and beatings of the Stakhanovites themselves. I have received information from someone who recently visited the Donbas that the miners were gravely unhappy about the movement and were pushing back against it. ... Beatings of Stakhanovites and *piatisotnitsy*[204] are quite frequent in the villages, but the true mood there will only become known when the field work season begins."[205]

---

[201] CAW, Oddz. II SG, sygn. I.303.4.1867, k. 238.

[202] Ibid., sygn. I.303.4.3144, k. 1555.

[203] See J. A. Getty and O. Naumov, *The Road to Terror: Stalin and the Self-Destruction of the Bolsheviks, 1932–1939* (New Haven: Yale University Press, 1999), 212–13.

[204] The name given to female collective-farm workers who followed Stakhanovite methods in the fields and harvested 500 quintals or more from one hectare. The name comes from the word *piatsot* (five hundred). It was this figure that Mariia Demchenko, a delegate from Kyiv oblast, claimed was the amount of her beet harvest. She quoted that number at the Second All-Union Conference of the Pioneers of Collective-Farm Labor. See V. Shmerling, *Mariia Demchenko* (Moscow: Molodaia gvardiia, 1936).

[205] CAW, Oddz. II Sg, sygn. I.303.4.3161, k. 109. On April 16, the head of the Kyiv consulate again emphasized that the Stakhanovite movement was not only failing to deliver, but was also being met with growing resistance from workers and peasants. Ibid., sygn. I.303.4.1867, k. 404.

In early 1936, in the Donbas's Rutchenkove mine no. 17-17 bis, an unannounced one-day workers' strike took place in protest of new, increased output norms. Sixty percent of the workers from one shift (the mine employed 3,400 workers on a three-shift basis) did not show up for work. The leaders were arrested and disappeared without a trace. One Polish citizen was arrested. His name was Józef Kiryk. He was sentenced to ten years in a labor camp for uttering the following sentence in public: "I was a Communist, but after seeing it all, I became a fascist."[206]

In early May 1936, Sośnicki wrote that, based on information that reached the consulate, clear resistance to Stakhanovite methods was evident in most of the Donbas mines. It could be seen in the workers' reluctance and their opposition, especially among those who were engaged in preparatory labor. That group was very unwilling to shift to contracts based on individual piecework.[207]

Sośnicki described the following event that took place on July 30, 1936. In one of the textile factories in Kharkiv, one worker, a cutter, was ordered to work according to Stakhanovite norms. The man replied that he was forty-five years old and would like to live for forty-five more years. If he was to work the Stakhanovite way, he would not survive five years. He was sentenced to five years in a labor camp. The consul added that "many similar examples could be cited."[208]

Sometimes this resistance was more marked. In the workshop of a machine-repair factory in Rutchenkove near Stalino, a bust of Stalin was damaged: the nose was broken off. The entire crew of 1,500 workers was assembled to find the perpetrator. He was not identified, whereupon the entire process ended in mutual accusations and a brawl.[209]

Needless to say, the all-powerful NKVD made sure that no incidents of "hostile counterrevolutionary activity" took place. Periodic waves of arrests of undesirable and suspect workers were organized in the factories. Even Communists were not spared. In mid-1936 alleged counterrevolutionary organizations were discovered and exposed in a few enterprises in Kharkiv: the Kharkiv Locomotive Factory (KhPZ), the Tiniakov Factory, and others. This "uncovering" was on the agenda of Kharkiv's Party Committee meeting on July 27–28, 1936. Stanisław Sośnicki reported on that meeting. It was not only allegedly

---

[206] Ibid., sygn. I.303.4.1967, doc. 33, n.p.
[207] Ibid., sygn. I.303.4.1867, k. 191.
[208] Ibid., k. 228.
[209] Ibid., k. 153-154; Ibid., sygn. I.303.4.1967, doc. 33.

counterrevolutionary activity that was a problem, but also the factory and city Party units that had "lost their Bolshevik vigilance."[210] He concluded that the reality was much different from the picture painted by Soviet propaganda. It had nothing to do with counterrevolutionary intentions but was all about protesting against and sabotaging the Stakhanovite movement. This sabotage was, in his opinion, not limited to the two factories named above, but was present to some extent in all the factories in his consular district. It must have assumed extraordinary intensity in the locomotive factory, judging from the fact that the authorities decided to fabricate the existence of a "harmful organization" within it.[211]

The opening salvo in the process of fabricating the existence of such an organization was the interruption of a meeting to support another state loan. A large group of workers began to chant anti-Stakhanovite slogans, e.g., that in no other country was the worker so heavily exploited as he was in the USSR. Seeing the growing antipathy among the workers, who were forced to attend another such meeting, the management decided to close the factory down. Arrests began after the meeting:[212] fifty workers were detained, twenty of them Communists.[213]

During the investigation that followed the "exposure" of the enemies in the Kharkiv Locomotive Factory, one of the arrested Communists was asked why he was engaged in sabotaging the Stakhanovite movement. He answered: "No worker in the long run, considering his current material conditions, can endure the disproportionately high Stakhanovite norms." Then he was asked why he, as a Communist, did not keep this opinion to himself and instead was spreading it openly among the workers. He replied: "Don't you know that this conviction is shared by nearly all of the workers?"[214]

---

[210] In the aftermath of the meeting, Smirnov, the Party secretary at the KhTZ, was fired for his lack of vigilance, that is, for failing to undertake the necessary measures to expose and punish the enemies. Sokolov, the Party secretary in Kharkiv, was also fired for letting the events at the KhPZ happen. AAN, MSZ, sygn. 6939, k. 132.

[211] Ibid., k. 132–35.

[212] Stanisław Sośnicki emphasized: "In such cases, the NKVD usually attempts to detect external interference, almost always from the Trotsky-Zinoviev direction, or from a foreign intelligence service, completely ignoring, at least officially, the possibility of dissatisfied workers self-organizing in reaction to what the authorities were doing, i.e., the actions that harmed their moral and material well-being" (Ibid., 136–37).

[213] Ibid., k. 135–36.

[214] CAW, Oddz. II SG, sygn. I.303.4.1867, k. 63.

3.3.4. Safety at Work

The excessive labor-output demands worsened the already poor safety conditions on the factory floor. In early 1936, as a result of the many breakdowns in the mines of the Artemvuhillia Trust, a number of shafts were completely decommissioned. In the Stalin mine, two mining sections caught fire following safety-regulation violations. In the Makiivvuhillia Trust mines, up to twenty breakdowns per day were reported.[215] Stanisław Sośnicki concluded: "Similar examples can be quoted ad infinitum, and all of them go to show that most of the Donbas mines are not prepared for the increased Stakhanovite output demand. A glaring example of that is the fact that, of 279 mines in the Donbas, one-quarter of them did not even fulfill their minimum plan."[216]

Soviet miners were constantly threatened with loss of health, or even life, because of the extremely bad safety conditions. Fatal accidents frequently occurred, but the press rarely wrote about them. In the Petrivka mine (Kharkiv oblast), sixty-seven miners died in February 1936, and in the Dzerzhynka mine of the Artemvuhillia Trust, eighteen died.[217]

The safety conditions were accurately captured by a former member of the Donbas managerial mining council, a German citizen, who was later expelled to his home country after five years of labor. That man said that if he was a safety inspector, he would close down practically all the mines in the Donbas.[218]

Because of lower labor efficiency, under-fulfillment of the plan, and the increased number of accidents, the authorities were forced to exclude many mines temporarily from the Stakhanovite movement. Sośnicki, in a dispatch on March 9, 1936 summarized the Soviet experiment as follows: "An enormous number of accidents, technological chaos, delayed work schedules, a return to *uravnilovka* [full egalitarianism] in the workers' wages and to pre-Stakhanovite methods of labor in numerous mines—this is the harvest after the first month of applying Stakhanovite methods to all the mines of the Donbas. Furthermore, it should be mentioned that many mines experienced a significant labor-force turnover. This figure reached 20 percent last month."[219]

---

[215] Ibid., sygn. I.303.4.1867, k. 149.
[216] Ibid.
[217] Ibid., k 153; see also: Ibid., sygn. I.303.4.1967, n.p., doc. 33.
[218] Ibid., k. 150.
[219] Ibid., k. 151.

A similar situation obtained in other branches of the economy where the Stakhanovite methods were applied, e.g., in the railways. According to the press, in the last two decades of July 1935, that is, just before the Stakhanovite movement began, 647 accidents were reported on the Catherinian railway, 520 in the Donbas, and 457 on the Southern railway. The most dangerous accidents happened in the Donetsk section: 376 cars and 6 locomotives were damaged in July 1935. The local press dubbed the Donbas railways "a cemetery of sick trains." The prescribed norm for the maximum number of out-of-order cars in that section was 1,200. Before July 1, 1935, that number was 2,500; on July 10 it was already 3,140; and on July 20 it was up to 3,725. Some railway stations in the Donetsk region were overflowing with broken cars. According to the press, the reasons behind this unfortunate state of affairs were poor work performance by railway employees, undermanned working posts, and insufficient supervision by the political and security personnel.[220]

After Petro Kryvonos's Stakhanovite methods were introduced in the railway sector, the opposite of the intended results occurred. The number of breakdowns and accidents increased. On April 6, 1936, Stanisław Sośnicki wrote to the Polish ambassador in Moscow that, since the start of the Kryvonos movement in the railways of his consular district, the number of accidents had increased. He reported two large accidents: one on March 28, 1936, near Belgorod, when a cargo train hit a passenger train, and five officials died, among other victims; and the second, on March 29, 1936, near Artemivsk, in which Aksinovich, the director of the communications and signaling branch of the Donetsk railway, Dmytruk, the director of the Debaltsevo section, and Burlakov, the head of the technical section of the Donetsk railway, were among the victims. The press was silent about these two accidents. According to Sośnicki, railwaymen who were among the visitors to the consulate said that railway accidents were a daily occurrence, while the press mentioned only the ones that were simply too big to hide.[221]

The Stakhanovite movement also failed in the "struggle to overcome departure delays" in the railways. Practically no train arrived at its destination on time. Some trains reached their destinations after delays of six hours or more. The train on the Baku-Shepetivka line only reached its final destination after such a delay. The passengers were thus unable to

---

[220] RGVA, f. 308 k, op. 19, d. 57, l. 91–92.
[221] CAW, Oddz. II SG, sygn. I.303.4.1867, k. 162–63.

catch the train leaving Shepetivka for Poland and had to wait another day for their connection.[222]

---

[222] Ibid., k. 57.

Chapter Four

The Great Purge

4.1. Kirov's Murder and a New Wave of Purges

As I noted above, the event that today is recognized as the symbolic beginning of the mass purges in the Soviet Union was the assassination of the Leningrad Party dignitary Sergei Kirov on December 1, 1934, by Leonid Nikolaev.[1] On the very same day, the Central Executive Committee (CEC) of the USSR passed a resolution instructing the country's judicial organs to conduct investigations, via streamlined, i.e., quicker, procedures, of persons accused of preparing or committing terrorist acts. The courts were ordered not to delay the execution of capital-punishment sentences and not to be "excessively" concerned with the sentenced persons' pleas for clemency, since the CEC "did not consider it possible to accept such pleas for consideration." In conclusion, the authors of the new instruction emphasized that the NKVD organs must proceed with the execution of prisoners sentenced to death immediately after the verdict was passed in court.[2]

Soon after the Kirov murder, the press made it known that several terrorist groups had been uncovered in Moscow and Leningrad.[3] Trials were launched and concluded.[4] On the very day after the murder of the Leningrad Communist Party leader, the authorities announced that it was impossible that Nikolaev alone was responsible for Kirov's murder, and that his assassination must have been ordered by much more significant players acting behind the scenes. At various assemblies in Kharkiv, the speakers (their speeches were broadcast on Kharkiv radio) emphasized that the shot that rang out in Leningrad was directed at the Communist

---

[1] For more information on this topic, see R. Conquest, *Stalin i zabójstwo Kirowa* (Warsaw: Gryf, 1989); idem, *The Great Terror: A Reassessment* (Oxford: Oxford University Press, 2008), 37–54.

[2] "W prezidiume TsIK Soyuza SSR," *Pravda*, December 4, 1934.

[3] See "V Narodnom Komissariate Vnutrennykh Del SSSR," *Pravda*, December 4, 1934. In early January 1935, Lieut. Józef Jedynak reported to the head of the *Dwójka* that in the USSR, in the aftermath of the Kirov assassination, 117 persons were charged and the search "for new counterrevolutionaries and plotters" was still ongoing. RGVA, f. 308 k, op. 6, d. 20, l. 11.

[4] For more information about the trials following the Kirov murder, see I. Zhukov, "Sledstvie i sudebnye protsesy po delu ob ubiistve Kirova," *Voprosy istorii*, 2000, no. 2, 33–51.

system as such, and that the origins of that crime should be sought in Warsaw, Berlin, and Tokyo.[5]

It soon became clear what the Bolsheviks' intentions were. They brought charges against a consul of "a certain small country" that was the puppet of "a much larger, stronger country." This consul was accused of supporting Leonid Nikolaev by financing him in the amount of five thousand rubles and promising that he would help him escape abroad after the deed.[6] The villain was the Latvian consul Georgs Bisseneks, and Germany was the "larger" country. Bisseneks was accused of supporting Kirov's murder only to make sure everything was in agreement with the old Soviet practice—that domestic enemies could not have acted on their own; therefore, they must have received support from abroad. Furthermore, the Latvian nationality of the assassin's wife (Milda Draule) could have led to an accusation against a representative of Latvia.[7] The Latvian consul was deemed a persona non grata by the Soviet government and forced to leave the USSR despite his resolute denial of having anything to do with Nikolaev.[8]

Alleged terrorists were also soon located in Ukraine, in the form of yet another "detected hostile group." Before examining the aftermath of the Kirov murder, it should be noted that purges and repressions applied to people with "questionable biographies," that is, those who were

---

[5] RGVA, 308 k, op. 4, d. 24, l. 211.

[6] See "Malenkii konsul i ego bolshie khoziaeva," *Pravda*, January 5, 1935; and "Posobniki i pokroviteli," *Izvestiia*, January 5, 1935. See also RGVA, f. 308 k, op. 6, d. 54, l. 34–38.

[7] Draule was Kirov's lover. It is likely that the murder was motivated by revenge, i.e., the husband took revenge on his wife's lover. Another factor to consider was the Soviet regime's non-obstruction of the assassination, and its immediate use of the event to initiate a new wave of Stalinist repressions. See Muzei Kirova, *Gibel' Kirova: fakty i versii*, http://kirovmuseum.ru/node/17.

[8] The accusations put forward by the Bolsheviks caused much confusion within the consular corps in Leningrad. A few consuls, including Eugeniusz Weese of Poland, asked the dean of the consular corps, the consul general of Denmark (Schröder), to ask the Soviet authorities for an explanation. The Danish consul did not. Instead, he invited all the consuls to visit him (on December 31, 1934) to discuss the circumstances surrounding the accusation put forward against one of them. During that meeting, it became known that Georgs Bisseneks had been informed by his legation in Moscow the day before that the Soviet government wanted him to leave within forty-eight hours. He was not told why he was being forced to leave. Based on this new information, most consuls were against any kind of inquiry until the situation was clarified. Schröder and most others were also against saying goodbye to Bisseneks at the railway station. Weese did not go there either. Schröder did not do anything to make the Soviet authorities explain the situation afterwards. RGVA, f. 308 k, op. 19, d. 53, l. 73–74.

associated with the government of the Ukrainian People's Republic or had belonged to parties other than the Communist Party, had begun in Ukraine a few years prior to the Kirov event. In the late 1920s and early 1930s, the well-publicized trial of the so-called Union for the Liberation of Ukraine (ULU) had taken place. The ULU was an utter fabrication invented by the GPU, whose mission was to eliminate the leading representatives of the Ukrainian intelligentsia. Forty-five people were accused, including the vice-rector of the All-Ukrainian Academy of Sciences, the literary historian and political activist Serhii Iefremov. At that time, Polish observers knew that the charges against those individuals (who were eventually sentenced) were not only unjustified but were completely absurd and designed to serve one purpose only: to remove hypothetical "Ukrainian nationalists" from any positions of influence on current affairs in Soviet Ukraine. Adam Stebłowski, the head of the Polish consulate general in Ukraine at the time, evaluated the official charges against the ULU in the following way: "One has the impression that Iefremov's and his comrades' guilt was limited merely to maintaining some degree of connection via correspondence with the national [i.e., pro-independence] Ukrainian diaspora and, perhaps, to some private conversations within the milieu of his old political associates about the current political situation in [Soviet] Ukraine and to some predictions they made about future developments. Many of the charges put forward by the GPU seem to originate purely in the realm of fantasy and to serve the peculiar goals of that institution."[9]

After the ULU trial was over, another wave of repressions followed. This time the trials were not publicized. In 1931 and 1932, Ukrainian activists who were members of Ukrainian leftist parties, as well as of the Communist Party of Western Ukraine (CPWU) were arrested. They were accused of being members of a so-called Ukrainian National Center. It was

[9] AAN, MSZ, sygn. 10042, k. 53–54. Jerzy Niezbrzycki's position with respect to the ULU case (in the document written during World War II quoted from earlier) is completely incomprehensible. He claimed that this organization in fact existed and that he was personally in touch with the alleged leaders, Serhii Iefremov and Andrii Nikovsky: "I was particularly interested in the German attention to nationality questions. At the time, I was in touch with the largest separatist organization of Ukraine, the so-called ULU (with Iefremov and Nikovsky as leaders). That organization had both direct and indirect influence: it was linked to the remnants of Shumskyism, already decimated at the time, and the insufficiently investigated (by Moscow) issue of separatism among the Ukrainian Communists, with Mykola Skrypnyk at the head; he committed suicide in 1934 [sic]." JPIA, ARW(JAN), sygn. 1, n.p.

with this organization that the GPU wished to see the well-known Ukrainian historian Mykhailo Hrushevsky affiliated. He had been the head of the Central Rada and the president of the Ukrainian People's Republic. The Polish diplomats had no knowledge, however, of the attempts to launch a political trial against him.[10] After the suicide of the education commissar, Mykola Skrypnyk, in July 1933, arrests began among the officials responsible for higher education and schooling who happened to work under Skrypnyk's oversight.[11] Many among the accused (and later sentenced) came from Poland, and they often crossed the border illegally. Initially, during so-called Ukrainization,[12] the system needed such people because they were usually educated, or at least they

---

[10] AAN, MSZ, sygn. 6938, k. 165–67.

[11] For more information about the political trials of 1930–33, see Kuśnierz, *Ukraina w latach kolektywizacji*, 255–95; idem, "Bolszewicki 'spektakl' w Charkowie, czyli proces Związku Wyzwolenia Ukrainy", *Wrocławskie Studia Wschodnie* 10 (2006): 145–67; A. Bolabolchenko, *SVU: Sud nad perekonanniamy* (Kyiv: Kobza, 1994); V. Prystaiko, Iu. Shapoval, *Sprava Spilky Vyzvolennia Ukraïny*, INTEL, Kyiv: 1995; V. Prystaiko and I. Shapoval, *Mykhailo Hrushevs'kyi i HPU-NKVD: Trahichne desiatylittia, 1924–1934* (Kyiv: Ukraina, 1996); and O. Rubl'ov and I. Cherchenko, *Stalinshchyna i dolia zakhidnoukraïns'koï intelihentsiï, 20-50-ti roky XX st.* (Kyiv: Naukova dumka, 1994).

[12] In the 1920s, the so-called policy of *korenizatsiia* was implemented in the Soviet Union. It was based on promoting official personnel from the region where an institution was located, or at least promoting those who spoke the local language. It was supposed to bring the Communists closer to the people, who approached them as just another foreign, Moscow-based power establishment. As a result of the policy of *korenizatsiia*, autonomous national-minority districts and village councils were established, schooling among national minorities was promoted, as was their literature and press. With respect to the Polish community, this policy resulted, for instance, in the creation of two such districts, one in Soviet Ukraine (named for Julian Marchlewski, 1925–35) and the other one in Soviet Belarus (named for Felix Dzerzhinsky, or Feliks Dzierżyński, 1932–37). In Ukraine, the policy was known as Ukrainization. The Kremlin tolerated it until the end of the 1920s. Even though the Bolsheviks never officially canceled the policy of Ukrainization, in practice it ended after the first wave of arrests among the Ukrainian intelligentsia (the ULU affair) in 1929. The suicide of Mykola Skrypnyk marks its end symbolically. Polish MFA officials accurately determined why the policy of Ukrainization was initiated at all: "It was a ploy that was designed to protect the Union [USSR] against pure Ukrainian nationalism; it was a tool of Soviet global policy directed at the world revolution they were dreaming about ... , and, in the short run, a tool for attracting national minorities to the Soviet project ... in neighboring countries—Poland, Romania, Czechoslovakia" (AAN, MSZ, sygn. 10000, k. 229). For more analysis of Soviet nationalities policy in Ukraine, as witnessed by the Polish MFA and military intelligence, see J. J. Bruski, "Między ukrainizacją a rusyfikacją: Sowiecka polityka narodowościowa na Ukrainie w ocenach dyplomacji i wywiadu II RP," *Prace Komisji Środkowoeuropejskiej PAU* 17 (2009): 7–27.

could speak Ukrainian. Later, when Stalinist policy grew more conservative, they became more of a hindrance. The worsening situation for these émigrés from Poland following the Kremlin's new anti-Ukrainization policy was noted by Jan-Karszo Siedlewski. In a report to the Polish legation in Moscow on December 30, 1933, he remarked that these individuals initially occupied many influential positions in Soviet Ukraine because there was a general shortage of highly educated cadres there. As Moscow's policy changed, and as "new" people appeared on the scene, the émigrés were no longer necessary and became top priorities on the arrest list. The diplomat wrote: "Taking into consideration the new anti-Ukrainization policy of the Party, [the Ukrainian émigrés from Poland] became not only no longer indispensable but also redundant, especially because they did not cease to claim special rights for the "martyr Ukrainians," who were persecuted in Poland for their beliefs and who, therefore, should be respected and revered. Their discontent, according to the GPU, could be heard, and heard too often, as criticism of the current regime, especially because it led to agitation and unrest among all the Ukrainian intelligentsia."[13]

In Soviet Ukraine, Kirov's murder provided another reason to do away with Communists from abroad. On December 18, 1934, the Soviet press reported that on December 13–15, 1934, an off-site session of the Military Collegium of the Supreme Court of the USSR reviewed the cases of thirty-seven individuals.[14] Most of those sentenced came from Poland (Eastern Galicia). They had come to the Soviet Union at different times. The Bolsheviks invented a story that they were part of a counterrevolutionary organization named the "Union of Ukrainian Nationalists." It was announced in the press that most of those arrested were in possession of revolvers and hand grenades at the time of their arrest; twenty-eight people were sentenced, by decision of the Central Executive Committee on December 1, 1934 (paragraphs 54-8 and 54-11 of the Criminal Code of the UkrSSR), to execution and forfeiture of property. The sentence was carried out immediately. The committed Communists from Lviv, Roman Skazynsky and Ivan and Taras Krushelnytsky, were among the executed.[15] The cases of the others, including the doyen of the

---

[13] AAN, MSZ, sygn. 6938, k. 13–14.

[14] "Prigovory Voiennoi Kollegii Verkhovnogo Suda Soiuza SSR w gor. Kieve po delam o terroristakh-belogvardeitsakh," *Pravda*, December 18, 1934.

[15] The following were also executed: Mykhailo Lebedynets, Roman Shevchenko, Anatolii

Krushelnytsky family, Antin, were postponed for further investigation, "due to the discovery of new facts."[16]

A few months later, on March 28, 1935, Antin Krushelnytsky[17] and Iuliian Bachynsky were sentenced to ten years in the Gulag by the Military Collegium of the Supreme Court of the USSR in Kyiv. The collegium was composed of Jan Rutman, Vasilii Ulrikh, and Ivan Golakov. In other trials, two of Antin Krushelnytsky's sons, Bohdan and Ostap, and his daughter Volodymyra were each sentenced to five years in the Gulag.[18] On March 27–28, 1935, another external session of the Military Collegium of the Supreme Court of the USSR in Kyiv sentenced seventeen people accused of participating in the activities of the "counterrevolutionary illegal organization of the Borotbists." Among them were Communist Party functionaries and non-Party members (writers).[19] As the accusation suggests, the charges were brought primarily against people who had been affiliated with the Ukrainian Party of Socialist Revolutionaries-Borotbists in the past.[20]

Karabut, Petro Sydorov, Hryhorii Kosynka-Strilets, Dmytro Falkivsky, Mykhailo Oksamyt, Oleksander Shcherbyn, Ivan Tereshchenko, Kostiantyn Burevii, Oleksii Vlyzko, Ievhen Dmitriv, Adam Bohdanovych, Porfyrii Butuzov, Ivan Butuzov, Volodymyr Piatnytsia, Iakiv Blachenko, Dominik Polevoi, Ivan Khoptiar, Petro Beretsky, Leonid Lukianov, Kostiantyn Pivnenko, Havrylo Protsenko, Serhii Matiiash, and Oleksander Liashenko.

[16] According to the NKVD, the following people, in addition to Antin Krushelnytsky, deserved investigation: Iuliian Bachynsky, Vasyl Mysyk, Vasyl Levytsky, Anna Skrypa-Kozlovska, Levko Kovaliv, Petro Helmer-Didushok, Oleksander Finytsky, and Herbert Stupin.

[17] Krushelnytsky was deported to a town called Medvezhia Gora (now Medvezhegorsk) near the White Sea Canal. His wife, Mariia, learned about it from a postcard he sent to her from Leningrad. RGVA, f. 308 k, op. 19, d. 56, l. 139 v. Antin Krushelnytsky and his three children were all executed in November or December 1937.

[18] Rubl'ov and Cherchenko, *Stalinshchyzna i dola*, 176–78, 314.

[19] The following people were sentenced to ten years in prison: Oleksander Polotsky, Mykola Liubchenko, Iurii Mazurenko, Levko Kovaliv, Mykola Kulish, Hryhorii Epik, Valeriian Polishchuk, Vasyl Vrazhlyvy-Shtanko, Valeriian Pidmohylny, Ievhen Pluzhnyk, Andrii Paniv, Volodymyr Shtanhelei, Petro Vanchenko, Hryhorii Maifet, and Oleksander Kovinka. Seven-year sentences were given to Danylo Kudria and Semen Semko-Kozachuk. See Iu. Shapoval, *Ukraïna 20-50-kh rokiv: Storinky nenapysanoï istoriï* (Kyiv: Naukova dumka, 1993), 163–66.

[20] The Borotbists were a Ukrainian political party that functioned during the years 1918–20. It was formed after a split in the Ukrainian Party of Socialists-Revolutionaries. The Borotbists were the left wing of that party, named for the newspaper they published, *Borot'ba*. In 1919, the Borotbists formed the Ukrainian Communist Party (of Borotbists),

The fates of the Krushelnytsky, Bachynsky, and Skazynsky families who had come to Soviet Ukraine mostly for purely ideological reasons, unfolded as follows. Before their sentences, the Krushelnytsky family was composed of Antin and Mariia and their five children: four sons (Ivan, Taras, Bohdan, Ostap) and a daughter, Volodymyra. The first three sons were married; Ivan's wife resided in Lviv and held Polish citizenship.[21] The first member of the family to immigrate to Soviet Ukraine was Volodymyra Krushelnytska. She came in December 1931 as a Polish citizen.[22] Influenced by her family, which had already adopted Soviet citizenship back in Lviv, Volodymyra then renounced her Polish citizenship and accepted a Soviet one. The PCfFA representative returned her passport to the Polish consulate on October 10, 1934. Before her trial, Volodymyra worked as an assistant to Dr. Krychevsky, who was an expert in infectious diseases. Her work was appreciated (e.g., she received a bonus payment in May 1933). A year later, Ivan Krushelnytsky, who was a Soviet citizen by then, joined her in Soviet Ukraine.[23] He was employed as an art history professor at one of the institutes in Kharkiv; his wife remained in Lviv. In May 1934, Antin and Mariia, together with Bohdan and his wife, Ostap, and Ivan's daughter—six-year-old Larysa—arrived in Kharkiv. Finally, on July 5, 1934, Taras, the fifth son of to immigrate, came to Kharkiv with his wife.[24]

Except for Ivan, the male members of the Krushelnytsky family were unable to find employment and survived by selling the items they had brought with them from Poland. Antin and Taras attempted to join the Writers' Union of Ukraine (SPU) but were refused. Only when their situation was becoming truly desperate did Antin Krushelnytsky decide

---

which cooperated with the Bolsheviks but advocated full independence for Ukraine. After pressure from the Bolsheviks, the Borotbists merged with the Communist Party (Bolshevik) of Ukraine in March 1920.

[21] According to the daughter Larysa Krushelnytska, her mother did not leave with her husband because of her health, but she wanted to join her family following her treatment. Once she learned about the arrests, however, she decided against leaving for the USSR. See L. Krushel'nyts'ka, *Rubaly lis… (Spohady halychanky)* (Lviv and New York: Vydavnytstvo M.P. Kots, 2001), 78.

[22] This date is the one in the indictment of February 4, 1935. See Iu. Shapoval et al, eds., *Ostannia adresa: Rozstrily solovets'kykh v'iazniv z Ukraïny u 1937–1938 rokakh* (Kyiv: Vydavnytstvo Fakt, 2003), vol. 1, 196. According to Polish records, she came to the Soviet Union on October 29, 1932. RGVA, f. 308 k, op. 19, d. 53, l. 136.

[23] According to his daughter, he came with his sister, Volodymyra; see Krushel'nyts'ka, *Rubaly lis*, 66.

[24] RGVA, f. 308 k, op. 19, d. 53, l. 136–37.

to write a letter to Pavel Postyshev, the CP(B)U second secretary, in early October 1934. He did not receive a reply, but soon after he was instructed to visit the SPU and was accepted as a member. Taras was also accepted to the municipal section of the SPU, where he served as a translator of German literature.

During the night of November 5–6, 1934, seven NKVD agents visited the Krushelnytskys' apartment. Two of them took Taras away immediately. The remaining five agents searched the apartment and then arrested Antin and Ivan. They were told they were going to be sent off to Kyiv. None of the other family members were allowed to see their arrested relatives. The women tried but failed to get an appointment with Postyshev. It was only from the newspapers that the women learned what happened to their men. During the night of December 14–15, Bohdan, Ostap, and Volodymyra were also arrested.[25]

Iuliian Bachynsky and his daughter, Olena, came to Soviet Ukraine as Polish citizens on November 26, 1933. The father found employment as one of the editors of the *Ukrainian Soviet Encyclopedia*. Their passports were issued by the Polish consulate in Berlin. In Ukraine, they resided as Polish citizens. During the night of November 5–6, Iuliian Bachynsky was arrested.[26]

Roman Skazynsky was a Ukrainian Communist from Lviv who worked as an editor at various newspapers. In 1926 he married Sofiia Skazynska. In 1932 he was arrested in the aftermath of the termination of *Sel'rob*.[27] He was released on January 5, 1933, and found employment as head editor of the Communist newspaper *Iliustrovana hazeta*. The newspaper ceased publication in July 1933, and Skazynsky worked only part-time after that. By the end of the year, he had secured employment at the weekly *Pratsia*, but it was impossible for him and his wife to support themselves on the 100 zlotys per month that he received for this work, plus what his wife made for some music tutoring. The Skazynskys received an offer from the Soviet consulate to live and work in the USSR. Encouraged by the prospects of development in Soviet Ukraine, Skazynsky accepted the offer and submitted an application for Soviet citizenship in late 1933. On December 14, 1933, he received a positive

---

[25] Ibid. Documents from Volodymyra Krushelnytska's investigation and trial were published in Shapoval et al., eds., *Ostannia adresa*, vol. 1, 196–99.

[26] RGVA, f. 308 k, op. 19, d. 53, l. 137.

[27] A pro-Soviet newspaper published in Lviv from 1927 to 1932.

response from the consulate. The couple then submitted a request to have their Polish citizenship revoked. Their request was accepted in May 1934.

On May 26, 1934, they entered Soviet Ukraine at the Zdolbuniv-Shepetivka border crossing. They were able to learn more about the state of "well-being in the Soviet paradise" on their very first day in the USSR. In Shepetivka, NKVD agents gave them tickets to Kharkiv and ten rubles to buy sheets for the bed in their train car. After they arrived in Kharkiv, they roamed the city looking for a place to stay; the local railway police showed no concern for their welfare. Finally they went to a MOPR[28] office and managed to secure a room at the Spartak Hotel, where they lived until September 7, 1934, paying twelve rubles per day. Later Skazynsky found employment as a literary editor at the Natsmenvydav (Publishing House for National Minorities), with a salary of 360 rubles. He also received contracts for translations from Russian into Polish from the Agricultural Farming House (Selkhozvydav). He translated books about horses and pigs and other agricultural topics.

The Skazynskys earned so little that they nearly starved and had to sell everything they had brought from Poland. Sofiia was hired at a Polish school as a teacher of music and rhythm, but she earned only eighty rubles per month. In Lviv she had graduated from a music academy (1918–22) and passed a teacher's proficiency exam, and from 1918 on she attended music institute. Her job in Soviet Ukraine was difficult because she did not know Russian, and her students spoke Polish poorly.

The only people the Skazynskys socialized with in Soviet Ukraine were the Krushelnytskys and Bachynskys. A few weeks after arriving in Kharkiv, Roman Skazynsky was summoned by the NKVD and invited to become an informant. As a Communist true believer, he refused. Nonetheless, he was told that he should continue to visit the Bachynskys and Krushelnytskys (and any other people with Galician roots). In due time, he was told, he would be asked who visited them and what the conversations were about. Skazynsky returned home heartbroken and complained about "how we poor Galicians are forced to spy on each other." A few days later, Iuliian Bachynsky (whom they had not known

---

[28] In Russian, Mezdhunarodnaia organizatsiia pomoshchi bortsam revolutsii—International Red Aid. Established in 1922 at the Fourth Congress of the Comintern, it was an organization that supported persecuted revolutionaries and their families. MOPR had branches in several countries. In Poland, it was known as Czerwona Pomoc (Red Help), and, after 1925, as Czerwona Pomoc w Polsce. It was disbanded in 1938, together with the Communist Party of Poland.

before) showed up at the Skazynskys' flat and announced that the NKVD had ordered him to spy on them, in the same way that Skazynsky had been told to spy on the Bachynskys and the Krushelnytskys.

Skazynsky was not able to enjoy the benefits of "building communism in the country of workers and peasants" for very long. He was arrested during the night of November 5–6, 1934, charged with planning an assassination attempt on Postyshev and Stanislav Kosior, and taken to a Kyiv prison. The day after his arrest, his wife was fired from her job. She did not see her husband again. On December 17, 1934, a janitor stopped by her home and told her that her husband had been executed. The evidence against him was two revolvers that were allegedly found at the Skazynskys' home during a search, together with other incriminating materials that the NKVD found. These materials purportedly served as evidence that Poland had sent the Skazynskys to the Soviet Union in order to kill Postyshev and Kosior.[29]

Both of the Krushelnytskys, as well as Skazynsky and Bachynsky, considered themselves to be ideal Communists, for which their actions in Poland should have served as a sufficient proof. As their families reported, they were never troubled by material difficulties, and they believed that everything was going to be fine.[30] Basically their only social interaction was among their own circle of émigrés. Besides, they were told even by the NKVD to maintain these interactions and report on them in-depth. Even while he was in the Kyiv prison, Antin Krushelnytsky constantly reiterated in his letters to his wife that he found the arrest rather bearable and that he was busy working on his novel *Bat'kivshchyna* (Fatherland), of which he had written seven hundred pages.[31]

I will return to the fate of these families in later sections of this chapter. What I want to describe first is what unfolded in Soviet Ukraine after the December trial, namely, the espionage scare, hysteria, and panic.[32] Three

---

[29] RGVA, f. 308 k, op. 19, d. 53, l. 135–38; and CAW, Oddz. II SG, sygn. I.303.4.2012, n.p., doc. 22. CAW, Oddz. II SG, sygn. I.303.4.5424, k. 12-23. See also *Hołodomor 1932–1933*, 647–54; and RGVA, f. 308 k, op. 19, d. 53, l. 177–82.

[30] RGVA, f. 308 k, op. 19, d. 53, l. 138.

[31] Ibid., d. 55, l. 133. Krushelnytsky took the manuscript with him when he was exiled. After his death, it was burned by the NKVD.

[32] This was another sign of the panic that spread among the Ukrainian intelligentsia. A year earlier they were shocked by the resolution of the joint session of the Central Committee and Central Control Commission of the CP(b)U, which declared that the main threat in Soviet Ukraine was local Ukrainian nationalism, which purportedly supported imperialist

weeks after the trial, the Polish vice-consul in Kyiv, Piotr Kurnicki, wrote to *Dwójka* headquarters about the Kirov murder and the subsequent arrests. He reported that those who had earlier been arrested for nationalism, Trotskyism, and related accusations were now scared to death. Many local professors, writers, and intellectuals, he wrote, literally had their clothes packed in their bags, awaiting their arrest at home. The news of the executions in Moscow and Leningrad led to veritable panic, visible, for instance, in the cases of residents expelled from their apartments for having had "the slightest trace of affiliation with the White Guard." A massive, sudden exodus from the larger cities into the countryside began. Kurnicki stressed that, as a result of the charges of cooperation with foreign intelligence services against those who were sentenced for Kirov's murder, people who had visited the Polish consulate at some point in the past became extremely anxious and did all they could to avoid any further contact with "representatives of the hostile bourgeoisie": "Almost no one visits us currently, apart from peasants and beggars," he wrote.[33]

Kurnicki also alluded to the exodus to the countryside. After the assassination, Soviet authorities began issuing orders for "uncertain elements" to leave the cities.[34] In Kharkiv, for example, two thousand people were put on the lists of those who had to leave the city and move to the northeastern regions of the USSR. Among the exiles were former industrialists, senior tsarist officers and officials, and landowners who had escaped repressions in the preceding period. In August 1935, Stanisław Sośnicki reported that the notice ordering a family to prepare for a long journey was only delivered a few days before their actual deportation.

---

interventionists. The following example, even if only anecdotal, is a telling illustration of the overall mood at the time. An engineer in Kharkiv, who had so far spoken Ukrainian on a regular basis, began speaking exclusively in Russian in offices and public spaces. He told his friends that he feared arrest; see AAN, MSZ, sygn. 6938, k. 12. "Nationalists" were sought and located with the utmost diligence. One of the "nationalists" expelled from the Party was the director of the education department in Zaporizhia, Berezovsky. He said the following during his city's Party unit session: "We are overloaded with papers asking us, what are you doing with respect to the Ukrainization issue? One time I replied: it is better to do nothing than to be mistaken. There is no strategy, not in the center, or in the oblast, on how to conduct Ukrainization in the future" (Ibid., sygn. 6710, k. 62).

[33] CAW, Oddz. II SG, sygn. I.303.4.1993, n.p., doc. 22 (1934).
[34] Conquest, *The Great Terror*, 45.

This meant that many people sold everything they had for virtually nothing just before leaving.[35]

Some eloquent reflections about the repressions that happened after Kirov's murder in Leningrad, and about the passive reaction of the world to the Bolsheviks' actions came from the second secretary of the Polish embassy in Moscow, Antoni Kałuski. As he had remarked at the start of the repressions, he had no doubt that innocent people would be among the victims. On December 11, 1934, he described the situation in the following way: "For the past ten days, we have been living in noxious fumes of innocently spilled blood… The revenge against innocent people was, on the one hand, ritual murder, some kind of pagan redress for the shadow cast by the murdered one—something that can be called monstrous mysticism, certainly a seeming paradox in a society of self-professed atheists. On the other hand, it is impossible not to see symptoms of a caveman's nervous breakdown; he is looking for affirmation of his own power by biting the neck of the first victim who crosses his path."[36]

In the next part of his analysis, Kałuski underscored how shocked he was by the absence of any moral reaction from the rest of the world, including the stance taken by the League of Nations, which did not respond at all to the events in the USSR. The decision of the dean of the diplomatic corps to lower the flag on the day of Kirov's funeral, at a time when it was known that the Bolsheviks' rage had already led to a series of executions, was something repulsive, in his opinion. Kałuski criticized the French ambassador and minister Paul Marchandeau,[37] who laid wreaths on Kirov's coffin at the time executions were underway. He also noted the cynicism that Maxim Litvinov displayed in Geneva, where he played the role of a peace emissary by offering to take on the difficult job of investigating the Marseille tragedy[38] with his "dirty" hands.

Kałuski also criticized the Polish press, which reacted to the Bolsheviks' behavior with excessive caution: "I understand that we cannot take the burden of worsening relations with the Soviets all upon ourselves, but it needs to be remembered that it was they who called us 'jackals' and

---

[35] RGVA, f. 308 k, op. 19, d. 57, l. 118.

[36] AAN, MSZ, sygn. 6753, k. 147

[37] Paul Marchandeau (1882–1968) was a French politician who in the 1930s served, in succession, as minister of the budget, finance, commerce and industry, finance again, and justice. When he visited the USSR, he was minister of justice.

[38] The assassination of Alexander I of Yugoslavia in that city. See Dullin, *Stalin i ego diplomaty*, 207.

'vermin,' not the other way round." Next he highlighted the fact that, during the Leipzig trial of Georgi Dimitrov and other Communists accused of setting the Reichstag on fire in Berlin in late 1933, the Bolsheviks were able to mobilize much international moral support to advocate their cause. "Is the Western world going to find something that will help us to resist this? Will it find the moral reserves to condemn this barbarism strongly enough?"[39]

The question was, however, purely rhetorical. It was futile to expect the world to react to the Soviet repressions, especially since it had not reacted to the Stalinist grain requisitions a few years earlier, as a result of which millions of peasants died from starvation. As it turned out soon, the repressions of émigré Communists from Eastern Galicia were merely a foreshadowing of what would soon unfold. The machine of repression was only warming up. Soon, it would target all social classes and groups — Communists, the NKVD, Red Army functionaries, and, most of all, ordinary citizens.

Most visitors to foreign consulates in the USSR, including the Polish ones, became extremely anxious and tried to avoid them at any cost. People visited the foreign posts only when there was a vitally important reason for doing so, as was the case for the families of the alleged terrorists murdered or deported by the Bolsheviks. After sentences were announced in the press, the wives, mothers, and daughters in the Skazynsky, Bachynsky, and Krushelnytsky families came to the Polish consulate pleading for Polish citizenship and the opportunity to return to Poland. Sofiia Skazynska was the first one to appear at the Kharkiv post, on December 26, 1934. She asked to have her Polish citizenship restored and for permission to return to that country. Her parents, Franciszek and Maria Kupczyńska, were still in Poland, residing in Lviv, at 7 St. Martin St. The consulate gave her permission to submit an application. After her husband was executed, she was evicted from her apartment and had to stay with the Krushelnytsky or Bachynsky families. She asked Polish officials to give her provisional material help. She spoke with Zdzisław Miłoszewski, a consular official and intelligence officer, and head of intelligence post M.13 (code name Oleg Ostrowski). After that conversation, Miłoszewski reported some significant pieces of information to the *Dwójka* that cast light on the arrests and death sentences in Soviet Ukraine, as well as on the circumstances of western Ukrainian Communists who had been deluded by the vision of a

---

[39] AAN, MSZ, sygn. 6753, k. 148–49.

"happy life" in the USSR and had decided to leave Poland for the USSR. Skazynska told him in detail the story of the Skazynskys' decision to leave Poland and emigrate to the USSR, and of the arrest and sentencing of her husband.[40]

After reading press reports from December 18, 1934, in which information about the execution of her husband was published, Sofiia Skazynska attempted to slit her wrists. Olena Bachynska saved her. On December 20, Skazynska was evicted from her apartment. Earlier she was visited by three NKVD agents and, in all likelihood, raped. That was the impression Miłoszewski had after talking to Skazynska: "She murmured something vaguely about being harassed." A janitor took away her husband's clothes right in front of her. After spending a few days with the Bachynskys and the Krushelnytskys, Skazynska came to the consulate with her plea to return to Poland, where she "would like to repay some people for what she had experienced here."

Miłoszewski wrote a positive recommendation supporting Skazynska's application. He asked the *Dwójka* to influence the municipal authorities in Poland to come to a quick decision. The head of post M.13 wrote that this would be to Poland's benefit as propaganda, especially because all the persons afflicted by the recent repressions would learn about it. Furthermore Miłoszewski emphasized that Skazynska could be useful for working "with our Ukrainians." Skazynska herself said that she could "be of significant benefit": she gave the last names of people with whom her husband had met and who had questionable contacts with the Soviet consulate in Lviv. The woman was absolutely positive of her husband's innocence, suspecting that it was some kind of vengeance on the part of "people from Poland." Upon her departure, Miłoszewski gave her a hundred rubles to help her get by.[41]

Stefaniia Krushelnytska, the wife of Taras Krushelnytsky, came next to the consulate to request permission and help to return to Poland. The consulate received a letter written in her support from her father, Franciszek Szuszkiewicz (who lived in Lviv, at 5 Kraszewski St.). Stefaniia Krushelnytska, in Consul Sośnicki's words, was in a state of unspeakable penury. Furthermore, she had recently given birth to a daughter. The child

---

[40] This information was initially included in Miłoszewski's report to the "East" Section of the Second Department, and later in the report, cited earlier, of the Polish consulate in Kharkiv from January 20, 1935.

[41] CAW, Oddz. II SG, sygn. I.303.4.2012, n.p., doc. 22.

was born on December 31, 1934, when her father, Taras Krushelnytsky, was no longer alive.

Another person who turned to the Polish consulate was the wife of executed Ivan Krushelnytsky, Olena Krushelnytska (née Levytska), a citizen of Poland residing in Lviv, at 19 Zadwórzańska St., with a plea to take her daughter, six-year-old Larysa Krushelnytska, out of the Soviet Union. The request was submitted through her lawyer, L. Krzymuski. Through the MFA's mediation, the consulate received a letter of approval from the voivodeship office in Lviv permitting Larysa to return to Poland.[42]

The Polish consulate allowed the above women to submit the relevant paperwork. However, visits from the wives of individuals charged with terrorism were, to say the least, awkward for the consulate, especially because the women had willingly renounced their Polish citizenship and their husbands were active Communists. Stanisław Sośnicki asked that, henceforth, the head of the East Section of the MFA issue relevant instructions on how to respond to the pleas of Sofiia Skazynska and other women. He emphasized that humanitarian principles obliged him to support those families, both in approving their requests to return to Poland and in issuing material help. He did not want to take that decision alone, however, because that issue "could provoke resentment, perhaps even suspicions, from the Soviet authorities." The consul asked the head of the East Section to issue detailed instructions on what the official stance should be toward Sofiia Skazynska and the Krushelnytsky family, both in terms of maintaining contact with them and in perhaps issuing financial support. He also asked whether he should send Skazynska's and Stefaniia Krushelnytska's requests to reinstate their Polish citizenship and allow their return to Poland to the voivodeship office in Lviv.[43]

A reply from the Polish MFA to Sośnicki's questions was not found in the archives, but the subsequent actions of the Polish consulate in Kharkiv and Ambassador Juliusz Łukasiewicz indicate that the MFA's reaction must have been positive. The East Section of the Second Department also responded positively to the idea of bringing the wives of the émigré Communists targeted with repression back to Poland. They shared

---

[42] RGVA, f. 308 k, op. 19, d. 53, l. 131.
[43] Ibid., l. 131 v.

Zdzisław Miłoszewski's opinion about the cases of Sofiia Skazynska and Mariia Krushelnytska.[44]

However, on March 9, 1935, Sofia Skazynska was arrested for "visiting the consulate and informing them about the Krushelnytsky family situation" and remained imprisoned in Kharkiv. At the time of her arrest, she was staying in Olena Bachynska's apartment.[45] There is no further information about Sofiia Skazynska in the Polish archives.[46] Larysa Krushelnytska writes of her in her memoirs.[47] Skazynska is described as a very energetic individual who visited her family often and expressed her outrage at the general malaise that was the predominant attitude in responses to Soviet repressions. "Why are you silent? You do not protest, you do not visit the Polish consulate!" she used to say. Larysa Krushelnytska reported that, after her arrest and sentencing, Skazynska "toured" the Soviet gulags until she managed to escape in 1940. She returned on foot, dressed in a quilted convict's jacket, to her apartment in Lviv, where she passed away.[48]

The Polish consulate in Kharkiv had no doubt that the executed and deported Communists had not engaged in the actions they were accused of in their indictments. From their conversations with the Bachynsky, Krushelnytsky and Skazynsky families, the Polish consular officials were convinced that none of the families had access to weapons. "Based on the testimonies of the accused, the consulate was unable to pin down the real reasons for the arrests and death sentences, as there was absolutely no evidence to be found that some kind of preparation for a terrorist act was underway."[49]

Following a conversation he had with Sofiia Skazynska, Zdzisław Miłoszewski theorized a few possible scenarios to explain the arrest of her

---

[44] CAW, Oddz. II SG, sygn. I.303.4.2012, n.p., doc. 63.

[45] RGVA, f. 308 k, op. 19, d. 55; Ibid., d. 57, l. 32.

[46] Oleksandr Rubl'ov, one of the most knowledgeable experts on Soviet persecution of the Ukrainian intelligentsia, does not mention any facts concerning her fate. See O. Rubl'ov, *Zakhidnoukraïns'ka intelihentsiia u zahal'nopolitychnykh ta kul'turnykh protsesakh (1914–1939)* (Kyiv: Instytut istorii Ukrainy NAN Ukrainy, 2004); and Rubl'ov and Cherchenko, *Stalinshchyna i dolia.*

[47] In her book, Larysa Krushelnytska used the name Marta instead of Skazynska's actual name. In an email exchange I had with her, Krushelnytska confirmed that Skazynska was certainly Sofiia, though they might have called her Marta at home. Larysa Krushelnytska, correspondence with the author, December 24, 2012.

[48] Krushel'nyts'ka, *Rubaly lis*, 91.

[49] RGVA, f. 308 k, op. 19, d. 53, l. 138.

husband and wrote: "It is a matter of fact that at the meetings organized in all the factories after the Kirov murder, it was constantly repeated that the people who had come from Poland to kill the local Communists had been annihilated. This was linked to the war-scare propaganda about an imminent Polish-German-Japanese invasion."[50]

Because none of the sentenced persons, except for Iuliian Bachynsky, held Polish citizenship, there were no formal grounds for representatives of the Second Polish Republic in the USSR to intervene in their cases. Bachynsky's case was different. Ambassador Juliusz Łukasiewicz himself intervened with the PCfFA in Moscow, demanding information about Bachynsky's fate. In the cases of Bachynsky and his daughter, as well in the case of the Krushelnytsky family, the Polish post in Kharkiv also intervened on several occasions. Despite these efforts, neither the Polish embassy nor consulate received any information about the accused. The Polish consul in Kharkiv, Stanisław Sośnicki, learned of the fate of Iuliian Bachynsky from his daughter Olena, who received a letter from the military prosecutor of the Ukrainian Military District on June 21, 1935. She informed Sośnicki that her father had been sentenced to ten years' imprisonment by the Military Council of the Supreme Court. Equipped with this information, Sośnicki went to see Mikhailov, the representative of the PCfFA in Kharkiv, on July 13, 1935.[51] The consul pointed to the fact that the behavior of the Soviet authorities was inappropriate, because "they knew about the embassy's and consulate's interest in Bachynsky's case and [yet] decided to inform [only] his daughter about it, completely ignoring the former." Sośnicki demanded to be told the reasons for the sentence and where Bachynsky was being detained. He protested against the "methods of arrest applied to Polish citizens, and against proceeding with their trials without making it possible for the consulate to see them and support them with legal expertise." Mikhailov agreed that Sośnicki was right about the inappropriateness of the actions of the Soviet judicial institutions and promised to contact the relevant authorities in Kyiv to ask for the reasons for the sentence.[52]

The consul also attempted to make it possible for Polish citizen Olena Bachynska, the daughter of Iuliian Bachynsky, to return to Poland. The

---

[50] CAW, Oddz. II SG, sygn. I.303.4.2012, n.p., doc. 22

[51] This is the date mentioned in the consulate's report, but the report itself is dated July 12, 1935, meaning that there is either a mistake in the date of the report's origin or in the date of Sośnicki's meeting with Mikhailov.

[52] RGVA, f. 308 k, op. 19, d. 57, l. 31.

Soviet authorities delayed their decision to issue an exit visa. The Soviet clerks made constant excuses, e.g., that their boss was absent and hence a decision could not be made. On March 16, 1935, Sośnicki intervened with Mikhailov in Bachynska's case. The Soviet official asked whether she had not happened to have been charged with some kind of criminal violation. Hearing these words, the Polish consul suspected that the Soviet authorities were unwilling to issue the visa, using charges of counterrevolutionary activity as an excuse.[53]

Olena Bachynska's case had a happy ending. After the Polish consulate made many attempts to intervene and after much time-consuming effort, she finally received an exit visa on July 13, 1935. According to the information the consulate received, she was scheduled to leave on July 18, 1935.[54]

Sośnicki also tried to help the child Larysa Krushelnytska. Because her closest family members had been arrested, and because her grandmother, Mariia Krushelnytska, was lying ill in a hospital, she became homeless and lived "in the streets" after the order to expel the Krushelnytsky family from Kharkiv was implemented. Sośnicki was unable to help her, however, because the authorities scrutinized every contact between the Krushelnytsky family and the consulate with utmost diligence. Instead Sośnicki asked Łukasiewicz to intercede with the Red Cross on Larysa's behalf. He felt this was the only organization that could help the little girl get to Poland, because she was a Soviet citizen.[55] Ultimately the Polish efforts were effective, and Larysa returned to Poland in late 1936.[56]

---

[53] Ibid., d. 55, l. 133.

[54] Ibid., d. 57, l. 32

[55] Ibid., d. 56, l. 139-139 v; d. 57, l. 32.

[56] Larysa Krushelnytska became a professor of archaeology and the director (later honorary director) of the Vasyl Stefanyk Scientific Library in Lviv (formerly the Ossolineum). Her memoirs, *Rubaly lis* (cited above), were published in 2001. The people who had the greatest influence on her decision to return, she wrote, were Marshal Piłsudski's widow, Aleksandra Piłsudska, and the head of the Moscow Political Committee of the Red Cross, Ekaterina Peshkova; see ibid., 109–10. Her memoir about the first days of the occupation of Lviv by both the Soviets and the Germans, in 1939 was published as L. Kruszelnyćka, "Mój Lwów," in *Europa nieprowincjonalna: Przemiany na ziemiach wschodnich dawnej Rzeczypospolitej (Białoruś, Litwa, Łotwa, Ukraina, wschodnie pogranicze III Rzeczypospolitej Polskiej) w latach 1772–1999*, ed. K. Jasiewicz (Warsaw and London: Rytm and Polonia Aid Foundation Trust, 1999), 117–23.

4.2. The Search for Trotskyites and Other "Enemies"

To justify its crimes, the Bolshevik system always had to fabricate the existence of some kind of domestic enemy. During the collectivization drive and the resulting famine, the main culprits for all misfortunes that befell the "country of peasants and workers" were, officially, the kulaks. Next the Stalinist state turned its attention to the Trotskyites, who purportedly were enemies hiding deep underground, spying for capitalist countries and following the orders of their intelligence services. "The search for hidden Trotskyites" began even before the Kirov murder,[57] continued during 1935, and had accelerated by the time of the first Moscow trial.

The term "Trotskyite" was, in the Stalinist system, a synonym for the greatest evil imaginable in the world.[58] The term implied a whole range of charges. This versatility was something that the Polish consul in Kharkiv, Stanisław Sośnicki, turned his attention to. On September 4, 1936, he wrote to the Polish ambassador in Moscow: "The term 'Trotskyite' in practice covers anything, including a bandit, a thief, a profiteer, a grifter, a nationalist, an anti-Stakhanovite, a careless clerk, a bad manager and director—in other words, anyone who can influence the functioning of the state apparat in a negative way."[59]

The Polish diplomats, consular officials, and intelligence officers who dealt with the problem of repressions against this broad category of Leon Trotsky's followers not only attempted to estimate their magnitude but also to discover their source and, hypothetically, to predict their consequences. It needs to be emphasized that the search for Trotskyites and other enemies in Ukraine (and in any other region of the USSR) was closely associated with events taking place in Moscow—that is, if

---

[57] On October 22, 1934, the Central Committee of the CP(B)U approved the document, prepared by the OrgBureau of the Central Committee, titled "On the Counterrevolutionary Activity of the Remnants of Nationalists and Trotskyites and the Support Given to Them by Rotten and Liberal Elements." The document stated that, despite increased vigilance in some areas, particularly in the scientific and educational spheres, remnants of the already vanquished faction of nationalists and Trotskyites continued their activities. Iurii Kotsiubynsky, the head of Soviet Ukraine's State Planning Committee, was named. He allegedly defended those elements, including a certain "Trotskyite" named Naumov. As a result, the Central Committee decided to remove those "hidden Trotskyites" from the Party, and Kotsiubynsky himself was fired from his post and removed from the Central Committee. See Shapoval, *Ukraïna 20-50-kh rokiv*, 181–82.

[58] K. Schlögel, *Terror i mechta: Moskva 1937* (Moscow: ROSSPEN, 2011), 101.

[59] CAW, Oddz. II SG, sygn. I.303.4.1867, k. 78.

"enemies" were discovered in Moscow, they also had to be present in the provinces. Various regions of Soviet Ukraine experienced a wave of arrests in 1935 and 1936, when individuals were charged with counterrevolutionary acts and Trotskyism.[60]

The Polish consulate in Kharkiv turned its attention to one such alleged Trotskyite organization. "A job of provocation, organized by a Trotskyite-nationalist group," was discovered at the October Locomotive Station of the Southern Railways. The main goal of that group was to "counteract all efforts aimed at restoring the good functioning of the railway sector." According to the NKVD, the leader of the counterrevolutionaries was the head of the depot and a former SR activist, Bohdanov, the son of a wealthy real-estate owner. In 1919 Bohdanov fought against the Bolsheviks on an armored train of the White Guard. He received his Party membership in 1930, after which he allegedly turned to counterrevolutionary activity in the Rodakovo depot, for which he was tried and acquitted. Next he was sentenced to one year in prison for causing a railway accident on the Limansky section of the Donbas railway but managed to avoid imprisonment. According to the indictment, the following individuals belonged to Bohdanov's group: Savchenko, Tkachenko, the provocateur hetmanite Kharchenko, Shurupov, Anisimov, Hrebenychenko, Zgiersky, Stetsenko, Kravanov, the hetmanite Voronko, Kovalenko, Onyshchenko, and others. That organization had purportedly already been created in 1927, when a Trotskyite group in the October depot resisted a Party policy as "local oppositionists." The main activist at the time was Tkachenko, but in 1934 Bohdanov became the leader and was supposedly "the real leader of the entire destructive operation in the Kharkiv railway hub." Bohdanov's people were allegedly scheduled during all the shifts at the station and aimed at damaging the locomotives by all possible means. They were also charged with secretly distributing anti-Soviet leaflets.[61]

---

[60] During the second half of 1935, compared to the same period in 1934, the number of cases investigated by special collegiums of the oblast courts grew by 95.9 percent; in the first half of 1936, that number (compared to the second half of 1935) grew by 20.8 percent. The Kharkiv collegium investigated 405 cases in 1935 and 796 in 1936; the Dnipropetrovsk collegium, 235 and 526, respectively; Donetsk, 358 and 534; Kyiv, 317 and 424; Chernihiv, 159 and 348; Vinnytsia, 170 and 268; Odesa, 133 and 256; and the Moldavian SSR, 27 and 81. See Shapoval, *Ukraïna 20-50-kh rokiv*, 181.

[61] RGVA, f. 308 k, op. 19, d. 58, l. 246–48

There were so many trials that in their reports to the embassy, the MFA, and the Second Department, the Polish consulates sometimes simply did not mention them. After the press released information[62] about the trial of "counterrevolutionaries and Petliura followers" in Kyiv, who, in the guise of being musicians and folk singers (bandura players), supposedly sowed ferment among the collective-farm workers, inciting them to destroy the crops, overwork the horses, abandon their work posts, and commit acts of sabotage. On October 30, 1935, the Polish embassy in Moscow asked the Polish consulate general in Kyiv to submit more information about that trial.

The head of the consulate replied that he had not directed the ambassador's and MFA's attention toward that particular trial in Kyiv because he did not consider it significant enough: "If a real, serious conspiracy or counterrevolutionary center was discovered, then they would either try to keep the entire thing secret or they would organize a huge public show trial. They would not, as has been done, merely publish a formal briefing in the judiciary column."[63]

Karszo-Siedlewski discovered no new facts apart from the ones that the press had made known. He did write, however, that the information published must have been much exaggerated, both in terms of the magnitude and significance of the operations of the aforementioned organization, and with respect to the purported existence of a secret printing house and library. He put forward the thesis that a group of outlaws, former tsarist officers who had nothing to lose, could possibly have been roaming the Ukrainian countryside making their living by singing and playing music. And while they were at it, after consuming some alcohol, they could have uttered anti-Soviet remarks and encouraged the peasants to commit sabotage; and, under the pretext of working for some kind of an organization, they could have pocketed any funds given to support the aims of that organization.[64]

The consul reiterated that, after the wide-ranging Party purges and firings of employees in all offices, institutions, and organizations, many people, indeed, found themselves living on the streets. Among them were likely ordinary rogues, frauds, idlers, and simply hapless fellows, and perhaps also a few from the old elites who had somehow survived until

---

[62] See "Zagadkowy proces kontrrewolucjonistów-petlurowców," *Ilustrowany Kuryer Codzienny*, October 22, 1935.

[63] RGVA, f. 308 k, op. 19, d. 58, l. 277.

[64] Ibid., l. 276–77.

the mid-1930s. People with nothing to lose would stop at nothing to earn some kind of living. Owing to the chaos prevailing in the Soviet administration, and thanks to false documents or after successfully changing their legal name, such persons succeeded in finding other employment, even after they were fired from a job. Sometimes they even managed to be appointed to influential Party or administrative positions. Such individuals were aware that they could be exposed at any time; hence they tried to accumulate as much money as they could illegally. When their true identity or their past was exposed and they failed to disappear quickly enough, a court trial took place, a fact that "could not have been hidden, but the societal impact of which was weakened because all the blame was put on the 'elements from hostile classes,' whose goal was not ordinary theft or graft, but undermining the authority of Soviet power."[65] Hence the Ukrainian press daily reported on all kinds of new abuses in the administrative organs of the cities, collective farms, various organizations, including Party ones, in municipalities, offices, factories, and railways.[66]

A key moment in the "struggle with Trotskyism" was the first Moscow trial, the so-called trial against the "Trotskyite-Zinovievite Terrorist Center," or the Trial of the Sixteen, held from August 19 to 24, 1936. Among the accused were the prominent Communist dignitaries Lev Kamenev and Grigorii Zinoviev, recent allies of Stalin in his struggle for power with Trotsky following Lenin's death—later known as the Left Opposition. They were charged with participating in the plot to assassinate Kirov and planning to assassinate other Party leaders. They were also accused of cooperating with foreign intelligence services.

A Polish observer was present at the trial. His name was Tadeusz Jankowski, and he was the chargé d'affaires of the embassy in Moscow. On August 26, 1936, he sent a confidential report, prepared by Stanisław Głuski, to the minister of foreign affairs. Before one could enter the courtroom, the Polish diplomat wrote, one's papers were checked five times. The audience in the courtroom did not hear a single bit of evidence that exemplified the counterrevolutionary activity of the accused. The only evidence in support of that claim were their own confessions. "Apart from Ivan Smirnov, all the other accused, including Kamenev and Zinoviev, humiliated and degraded themselves to the limit, perhaps

---

[65] Ibid., l. 277–78.
[66] Ibid., l. 278.

hoping that this behavior would help to mitigate their sentence. They displayed feelings of repentance, genuine or not, admitted to committing all the acts they were accused of, and apologized profusely in a typically Russian way, but also denounced and accused each other, flattered and praised the prosecutor and the court, and threw the worst possible light on their own underground organization. In other words, they were *plus catholique que le pape* [more Catholic than the pope]. One had the impression that NKVD agents were among the accused. Their sole role in court was to inform against their accomplices, e.g., the accused Reinhold."[67]

After hearing the final speeches of the accused on August 22 and 23, 1936, Jankowski concluded that there was nothing new or interesting in them: "The utter moral collapse of the spirits of the accused was even more markedly visible, apart from Smirnov. Quiet voices among the Soviet audience could be heard saying, *eto dazhe protivno slushat'* — that it was actually repugnant to hear those speeches." Evaluating the trial itself, Jankowski wrote: "Many claims by the prosecutor, upon which his indictment is based, seem greatly exaggerated or simply ungrounded, e.g., the alleged participation in the Kirov murder plot." As someone astutely pointed out, many of the accused had been in jail for the past few years; hence, it was difficult to conceive that they could have directed terrorist operations from there. The authors of the report stated that the prosecutor's claim that the accused not only thought and spoke about the Terror but also engaged in it (even if no instances of such behavior were mentioned at all), was ridiculous. Another similarly absurd claim struck the Polish observers, namely: how it was possible that, according to the indictment, the accused had been engaged in preparations to assassinate Stalin and other Communist dignitaries since 1932 but failed to implement a single one of them, even against politicians of secondary importance. In conclusion, the authors of the report wrote that this trial was meant to scare all the skeptics in the Party and to ensure that they never thought about criticizing the regime again. They accurately predicted that this issue would not disappear from the agenda, and that "new political trials" were very likely to be seen soon.[68]

---

[67] Furthermore, in reports about the contemporary geopolitical situation that the Second Department prepared, it was emphasized that "The behavior of the accused is a shining example of the extreme moral degradation of the old Bolshevik leaders and their collaborators" (CAW, Oddz. II SG, sygn. I.303.4.3165, k. 17).

[68] Ibid., sygn. I.303.4.3160, k. 1–9. Jankowski included similar impressions in his book about

In keeping with Bolshevik tradition, this public trial was a loud spectacle of hatred directed against "despicable enemies." It prefigured a whole series of new arrests of "less significant" affiliates of the "Trotskyite-Zinovievite Terrorist Center."[69] This campaign, needless to say, did not spare Soviet Ukraine. On September 19, 1936, the head of the NKVD, Genrikh Yagoda sent a list of 585 alleged participants in a counterrevolutionary Trotskyite organization to Nikolai Yezhov. They were arrested in Moscow, Leningrad, and Gorky oblasts and in Ukraine. The prisoners were divided into four groups according to which category of punishment they were to receive:
I – the death penalty (326)
II - 10 years' imprisonment (163 persons)
III - 8 years' imprisonment (42 persons)
IV - 5 years' imprisonment (54 persons)
    In Soviet Ukraine, each category included the following numbers of prisoners:
I – the death penalty (44)
II - 10 years' imprisonment (7)
III - 8 years' imprisonment (4)
IV - 5 years' imprisonment (0)[70]
    Soon thereafter, the NKVD pieced together a fabricated "Ukrainian Trotskyite Center," which was supposedly founded by the Ukrainian Communist Iurii Kotsiubynsky on Iurii Piatakov's orders. Kotsiubynsky served inter alia, as the deputy head of the Council of People's Commissars of Ukraine and the head of the State Planning Committee of Soviet Ukraine. In November 1934, he was dismissed from his posts for "abandoning his vigilance against Trotskyite elements."[71] Kotsiubynsky

---

the USSR that he wrote in London in 1953; see T. Jankowski, *Studium ZSRR: Dzieje wewnętrzne, Ustrój, Polityka zagraniczna* (London: Szkoła Nauk Politycznych Społecznych, 1953), 184–85.

[69] Soon after the trial, the Polish embassy in Moscow informed Foreign Minister Józef Beck of its aftermath: that arrests were still underway and that, based on press reports, there were 50 Trotskyite organizations discovered throughout the USSR at the time. AAN, MSZ, sygn. 6939, k. 263.

[70] RGASPI, f. 671, op. 1, d. 225, l. 1–27.

[71] Rumors of Iurii Kotsiubynsky's arrest reached foreign posts rather quickly. On December 2, 1934, the Polish ambassador was informed about the arrest by both Jan Karszo-Siedlewski and Stanisław Sośnicki. What Sośnicki knew had been verified at a reception organized by the Polish consulate: the German and Italian consuls confirmed the news. The German consul said that Kotsiubynsky's family had already left for Moscow. RGVA, f. 308 k, op. 4, d. 24, l. 213. Nearly two weeks later, on December 15, 1934, Piotr Kurnicki

thought the accusations must be a mistake and traveled to Moscow, where he was arrested and then, in February 1935, sentenced to five years in prison. In October 1936, he was transferred to Kyiv, where he was accused of directing the "Ukrainian Trotskyite Center" and sentenced to death in March 1937.[72]

At the same time, arrests of less prominent Party members, clerks, and workers were underway. Individual Party members had their biographies carefully scrutinized to determine whether they had any contacts in the past with the newly discovered "enemies of the people." To become a Trotskyite, or a different kind of an enemy, saboteur, or counterrevolutionary, one could, for instance, fail to fulfill production quotas if one was an administrator, manager, or engineer; or disrupt the Stakhanovite movement if one was a worker. To become a saboteur, it was enough for a worker to fail to display enthusiasm for the new movement. This was something that Stanisław Sośnicki emphasized in his informative and analytical report, "Counterrevolution and the First Anniversary of the Stakhanovite Movement," addressed to the ambassador in Moscow: "As if a side note to the preparations to celebrate the first anniversary of the Stakhanovite movement, repressions in this consular district have affected virtually all spheres of economic life. Those actions have targeted mostly particular factories, but they were called a struggle with the remnants of the Trotsky-Zinoviev counterrevolution. These remnants have been very actively suppressed for over two years, but now they have suddenly come alive again, reappearing everywhere. This state of affairs was discovered following acts of sabotage perpetrated against the Stakhanovite movement, and since this movement was introduced into every area of economic and social life, the enemies, again called the Trotsky-Zinoviev counterrevolution, thus have appeared everywhere, too."[73]

In his report, Sośnicki posed the thesis that the main reasons behind the new wave of anti-Trotskyite repressions were the country's poor economic conditions and the subsequent need to find the proverbial

---

wrote that rumor had it that Kotsiubynsky's arrest was associated with the "wave of the Trotskyites' exposure" (AAN, MSZ, sygn. 6938, k. 180).

[72] In 1956 the Military Collegium of the Soviet Supreme Court reinvestigated the issue and concluded that Kotsiubynsky was arrested without grounds, and he was rehabilitated. On April 28, 1957, the Central Committee of the Communist Party of Ukraine reinstated him as a Party member posthumously. See TsDAHOU, f. 39, op. 4, spr. 103, ark. 8–9, ark. 56–63; and I. Shemshushenko, ed., *Zhertvy represii* (Kyiv: Iurinform, 1993), 56–63.

[73] CAW, Oddz. II SG, sygn. I.303.4.1867, k. 54.

scapegoats who could be blamed for all economic shortcomings. The consul was correct in suggesting the following rationalization for how these "enemies" were found: "When it comes to the working class as a whole, they look for 'saboteurs' who resist the new exploitative methods of the Stakhanovite movement. At the same time, anyone who does not fulfill the excessive quotas, which are beyond his capacity, earns this title. If the enterprise as a whole does not fulfill the quotas, the director is also found guilty; this way, both the worker and the director become agents of the Trotsky-Zinoviev counterrevolution."[74] Each anti-Stakhanovite thus became an enemy of the Soviet state and "had to be condemned as a counterrevolutionary Trotsky-Zinoviev and foreign-intelligence agent for the greater good of Communist society."[75]

Sometimes the authorities did not have to bother to uncover "hidden saboteurs," because open workers' rebellions also did take place. They were directed against the exploitative methods of the Stakhanovite movement or against the compulsory signing of a "voluntary" agreement to have a part of one's wage deducted to sponsor a state loan, to help the victims of the Spanish Civil War, and so on.[76]

Polish diplomats and consular officials also tried to estimate the number of arrested persons based on their own sources. They did not have, and could not have had, accurate data, but even the fragmentary information they received allowed them to sketch a general picture of the new Soviet reality, in which terror was ubiquitous, people disappeared without a trace during the night, and arrests and executions happened daily. Soon after the first Moscow trial, on September 18, 1936, Jan Karszo-Siedlewski informed the ambassador about the consequences of that trial and of the (by then) typical propaganda campaign in Soviet Ukraine. He wrote that over the past few weeks several thousand people had been dismissed from their jobs and arrested. He quoted the figure of 7,000 to 8,000: 2,000 in Kyiv and Dnipropetrovsk, and at least 500 in Odesa. Most of them, he held, were deported to Kazakhstan.[77]

Stanisław Nawrocki (code name Narcyz Napiórkowski, the head of intelligence post E.15) also tried to estimate the magnitude of the repressions in Ukraine. In his analytical and observational reports, he estimated the number of people arrested for Trotskyism and tried to

---

[74] Ibid., k. 62.
[75] Ibid., k. 65.
[76] For more information about one such rebellion, see chapter 3, section 3.3.1.
[77] AAN, MSZ, sygn. 6669, k. 14.

convey the social atmosphere prevalent in the Kyiv consular district after the first Moscow trial. On September 7, 1936, he wrote to the Second Department that "a high level of unease associated with the very numerous arrests among the Trotskyites could be detected among the urban population." He quoted figures that he obtained, he claimed, from a credible source; they were similar to the ones quoted by Karszo-Siedlewski, according to whom 2,000 people were arrested in Kyiv as Trotskyites.[78]

Five days later Nawrocki prepared a report, titled "About the Ukrainian Events," in which he wrote that the arrests of Trotskyites began on the second day of the Kamenev-Zinoviev trial[79] and were enveloped in secrecy. The arrests were conducted mainly at night. After two to four days of detention those arrested were transported in prison vehicles or escorted by armed guards on foot to the railway station, where they were loaded onto train cars and dispatched to the east. Without indicating his source, Nawrocki quoted the following figures: 2,500 persons arrested in Dnipropetrovsk oblast (2,000 from Dnipropetrovsk, Zaporizhia, and Kryvyi Rih); in Kyiv oblast, 2,200 (in Kyiv, 2,000; from outside the city, 200); in Odesa oblast, approximately 800; in Chernihiv oblast, about 700; and in Vinnytsia oblast, 200. In total, 6,500 persons were arrested, not counting the Donbas and Kharkiv oblast.[80] The Polish agent also mentioned, in passing, that employees of sixteen Ukrainian newspapers, mostly senior editors, their deputies, and secretaries, were also arrested. Identical operations were also conducted within the Party and state apparats and among the managers of industrial enterprises and collective farms.

Characteristically, the author of the report, while quoting figures on the number of arrested persons, put forward the thesis that there did indeed exist a serious resistance movement within the Communist Party—Trotskyism. For him the mass arrests were proof that so-called Trotskyism "had began to outgrow the [authorities'] ability to control it by ordinary means": "I think that the recent arrests will not result in eradicating the oppositional mood within the Ukrainian Party." The author truly believed, it seems, that the Communists actually faced a Trotskyist opposition and had decided to go ahead with radical measures

---

[78] CAW, Oddz. II SG, sygn. I.303.4.1956, n.p., doc. 21.

[79] That is, on August 20, 1936.

[80] A *Dwójka* analyst had doubts about these figures and asked that where they were from be specified.

such as mass arrests, which was something they "had been forced to postpone no longer."[81]

Nawrocki's opinion was not supported by anyone else. Other Polish observers had no doubt that not only were the trials a farce and the accused persons not guilty, but that there was also no substantial oppositional movement to speak of in the USSR. The new wave of repression was aimed at "cleansing Soviet society under construction" of all possible enemies, even if those same enemies "did not realize that they were the enemies of the people" or "Trotskyites," whether active or hypothetical.

Jan Karszo-Siedlewski did not doubt the true nature of the arrests. A few days before the first Moscow trial, on August 14, he wrote a letter to the ambassador in which he explained the cause of the "anti-Trotskyite hysteria" as he saw it. He believed that Moscow had to remind the local centers of power that the purge "that had already been underway in practice for a long time, disguised as the verification and replacement of Party cards and documents," had to come to its conclusion. This campaign, he held, was launched to make sure that "even the dumbest Party activists in the provinces finally understood what this business was all about." The Polish diplomat was also right to remark that those arrested posed no danger to the regime whatsoever. If they in fact did pose it, the Bolsheviks would surely not make that information public.[82]

He further elaborated on his views four days later in a paper prepared for the *Dwójka*: "This trial, as well as the surrounding campaign in the press, which is still ongoing, further bolsters my belief that nothing in particular has been recently discovered. Instead all kinds of misdeeds by various people from various periods, which had been meticulously catalogued over a long time, are being used—now that the right moment has come—for domestic propagandistic purposes to strengthen the

---

[81] CAW, Oddz. II SG, sygn. I.303.4.1956, n.p., doc. 32. Nawrocki provided other (fragmentary) data about the scale of the repressions. In the *Situation in Ukraine* report from February 14, 1937 "based on a credible source," he wrote that between January 20 and February 14, 1937, 1,500 to 2,000 persons were arrested in Right-Bank Ukraine, 75 percent of them in Kyiv oblast. In his next report on March 23, 1937, he wrote that the arrests had suddenly stopped in early March. Referring again to a credible source "verified on numerous occasions," he reported that in January, February and in early March, 4,500 to 5,000 Party members in Right-Bank Ukraine were arrested, 70 percent of them in Kyiv oblast, 15 percent in Vinnytsia oblast, 10 percent in Odesa oblast, 5 percent in Chernihiv oblast. Ibid., n.p., no document number.

[82] Ibid., sygn. I.303.4.3161, k. 343.

Stalinist regime by eradicating all uncertain elements that could become focal points of opposition in the future, which was something that the regime considered particularly undesirable and dangerous when all means and all forces had to be mobilized for war, which is something they are clearly getting more afraid of and are preparing themselves for, as if it were going to break out soon."[83]

Stanisław Sośnicki, the Polish consul in Kharkiv, painted a similar picture of the situation. In a paper written for the ambassador, "Purges in our Consular District from September 4, 1936," he emphasized that the trial of Zinoviev, Kamenev, and others had accelerated the wave of arrests. The key to understanding the purge was rooted in the fact that it applied to everyone who had the wrong kind of past biography, or to those who had already been penalized, not necessarily by the Party or by the law, but, for instance, administratively. Now it turned out that they were Trotskyites following the orders of some unidentified dark forces: "These arrests and scoldings are of a mass nature, do not spare a single administrative or 'social' area of life, nor do they spare the Party. If, in a particular sector, no well-known persons can be identified so as to be unmasked, then some old crimes and old names are dug out of the archive, refreshed, and placed in charge of a new group of criminals in a particular town or economic unit."[84]

If an "enemy of the people" was "uncovered," then his identity was made public in the press, on the radio, or at mass meetings. His biography was presented so as to provide unquestionable evidence that, in the past, this "uncovered enemy" had been a proponent of Trotsky or some other serious opponent of the Soviet regime. If the alleged "enemy" himself or herself was not conspiring now with the Trotskyites or other counterrevolutionary elements, then "surely" his relatives or close friends were.[85]

One typical example demonstrating how the mechanics of uncovering "the enemies of the people" worked was the case of the head of the city council in Dnipropetrovsk, Mykola Holubenko. Having already been removed from his post for administrative violations in 1935, when the "Trotskyite psychosis" began and "Trotskyites were uncovered" everywhere, he was declared as none other than a Trotskyite counterrevolutionary. Holubenko purportedly organized an entire

---

[83] Ibid., sygn. I.303.4.1985, doc. 35 (1936), n.p.
[84] Ibid., sygn. I.303.4.1867, k. 78.
[85] Ibid., k. 82.

counterrevolutionary group within the city's administration.[86] Typically, all the officials who were involved had a record of some sort of misdemeanor, e.g., financial misdeeds that contributed to the failure to fulfill the plans.[87]

Another victim of the witch hunt was the director of the Kryvorizhstal industrial complex, Iakov Vesnik, who had been lauded by the Soviet authorities only a year earlier (among other accolades, he received the Order of Lenin). Vesnik was charged with "rotten liberalism," which was manifested in his defense of enemies of the Party whom he decided to employ in the enterprise he directed. In August 1936, the Party Committee in Kryvyi Rih expelled him from the Party because he was the patron and manager of one of the sixteen accused in the first Moscow trial, the commercial director (in 1934 and 1935) of Kryvorizhstal, Efim Dreitser, who was executed after the trial. Vesnik was also accused of supplying financial aid to "class enemies."[88]

Sośnicki provided many similar examples from his consular district so typical of the mechanics of "searching for Trotskyites and other enemies."[89] Later he once again put forward the supposition[90] that the basis for the Kremlin's policy, despite all the "political camouflage colors," was economic in nature, i.e., the failure of particular factories and industrial sectors to fulfill the production quotas, the unfavorable attitude of the workers brought about by their miserable living conditions, and the like.[91] The repressions were designed to scare and mobilize the Soviet people to work more effectively. Sośnicki also wrote that other reasons apart from the economy, that motivated Stalin to go ahead with the purges were the November elections and the introduction of the new constitution.[92]

From January 23 to 30, 1937, another trial took place in Moscow, the "Parallel Anti-Soviet Trotskyite Center" trial, or the Trial of Seventeen. The main accused figures were Party dignitaries who had been members of the opposition in the past, such as Karl Radek, Iurii Piatakov, and Grigorii

---

[86] Mykola Holubenko was arrested and executed in February 1937; see hainyzhnyk.in.ua/doc2/1937%2802-06%29.spysok_pidsudnyh.php.

[87] CAW, Oddz. II SG, sygn. I.303.4.1867, k. 78–79.

[88] Ibid., k. 81. After the commissar of heavy industry, Sergo Ordzhonikidze, intervened, Vesnik was reinstituted as a Party member ten days later. He was arrested again on July 10, 1937, and shot on November 17. See www.centrasia.ru/person2.php?&st=1173735940.

[89] CAW, Oddz. II SG, sygn. I.303.4.1867, k. 81–86.

[90] See the report by Stanisław Sośnicki from August 17, 1936, cited earlier.

[91] CAW, Oddz. II SG, sygn. I.303.4.1867, k. 86.

[92] Ibid.

Sokolnikov. Of course, all the charges were fabricated. The trial was a farce. Indicative of this was the fact that even before the official sentences were uttered in the courtroom, the news that the accused would be executed were provided to the American press.[93]

The Polish embassy staff in Moscow tried to make sense of Stalin's motivation for organizing yet another political show trial. They came to the conclusion that it was a continuation of his dispute with Trotsky, who, after the first Moscow trial, wrote a popular book condemning Stalin, *La Révolution trahie*, published in Paris in 1936.[94] Trotsky claimed that Stalin betrayed the revolution's ideals, while Stalin—the embassy believed— attempted, with the Trial of Seventeen, to support a contrary thesis: that his government was the last bastion of socialism and that he was defending it against the restoration of capitalism, purportedly being prepared by Trotsky. It was "telling" that it was Trotskyism, not Hitler or fascism, that was identified as the main enemy: "Neither Hitler nor fascism, but Trotsky and his Fourth International, judging from this trial, seem to be the main enemy of the USSR."[95]

The head of the Second Department of the Main Staff, Colonel Tadeusz Pełczyński, came to a similar conclusion. He deduced, accurately, that it was impossible to understand the nature of the purge without considering the ongoing ideological strife between Trotsky and Stalin. This was an old, well-established dispute: was it possible to build socialism only in one country or not? Stalin thought that it was and decided to go ahead with the giant industrialization drive in the USSR. Trotsky believed that this task was impossible without the victory of a global revolution. The Spanish Civil War revitalized their dispute. The followers of Trotsky (the newly formed Fourth International) accused Stalin of insufficient support for the Spanish Republicans, which was fatal for the revolutionary cause in Spain. Pełczyński held that it was for the sake of winning that ideological struggle that the Trials of the Sixteen and the Seventeen were organized. They were designed to show how cynical and strongly connected to German intelligence the Trotskyite organizations were, thus discrediting and disarming them.[96]

---

[93] Dullin, *Stalin i ego diplomaty*, 209.

[94] English translation: *The Revolution Betrayed: What Is the Soviet Union and Where Is It Going*, originally published in 1937.

[95] AAN, MSZ, sygn. 6652 A, k. 10–11

[96] CAW, Oddz. II SG, lecture titled "Russia" given by the head of the Second Department of

Let us return to the theory put forward by the Polish diplomats in Moscow. We can agree with their explanation of the reasons behind the trial. One might also agree with their other theories, such as: that Stalin intended to get rid of all potential opposition as a prevention—to eliminate the remnants of the Bolshevik old guard, to turn the fictitious Trotskyite followers into scapegoats and blame them for the difficulties experienced in all sectors of the economy and for the accidents in factories and on the railroads. Another reason was to mobilize Soviet society to resist likely penetration by German and Japanese agents, who purportedly cooperated with Trotsky. Moreover, the embassy correctly predicted that Stalin was preparing another series of arrests and trials, this time against the "Right deviation" led by Nikolai Bukharin.[97] Other theories are debatable, however. According to Ambassador Grzybowski, who signed the document, "the zeal with which the Trotskyist opposition was suppressed" was proof of the fact that "oppositional moods were on the rise everywhere across the USSR." The data from Kyiv, Kharkiv, and Tbilisi was supposed to support this claim. They suggested that the arrests were very numerous and affected citizens from all social groups—from ordinary workers to university professors and Party dignitaries. The ambassador based his theory on the statement made at the end of the second Moscow trial by Karl Radek: "The Trotskyite organization has become the center of all counterrevolutionary forces in the country," and there were "half-Trotskyites" and "quarter-Trotskyites" who helped the "hundred-percent Trotskyites."[98] Radek's words, uttered in front of a Soviet court, should not be taken at face value. At the time, the accused pleaded guilty to all manner of sins, as the NKVD asked them to do. In addition to the data about the arrested Trotskyites that the ambassador quoted (which he received from the Polish consulates), other, more precise data were also available about the mechanisms that governed "the search for Trotskyites."[99] Those theories were somewhat similar to the ones Stanisław Nawrocki presented after the first Moscow trial: if arrests

---

the Main Staff during a course for higher-ranking military officers in Rembertów, December 1, 1937, k. 13. Piotr Kołakowski gave me the document (without the sygn. number).

[97] AAN, MSZ, sygn. 6652 A, k. 12–14; the same thesis was repeated in the next report, on February 9, 1937.

[98] Ibid., k. 11–12.

[99] See the previously cited reports by Stanisław Sośnicki on August 17 and September 4, 1936.

related to Trotskyism were underway, then it followed that some kind of Trotskyite, i.e., anti-Stalinist, opposition, must exist.[100]

When one ponders the question of whether any kind of opposition did in fact exist in the USSR at the time, all that could really be considered as opposition was deeply hidden intellectual opposition. At the time, the all-seeing NKVD was present virtually everywhere, making any kind of open oppositional activity barely thinkable. Citizens were persecuted, arrested, deported, and shot not for being active oppositionists, but for being potential ones—a peculiar kind of preventive repressive strategy. The logic behind the actions undertaken by the Stalinist regime was as follows: if someone had belonged, for example, to a circle of Trotsky sympathizers in the past, then, no matter how much he tried to pass for an honest Soviet citizen later, deep down he must have remained a follower of Trotsky and hostile to the Stalinist line. He had to be liquidated because, if a war broke out, such a citizen's behavior would be particularly unpredictable.

Jan Karszo-Siedlewski produced analyses of the second Moscow trial and similarly accurate predictions about future developments. On many scores, he agreed with Ambassador Grzybowski. On January 23, 1937, Karszo-Siedlewski wrote that the difficult economic situation was the main cause for the trials. The diplomat predicted that the USSR "had entered a new, likely long, phase of a harsh police state and state-executed terror as a means of forcing Soviet citizens to work harder and be more submissive."[101]

In a subsequent report to Grzybowski, dated February 1, 1937, Karszo-Siedlewski claimed that the Stakhanovite campaign, the Spanish Civil War, and the Sixteenth Congress of Soviets in the USSR had all been child's play compared with the campaign initiated by the Moscow trial. According to the diplomat, everything about the trials suggested that the struggle with Trotskyism was "a whole new political, economic, and social-educational program, oriented toward mobilizing Soviet society, mostly against Germany and Japan." The goal was to convince Soviet society that war was inevitable even if the USSR did not want it, and that it was going to be started by Japan and Germany. Both Japan and Germany were readying themselves for it through the recently uncovered

---

[100] This trope was examined further, in reaction to the third Moscow Trial, in the informational bulletin *Polska a Zagranica*, no. 4, April 4, 1938; see later sections in chapter 4.

[101] CAW, Oddz. II SG, sygn. I.303.4.1867, k. 509-510.

Trotskyites. Germany was ready for war and would be supported by Japan, Poland, and Italy.

The Polish diplomat wrote that there were a few motives behind this new campaign. First of all, Soviet society's attention had to be diverted away from the daily struggles of existence. Second, it was "the intention of Stalin's clique" to blame Trotskyites for all the failures in the economic sphere and the numerous accidents in mines, factories, and railways. Third, it was Stalin's real worry that the Trotskyite movement was developing not only in the USSR, but also in Spain, Mexico, France, and Czechoslovakia and that it could bring together the "old Bolsheviks," the founding fathers of the revolution. In the end, Jan Karszo-Siedlewski wrote once again that he thought the main reason behind the repressions in the USSR was the difficult economic and political situation. "Only if the harvest this year is sufficient, and the international situation clears up a little bit, can domestic relations then perhaps be relaxed."[102]

Another important moment in the development of the Stalinist purges was the so-called case of Marshal Mikhail Tukhachevsky.[103] Iona Iakir,[104] the commander of the Kyiv Military District, was also arrested and executed along with Tukhachevsky. Another wave of arrests of Red Army cadres and alleged associates of Tukhachevsky took place soon thereafter. Among the high-ranking Party officials who were somehow linked to Soviet Ukrainian affairs, Vsevolod Balytsky[105] of the NKVD in Soviet Ukraine, was one of those arrested shortly after the Tukhachevsky trial.

---

[102] Ibid., k. 516–19, 526. In the secret MFA bulletin *Polska a Zagranica*, no. 4 (February 15, 1937), the February 1, 1937 report from Jan Karszo-Siedlewski was attached to an article about the Trotskyites' trial; AAN, MSZ, sygn. 117, k. 74–84.

[103] The trial took place on June 11, 1937. All of the accused—Tukhachevsky, Iakir, Jeronimas Uborevičius, August Kork, Roberts Eidemanis, Boris Feldman, Vitalii Primakov, and Vytautas Putna—were sentenced to death and executed immediately.

[104] Iona Iakir (1896–1937) was a prominent Red Army commander who was put in charge of the Ukrainian (1925–37) and Kyiv (1935–37) Military Districts. TsDAHOU, f. 39, op. 4, spr. 241, ark. 34.

[105] Vsevolod Balytsky (1892–1937) was the head of the GPU (1923–31) and NKVD (1924–30) in Soviet Ukraine; the deputy head of the OGPU for the entire USSR (1931–34); a special emissary in Soviet Ukraine (November 1932–February 20, 1933) sent to ensure that the Kremlin's grain-requisitioning and delivery policy was implemented; the plenipotentiary and head of the OGPU there (February 21, 1933–July 1934); the head of the NKVD in Soviet Ukraine (July 1934–May 1937); and the director of the NKVD administration in the Soviet Far East (May 11–June 19, 1937). He was arrested on July 7, 1937, sentenced to death on November 27 in Moscow, and executed that very day. TsDAHOU, f. 39, op. 4, spr. 10, ark. 3. See also Iu. Shapoval and V. Zolotar'ov, *Vsevolod Balyts'kyi: Osoba, chas, otochennia* (Kyiv: Stylos, 2002).

Balytsky admitted that he was a participant in "Ukrainian Center of Conspiracy in the Army" together with Iona Iakir and other Party dignitaries, such as Mykola Popov,[106] Ilia Shelekhes,[107] Evgenii Veger,[108] and Mykola Demchenko.[109] Iakir purportedly recruited Balytsky.[110] Tukhachevsky was charged with treason and cooperation with German intelligence.[111] After the trial, the Polish vice-consul in Kyiv, Adam Koch, informed the Polish ambassador in Moscow that during the two nights of June 10–11 and 11–12, 1937, arrests of high-ranking military officers were conducted in Kyiv, including the commander of the city, Golubkov. According to the information the vice-consul received, the arrests of officers were conducted in the garrisons in Berdychiv and Zhytomyr.

---

[106] Mykola Popov (1891–1938) served as the agitation and propaganda secretary of the Central Committee of CP(B)U between 1933 and 1937. Between 1936 and 1937, he was a member of the CP(B)U's Politburo. He was arrested in June 1937 and executed in February 1938. Popov's rehabilitated in March 1956. TsDAHOU, f. 39, op. 4, spr. 161, ark. 7.

[107] Ilia Shelekhes (1891–1937) headed the Kharkiv Oblast and City Soviets (March 1933–May 1934) and was a member of the CP(B)U's Central Committee (April 1933–July 1937); the deputy head of Soviet Ukraine's Council of People's Commissars (April 1934–July 1937); and a candidate member (April 1933–May 1936) and full member (May 1936–July 1937) of the CP(B)U's Politburo. He was arrested on June 23, 1937; sentenced to death on September 2, 1937, and executed the next day. See www.mke.su/doc/ShELEKhES%20IS.html.

[108] Evgenii Veger (1899–1937) was the first secretary of the CP(B)U in Odesa oblast (February 1933–July 1937), a member of the CP(B)U's Central Committee, and a candidate member of its Politburo from February 1933 to June 1937. He was arrested on June 25, 1937 and executed on November 27, 1937. TsDAHOU, f. 39, op. 4, spr. 27, ark. 1–2.

[109] Mykola Demchenko (1896–1937) was a member of the CP(B)U's Central Committee (1927–37); the people's commissar of agriculture of Soviet Ukraine (1929–32); the Party's first secretary in Kyiv oblast and city (1932–34) and Kharkiv oblast and city (1934–36); a candidate member (1928–31) and member (1931–37) of the CP(B)U Politburo; and the USSR's deputy people's commissar of agriculture (1936–37) and people's commissar of state farms (1937). He was arrested on 22 July 1937, sentenced to death on 29 October 1937, and executed in Moscow. TsDAHOU, f. 39, op.4, spr. 56, ark. 1-19.

[110] A. Iakovlev et al, eds., *Lubianka: Stalin i Glavnoe upravlenie gosbezopasnosti NKVD. Arkhiv Stalina. Dokumenty vysshikh organov partiinoi i gosudarstvennoi vlasti. 1937–1938* (Moscow: Mezhdunarodnyi fond "Demokratiia," 2004), 257–58.

[111] For more information about the Tukhachevsky trial and the purges that followed, see P. P. Wieczorkiewicz, *Sprawa Tuchaczewskiego* (Warsaw: Gryf, 1994); idem, *Łańcuch śmierci: Czystka w Armii Czerwonej 1937–1939*, (Warsaw: Rytm, 2001); Conquest, *The Great Terror*, 182–213; and O. Suvenirov, *Tragediia RKKA, 1937–1938* (Moscow: Terra, 1998).

After the officers were detained, their families were immediately evicted from their apartments.[112]

The accusations Soviet prosecutors made and the trials they organized had nothing to do with reality. The Polish MFA had no doubt that there was no conspiracy to speak of—that it all had to do with Stalin's desire to remove all his potential opponents. After Jan Szembek received information about Tukhachevsky's and the other arrests, he sent an encrypted message, first to the Polish embassy in Tokyo and then to other Polish embassies, in which he rejected the possibility that the official Soviet story of the accused being involved in espionage was true. He believed that Stalin's main motive was to strengthen his own position and eliminate internal opposition to "the overall difficulties of the system close by in the background." The mood of opposition in the Red Army, Szembek speculated, created the possibility for a coup d'état.[113]

During his lecture to high-ranking military leaders in Rembertów on December 1, 1937, Tadeusz Pełczyński emphasized that the Tukhachevsky case had nothing to do with protecting the military against the Party's influence. The accused individuals were sentenced because they represented the war camp, criticized Stalin's opportunistic foreign policy, and requested determined measures "even if they were going to provoke a major military clash."[114]

Another interesting opinion was voiced by Lieutenant Colonel Antoni Szymański, the Polish military attaché in Berlin. He reflected on the German military command's reaction to Tukhachevsky's execution on June 17, 1937, after a conversation with Lieutenant Colonel Walter Scheller, one of the most qualified German officers in the field of Soviet affairs, according to Szymański: Scheller was the head of the foreign section in the HQ (*Wehrmachtsamt*) of the war ministry. Szymański reported on the conversation to the head of the *Dwójka*. Scheller had reported directly to Field Marshal Werner von Blomberg about the executions of Tukhachevsky and other high-ranking officers. The marshal's response was that Stalin had "executed his best and only leaders, whose posts will be inherited by military amateurs."[115]

---

[112] CAW, Oddz. II SG, sygn. I.303.4.1867, k. 613.

[113] AAN, MSZ, sygn. 6669, k. 52; Ibid., k. 53.

[114] The lecture "Russia" by the head of the Second Department of the Main Staff at a course for high-ranking military officers in Rembertów, December 1, 1937, k. 17–18.

[115] CAW, Oddz. II SG, sygn. I.303.4.3181, k. 58–59.

Lieutenant Colonel Scheller maintained a quietly welcoming attitude toward the recent events in the USSR. About what he had to say, Szymański wrote, "one could detect the overall mood present among the military leadership of the Reich." The assessment of the mass arrests and executions in the USSR within German military circles was that it was "a manifestation of overall internal decay, [a measure that] was going to make it impossible for the Russians to intervene in foreign affairs in the next several years." Scheller said that Germany did not share the opinion of the former Japanese military attaché in Moscow, Colonel Hikosaburo Hata, that the executions and the trials would strengthen the Soviet forces.[116]

Military Attaché Szymański also described the reactions of other foreign representatives in Berlin to the Tukhachevsky trial. The British and French representatives had no particular opinion on the subject. The military attaché of Czechoslovakia fully trusted his Soviet colleague and believed that cooperation between the executed Soviet military officers and the Germans was a fact.[117]

The deaths of Marshal Tukhachevsky and the other Soviet military leaders initiated a wave of massive purges within the Red Army, which, of course, could not have had a positive impact on the army's capacity for military action. According to official data, 33,947 military officrs were dismissed from their posts during 1937–38, and 7,280 of them were arrested.[118] Such precise data was something that neither the Polish nor any other intelligence service had access to. Knowledge of the disappearance of the highest-ranking leaders was something that was available[119] simply because their absence was so evident.[120] In general, however, obtaining any kind of information about the internal situation in the Red Army became extremely difficult. In communiqué no. 1, dated

---

[116] Ibid., k. 59.

[117] Ibid., k. 60.

[118] Petrov and Jansen, "Stalinskii pitomets" 84.

[119] In addition to the execution of three of the five marshals (Vasilii Blücher and Aleksandr Egorov were executed along with Tukhachevsky), the same happened to six of the twelve members of the Supreme Military Council and to all the commanders of the military districts. By the end of 1938, only 39 percent of the officers who had been in their posts in early 1937 remained. See Wieczorkiewicz, Łańcuch śmierci, 93–178; P. Kołakowski, Czas próby, 28; A. Pepłoński, Organizacja i działalność Referatu "Wschód" Oddziału II Sztabu Głównego WP (Warsaw: Wyd. Urząd Ochrony Państwa, 1994), 118; Włodarkiewicz, Przed 17 września, 194; and Musiał, Na Zachód, 293–97.

[120] RGVA, f. 464, op. 1, d. 2427, l. 11–12.

July 1938, about the Armed Forces of the Soviet Union by the Second Department of the Main Staff, which its head, Colonel Pełczyński, sent to the most important Polish state figures and institutions responsible for national security, we read: "The purge conducted in the army is being carefully hidden from the eyes of those who should not be seeing it. Hence we have very fragmentary data about it. They allow us to conclude, however, that the scale of the current purge is significantly larger than anything that the Soviet army has seen so far."[121]

As a result of the purge, new and inexperienced officers were promoted to higher posts. They often lacked the necessary qualifications.[122] The only criterion critical to an officer's promotion was whether he supported the Stalinist policy and contributed to annihilating its enemies sufficiently. As pointed out in military communiqué no. 1, Brigade Commander (KomBrig) Ivan Evseev was a good example of this process. When he was merely twenty-seven years old, he became a general.[123]

The purges and promotions of young, inexperienced officers were, from Warsaw's point of view, taken to imply a weakening of the Red Army. In the same report, we read: "these kinds of personnel changes must have a negative influence on the level of the troops' military training, discipline, and quality of provisioning."[124]

Polish intelligence officers examined the purges in the Red Army and concluded that it had lost the capacity for major offensive action. In a lecture Colonel Józef Smoleński, Pełczyński's successor as head of the *Dwójka*, gave in a course for high-ranking military leaders in Rembertów on November 29, 1938, he said: "The current crisis has clearly affected the armed forces of the USSR. The Red Army's value has been undermined through the decapitation of its experienced leadership and the introduction of collective command."[125] Next Colonel Smoleński said that "under these conditions, it becomes clear that the overall capacity of the USSR in 1938 has further decreased." He pointed to the Czechoslovak

---

[121] Ibid., l. 11.

[122] See Wieczorkiewicz, *Łańcuch śmierci*, 998–99.

[123] RGVA, f. 464, op. 1, d. 2427, l. 13–14. General Evseev was born in 1910. He joined the army in 1929, earlier than was written in the communiqué. He took part in the Spanish Civil War. During World War II, he first commanded an air force corps, then the Caucasian Front of Anti-Aircraft Defense. See Wieczorkiewicz, *Łańcuch śmierci*, 999.

[124] RGVA, f. 464 k, op. 1, d. 2427, l. 14. The Polish press also covered this issue. See Romanek, *Totalitaryzm sowiecki w ocenie*, 102–3.

[125] RGVA, f. 464 k, op. 1, d. 3018, l. 22.

crisis as evidence supporting this thesis. At the time, the USSR did not do anything beyond saber rattling. "In conclusion, the USSR's stance during the last European crisis left no illusions about the real capacity of that country, both among its friends and enemies."[126]

On July 23, 1937, Jan Karszo-Siedlewski wrote to the ambassador in Moscow that "he did not intend to analyze the reasons that encouraged Stalin to go ahead with such a radical purge of the Party apparat." The reasons were numerous, the diplomat wrote. At this stage, it was impossible to decide which one of them was decisive: "Only more precise, verified knowledge could decide in favor of this or that thesis, but this knowledge seeps through to the public domain very slowly, and we will have to wait before we put together the right kind of diagnosis."[127]

Karszo-Siedlewski categorically denied that there was any kind of conspiracy present in Soviet Ukraine and stated that most of the arrested Party dignitaries never belonged to any oppositional group or ever committed any wrongful acts—and, in any case, "cannot be considered responsible for some offenses they are charged with; if there were any failures they played a part in, they were caused by the systemic conditions created by the Stalinist regime."

Then, however, in contrast to the caution he displayed in the first part of his analysis, Karszo-Siedlewski tried to explain Stalin's decision to go ahead with the purges. The diplomat wrote that one must not ask the question "why he took this particular step," but rather "what this step is supposed to achieve." He elaborated on this distinction in the following way. In the domestic situation that he had created, Stalin perceived "the necessity to implement a series of far-reaching measures or reforms of social or economic nature, for which the ground has to be cleared beforehand and the opinion of his own citizens suitably preformed." Consequently, not only opposition but any kind of criticism, especially if coming from the old Bolsheviks, could be harmful to the regime, and this explained their liquidation.[128]

A month later, on August 21, 1937, Karszo-Siedlewski sent a report to Ambassador Grzybowski, that dealt with "the general situation in Soviet Ukraine.[129] He wrote that the purpose of the purges had become more

---

[126] RGVA, f. 464 k, op. 1, d. 3018, l. 23.

[127] CAW, Oddz. II SG, sygn. I.303.4.1867, k. 695.

[128] Ibid., k. 696.

[129] As mentioned in chapter 2, in his letter to the Second Department two days later (August

evident. According to him, the purpose was to remove the more independent and influential people from the Party and government apparat, especially those who could refer to their actions during the revolutionary period to justify their right to criticize the government's current measures. "The campaign to uncover the deleterious activity of the enemy of the people became a scarecrow that, similar to the Stakhanovite movement back in the day, was designed, on the one hand, to increase the people's production efficiency, and, on the other, to suppress awareness of the scale of abuse and the already widespread negligence within the Russian nation, both in professional obligations and for the personal necessities of life."[130]

Karszo-Siedlewski's prior beliefs about the purge were confirmed by the trip he made around Soviet Ukraine (he visited, among others, Zhytomyr, Berdychiv, Vinnytsia, Balta, Odesa, Mykolaiv, Kherson, Simferopol, Sevastopol, and Yalta) from August 9 to 19, 1937, when he had the opportunity to talk with ordinary people. He was able to outsmart the NKVD agents tailing him and lost them en route from Kyiv to Odesa. He wrote: "One is under the impression that Stalin was victorious in this campaign. He was able not only to expel some inconvenient people from the Party apparat, but ... also to replace them with new ones, young and fully submissive to his will. Most importantly, this process has been completed without any major upheavals that would normally have been seen as unavoidable in any normal European country where logical reasoning still abides. Once again I believe that Stalin knows his people very well and he knows exactly what he can afford. The reorganized, or, to be more precise, the newly organized, managerial apparat of the Party, the military, the state administration, and the economy still operate normally, not worse and not much differently, but they are more afraid now; thus they have become more cautious and leery of any kind of initiative."[131]

The fact that Stalin was a "skillful psychologist" was something Karszo-Siedlewski had already noted. On August 1, 1937, he wrote in a

---

23, 1937), Karszo-Siedlewski called this report "the essentials of his views on the Soviet Union and the group of people that rules it." He stressed: "It is a kind of last will and testament of mine in the field of Soviet affairs, and, at the same time, my last report before I return to Warsaw [the diplomat did write a few more reports in September 1937, after his return to Warsaw], unless something extraordinary happens, which I doubt" (Ibid., sygn. I.303.4.1985, doc. 22 [1937]).

[130] Ibid., sygn. I.303.4.1867, k. 624.

[131] Ibid., k. 626.

letter to Ambassador Grzybowski: "Stalin is a good psychologist, who knows the Russian nation very well and counts on its passivity and the generally low intellectual level among the masses, thus calculating accurately how far he can execute his dictatorial will without meeting resistance. Here I would like to turn your attention to the fact that during the excessively rash collectivization drive of 1932–33 [*sic*], Stalin found himself in a no less difficult situation and, when it came to Ukraine, surely in a much more difficult one than the current one, and somehow he was able to muddle through it, even if all of us who observed those events directly were under the impression that the entire USSR, and Stalin himself, was on the edge of the abyss. Currently it also seems that he has won this campaign as well, or, at the very least, that he has temporarily strengthened his domestic political position."[132]

From March 2 to 13, 1938, the last public show trial took place in Moscow—the trial against the "Anti-Soviet Bloc of Rightists and Trotskyites," or the Trial of the Twenty-One. Among the accused were Nikolai Bukharin, Stalin's ally in the struggle with the so-called Left Opposition; Alexei Rykov, the former chief of the Council of People's Commissars of the USSR; and Genrikh Yagoda, Yezhov's predecessor as head of the NKVD.

There is the least amount of information in the Polish archives about this trial compared to the previous two trials. The reports of the *Dwójka* and the MFA are not numerous. The *Dwójka's* report of April 21, 1938 stated that the reason for this trial was similar to that of the two previous trials: it was rooted in the "nexus of the growing conflict between Stalin and Trotsky to win support of the international proletariat; in the domestic arena, it was Stalin's reaction to the anomalies of Soviet life, which grew in intensity during the recent political crisis in the Party."[133] Why was the emphasis distributed in this way? The authors of the report noted that, in 1937 Stalin's goal of compromising Trotsky and his Fourth International had not been achieved. The campaign that began in 1936 and was continued in 1937 during the great Moscow show trials resulted in growing strife between the Stalinists and the Trotskyites, but it did not lead to a defeat of the Fourth International. Furthermore, in order to acquit himself of the charges of betrayal of the world revolution, Trotsky staged a political trial that was a direct response to Stalin's actions. In that trial,

---

[132] Ibid., k. 668,

[133] RGVA, f. 464 k, op. 1, d. 2424 A, l. 1b; see also Ibid., d. 3018, l. 4–5.

which took place in New York, Trotsky played the role of the accused and, relying on witnesses and substantial evidence, proved that the charges brought against him were groundless. As a consequence, an international commission composed of well-known American leftist activists, among whom there were no Trotsky followers, came to the conclusion that the Moscow trials were staged and that Trotsky was not guilty of the charges brought against him. Moreover, Trotsky wrote a book titled *Stalin's Crimes*.[134] In response, Stalin decided to engineer another trial in which Trotsky remained the main culprit. Of those accused physically present in Moscow, Nikolai Bukharin was the main figure.

The other reason behind the trial was economic, that is, blaming Bukharin and other alleged agents of foreign-intelligence services for the economic failures. They were charged with acting on orders from foreign powers to damage the Soviet economy.[135]

Based on the MFA's information bulletin *Polska a Zagranica* (Poland and Abroad) no. 5 (April 4, 1938), it is possible to conclude that the MFA interpreted this trial as they had the previous ones—as a continuation of Stalin's struggle with the old Bolshevik guard. However, the demeanor of the main person accused in this trial, Nikolai Bukharin, became famous because it differed from how most of the other victims behaved. He openly debated, even criticized, the charges brought against him. The *Dwójka* took note of his behavior, and it was covered in the information bulletin of the MFA: "Bukharin's speech made quite an impression in the courtroom,"[136] they reported.

Of course, the Polish analysts had no doubt that this trial, like the previous ones, was a sheer farce, even if the possibility did exist that Bukharin or any of the other accused could have seized power if a Kremlin coup took place. Bukharin's stance was certainly a novel one. He did not, as his predecessors had, submissively plead guilty to all the charges brought against him, but started to debate them. Others among the accused, for example Genrikh Yagoda and Khristian Rakovsky, rejected some of the charges. Their attitude, coupled with other external voices questioning the charges, as was noted in the bulletin, "further strengthened our belief that the alleged facts and circumstances presented in this trial, similarly to what happened in all the previous ones, were pure

---

[134] Polish translation: L. Trocki, *Zbrodnie Stalina* (Warsaw: Biblioteka Polska, 1937).
[135] RGVA, f. 464 k, op. 1, d. 2424 A, l. 1, 6–7.
[136] AAN, MSZ, sygn. 119, k. 177; see also RGVA, f. 464 k, op. 1, d. 2424 A, l. 16.

fantasy that had nothing to do with reality. The old 'method' has not changed."[137]

As with the previous trials, economic reasons were mentioned as one of the causes. The authors' belief was that one of Stalin's motives was to blame the "enemies of the people" for all kinds of economic problems: "Stalin intended to divert the people's discontent caused by all the Kremlin's shortcomings; according to the old recipe, he wanted once more to make the people believe that those shortcomings were caused by a conscious and systematic campaign of sabotage run by elements hostile to the Soviet state, that is, the opposition. Stalin wanted to kill two birds with one stone, i.e., to absolve himself of responsibility and to morally discredit the opposition. The opposition became the sole guilty actor and the scapegoat for all the economic difficulties of the Soviet state."[138]

The authors of the bulletin ridiculed the charges brought against the accused, such as: the preparation of terrorist acts, espionage for capitalist countries (Germany, Japan, Great Britain, Poland, the United States, Italy), or the desire to overthrow the Communist system. At the same time, the authors believed that the existence of this process meant that "a serious, even if disorganized" opposition composed of people occupying higher posts in the Party, government, army, trade unions, and co-ops did exist.[139] This thesis was, of course, exaggerated. Bukharin and Rykov used to be Stalin's opponents (the Right Opposition), but after they condemned their factional activity in 1929,[140] they no longer engaged in any serious actions directed against Stalin. People from various walks of Soviet life were brought together just because at some point in the past they had not shared Stalin's opinion. This fact alone could not serve as evidence that those people formed some kind of oppositional group at the time of their

---

[137] AAN, MSZ, sygn. 119, k. 178–81.

[138] Ibid., k. 183–84.

[139] Ibid., k. 181–83.

[140] In February 1929, a joint session of the Politburo and the Central Commission of Control supported Stalin in his struggle against the Bukharin group. In April 1929, Bukharin and Tomsky were dismissed from their editorial posts at *Pravda* and in the Comintern. In November 1929, the plenum of the CC removed Bukharin from the Politburo, and Rykov and Tomsky received a warning that "if their activity was going to be directed against the main line of the Party," then appropriate measures would be taken against them. On November 25, 1929, Rykov, Bukharin, and Tomsky issued a statement, published in *Pravda* a day later. All three agreed with the Party line; *Pravda*, April 4, November 18 and 26, 1929.

arrest, and certainly not that they were engaged in planning a "palace coup."

The figure that linked the Moscow center with Ukraine was Hryhorii Hrynko, the commissar for finance of the USSR from 1930 to 1937. In the past, he had been a member of the Ukrainian party of Borotbists, and later he was charged with being one of the leaders of the Oleksander Shumsky group.[141] After that group was disbanded, Hrynko, allegedly with the assistance of Panas Liubchenko, joined a new organization, whose purpose, just as every other Soviet indictment stated, was to win independence for Ukraine.[142]

To sum up, the Polish foreign service, especially its diplomats, generated fairly accurate analyses and predictions about the causes of the purges that targeted Party members and other social groups (more details will be discussed in later parts of this chapter). One exception to their accuracy was the overestimation of the significance of the real opposition against Stalin. Other than that, their opinions about the nature of the Stalinist Terror were principally correct, if not at all particular junctures. Stalin's main goal was to eliminate his potential rivals and opponents, both in the Party and in society as a whole. This theme is pursued quite often in the Polish reports, even if they were not entirely clear on the issue that it was not only Stalin's personal power that was at stake during the purges, but also, de facto, war preparations. The exception to this rule was Jan Karszo-Siedlewski's remarks about the Soviet system as a whole.[143]

---

[141] Oleksander Shumsky (1890–1946) was the commissar for education in Soviet Ukraine (1924–27) and a proponent of greater autonomy and independence of the republic and the CP(B)U from Moscow's influence. His views (so-called Shumskyism) were condemned as nationalist, and in 1927 he had to resign from his post and leave Ukraine. He was arrested in Leningrad on May 13, 1933, charged with heading a counterrevolutionary organization called the Ukrainian Military Organization (UMO), and sentenced to ten years in the Gulag, even though he did not plead guilty. Immediately after the sentence, Shumsky began fighting to win his freedom back. After many appeals and letters (including to Stalin), his labor-camp sentence was changed to exile in Krasnoiarsk. In October 1937, he was arrested again for alleged counterrevolutionary activity. After two years, in November 1939, the investigation was closed, but his old sentence (the UMO case) remained valid. His deportation came to an end in 1943, and he spent the next three years in a hospital. In June 1946, he arrived in Saratov. Following a failed suicide attempt, he embarked on a trip to Kyiv but died en route on September 18, 1946. See Shapoval, *Ukraïna 20-50-kh rokiv*, 134–44; and Kuśnierz, *Ukraina w latach kolektywizacji*, 292.

[142] AAN, MSZ, sygn. 119, k. 187–88.

[143] See chapter 2 section 3.

Stalin wanted to make Soviet society more united, for example by eliminating "fifth columns," which, according to him, were composed of members of the national minorities and all those who had the "wrong kind" of social background or been previously politically involved, and could become "activated" against the state in the event of a war with one of the capitalist countries.[144]

Of importance in the Polish analyses of reasons for the purges were economic difficulties. In retrospect, in conjunction with the insights gleaned from Soviet archives, it needs to be emphasized that economic problems were not the most important cause of the Great Terror. Even so, repressions were also considered helpful in providing an explanations and perhaps in solving some economic problems. The harmful activities of the alleged "enemies of the people" were often given as explanation for all kinds of problems in everyday existence. Stalin had new scapegoats at his disposal, who could be blamed for the failure to fulfill apartment construction plans, insufficient supplies for the cities, and the scarcity of the most basic products, such as clothing, shoes, furniture, bicycles, flashlights, chairs, tables, children's goods, nails, and so on. The sentenced "enemies of the people" purportedly acted on the orders of countries hostile to the USSR. The terror perpetrated against those enemies also served as a means of mobilizing society. The important ideological struggle with Trotsky and his foreign proponents should also not be forgotten. The trials were designed to highlight the connections between the worst enemies of the "happy proletariat" and Leon Trotsky and his followers at the forefront.

Ambassador Wacław Grzybowski wrote in a November 15, 1937 report to the MFA that, based on reports he received and on his own observations, the terror in the USSR had two goals. The first was to eliminate all real and potential enemies of the regime. The ambassador's analysis did not go beyond the issue of Stalin's personal struggle for power; he did not see that the purge as a whole was also part of preparing the USSR for a future war. The second goal, according to Grzybowski, was to "attempt to repair and mobilize the bureaucratic and economic apparat, the sole actor now deciding the success or failure of Stalin's authoritarianism." This "repair" was supposed to be accomplished by replacing the old Bolsheviks with new people, who knew no system

---

[144] See Kuromiya, *Głosy straconych*, 12–13; idem, "Stalin's Great Terror and International Espionage"; and Vasyliev, "Vplyv 'velykoho teroru,' " 54.

apart from the one in which they grew up. Grzybowski also expected, wrongly, that the changes taking place in the USSR were bound to have a negative impact on its international position: that is, its relations with democratic countries could be damaged and Moscow's isolation could increase.[145]

As Marek Kornat has noted, Grzybowki's opinions did not differ from the ones voiced by the leadership of the MFA—Minister Józef Beck, Jan Szembek, Tadeusz Kobylański, and Stanisław Zabiełło.[146] The MFA embraced the same point of view (which the Second Department also shared), which meant that the most important goal of the purges—war preparation, understood as the elimination of the highest possible number of hypothetical internal enemies before its outbreak—was not one they appreciated. The secret informational bulletin *Polska a Zagranica*, no. 3, from March 9, 1938, included an article titled "The USSR on the Eve of 1938." On the motives that drove Stalin to initiate the mass purges, the authors wrote that the causes of such "a brutal and radical showdown" were multifold but could be reduced to one common denominator: Stalin was anxious that his old comrades, who had helped him to take power, could, for "ideological or opportunistic" reasons, turn against him. Stalin worried that "a danger could arise in the midst of that group that could threaten his personal position," the authors wrote. "For as long as Stalin had to wage a war against his opponents without having his own position secured, he had to rely on complicated maneuvers and limit himself to removing them from top positions, perhaps including deportation. Currently, with the rudder of power firmly in Stalin's grip, what we are seeing is the logical conclusion of all authoritarian regimes," they wrote, "i.e., the physical elimination of the dictator's enemies and competitors, the removal of powerful individuals who could focus the opposition, discrediting them and their ideology by means of treason charges in order to scare all those who were thinking about resisting his will, or even those who were inclined to evaluate his political tactics independently." The MFA, akin to what the Polish diplomats working in the USSR were writing, believed that the cause for the purges was to be found in economic considerations, i.e., in the "desire to make the economic life of the country more efficient."[147]

---

[145] AAN, MSZ, sygn. 6669, k. 27–34.
[146] Kornat, *Polska 1939 roku*, 214.
[147] AAN, MSZ, sygn. 119, k. 63–65.

Finally, it is worth mentioning that the Polish press held similar views on the Great Purge as the ones shared by the MFA and Polish military intelligence. Generally, no one believed the charges brought against the accused. Among the several explanations given for Stalin's actions, the following were frequently cited: Stalin's desire to discredit Trotsky; to divert society's attention away from economic problems, explaining those problems as the purported activity of enemies who had to be eliminated; and to make society anxious about looming foreign aggression, which was calculated to encourage mobilization in favor of war.[148]

4.3. Repressions of Communist Dignitaries

The January 1938 plenum of the Central Committee of the All-Union Communist Party issued a decree titled "On the mistakes of Party units in the process of removing Communists from the Party, on the formalistic-bureaucratic attitude with respect to the appeals of the individuals removed from the Party, and on the means to eliminate these shortcomings."[149] It ended the massive repressions against Party members that had begun in 1934 and continued with varying intensity since. The decree announced that the plenum wished to turn the attention of Party units and their heads to the fact that, during the purge of "Trotskyite-rightist agents of fascism" from the Party, many mistakes were made that now made it difficult for the Party to get rid of hypocritical members (*dvurushniki*), spies, and wreckers. "It is high time to understand that Bolshevik vigilance was about the ability to uncover the enemy no matter how cunning and able he was, no matter what his disguise was, but it was not about the wholesale removal of tens or hundreds of members who happened to be at hand, 'just to be on the safe side' and without proper investigation [*razbor*]." In other words, the policy of mass expulsions from the Party was criticized, and the blame for these "excesses" — apart from the "traditional enemies," such as disguised (*zamaskirovannye*) "enemies of the people," hypocrites, wreckers — was put on the "camouflaged Communists-opportunists" who, as described earlier, "were trying to

---

[148] For more information on this topic, see Tokarz, "Interpretacje genezy 'Wielkiej Czystki' "; and idem, "Architekt terroru," 144–54.

[149] "Ob oshibkakh partorganizatsii pri iskliuchenii kommunistov iz partii, o formal'no-biurokraticheskom otnoshenii k apellatsiiam iskliuchonnykh iz VKP(b) i o merakh po ustraneniiu etikh nedostatkov: Postanovlenie Plenuma TsK VKP(b)," *Pravda*, January 19, 1938.

distinguish and promote themselves by removing [the Communists] from the Party, by repressing Party members. Taking this opportunity, they are trying to defend themselves from the possible accusation of the lack of vigilance by applying repressions en masse against Party members."[150]

Before the repressions of Communist Party members could be considerable limited by the January 1938 decree, the number of Party and government members who had already been accused of perpetrating "crimes" and shot after suitable evidence was "obtained" was very high. The fabrication of new scandals and conspiracies took place by forcing the accused to submit self-accusatory confessions, usually through physical coercion. In these confessions, the prisoners not only pleaded guilty to various, sometimes quite odd or downright unbelievable counterrevolutionary actions, but they were also forced to name their associates. When the accused persons were tortured, they were forced not only to confirm names that the NKVD officials asked them about, but also to confess the names of "associates" themselves, such as the people who purportedly recruited them to join this or that so-called criminal organization, or the ones they had allegedly recruited to work for that organization. New "enemies of the people" were uncovered this way, as were entire "spy networks" and "anti-Soviet groups." Normally, "enemies of the people" were to be found in close vicinity to the accused — at work or among family members or friends.[151] During the

---

[150] Ibid.

[151] The manner in which the Soviet security apparat fabricated the "existence of anti-Soviet groups" is accurately described in a statement made by I. Hladky, an official in the Soviet Ukrainian People's Commissariat for Agriculture. Arrested in 1938, he remembered those events many years later: "They took me for a hearing in the evening. I entered the cabinet. The investigator had a large file on the table. I understood the file was not on me, but a psychological game had begun nonetheless. He browsed the file, looked at me, and feigned surprise when looking at how bad my 'misdemeanours' were, exclaiming 'ohs' and 'aha.' A curse word was hanging in the air. Then the investigator stood up and hit me hard [with his fist]. I fell back. He raised me and took me back to the table. 'Here's the paper, write here. Who recruited you?' I was not allowed to sleep for three nights. The same scenario was repeated over and over again. It was unbearable. I began to hallucinate. Finally, I don't know why, I sat down and began to write. They gave me some food, allowed me to sleep. When I was summoned again to take one more look at my notes, I could not believe my eyes. There were names of my friends written down on the paper in my handwriting. I was in such a state that I could not remember how I had done it. No,

period of heightened purges and terror, no one could be sure of his or her fate. A dignitary, or a rank-and-file Party member who was promoted thanks to the fact that his predecessor was arrested and charged with being "the enemy of the people," could also be arrested at any time. In the March 9, 1938 issue of the information bulletin *Polska a Zagranica*, the following apt remark was included: "Some kind of failure in a field where action was required by the authorities, a failure whose roots were deep in the previous period, or some kind of an ambiguous moment in the thick volumes of investigative documents produced daily in the prisons of the GPU [*sic*], leads to yet another downfall of a newly appointed dignitary; his place is taken by increasingly less experienced and less prominent activists.... At first anyone who had any kind of close association with the already eliminated enemy of the people is arrested or deported. Next some very old cases are dug up in the GPU archives, and those people who had committed any misdeeds offending Soviet authority over the past two decades, even if they had become the most loyal among Stalin's subjects since then, are targeted."[152]

The climate of purges and terror bred uncertainty and agitation among the Soviet Party and state apparat. No one could be sure that the NKVD was not busy fabricating a case against him at the moment. Anyone could be suddenly accused of counterrevolutionary deeds, thrown out of the Party, and perhaps arrested and shot. In June 1937, Consul Tadeusz Brzeziński saw the representative of the PCfFA in Kharkiv, Pavel Nekunde, and noticed that the Soviet official was clearly agitated and uncertain of his own fate, a typical phenomenon within the entire Soviet apparat at the time. Nekunde did not hesitate to share his thoughts with the consul and said that his professional position could soon see some major changes, "because everything was possible in this system."[153]

Employees of the Polish posts in the USSR tried to estimate the magnitude of the number of arrests in their reports. They could not do so

---

this cannot happen this way, I thought, I tore everything to pieces. Of course, what followed was a scandal and threats." Cited in Shapoval, "Peredden' i apohei Velykoho teroru," 477.

[152] AAN, MSZ, sygn. 119, k. 67–68.

[153] Ibid., sygn. 6669, k. 56. Nekunde's forebodings were not groundless. He was arrested on December 10, 1937, and sentenced to execution on February 17, 1938. The sentence was carried out. See www.centrasia.ru/person2.php?&st=1255467340.

precisely, of course, because they had no access to the relevant data. This was especially true for their estimations of the purges within the NKVD apparat. Essentially no major analysis of the purges in the NKVD organs can be found in the Polish records, not only in Soviet Ukraine but also from the entire USSR. In general, no information about this issue can be found at all.[154] On the other hand, Polish observers had no problem finding out who from among the highest echelons of power was arrested. It was enough to follow the press daily or take note of those who were absent from major public events. The first hint was that a given figure was no longer mentioned in the press, almost as if that person had never existed.[155] After some time, a longer publication or a

---

[154] On April 6, 1937, Tadeusz Jankowski, the chargé d'affaires at the Polish embassy in Moscow, signed a report prepared by Stanisław Głuski and addressed to Minister Józef Beck. In the report, Głuski informed the head of the MFA that, on April 3, 1937, the former head of the NKVD, Genrikh Yagoda, was suddenly dismissed from his post as commissar of communications in the USSR and that his case was under investigation. It was "the sensational news of the day here," bigger even than the dismissal of long-time deputy commissar of the PCfFA, Nikolai Krestinsky. Głuski wrote that after Yagoda's dismissal as head of the NKVD, it seemed that he "would see the end of his days" in the post of communications commissar. Trying to guess the motives that lay behind Yagoda's dismissal, "it seemed unlikely that some new facts about Yagoda's criminal activity were found, facts that were not known a year ago." The report's author was also not able to predict whether Yagoda was going to be judged in a show trial or whether he would be sentenced quietly. He believed that Yagoda's arrest was "an educational measure" for other Communist dignitaries and an example for the masses, demonstrating that no one was above punishment if he committed a crime. AAN, MSZ, sygn. 6652 A, k. 26–27. The Polish embassy in Moscow reported on Yagoda's arrest a few days after the fact, which took place on March 29, 1937. It was only two days later that Stalin's signature found its way to the relevant Politburo document sanctioning the arrest of the former commissar. RGANI, f. 89, op. 48, d. 2, l. 1. See also Petrov and Jansen, "Stalinskii pitomets", 74.

[155] Nikita Khrushchev described this situation accurately in his memoirs. He wrote of the "disappearance" of Stanislav Kosior, head of the CP(B)U (1928–38), who later become deputy head of the Council of People's Commissars of the USSR: "When Kosior was summoned to Moscow, it soon turned out that the radio station that was named after him was no longer named after him but was simply called the Kyiv radio station. It was a signal that Kosior was gone. It was this signal that let me know that Kosior was arrested" ("Memuary Nikity Sergeevicha Khrushcheva," Voprosy istorii, 1990, no. 6, 82). In this context, the news published in Pravda on April 29, 1938 should be mentioned. A collective farm named Bezbozhnik (the Godless) in Vagharshapat raion in Armenia nominated Kosior as their candidate to the Supreme Soviet of the USSR. Four days later, on May 3, 1938, Kosior was arrested and disappeared without a trace. His name was never mentioned in the press. On May 15, 1938, Pravda published the names of the main

brief mention might appear in the papers that "an enemy of the people has been unmasked," even if that person had been a leading Communist activist just a few days before. "When a person disappears, nothing is published about him and no name of his successor is announced. Only later (after instructions from Moscow), a publication appears announcing that this or that person was an enemy of the people," Karszo-Siedlewski wrote to Ambassador Grzybowski on August 1, 1937.[156]

This was the case, for instance, with the head of the Council of People's Commissars in Soviet Ukraine, Mykhailo Bondarenko, who served in that post between August 30 (after Panas Liubchenko's death) and October 13, 1937. On that day, he was arrested on a typical charge of belonging to an anti-Soviet terrorist Trotskyite organization; on February 10, 1938, he was executed.[157] The foreign consular corps in Ukraine noticed Bondarenko's absence, of course. Two and a half weeks later, on October 30, 1937, Adam Koch informed Ambassador Grzybowski of Bondarenko's arrest and of the arrest of the second secretary of the Central Committee of the CP(B)U, Serhii Kudriavtsev:[158] "There is no official confirmation of the last two arrests, but people talk about them in the city quite loudly. These unverified rumors seemed to find their confirmation in the fact that neither Kudriavtsev nor Bondarenko were nominated as candidates in the elections, while all the other Party secretaries from other oblasts had already been 'appointed' as representatives of the people."[159]

Koch noted that another piece of evidence confirming the speculation about Bondarenko's arrest was the fact that there was not a single

---

candidates to the Supreme Soviet from Ukraine, but Kosior was not among them. Nothing was written about his candidacy from Armenia either. See *Pravda* April 29, 1938 and May 15, 1938.

156 CAW, Oddz. II SG, sygn. I.303.4.1867, k. 664.

157 Mykhailo Bondarenko (1903–38) was rehabilitated in April 1956. For more information, see, for example, "Kerivnyky uriadiv Ukraïns'koï Radians'koï Sotsialistychnoï Respubliky, Bondarenko Mykhailo Illich," www.kmu.gov.ua/control/uk/publish/article?art_id=1261349&cat_id=66125.

158 Serhii Kudriavtsev (1903–38) served as the second secretary between September 26 and October 13, 1937, when he was arrested. He was sentenced and executed in April 1938. See, e.g., V. Vasyliev, "Kudriavtsev Serhii Oleksandrovych," *Instytut istoriï Ukraïny Natsionalnoï akademiï nauk Ukraïny,* www.history.org.ua/index.php?encyclop &termin=Kudryavtsev_S.

159 CAW, Oddz. II SG, sygn. I.303.4.1867, k. 672–73.

governmental decree signed by him after October 8, 1937.[160] On November 13, 1937, Koch wrote: "It is difficult to speak of the arrests of Party or government dignitaries because the information about them does not trickle down the same way it does when ordinary citizens are arrested. What must be spoken of instead are events, changes, appointments, or dismissals to and from official posts. Nonetheless, in many cases, one can reasonably surmise that an arrest has taken place. The events in this sphere over the past dozen or so days were quite impressive. There is no official confirmation of Bondarenko's and Kudriavtsev's dismissal, but a number of new facts (their absence at the military parade) confirm the information included in the recent report."[161] Koch also mentioned the disappearance of Volodymyr Zatonsky, who was dismissed from his post as people's commissar of education of Soviet Ukraine on November 3, 1937.[162] Another dignitary he wrote about was Vladimir Neverovich, who was ordered to come to Moscow, together with his wife, on the night of November 27–28, 1937. No one within the consular corps in Kyiv had any doubt that he had been arrested.[163]

Officials from the Polish consular and intelligence posts also reported on other cases of repression against high-ranking Communist dignitaries. They did not hesitate to include rumors, too. The head of post X.37, Jerzy Kamiński, wrote on August 1, 1937, about rumors that he heard about Vsevolod Balytsky, the former chief of the Soviet Ukrainian NKVD. One of them had it that he had escaped to Japan by airplane, but Kamiński thought this was highly unlikely. He thought that Balytsky had been arrested.[164] He was right; we now know that the head of the Soviet Ukrainian NKVD was arrested on July 7, 1937, imprisoned, sentenced, and then shot on November 27, 1937.

On August 21, 1937, Jan Karszo-Siedlewski wrote to the ambassador that the most recent wave of arrests included such dignitaries[165] as Andrii

[160] Ibid.

[161] Ibid., k. 651.

[162] Volodymyr Zatonsky (1888–1938) became the people's commissar of education in Soviet Ukraine after the suicide of Mykola Skrypnyk and served in that post between 1933 and 1937. He was arrested in 1937, executed in July 1938, and rehabilitated in 1956. TsDAHOU, f. 39, op. 4, spr. 72, ark. 1-1a.

[163] CAW, Oddz. II SG, sygn. I.303.4.1867, k. 651.

[164] Ibid., sygn. I.303.4.2101, doc. 88, n.p.

[165] All of them were designated by the NKVD for the so-called second trial of Borotbists. See Shapoval, *Ukraïna 20-50-kh rokiv*, 223–40.

Khvylia,[166] Marko Vasylenko,[167] Vasyl Poraiko,[168] and V. Krykh.[169] He also mentioned that in the final days of July 1937, the representative of the PCfFA, Adolf Petrovsky (Piotrowski), was arrested, but this fact remained unverified[170] because Petrovsky had been sick for quite a while. In fact, he was arrested, under NKVD order no. 00485, the order that initiated the anti-Polish operation. On September 1937, Petrovsky pleaded guilty to the charge of espionage activities for Poland.[171]

The Polish diplomat also wrote about the rumors that Stanislav (Stanisław) Kosior was dismissed together with Panas Liubchenko and Volodymyr Zatonsky.[172] Those rumors turned out to be true. Kosior was head of the CP(B)U until January 1938, when he was promoted to the position of deputy head of the Council of People's Commissars of the USSR.[173] On May 3, 1938, however, he was arrested on the charge of belonging to the Polish Military Organization.[174] He was executed on

---

[166] Andrii Khvylia (1898–1938) was a CP(B)U figure, famous for his struggle against "Ukrainian nationalism" after Skrypnyk's suicide. He prepared a "reform" of the Ukrainian language to make it more similar to Russian. He was arrested in August 1937 and executed in February 1938. See ibid., 225–32.

[167] Marko Vasylenko (1895–1937) was a Party and state functionary in Soviet Ukraine, the head of Kyiv Executive Committee and people's commisar of finances. He was arrested in August 1937 and executed in October 1937. See S. Bilokin, "Holod (urywok iz statti)," http://zdibrova.narod.ru/base/annousements/bkgpdf.pdf.

[168] Vasyl Poraiko (1888–1937) was a Party and state functionary in Soviet Ukraine: from 1927 to 30 he was the people's commissar of justice and prosecutor general, and during 1930–37 he was deputy head of the Council of People's Commissars in Ukraine. He was arrested in August 1937 and shot in October 1937. In March 1957, he was rehabilitated. See Amons, "Represovani heneralni prokurory URSR," *Ukraïns'ka asotsiatsiia prokuroriv*, http://www.uap.org.ua/ua/journal/1_8.html?_m=publications&_t=rec&id=15343.

[169] V. Krykh was the people's commissar for the state farms in Soviet Ukraine.

[170] CAW, Oddz. II SG, sygn. I.303.4.1867, k. 625.

[171] More information about the NKVD's Polish operation no. 00485 will be provided later in this chapter.

[172] CAW, Oddz. II SG, sygn. I.303.4.1867, k. 625.

[173] *Pravda*, January 20, 1938.

[174] Stanislav (Stanisław) Kosior's brother, Kazymyr (Kazimierz), accused him of espionage activity. When he learned of this, the former leader of the Ukrainian Bolsheviks wrote a slavish letter to Stalin on April 30, 1938, in which he condemned his brother as an enemy and swore that he had never belonged to any organization that was hostile to the Soviet state. This was one of the many letters at the time written by (not so long ago) Communist leaders, who suddenly found themselves in an NKVD prison or knew that they were about to end up there. Here's a fragment of Kosior's letter: "Since yesterday, I've been living with this horrifying burden of suspicion and the lack of trust toward my person. Please imagine what a person like me must be going through, someone who does not

February 26, 1939.[175] Liubchenko survived a mere nine days after the date of the Polish diplomats's report. The August 1937 plenum of the Central Committee (CC) of the Communist Party (Bolshevik) of Ukraine witnessed violent verbal attacks of Liubchenko's person, with all kinds of accusations of counterrevolutionary crimes. Liubchenko realized that his

---

recognize any fault in his behavior, someone who has always been faithful to the Party and personally to you, Comrade Stalin. Of course, I realize that my brother's arrest might have cast some shadow over my person. It was a very emotional experience for me. But the subsequent turn of events has taken me completely by surprise. I swear on my life that not only did I know nothing, but, moreover, I had no grounds whatsoever to suspect anything about Kazymyr Kosior's true character. He was never close to me. I have practically never (during the entire revolutionary period) spoken with him seriously. We were never close to each other. He found himself in Ukraine accidentally (but I could and should have prevented it). I knew nothing about his acquaintances, whom he met, who his friends were. Even in Kyiv we did not see each other. And we were not close to each other. I have reviewed everything in my memory, I have checked whether I might have heard some bad word about him, about Kazymyr, but there was nothing I could find. Why he invented all this is something I struggle to understand. Comrade Stalin, all this is fabricated by Kazymyr Kosior from the beginning to the end. I live by the hope and certainty that my truth will be stronger than the enemy's lies. I have never lied, I have never indulged in an ambiguous approach to the Party and its policy. Hence my certainty that no one can incriminate me with anything and that the truth is fully on my side. It is very hard for me to come to terms with what has happened. The Politburo did not find the time to summon me and ask me personally. This is an unbearable burden to me. But I understand the situation and I should submit to what is about to happen, if the decision has been made. I ask you, Comrade Stalin, and all the other Politburo members, to give me a chance to explain myself. Please acknowledge the fact that I have become a victim of a hostile slander, which, I am certain, will be very easy to discredit if the investigation is detailed and careful. Sometimes it all seems like a bad dream. I cannot believe that the Party has lost trust in me. I did not deserve that. Anyone can see for himself, a glance at my political and personal life is enough. I live, confident that the truth will prevail, that the Party, and you, Comrade Stalin, will be able to evaluate people properly, even in the most difficult condition, which I have seen you do more than once. I will wait until distrust of my person and the horrible accusation thrown at me fade away. If I had made mistakes, I swear, once again, that I served my Party honestly, disinterestedly, and till the end. April 30, 1938. RGASPI, f. 558, op. 11, d. 754, l. 124–34. Kosior shared the fate of his fellow dismissed dignitaries: he did not manage to avoid capital punishment. For a long time he did not plead guilty, but was finally broken by the NKVD. Kosior's wife, Elizaveta, told Roza Alikhanova (the wife of Georg Alikhanov, a Comintern activist and one of the founding fathers of the Communist Party of Armenia) how her husband was broken. His sixteen-year-old daughter, Tamara, was brought to the room he was detained in and was raped in front of him. After that Kosior signed everything they wanted him to sign. His daughter committed suicide after she was allowed to leave the prison. See R. Miedwiediew [Medvedev], *Pod osąd historii: Geneza i następstwa stalinizmu*, vol. 1 (Warsaw: Bellona, 1990), 475.

[175] Kosior was rehabilitated in March 1956; TsDAHOU, f. 39, op. 4, spr. 100, ark. 1–3.

time was up. On August 30, 1937, during a break between plenum sessions, he went home, where he shot his wife and then himself.[176]

Earlier, rumors were rife that Pavel Postyshev's wife, Tetiana Postolovska, had been arrested. On February 14, 1937, Stanisław Nawrocki submitted unverified information to the *Dwójka* that she had been arrested on February 9, 1937.[177] This news was premature, but it shows that rumors of Posyshev's imminent downfall were on the rise. Postolovska served, among other positions, as the director of the Ukrainian branch of Lenin's museum. In the aftermath of the well-known Nikolaenko case,[178] she was dismissed from her directorial post on February 17, 1937. Nevertheless, this event heralded the downfall of Postyshev, one of the most influential figures in Soviet Ukraine. In March 1937, he was removed as second secretary of the CC CP(B)U and head of the Party in Kyiv oblast and dispatched to serve as first Party secretary in

---

[176] Panas Liubchenko (1897–1937) was the chair of Soviet Ukraine's Council of People's Commissars (1934–37). See, for example, R. Pirog, "Kak pogib predsedatel' sovnarkoma Ukrainskoi SSR P.P. Liubchenko," *Izvestiia TsK KPSS*, 1990, no. 10; "Kerivnyky uriadiv Ukraïns'koï Radians'koï Sotsialistychnoï Respubliky: Liubchenko Panas Petrovych," http://www.kmu.gov.ua/control/uk/publish/article?art_id=1261316.

[177] CAW, Oddz. II SG, sygn. I.303.4.1956, n.p. She was in fact arrested on 21 February 1938.

[178] P. T. Nikolaenko was a doctoral candidate at the Kyiv Institute of History. Like many others, she succumbed to the overwhelming pressure to "uncover the enemies of the people" and started to write denunciations of her superiors, Party members, and officials. She wrote a few thousand (*sic*) denunciations. In his memoirs, Khrushchev called her crazy and wrote the following description after she came to meet him after he had become the head of the CP(B)U. "She started talking about the enemies of the people. It was simply insane. She considered all Ukrainians to be nationalists, they were all Petliura followers in her eyes, they all should have been arrested" (later she also wrote denunciations of Khrushchev). No one would have attached any importance to Nikolaenko, because thousands of people were behaving in the same way, had she not attracted the attention of Stalin himself. Earlier Lazar Kaganovich met with her in Kyiv, and it was he who reported on her activity to Stalin. Stalin, in turn, talked about Nikolaenko at the February–March 1937 plenum, which, by the way, initiated the mass purge of the Party and the NKVD. He mentioned her because she had attacked Postyshev and Kyiv's Party organization. Postyshev threw her out of the Party, in part because she wrote denunciations of him. Stalin used Nikolaenko to sketch the future line of the Party and as encouragement for the rank-and-file to follow her. He said that she was a whistle-blower (on multiple occasions) who signaled that things were not right in the local Party unit, but no one paid attention to her; on the contrary, she was removed from the Party. It was only thanks to the intervention of the central Party organs that the problem was finally addressed. Stalin said that it was Nikolaenko who was right, not Kyiv's Party organization. See RGASPI, f. 81, op. 3, d. 224, l. 39-40, and d. 223, l. 141–60; "Memuary Nikity Sergeevicha Khrushcheva," 70–71; and O. Khlevniuk, *1937-i: Stalin, NKVD i sovetskoe obshchestvo* (Moscow: Respublika, 1992), 107–8.

Kuibyshev oblast. In February 1938, Postyshev and his wife were arrested and later shot (Postolovska in August 1938, and Postyshev in February 1939).

4.4. The Social Climate and the Attitude toward the Repressions of Party Members

4.4.1. Fear, Passivity, and Apathy

The head of the Second Department of the Polish Main Staff, Colonel Tadeusz Pełczyński, wrote in a April 1938 report on the domestic situation in the USSR, just as the dynamics of the purge had reached their zenith: "The prevailing, typical attribute of the gray masses of Soviet citizens is fear and conformity, making any kind of assessment or description of the social climate very difficult. They hide their thoughts and emotions in front of everyone, including their families."[179] In turn, Colonel Józef Smoleński wrote about how difficult it was for foreigners in the USSR to obtain any information: "During their stay in the USSR, most foreigners were, by default, approached as spies. A Soviet citizen who encounters a foreigner will immediately be interrogated by GPU [NKVD] functionaries. The few foreigners who have been able to make it through the 'Chinese Wall' of bureaucratic obstacles and get into Soviet Russia, or who have perhaps spent a few months there, usually cannot boast that they discovered any significant or interesting facts. In particular, anything linked to the military forces is surrounded by a very high wall of secrecy. A Soviet citizen, a worker or an intellectual, a collective-farm worker or an individual farmer [edinolichnik], a civilian or an army man, never talks about military affairs in public."[180] In his September 4, 1939 report to the Polish minister of military affairs, the military attaché in Moscow, Colonel Stefan Brzeszczyński, also gave the impression that it was extremely difficult in the USSR to obtain intelligence information, and military intelligence in particular. "In the USSR, literally everything," he wrote, "was surrounded by deep secrecy, and this secrecy was guarded not only by all kinds of authorities but by the civilians too, consciously or not, out of fear of the GPU."[181]

There was much truth in these claims. The Soviet authorities constantly warned their citizens that the country was threatened by

---

[179] RGVA, f. 464 k, op. 1, d. 2424 A, l. 112.
[180] Ibid., d. 3018, l. 13.
[181] As quoted in R. Majzner, *Attachaty wojskowe Drugiej Rzeczypospolitej, 1919–1945: Strukturalno-organizacyjne aspekty funkcjonowania* (Częstochowa: Wydawnictwo Akademii im. Jana Długosza, 2011), 355.

foreign intervention, that spies, foreign and domestic, were everywhere. A brief visit to a foreign post, or even a random encounter with an employee of a foreign consulate, inevitably led to an interrogation by the NKVD—and often to arrest and sentencing. Mass repressions were underway, and "cooperation with foreign intelligence" was a frequent charge. Considering these facts, it is not surprising that Soviet citizens were extremely cautious about voicing their thoughts and feelings about the Stalinist system, especially to representatives of the "bourgeoisie." Nonetheless, Polish diplomats, consular officials, and military intelligence officers tried, to the best of their abilities, to assess the response of Soviet society toward the repressions and terror, as well as the Communist system as such.[182] Contrary to what Colonel Smoleński feared, they were able to collect considerable significant and interesting information. Since censorship was strictly enforced in the USSR, their only sources of information were their own observations and the conversations they were able to have. They observed Soviet citizens in stores and in the lines in front of the stores, in public parks, in the streets, and during public parades. One often had to be skillful about getting lost in the crowd, which was something the Polish observers, especially Stanisław Suchecki, successfully mastered. Conversations with visitors to the consulates produced many interesting details, too. As the repressions grew in intensity, such conversations became rare. At the same time, the number of provocateurs among the visitors grew. It is worth pointing out a certain pattern: when Soviet citizens felt they were in a relatively safe space, e.g., the consular post of a foreign country, they often vented, expressing their resentment toward both the Stalinist terror and the system as such and its mainstays.

Even before the first Moscow trial, Stanisław Suchecki noted that the Kharkiv proletariat was immersed in a gloom brought about by exhaustion, the difficult conditions of daily life, and a quiet resentment of the Soviet policy that, instead of meeting the basic and vital requirements of existence for the population, favored military expansion and massive rearmament. The population was, in theory, aware of these facts but remained silent, since any criticism was immediately stifled. In a conversation with locals, the head of intelligence post E.10 was told that, if the Soviet authorities had opened the country's borders, then at least

---

[182] For more on information about military issues collected by the Polish military intelligence, see Kołakowski, Czas próby, 193–251.

half of the population would have left. This statement was no doubt an exaggeration, but it did reflect the people's feelings about the system.[183] In spite of that, Suchecki did not notice any nostalgia for the previous system. All that the people wanted was to see their living conditions improved. They also wished the NKVD terror was gone: "the causes for popular discontent had no deeper ideological or political grounds, meaning that the mood of the masses can change very quickly, for instance, when their material conditions change for the better."[184]

In one of the Polish analyses of the general state of Soviet Ukrainian society, we read: "The overall mental state of most of the ordinary citizens of [Sovet] Ukraine, tormented by systematic undernourishment and fear of death, was characterized by a half-educated man, a former primary school teacher, in the following way: 'People want to live without this constant struggle for survival, they want to have their own garden, a bee house, they want to be building their own little household.' " Apart from these basic concerns, the authors wrote, there were other feelings, more serious and more militant, but they were localized, fragmented, not aggressive enough, and hence not really dangerous from Moscow's point of view.[185]

Stanisław Suchecki noticed one other characteristic that reflected the attitude of ordinary Communists toward the terror. In the process of "uncovering" Trotskyites, many intrigues were launched, including domestic ones, the purpose of which was to discredit one's colleagues and promote one's own position. Some people did not feel comfortable in this atmosphere of "constantly proving one's vigilance," i.e., participating in the act of permanently spying on one's colleagues or informing the authorities about anything that could be considered suspect. But they were afraid to let their uneasiness with this situation be known. A local Communist, a man who worked as an educator in a village near Chuhuiv (Kharkiv oblast), told Suchecki that he would gladly resign from the Party, because he was disgusted by constant "trifles and banalities [*skoki i drobiazgi*]." He was afraid to do so, however, because this could cost him his salary (600–700 rubles per month) and might also lead to "them [the NKVD] sending in a file and deporting me somewhere [*prishliut delo i soshliut kuda-nibud'*]," and he had a wife and children."[186]

---

[183] Ibid., f. 308 k, op. 19, d. 63, l. 47.
[184] Ibid.
[185] Ibid., d. 58, l. 146.
[186] Ibid., d. 63, l. 187.

The examples cited above accurately reflected both the people's needs and their generally passive attitude toward the regime, not only in Ukraine, but in the USSR as a whole. The social climate was such that people intimidated by terror did not voice political demands. They wanted to see relative stability in the areas of economic and personal security: they dreamt of the day when they would no longer have to worry about how to obtain their daily bread, and when the atmosphere of constant, all-encompassing terror would finally disappear.

After the first Moscow trial, Jan Karszo-Siedlewski noticed that the ubiquitous terror silenced all voices of discontent.[187] When Adam Koch wrote about the living conditions of Soviet citizens, he in turn emphasized that the permanent anxiety about arrest meant that people could not be occupied with voicing their discontent: "Ceaseless anxiety over one's fate and possible arrest is a very effective antidote against worrying about one's economic requirements. What benefit could satisfying the latter bring if one did not know if one could still enjoy them tomorrow? Hence most residents of Kyiv and other cities considered them [economic issues] a minor priority compared to worrying about their personal liberty."[188]

4.4.2. The Attitude toward Repressions of Communists

The overall attitude toward the repressions within the high-ranking Communist leadership can be summarized as follows: when repressions were applied "to those at the top," people were not overly worried, nor were they very interested. Occasionally that this or that Bolshevik was done away with brought them some kind of perverse satisfaction. All this changed when the repressions began to affect ordinary citizens—a topic I will discuss in the next part of this book. Occasionally ordinary people did not hide their attitude toward the bleakness surrounding them, despite the price they could pay for this, including arrest and execution.

Officials from the Polish foreign service emphasized that most people were mostly indifferent to the repressions that took place in the Party, state, and military apparat, based on the data they received from their informants and visitors to the consulate, or from their own observations, primarily of people standing in lines or using public transportation. Occasionally some outward manifestations of resistance were observed. These were expressed at the mass meetings sometimes organized by the

---

[187] AAN, MSZ, sygn. 6669, k. 14.
[188] Ibid., sygn. 9515, k. 54.

Bolsheviks. During such meetings, the crowd was expected to demand the death penalty for "the enemies of the people" or display joy after hearing that such sentences had been carried out.

Two days before the first Moscow trial began, Consul Stanisław Sośnicki emphasized in his report to the ambassador, "Counterrevolution and the First Anniversary of the Stakhanovite Movement," that most people awaited the trial with indifference, despite the big propaganda campaign surrounding it. They continued to focus on their own personal problems, of which there was no shortage in the Soviet system. "The mood of the working masses has evidently cooled down, and most displayed indifference to everything initiated by the authorities to achieve this or that objective. The struggle for daily bread takes priority among the working masses."[189] Indeed, as has been stressed, what people wanted most of all was piece of mind and relative stability.

Based on his observations and casual conversations, Stanisław Suchecki noticed that the Zinoviev-Kamenev trial caused a sensation, but it was difficult to discern either compassion for the alleged perpetrators or "genuine outrage" at their deeds. In several instances, the head of intelligence post E.10 did note that his interlocutors betrayed, by their words or their tone, regret that the assassination attempt the accused had planned in Moscow had failed.[190]

Nothing changed after the second Moscow trial. Jan Karszo-Siedlewski wrote to the Polish ambassador in Moscow on February 1, 1937: "The local society displays little interest in or reaction to those arrests [of the Trotskyites], approaching them as the settling of internal Party scores and misunderstandings and having no consequences in other areas of life."[191] According to the diplomat, Soviet society did not question the very fact of there being oppositional activities organized by the so-called Trotskyites. "Now, it is difficult to say," he wrote, "what the average Soviet citizen thinks about it all; he is so anxious and so terrorized that he is afraid of his own shadow. I do have evidence that allows for the conclusion that most of Soviet society of a lower intellectual or moral level believes this whole Stalin-fabricated affair about the anti-Soviet activity of the 'Trotskyites,' which is something that Moscow wanted to achieve."[192] This was where Karszo-Siedlewski felt a threat to the authorities did lurk,

---

[189] CAW, Oddz. II SG, sygn. I.303.4.1867, k. 66, CAW.

[190] RGVA, f. 308 k, op. 19, d. 63, l. 185.

[191] CAW, Oddz. II SG, sygn. I.303.4.1867, k. 523.

[192] Ibid., k. 521–22.

because if most of the population really did believe in this huge conspiracy, then it would, of necessity, have started doubting the effectiveness of the NKVD—i.e., if the Trotskyite network had really operated for so long and so extensively.[193] Karszo-Siedlewski's judgment, in this instance, seems too speculative. The average citizen was more than sufficiently afraid of the NKVD and certainly did not believe in any "decreasing effectiveness" of that institution.

After the Tukhachevsky Case was over, Karszo-Siedlewski once again shared with the ambassador his impressions on July 23, 1937 of society's attitude toward the arrests: "The indifference with which [Soviet] Ukrainian society has reacted to the purges and arrests currently underway is the most surprising phenomenon. After all, only yesterday its victims were dignitaries, or even national heroes. Sometimes one has the impression that all of this must be taking place outside the Soviet Union, while life in the country has stayed in 'business as usual' mode. Among Party and government cadres, the mood must certainly be different, but we have no insight into their lives because Party discipline, not to mention the general distrust, makes it impossible for that mood to reach the outside world. The broad working and peasant masses care little for these events, and understands them even less. The negative outcomes of these events do not bother them, as they are considered internal score-settling within the ruling circles."[194]

Adam Koch had a similar impression. On October 30, 1937, he wrote that the purge that took place in the summer of 1937 applied mostly to Party members and officials. Hence "the broad masses overall assumed an indifferent attitude, as if all these events took place outside the sphere of their interests."[195] Earlier, just after the sentence in the Tukhachevsky Case was announced, Koch attempted to assess popular reaction to his execution, the fates of Iakir and the other generals, and the recent arrests in Soviet Ukraine (e.g., of Vsevolod Balytsky). The Polish vice-consul did not notice the slightest trace of interest in those events, not to mention deeper feelings such as sadness or despair: "It seems that people keep on living their lives as if the current events took place completely outside the sphere of their interests. What struck me was the unusual absence, especially on a holiday, of officers and soldiers in the streets, even when

---

[193] Ibid., k. 522.
[194] Ibid., k. 696–97
[195] Ibid., k. 677.

one takes into consideration the fact that the city garrison is out at a summer camp."[196]

The reaction on the streets of Moscow to the purges was identical. Colonel Konstanty Zaborowski, the military attaché in Moscow, informed the *Dwójka* about the passivity of the people and their lack of response to the arrests of the Soviet generals. In a letter dated June 15, 1937, Zaborowski tried to illustrate the attitude of ordinary citizens to the purges and the Tukhachevsky Case. He reported that he did not notice that anyone in the streets seemed concerned with the issue. Russian drivers said that the generals got what they deserved, while workers and some railway employees said that it could not have any negative impact on their own situation. "With this kind of society and these kinds of attitudes, one will likely be able to continue with various experiments for quite some time. Everyone is used to the fact that they devour one another at the top. No ordinary citizen has any love for those at the top. Everyone thinks only about whether his situation will be better or worse. Apathy, dullness, and a peculiar kind of mouse psychology [abound]—everyone is ready to hide in their nooks and they all have plenty, plenty of endurance."[197] Zabrowski continued: "All evidence goes to show that thus far Stalin has everyone and everything firmly in his grip (*Stalin mocno trzyma za 'pysk' wszystkich i wszystko*).... His position only grows stronger, while Soviet society and his instruments of power—the Party, the GPU [NKVD], the army—receive one heavy blow after another."[198]

4.4.3. Word-of-Mouth Counter-Propaganda and Other Signs of Resistance

Indifference, as virtually all the Polish reports emphasized, was typically the attitude most Soviet citizens assumed when confronted with repressions levied against Communists. Some signs of disagreement were observed nonetheless, and Polish officials reported on them as well. They were usually limited to pejorative verbal comments about the repressions, living conditions, or the system as a whole. Representatives of the Second Polish Republic occasionally witnessed such moments.

On September 11, 1935, the head of intelligence post G.27, Ludwik Michałowski, wrote a report about the mood of Soviet society. He began

---

[196] Ibid., k. 613–14.
[197] Ibid., sygn. I.303.4.3181, k. 55.
[198] Ibid., k. 55-56.

by reminding his readers that the lack of any oppositional press combined with repressions made it very difficult to obtain relevant information on this topic. Soviet people indulged in some honesty only when they were absolutely sure that this would not entail repression, i.e., inside a consulate. Michałowski cited some stories and reiterated that he was positive of their authenticity. The wife of engineer Kuznetsov, the technical director of the Stal enterprise in Kharkiv, told Michałowski that when her husband received a portrait of Sergo Ordzhonikidze with a dedication, she said—only in the presence of people she could trust—that she would not allow the portrait of this bandit to hang in her apartment. Her husband said that the person who gave him the portrait occasionally visited his apartment when he was in Kharkiv and would thus notice its absence. His wife replied that he could hang it in his cabinet, adding that having to look at one of the country's oppressors was unbearable to her.

The wife of Petrushevych, a technical director in a Kharkiv sugar-refinery complex, said that she would donate all she had to a mausoleum for Stalin. She prayed he would die soon, because only then would any radical changes be possible. Petrushevych's daughter, however, who worked in the Kharkiv Electromechanical Plant, told Michałowski that the Soviet system provided more opportunities for young people than the capitalist system did. She was unable to answer Michałowski's question about how she would be able to survive only on her salary without her father's help.

A cashier at a railway station, a Communist named Sviridova, told Ludwik Michałowski that she would give up everything if she could only get a passport to leave the country. A porter at a railway-cargo station gave the following reply to Michałowski's remark that "affluent life" was within reach: "Yes, certainly, affluent life is so widespread in the Soviet country that no one can find it anymore" (*Da, verno, zazhitochnaia zhizn' tak shiroko rozlilas' po sovetskoi strane, chto ei nikto naiti ne mozhet*).[199]

As already mentioned, Stanisław Nawrocki informed the *Dwójka* about public instances of word-of-mouth resistance—something that could relatively easily be heard while listening to Soviet people talking when they were waiting in lines. On September 7, 1936, he wrote that people in queues, a permanent feature of the "happy" Soviet landscape, were grumbling, which was "already a lot, considering Soviet conditions." A joke about what the acronym "USSR" (Russian: SSSR) really meant was

---

[199] CAW, Oddz. II SG, sygn. I.303.4.1968, n.p., doc. 68.

making the rounds of the city: it meant <u>S</u>mert' <u>S</u>talina <u>S</u>paset <u>R</u>ossiiu (Stalin's Death Will Save Russia).[200]

On October 28, 1937, *Dwójka* agent Jerzy Kamiński talked with an old waiter in a "below par" restaurant on Stalin Street in Kharkiv. The waiter told him that he often overheard conversations among young people after they had had a drink or two and knew that they were dissatisfied with the current system. He was once told: "Dear old man of ours, we have not seen real life, and we will now probably never see it" (*Ekh, papasha, ne vidali my zhizni nastoiashchei, da veroiatno teper' i ne uvidim*).[201]

Even functionaries in the Soviet policing and security organs expressed discontent. An army office in the center of Kharkiv dealt with sending demobilized soldiers home or to their new place of employment. Each soldier received 10 to 30 rubles for his journey. One day (in mid-1935) the soldiers made it known that they were outraged by the fact that they were ordered to travel to places from which their families had already been deported, and that they were left without any financial means to carry on. In the aftermath of their protest, the office was moved from the center to a less prominent spot in Kharkiv.[202]

---

[200] Ibid., sygn. I.303.4.1956, n.p., doc. 21.

[201] Ibid., sygn. I.303.4.2101, n.p., doc. 115.

[202] RGVA, f. 308 k, op. 6, d. 21, l. 288. The head of intelligence post H.12 in Moscow, Gustaw Olszewski, also provided interesting details. He witnessed a scene in a park in Moscow, when an NKVD soldier addressed his colleagues with the phrase "it's not good, comrades," pointing to the worn-out shoe on his foot. His comrades confirmed his observation after they looked over their own clothes. The NKVD soldier had spoken out loud in a public space. A large audience heard his complaints. The head of intelligence post H.12 gave other examples of "the mood on the street." Another incident took place at Maxim Gorky's funeral. Traditionally at such an event, delegations from institutions and enterprises showed up with flag-bearers (groups of up to twenty people). Attendance was mandatory. One of the female delegates complained to the participants walking next to her that she had to waste her entire day because of the funeral. Because of it, streetcars and buses were canceled, or their routes were changed. People damned this circumstance in public. "The population's masses," Olszewski wrote, "were completely uninterested in the funeral: they did not notice it or pretended not to know anything about it." Olszewski also described people's attitude to the athletes' (*fizkul'turniki*) parade. He observed that working-class youth did not show any enthusiasm, were undisciplined and tired of the multiple exercises preceding the parade. They were forced to participate in the preparatory exercises, which officers supervised. Children from schools, however, were very disciplined and full of enthusiasm. As a consequence of the ceremonies, municipal communications malfunctioned and people voiced their displeasure loudly. For example, one group of the exercise participants hailed a bus that was en route, and the bus had to stop. The passengers got impatient, and one of them finally burst out, "Damn! When will

Cases of more violent and nonverbal acts of resistance to the lies propagated daily by the Bolsheviks also took place. In December 1934, after the Kirov murder, the entire USSR experienced a wave of mass gatherings "in support" of the Stalinist line and to demand the death penalty for Leonid Nikolaev, Grigory Zinoviev, and Lev Kamenev. Those meetings did not always take place according to plan. One of the workers from the Kharkiv Locomotive Factory spoke: "Why do you even ask us [about our opinion]? Some time ago you killed 28 persons,[203] among whom, I am sure, there were citizens of foreign countries. Back then you did not ask us about anything, nor did you inform the consulates. Why are you so meticulous with respect to our own people? Why do you need our permission or demands? If we vote not to kill them, you will do it anyway." This worker was immediately arrested. The press reported on the "enthusiastic acceptance of the motion" after the gathering. The worker's speech was, of course, passed over in silence.[204]

In mid-1935 slogans with the following words appeared on the walls of the Kharkiv *torgsin* stores one day: TORGSIN—"Tovarishchi, Organizuites', Rossiia Gibnet, Sovety Istrebliaiut Narod" [Comrades, Organize, Russia Is Dying, the Soviets are Annihilating the People]. The police washed off the signs immediately.[205]

Jerzy Kamiński also reported some cases of "counterrevolutionary attitudes" to the *Dwójka* based on information he received from his informants. In a report on February 18, 1937, the head of post X.37 wrote that his informant Lucyna Grekowa[206] told him that a certain man named Lasko, the director of the assembly section at the Kharkiv Agricultural Machine Plant, was killed because he reported on his colleagues and was particularly aggressive in his speeches against the workers who were accused of Trotskyism.[207]

On July 2, 1937, Jerzy Kamiński reported on the information he received from his informant C-3, whose real name was Cezaria Talko.[208]

---

this mess come to an end!" even though an NKVD agent and a policeman were in close proximity. He left the bus, shutting the door behind him. Ibid., op. 19, d. 66, l. 17

[203] The December Trial in Kyiv (December 13–15, 1934).

[204] CAW, Oddz. II SG, sygn. I.303.4.2012, n.p., doc. 22.

[205] RGVA, f. 308 k, op. 6, d. 21, l. 288.

[206] She was paid 50 zlotys for her information.

[207] CAW, Oddz. II SG, sygn. I.303.4.2101, n.p., doc. 180.

[208] Talko received financial rewards for her services. In the records from post X.37 in Kharkiv, there is a signed receipt for 400 rubles (April 15, 1937) that Talko received for delivering a passport.

At a gathering at the glass factory in Merefa near Kharkiv organized to condemn Marshal Tukhachevsky, one of the workers said that they should not be afraid of the landowners (*pomeshchiki*) and capitalists anymore, "because back in the day one worked for one of them, while today there are more people doing nothing else besides waiting to get their wallets filled." Another worker complained that the new generation chased after sinecures, and it was unclear who was going to do the work when the old people died out. The NKVD detained both workers after the meeting. When Skulachenko, the son of the head of the mechanized troops of the Kharkiv Military District, learned that Tukhachevsky and Iakir had been arrested (Iakir's son was a student at his school, no. 1), he said that Stalin himself would be arrested next time. The head of post X.37 post also reported that the mother-in-law of a Communist told him that children were very saddened by Marshal Semen Budenny's fate when they thought the founder of the Red Cavalry had also been shot.[209]

On July 18, 1937, informant C-3 told Kamiński that, in association with the new defense loan issued by the state, a gathering had taken place at the glass factory in Merefa, during which some workers shouted that they had had enough of price increases. In the scuffle that ensued, Stalin's portrait was dropped and torn apart. The NKVD immediately arrested several of the perpetrators. The factory's newspaper, *Chervonyi shkloduv*, never mentioned the event.[210]

It should be mentioned here that Kamiński suspected, justifiably, that his two informants—Grekowa and Talko[211]—were NKVD informants.

---

[209] CAW, Oddz. II SG, sygn. I.303.4.2101, n.p., doc. 60.

[210] Ibid., doc. 155

[211] On July 3, 1937, Kamiński described the two women: "Lucyna Grekowa was a physician, aged 40-45, Polish. She had female friends in all the military factories in Kharkiv. She delivers general information, i.e., the kind that can be easily explained if one knows the right people. She never, and she had many occasions, gave me any valuable information, e.g., the names of military commanders. As previously mentioned, her cooperation was probably tolerated by the NKVD, perhaps even imposed upon her by them... She is interested in consular affairs and in our own interests. Meetings take place in her apartment, very rarely in our office." Grekowa lived in Kharkiv at Baseina St., 28/4; her phone number was 7-72-90. Kamiński described Cezaria Talko as follows: "Polish by origin, approx. 40 years old. She lives in Merefa, works at the local steelworks. She lived with her husband and three children (according to her own information) in exile in Solovki [the Solovets Islands]. Together with her children, she got out illegally, and her husband allegedly made it into Poland, illegally as well. She came to the consulate for the first time in 1937 and asked whether [we] had any information about her husband.

Some of the news they provided could have been exaggerated or untrue. But the information about the events described here cannot be dismissed as false, because instances of such local "rebellions" did take place, even if infrequently, and are reflected in NKVD records.[212] The NKVD also reported on finding leaflets that painted Tukhachevsky as a "hero" and Stalin and his NKVD as executioners.[213]

4.4.4. Waiting for War

The Polish reports suggest that Soviet citizens, who were suffering from Bolshevik barbarity, persecution, and penury, saw the coming of war with the capitalist world as an end to their misery. Fear of war was one of the favorite motifs of Soviet propaganda, especially during the second half of the 1930s.[214] The war would, of course, be started by "the fascists, who were just waiting to seize Soviet land." In his September 18, 1936 report "The Current Situation in Ukraine," Stanisław Nawrocki wrote that he believed the Soviet people were expecting a war with "the fascists" to break out soon. He mentioned that the word "fascist" held positive associations: "I noticed that in all cases when war was mentioned, my

---

Altogether she visited the consulate three times. She has a false passport that she got from an NKVD agent she knew in the past." According to Polish intelligence, the news she delivered was exaggerated, e.g., about the mood of the population, about untrue train accidents. For documents she delivered, she received 450 rubles. One other contact was described in Kamiński's report, the German consular official Hermann Strecker: "39 y.o., a German consular official, he finished high school in Kharkiv before the revolution. Very cunning. Interesting. A complete amateur in military affairs. Knows the local conditions very well and has many contacts, but he cannot rely on them now (the anti-fascist attitude of the local authorities). He likes to drink. He can be useful if one maintains good (friendly) relations with him. He might know a lot in terms of moods and rumors, but not so much about industrial or military affairs" (Archiwum Instytutu Pamięci Narodowej w Warszawie: zespół: Ministerstwo Bezpieczeństwa Publicznego w Warszawie, sygn. IPN BU 1572/1169, n.p.).

[212] See Wieczorkiewicz, Łańcuch śmierci, 90.

[213] Ibid.; see also Kuromiya, Głosy straconych, 152.

[214] See, for example. *Pravda*, August 1, 1938; "Provokatory voiny," *Pravda*, February 11, 1938; "Pravotrotskistskie bandity—podzhigateli voiny," *Pravda*, March 7, 1938; "Fashizm eto voina! Sotsializm—eto mir!," *Pravda*, August 1 1938; "Vsiakaia popytka podzhigatelei voiny narushyt' granitsy nashei rodiny vstretit sokrushytel'nyi otpor," "Sovetskii narod i Krasnaia Armiia, splocheny vokrug partii Lenina-Stalina i pravitel'stva, gotovy nanesti provokatoram voiny unichtozhaiushchii udar," *Pravda*, August 3, 1938. See also the caricatures published in *Pravda* on May 1, 1937. The idea of future foreign aggression gave birth to many popular films, e.g., *Rodina zovet* (Mosfilm, 1936, dir. Aleksandr Macheret); *Granitsa na zamkie* (Soiuzdetfilm, 1937, dir. Vasilii Zhuravlev); *Esli zavtra voina* (Mosfilm, 1938, dir. Efim Dzygan); and *Na granitse* (Lenfilm, 1938, dir. Aleksandr Ivanov).

interlocutors (Ukrainians) were not afraid of it; on the contrary, they wanted it to happen because they hoped it could overthrow Soviet rule. This view is very widespread here."[215]

This particular view—that both urban and rural citizens universally hoped for war as the only possible salvation from Bolshevik rule—was frequently noted in the Polish reports. In August 1935, Consul Stanisław Sośnicki remarked that the opinion that only foreign intervention could change things could be heard more and more often: "As soon as border skirmishes begin, then we will murder these Communists here," the Polish consul once heard. A German engineer who was deported back to his country after a few years in the USSR was passing through Zdolbuniv where he shared his opinion about Soviet society with the Polish authorities. Based on his observations, he concluded that the Soviet population was not satisfied with the regime: "Most people are waiting for war as an opportunity to get rid of this regime."[216] Stanisław Suchecki paid attention to this same fact. The head of intelligence post E.10 did not notice such attitudes in Kharkiv directly, but he received reports from the field that rural residents were so unhappy with the misery they had to endure in the collective farms, which local authorities administered, that they expected the Poles or the Germans to arrive, reinstate private agricultural property, and restore normal conditions of life.[217]

On April 27, 1936, Ludwik Michałowski reported back to intelligence headquarters that Soviet propaganda was making use of the recent wave of strikes in Poland. This news of the strikes did not make a good impression on the people that he spoke with, for whom those events were a sign of weakness: "From my conversations with local citizens, it follows that they are losing faith in Europe. They think the continent is either blinded or truly weak and helpless when confronted with the organizational and military might of the Soviets. They believe only Hitler is capable of doing something. They also express regret that the Marshal [Piłsudski] is no longer with us in Poland."[218]

Michałowski mentioned that what the Polish press was publishing helped the Soviet cause, because one did not have to look very hard to find something anti-Polish to write about.[219] What Michałowski had in

---

[215] CAW, Oddz. II SG, sygn. I.303.4.1956, n.p., doc. 32.
[216] Ibid., d. 22, l. 224–25.
[217] Ibid., op. 19, d. 63, l. 49.
[218] CAW, Oddz. II SG, sygn. I.303.4.1967, doc. 67; see also RGVA, f. 308 k, op. 19, d. 63, l. 33.
[219] CAW, Oddz. II SG, sygn. I.303.4.1967, doc. 67.

mind were the quotations that the Soviet press took from the Polish press that highlighted the various problems the second Polish Republic was experiencing, such as the aforementioned strikes, overall poverty, and the predicament of the national minorities.[220] The Soviet press enjoyed publishing such material taken not only from the Polish press but from any other country[221] where any negative aspects of capitalism were under scrutiny. The Bolsheviks presented the reprinted material as evidence that the situation of the workers and peasants in capitalist countries was "hopeless," and, furthermore, they remarked that these kinds of problems were unknown to the "happy" Soviet citizen.

4.5. Mass Repressions during the Yezhovshchina

The Yezhovshchina refers to the mass repressions against ordinary citizens that were based on various operational orders of the NKVD under Nikolai Yezhov: 00447 was the kulak operation;[222] 00485, the Polish operation;[223]

---

[220] See, e.g., "Holod, bezrobittia, vyrodzhennia: Zhakhlyve stanovyshche trudiashchykh u Polshchi," Visti, January 21, 1936; "Mezhdunarodnyi Iunosheskii den'," Pravda, October 6, 1937; L. Janusz, "Bez khleba, bez prav," ibid.; "Nishcheta i golod v derevniakh Pol'shi: Fakty i dokumenty iz pol'skoi burzhuaznoi pechati," Pravda, September 14, 1937; B. Kolesnikov, "Vseobshchaia krest'ianskaia zabastovka v Polshe," ibid.; "Schastlivaia zhizn' kolkhoznoi derevni," Pravda, September 29, 1937; and "Komediia 'vyborov' w Pol'she," Pravda, October 15, 1938.

[221] A. Klimov, "Samoubiistva w 'Tretei imperii,'" Pravda, March 13, 1937; "Zhizn' ital'ianskoi molodezhi (fakty, tsifry, dokumenty)," Pravda, September 6, 1937; "Zhizn' iaponskoi molodezhi (fakty, tsifry, dokumenty)," ibid.; P. Poliakov, "Rost bezrabotitsy v stranakh kapitala," Pravda, February 19, 1938; "Nishcheta i golod ital'ianskikh trudiashchikhsia," Pravda October 23, 1938; "Nuzhda i bezrabotitsa tekstilshchikov Anglii," Pravda, October 20, 1937; "Golodnye pokhody indiiskikh krest'ian," Pravda, April 8, 1938; and "Nishcheta rabochikh na Iamaike," Pravda, April 9, 1938.

[222] For information about the 00447 operation, see M. Junge, G. Bordiugov, and R. Binner, Vertikal' Bolshogo terrora: Istoriia operatsii po prikazu NKVD nr 00447 (Moscow: Novyi khronograf, 2008); S. A. Kokin and M. Junge, eds., Velykyi teror v Ukraïni: "Kurkul's'ka operatsiia" 1937–1938 rr. (Kyiv: Vydavnychyi dim "Kyievo-Mohylians'ka akademiia," 2010), 2 vols.; and V. Nikol's'kyi, "Represii za 'limitamy' (1937–1938 rr.)," Ukraïns'kyi istorychnyi zhurnal, 2006, no. 3: 210–23.

[223] For information about the 00485 operation, see N. Pietrow, "Polska operacja NKWD," Karta, 1993, no. 11; S. Stępień, ed., Polacy na Ukrainie: Zbiór dokumentów, part 1, 1917–1939, vol. 3 (Przemyśl: Południowo-Wschodni Instytut Naukowy, 2001); Bednarek, Kułakowski, Kokin et al., eds., Polska i Ukraina w latach trzydziestych–czterdziestych XX wieku, vol. 8; and N. Petrov and A. Roginskii, "The 'Polish Operation' of the NKVD, 1937–8," in Stalin's Terror: High Politics and Mass Repressions in the Soviet Union, ed. B. McLoughlin and K. McDermott, (Houndmills, Basingstoke, Hampshire and New York:

00439, against Germans,[224] 00486, the repression of the wives and children of people already sentenced;[225] and others. These operations began during July and August 1937.

NKVD records offer estimates of the magnitude of the tragedy that unfolded in the Soviet Union. On the Soviet Ukrainian NKVD's balance sheet of individuals arrested and shot between 1935 and 1940, the total is given as 249,062 people sentenced and 127,917 shot[226] (see table 8). Between 1936 and 1938, 220,060 were sentenced and 127,588 were shot. In 1964, the Ukrainian KGB quoted similar data for 1936 through 1938: 211,503 arrested and 122,414 shot.[227]

Table 8. Number of persons sentenced and shot in Soviet Ukraine, 1935–40

Year	Number of sentenced individuals	Number sentenced to capital punishment
1935	18,422	137
1936	14,038	177
1937	130,512	67,767
1938	75,510	59,644

Palgrave Macmillan, 2003), 153–72. See also the nonacademic work by M. Łoziński, *Operacja polska: Stalinowska zbrodnia na Polakach w latach 1937–1938* (Kłodawa: Drukarnia Braci Wielińskich, 2008).

[224] For information about the persecution of the German minority, see A. Daniel, L. Ieromina, E. Zhemkova et al., eds., *Repressii protiv rossiiskikh nemtsev: Nakazannyi narod. Po materialam konferentsii "Repressii protiv rossiiskikh nemtsev v Sovetskom Soiuze v kontekste sovetskoi natsionalnoi politiki" provedennoi Nemetskim kul'turnym tsentrom im. Goethe v Moskve sovmestno s Obshchestvom Memorial, 18–20 noiabria 1998 goda* (Moscow: Zvenia, 1999). See also L. Iakovleva, B. Chyrko, and S. Pyshko, eds., *Nimtsi v Ukraini, 20-30-ti rr. XX st.: Zbirnyk dokumentiv z derzhavnykh arkhiviv Ukraïny* (Kyiv: Instytut istoriï Ukraïny, 1994).

[225] For information about this topic, see T. Vrons'ka, "Stalins'ka henderna polityka u dobu 'Velykoho teroru' (1937–1938 rr.)," *Z arkhiviv VUChK-GPU-NKVD-KGB*, 2009, no. 1 (32): 137–75; and idem, *Zaruchnyky totalitarnoho rezhymu: Represiï proty rodyn "vorohiv narodu" v Ukraïni (1917–1953 rr.)* (Kyiv: Instytut istoriï NAN Ukraïny, 2009). See also A. Iakovlev, ed., *Deti GULAGa, 1918–1956* (Moscow: Mezhdunarodnyi fond "Demokratiia," 2002), 225–375.

[226] HDASBU, f. 42, spr. 35 A, ark. 11.

[227] Ibid., ark. 5.

1939	7,370	147
1940	3,210	45
Total	249,062	127,917

Source: HDASBU, f. 42, spr. 35 A, ark. 11.

Many more people were arrested. According to official data, 24,934 individuals were arrested in 1935, and 15,717 in 1936. This figure increased dramatically during 1937 and 1938 (159,572 persons in 1937 and 88,966 persons during the first half of 1938).[228] All told, in 1938, 108,006 persons were arrested. When the Great Terror ended, the annual number of arrests returned to the pre-1937 level: 12,000 persons were arrested in 1939.[229] In Soviet Ukraine, in 1937–38 more than 31 percent of all those arrested were arrested in the so-called nationalities operations; 18 percent, in the 00447 operation; and 16 percent, for membership in a "bourgeois-nationalist organization."[230]

Employees of the Polish diplomatic and consular posts did not know about these specific NKVD orders, but they had a good overall sense of the situation. As early as in February 1937, Ambassador Wacław Grzybowski predicted that the repressions that he could see at the time would soon be expanded to include youth and all social classes.[231]

Soviet reality was such that anyone, for whatever reasons, and at any time could be arrested. The Russian writer Ilia Ehrenburg reflected many years later on his survival during the Stalinist Terror and purges: "I lived in an era when the fate of a man was not like a game of chess but like a lottery."[232]

Most residents of the Bolshevik state at the time suffered from extreme and permanent anxiety. Not even closest family members could be trusted. Just how extreme that anxiety was is described in numerous memoirs written by those who witnessed the events. Ivan (Jan) Sawicki, a

---

[228] Ibid., spr. 35, ark. 2-3; see also Iu. Shapoval, "Peredden' i apohei Velykoho teroru," in V. Lytvyn and V. Smolii, *Politychnyi teror i teroryzm v Ukraïni XIX–XX st.: Istorychni narysy* (Kyiv: Naukova dumka, 2002), 469.

[229] HDASBU, f. 42, spr. 35 A, ark. 2-3.

[230] Vasyliev, "Vplyv 'velykoho teroru,' " 53–54.

[231] AAN, Ambasada RP w Moskwie, sygn. 41, k. 9–10.

[232] Quoted in M. Heller, *Maszyna i śrubki: Jak hartował się człowiek sowiecki* (Paris: Instytut Literacki, 1988), 60.

Pole who lived in what is now Khmelnytskyi oblast, recollected after
many years: "Fear was so great that people could no longer control
themselves. It was enough for a policeman to pass by and I was shaking
completely up and down, my hands and chest trembling, [and] I became
sort of paralyzed. That feeling has remained with me until today ... When
a policeman passes by, I try to avoid him the best I can so that my gaze
would never fall upon him again."[233] Mieczysław Łoziński, who survived
the terror, wrote many years later: "I have remembered those dark days
my entire life. In my house, in the house of my parents, those years were
filled with anxiety. The atmosphere of fear and the sad, dead silence.
Nights were particularly fearsome. The faintest sound could cause the
entire family to be wide awake. In the kitchen, next to the oven, there lay
a bag filled with crackers in case they came to arrest our father again[234] on
the troika's recommendation, so that he could take it with him for his last
journey."[235]

As noted above, so long as the repressions extended only to the Party
apparat, and did not apply to ordinary citizens, most of those citizens did
not care much about the Party officials. This changed as soon as the
repressions extended beyond the Party. Polish observers paid attention to
this shift. In his report on October 30, 1937, Vice-Consul Adam Koch
wrote: "The current situation has changed a bit. The arrests underway
now apply also to common citizens to a serious extent. Any one of them
could fall into the NKVD's hands at any time. Among ordinary people one
can detect a certain kind of arrest anxiety. On the other hand, there is a
kind of apathy or resignation caused by helplessness and the inability to
defend oneself. The only way to defend oneself, and only partially
successfully, was to generate an atmosphere of general and utter distrust
and unbelief around oneself. It is now normal that a husband does not
trust his wife and parents are wary of speaking out when their children
are present. Can this atmosphere be otherwise when, according to
statements a few residents of Kyiv have submitted, there is not a single
apartment building in a typical Kyiv block where at least one resident has
not been arrested?"[236]

One denunciation was enough to bring about someone's arrest. Still,
some Communist dignitaries criticized regular Party members,

---

[233] Dzwonkowski, *Głód i represje wobec ludności polskiej*, 202.
[234] Łoziński's father spent five years in the Gulag and returned home in 1937.
[235] Łoziński, *Operacja polska*, 107.
[236] CAW, Oddz. II SG, sygn. I.303.4.1867, k. 677.

complaining that the number of denunciations they had delivered to the relevant authorities was too low. In the January 1938 resolution of the CC plenum, an example of "the enemy of the people" was given. The person was the former secretary of Kyiv Oblast's Party Committee, Serhii Kudriavtsev, arrested in October 1937. At Party meetings he provocatively asked the Communists who tried to speak up the following question: "Have you written a statement [*zaiavlenie*] on [against] anyone?" As a result of "this provocation," nearly half of the members of the Party in Kyiv would soon have a "statement" submitted against them with the relevant authorities. Most of those statements were either false or downright provocative, the plenum's resolution concluded.[237]

Occasionally a particular denunciation was the product of the zeal with which the Soviet authorities encouraged their citizens to inform the NKVD about anything that seemed suspect. In other words, the Soviet citizen was expected "to cooperate [inform] with the NKVD," i.e., effectively become an NKVD agent.[238] Sometimes a denunciation was the result of a citizen's anxiety that he was "not vigilant enough since he had not yet discovered a single enemy of the people." This lack of results could seem suspect since, if one read the Soviet press, one had the impression

---

[237] *Ob oshibkakh partorganizatsii pri iskluchenii kommunistov iz partii.*

[238] The front-page editorial in *Pravda* on March 11, 1938 ("Chest' i slava sovetskoi razvedke") mentions the "love" of the Soviet people for the NKVD and its chief, Yezhov: "Our NKVD officers [*narkomvnudeltsy*] rely in their work on the multimillion [large] brave and patriotic Soviet people. Soviet intelligence includes not just intelligence officers, but also the millions of working people, who have learned what Bolshevik vigilance is and how to uncover the enemies of the people. The working masses realize that by helping the NKVD, they help themselves. They realize that the NKVD's work is an important part of the overall effort of the working class, of socialism." See also, e.g. N. Rubin and I. Serebrov, "O podryvnoi deiatel'nosti fashystkikh razvedok v SSSR i zadachakh bor'by s neiu," *Pravda*, July 29 and 30, 1937. In addition to encouraging ordinary citizens to write denunciations of the (largely imaginary) enemies of the people, Soviet intelligence made sure that anyone who had any contact with representatives of foreign countries could be employed for intelligence gathering. It was particularly true of those Soviet employees who traveled abroad on duty —for Aeroflot, on trade missions, or the few tourists who allegedly obtained information of a military, political, or economic nature. In 1932 a special instruction appeared for Soviet tourists, in which they learned that "tourist intelligence" was a duty for all of them. The instruction specified how it should be done: one should contact the locals, initiate conversations with them, attend parties, exploit their interlocutor's weaknesses, i.e., alcohol abuse, and visit strategic places, such as airports, seaports, or military garrisons. See A. Krzak, *Kontrwywiad wojskowy II Rzeczypospolitej przeciwko radzieckim służbom specjalnym, 1921–1939* (Toruń: Wydawnictwo Adam Marszałek, 2007), 144–45.

that all kinds of "enemies of the people" were lurking behind every corner: Trotskyites, spies, saboteurs, or former kulaks "heroically uncovered by the Soviet patriots." A denunciation could have been made for more prosaic reasons. It could have been an act of ordinary vengeance caused by interpersonal relations with a neighbor, a family member, a superior at work—with any person against whom someone held a grudge. In the document, cited previously, about the purge in the Kharkiv consular district dated September 4, 1936, Consul Stanisław Sośnicki touched upon this issue of denunciations. He emphasized that this practice was influenced by the inequalities between the poor and the more affluent, which sparked resentment: "This is the backstory behind the strife fought by means of mutual smearing and the worst kind of informing of one against another."[239]

On September 10, 1936, Suchecki wrote: "Monstrous stupidities take place in connection with the search for and uncovering of Trotskyites. Anonymous denunciations are flooding the GPU [NKVD], as they say, because people grab this opportunity to settle their old scores through the GPU. Of course, the GPU takes advantage of all these denunciations because it has to demonstrate how vigilant and zealous it is. This entire situation only strengthens the GPU."[240]

Particularly disturbing were the denunciations by Bolshevik-educated children who informed on their parents. The most infamous was the case of Pavlik Morozov. He informed on his father, who was soon afterwards arrested for hiding grain. After Pavlik's family learned about his deed, they murdered him. Soviet propaganda soon made a hero out of Pavlik, and he became a role model for the Soviet system. A brief perusal of the Soviet press shows that Pavlik found his followers. This aspect of the denunciation frenzy was something that Władysław Michniewicz focused on. In May 1935 he wrote: "Even children are not immune [to this depravity]. After some misunderstanding, children inform on their parents, and if the parents have no proletarian background, they can be in serious trouble."[241] Stanisław Suchecki wrote: "Relations between parents and children are often unbearable. In the event of a quarrel, children report on their parents, who are then punished by the authorities."[242]

---

[239] CAW, Oddz. II SG, sygn. I.303.4.1867, k. 82–83.
[240] RGVA, f. 308 k, op. 19, d. 63, l. 186.
[241] CAW, Oddz. II SG, sygn. I.303.4.1926, doc. 77, n.p.
[242] RGVA, f. 308 k, op. 19, d. 63, l. 33.

As the terror grew, citizens "grew more vigilant"; in other words, the number of denunciations grew. Though usually groundless, these denunciations often could turn into a death or Gulag sentence for innocent people.

The fact of there being no denunciation against a person on file at the NKVD did not guarantee her or his safety. One careless word, however innocent or ironic, about matters in the "happiest and most democratic country in the world" could be enough. The head of intelligence post E.10 in Kharkiv wrote in mid-1936 that a worker had been arrested at 2:00 a.m. in his apartment. The worker, who worked at the Shevchenko factory, had said the following in public: "Stalin's life is much better, so why should he even care about us?" (Kuda to luchshe Stalin zhivet, emu do nas dela net?).[243] What happened to that worker no one knew.

Other circumstances under which one could be arrested were: the wrong ethnic or class origin of one's family, or even the wrong name;[244] links to the church; relatives abroad or receiving letters from abroad, and contacts, even accidental, with a foreign diplomatic or consular post.[245] Polish diplomats paid attention to all these factors. In his October 30, 1937 report to Ambassador Grzybowski, Adam Koch remarked that it was enough to receive a letter from abroad to have one's apartment searched and to be arrested: "The situation has gone so far that people who receive letters from their relatives abroad decline to accept them, fearing espionage charges."[246]

Other Polish reports also mentioned the unpleasant consequences and difficulties awaiting those who received correspondence from abroad. In August 1937 the intelligence service of the Border Protection Corps received information from an Italian specialist returning from the USSR that all the letters from abroad arriving to recipients in the USSR had to be picked up personally after showing one's ID, and packages of any kind had to be opened at the post office in front of the recipient.[247] One month later military intelligence gathered similar data with respect to the

---

[243] Ibid., l. 46–47.

[244] A navy officer was dismissed from his post in Novorossiisk. His father was named Ernest (i.e., his patronymic was Ernestovich), meaning that he must have had German origins—and therefore meaning that he must have remained in touch with foreign countries. This contact was enough for the NKVD to initiate repressions. CAW, Oddz. II SG, sygn. I.303.4.1867, k. 676.

[245] Hiroaki Kuromiya wrote about several similar cases; see his Głosy straconych, 146–63.

[246] CAW, Oddz. II SG, sygn. I.303.4.1867, k. 676.

[247] ASG, Dowództwo KOP, sygn. 541/566, k. 69.

correspondence restrictions in the USSR. Addressees who lived in the provinces (in Kurne and Holovanivsk raion) and received mail from abroad were summoned to the post office, where they could pick up their letters after providing proof of their identity. In Kyiv mail from abroad was still delivered directly to private addresses, but there were cases of nondelivery. Instead, the mail was returned to senders with the notice "the receiver did not accept the letter."[248]

Over time, more and more similar news reached the Polish posts. On December 2, 1937, the head of intelligence post G.27 shared the following information with the *Dwójka*: "We have a confirmation (Kyiv), that the [mail] recipients were summoned to the post office, their IDs were checked, [and] they had to fill out surveys (their class background was also questioned). Correspondence from abroad is the cause of recent arrests of ordinary citizens. Our visitors are constantly pleading for a general announcement to be made in our country [Poland] so that people know they should not send mail to the USSR, because 'they cause a lot of harm.'"[249]

Staff at the Polish Ministry of Interior Affairs alerted the MFA to this practice on December 13, 1937. They warned the MFA that, based on confidential information they had received, the Soviet authorities had increased their surveillance of mail reaching the USSR from Poland. The addressees of such mail were called in for interrogations and dismissed from their jobs.[250] The voivodeship office in Navahrudak [Nowogródek] received information from a female resident of Baranavichy county in Navahrudak voivodeship that she had received a letter from her mother in the USSR warning her not to write to her mother too frequently, because her mother was being interrogated by the Soviet authorities for that reason.[251]

As I discussed in the first chapter, having any contact with the consulates could have serious repercussions, even if the nature of that contact was purely formal. The atmosphere of terror was so invasive that

---

[248] Ibid., k. 52.

[249] CAW, Oddz. II SG, sygn. I.303.4.1968, doc. 41.

[250] AAN, MSZ, 6755 A, k. 206. Because of the mass repressions in the USSR, Polish citizens, and especially those of Ukrainian ethnicity, began to write letters to the Soviet consulate in Lviv asking about the fate of their relatives. They also came in person. The Soviet consulate received hundreds of such letters. In 1938, 96 people from Lviv voivodeship alone came to the consulate with this issue in mind. Their requests were usually either ignored or they received the response, "this person left and his/her whereabouts are unknown" (Rubl'ov, *Zakhidnoukraïns'ka intelihentsiia*, 309).

[251] AAN, MSZ, 6755 A, k. 205.

Soviet citizens who were acquainted with Polish officials tried to avoid their gaze.[252] This state of affairs applied not only to ordinary Soviet citizens, but also to some officials who had to remain in touch with foreigners because of the nature of their work. They were also extremely anxious about such encounters. Consul Tadeusz Brzeziński described one such Soviet official, with whom he had to schedule a business meeting, as "primitively distrustful" (*"prostacko nieufni"*). One needs to remember that what appeared to him as unreasonable distrust could be felt by his Soviet interlocutors, justifiably, as being in mortal danger. Soviet officials such as Pavel Nekunde or Adolf Petrovsky, whose job it was to be in touch with the foreign diplomatic corps on a regular basis, pleaded guilty to charges of espionage for foreign powers and acknowledged their work relationships to be treasonous. What other reaction, then, could be expected from an ordinary, local Soviet clerk who had to meet with the Polish consul because it was his professional duty? He must have been well aware that, sooner or later, the wrong kind of report would find its way to an NKVD office, and his professional relationship would then be defined as a "treasonous relationship."

This fear was well justified. The Bolsheviks, after all, found any reason, whether serious or completely made up, good enough to accuse this or that person of committing an anti-Soviet crime and to arrest and execute him. The Soviet people dreaded the sight of an NKVD car parked near their apartment at night. This could herald that soon there would be a knock on their door from an NKVD agent with an arrest order. NKVD cars, often dubbed "black ravens" (*chorni vorony*) were a permanent nightly feature "of the most democratic country in the world." As early as September 1936, the head of intelligence post E.10 wrote: "No one is sure anymore whether a *black raven* filled with *gepisty* [NKVD men] is not going to visit him the next night. There is virtually not a single day without an arrest, one hears about them constantly at least a few dozen—arrests of 'Trotskyites' who—so they say—are wrecking the plan and sabotaging 'the Stakhanovite movement' or displayed some 'hesitation' with respect to the correctness of the Party line. People are at loss to understand where it is all heading and what sorts of consequences are awaiting them."[253]

As the repressions intensified, so did the atmosphere of terror. On August 13, 1937, *Dwójka* agent Jerzy Kamiński wrote: "In the last few days,

---

[252] See chapter 1, section 1.2.2.
[253] RGVA, f. 308 k, op. 19, d. 63, l. 187.

the arrests have assumed a truly epidemic scale. Many citizens tremble, fearing arrest as night comes. One night two weeks ago, about thirty persons were taken away from a house where technical experts reside. Arrests among workers usually have a political background, e.g., careless words uttered publicly, the wrong kind of contacts, or a background of "wrecking"—bad production quality, not taking enough care of one's workplace, etc."[254]

Adam Koch reported to Ambassador Grzybowski about the mass arrests on several occasions. On October 30, 1937, he remarked: "The fact of arrests among ordinary people is confirmed by the numerous NKVD cars parked in front of residential houses at night. People woken up in the middle of their sleep are transported to the Lukianivka prison."[255]

In another report on November 13, 1937, Koch reported: "The intensification of arrests among ordinary citizens has not abated. The NKVD cars keep on driving at night with the same frequency [and] the lines of people waiting in front of the Lukianivka Prison are just as long as they were in October, despite the fact that significant quantities of prisoners have already been driven away. The omnipresent terror continues. It is enough for someone on a streetcar to say 'zhit' stalo luchshe, zhit' stalo veseleie' [life has become better, life has become merrier][256] to be accused of irony, antigovernment agitation, and sowing discontent (this actually happened on tram no. 18 on November 4, 1937)."[257]

On November 26, 1937, the vice-consul wrote about the political situation in Soviet Ukraine in general and concluded that the intensity of political arrests had not abated but remained at the same level, both in the cities and in the countryside. Information he received from a Soviet lawyer named Goldman helped give him a sense of the scale of the arrests. In the first ten days of November 1937, it was estimated that around thirty thousand prisoners were being held in Odesa's prisons. During the previous two and a half months, three transports filled with prisoners sentenced to deportation left Odesa each week, i.e., approximately three thousand persons per month.[258] Koch emphasized that the data he

---

[254] CAW, Oddz. II SG, sygn. I.303.4.2101, doc. 89.

[255] Ibid., sygn. I.303.4.1867, k. 673.

[256] Stalin's famous saying.

[257] CAW, Oddz. II SG, sygn. I.303.4.1867, k. 650–51.

[258] Other data from Koch's report: several dozen doctors, including Professor Korovytsky, were imprisoned in Odesa; on November 13, 1937, 1,300 wives of men who had already

received suggested that prisons were overflowing nearly everywhere (with up to forty people in one cell)—in Stalino, Vinnytsia, Zaporizhia, Berdychiv, Kamianets-Podilskyi, Uman, Zhytomyr, Fastiv, and Chernihiv.[259]

Koch was right to point out that the confessions the authorities wanted to hear from those imprisoned—e.g., whom to arrest next—were obtained very quickly. The most common way of obtaining these confessions was torturing the prisoner for as long as necessary.[260] Most prisoners, under pressure of beatings or other "interrogation methods practiced by the NKVD," gave up and submitted the statements the NKVD wanted. The vice-consul described one such method: "According to the information we have received from several sources, prisoners suffer hunger in nearly all the prisons in an identical way: one person is given 400 grams of bread per day and a cup of tea (a bucket of tea is shared by approx. 60 people). Unsurprisingly, the prisoners, especially because they were aware that they were going to be deported to Kazakhstan or to Siberia anyway, confessed whatever the prosecutor or the NKVD wanted them to confess, after which they awaited deportation more calmly, since they expected the conditions [of deportation] to be better than those in their current place of imprisonment."[261]

Koch tried to answer the question of how long the mass repressions were going to last. He concluded that, so far, there were no signs "that this abnormal state will somehow be changed; on the contrary, there are signs indicating that the purge of those higher in the hierarchy has not yet ended." As evidence, Koch quoted some recent press articles that vilified the "as yet remaining enemies of the people."[262] He was convinced that

---

been arrested were taken away from Kyiv; on November 17, three transports with deportees left Kyiv (about 6,000 persons); 500 persons were arrested in Dnipropetrovsk during the previous two months; and there were 300 prisoners in the Nikopol prison.

[259] CAW, Oddz. II SG, sygn. I.303.4.1867, k. 688–89. Other Polish officials also reported on the overfilled prisons. Jerzy Kamiński wrote about the prisons in Artemivsk. There were up to 30 people in one cell. Ibid., sygn. I.303.4.2101, n.p., doc. 127.

[260] T. Snyder, *Skrwawione ziemie: Europa pomiędzy Hitlerem a Stalinem* (Warsaw: Świat Książki, 2011), 117. Nikita Petrov has written about the "investigative methods" used by Stalinist interrogators. He also describes in detail some of the people who were in charge of investigations; see N. Pietrow, *Psy Stalina* (Warsaw: Demart, 2012).

[261] CAW, Oddz. II SG, sygn. I.303.4.1867, k. 689

[262] He mentioned the deputy commissar for domestic trade, Molodchenko; the director of the Dentistry Institute, Dubrovsky; the entire phone management board; the director of the Pedagogical Institute in Hlukhiv; the board of the Jewish section of the Union of Writers of Ukraine; and the head of the Kyiv fruit trade agency.

the arrests would not stop before December 12, 1937. This was the date scheduled for the elections to the two chambers of Soviet parliament, the Soviet of the Union and the Soviet of Nationalities. One thing was certain, and that was that the end of the purge could not be predicted: "Given this state of affairs, and given that so many issues are beyond our reckoning, no analysis of the situation in [Soviet] Ukraine can be made on the basis of which one could put forward positive theses about what will unfold in the period after the purges and mass arrests are over."[263]

Arrests and deportations continued in full force both before and after the December 12, 1937 elections. In January 1938, Colonel Tadeusz Pełczyński informed the most important individuals responsible for Polish national security: "The echoes that reach us from many directions speak about unspeakably crowded prisons and very numerous, systematic transports carrying deported prisoners to Kazakhstan and Siberia."[264] He shared information that he obtained. In Kyiv's Podil district druring the night of December 13–14, 1937, mass arrests took place. Breaking with traditional procedure, a portion of the group arrested had to walk to the prison because no more vehicles were available. A special investigative commission arrived in Toporyshche (north of Zhytomyr) because one of the voters wrote an offensive remark on the voting ballot. Then nearly the entire village was deported. In Dnipropetrovsk, during the night of December 7–8, nearly three thousand people were arrested, while in Zhytomyr about nine thousand were. Mass arrests were also conducted in Odesa, Tyraspil, and Stalino.[265]

The intensity of the terror did not abate during the following months. The atmosphere of distrust, all-encompassing fear, and uncertainty about what tomorrow would bring was aptly captured in an article published in the informational bulletin of the MFA, *Polska a Zagranica*, no. 3, on March 9, 1938: "Terror has become one of the principal methods of governance, the only stimulant that drives the command economy forward and the sole means of keeping the society, which is, in general, unhappy with the currently prevailing regime, submissive. The wave of terror is fueled by the strangest kinds of denunciations and self-denunciations so typical of the Russian [i.e., Soviet] psyche. This creates an odd mixture of truth, appearances, and lies, which, in the eyes of the

---

[263] Ibid., k. 690–91.
[264] RGVA, f. 464 k, op. 1, d. 2424, l. 73.
[265] Ibid.

authorities, definitively blurs the border between fake denunciations and real guilt. Any incautious word about current Soviet reality passed on to the authorities by the omnipresent eavesdropping ears leads to, in the best possible scenario, a deportation order to the distant provinces of Turkestan or Siberia. The current atmosphere of intimidation and danger trumps everything seen in the USSR thus far, including the bloody days of War Communism. Back in those days, at least one knew who the enemy was and for what. No one can be confident of seeing tomorrow today."[266]

The Great Terror finally ended when the "bloody dwarf," Nikolai Yezhov, was removed as people's commissar of the NKVD in late November 1938. Mass repression came to an abrupt halt, a fact that third-party observers noticed. For the head of the Polish consulate general in Kyiv, Jerzy Matusiński, the most immediate proof of the thaw was the fact that the first two months of 1939 brought only one personnel change within the top cadres of the government and Party bureaucracy in Ukraine. This one exception was the disappearance—"a very quiet one"— of Aleksandr Uspensky, the head of the Soviet Ukrainian NKVD in 1938. "The whole issue has been silenced to such an extent that a new head of the NKVD has not been appointed yet. Kobulov has been formally appointed, but merely as the deputy people's commissar.[267] Uspensky's dismissal can be read as a sign of a thaw, similar to—on the pan-Union level—Yezhov's dismissal."[268] The diplomat continued: "If we compare this state of affairs with what was happening a year ago and during the previous year perhaps—when arrests also took place, often on a massive scale among ordinary citizens, parallel to the purge done in the Party and the elimination of numerous dignitaries from the top echelons in the Party and in the government—the difference is noticeable."[269]

---

[266] AAN, MSZ, sygn. 119.

[267] Amaiak Kobulov, together with his older brother Bogdan, were among the closest associates of Yezhov's successor, Lavrentii Beria. From December 7, 1938, Kobulov was the first deputy head of the NKVD in Soviet Ukraine until the end of August 1939. In September 1939 he was sent to Berlin as the NKVD *rezydent* (code name Zakhar). During his absence his position in Soviet Ukraine remained vacant. After he returned to the USSR in July, he served at numerous top NKVD posts. After Stalin's death, he was arrested and sentenced to death. He was executed on February 19, 1955. See Pietrow, *Psy Stalina*, 102–13.

[268] AAN, MSZ, sygn. 6711, k. 7–8.

[269] Ibid., k. 8.

When Matusiński wrote about "the mysterious disappearance" of Uspensky, he was not aware of the details. When Uspensky was summoned to Moscow to be, as it was said, promoted, he expected that he was going to be arrested instead and he decided to fabricate his own suicide. He left a letter in his office in which he wrote that his corpse could be found in the Dnipro River. Then he boarded a train headed for Voronezh and using falsified documents traveled across the USSR. Ultimately, Uspensky was arrested in Miass, Chelyabinsk oblast, on April 16, 1939. He confessed that he had "participated in a counterrevolutionary organization and was a spy working for Germany" and was executed in January 1940.[270]

4.6. Repressions in the Countryside
4.6.1. Public Trials
The Central Committee (CC) of the All-Union Communist Party (of Bolsheviks) issued an instruction on August 3, 1937, to all the secretaries of oblast, krai and republican Central Committees advising them to launch two or three public political trials in each oblast of so-called enemies of the people who were "wreckers in the agricultural economy." These trials had to be publicized widely in the press. On September 10, 1937, a similar resolution was issued by the Central Committee and the Council of People's Commissars directed against "wreckers in the grain storage economy"; on October 2, 1937, another resolution was made against "wreckers in the animal farming economy." Two or three trials were suggested by the first resolution, and three to six by the second.

A September 11, 1937 resolution of the Politburo recommended that the persons arrested in cases of "counterrevolutionary wrecking and sabotage" should be informed of the indictment one day (24 hours) before the court trial began. No appeals were permitted, and death sentences were to be implemented immediately after the clemency pleas were rejected.[271] The actual trials were launched quite quickly. By January 4, 1938, seventy-two show trials had been completed in Soviet Ukraine. Of

---

[270] Aleksandr Uspensky (Ukr. Oleksander Uspens'kyi) (1902–1940) was an NKVD officer; from January 25 until November 14, 1938, he was head of the NKVD in Ukraine. See V. Zolotar'ov, *Oleksandr Uspens'kyi: Osoba, chas, otochennia* (Kharkiv: Folio, 2004). See also "Memuary Nikity Sergeevicha Khrushchova," *Voprosy istorii*, 1990, no. 5: 63–64.

[271] RGANI, f. 89, op. 48, d. 12, l. 1; V. Danilov and R. Manning, eds., *Tragediia sovetskoi derevni: Kollektivizatsiia i raskulachivanie. Dokumenty i materialy v 5 tomakh, 1927–1939* (Moscow: ROSSPEN, 2004), vol. 5, *1937–1939*, book 1 (1937), 300–302, 394, 452, and 486.

the 399 persons sentenced, 238 were executed and 161 were sentenced to ten years in prison. Seventeen of the seventy-two trials pertained to "wrecking" in agriculture (52 people were sentenced to death, and 38, to ten years in the Gulag). Twenty-seven trials covered "wrecking" in animal farming (110 were sentenced to death and 55, to ten years in the Gulag). Another twenty-seven trials were run in the *zagotzerno* (grain processing) apparatus (72 were sentenced to death and 70, to the Gulag); and one trial was organized in the coal industry, in which 6 persons were sentenced to death and one to the Gulag.[272]

Of course, the "wreckers" could not have acted alone but at the instigation of foreign-intelligence services. Nothing new or different unfolded in these trials compared with the old scenario. The command center for those operations was purportedly located in Poland and Germany. On June 13, 1938, at the Fourteenth Congress of the CP(B)U, the Party's boss, Nikita Khrushchev, said: "The enemies did all they could to destroy our collective farms. The problems [Soviet] Ukraine experienced during collectivization were masterminded by Piłsudski and the German fascists. The enemies sensed what kind of power the collective farms could deliver for Ukraine, the peasantry, [and] the socialist state. Therefore they did all they could to destroy the collective farms under construction, to organize sabotage, provocations, and thence to destroy the collective agriculture, devastate it, to sow discontent among our peasants. We had destroyed nearly all the enemies, but some hostile roots have remained, and it would have been a mistake to believe that we have already done all that had to be done. We need to be vigilant, always ready for battle, ready for the merciless treatment of spies and traitors. We will defeat them and finish them off completely."[273]

Unsurprisingly, the new campaign could not escape the attention of the Polish foreign services, especially because they were indirect targets of this new spy-hunt paranoia. Jan Karszo-Siedlewski's remarks during a conversation with Vladimir Neverovich on September 14, 1937, demonstrated just how immense the witch hunt about anything related to Poland was: "It is my impression that when I go for a walk in the field or when I go to pick mushrooms in the forest, people I meet on the way, after

---

[272] HDASBU, f. 42, spr. 33, ark. 30–31. Polish intelligence had only fragmentary data about the scale of the trials and sentences. According to Colonel Tadeusz Pełczyński's data from April 21, 1938, twenty-seven trials had been completed in Soviet Ukraine, resulting in 118 sentencings. See RGVA, f. 464 k, op. 1, d. 2424 A, l. 116.

[273] Quoted in Vasyliev, "Vplyv 'velykoho teroru,' " 45.

they had read what is published in the Soviet press, would tell each other that the Polish consul is on his way to set the forest aflame or wreck some tractors."[274]

It needs to be emphasized that the NKVD treated the Polish diplomat as a spy (as they did most foreign representatives in the USSR) serving as an intermediary keeping Polish intelligence in touch, for example, with the head of the Soviet Ukrainian Council of People's Commissars, Panas Liubchenko. The head of the NKVD of the Ukrainian SSR, Izrail Leplevsky,[275] wrote to Nikolai Yezhov in a September 21, 1937 report on the implementation of Polish operation no. 00485 that Consul Karszo-Siedlewski relied on the spy network built by Adolf Petrovsky, the representative of the PCfFA,[276] "to manage the Ukrainian nationalist organization in such a way that it served Poland's interest."[277] The Polish diplomat, according to the NKVD's account, served as a kind of protector of the Ukrainian agents within the highest echelons of power. As I have already pointed out, Karszo-Siedlewski did work for the *Dwójka*,[278] but the charges the NKVD fabricated—that he maintained espionage contacts with Petrovsky and other representatives of the PCfFA, such as the deputy representative, Mikhail Yushkevich, or Petrovsky's secretary, Bredenko,

---

[274] CAW, Oddz. II SG, sygn. I.303.4.1867, k. 710.

[275] Izrail Leplevsky (1896–1938) had been a Chekist since 1918. On June 14, 1937, Yezhov appointed him commissar for internal affairs in Soviet Ukraine. He implemented massive repressions for half a year until he was dismissed in January 1938 and summoned to Moscow. Leplevsky was arrested in April 1938 and executed on July 28, 1938. See N. Petrov and K. Skorkin, *Kto rukovodil NKVD, 1934–1941: Spravochnik* (Moscow: Zvenia, 1999); quoted in www.memo.ru/history /NKVD/kto/index.htm.

[276] During an interrogation held on September 1, 1937, Adolf Petrovsky confessed that he was an agent of the *Dwójka* and that his activity revolved around being an intermediary between Panas Liubchenko and Jan Karszo-Siedlewski. This mediation allegedly involved passing sealed packages between the two. Moreover, Petrovsky confessed that after he arrived in Ukraine at the end of 1934, at one meeting with Jan Karszo-Siedlewski the diplomat told him that Liubchenko was a major Ukrainian nationalist activist with close ties to Poland. Allegedly Warsaw gave him "a special task in the counterrevolutionary and espionage field." The goal was to detach Ukraine from the USSR. Liubchenko purportedly told Petrovsky that he supported Polish operations inside the Red Army so that it would suffer defeat in a war with Poland. See Rubl'ov and Rubl'ova, *Ukraïna–Pol'shcha 1920–1939 rr.*, 512–16; and Stępień, *Polacy na Ukrainie*, vol. 3, 79–180.

[277] Bednarek et al., eds., *Polska i Ukraina w latach trzydziestych-czterdziestych XX wieku,*vol. 8, pt. 1, 565–67.

[278] A survey of his cooperation with the *Dwójka* is in M. Kruszyński, "O współpracy konsula Jana Karszo-Siedlewskiego," 169–78.

or with Liubchenko himself — were absurd and groundless. It is enough to remind readers how problematic it was for the Polish foreign service to settle any issue, however immaterial, via the PCfFA. The charges were nonetheless typical of the sort that the NKVD fabricated to justify the massive crimes perpetrated in the USSR at the time. One does not need to engage in any advanced research to demonstrate that the PCfFA representatives had to meet with foreign diplomats, given the very definition of their service. They had to talk with diplomats and organize meetings with the relevant Soviet authorities — generally to serve as intermediaries between the entire foreign diplomatic corps and the Soviet administration. All this normal work was retrospectively defined as "conducting espionage activity" or "transmitting espionage materials." Pressured by the NKVD's interrogation methods, most PCfFA officials sooner or later pleaded guilty to all — even to the strangest — crimes and operations they purportedly committed against the Soviet state. When it comes to any intelligence activity Karszo-Siedlewski conducted, this was essentially limited to writing observational reports that only rarely, and insignificantly, differed from the ones he submitted to the MFA.[279]

Let us return to the September 14 conversation between Karszo-Siedlewski and Neverovich. After they had dealt with professional business, the diplomat said that he considered the conversation over, but he still wished to hear (unofficially) Neverovich's opinion about recent articles in the press that had smeared Poland's good reputation by suggesting that Warsaw was responsible, together with Berlin, for masterminding and leading the organization that engaged in destruction of Soviet Ukrainian agriculture (damaging crops, killing cattle, wrecking tractors). More specifically, he asked Neverovich whether the authors of those articles really believed in what they wrote. If they did, he said, it demonstrated how brainwashed they were; if they did not, he asked, what then was their reason for inciting the Soviet people against Poland while, on the international forum, the Soviet Union claimed it wanted peace? As was typical, the Soviet official dodged the question.[280] With respect to the

---

[279] This of course did not mean that Polish intelligence did not use consular posts as a cover for its operations. In the Ran Affair (mentioned in chapter 1), the Polish intelligence officer Stefan Kasperski (code name Albert Ran), who was caught red-handed, had supplied the Soviet side with arguments further convincing them that the USSR was surrounded by spies, inside and outside.

[280] CAW, Oddz. II SG, sygn. I.303.4.1867, k. 709–10.

trials against the so-called village wreckers that were recently organized in the USSR, Karszo-Siedlewski was certain that no sabotage-oriented organization existed and that it was a product of the regime's imagination. "In reality there was no single organized campaign in Soviet Ukraine that was anti-Soviet in general or, more specifically, oriented toward wrecking and sabotage in industry and agriculture."[281]

The diplomat was absolutely right. Most of the so-called sabotage, purportedly performed by "disguised enemies," that led to losses in crops and cattle were the products of some intrinsic features within the Communist system. For example, the alleged acts of sabotage were really caused by the lack of animal fodder, insufficient training of workers, bad quality of grain storage, and so on. Such cases happened regularly. On January 14, 1936, thanks to radio interception, Polish intelligence received information about the very high death rate among horses in Stalino and Makiivka raions (Donetsk oblast). The cause was the shortage of the right kind of fodder. The horses were fed with pressed hay and chaff completely drenched with water. The fodder had been stored for too long, and it was already rotten when the horses were fed it.[282]

Four days after the conversation with Nemerovich, Jan Karszo-Siedlewski prepared a report in which he dealt with Soviet propaganda one more time. This time the propaganda had suggested that Poland had something to do with counterrevolutionary occurrences in Soviet agriculture. He pointed out that at all recent mass gatherings, even in the villages and collective farms, the propagandists claimed that Poland was readying itself for war with the USSR. The diplomat stressed that this campaign was something that should not be taken lightly in Poland. He suggested that a diplomatic campaign had to be initiated in response, but also that the popular press (he mentioned the publication *Ilustrowany Kuryer Codzienny*), as well as the pro-government *Gazeta Polska*, should not neglect to react to those assertions. He even suggested a title for an article—"Na złodzieju czapka gore (loosely translated, "the ones who are really responsible are blaming others for the crime"). Karszo-Siedlewski believed that the issue of the Soviet military build-up should be made clearer to the Polish public—i.e., the increased number of military garrisons, airports, and strategic highways near the Polish border—"the

---

281 Ibid., k. 680–86.
282 RGVA, f. 462 k, op.1, d. 69, l. 103. In his memoirs, Nikita Khrushchev described the mechanism of uncovering the "wreckers" in agriculture. See "Memuary Nikity Sergeevicha Khrushcheva," *Voprosy istorii*, 1990, no. 5: 60–63.

rapidly growing number of which cannot be explained by defensive objectives alone."[283]

Vice-consul Koch analyzed the aforementioned agricultural trials in a few of his reports as well. In addition to providing factual information about how many trials took place, he ventured the thesis (after some hesitation) that the main culprit behind the offenses that particular individuals were charged with was the system itself. It was the system that caused the huge organizational mess and neglect, which in turn led to losses in cattle and to the general disrepair of agricultural machinery. On October 30, 1937, Koch mentioned that five trials were underway for managers in the *zagotzerno* agency. They were charged with the act of willfully spreading infection among cattle, neglecting to do the work necessary for proper beet cultivation, and so on. The trials focused on the kinds of agricultural activity where "major work intensification at a certain time period" was a necessity. Koch also wrote that the trials were aimed at "encouraging" the peasants to do their work more diligently, and he predicted that new trials could be expected, because "some areas of agricultural activity (especially ploughing) exhibited very noticeable shortcomings."[284]

A month later, on November 28, 1937, Koch wrote to the ambassador informing him that seven trials of the *zagotzerno* agency employees had already taken place. Another, major and collective, trial was supposed to start on November 27. The list of the accused included the head of the Ukrainian *zagotzerno* agency, his deputy, and the heads of the regional centers in Kyiv, Bila Tserkva, and Uman. The accused were presented with the standard charges—spreading disease or poisoning cattle, which was dangerous also for human beings; infecting the grain stored at the *zagotzerno* depots with viruses; and poor storage of grain, which led to damp conditions, rotting, etc. Evaluating the charges and the trials, Koch concluded that in some cases the human factor was responsible for the losses. "However, we do not know whether it is a person who does it willfully because he has nothing to lose, or a person (as in the case of veterinary doctors) who has not been sufficiently trained, or due to a true error of judgment.[285] He wrote later: "In other cases it is the system as such, i.e., poor organization or the high rotation of cadres, that is really

---

[283] CAW, Oddz. II SG, sygn. I.303.4.1867, k. 709–13.
[284] Ibid., k. 674.
[285] Ibid., k. 717.

responsible for the losses, not an individual human being. Is the current director of the *zagotzerno* agency (the previous one was executed in mid-October) really personally responsible for the fact that both the collective farms and the sovkhozes deliver mostly damp, or even overgrown, grain? Is the current director of the *zagotzerno* agency in Chernihiv responsible for the fact that, back in the day, a technician built the silos in such a way that there is no air circulation in the building to keep the grain dry?"[286]

4.6.2. NKVD Operation no. 00447

Most repressions in the agricultural sector were implemented under the heading of the so-called kulak operation. In terms of the number of victims, it was the largest operation performed during the Yezhovshchina. On July 30, 1937, the NKVD issued operational order no. 00447, which specified what kind of measures awaited the former kulaks but also was directed against criminals and "the anti-Soviet element."[287] The Politburo of the Central Committee confirmed the NKVD's order during its session on the following day.[288] Order 00447 applied to former kulaks who had already returned home after surviving their original deportation sentence, to other kulaks who had avoided the Gulag so far or had escaped, and to those who were still imprisoned or in the Gulag. "The anti-Soviet element" was divided into two categories. The first included "all of the most hostile elements," who were earmarked for immediate arrest and, after their case was investigated by the so-called troika, execution. The second category included "less active but nonetheless hostile elements." They were prescribed a sentence of eight to ten years in a Gulag camp. NKVD order no. 00447, approved by the Politburo, assumed that more than 250,000 people would be arrested in the entire USSR and 80,000 would be executed. In Soviet Ukraine, 28,800 individuals were scheduled to be arrested, 8,000 of them in the first category, and 20,800 in the second.[289]

The operation began on August 5, 1937, and lasted until mid-1938. It exceeded the original quotas significantly.[290] During the course of the

---

[286] Ibid.

[287] Iakovlev et al., *Lubianka: Stalin i Glavnoe upravlenie*, 273–81.

[288] Ibid., 281–82.

[289] Ibid., 273–81.

[290] In an NKVD report dated March 1, 1938, the number was revised up to 657,868 people, compared to the original figure quoted in the 00447 order, and the quota of death

operation, local NKVD organs asked—sometimes a few times—the center to increase the limits (contingents or quotas) of allowed repressions. These did increase with time. The head of the Soviet Ukrainian NKVD, Izrail Leplevsky, sought to increase those numbers, as seen by the following quote from a letter typical of those he sent to Yezhov: "I report that the quotas you indicated for Ukraine, based on order no. 00447, that is, 24,150 persons for the first category and 47,800 persons for the second category, have been exhausted. In accordance with your telegram no. 50194 from December 11, 1937, I am asking you to approve the extra quotas of 6,000 for the first category and 10,000 for the second category."[291] After he received an endorsement from Moscow, he immediately instructed his NKVD agents that the limit was of an approximate, not a strict, nature. He ordered the troikas to increase their efforts and rebuked his subordinates for excessive leniency, such as relegating people who were too old or disabled for physical labor in a Gulag camp to the second category.[292]

The Polish MFA and intelligence services, as well as representatives of other foreign countries, were not aware of NKVD order 00447. They had no knowledge about the scale of the operation. The NKVD conducted its operations in secrecy, and no one was informed of the sentencings, even the sentenced persons themselves.[293] Their families were also not informed about their whereabouts but were left to believe, naively

---

sentences was updated to 319,089. Up to that point, 270,656 people from the first category and 341,816 from the second category had been sentenced, and, in Ukraine, 31,417 and 48,868, respectively. The numbers of so-called former kulaks in those counts were as follows: 115,378 and 148,507 in the entire USSR, and 15,636 and 22,502 in Soviet Ukraine. According to the records of the Soviet Ukrainian NKVD with respect to their operational work between October 1, 1936, and July 1, 1938, 64,634 former kulaks were arrested in 1937 (this figure included not only those who were arrested based on order no. 00447, but also everyone else who was classified as "a former kulak" in their social-background rubric), and in the first half of 1938, 27,161 were arrested. According to NKVD data, 111,675 people were arrested during 1937–38 as a result of operation 00447 in Soviet Ukraine, and of those 51,400 were classified as former kulaks. Of them, 109,469 people were sentenced: 49,831 of them were classified as former kulaks, 11,655 as criminals, and 48,433 as "other counterrevolutionary elements." See HDASBU, f. 42, spr. 35, ark. 2–3; Danilov and Manning, *Tragediia sovetskoi derevni*, vol. 5, book 2, 56–61; and R. Kuśnierz, "Przemoc systemu komunistycznego wobec chłopów w latach 1929–1939 (na przykładzie Sowieckiej Ukrainy)," in *Ofiary imperium: Imperia jako ofiary. 44 spojrzenia/Imperial Victims: Empires as Victims. 44 Views*, ed. A. Nowak (Warsaw: IPN-KŚZpNP and Instytut Historii PAN, 2010), 438–39.

[291] HDASBU, f. 42, spr. 32, ark. 108.

[292] See, e.g., ibid., ark. 55–78, 80–93, and 99–107.

[293] Snyder, *Skrwawione ziemie*, 106.

perhaps, that the trial was still ongoing and that their relative was still alive. The mothers, wives, and daughters of those sentenced did not fully comprehend what the clause "sentenced without any rights to correspondence" really meant. They wrote letters to the highest authorities in the USSR claiming that the accused was certainly innocent, that a horrible misunderstanding must have taken place. The truth about what happened to their loved ones reached their families only after many years—after Khrushchev's thaw or even much later, during Perestroika.

The kulak operation was not accompanied by the usual propaganda campaign. There was no news of the kulaks regathering strength and plotting against Soviet power again. In 1937 and 1938, what was predominant in the Soviet press was the agenda of fighting against "the enemies of the people," i.e., the Trotskyites, Zinoviev and Bukharin followers, as well as other "less dangerous" internal enemies (Party and state bureaucrats, negligent workers, thieves). "Spies" who purportedly cooperated with foreign powers were also among the main targets. Kulaks were not mentioned, other than in a purely historical context, when events from the past were discussed—from the tsarist period or from before the collectivization drive of the early 1930s, when peasants deemed as kulaks by the Bolsheviks were considered to be "leeches who sucked the blood of the workers" and were blamed for all the difficulties Soviet agriculture experienced.[294]

News about the terror and repressions against the "kulaks" could not have reached the Polish posts immediately. On October 30, 1937—that is, at the end of the third month of operation 00447—Adam Koch informed the ambassador in Moscow that the situation in the countryside was different than that in the cities, as there were no "mass arrests and the kind of political atmosphere that looms large over Kyiv."[295] He even wrote that the situation in the countryside was much better than in the previous year: "The wage consisted on average of 4 kg of grain and 0.80–1.20 rubles for one *trudoden'*, which was a lot considering Ukrainian conditions; hence, the overall mood of the rural population, who look purely through the prism of bread, is better than last year."[296]

---

[294] R. Kuśnierz, "Sowieckie ustawodawstwo wobec kułaków," in *Społeczeństwo a władza: Ustrój, prawo, idee*, ed. J. Przygodzki and M. J. Ptak (Wrocław: Kolonia Limited, 2010), 753.

[295] CAW, Oddz. II SG, sygn. I.303.4.1867, k. 678.

[296] Ibid.

However, two weeks later Polish officials finally received news of the much more tragic situation in the Soviet countryside. Still, they had no idea of the cause for such massive repressions. In a message to the ambassador dated November 13, 1937, the vice-consul wrote: "Apart from the arrests that we know about in Kyiv, one needs to mention the much greater scale of arrests in the provincial cities (we hear that there is a shortage of prison space in Odesa) and in the countryside, e.g., in the southern part of Vinnytsia oblast and in the northwestern part of Ukraine. The causes of those arrests in the countryside are still largely unknown; they have taken place without any show trials preceding them, and they did not apply to individuals, so far, but to larger groups of peasants."[297]

The Polish authorities responded to the new wave of repressions in a way that was informed by their experiences during the years 1929–33, when the Soviet Union saw a mass exodus (or at least an attempt to flee) of peasants whose households had been confiscated as a result of collectivization. They wondered whether the situation was going to develop in the same direction. Captain Zborowski, the chief of the Autonomous Information Agency of Corps Regional Command no. 9 in Brest, asked the administration of the counties in his district (Baranavichy, Brest, Siedlce, Pinsk, Drohiczyn, Kosava) to report whether any foreigners deported from the USSR had found their way there.[298] He received replies from Drohiczyn (December 28, 1937) and Kosava (January 12, 1938) that no such people had been seen.[299] The fact that only a few people were able to make it out of the USSR was because of completely different circumstances in 1937 and 1938 than had existed during the collectivization drive, especially in its early period (1929–30). First of all, the kulak operation had a narrower reach than the mass collectivization and dekulakization drives. Furthermore, since 1935 the Bolsheviks had been implementing a systematic policy of "cleansing" the borderlands by deporting the "uncertain" population (mostly ethnic Poles and Germans) and settling "certain" populations there from central and eastern Soviet Ukraine.

---

[297] Ibid., k. 651.
[298] Ibid., Samodzielny Referat Informacyjny DOK nr IX Brześć nad Bugiem, sygn. I.371.9/A.152, n.p.
[299] Ibid.

4.7. Repressions of Polish People[300]

The Great Purge also encompassed the mass persecution of national minorities and other foreign nationals who resided in the USSR at the time. Many operations against nationalities were conducted during the Yezhovshchina. The largest one, in terms of the number of victims (shot dead or deported to a Gulag camp), was the Polish operation. Polish diplomats, consular officials, and intelligence services informed Warsaw about the repressions against Poles, Germans, Greeks, Bulgarians, Czechs, and Austrians, but of course they were most concerned with the fate of their fellow compatriots, about whom they wrote numerous reports.[301] The persecution of the Polish minority in Ukraine in the 1930s, especially during the most violent period of the Yezhovshchina, has been covered quite extensively in the historiography.[302] Various aspects of those repressions have been carefully examined: the causes, the mechanisms of implementation, and their consequences. One very important aspect, however, has not been studied: the question of the extent to which the Polish diplomatic and consular corps were aware of the plight of the Polish minority, and, if so, how successfully they engaged in efforts to help alleviate it. This topic has received tangential attention in the

---

[300] Parts of this section have already been published; see Kuśnierz, "Próby interwencji dyplomacji polskiej," 143–68; and idem, "Represje wobec Polaków na Ukrainie," 67–79.

[301] As mentioned, I published these documents in my book "Nas, Polaków, nie ma kto bronić..."

[302] See, e.g., Iwanow, Polacy w Związku Radzieckim; idem, Pierwszy naród ukarany; W. Lizak, Rozstrzelana Polonia: Polacy w ZSRR, 1917–1939 (Szczecin: Prywatny Instytut Analiz Społecznych, 1990); Pietrow, "Polska operacja NKWD," 24–44; Kupczak, Polacy na Ukrainie; T. Ieremenko, Pol's'ka natsional'na menshyna v Ukraïni v 20-30-ti roky XX stolittia (Kyiv: Instytut istoriï Ukraïny NAN Ukraïny, 1994); I. Vynnychenko, Ukraïna 1920–1980-kh: Deportatsiï, zaslannia, vyslannia (Kyiv: "Rada," 1994); O. Rubl'ov and V. Repryntsev, "Represiï proty polakiv v Ukraïni u 1930-ti roky," Z arkhiviv VUChK-GPU-NKVD-KGB, 1995, no. 1/2; and Stroński, Represje stalinizmu. See also S. Stępień, ed., Polacy na Ukrainie:. Zbiór dokumentów, part 1, 1917–1939, vols. 1, 2, 3, 5 (Przemyśl: Instytut Południowo-Wschodni, 1998, 1999, 2001, 2005); Bednarek et al., eds., Polska i Ukraina w latach trzydziestych-czterdziestych XX wieku, vol. 8; T. Sommer, ed., Rozstrzelać Polaków: Ludobójstwo Polaków w Związku Sowieckim w latach 1937–1938. Dokumenty z centrali (Warsaw: Biblioteka Wolności, 2010); "Pamięć wielkiej zbrodni: 75 rocznica 'operacji polskiej' NKWD: Ankieta historyczna (Nikita Pietrow, Hiroaki Kuromiya, Krzysztof Jasiewicz, Marek Jan Chodkiewicz, Bogdan Musiał, Tomasz Sommer, Jerzy Bednarek, Jan Jacek Bruski, Marek Kornat, Henryk Głębocki), Arcana, 2012, no. 4–5, 58–79. See also N. Iwanow, Zapomniane ludobójstwo...; T. Sommer, ed., Dzieci operacji polskiej mówią: 45 relacji (Warsaw: 3 S Media, 2013); and T. Sommer, Operacja antypolska NKWD 1937–1938 (Warsaw: 3S Media, 2014).

historiography of the Polish minority in the USSR;[303] the predominant supposition is that Polish diplomats were essentially not interested in the fate of the persecuted ethnic Poles, with the exception of the Catholic Church.[304]

Analysis of hitherto unpublished materials of the Polish MFA and the *Dwójka* allows for a thesis that such claims are only partially justified. The representatives of the Second Polish Republic tried to help not only the clergy and Catholic parishes, but also persecuted "ordinary" Poles. Of course, their efforts were not systematic; they were not part of a broader Polish foreign policy, but rather belonged to each consul's individual discretion and initiative within his consular district. An example of such activity can be seen in the approach of Jan Karszo-Siedlewski, the head of the consulate general in Kyiv and a counselor to the embassy in Moscow. After receiving an increasing volume of news about the terror, arrests, and deportations directed against the ethnic Polish population, he not only tried to direct the ambassador's attention to that problem, but also, in 1935, raised that issue with the relevant authorities in Soviet Ukraine. Finally, he managed to meet with the head of the Soviet Ukrainian NKVD at the time, Vsevolod Balytsky.

Before describing that meeting between Karszo-Siedlewski and Balytsky, a few words need to be said about the Soviet measures with respect to the de-Polonization process of the USSR's western border area. Those developments worried the Polish consulates greatly. Between February 1 and 9, 1935, 2,000 families (681 of them were Polish) were deported from the Ukrainian oblasts bordering on Poland to the White Sea Canal area. On January 23, 1935, the Politburo of the CP(B)U ordered the resettlement of 8,300 peasant families (Ukrainian, Polish, German and others[305]) for "national security reasons." Their place was to be taken by 4,000 "outstanding" collective-farm workers from Kyiv and Chernihiv oblasts. The deportations were conducted between February 20 and March 10, 1935. Later, on September 8, 1935, the NKVD issued an order to deport from Marchlewski raion in Volhynia (Pol. Marchlewszczyzna) 350 families (1,668 individuals) who were "a hostile and uncertain element." Following the November 4, 1935, decisions of the Politburo of the CP(B)U and the Soviet Ukrainian Council of People's Commissars of December

---

[303] See Stroński, *Represje stalinizmu*, 261–73; and Iwanow, *Pierwszy naród ukarany*, 244–54.

[304] H. Stroński, "Losy ludności polskiej," 256, 270.

[305] Among them were 3,434 Ukrainian families, 2,866 Polish, 1,903 German, and 126 others.

1935, 1,100 Polish families from twelve raions in Vinnytsia oblast were deported to Kharkiv and Donetsk oblasts in mid-January 1936.[306] The next and final stage of this process were deportations to Kazakhstan; in the second half of 1936, 11,494 Polish families (almost 70,000 people) were deported to Kazakhstan from Kyiv and Vinnytsia oblasts.[307]

After the deportations started, the Polish consulates were flooded with letters from the victims, who wrote that their property had been confiscated, that their household was burdened with excessive or unjustified taxation, or that they were unlawfully held in detainment or had already been deported. Some of these Poles visited the Polish consular posts seeking help. This step often led to their arrest. Information about deportations of Polish people from Soviet Ukraine was also gathered by Branch no. 5 of the *Dwójka* in Lviv.[308]

In all cases, when the Polish people came to seek help in the consulates, there was nothing that Polish officials could do because, technically, they were dealing with Soviet citizens. The Soviets did not recognize the claim that those people belonged to a Polish national minority, and each communication, even a verbal one, on this topic was met with the reply that it was an unacceptable form of interference by a foreign power into Soviet internal affairs. Ethnic Germans who resided in Soviet Ukraine experienced a similar plight, but there was nothing the German consulates could do to defend them.[309]

Jan Karszo-Siedlewski was particularly interested and active in intervening on behalf of the persecuted Polish minority. In part, his involvement was because the deportations took place in the borderlands, i.e., in his Kyiv consular district. But the most important factor, evidenced by his numerous letters to the ambassador and the MFA, was his personal empathy for the Polish community (*polskość*), which the Bolsheviks threatened with liquidation. Based on the archival materials produced by the Polish consulate in Kharkiv, it can be deduced that the Kharkiv post did not pay as much attention to these matters as did the Kyiv post. Consul Stanisław Sośnicki did not undertake any special efforts, unlike Counselor Jan Karszo-Siedlewski, to defend the persecuted Polish

---

[306] Stępień, *Polacy na Ukrainie*, vol. 1, 276–78 and 280–81; Stroński, *Represje stalinizmu*, 178–87; T. Martin, "The Origins of Soviet Ethnic Cleansing," *The Journal of Modern History* 70, no. 4 (1998): 848; and Ieremenko, *Pol's'ka natsional'na menshyna*, 62.

[307] This topic will be explored in this chapter.

[308] See, e.g., RGVA, f. 308 k, op. 6, d. 22 and f. 462 k, op. 1, d. 70, l. 54.

[309] See ibid., f. 308 k, op. 19, d. 53, l. 160 and d. 54, l. 11.

community. All Sośnicki did was inform the embassy and the MFA, based on data he received, where in his consular district the Poles deported from western Soviet Ukraine were located and in what conditions they found themselves. On August 2, 1935, Sośnicki wrote to Ambassador Łukasiewicz: "In the past months, 800 Polish persons from the Horodok (east of Husiatyn) and Kamianets-Podilskyi areas were resettled in Kupiansk raion of Kharkiv oblast. This population was transported by means of five trains and relocated in certain villages that had been emptied after the famine [of 1932–33] or following deportations to other parts of the USSR." Sośnicki reported that the deported people were allowed to take only the most necessary personal belongings with them and were prohibited from maintaining any contact with the areas they were forced to abandon. "Some of them ran away back to their old homes, but we do not know what their fate currently is."[310]

The consulate in Kharkiv received, perhaps by mistake, a letter from one of the deportees about the conditions that the Poles deported from the western borderlands of Soviet Ukraine faced. The consulate delivered a copy of that letter to the ambassador in Moscow. Here is its translation:[311]

"Dear brother and sister-in-law,
We have reached our destination to where they deported us. We have been relocated to some houses with pigsties and small orchards, but this is of no significance or interest to us, because it is very far (27 kilometers from the railway station). The houses are in the steppes—you know what we are talking about. There is no forest, just the earth and the sky, a lot of houses are unoccupied, there is no fuel for heating apart from hay. Mother is very sick, father is gravely ill, everything aches, [we have] cramps all over our bodies, we do not have any work or income, there are no factories or towns nearby, [and] no one is capable of earning a single penny. We only have what we have taken with us, that is, one cow and one small pig; we took some potatoes but they all froze [and are useless]; it is very difficult to buy them here because we have no money and they are very expensive. A bucket of potatoes costs 18 rubles in the market. There have been crop failures and terrible droughts in this village, but the soil is decent, black-earth. There are only eight families here from

---

[310] Ibid., d. 57, l. 115.

[311] The letter was written in a specific dialect used by the Polish diaspora in that region. It differed significantly, especially stylistically, from the more standard Polish used in Poland at the time.

our old village of Lodzianivka ... The train that took us here was a cargo train, it was very cold; all us are very sick, Monyzh was very sick, but he is a little better now; we do not know what's going to happen next. Mania remained in Baranivka, she was supposed to marry Kolczewska's son, but after what has happened recently we do not know what's next ... The house and everything else have been nationalized. We left our house on March 3 and got here on Ash Wednesday at 10:00 p.m. Dear brother-in-law, we got your letter on our way in Polonne—it was received by the head of the collective and he gave it to me at the Polonne railway station, the one you wrote on February 7, 1935. We are very grateful that you do not forget about us because no one else remembers, because everyone has disappeared somewhere in the big wide world. Warm greetings to you and your family from your brother-in-law, sister, and children. Our new address is Dnipropetrovsk oblast, Nova Praha raion, Dubove settlement no. 2."[312]

The Polish consulate general in Kyiv followed the Stalinist repressions within the Polish community much more closely than did the Kharkiv consulate. Jan Karszo-Siedlewski tried to present to the Polish embassy in Moscow the most comprehensible picture possible of that policy, as well as to undertake to help the persecuted community, even as he realized that it would be extremely difficult to achieve any tangible results. On March 23, 1935, he prepared a very informative analytical paper and sent it to the ambassador in Moscow. It was on the policy of liquidating the Polish "element" in Soviet Ukraine. He wrote: "It is my duty to report to you, Mr. Ambassador, once again, that the repressions and arrests of the Polish population in the borderlands of Kyiv and Vinnytsia oblasts are taking place on a massive scale. The developments that I wrote about in my reports from January, February, and early March have not ceased; on the contrary, they have been on the rise in the past few weeks. These arrests often lead to the mass deportation of entire families from Soviet Ukraine. The villages and towns of the raions bordering Poland are systematically cleansed of the remnants of the Polish population, deported to an unknown destination. Oftentimes parents and children, wives and husbands, are separated, etc. All this happens under the heading of collectivization, which has accelerated rapidly again in the past few weeks, particularly in Vinnytsia oblast, or under the guise of participating in the espionage campaign. It is enough to undertake any

---

[312] RGVA, f. 308 k, op. 6, d. 54, l. 69.

actions toward making one's travel to Poland possible, or just to visit the consulate, to earn such charges, or sometimes there is no reason for them whatsoever. The persecution of Catholic churches has also increased, which is something I have already reported."[313]

The next part of Karszo-Siedlewski's report is a desperate outcry: no efforts, either in Kyiv or in Moscow, can save the persecuted compatriots, because the Bolshevik authorities have prepared a meticulous plan of eradicating the Polish element from the Soviet areas bordering on Poland, and they have been implementing it with determination. The diplomat wrote that he could do nothing to help the persecuted people, because they were Soviet citizens. All of his intercessions had been futile: "I also do not believe that any diplomatic intervention [in Moscow] will be effective. Where a certain prearranged system has taken hold, managed by people with ill will, no verbal interventions or explanations can help. What we are dealing with in [Soviet] Ukraine is an enemy who still puts on a mask, but who [we should have no doubts] really hates us and tries, wherever he can, to destroy the remnants of Polishness on his territory; [we are dealing with] an uncouth brute (*bezceremonialny cham*), who recognizes only sheer force [as a factor in politics]."[314]

The only way to try to change the Soviet policy directed against the ethnic Polish community of the USSR, Karszo-Siedlewski believed, was to mirror similar repressive measures at home. "Hence only through legal, but clear, repressive measures from our side applied against Soviet citizens, or against Polish Communists, can we hope to defend our interests in [Soviet] Ukraine, of course all within the limits imposed by the overall political situation and the Polish-Soviet Non-Aggression Pact." As an example of such retaliatory measures he quoted a ban on making any financial transfers to the USSR, either from private individuals or from institutions. The justification for this measure could be the principle of mutuality, since the Soviet side made it impossible to make any financial transfers in rubles or (hard) currencies across the Soviet border. The diplomat stressed that large amounts of money were involved and that the Soviet authorities "were currently very sensitive to everything that could hurt their finances."[315]

---

[313] Ibid., l. 52.
[314] Ibid., l. 52–53.
[315] Ibid., l. 53.

In a letter, Karszo-Siedlewski also suggested that a new agreement be made with the Soviet government, according to which both sides would inform each other immediately about each case of an arrest of a citizen of the other country on their respective territories. This proposal, unfortunately, was not included in the Polish-Soviet consular agreement, even though a similar agreement was signed by the USSR and Germany. Such an arrangement would have speeded up and rendered more effective the efforts of the Polish consulates in the USSR to support any arrested Polish citizen. The diplomat suggested that such an agreement should be concluded after he had intervened with the PCfFA representative in support of a Polish citizen named Tkaczenko, who was arrested in Kyiv in early February 1935 and had turned to the Polish consulate for help. This person was not found in the records of the Polish consulate; hence, the head of the consulate asked the PCfFA representative to confirm that Tkaczenko was really a Polish citizen. He did not receive an answer until March 13, 1935, when the PCfFA informed him that they had to verify whether a given person was a Soviet or foreign citizen on an individual basis (i.e., there was no systematic way to check); furthermore, there was no agreement with Poland that would oblige the Soviet side to provide such information within a specified period of time.

In response, Karszo-Siedlewski told the PCfFA representative that if he had to wait a few months (as he usually did) to learn whether the arrested person in question was a Polish citizen or not, and only then be able to intervene in her support, then he should give up his right to do so altogether. He also said that he felt compelled to inform Warsaw that he considered the (legal) protection over Polish citizens on Soviet territory to be illusory. Adolf Petrovsky promised to get in touch "with the decision-makers" to ensure they were able to provide such information in the event of an arrest as quickly as possible—to allow the consulate to receive an answer to an inquiry within a week.[316]

Aside from his letters to the ambassador and the MFA, Karszo-Siedlewski also raised the issue of the persecution of the Polish community in Soviet Ukraine during his conversations with Petrovsky, the representative of the PCfFA, and Petrovsky's secretary, Bredenko, in January and February 1935. For instance, he did so in early February 1935. Petrovsky was absent, since he was a deputy at the all-Soviet Party Congress and remained in Moscow, but Karszo-Siedlewski was received

---

[316] Ibid., l. 49.

by Bredenko. After listening to what the Polish diplomat had to say, Bredenko cynically replied that it was impossible that someone would be arrested merely for visiting or staying in touch with the consulate or for expressing his desire to travel to Poland. There must have been other reasons for that person's arrest, about which he would try to obtain more information, he said. Karszo-Siedlewski did not expect to receive any such information, but even so, he wrote, this conversation marked some progress because Bredenko listened through to the end and did not interrupt him by saying that he was meddling in internal Soviet affairs. During their conversation, the Polish diplomat also said that he regretted that he could no longer stay in touch, even only socially, with the Soviet Ukrainian NKVD chief, Vsevolod Balytsky, "who perhaps was not aware of the many excesses committed by his subordinates." He said that the employees of the Polish consulates felt more isolated from local society than ever, and that Soviet citizens feared seeing them. He also mentioned that he noticed the very unfavorable stance of the Soviet authorities toward Poland. He was very skeptical, however, that Bredenko would report on this conversation and its topics to anyone.[317]

On February 20, Karszo-Siedlewski met with Petrovsky after the latter returned from Moscow. The main issue on the agenda was the mistreatment of ethnic Poles in the USSR who wished to immigrate to Poland. Petrovsky "was not able to deny that such cases did take place or to give a satisfactory guarantee that they would not happen again," preferring instead to talk vaguely about the general state of Polish-Soviet relations.[318] Realizing that his conversations with the representatives of the PCfFA were ineffective, the diplomat began requesting (systematically) a meeting with Vsevolod Balytsky.[319] He was unsuccessful initially, but after many attempts and requests, he received word that Balytsky would receive him at noon on March 31, 1935, at NKVD headquarters. The meeting lasted one hour. The only other person present was Petrovsky. It is remarkable that this meeting between a Polish diplomat and a high-ranking NKVD official was, until recently, unknown of and so not covered

---

[317] See CAW, Oddz. II SG, sygn. I.303.4.3145, k. 167–68.

[318] RGVA, f. 308 k, op. 19, d. 54, l. 43–45.

[319] Karszo-Siedlewski made attempts previously to meet with Balytsky and other members of the Soviet Ukrainian government. See Rubl'ov and Rubl'ova, *Ukraïna-Pol'shcha 1920– 1939 rr.*, 449.

in the historiography.[320] It deserves attention, if only for this reason. During that meeting, Karszo-Siedlewski placed on the agenda the persecutions and deportations that the Polish community was suffering, the obstacles that Poles who wanted to leave the USSR (for Poland) faced, and the inappropriate behavior of NKVD agents toward employees of the Polish consulate. Balytsky greeted his Polish guest very courteously. He started out by saying, "I thought that you, sir, had an issue you wanted to discuss with me." Karszo-Siedlewski said he had no particular issue at that moment that he wished to discuss with Balytsky personally, but that he was happy he had the opportunity to get to know him and to establish a relationship with a member of the Soviet Ukrainian government responsible for the most important commissariat, the one on which all consular matters depended. Balytsky replied that, in fact, the Pole had the opportunity to raise all such issues with Petrovsky. Karszo-Siedlewski replied that, yes, he could raise those issues, but he could not address them effectively because most of them were ignored; furthermore, his private conversations with Petrovsky were treated by the Soviet Ukrainian government as official requests. Moreover, in the conversations with Petrovsky, the suspicion was raised that the counselor was meddling in the internal affairs of a foreign power, whereas he only wished to deliver an amicable reminder to his colleague that local security organs were committing certain excesses in their operations.

In the next part of the conversation, the Polish diplomat proceeded to describe the difficult conditions of the Polish community in Soviet Ukraine; he quoted the facts about mass repressions, arrests, deportations of entire villages from Ukraine, and instances of family separations. Balytsky asked for specific examples, which he would investigate and clarify. Karszo-Siedlewski replied that he had three and a half years of experience of working in the field of Soviet affairs, and he was not going to cite specific examples because these could always be explained away by one circumstance or another. He said that his knowledge was based on multiple observations and verified information.

Balytsky replied that the Polish diplomat was exaggerating and there was no mass deportation of ethnic Poles from Soviet Ukraine, while the resettlement operation in the areas that bordered Poland had been underway for several years already and was not an act of political

---

[320] I wrote about this meeting in two articles; see Kuśnierz, "Próby interwencji dyplomacji polskiej," 153–55, and "Represje wobec Polaków na Ukrainie," 70–71.

repression but an economic measure aimed at moving people from less to more fertile farmland. The commissar's arguments did not convince Karszo-Siedlewski, but he noted that if they were indeed the goals of the Soviet Ukrainian government, then he hoped that Balytsky was going to investigate the matter and put a halt to the mass deportations and executions of ethnic Poles, because these were "a clear abuse of power by the local authorities, who, after having listened to their Party and government leaders talk about increasing vigilance for such a long time, now wanted to display their ardor."

The next issue raised was the problem of making it difficult for ethnic Poles to emigrate from the USSR to Poland. "They have to wait about a year for a Soviet decision, which is usually negative. The mere fact of appearing at a Polish consulate attracts suspicions against that person, not to mention surveillance and, not infrequently, arrest," held Karszo-Siedlewski. He gave the example of a fifteen-year-old boy, Ignacy Sujkowski,[321] who, when he expressed his desire to return to Poland to reunite with his father, was arrested and charged with espionage. Balytsky said that willful espionage was impossible in this case and instructed his secretary to investigate the matter (Karszo-Siedlewski witnessed this). Balytsky replied that the caution with respect to individuals who visited foreign consulates was connected to the fact that many enemies of the Communist system were still present in the USSR and brought false and harmful information to the consulates. Karszo-Siedlewski replied that he did not need such information, and that any individuals who came with such news to his consulate were equally suspect, as was the information they provided.

---

[321] Ignacy Sujkowski (born in 1919) was the son of a Polish citizen, Józef Sujkowski, who lived in Poland and had been trying for several years to facilitate the return of his son. Ignacy Sujkowski was a Soviet citizen who lived in Zhupanivka, a village in Korosten raion, and he spoke Polish well. As a result of his father's efforts, Ignacy Sułkowski visited the Polish consulate in Kyiv twice. He was accused of espionage by the NKVD in Korosten in early January 1935 and was taken away to an unspecified destination after spending two weeks under arrest in Korosten. Karszo-Siedlewski tried to intercede by sending a note to the PCfFA representative. The latter did not reply. It was only after a personal intervention by Karszo-Siedlewski that a note was delivered to the consulate on March 14, informing him that Sujkowski was a Soviet citizen, meaning that it was impossible for the consulate to receive any information about him. In a phone conversation, the PCfFA representative said that Sujkowski had been arrested for espionage and deported. RGVA, f. 308 k, op. 6, d. 54, l. 50–51.

Karszo-Siedlewski asked what purpose lay behind making it difficult for ethnic Polish families in the USSR to be reunited with their families in Poland. Why were children and parents, wives and husbands, the young and the elderly, prevented from reuniting? He gave the example of Moscow, where the Polish side issued certificates allowing ethnic Poles to settle in Poland and the Soviet authorities issued them exit visas, but the Soviet Ukrainian administration did not recognize these visas. At this point, the PCfFA representative, Petrovsky, supported Karszo-Siedlewski and suggested that this simplified procedure applied to certain groups of persons, not only to ethnic Poles, but also to ethnic Germans. Balytsky replied that if this procedure was practiced in Moscow, he did not see any reason why it should not be extended to Soviet Ukraine as well. He promised to issue relevant instructions to his subordinates in the NKVD. He added that he personally was not bothered by the fact that some children and elderly wanted to reunite with their families in Poland, nor by anyone who was hostile to the Soviet state and wanted to leave the country.

Next, Karszo-Siedlewski raised the case of the consulate's janitor, Aleksander Łaszcz,[322] his wife, and their child. The case had been ongoing for two years already, without success. Balytsky replied that he was going to look into it and would inform the counselor soon. Finally, jokingly, his Polish guest raised the issue of the shadowing (by the NKVD) of his own person and other employees of the consulate, and the isolation of his post brought about by the persecution of visitors (who were afraid to greet Polish officials in the streets). He specified that he had nothing against some form of surveillance as such, since he had nothing to hide, but he was worried about the specifics of its implementation, which should not "make it difficult to carry on with life." Balytsky replied that the goal of

---

[322] Aleksander Łaszcz had worked as a watchman at the Polish consulate in Kharkiv since February 1933. He was a (church) organist by training. He fell ill and was unable to carry on with his duties. This meant that it would be impossible for him to find a new job in the Soviet Union. His family was back in Poland (where he owned some land), and they were ready to take care of him. Łaszcz, his wife, and an 18-month-old daughter received Polish citizenship, after which, on February 28, 1934, he applied to the All-Ukrainian Central Executive Committee to allow him to renounce his Soviet citizenship, which would, in turn, allow him to get an exit visa. The committee rejected his application, which he learned on April 29, 1934. On May 8, 1934, Jan Karszo-Siedlewski sent a note to the representative of the PCfFA in Kharkiv, Ignatii Kalina, asking for a quick decision in Łaszcz's favor. He had spoken personally with Kalina about the case on May 5. On May 7, the vice-consul, Eugeniusz Weese, also brought up the issue in a conversation with Kalina's deputy, Bredenko. Ibid., op. 4, d. 24, l. 73.

these operations was to provide security and prevent the class enemy from acting, as had happened to the German consul, Fritz von Twardowski, who had been the target of an assassination attempt in Moscow. Balytsky promised to instruct his subordinates to allow the Polish officials "to live in peace."

The conversation took place in a friendly atmosphere. Both interlocutors expressed their desire to meet again soon.[323] Karszo-Siedlewski considered the meeting "a continuation of efforts to make the plight of ethnic Poles residing in Soviet Ukraine more bearable."[324]

As it soon turned out, all of Balytsky's promises and assurances were worth very little. The persecution of ethnic Poles did not stop, but actually gradually increased. On October 25, 1935, Jan-Karszo Siedlewski reported that "Losses among the Polish community of Right-Bank Ukraine are simply innumerable."[325] He had been encouraged by Balytsky's and Petrovsky's assurances that a certain number of applications from ethnic Polish elderly and children would be dealt with positively and quickly. He thus decided to send off some overdue cases to the Soviet authorities. On October 29, 1935, in a two-hour conversation with Petrovsky, he referred to their joint meeting with Balytsky. He said that, apart from a few exceptions, nothing had been done in the past half-a-year to make it easier for the suffering Polish community, especially children and the elderly, to reunite with their families in Poland. Apart from a few specific cases, the general problem of persecution of the Polish community in Soviet Ukraine had not been addressed. The counselor also raised the issue of the anti-Polish campaign in the Soviet Ukrainian press and the statements of a few high-ranking Communist dignitaries (he mentioned Mykola Popov) about the alleged alliance between Poland and Germany against the USSR. This campaign led to the Soviet Ukrainian administration's negative attitude toward Poland. He also raised the issue of its persecution of Catholic priests and the closing of Catholic churches.[326] Petrovsky promised that soon, after the anniversary of the October Revolution (November 7–8), he would personally push through the applications of some (important for the Polish side) elderly individuals and children, as well as locate a Catholic priest.[327]

---

[323] CAW, Oddz. II SG, sygn. I.303.4.3145, k. 588–94.

[324] Ibid., sygn. I.303.4.1985, n.p., doc. 6 (1935).

[325] Ibid., sygn. I.303.4.3144, k. 1359.

[326] For more information on this topic, see chapter 5.

[327] CAW, Oddz. II SG, sygn. I.303.4.3144, k. 1405–1407.

The results were insignificant. The diplomat wrote on November 8, 1935, in a letter to the ambassador: "Balytsky ordered his subordinates to deal positively with three or four cases that he thought we really cared about, e.g., the Łaszcz case.[328] He demonstrated a personally favorable attitude toward me, an act of courtesy, but he did nothing else. All the other applications, despite the notes expressing urgency from our side, did not move forward an inch, and, in a few cases of small children, we received a rejection without any explanation."[329]

Karszo-Siedlewski's intercession with Petrovsky led to positive outcomes only in a few cases. A priest was indeed found. On November 21, 1935, Petrovsky informed the Polish consulate that a priest from Kharkiv had received permission to conduct masses in Kyiv. However, the essential issue of enabling ethnic Poles to return to their ancestral homeland remained unaddressed. A simplified procedure of issuing exit visas (which the Polish diplomat had suggested) was rejected, and thus the only way to be able to renounce Soviet citizenship was to apply and submit the necessary documents to the All-Ukrainian Central Executive Committee.[330]

On November 26, 1935, Petrovsky announced that the Soviet Ukrainian authorities had definitely rejected the applications of Polish children whose parents were in Poland, and he recommended a diplomatic intervention in Moscow to address this issue. He cited one rationale for that decision, namely, that a positive decision could have encouraged many people to flee to Poland. Hearing this argument, the head of the consulate general in Kyiv could not refrain from making the comment that, since the authorities were so afraid of a mass exodus to Poland, which would have been very dangerous for them at the time, this was indirect evidence of the truthfulness of the claim that he had made in the presence of Balytsky—namely, that many ethnic Poles were either being persecuted or living in extreme poverty. After all, no one would flee from a place where they were doing well. He thanked Petrovsky for permitting the priest from Kharkiv to perform his clerical duties in Kyiv

---

[328] Jan Karszo-Siedlewski informed the ambassador on May 20, 1935, that, as a result of the promise Balytsky made during their conversation on March 31, 1935, the latter had instructed his subordinates to issue exit visas for Aleksander Łaszcz, his wife, and his child. According to the report, Łaszcz and his family were scheduled to leave for Poland on May 21, 1935. RGVA, f. 308 k, op. 19, d. 56, l. 61.

[329] CAW, Oddz. II SG, sygn. I.303.4.3144, k. 1404–1405.

[330] Ibid., k. 1524–25 v.

as well, but he noted that this decision could not really address people's needs, because it was very difficult, in practice, to be in charge of two very distant parishes—one in Kharkiv and one in Kyiv.[331]

As evidenced by the facts presented here, intercession of all sorts, even those made at the very top of the NKVD, did not improve the Polish community's situation in Ukraine. Its members often did not speak Polish, but they were aware of their roots and cultivated Polish traditions and customs.[332] They became convinced that Polish diplomatic and consular posts in the USSR were not interest in their plight. That sentiment is reflected in a letter written in Ukrainian by Jan Paciórkowski of Vinnytsia to the Polish consul in Kyiv. The sender accused the representatives of the Second Polish Republic of complete inaction with respect to the persecuted Polish priests and the liquidation of Polish churches. He went so far as to charge them with "selling out" to the Bolsheviks: "There must be some kind of meanness of character among our Polish representatives, [for] there can be no other explanation. We have written to our ambassador in Moscow, but he has not replied. We think that all of you have sold us out, and there is no one to defend us, the Poles. If only there was a chance to go to Poland and ask our lord [President Ignacy] Mościcki for help, but there is none. We ask you to help us to open the church in Vinnytsia and to send [us] a priest."[333]

The direction of the (anti-) Polish policy was orchestrated within the Kremlin and implemented locally without the slightest modification. As Aleksander Stpiczyński, a clerk in the Polish consulate in Kyiv and the head of intelligence post F.8, informed his superior in the intelligence hierarchy (Władysław Michniewicz, B.18) in a general report on September 1935 (written on October 14, 1935): "The plight of the Polish community in [Soviet] Ukraine gets worse and worse daily. The numerous persecutions of ethnic Poles create an atmosphere of doom and gloom, which is reflected in the sudden decrease in the number of visitors to the

---

[331] Ibid., k. 1525–25 v.

[332] An informant of *Dwójka's* Branch no. 5 in Lviv, a long-time resident of Soviet Podilia, reported on the mood of the local ethnic Polish diaspora: "The sense of patriotism [toward independent Poland] they feel is very strong. Many Poles have Polish books written by various authors, but in particular, by Mickiewicz, Sienkiewicz, and Orzeszkowa. These books make the rounds among families and they are being read avidly." The informant believed that it was desirable to deliver more books to Soviet Ukraine, but only those published before World War I, because the presence of newer books could lead to persecution. RGVA, f. 308 k, op. 6, d. 22.

[333] CAW, Oddz. II SG, sygn. I.303.4.1927, doc. 84, n.p.

consulate. The few who are still coming admit that it is only greater necessity that has forced them to undertake that step."[334]

On November 8, 1935, Jan Karszo-Siedlewski sent a report about the conditions of the Polish community in Soviet Ukraine: "[Their] situation is becoming increasingly difficult. The ethnic Poles who resided in the larger clusters of the Polish population in the villages of Right-Bank Ukraine have been nearly completely annihilated, which was something that the Soviet authorities were unable to achieve earlier through the rapid collectivization drive, which ruthlessly broke the resistance of the Polish peasant and his inborn antipathy toward collective property. This has been recently achieved through an organized campaign launched in the fall of this past year; it was targeted at removing and eliminating the Polish element."[335]

The counselor remarked that the worst plight was suffered by the remnants of the old Polish intelligentsia and, most importantly, those who came from Poland or who had families there and maintained contact with their home country and tried to return to Poland, often by asking the consulate the help them. The level of suspicion directed against those individuals increased daily. Despite the extreme likelihood of arrest, these people frequently turned to the consulate for financial help because they faced starvation. In the earlier period, the Kyiv post had twenty to thirty visitors per day, but after the intensity of persecution increased, this number fell to a few visitors per day, all of whom came to ask for financial help.[336]

A light at the end of the tunnel, in Karszo-Siedlewski's view, that gave some hope that the Polish government's stance on the persecution of the Polish community in the USSR would change was the news article by Jan Otmar Berson, "Polacy w Sowietach" (Poles in the USSR), published on December 27, 1935, in the pro-government *Gazeta Polska*. As the title suggests, it dealt with the dire condition of the Polish community in the USSR. The conunselor hoped that this article would be seen as a kind of warning by the Polish government reminding Moscow that Poland cared about the fate of ethnic Poles in the USSR, and that it was only its desire to maintain good neighborly relations that prevented the Polish government from intervening officially. On January 4, 1936, Karszo-

---

[334] Ibid., sygn. I.303.4.1926, doc. 255, n.p.
[335] Ibid., sygn. I.303.4.3144, k. 1403.
[336] Ibid., k. 1403–1404.

Siedlewski wrote a letter about this issue and sent it to Tadeusz Kobylański, the head of the consular department of the MFA. He asked whether Berson's article had been coordinated beforehand with the MFA, or whether it was written by Berson on his own initiative. Hoping that he was right about the article, the counselor wrote: "I would be very happy if my supposition was correct, because the plight of the Polish community in Ukraine is becoming increasingly difficult and the attitude of the [Soviet] Ukrainian authorities is increasingly hostile."[337]

Karszo-Siedlewski's illusions about the MFA's stance were dispelled away a few days later when Foreign Minister Józef Beck touched upon various issues in his exposé, such as the Italian intervention in Ethiopia, relations with neighboring countries, and the persecution of the Polish minority—but only in Czechoslovakia(!). The incomparably greater level of persecution in the USSR, including the public anti-Polish statements noted above, was something that Beck decided to pass over in silence. On January 19, 1936, Karszo-Siedlewski wrote another letter to Tadeusz Kobylański, in which he reported the reaction in the Soviet press to the exposé; he said that he "completely understands and shares the motivations that made Minister Beck treat the Soviet issue so vaguely" and skip over the problem of the persecuted Polish community altogether, but he also remarked that "it did not change the fact that the minister's intentions were completely misunderstood in the Soviet Union."[338]

It seemed strange to Karszo-Siedlewski that the issue of the persecution of the Polish community in the USSR was not raised, even in a most general way, by a single Sejm member: "Why couldn't some appropriate place [for this issue] be found in the speeches of PM Walewski or PM Surzyński, who, since they spoke about the Comintern, could somehow have responded to the hostile speeches of Molotov or Liubchenko, or generally to the anti-Polish sentiment of the Soviet press? Since this issue has also not been raised by any member of the Polish press—even in the opposition newspapers, which could have afforded

---

[337] Ibid., sygn. I.303.4.1867, k. 354.

[338] The fact that Józef Beck did not mention the USSR specifically in his exposé and did not respond to Molotov's speech, in which the commissar claimed that "Poland, together with the Japanese-German military bloc, is preparing for war against the socialist state," made the Bolsheviks furious. A journalist for the Soviet Ukrainian newspaper *Visti* wrote that Beck's move "was aimed at hiding the fact of collaboration with Germany and Japan in preparing anti-Soviet projects." Tadeusz Jankowski, a counselor at the Polish embassy in Moscow, and Jan Karszo-Siedlewski both sent detailed reports to Warsaw about how the Soviet press reacted to Beck's speech. AAN, MSZ, sygn. 6790, k. 35 i nn.

criticizing the Soviet authorities more easily—all this contributes to the impression that Polish public opinion is either completely uninformed about this issue or indifferent, to say the least."[339] At the end of his letter, he assured his readers: "When it comes to my own behavior in my field [of operations], I fully comply with the instructions received from Warsaw, that is: I do not react to any of the local anti-Polish assaults and speeches and I do not raise this issue even in private conversations with the PCfFA representative, Petrovsky, whom I last saw on December 26, 1935. It is a little easier now, since currently we do not have any serious consular matters that would require more serious intervention.... The local administrative authorities attempt to be polite toward us, but it is perhaps redundant to mention that the unfavorable, even hostile, attitude of those authorities to the ethnic Poles residing in Soviet Ukraine has neither improved nor changed."[340]

The evidence demonstrates that, among the relevant authorities of the Second Polish Republic, there was no significant interest in the issues affecting the Polish community in the USSR. There was no reaction, and there was certainly no placement of this issue on the Polish-Soviet bilateral relations agenda. Moreover, the Polish authorities did not want to open the Polish border to ethnic Poles residing in the USSR. In August 1936, Stanisław Eska, a counselor to the Polish embassy in Moscow and the head of the consular department in Moscow, prepared a document titled "Instrukcja prawno-konsularna dla urzędów konsularnych RP w ZSRR" (Legal-consular instruction for the Polish consular posts in the USSR). The instruction stated that the arrival of Soviet citizens, even those who had the right to Polish citizenship, in Poland[341] was, in general, undesirable, whatever the reason, and could only be tolerated under special circumstances. Polish consulates were forbidden to allow their decisions to be guided by humanitarian principles when evaluating applications from "Soviet Poles" who wanted to emigrate to Poland.

Those who were interested in applying for Polish citizenship could usually be divided into two categories. The first group was composed of

---

[339] CAW, Oddz. II SG, sygn. I.303.4.1867, k. 368.

[340] Ibid., k. 368–68 v.

[341] The bill on Polish citizenship passed on January 20, 1920 stated that citizens of other countries, who, after their immigration to Poland, submitted evidence of their Polish background at their local administrative office, together with a statement that they wanted to become Polish citizens, and renounced foreign citizenship, would receive Polish citizenship.

former Austro-Hungarian prisoners of war who came from the counties and cities of the former Austrian area that became part of the Second Polish Republic after the First World War. The second group consisted of persons who entered the USSR illegally. With respect to the first group, the instruction was simple: "We need to adopt a working principle that each such new application does not stem from a sense of duty toward the fatherland, but from the worsening material condition of the applicant or from his conflict with the Soviet authorities. Making it easier for the unemployed element, further demoralized by the conditions prevailing in the country of militant Communism, needs to be considered as unconditionally deleterious and unacceptable. We need to remain skeptical with respect to this group of persons and—excluding some exceptional cases—not be swayed by humanitarian considerations."[342] Such persons were requested to present a document from the Soviet authorities stating that they had not acquired Soviet citizenship. In most cases, applicants were not able to obtain such a document, making it impossible for them to have their application considered. Only in exceptional cases, when the return of an individual was considered justified by the consulate, was the instruction allowed for the consular post to turn to the PCfFA or their representatives in the city of their operations with an inquiry as to whether such a person was considered a foreigner (in the USSR) or not. If the answer was negative, then they should ask when and in what circumstances the person had acquired Soviet citizenship. Only after all this documentation was received could the consulate forward it to the authorities in Poland, together with a statement about why they considered it desirable for the particular individual to return to Poland.[343]

Those who crossed the border illegally and wanted to return to Poland were to be approached with the utmost skepticism. There were certain mitigating circumstances that could have helped an individual to get to Poland, such as the "non-discrediting circumstances" of his departure, for example, unemployment or family issues. With respect to that category of persons, consulates were required to ask the local authorities in Poland for their opinion and to ask for documentation with respect to the individual

---

[342] AAN, MSZ, sygn. 11697, k. 2.

[343] The local county authorities in Poland were often against repatriation, quoting various reasons such as "Communist beliefs," "record of anti-state activity," or the lack of means to support oneself in Poland. See Skóra, "Organizacja i działalność służby," 277.

in question. The applicant also had to submit a statement from the Soviet authorities confirming that he had not acquired Soviet citizenship.

The instruction also spoke about Polish citizens who entered the Soviet Union legally. They were to be given all possible protection and support. If needed, the consulates had to intervene in their cases with the relevant Soviet authorities.[344]

This instruction was implemented rigorously, which in practice meant that the passport-issuing activity of the Polish consulates in the USSR came to an end.[345] Given this particular instruction of the Polish government, there was not much that the Polish foreign service could do apart from reporting on the increasingly worsening position of the Polish community in the USSR. In May 1936 another deportation campaign from Kyiv and Vinnytsia oblasts to Kazakhstan began affecting 11,494 Polish and, 3,506 German families.[346] On July 16, 1936, Jan Karszo-Siedlewski wrote a report to the MFA in which he said that the Polish community in Soviet Ukraine has been completely annihilated or deported over the past year, meaning that currently "Polishness, understood as coherent clusters of Polish population, needs to considered virtually nonexistent; there is nothing left [of the former community] still to be destroyed."[347]

The increase in persecution of the Polish community was something that military intelligence monitored. On September 11, 1936, the *Dwójka* instructed its agents to collect information about the attitude of the Bolshevik authorities toward Poles—both citizens of Poland (including Communists) and Soviet citizens who were ethnic Poles. The instruction requested specific information about unfolding events.[348]

Military intelligence did all they could to gather relevant information. On December 23, 1936, the head of Kyiv-based intelligence post no. E.15, Stanisław Nawrocki, prepared a report that dealt with deportations of ethnic Poles from Soviet Ukraine. It was based, he wrote, on "numerous pieces of information supplied by casual informants": "We have concluded, with all certainty, that between August and November the Soviet authorities were engaged in an intensified campaign of deporting

---

[344] AAN, MSZ, sygn. 11697, k. 3.

[345] Skóra, *Służba konsularna*, 721.

[346] They were deported to Karaganda and northern Kazakhstan oblasts. GARF, f. R-9479 s, op. 1 s, d. 54, l. 6.

[347] CAW, Oddz. II SG, sygn. I.303.4.1867, k. 486.

[348] Ibid., sygn. I.303.4.1956, n.p., doc. 22; sygn. I.303.4.1967, n.p., doc. 114; and sygn. I.303.4.1982, n.p., doc. 29.

ethnic Poles from Right-Bank Ukraine. We have the following data: about 450 Polish families were deported from Kamianets-Podilskyi oblast (mostly from Chemerivtsi raion). About 4,000 ethnic Poles were deported from Novohrad-Volynskyi okruha (from the territory of the former Marchlewszczyzna Polish autonomous raion). We have also received information about deportations of ethnic Poles out of Shepetivka and Proskuriv raions. Most of them have been resettled in Kazakhstan. The time that the Soviet authorities allotted for journey preparation [for those who learned they were about to be deported] was ten days. Some farming supplies were given for the journey, e.g., three families received two horses, one plough, and one wagon."[349]

Persecution of Poles was also underway in Left-Bank Ukraine. On May 30, 1936, Stanisław Sośnicki, the Polish consul in Kharkiv, wrote to the ambassador: "I would like to inform you, sir, that the persecution of ethnic Poles in my consular district has recently been launched again. Polish families and Polish citizens are constantly under NKVD surveillance and summoned for interrogations. The reason for this behavior by the authorities is the correspondence that those persons maintain with their relatives in Poland. In industrial centers, Poles are accused of talking with German workers. In the Dzerzhinsky factory in Dnipropetrovsk, several hundred Poles were arrested."[350]

A few days after he wrote this report, Sośnicki learned that a Polish worker in the Dzerzhinsky factory in Dniprodzerzhynsk (Kamianske) was sentenced to two years in a Gulag camp because he had dared to make a toast in public to the well-being of Poland and to Marshal Piłsudski.[351]

With the operational order of the head of the NKVD dated August 11, 1937 (no. 00485),[352] the so-called Polish operation began. As a result, 54,011 people were arrested in Soviet Ukraine, of whom 39,322 were Poles. The number of them sentenced was 39,670, 33,447 of them to capital punishment.[353] The Polish operation was the second most repressive

---

[349] Ibid., sygn. I.303.4.1956, n.p., doc. 96,

[350] Ibid., sygn. I.303.4.1867, k. 208–9.

[351] Ibid., k. 214.

[352] The content of the order is translated into Polish in Pietrow, *Polska operacja NKWD*, 27–29; and in Bednarek, et al., eds., *Polska i Ukraina w latach trzydziestych-czterdziestych XX wieku*, vol. 8, part 1, 257–63.

[353] HDASBU, f. 42, spr. 35, ark. 9, 13. Oleksandr Rubl'ov and Volodymyr Reprentsev gave the following figures: 56,516 arrested (44,467 of Polish ethnicity) and 39,644 sentenced; see Rubl'ov and Repryntsev, *Represiï proty polakiv*, 40. In the entire USSR, ca 140,000 Poles were sentenced; see Pietrow, *Polska operacja NKWD*, 32, 40.

campaign in terms of the number of victims (after the kulak operation, in terms of the number of death penalties and Gulag sentences) that the Bolsheviks organized during the period of the Great Terror. What is remarkable is the fact that an ethnic Pole was much more likely than the average Soviet citizen to suffer persecution. Ethnic Poles made up merely 0.4 percent of the total Soviet population, yet during the period of the Great Terror, they were forty times more likely to perish than other Soviet citizens.[354]

Data from the Navahrudak voivodeship office confirms the magnitude of the repressions of ethnic Poles in the USSR. Registered letters sent from Poland to the USSR were returned to the sender 75 percent of the time, with notes such as "addressee has left and his whereabouts are unknown" or simply "not accepted." Usually letters were not returned at all.[355] On August 15, 1937, *Dwójka* agent Jerzy Kamiński wrote the following note: "Recently we have been receiving reports about persecutions of Polish people, and Polish citizens in particular: their passports are taken away, [and] the citizenship of those who have not been arrested yet is being questioned."[356]

On October 30, the deputy consul in Kyiv, Adam Koch, wrote that virtually no Poles visited the consulate on personal business. All those who had maintained any kind of contact with foreign consulates had been either arrested or deported.[357]

A few weeks later, on November 26, 1937, Koch reported: "Mass arrests and immediate deportations of ethnic Poles and Germans have been conducted over the past month. A few examples: All the Polish workers (40) of the sugar refinery in Pohrebyshche (together with their families) have been arrested and deported; in Ruzhe (?) raion, two entire Polish villages have virtually been deported wholesale; in the detention cells of Poltava there were over 2,500 detainees as of November 10, almost all of them of Polish or German ethnicity; in Kyiv, large numbers of Poles, Germans, Italians, [and] Czechs have been arrested. Another related wave of arrests targeted people who maintained some form of correspondence abroad. Recently we registered a few cases of immediate arrest after an occurence of receiving mail from abroad. These two rationales behind the

---

[354] Snyder, *Skrwawione ziemie*, 125–26; see also H. Kuromiya, "Stalin, Poles, and Ukrainians," in *Ofiary imperium*, ed. Nowak, 424.

[355] AAN, MSZ, sygn. 6755 A, k. 205.

[356] CAW, Oddz. II SG, sygn. I.303.4.2101, n.p., doc. 90.

[357] Ibid., sygn. I.303.4.1867, k. 676.

arrests and deportations seem justified from the point of view of the current policy of the regime. The isolation they are trying to implement can only be achieved through ruthlessness, [and] hence all the elements that can hinder their efforts must be removed one by one: foreigners, consulates, finally people who have any kind of a link, material or psychological, with a foreign country. Practically all foreigners have been removed, and we can expect that within a few months there will be not a single foreigner in all of [Soviet] Ukraine."[358]

The question as to what pushed the regime to pursue such a policy with respect to foreigners was the following: "It can be concluded that the government wants to build a Chinese wall that would prevent any information leaving the country and prevent, at the same time, even the faintest echo of world events from reaching the USSR."[359]

Koch was right in his assessment. The Soviet waves of repressions of national minorities certainly limited the operational potential of the foreign intelligence services and the Polish one in particular, for whom ethnic Poles in the USSR constituted a natural base of support.[360] Of course, most of the arrested and persecuted Poles did not engage in any activity that could be described as anti-state.[361] Very few of the persecuted Poles could even have met with a Polish consul. Those who did visit a consulate and reported on what they knew usually spoke about their daily lives, the condition of their compatriots in a given town, the repressions they suffered, and so on. The principle that motivated Stalin, however, was simple: it is better to execute a large number of people (as a preventive

---

[358] Ibid., k. 687–88.

[359] Ibid., k. 688. Similar formulations could be found in the MFA's information bulletin *Polska a Zagranica*: "Along all the Soviet borders, both European and Asian, a mass expulsion of the local population is taking place so that an uninhabited strip of land can be created making it impossible for any Soviet citizen to come in contact with foreign countries. The Soviet authorities aim to eliminate any possibility of foreign penetration into their territory; the only channels of contact with the outside world that remain open (and strictly controlled) are those that allow them to keep their own propagandists and political campaigns running. The Soviet worm, not confident in its own strength and fearing the outside world, is trying to hide deeper and deeper in the ground. It does not abandon its fundamental principles of [Communist] foreign policy. It is increasingly hopeless in many sectors, but the Soviet government does not stop struggling for their realization, and it is doubtful that they will ever be abandoned." AAN, MSZ, sygn. 119, k. 90–91.

[360] See M. Jabłonowski and J. Prochwicz, *Wywiad Korpusu Ochrony Pogranicza, 1924–1939* (Warsaw: Aspra-Jr, 2003/2004), 89, 94, 167; and Misiuk, *Służby specjalne*, 67.

[361] See Snyder, *Skrwawione ziemie*, 127.

measure), even if a significant number of them are completely innocent, than to allow one potential, hidden enemy to survive and, in the right conditions, become visible again and be in a position to harm the Soviet regime.

During the Yezhovshchina, the employees of the Polish posts in Soviet Ukraine essentially intervened only in individual cases of Polish citizens who suffered persecution by the NKVD. Usually their efforts were of little benefit. After such cases were investigated on the spot, they were forwarded to the ambassador in Moscow for "consideration" whether to intervene in Moscow and contact the Red Cross to provide immediate relief. Consul Tadeusz Brzeziński wrote about one such case to Ambassador Wacław Grzybowski. On March 19, 1937, he sent a note about two Polish citizens—Józef Leżański and Jan Kowalczuk—in the city of Stalino. They were sentenced for espionage to nine and ten years of prison, respectively. Leżański appealed to the Soviet Supreme Court, and his sentence was reduced to six years. Kowalczuk's appeal, at the time of the Polish official's visit (see below), was still awaiting a reply. Leżański and Kowalczuk, who came to the USSR from Canada in 1931, worked as highly skilled workers before, ultimately, like many other foreigners, falling victim to Stalinist repressions.[362]

After the consulate received permission from the Soviet authorities to see the two sentenced Polish citizens, Consul Brzeziński dispatched Jerzy Kamiński, a consular official and a *Dwójka* agent, to see them in a Stalino prison on March 17, 1937. There, in the presence of the commander of the prison, his deputy, and an NKVD lieutenant, Kamiński was able to meet with the two prisoners. Since there was no translator in their company, the NKVD agent advised Kamiński to speak only in Russian and categorically forbade him to raise any issues related to the circumstances of their arrests, the investigation, and their trial, threatening that he would interrupt the meeting if such issues were discussed. Józef Leżański was brought in first (the meeting lasted forty minutes). He had no relatives in the USSR; his parents lived in Poland. At the beginning of the conversation, Leżański examined Kamiński's passport very carefully. Kamiński noted later: "It looked like he was prepared for any kind of surprise, initially his gaze was full of distrust, but this changed after he saw my passport." Leżanski did not talk much, saying only that he had submitted an appeal to the All-Ukrainian Central Executive Committee. He asked that his parents not be

[362] CAW, Oddz. II SG, sygn. I.303.4.1867, k. 264–65.

told of his arrest, and he complained about the lack of money and clothes. He mentioned that he had stomachaches. Kamiński gave him 50 rubles that he had received from the consul for that purpose. At the end, Leżański asked that the consulate help him. He repeated several times that he wanted to be free and that he would have a lot to talk about, but could not speak openly there.

The second arrested Pole—Jan Kowalczuk—was brought in next. He was married,[363] and his wife had accepted Soviet citizenship in Lviv. She was arrested a month and a half before his own arrest (he was arrested on September 22, 1936). They had an eight-year-old daughter, who was "protected by the hand of the state" at the time. The meeting lasted fifty minutes. Kowalczuk was more talkative than Leżański, enough so that Kamiński was worried the NKVD agent would interrupt their meeting. Kowalczuk announced that he wanted the investigation to be reopened because he was innocent. He complained about the lack of qualified legal support during the investigation and court trial, and about poor conditions in the prison. He also complained that he had received no receipt for the money and belongings that were taken away from him when he was arrested, and that he had to sleep on a single bench with another prisoner, which was an improvement compared to sleeping right on the floor, which was what happened to him initially. Kowalczuk said that he was going to write to the consulate with the request that his daughter be cared for by making it possible for her to return to Poland to stay with a relative, Justyna Soroka, who resided in Torchynivtsi, Sambir county. At the end of the conversation, he asked the consulate to intervene on his behalf.[364] There is no other information about Leżański and Kowalczuk in the Polish archives. One example that demonstrates the attitude of local Soviet authorities toward the attempts at intervention that Polish consular officials made in defense of Polish citizens is the case of Professor Ernest Werber. Werber had been arrested on September 2, 1937, in Odesa. The Polish consulate general in Kyiv was informed about this only in November 1937. On November 13, 1937, the consulate sent a note to a PCfFA representative requesting an explanation. On November 19, 1937, the consulate received the answer that the representative had asked the relevant Soviet authorities to provide an explanation. No response

---

[363] Kamiński wrote that Kowalczuk expressed hatred toward his wife, claiming that he would divorce her if their child was not there.
[364] CAW, Oddz. II SG, sygn. I.303.4.1867, k. 266–72.

came, however, forcing the consulate to send reminders about Werber's case once a month for four months, on January 5, February 2, March 3, and April 9, 1938. No answer arrived, and the consulate wrote again on November 17, 1938 to remind the authorities that the case has not been resolved for over a year. In reply, the PCfFA representative Vidiakin wrote that he had sent a reply on May 15, 1938, and opined that the Polish officials had a disorganized mail department.

Vice-consul Adam Koch discounted the possibility that Vidiakin's reply could have been missed because of negligence. He said that there was no point in replying seriously to such a suggestion because it would be ineffective anyway and the consulate would then receive an even more offensive response, to which it could also not reply because it was impossible "to compete with the Soviet authorities in their lack of good manners." The only action that the head of the Polish consulate in Kyiv, Jerzy Matusiński, could undertake was to ask the embassy in Moscow to intervene with the PCfFA directly.[365]

The Polish MFA and military intelligence certainly had extensive knowledge and a firm awareness of the repressive Bolshevik policy against ethnic Polish people in the USSR — both Soviet and Polish citizens. They knew about deportations and mass arrests. However, neither the Polish diplomats nor Polish military intelligence knew what exactly had happened to those arrested during the years of the Great Terror. They suspected that after the arrests, deportation to Kazakhstan or Siberia had taken place. In the Polish archives there is no information that this planned mass crime against innocent people had been taking place. There one can not find an attempt to provide a particular number of arrested people, but only fragmentary data pertaining to individual towns or workplaces. However, it should be emphasized that the secret services and diplomats of other countries did not have such information either. This was the best proof of the brutal effectiveness of the Communist regime in hiding the truth about its essence.

Jan Karszo-Siedlewski intervened on numerous occasions to defend the persecuted Polish diaspora, including with the head of the Soviet Ukrainian NKVD, Vsevolod Balytsky. The Polish government, however, wanted to maintain proper relations with the Bolsheviks[366] and largely

---

[365] Ibid., k. 790-791.
[366] The cornerstone of Polish policy toward the USSR was the Non-Aggression Pact of 1932, which was renewed in 1934.

refrained from undertaking any action concerning the persecution of the Polish community in the USSR, recognizing this crime as an internal Soviet affair. The Polish government was also motivated by reasons of security: it feared an influx of fellow Poles who were "contaminated with Communism." The few attempts at intervention that the Polish side made turned out to be ineffective in any case. The state of the Polish community in the USSR did not improve during the period of relatively proper Polish-Soviet relations in the mid-1930s. The remark Piotr Kurnicki made in 1933 was correct: "Because the Soviet Union treats the Polish minority as its exclusive property, even the best official relations with Poland cannot, in my opinion, have any positive impact on their condition in [Soviet] Ukraine."[367]

4.8. Persecution of Other Nationalities

As noted earlier, Polish foreign-service officials and intelligence agents also reported from time to time on the persecution of other nationalities residing in Soviet Ukraine. Usually this reporting was "in addition to" the main topic of their interest—the fate of the Polish people—or occurred when analyzing Stalinist nationalities policy in general or after having conversations with diplomatic or consular representatives of other countries.

The most frequent interlocutors were the representatives of the German consulates. In the East Section (Referat "Wschód"), as its head Jerzy Niezbrzycki recollected, there was "a giant [paper] data base with specially marked subsections on German intelligence on Russia." However, Niezbrzycki, the long-time head of the Referat Wschód, did not have a high opinion of the value of information gathered by German intelligence, which was based primarily on interviewing Germans who had or were leaving the USSR. They were not able to say much about the environment that surrounded them, apart from narrating their own personal experiences from the period of the first five-year plans.[368] Representatives of Japan and Italy were spoken to a little less frequently. Amicable relations were maintained with these three countries. The least friendly relations were with representatives of the Czechoslovak consulate in Kyiv. Nothing is known about the existence or quality of relations with the Turkish post in Odesa.

---

[367] Ibid., sygn. I.303.4.1859, doc. 68, n.p.
[368] JPIA, ARW(JAN), sygn. 1, n.p.

Except for the arrests of Polish Communists in the NKVD-fabricated case of the Polish Military Organization (1933–34), broader persecutions of foreigners who resided in the USSR began after the Kirov murder. Some of them were arrested (Germans in particular), others were told to leave the "country of workers and peasants." According to data the *Dwójka* gathered, 458 foreigners were expelled during the last quarter of 1935: 300 Germans, 56 Italians, 35 Czechoslovaks, 28 Austrians, 7 Swiss, Yugoslav, Dutch, and Hungarians each, and 4 Frenchmen and citizens of the Free City of Gdańsk each, and one Swede, one Dane, and one Argentinean.[369]

Many foreigners decided to leave of their own accord. This group included farmers who had not yet been collectivized, as well as industrial workers who, because of the increasingly hostile attitude of the Soviet system to foreigners and because of worsening living conditions, decided to return to their country of origin. The number of visitors who wanted to enter a German consular post was very high. The German consul in Kharkiv had to provide sleeping spaces in his building; on May 19, 1935, for example, 50 Germans returning to Germany spent the night at that post.[370]

The Polish consulates gathered data pertaining to the arrests of foreigners. According to data gathered by the Kharkiv post, in the last two weeks of September 1935 eight German engineers (who were citizens of Germany) were arrested within the area of that consular district. All eight were charged with counterrevolutionary activity. The German post intervened with a PCfFA agent, but to no avail.[371] *Dwójka* agent Jerzy Kamiński in a report written on February 18, 1937, based on information received from "a casual informant," stated that sixty Germans had been arrested in Horlivka. All were Soviet citizens. He learned from Hermann Strecker that 600 ethnic Germans who were also Soviet citizens had been arrested in the Donbas; most of them were being held in the NKVD building in Artemivsk.[372]

As the Great Terror began, in 1937, repressions became massive and systematic in nature. The second largest nationality operation run by the NKVD, in terms of the number of victims, in the USSR as a whole and in Soviet Ukraine, was the German one. Consequently the largest amount of archival material available in the Polish archives after that on the Polish population obviously pertains to ethnic Germans. The German operation

---

[369] RGVA, f. 464 k, op. 1, d. 2424, l. 71.

[370] Ibid., f. 308 k, op. 19, d. 56, l. 58.

[371] Ibid., d. 58, l. 77.

[372] CAW, Oddz. II SG, sygn. I.303.4.2101, n.p., doc. 181.

was chronologically the first of the NKVD's nationality operations. On July 25, 1937, Nikolai Yezhov signed operational order no. 00439. According to that document, the arrests of German citizens who were working (or had once worked) at Soviet military or railway enterprises were scheduled to begin on July 29, 1937. The operation was to last five days. Political émigrés from Germany were to be arrested only if they kept their German citizenship. For each German political émigré who accepted Soviet citizenship, the local NKVD branch was ordered to open a personal file, start gathering compromising material "on him," and send it to Yezhov by August 5, 1937 so that he could make a decision about that individual's arrest.[373]

The Soviet regime did not limit itself to arresting those individuals specified in order 00439. Starting in the fall of 1937, operations were extended to include German citizens who worked in other Soviet enterprises and to ethnic Germans who were Soviet citizens. By November 1937, 65,000 to 68,000 people had been arrested in the entire USSR, and about 55,000 of them were sentenced (42,000 were executed). Only one-third of those who were sentenced under order 00439 were of German nationality.[374] The result of those operations in Soviet Ukraine were as follows: 23,036 individuals were arrested, 20,520 of whom were of German nationality;[375] 11,470 people were sentenced; and 10,233 of them were executed.[376]

The German foreign service could not remain indifferent to what the Stalinist regime was doing to German citizens and ethnic Germans who resided in the USSR at the time, and it tried to gather information on the number of arrests. Naturally, the information about ethnic Germans who were Soviet citizens could not have been accurate. More precise data could be obtained about those individuals who remained German citizens after they arrived in the Soviet Union legally, most often to work in a Soviet enterprise.[377]

---

[373] Iakovlev et al., *Lubianka: Stalin i Glavnoe upravlenie*, 271–72.

[374] Petrov and Jansen, *"Stalinskii pitomets"*, 110.

[375] HDASBU, f. 42, spr. 35, ark. 8–10.

[376] Ibid., ark. 14.

[377] According to data the German consulate general obtained in Kharkiv in mid-1935, there were 2,900 German citizens remaining in Soviet Ukraine: 1,400 in the German consular district based in Kyiv; 1,100 in the Kharkiv district; and 400 in the Odesa district. RGVA, f. 308 k, op. 19, d. 56, l. 113.

Polish officials received some information about the repressions resulting from NKVD order no. 00439. Agent Jerzy Kamiński informed Jerzy Niezbrzycki that, between July 31 and August 11, 1937, seventeen Germans were arrested.[378] By October 1, 1937, German records registered 382 German citizens who were in Soviet prisons. Eighty of them had been arrested in Donetsk, Dnipropetrovsk, and Kharkiv oblasts.[379] On October 22, 1937, Kamiński wrote that he had received information the day before that six German citizens had been arrested. He stressed that the arrests of ethnic Germans who were Soviet citizens were part of a separate but concurrent operation.[380]

In Adam Koch's analysis of October 30, 1937, he made use of information acquired from German and Italian sources. Koch learned from the German consulate in Kyiv that about fifty German citizens were in prisons within the Kyiv consular district. In October 1937 expulsions of Germans from the USSR increased and reached the number of approximately 100 people, i.e., 80 percent of all expelled foreigners at the time.[381] Adam Koch also mentioned that, independently of the repressions against "ordinary" foreigners (workers, specialists), all foreign professors working at Kyiv institutions of higher education were either arrested or expelled. The last of them, Professor Meyer, a German citizen, was arrested on October 26, 1937.[382]

On November 13, 1937, Koch informed Ambassador Grzybowski that the German consulate in Kyiv had reported that of 300 German passports stored at the consulate ten months earlier, only 130 remained. This meant that 170 individuals had left the USSR. Most of the 130 German citizens who remained were scheduled to leave by the end of 1937.[383] From the total figure of over 1,000 Austrian citizens who had resided in Kharkiv, 700 left for Austria, 200 joined the Republican military forces in Spain, 200 were arrested, and 20 were allegedly hiding inside the Austrian embassy in Moscow. The last piece of information was unverified; hence Koch asked the ambassador to investigate this, as it would help to evaluate the credibility of the informant who provided the information. Finally, the

---

[378] CAW, Oddz. II SG, sygn. I.303.4.2101, n.p., doc. 90.
[379] Ibid., doc. 127.
[380] Ibid.
[381] Ibid., sygn. I.303.4.1867.
[382] Ibid., k. 676.
[383] Ibid., k. 654.

vice-consul mentioned the compulsory emigration of the few remaining Czechs, Yugoslavs, and Hungarians from the USSR.[384]

Conversations with representatives of other consulates did not lead to valuable information about the persecutions of national minorities. There were very few Italians, and even fewer Japanese, in Soviet Ukraine. As stated earlier, the most productive relations were with the representatives of Italy, Japan, and Germany. In Koch's report in October 1937, he also cited some data from the Italian consulate. He wrote that only a few Italian citizens had recently been arrested in Soviet Ukraine, and in October 1937 ten Italian citizens were expelled from the USSR. Because the Soviet authorities had not extended permission to stay to other Italian citizens, the Italian authorities expected that about sixty Italian citizens were going to leave Soviet Ukraine within the next two months. According to unconfirmed information, the NKVD had arrested all Communists who were Czechoslovak citizens. Other citizens of that country (non-Communists) were initially fired from their jobs, and they were eventually forced to leave altogether. Koch's comment on this was: "This method is still more elegant than the measures applied to citizens of other countries."[385]

This data was, needless to say, far from precise. Furthermore, the Polish foreign service did not pay close attention to the fate of other nationalities who suffered from Stalinist repression. The persecution of national minorities, as well as other mass repressive campaigns, finally came to an end with the dismissal of Yezhov from his post as head of the NKVD. On November 26, 1938, based on the resolution of the Central Committee and the Council of People's Commissars of November 17, 1938 (titled "On the Arrests, Prosecutorial Surveillance and Investigations, and Distortions in the Operations of the Organs of the NKVD and Prosecutors"), Yezhov's successor, Lavrentii Beria, issued operational order no. 00672, which canceled all previous NKVD orders (00439, 00447, 00485, 00486, and others).[386] Even if most of the repressive actions were officially over, the negative feelings toward foreigners in the USSR remained. In the March 9, 1938 issue of the MFA's information bulletin *Polska a Zagranica*, which dealt with events in the Soviet Union in 1937 and 1938, the MFA accurately predicted, even then, that even if the repressive

---

[384] Ibid., k. 655.
[385] Ibid., k. 675.
[386] RGANI, f. 89, op. 73, d. 18, l. 1–10.

campaign against foreigners in the USSR were to come to an end one day, the general attitude of suspicion and hostility was there to stay for much longer.[387]

---

[387] AAN, MSZ, sygn. 119, k. 70.

Chapter Five

Religious Persecution

5.1. "Religion Is the Opium of the People"

"Religion is the opium of the people," said Marx and later Lenin, who had an opportunity to test this theory in practice. The Bolsheviks wanted to create a state that was radically different from any system of governance known in the civilized world, meaning that they were hell-bent on getting rid of all the remnants of the old system. The most important component of the old system, they believed, was faith in God.[1] Deriving from that faith were certain traditional values, such as respect for one's parents, family, and private property. All this had to be uprooted in order to clear the ground for the new "Soviet man" liberated from the "old anachronisms," a man faithfully loyal to the Party, its leaders, and the "new" values. The Bolsheviks knew that the human psyche was such that people had to believe in something. Consequently they eradicated religion in their country and promoted atheism. On the other hand, they initiated a quasi-religious cult of personality and a "faith" in constructing "a Bolshevik paradise" on earth—"a happy, most just" social system that guaranteed a blissful, affluent life for peasants in the collective farms, workers in the factories, and schoolchildren. Women were promised "liberation from the kitchen." The Bible was replaced with a secular cult of leaders—Lenin, then Stalin. It is enough to mention the tales "of heroism and incredible feats" of the young Vladimir Ulianov, soon to be the brave revolutionary and leader Vladimir Ilich Lenin, a man who became the role model for Soviet schoolchildren. As Roman Dzwonkowski emphasized, the Soviet state was atheist in principle, but it became de facto a form of theocracy *par excellence*. All citizens who occupied an official post at any level had to abide by the principle of nonbelief in God.[2]

---

[1] Lenin said: "All contemporary religions and churches, all religious organizations, are considered by Marxism a tool of bourgeois reaction, serving in its defense and for the exploitation and dumbing down of the working class." Cited in Dzwonkowski, *Kościół katolicki w ZSSR*, 60.

[2] Idem, "Sowieckie państwo wyznaniowe," *Roczniki Nauk Społecznych* 25, no. 1 (1997): 298. As Dzwonkowski emphasized, even the French ambassador in Moscow, François Alphand,

In 1937 journalist Emelian Iaroslavsky clearly articulated this thrust of Communist ideology: "Communists recognize religion as an evil that has to be suppressed by persuasion, by propaganda... Communists, through their anti-religious and cultural-educational propaganda, through all of their efforts, help the working classes to overcome the anachronism of the past, the ideology alien to a scientific approach to life, to break away from the false, illusory beliefs in an afterlife, gods, goddesses, saints, angels, devils, paradise, and hell. *Bolsheviks help those who work here, in this life, to build a happy, joyous life for everyone* [author's emphasis]."[3] As Aleksandra Leinwand put it, the bright future the Bolsheviks promised was to be delivered here and now, but first one had to eliminate the still existing relics of the past.[4]

The family as an institution was a serious obstacle to the "Communist modernization" of society. The new Communist family was supposed to replace the traditional family. Soviet children were told that the Communist Party was their true family. Pavlik Morozov was held up as the role model for the kind of devotion expected of them. Volodymyr Zatonsky, the people's commissar for education of the Ukrainian SSR in the 1930s, offered a clear statement of the new Bolshevik values in August 1930, during a demonstration against "bourgeois upbringing." In his speech before fifteen thousand children who marched in front of the government of Soviet Ukraine, he called upon them to resist religion and submit "to your new family, the Communist Party, which is going to replace the bourgeois family for you."[5] The mechanisms of Soviet anti-family propaganda were clearly reflected in the Soviet film *Esli zavtra voina* (*If War Breaks Out Tomorrow*), released by Mosfilm in 1938. In the film, after a military invasion of Russian territory, Soviet people are called to join the army. Everyone wants to fight, including mothers with little children. Anna Ivanova is one of them. After she enlists at her factory to go to the front, one of her female colleagues reminds her that she has a

---

who was generally not familiar with the condition of the Catholic Church in the USSR, accurately assessed the direction of Soviet policy on religion in a report he sent back to Paris on July 20, 1934. He wrote that the Communists were introducing "a new religion, naturally to the exclusion of all the other ones" (ibid).

[3] E. Iaroslavskii, "Tserkov' i gosudarstvo," *Pravda*, September 5, 1937.

[4] A. Leinwand, *Sztuka w służbie utopii: O funkcjach politycznych i propagandowych sztuk plastycznych w Rosji Radzieckiej lat 1917–1922* (Warsaw: Instytut Historii PAN and Mazowiecka Wyższa Szkoła Humanistyczno-Pedagogiczna, 1998), 197.

[5] Kuśnierz, *Ukraina w latach kolektywizacji*, 120.

son. Ivanova replies: "Don't worry, he will not become an orphan. He will grow up a Bolshevik."

The Bolsheviks wanted to eliminate religion from the moment they took power.[6] Stalin returned to this issue in 1929 with the intention of resolving it once and for all. Along with the assault on the peasantry, a great number of churches were closed down, arrests decimated the clergy, and secular assisting personnel were scared away from serving their religious communities with threats and repressions.[7] The Ukrainian Autocephalous Orthodox Church was suppressed altogether.[8] The second

---

[6] A decree of the Council of People's Commissars on January 23 (February 2 NS), 1918, "on the separation of the church from the state and the school," disenfranchised the clergy (the so-called *lishentsy*) and banned religion classes for students who were not at least eighteen years old. In February 1922, a decree was passed according to which all "houses of prayer" were obliged to relinquish all valuables containing gold, silver, and other precious metals and transfer them to a hunger-relief fund. A decree on April 8, 1929 banned religious organizations from: establishing "self-help societies"; providing material help to their members; organizing prayer meetings for children, youth, and women; opening libraries and reading rooms; and establishing social-aid facilities. The clergy and accompanying personnel were also banned from residing in city centers and near churches. In 1930, due to "the shortage of paper for daily newspapers," a decree was issued that obliged individual citizens and "houses of prayer" to surrender copies of the Bible, religious literature, and prayer books to the authorities. See Dzwonkowski, *Kościół katolicki w ZSSR*, 63, 66, 100; J. Wróbel, "Polityka ZSRR wobec kościoła katolickiego w latach 1917–1939," in *Polacy w kościele katolickim w ZSSR*, ed. E. Walewander (Lublin: Wydawnictwo KUL, 1989), 89; and R. Conquest, *Zhnyva skorboty: Radians'ka kolektyvizatsiia i holodomor* (Kyiv: Lybid', 1993), 228–30.

[7] For more information on the Bolshevik struggle with religion, see, in addition to the publications cited in the previous note: R. Dzwonkowski, SAC, *Losy duchowieństwa katolickiego w ZSSR, 1917–1939: Martyrologium* (Lublin: TN KUL, 1998); idem, "Stan badań nad historią Kościoła i życiem religijnym katolików obrządku łacińskiego w ZSRR (1917–1990)," in *Mniejszości polskie i polonia w ZSRR*, ed. H. Kubiak, T. Paleczny, J. Rokicki, and M. Wawrykiewicz (Wrocław-Warsaw-Kraków: Zakład Narodowy im. Ossolińskich, 1992), 103–18; M. Iwanow, "Kościół katolicki w ZSRR wobec radzieckiej polityki wyznaniowej 1921–1938," in *Chrześcijaństwo w ZSRR w dobie pierestrojki i głasnosti: Materiały z sesji Eklezjologiczno-Mitologicznej, Pieniężno 28–30 IX 1989*, ed. W. Grzeszczak, SVD, and E. Śliwka, SVD (Warsaw-Pieniężno: Verbinum, 1992), 89–129; idem, "Kościół najbardziej prześladowany," *Więź*, 1990, no. 2-3: 23–37; R. Kuśnierz, "Walka z religią na Ukrainie w latach trzydziestych," *Więź*, 2004, no. 6: 115–25, F. Rzemieniuk, "Obraz diecezji kamienieckiej w latach 1918–1939," *Przegląd Wschodni* 29, no. 1 (2002): 119–35; H. Stroński, "Skazany na milczenie: Kościół rzymsko-katolicki na Ukrainie Radzieckiej w latach 1920–1930," *Więź*, 1996, no. 10: 96–119; and J. Wróbel, "Likwidacja: Polityka ZSRR wobec kościołów i religii w latach dwudziestych," *Przegląd Powszechny*, 1990, no. 3: 355–68.

[8] See, for example, R. Kuśnierz, "Próba kościelnej niezależności: Ukraińska Autokefaliczna Cerkiew Prawosławna (1919–1936)," *Więź*, 2006, no. 6: 107–13; "Represovana UAPTs:

half of the 1930s in the USSR was a time when organized religions were being "finished off." By the end of the 1930s, all Catholic churches in Ukraine were closed down, as were 75 to 80 percent of all Orthodox churches (approximately 8,000). In Kyiv oblast, just two places of worship remained of the earlier count of 1,710; all twenty-eight of the monasteries were closed; and only three priests remained of the original count of 1,425. Not a single bishop remained active in Soviet Ukraine.[9] By the end of October 1937, the NKVD troikas had sentenced 2,341 clergymen of various denominations, as well as secular persons who were in some way affiliated with places of worship (Russian *tserkovniki*), of whom 1,252 were sentenced to death; and 1,028 *sektanty* (believers who did not belong to the officially recognized religions)[10] were also sentenced, 400 of them to death (see table 9).[11]

Table 9. The number of *tsesrkovniki*, and *sektanty* sentenced by NKVD troikas in Soviet Ukraine as of October 1937

Oblast	Number of sentenced *tserkovniki*			Number of sentenced *sektanty*		
	All	Category I	Category II	All	Category I	Category II
Kyiv	641	320	321	163	73	90
Kharkiv	354	252	102	176	89	87
Dnipropetrovsk	82	36	46	74	14	60
Donetsk	324	173	151	199	57	142
Odesa	398	234	164	11	60	51
Vinnytsia	357	147	210	326	73	253

Politychni represii proty sviashchennykiv Ukraïns'koi Avtokefal'noï Pravoslavnoï Tserkvy (1919–1938); Za dokumentamy Haluzevoho derzhavnoho arkhivu Sluzhby bezpeky Ukraïny," *Z arkhiviv VUChK-GPU-NKVD-KGB* 2005, no. 1/2 (24/25), vol. 1, passim; 2006, no. 1/2 (26/27), passim; "Sviashchennyky Ukraïns'koi Avtokefal'noï Pravoslavnoï Tserkvy pid represyvnym tyskom totalitarnoho rezhymu," *Z arkhiviv VUChK-GPU-NKVD-KGB*, 2007, no. 1 (28), 13–34; I. Prelovs'ka, "Peresliduvannia ta likvidatsiia UAPTs (UPTs) (1921–1938 rr.): Ohliad arkhivno-kryminal'nykh sprav HDA SB Ukraïny ta TsDAHO Ukraïny," *Z arkhiviv VUChK-GPU-NKVD-KGB*, 2009, no. 1 (32): 26–48.

[9] I. Prelovs'ka, "Peresliduvannia ta likvidatsiia," 30–31.

[10] In Soviet nomenclature, a *sektant* was anyone who belonged to a non-hierarchical church, e.g., Baptists, Jehovah's Witnesses, etc.

[11] HDASBU, f. 42, spr. 32, ark. 43. See also O. Bazhan, "Represiï sered dukhovenstva ta viruiuchykh v URSR v chasy 'velykoho teroru': Statystychnyi aspekt," *Z arkhiviv VUChK-GPU-NKVD-KGB*, 2007, no. 2 (29): 14.

Chernihiv	26	7	19		-	
Moldavian ASSR	11	8	3			
Kamianets-Podilskyi	78	32	46	75	30	45
Mykolaiv	43	29	4			
Poltava	27	14	13	4	4	
Total	2,341	1,252	1,079	1,028	400	728

Source: HDASBU, f. 42, spr. 32, ark. 43; Bazhan, "Represiï sered dukhovenstva," 14.

In the final two months of 1937, there was a significant increase in the number of sentencings. As of January 4, 1938, the NKVD troikas had sentenced 6,368 priests, *tserkovniki*, and *sektanty* altogether; there were 3,855 Germans and 1,818 Poles among the sentenced (see table 10).[12]

Table 10. The number of priests, *tserkovniki*, and *sektanty* sentenced by NKVD troikas as of January 4, 1938

Oblast	The number of priests, *tserkovniki*, and *sektany* sentenced
Kyiv	1,063
Donetsk	664
Kharkiv	721
Odesa	628
Dnipropetrovsk	278
Vinnytsia	981
Chernihiv	159
Zhytomyr	516
Mykolaiv	232
Kamianets-Podilskyi	504
Poltava	366
Moldavian ASSR	256
Total	6,368

Source: HDASBU, f. 42, spr. 33, ark. 39.

---

[12] HDASBU, f. 42, spr. 33, ark. 39.

5.2. Polish Consular and Church Initiatives to Protect the Future of the Catholic Church

The Polish consulates tried, actively and unofficially, to help Polish religious communities from the very beginning of the Bolshevik regime.[13] This help was mostly in the form of delivering funds that could be used to cover the taxes and other burdens the Soviet authorities imposed on religious institutions. If those fees were not paid, the church was immediately closed down. Financial support was also delivered, to a lesser degree, to particular priests. This support was particularly indispensable between 1929 and 1930, when the new campaign to eradicate organized religion in the USSR was initiated.[14]

Support was also provided in the subsequent period. Father Alois (Alojzy) Schönfeld, who was arrested in July 1935, told the NKVD, who interrogated him on November 2, 1935, that Jan Karszo-Siedlewski offered him support for the renovation of his church. They had met for the first time at the Polish legion cemetery in 1934. It was then that the diplomat asked whether the priest needed some help. The priest replied that the roof of his church was leaking and needed repair. The estimated cost, the priest said, was around 18,000 rubles. Karszo-Siedlewski replied that he was going to see what could be done. In early 1935, he visited Father Schönfeld in his apartment and said that it could be done—that he would take care of dealing with the Soviet authorities to get a construction permit and of transferring the money (the funds could not be transferred via

---

[13] See, for example, Dzwonkowski, *Kościół katolicki w ZSSR*, 301–34; idem, "Władze II RP," 137–58; Rosowski, "Polska dyplomacja w obronie Kościoła rzymskokatolickiego," passim.

[14] In early January 1930, Kharkiv's only Catholic church at the time was ordered to pay 700 rubles of rent by mid-January. The local Catholic community managed to collect 200 rubles. The consulate general in Kharkiv asked the embassy in Moscow to help in covering this additional expense. The embassy, in turn, asked the MFA. The MFA agreed but remarked that those funds had to be transferred covertly, because, first of all, the Bolsheviks could always impose a new tax and, second, they could interpret this transfer as intervening in their internal affairs. The MFA also advised keeping contact between Polish officials and the clergy to a minimum, to protect the latter. At the same time, the Polish MFA wrote a letter to Cardinal Primate August Hlond with the question whether this sum could be returned. On February 27, 1930, the primate's office replied that the Church could not cover this expense in Kharkiv because they did not have a fund to support Catholic communities abroad, but that he was going to try (covertly) to find some funds to support the Catholic Church in the Far East (*sic*). See Kuśnierz, *Ukraina w latach kolektywizacji*, 249–50. More details about the support provided by the Polish Catholic Church to the Church in the USSR will follow later in this chapter.

official channels). The consulate financed the full renovation expenditure of 45,000 rubles. Father Schönfeld also received, at various times, a total of 3,700 rubles from Karszo-Siedlewski. Almost all the money was spent to cover Soviet taxes, but the priest accepted 300 rubles to cover his own expenses as compensation for a prayer service he conducted at the tombs of the Polish Legion soldiers.[15]

Jan Karszo-Siedlewski not only was personally engaged in providing assistance to the Catholic churches and priests in the Ukrainian SSR; he also directed Ambassador Łukasiewicz's attention to the issue, urging him to inform Warsaw about the results of the Bolshevik policy and advocating that the Polish government do something to protect the Catholic Church, which was the most significant foundation of Polishness in Soviet Ukraine. Karszo-Siedlewski also directed Foreign Minister Beck's attention to this problem. A paper by the consulate (August 30, 1935) stated: "The catastrophic condition of the Catholic Church in Ukraine, a result of the systematic Soviet anti-religious policy, cannot be something to which the Christian world remains indifferent."[16]

One day later, Karszo-Siedlewski wrote to Beck: "The situation is indeed catastrophic, and if there is no strong pressure from the outside very soon, then in a few weeks it will be altogether too late to rescue anything." The diplomat emphasized that, as a Calvinist, he did not care about this issue from a religious point of view, but rather from a Polish national interest point of view, because the Catholic Church was the most important bastion of Polishness in Ukraine.[17]

A few months later, on September 29, 1935, Karszo-Siedlewski wrote to the ambassador once again: "I consider it my duty to turn your attention, Mr. Ambassador, to the desperate condition in which the Catholic Church finds itself in Soviet Ukraine. I have raised this issue in a telegram and in detail in my report on August 30 (this year, nr 15/Ukr/4/Tjn). As I predicted, this condition is worsening day by day. Kyiv, the largest and most important center of Polishness in Ukraine, has remained without a priest since July 29 (this year), i.e., since priest Schenfeld [*sic*] was arrested. This has had a catastrophic influence on the entire parish, and the attendance rate in the church has declined steadily.

---

[15] "Vlada i kostel v Radians'kii Ukraïni, 1919–1937 rr.: Rymo-katolyts'ka Tserkva pid represyvnym tyskom totalitaryzmu," *Z arkhiviv VUChK-GPU-NKVD-KGB*, 2003, no. 2 (21): 297–98. There are no Polish documents that confirm Schönfeld's statements.

[16] AAN, SG, sygn. IV/6, k. 543.

[17] Ibid., MSZ, sygn. 2821, k. 42.

The situation is no better in the countryside, because all the priests who were able to run their parishes (those who had enough administrative authority) have been removed, arrested, and possibly deported. The exception to this rule is the priest in Kharkiv, but he is not able [alone] to take care of the Catholic parishes in Right-Bank Ukraine. The Polish government should not remain indifferent to this issue, because the Catholic Church is perhaps the most serious factor in maintaining patriotic feelings among the Polish community. Once again, I report that the issue is urgent, because soon there will be nothing left to be rescued."[18]

The Polish government tried to respond through unofficial channels. On November 8, 1935, the vice-director of the Political Department of the MFA, Tadeusz Gwiazdowski, sent a note, prepared by Xawery Zaleski on October 26, 1935, to the Polish embassy in Washington. In it Zaleski described the persecution suffered by the Catholic and Evangelical churches in the USSR. He requested that he be allowed to distribute the paper as widely as possible, especially among influential Evangelical and Catholic figures and institutions in the United States. He emphasized that this had to be done carefully and that the fact that official Polish authorities played a role in distributing that information had to be kept secret.[19] Earlier, without any instructions, the MFA forwarded Zaleski's note to the Polish embassy to the Vatican.[20]

As has already been noted, the Catholic Church in Poland also helped the Church in the USSR. The Polish Catholic press (particularly *Przegląd Powszechny*), as well as the scientific and popular press, was interested in the fate of the Catholic Church in the USSR. Furthermore, 150 Catholic priests in Poland came from parishes in the USSR, and a few dozen of them had spent some time in the Gulag.[21]

Subsequently, primates of the Polish Catholic Church—Cardinals Edmund Dalbor and August Hlond—transferred certain amounts of money to help Catholic priests in the USSR.[22] On July 22, 1934, in a private conversation with a counselor to the Polish embassy in Moscow, Primate August Hlond promised to send 500 zlotys per month to support Catholic

---

[18] RGVA, f. 308 k, op. 19, d. 58, l. 21.

[19] AAN, MSZ, sygn. 2821, k. 88.

[20] Ibid., k. 81

[21] Dzwonkowski, *Kościół katolicki w ZSSR*, 335–41.

[22] See idem, "Represje wobec duchowieństwa katolickiego w ZSRR 1918–1939," in *Skazani jako 'szpiedzy Watykanu': Z historii Kościoła katolickiego w ZSRR 1918–1956*, ed. R. Dzwonkowski, SAC (Ząbki: Apostolicum, 1998), 35.

priests in the USSR. In February 1935, Primate Hlond, through the mediation of a former counselor of the Polish embassy in Moscow, Alfred Poniński, sent 1,500 zlotys to support the priests imprisoned in Soviet Gulag camps. Hlond remained in constant touch with the MFA, who informed him of the measures of support undertaken to help the Catholic Church in the USSR, as well as of the general state of the Church in the "Bolshevik paradise." Father Teofil Skalski,[23] who knew Soviet conditions all too well, also tried to support the persecuted priests. Through the mediation of Stanisław Eska, he managed to provide material support to at least thirty-five imprisoned priests.[24]

5.2.1. The Annihilation of the Church

Financial help from both Polish officials and the Church did not save the Catholic Church in the USSR from total annihilation, nor did the interventions of the Polish officials with the PCfFA.[25] The number of active priests and open churches decreased every year in the USSR. According to data from the Polish consulate in Kyiv, in 1928 there were 102 functioning Catholic churches (at the parish level) in Kamianets diocese. This figure did not include minor churches and chapels. Forty-one priests were serving those parishes. In Zhytomyr diocese, the respective figures were 107 and 40. In Left-Bank Ukraine, one church was open in each of the following cities: Kharkiv, Dnipropetrovsk, Poltava, Mariupol, Romny, Stalino, Makiivka, Kamianske, Slaviansk, and Kremenchuk; and in the

---

[23] Father Teofil Skalski (1877–1958) was an apostolic administrator in the Łuck-Zhytomyr diocese. He was arrested by the Bolsheviks on several occasions, the last time in 1926, and sentenced in 1928 to ten years in a Gulag camp. On September 15, 1932, in the last exchange of prisoners between Poland and the USSR, he and seventeen other priests were in the group of fifty-one Poles who left the USSR. During the years 1933–39, Skalski was a parson in the cathedralic parish of Lutsk. After the Soviet invasion, he left Lutsk and found himself under the German occupation. Thanks to the intervention of Cardinal Adam Sapieha, Skalski came to Kraków. He spent two years in Nowy Targ, after which he became a parishioner in Mszana Dolna, where he died. See Dzwonkowski, *Losy duchowieństwa katolickiego*, 436–38; and "Vlada i kostel," 424–26. Father Skalski wrote an informative memoir about his time in the USSR: *Terror i cierpienie: Kościół katolicki na Ukrainie, 1900–1932. Wspomnienia* (Lublin, Norbertinum, 1995).

[24] Rosowski, "Polska dyplomacja w obronie Kościoła," 282–83.

[25] The territory of Soviet Ukraine included Mahiliou archdiocese (Kharkiv; the archdiocese extended mostly to European Russia and eastern Belarus), and the following dioceses: Kamianets-Podilskyi (southwestern Ukraine), Zhytomyr (northern Ukraine and the Kyiv district), and Tyraspil (southern Ukraine; this diocese also included the Volga region). See Dzwonkowski, *Losy duchowieństwa katolickiego*, 67–69.

colony Luxemburg.[26] Many of those priests were arrested in the following years (see table 11).

Table 11. The number of Catholic priests arrested in Soviet Ukraine, 1926–32, according to data obtained by the Polish consulate in Kyiv

Year	Priests arrested
1926	11
1927	8
1928	2
1929	2
1930	49
1931	3
1932	2

Source: AAN, SG, sygn. IV/6, k. 546–47.

As a result of the mass arrests of priests in 1930, there was a significant drop in the number of open churches. In 1930 their number was only about a third of what it had been the year before. In Left-Bank Ukraine, nine of the eleven churches were closed. In 1934 only twenty-five priests were active in Right-Bank Ukraine—nine in Kamianets-Podilskyi diocese and sixteen in Zhytomyr diocese. In 1935, only five of them remained (three had died, ten were arrested, two were sick and unable to work, five saw their rights to serve taken away).[27] In Left-Bank Ukraine in 1935, only two priests remained—Leonard Gaszyński in Kharkiv and Wincenty Skwirecki in Dnipropetrovsk. Gaszyński was arrested on August 12, 1937, and Skwirecki, according to various sources, either in 1936 or in 1937.[28]

---

[26] AAN, SG, sygn. IV/6, k. 546.

[27] Kuśnierz, *Ukraina w latach kolektywizacji*, 251.

[28] RGVA, f. 308 k, op. 19, d. 57, l. 263. There is no detailed information available about Father Wincenty Skwirecki. According to Roman Dzwonkowski, it is likely that he was murdered in 1936. Consul Tadeusz Brzeziński reported that the priest was arrested in July 1937. On September 7, 1937, the consul went to Dnipropetrovsk and concluded that a Catholic church (popularly known as the Polish church) on the main (Marx) boulevard had been closed down. Religious services no longer took place. "From what I could learn," Brzeziński reported, "the closure of the church took place about five months ago, [and] Father Skwirecki aka Sworowski was arrested by the NKVD two months ago" (AAN, MSZ, sygn. 2823, k. 118). There is much more information available about Father Leonard Gaszyński. In contrast to Father Schönfeld, after he was arrested, Gaszyński pleaded guilty to "conducting wide-ranging anti-Soviet activity strictly associated with

As mentioned earlier, Father Alois Schönfeld was arrested in 1935. The Kyiv NKVD accused him, together with seven other priests and eleven *sektanty*, of participating in a "counterrevolutionary fascist organization of Roman Catholic and Uniate priests in Right-Bank Ukraine."[29]

The arrest of the only Catholic priest in Kyiv made it impossible for Polish officials to practice their religion. This was a violation of Article VII of the Treaty of Riga. Jan Karszo-Siedlewski attempted to intervene to protect the priest. Soon after Father Schönfeld's arrest, Karszo-Siedlewski contacted the PCfFA for an explanation as to why the priest was put in prison. He received the formulaic reply that the priest was arrested for "anti-state activity confirmed by concrete facts." Not satisfied with this answer, on August 4, 1935 the Polish diplomat wrote a letter to People's Commissar of the NKVD Vsevolod Balytsky. In it, he reminded Balytsky that in their March meeting he had expressed his readiness to become interested in "particular cases" of repressions against Polish people. Karszo-Siedlewski considered the arrest of the priest of the two Catholic churches in the capital of Soviet Ukraine (on the night of July 28–29, 1935) to be such a case. The head of the Polish post in Kyiv assured Balytsky that the priest was not engaged in any anti-state activity and could not have been engaged in anything that conflicted with Soviet laws. He expressed

---

the Polish intelligence service" from the moment Soviet power was in place until his very arrest. He was forced to confess that, under cover of, for example, rosary prayer circles (*kółka różańcowe*), their members were conducting anti-Soviet activity. Father Gaszyński said that he was permanently in touch with the leaders of the Polish consulates in Kharkiv. Consul Adam Stebłowski allegedly gave him the mission of creating an extensive nationalist organization among ethnic Polish Catholics. Gaszyński confessed he had accepted the mission. This was supposed to be a large organization, according to him (he gave the NKVD nineteen names, saying that he could not remember many others). Gaszyński also pleaded guilty to delivering espionage information that captured the mood of Soviet society. He said that espionage contacts were also maintained with Stebłowski's successors in Kharkiv. Father Gaszyński was shot on October 12, 1938. Eleven of his parishioners were executed along with him. On August 22, 1958, Father Gaszyński and his fellow parishioners were rehabilitated. See AAN, MSZ, sygn. 2823, k. 114; Dzwonkowski, *Losy duchowieństwa katolickiego*, 238–39, 439–40; and "Vlada i kostel," 353–61 and 383–84.

[29] Father Schönfeld was arrested on July 28, 1935 (Karszo-Siedlewski and R. Dzwonkowski both give a different date: July 29). He did not plead guilty of "conducting counterrevolutionary activity," even if he did recognize that his beliefs and upbringing did not make him a Soviet man. On May 14, 1936, he was sentenced to five years in the Gulag. He served his sentence in a camp in Karaganda (Kazakhstan), where he died on April 6, 1938. He was rehabilitated on August 8, 1989. See Dzwonkowski, *Losy duchowieństwa katolickiego*, 430–32; and "Vlada i kostel," 295 and 432.

his hope that Schönfeld's arrest must have been caused by a misunderstanding or a mistake. Hence, he asked for Balytsky's personal intervention in the priest's case to prevent the sentencing of an innocent man. In the end, Karszo-Siedlewski suggested, perhaps a bit craftily, that he feared that the priest's arrest might have been a provocation carried out by "elements who wished to discredit the USSR abroad; foreign countries [after all] believed that the USSR, in accordance with the multiple reassurances and utterances of its leaders, persecuted no organized religion on its territory."[30]

Those arguments did not convince Balytsky, and Karszo-Siedlewski received no answer. Nonetheless, the Polish diplomat did not stop intervening in Schönfeld's case or in the cases of other persecuted priests. On October 29, 1935, he held a conversation with Adolf Petrovsky, which was mostly about the persecution of the Polish community in Soviet Ukraine in general,[31] and of the Catholic clergy in particular. Karszo-Siedlewski said he was never going to believe that the true cause for all the arrests was anti-state activity. They were, he thought, part of the systematic effort to annihilate organized religion, scheduled to take place during the Second Five-Year Plan. He touched upon the arrest of the rector of St. Alexander's Parish, Father Alois Schönfeld. He said that there was no one left to serve as a priest for the consulate officials and workers, which was a breach of Article VII of the Treaty of Riga, which guaranteed that the Polish foreign service would be allowed to practice their religion in the USSR. A new parson could not be appointed, because there was no single clergyman senior enough who had not already been arrested. The PCfFA representative promised to raise this issue with the relevant authorities, to try to find a priest to serve in the Kyiv parish and address other problems that his Polish interlocutor mentioned.[32]

After a few weeks, Father Leonard Gaszyński from Kharkiv received permission to celebrate masses in Kyiv.[33] However, it was difficult to imagine one person being able to run two parishes simultaneously that were so remote from each other. Christmas and New Year's Day of 1935 were celebrated without a priest. It was only in December 1936, after much effort by Karszo-Siedlewski, that a priest from Rostov-on-Don was delegated to serve in Kyiv permanently. His name was Zygmunt

[30] AAN, MSZ, sygn. 2821, k. 44–45.
[31] This conversation was partially covered earlier, in chapter 4, section 7.
[32] CAW, Oddz. II SG, sygn. I.303.4.3144, k. 1405–7.
[33] Ibid., k. 1524–25.

Kwaśniewski. He first appeared in Kyiv in May 1936. Karszo-Siedlewski obtained permission for him to stay for two weeks. Father Kwaśniewski served his first mass there on May 3 (Polish Constitution Day), 1936; it was the first mass there in nine months. According to the consulate, the church was extremely overfilled. On May 12, 1936, Kwaśniewski celebrated a mass in memory of Marshal Piłsudski. Attendance was limited to the employees of the Polish consulate in Kyiv.[34]

Father Kwaśniewski was not given the opportunity to serve in the Soviet Ukrainian capital for long. During the night of August 2–3, 1937, NKVD agents entered his apartment. In all likelihood, a denunciation had been filed against him that he possessed foreign currency, gold, or other valuables. The agents' thorough search lasted six hours. The wooden floorboards were removed. Apart from 1,200 rubles, nothing else of importance was found. The money was confiscated, and no protocol documenting the search was provided. Nevertheless, the priest was arrested. In addition, the sexton's apartment was also searched thoroughly. The NKVD agents even dug up the dirt floor in the basement.[35]

Besides Father Kwaśniewski, other individuals associated with the Church were also arrested. On June 4, 1937, the head of St. Nicholas's Church management board, Sambor, was arrested. On May 29, an elderly lady (Adamowiczowa was her surname) who helped to beautify the altars was arrested. She visited Father Kwaśniewski often, and he visited her.[36] During the next week, all the members of the church's management board were arrested and during the night of June 26–27, 1937 all three remaining members of the board of St. Nicholas's Church were arrested. A thorough search was conducted. The treasurer was taken away, as were all the records pertaining to the finances of the parish. The only person left to take care of the church was a female janitor (a local beggar), who kept all the keys.[37]

The consulate general correctly predicted that after Father Zygmunt Kwaśniewski was arrested, the Soviet authorities would not allow another priest to relocate to Kyiv to perform religious services, which inevitably

[34] Ibid., sygn. I.303.4.1867, k. 449. A similar mass (a prayer for Piłsudski's soul) took place in Leningrad, but it was open to the public, and many people came to St. Catherine's Church there. Ibid., sygn. I.303.4.3161, k. 228.
[35] Ibid., sygn. I.303.4.1867, k. 594.
[36] Ibid., k. 595.
[37] Ibid., k. 615–16.

would lead to the closure of the two Catholic churches in the city. The Polish consulate did allow for the possibility of Father Kwaśniewski's release. If that were to happen, then his work would likely "benefit the NKVD," or so they supposed.[38]

According to the Polish post, once Father Kwaśniewski had been arrested, one could expect pressure to be exerted upon particular individuals who still took part in religious practices in order to stop them; and in the provinces, the local communities could expect their few remaining churches to be closed down, assigned a different (other than religious) purpose, or simply destroyed. These predictions turned out to be true. News of church closures, or of the arrests of the few remaining priests and of believers, arrived from various localities in Soviet Ukraine.[39] The practice of closing down houses of worship was a central feature of Bolshevik religious policy. The most frequent reason for their liquidation was underpayment of taxes. Other reasons included, for example, local authorities "borrowing" churches during the harvest from their religious administrators, allegedly for a brief period, tin order to store grain in them. These places of worship were never returned to their original owners.[40]

The Polish consulate also assumed, but incorrectly, that St. Alexander's Church would soon be torn down in association with the reconstruction

---

[38] Ibid., k. 599–600. In 1927, Father Kwaśniewski had been forced to cooperate with the Soviet authorities. This fact did not protect him from arrest in 1930, when he was sentenced to five years in the Gulag. After his release, he could not return to Proskuriv, where he had worked before 1930, and he settled in Rostov-on-Don, from which he moved to Kyiv. After his second arrest in 1937, he pleaded guilty to "espionage activity" on behalf of the Polish Republic and to recruiting about a dozen new members for it from Kyiv and Vinnytsia oblasts. In September 1937, Father Zygmunt Kwaśniewski was executed. See Dzwonkowski, *Losy duchowieństwa katolickiego*, 317–20; "Vlada i kostel," 396–97; Bazhan, "Represiï sered dukhovenstva," 12; and Kuromiya, *Głosy straconych*, 58–60.

[39] In August 1935, a priest was arrested in the village of Modra, near Radomyshl, and transported to Kyiv. On August 11, 1935, in the village of Mishchantsi, near Radomyshl, Komsomol activists demolished the interior of the church, including the figures of saints, paintings, and altars. RGVA, f. 308 k, op. 19, d. 57, l. 309. Before Christmas 1935, the Catholic church in Uman was closed down and pillaged. Father Jan Przysiecki (born in 1859) remained without any means of support and "literally starved." AAN, MSZ, 6939, k. 21. According to Roman Dzwonkowski, Przysiecki was the last Catholic priest in Soviet Podilia and Volhynia to remain free. He was arrested, likely, in the second half of 1937. His subsequent fate is unknown. See Dzwonkowski, *Losy duchowieństwa katolickiego*, 400–401.

[40] CAW, Oddz. II SG, sygn. I.303.4.1867, k. 354.

of Kyiv.[41] This assumption was not groundless. The so-called reorganization of the Soviet Ukrainian capital led to the destruction of many churches, and it seemed the next logical step would be to tear down St. Alexander's Church in the center of the city.[42] But this was not the case. Following Father Kwaśniewski's arrest, both St. Alexander's and St. Nicholas's Church were still open on Sundays and holidays. The faithful prayed in them without a priest. Judging from a letter from the head of the consulate general in Kyiv, Jerzy Matusiński, to the embassy in Moscow on May 15, 1937, both churches were probably fully closed down in May 1938.[43]

Jerzy Matusiński officially protested when these last two Catholic churches in Kyiv were closed, but the PCfFA representative, Vidiakin, replied that the residents of Kyiv had expressed such a desire—a desire that justified the All-Union Central Executive Committee's decree ordering their closure.[44] St. Alexander's Church was initially turned into a worker's hostel. In 1952, it became a planetarium. In 1982 the planetarium was moved elsewhere, and the church remained empty and deteriorated. It was reopened as a Roman Catholic parish and cathedral in 1991. In St. Nicholas's Church, the Bolsheviks organized some storage depots; since 1979 organ concerts have been held in it. Religious services have been taking place there since 1991, but the church has not been reinstated as a Roman Catholic parish.

---

[41] Ibid., k. 600.

[42] This was associated with the process of moving the capital of the Ukrainian SSR from Kharkiv to Kyiv in 1934. Victims of Kyiv's "reconstruction," i.e., the erection of the Sovnarkom and CC CP(B)U buildings, were numerous historic monuments. St. Michael's Golden-Domed Monastery (eleventh-twelfth centuries) was demolished, and the Holy Trinity Church (twelfth century) was also ruined. The seventeenth-century Epiphany Brotherhood Monastery in Kyiv's Podil district was another victim; a park for entertainment and relaxation was built in its place. The twelfth-century Dormition Church was also destroyed in that district, as were many other churches. See I. Vlasovs'kyi, *Narys istorii Ukraïns'koï Pravoslavnoï Tserkvy*, vol. 4, part 1, *Ukraïns'ka Pravoslavna Tserkva Kyïvs'koho patriarkhatu* (Kyiv: Lybid, 1998), 296–97; O. Rybliuk, "Demokratyzatsiia suspil'noho zhyttia iak faktor natsional'no-relihiinoho vidrodzhennia," in *Istoriia relihii v Ukraïni: Tezy povidomlen' Mizhnarodnoho kruhloho stolu (Lviv, 3-5 travnia 1995)* ed. V. Haiuk, I. Dashkevych, L. Morovs'ka et al (Kyiv and Lviv: [s.n.], 1995), 385.

[43] AAN, MSZ, sygn. 11084, k. 13.

[44] Ibid., sygn. 2824, k. 33. See Dzwonkowski, *Kościół katolicki w ZSSR*, 329; and Rosowski, "Polska dyplomacja w obronie Kościoła," 285.

Persecution of organized religion was the same in Soviet Ukraine as it was in all the other regions of the USSR. Arrests were underway in Soviet Belarus and Russia. On May 3, 1937, the last remaining Catholic priest in Moscow, Michał Cakul, was arrested. He was the parson for two Polish churches, St. Peter and Paul's and Holiest Mother Mary's.[45] This meant that the employees of the Polish embassy had no possibility to practice their religion. Ambassador Wacław Grzybowski asked Foreign Minister Józef Beck to intervene and make sure a Catholic priest was present for worship purposes. Grzybowski saw two ways to proceed. The first one was to relocate a local priest. The second was to send a priest from Poland who would apply for permission to offer religious services in other Soviet cities where Polish posts were present. At that time, the embassies of France, Italy, and the United States had their own chaplains.[46]

A few weeks later, Grzybowski received an answer from Jan Szembek, who shared the opinion that a priest had to be found but suggested that first one should be sought within the Polish communities in the USSR, especially in Minsk and Kyiv.[47] The intentions of the Polish MFA were clear. The goal was to increase the scope and freedom to maintain contact with the local Polish communities. However, at the time all the Polish priests had already been imprisoned. Grzybowski tried to follow the instruction and attempted to intervene with the Soviet authorities to find priests for the embassy and consulates, but he failed to achieve any results. For the last time, in August 1938, the Polish ambassador in Moscow broached this subject with the deputy people's commissar for foreign affairs, Vladimir Potemkin. Potemkin assured Grzybowski that a search was underway. These promises turned out to be empty words.[48]

5.3. The Persecution of Other Religions.
5.3.1. The Orthodox Church

In addition to the Catholic Church, all other organized religions in the USSR suffered persecution at the time. They included all the Orthodox

---

[45] According to data from the Polish embassy, Father Cakul was sentenced to ten years in a Gulag camp, based on article 58, paragraphs 10 and 11 of the criminal code of the RSFSR, for propaganda and agitation against the Soviet state. AAN, MSZ, sygn. 2823, k. 136. Roman Dzwonkowski, SAC, maintains that Cakul was sentenced and executed; see his *Losy duchowieństwa katolickiego*, 186–88.

[46] AAN, MSZ, k. 133–34.

[47] Ibid., k. 131.

[48] Dzwonkowski, *Kościół katolicki w ZSSR*, 331.

denominations, Lutherans, Judaists, and so on. Tellingly, the desperate followers of those religions saw a foreign diplomatic post as the only institution left that could still exert pressure on the Soviet authorities to abide by the articles of their own constitution, which guaranteed religious freedom. Residents of the village of Bozhykivtsi in Zatonsk (now Vinkivtsi) raion, Vinnytsia oblast, sent a letter to the Polish consulate in Kyiv (without a date or the consul's name). The letter was signed on behalf of the community by the representative of the religious congregation, Vasyl Shvets.

In the undated letter, Shvets informed the consulate that the head of the village soviet had closed the Orthodox church and persecuted those who believed in God. The church had submitted all payments properly and had no debts, but despite this the head of the soviet did not let anyone enter the church. The believers turned to the prosecutor and received the reply that the authorities were not in a position to close the church down. People brought this letter the head of the village soviet; he replied that "one could wipe one's rear with it" and tore it to pieces. He added that he was not going to open the church and everyone was going to be tried in court. Shvets wrote that the constitution guaranteed freedom of religion. Where was he supposed to complain now? When people wrote letters describing recent developments to the authorities, they received a reply stating that what they described was not true, that such events (closures of churches) actually took place in Poland. Vasyl Shvets ended his letter to the consul thus: "Village authorities have closed down Orthodox churches in all the nearby villages. They remove and throw down crosses from the roofs of Orthodox and Catholic churches and install red flags in their place. They enter Orthodox churches, demolish the paintings, the Holy Gospel, [and] they ridicule the holy place." Shvets asked for help and counsel. He also asked the consulate to inform other foreign consular posts in Kyiv of their problems and to encourage them to defend places of worship and faith in God. He wrote that if the consul did not believe him, he should send his representative to investigate locally.[49]

Employees of the Polish embassy and consulates attempted to estimate the scale of persecution against the clergy and believers of religions other than Catholicism. As previously noted, after the Kirov murder, the deportation of "uncertain elements" began. Clergymen were

---

[49] RGVA, f. 308 k, op. 6, d. 54, l. 168–68 v.

among them.[50] Systematic repressions continued. According to research the Polish consulate in Kharkiv conducted, in April 1936 only seven Orthodox churches were open in the city, three of them belonging to the Living Church (*Zhyva tserkva*),[51] two to the Russian Orthodox Church, and one each to the Old Believers and the Armenian Apostolic Churches. But in 1925, there were twenty-eight Orthodox churches in the city. The Living Church was managed directly by the Soviet authorities, while the two Russian Orthodox churches were under Archbishop Innokentii, who theoretically was a subordinate of the Moscow metropolitan, Sergei. There was no church in the center of the city; all of them were on the outskirts.[52] The consulate could not, however, provide precise data with respect to the number of Orthodox priests and churches in the countryside because they had either been destroyed or turned into silos, depots, clubs, and the like. The percentage of open Orthodox churches in the villages was very low, the consulate concluded.[53] Jan Karszo-Siedlewski also did not even give an approximate number of open Orthodox churches and active priests because, as he pointed out, even the Soviet authorities did not have such data.[54]

In the 1930s, a majority of the Orthodox priests who remained active were essentially NKVD agents or, if not technically agents, completely dependent on the NKVD.[55] Consul Sośnicki emphasized that Metropolitan Innokentii was in practice fully subordinate to the NKVD: he acted strictly in accordance with instructions written by the municipal and oblast authorities, regardless of the seeming independence of Metropolitan Sergei (e.g., in writing sermons and letters to the believers) who was also dependent on the NKVD. If the Soviet security services were able to control the senior authorities of the Orthodox Church, they could certainly

---

[50] Ibid., op. 19, d. 57, l. 118.

[51] The Ukrainian Synodal Church, often called Living or New Church, split off in 1922 from the Russian Orthodox Church. The Soviet secret service was, of course, vitally interested in the split, since it weakened the traditional church. In Ukraine it operated from 1925 until 1946. Pimen Pegov was its head. For more about the split, see O. Tryhub, "Rozkol iak forma borot'by DPU USRR iz pravoslavnoiu tserkvoiu v Ukraïni (1922–1927 rr.)," *Z arkhiviv VUChK-GPU-NKVD-KGB*, 2009, no. 1 (32): 10–26.

[52] CAW, Oddz. II SG, sygn. I.303.4.3161, k. 277, 279.

[53] Ibid., k. 280.

[54] Ibid., sygn. I.303.4.1867, k. 428–29.

[55] It had not been a marginal phenomenon previously; e.g., in the exarchate of the Ukrainian Orthodox Church (*tikhonovtsy*), there were 30 secret informants in 1923, 84 in 1926, and 82 in 1928. The same numbers of secret informants were present in the Ukrainian Synodal Church during those years. See Tryhub, "Rozkol iak forma," 20.

do so with respect to rank-and-file priests. Priests often faced a choice: either they were dismissed from their parishes, arrested, deported, and even shot; or they became tools of the NKVD. The second choice offered a relatively stable existence for them and their families. If they chose the second, they often found themselves forced to voice absurd theses. Protopope O. Pospelov, and other priests who followed him, announced that the people supported Soviet power—that it was not only legitimate but also established by God [sic], and that "the results achieved by the Soviet system were an indicator of how much of God's grace was granted to it." No less ridiculous events followed from such an absurd "theory"; for example, in the town of Dobrianka in Chernihiv oblast, a local priest called upon the population to give thanks to God for "supplying the USSR with a new constitution."[56]

Consul Stanisław Sośnicki claimed that all the Orthodox priests and bishops who had avoided arrest and remained at their posts must have been NKVD agents. Their material conditions of existence, understandably, were better than those of the priests who had been removed from their parishes. Their income exceeded 1,000 rubles per month. Furthermore, priests paid 300 rubles in taxes annually, while deacons paid 150 rubles. Moreover, Orthodox churches in Kharkiv paid a tax of 30 to 40 thousand rubles annually.[57] The position of unemployed priests was much worse. There were about 100 of them in Kharkiv. They lived in utter penury, begging for help wherever they could, including in front of Catholic and Lutheran churches. They were left without work after the Orthodox churches were closed,[58] and, in order to be eligible for employment, they had to write a statement that they had "renounced all religious superstition." Those who could not do this had to beg to survive.[59] Even though the Bolsheviks controlled the priesthood, they subsequently led a policy of eliminating religion from the universe "of the new Soviet man." In addition to the practices described above, Communists tried to foment antagonism between churches. The priests of the Living Church called upon their faithful to stop attending

---

[56] CAW, Oddz. II SG, sygn. I.303.4.1867, k. 598.

[57] Ibid., sygn. I.303.4.3161, k. 278

[58] On May 30, 1936, Consul Sośnicki noted that the last church in Volchansk, 70 kilometers from Kharkiv, had been closed. After they learned of the decision, local people came to the church and prayed and wept. After the church was closed down, the authorities ordered the two priests to have their beards cut. CAW, Oddz. II SG, sygn. I.303.4.1867, k. 213.

[59] Ibid, sygn. I.303.4.3161, 277–78.

Orthodox churches. Orthodox priests were forbidden, under threat of deportation, to actively evangelize beyond their former group of parishioners.[60]

5.3.2. The Persecution of Lutheran Pastors and Jewish Rabbis

Bolsheviks subsequently eliminated clergymen and believers of other, smaller religious denominations, including those of the Lutheran Church and the Judaic faith. This persecution began in the late 1920s, at the same time as the persecution of the Catholic and Orthodox Churches, and continued during the 1930s. The aim was to eradicate these religions completely. The Lutheran Church was officially liquidated in the USSR in 1937 (See table 12).

Table 12. The number of Lutheran pastors in the USSR, 1929–37[61]

Year	Number of pastors arrested	Number of pastors remaining
1929	8	-
1930	15	83
1931	2	-
1932	-	53
1933	4	41
1934	15	39
1935	14	14
1937	7	9
1938	10	0

Source: O. Litzenberger, *Evangelichesko-luteranskaia tserkov' i sovetskoe gosudarstvo (1917–1938)* (Moscow: Gotika, 1999), 277.

There are not many records about the Lutheran Church in the Polish records. A report from the Polish consulate in Kyiv emphasized that "The position of the Lutheran Church in Soviet Ukraine is equally as tragic as it is for the Catholic Church, as described in [our] report from August 30,

---

[60] Ibid., k. 279.

[61] In the entire interwar period, of the total number of 352 Lutheran pastors in the USSR, 130 were persecuted, arrested, and sentenced. About 100 of them spent many years in a Gulag camp, 22 died there, 15 were executed, and 4 went missing. Over 100 pastors left the USSR, about 70 in 1917–25, about 30 in 1925–38, 7 in the early 1930s, and 2 in the 1970s. O. Litzenberger, *Evangelichesko-liuteranskaia tserkov' i sovetskoe gosudarstvo (1917–1938)* (Moscow: Gotika, 1999), 277.

[19]35."[62] The motivations in this case were much the same as with that of the Catholic Church. First, the Bolshevik stance on religion, in principle, brought about persection; second, relations between the USSR and the Third Reich was a further influence. The worse those relations became, the greater the distrust with which Soviet authorities approached anything associated with Germany in their country, including Protestants, most of whom were German by ethnicity. This could be seen clearly in early 1935, when many Lutheran priests ministers were arrested for the intermediary role they played in transferring support, mostly financial, from aid committees in Germany to Soviet ethnic Germans.[63]

The Lutheran Church in Soviet Ukraine was divided into two synodal administrative districts uniting particular Evangelical Lutheran congregations: northern Ukraine and Zaporizhia. The first one was composed of six communes: Kharkiv, Kyiv, Poltava, Dnipropetrovsk, Luhansk, and Bilovezhi in Dmytrivka raion. The Zaporizhia district included twelve communes: Iosypivka (Karl-Marx raion), Shydlovo (Hryshyne raion), Kronau (Vysokopillia raion), Ludwigstal (Luxemburg German raion), Hochstädt (Molochansk raion), Eugenfeld (Kyzyirsk [Melitopol] raion), Tersianka (Novomykolaivka raion), Neu-Stuttgart (Melitopol raion), Grunau near Zaporizhia, Mariupol, Berdiansk, and Sumy. Fourteen pastors served in those communes.[64]

Jan Karszo-Siedlewski informed the Polish envoy in Moscow that during the night of January 15–16, 1934, the pastor who was the head of the Lutheran Church in Soviet Ukraine was arrested. At the time, he was the sixth Lutheran pastor to be arrested.[65]

There was a massive wave of arrests of Lutheran pastors in 1934 and 1935. On May 17, 1935, a death sentence was passed during the trial of Simon Kludt from Friedenstal near Zaporizhia. He was sentenced for counterrevolutionary activity and Hitlerite propaganda.[66] Pastors Woldemar Seib from Dnipropetrovsk and Friedrich Deutschmann from Eugenfeld (Melitopol raion) were sentenced to death. They were accused of recording the addresses of German citizens in Soviet Ukraine who were starving and sending the addresses to Germany, asking for financial help. According to the Bolsheviks, this money was later used for Hitlerite

---

[62] AAN, SG, sygn. IV/6, k. 553.
[63] Ibid.
[64] Ibid., MSZ, sygn. 2821, k. 69.
[65] Ibid., sygn. 6938, k. 24–25.
[66] RGVA, 308 k, op. 19, d. 56, l. 113.

propaganda and creating Hitlerite cells among Soviet ethnic Germans. The pastors were accused of maintaining contacts with the German consulate in Kharkiv, which supposedly gave them money for counterrevolutionary activity. "Sending the addresses of the starving Germans to Germany, according to the Soviet authorities, supposedly discredited the official Soviet statements about the nonexistence of famine in Ukraine," Consul Stanisław Sośnicki wrote, informing the ambassador in Moscow about the reasons for those arrests.[67]

The sentencing of Seib and Deutschmann to death received much attention abroad. Representatives of all the religious communities in Geneva submitted a protest against those events to the League of Nations on May 17, 1935. They asked France's Prime Minister Pierre Laval to intervene with the Soviet government. The letter of protest was published in Swiss newspapers hostile to the Soviet regime.[68] The campaign was effective to the extent that both Seib's and Deutschmann's death sentences were reduced to ten years of deportation to the Gulag.[69]

In September 1935, the Polish consulate in Kharkiv reported on data they possessed about the Lutheran Church. On the day the report was finalized, all fourteen active Lutheran pastors, except for Albert Mayer from Kharkiv, were arrested and deported to the Gulag. Pastor Simon Kludt was executed.[70] Likewise, according to data the Polish post in Kyiv gathered, four pastors were active in Soviet Ukraine in 1935: Mayer, Vogel from Odesa, Wilhelm Frank from Kassel (Odesa oblast), and Domres from Zhytomyr, who constituted the so-called Bolshevik "Freireligiose Gemeinde."[71]

In September 1936, the Polish embassy in Moscow informed the MFA about the arrests of rabbis. They reported that this was a widespread phenomenon in Soviet Belarus and Ukraine. Those arrests were related to the arrest and sentencing (to five years of prison) of the chief rabbi of Rostov (the son of the chief rabbi of Moscow) for staying in touch with the rabbi of Lepaja, who had left the USSR earlier and conducted anti-Bolshevik propaganda from Lepaja. The real reason for his arrest was

---

[67] Ibid., l. 59.
[68] AAN, MSZ, sygn. 2821, k. 18; Ibid., k. 17.
[69] RGVA, 308 k, op. 19, d. 56, l. 113, l. 134.
[70] AAN, MSZ, sygn. 2821, k. 69.
[71] Ibid., SG, sygn. IV/6, k. 553-554; these names can be found in the MFA note. See ibid., MSZ, sygn. 2821, k. 87.

because he received money via the USSR State Bank from the rabbi of Lepaja to sponsor a Jewish religious academy.[72]

5.4 Participation in Religious Practices

As the Polish consuls observed, despite repressions of the clergy and the personnel assisting them, until the operations against nationalities were launched the attendance at religious events in churches continued to grow. This was particularly true for the larger communities of Poles, such as those who lived within the area of the Kyiv consular district.

In 1936, despite the fact that Father Alois Schönfeld had been arrested, the attendance rate in houses of worship in Kyiv was very high. The so-called May services were particularly popular among the local Polish community. The Stalin Constitution of 1936 had an influence on the number of religious devotees attending churches, both Catholic and Orthodox. Before that constitution was officially adopted, there was a major propaganda campaign to explain its "advantages." In theory, the Stalin Constitution guaranteed everyone's freedom of faith and of religious practice. Initially the devout approached this article with caution, but they eventually accepted as literal truth. They believed the Communists were about to end religious persecution. So they demanded that the places of worship that had been taken away from them be returned. They clearly must have forgotten that they were dealing with people who had passed the "most liberal constitution in the world" but kept how to interpret it entirely within their own discretion.

Polish consular officials noted high attendance at religious services, both in Catholic and Orthodox churches. In April 1936, Consul Sośnicki noticed a higher than usual tendency among Soviet people to attend Orthodox churches. He believed the cause was the increasing poverty among the people, who sought some relief, at least in spiritual terms, in religion. He wrote that, on the one hand, the authorities did not create any difficulties for holding Orthodox religious practices because they realized that the priests were going to die out soon anyway, which would inevitably lead to the closing of churches; on the other hand, they made sure the influx of new faithful did not grow out of control. They systematically reduced the number of open churches for any reason, or none whatsoever.[73]

---

[72] Ibid., MSZ, sygn. 6939, k. 259–60.
[73] CAW, Oddz. II SG, sygn. I.303.4.3161, k. 279. The Polish embassy in Moscow reported that repairs to some Orthodox churches were permitted. For example, in the summer of 1935 the Cathedralic Church in Moscow was renovated. AAN, MSZ, sygn. 6939, k. 259–60.

During Easter 1936, Orthodox churches were overflowing with devotees. The crowds were so great that the police were ordered to regulate the flow of people. Typically, antireligious meetings took place in factories, clubs, and so on, but many of those who attended such gatherings went to their church after they were over, and they received Holy Communion the next day. Many young people attended religious services.[74]

Staff at the Polish consular post in Kyiv reported that Father Zygmunt Kwaśniewski was "immensely effective" in attracting people to his church. This was, they believed, the reason why he was arrested. On Sundays, the number of devotees could reach two thousand, and four to five thousand attended the Resurrection Mass that was held in St. Nicholas's Church. Not all attendees were able to fit inside the church, and some had to stand on the stairs outside. On Sundays and holidays, from thirty to fifty baptisms took place, with about ten on a regular day. Many weddings took place in the two Catholic churches of Kyiv. Baptisms and weddings were organized not only for local parishioners, but also for devotees from distant places such as Odesa, Shepetivka, Kamianets-Podilskyi, and Poltava. May services attracted as many as seven hundred to a thousand people.[75] The Bolsheviks tried all they could to limit the number of people who observed religious practices. Many NKVD agents went to church. Organ music was prohibited in St. Alexander's Church starting from May 1937. On May 30, some unidentified men were seen taking photographs of the faithful as they were leaving the church.[76] As noted, May services were extremely popular. In response, the Bolsheviks issued a ban on masses in the evenings in June, allowing only morning services to be held.[77] This was how they tried to prevent people who worked morning shifts, as well as youth and children, from attending church. When these measures turned out to be ineffectual, to solve the problem they then decided to arrest Father Kwaśniewski.

The Polish consulate general in Kyiv noticed, based on both data quoted here and on other information, that, despite this persecution of religion, "people came to meet God" anyway. This was particularly true of the rural population: the most outward sign of their religiosity was the fact that people tended to celebrate Sundays and religious holidays,

---

[74] CAW, Oddz. II SG, sygn. I.303.4.3161, k. 279.

[75] Ibid., sygn. I.303.4.1867, k. 596.

[76] Ibid., k. 595–96.

[77] Ibid., k. 597.

whereas they worked on the official, Bolshevik-made holidays. This picture was a bit different in the cities. "The urban population was targeted by Bolshevik propaganda," the Polish post reported, "particularly with regard to materialism and material welfare, the basis for the new faith. This 'faith' must have failed completely though, because not only was material well-being nowhere to be seen, it was hard for ordinary people to obtain their daily bread. One cannot conclude, however, that, even if the urban-industrial population does not subscribe to the new religion, it automatically reverted back to faith in God. No, they were left hanging in the vacuum of nonbelief. But some part of the urban population—albeit very small—has begun to betray signs of returning to faith in God."[78]

In the smaller Polish communities, the already limited group of those who participated in Catholic religious services further diminished after the priest was arrested. Consul Tadeusz Brzeziński wrote that the arrest of Father Gaszyński in Kharkiv caused great anxiety among the local Poles, which was reflected in the lower number of devotees (men in particular) seen in the church. On Sunday, at the hour that the mass normally began when Father Gaszyński was present, several dozen people were present nonetheless. They prayed and sang religious songs without their priest. After one hour a service took place, conducted by a Turkish citizen in the Armenian liturgical style.[79]

---

[78] Ibid., k. 597.
[79] AAN, MSZ, sygn. 2823, k. 115.

Chapter Six
Soviet Propaganda

6.1. Propaganda and Reality

"The contrast between the fictional world of the revolutionary tale and real life is striking."[1] These were the words of Ambassador Wacław Grzybowski. They reflect the nature of "parallel reality" in the Soviet Union—the one propaganda constructed, and the one people lived—very well. An important feature of the Stalinist regime, as Andrzej Chojnowski wrote, was not only terror, which was at the heart of the new order, but also "the monstrous lie that cast the residents of the totalitarian empire into the world of fiction constructed by propaganda."[2]

Given the uniqueness of the Soviet state, which operated in parallel realities throughout its entire duration, the authors of the Polish consular, diplomatic, and intelligence reports that were delivered to their superiors in Moscow or Warsaw by definition had to compare the Kremlin's official position with their own observations. Issues of propaganda have in part already been discussed in the sections of this book that described the Stakhanovite movement,[3] but other Polish analyses have also treated the issue of propaganda in general, and it is this aspect that I would like to examine in this chapter.

Soviet propagandists clung closely to their instructions on how to present both the domestic and the outer world. Aspects of the former, the "happy life" and "achievements" of Soviet socialism, were praised in all possible ways. The latter, of course, was dominated by pictures of miserable, desperate, and hungry workers in the West, of the depopulation and hopelessness intrinsic to capitalism. Creating the fictitious reality of the alleged wealth and happiness of Soviet society took place under Stalin's own guidance: "Our proletarian revolution," he said, "is the only revolution in the world that has delivered not only political results for the people, but also material results ... Our revolution is the only one that has liberated the people from the fetters of capitalism while

---

[1] AAN, Ambasada RP w Moskwie, sygn. 41, k. 5.
[2] A. Chojnowski, *Ukraina* (Warsaw: Trio, 1997), 107.
[3] See chapter 3, section 3.

providing the necessary conditions for a wealthy life. Here lies the source of the power and invincibility of our revolution."[4]

The speech by the head of the Soviet Ukrainian Council of People's Commissars, Mykola Marchak, may be cited here as the epitome of Soviet propaganda. On February 20, 1938, at the fifth session of the republic's Central Executive Committee, he touched on the issue of electoral rights in the context of the Supreme Soviet of the Ukrainian SSR. He said: "Right on the border of two worlds, socialist and capitalist, mighty Ukraine stands, an irremovable, integral part of the great USSR. The two worlds are in a bitter conflict. In gentry-owned Poland, in fascist Germany, and in other capitalist countries, millions of workers suffer under the yoke of political lawlessness and inhuman exploitation. The workers and peasants of Western Ukraine are under a double amount of pressure. The peasantry of Western Ukraine has long forgotten what sugar tastes like. Butter, kerosene, matches, and salt are a rarity in peasant life there." Next, Marchak spoke about the Ukrainian peasants in Poland who "looked across the border with jealousy": "With a gaze filled with hope for a better future, the workers of Western Ukraine look at living conditions in the Soviet country under the sun of a Stalinist constitution."[5]

Jan Łagoda, who was in Soviet Ukraine in early February 1936 thanks to Jan Karszo-Siedlewski, had the opportunity to observe a session of the Central Executive Committee. He took notes on some of the more interesting speeches. A representative of Proskuriv raion said that his raion had fulfilled all the obligations it had with respect to the state, while in Poland peasants were allegedly forced to sell "their last cow" to pay their taxes. Collective-farm workers in Soviet Ukraine were leading a happy and merry life, while in Poland they cut one match into four pieces; there exist special machines that do that, he said. A representative from Iampil, on the left bank of the Dnister River, boasted that his town had installed an electricity generator to provide street lighting: "Let the Romanian people squint their eyes while they watch our affluent life."[6]

On April 3, 1937, the newspaper *Bil'shovyk* published a letter from T. Goldfarb, a participant in an international piano competition held in Warsaw. She reflected on her impressions during a train journey from the USSR, via Shepetivka, to Poland. The Polish consulate in Kyiv translated

[4] "Pod znamenem partii Lenina-Stalina," *Pravda*, November 7, 1938.

[5] "Doklad tov. N.M. Marchaka o proekte 'Polozhenie o vyborakh v Verkhovnyi Sovet USSR,'" *Pravda*, February 21, 1938.

[6] AAN, MSZ, sygn. 9514, 130–32.

the letter and sent it back to Warsaw. This was the picture she painted of the "misery" in Poland and of the "happiness" in the USSR: "Even at the first train station, I saw a different world, different customs. That was capitalist Poland torn by an economic crisis, a country where millions live in penury and hunger, without employment. Our press writes a lot about how Polish workers, peasants, intelligentsia, live. For me, a [female] citizen of the Soviet Union, a permanent resident of the beautiful city of Kyiv, a person who is twenty-two years old, the journey to a different world was very informative. In Warsaw I saw the poverty of the outskirts and the luxury of the wealthy districts. There are a lot of goods in the stores, the shop windows are very appealing, but there are only a few buyers inside. There is no money, people earn too little to be able to afford purchases. Hence the stores are empty. Just across the border I saw poor Polish villages, fields in deplorable conditions. One can see the humiliation [of the common people] reflected everywhere. When you compare the two worlds, the two systems, you notice things you would have not otherwise seen. You realize how joyful it is to be a citizen of the Soviet country, our fatherland, where human dignity is fully appreciated. Many academics told us they would consider it great if they could work and study in the USSR. This was something also said by musicians, who suffer from high unemployment. I was at a reception at the home of a professor, a leading composer; he lives in very modest conditions, not to say poverty."[7]

This was the sort of content served up by the Soviet press. A reader who lived in the "Soviet [informational] ghetto" had exclusive access to such, and only such, news. The Soviet totalitarian system made sure that no unauthorized information made it into the "Soviet paradise" that would harm the meticulously constructed picture of "the most progressive country in the world." Soviet radio stations jammed foreign broadcasts, in particular those aired from Poland. In Kyiv, one could hear, at any time during the day, Warsaw Radio Station, which was equipped with a very strong American Emerson transmitter. No other station could be heard until 10:00 p.m. Polish time (midnight Moscow time). Only after midnight, when Soviet radio stations stopped transmitting, could one hear other Polish radio stations. Radio stations from Lviv, Vilnius, and Poznań could

---

[7] CAW, Oddz. II SG, I.303.4.1867, k. 550–50 v.

be heard clearly; but the Polish consulate could never hear transmissions from Katowice, Łódź, or Kraków.[8]

The Soviet authorities cared about creating a positive image of the USSR as a democratic country, a country that respected civil liberties. For this reason, as well as for strategic reasons, some cities issued (preventatively) a ban on photographying public places, and one could not be in the streets with a camera in hand.[9]

When an important event was about to take place, for instance the visit of an important foreign person, the Bolsheviks were often able, for propaganda purposes, to transform the gloomy Soviet landscape very quickly into something that looked like a role model.[10] On June 15, 1935, Foreign Minister Edvard Beneš of Czechoslovakia came from Kharkiv to Kyiv (he had visited Leningrad earlier). Just as Édouard Herriot was shown a country full of "happy and well-nourished people" while the famine had already reaped its horrendous harvest, the Soviets showed Beneš around the Kyivan Caves Monastery to convince him that the USSR was a country of religious freedom. Piotr Kurnicki witnessed Beneš's visit and the Soviet preparations for it. He wrote that it was characteristic that all antireligious posters had been removed from the area of the monastery, and the "interior of the church was restored to its old appearance to make it seem as if a mass had taken place there yesterday. Around the monastery one could see a few priests at the time of his visit, and, moreover, a few monks, who have not been seen there for a long time."[11]

Any problematic information that could hurt the image of "progress" in the USSR was either whitewashed or dismissed. During his journey to the Donbas in November 1935, Stanisław Sośnicki, the Polish consul in Kharkiv, saw a crowd of people in Stalino at 8:00 a.m. They had gathered in front of a cooperative just across from the hotel. He asked the member of the local executive committee who those people were and why they were standing in line. He was told that there was a sale on *torgsin* goods. Later, Sośnicki learned that a few dozen pairs of rubber shoes had been delivered to the cooperative, and the people were trying to get a hold of them immediately. The police later dispersed the crowd. A similar scene

---

[8] RGVA, f. 308 k, op. 19, d. 53, l. 139.

[9] CAW, Oddz. II SG, sygn. I.303.4.2101, n.p.

[10] For example, when Édouard Herriot visited the Soviet Union during the famine of 1933. See Kuśnierz, *Ukraina w latach kolektywizacji*, 183–89.

[11] RGVA, f. 308 k, op. 19, d. 56, l. 132.

played out in front of another store the next day when a bunch of warm shirts were delivered.[12]

The Soviets emphasized that many social problems that plagued capitalism (unemployment, lack of social security, poverty, prostitution) did not exist in the USSR. How exactly one of these — prostitution — was being eradicated in the USSR was a process that Captain Jan Szyndler, an employee of the Polish mission in Moscow, observed. On June 3, 1936, together with other foreign guests, he visited a model correctional facility for prostitutes. The tour was given by the director, who praised Stalin's protection of the people and said that the Soviet authorities had eradicated the root causes of prostitution: "The struggle is over, the victory is complete. The causes of prostitution — unemployment, exploitation, political and civic ignorance — have been removed by the Soviet authorities, and the well-being and support provided to the citizens by the Party and the government have created a situation in which, in Moscow, there are only twenty to thirty prostitutes per four million residents."

Five similar facilities existed in the region. All of them would be soon closed because, in the director's words, there would be no prostitutes left. There were 130 former prostitutes at the facility Szyndler visited. In the morning, they engaged in rehabilitation and studies, and they worked in the evening. The minimum salary was 150 rubles; some Stakhanovites earned between 300 and 500 rubles. Each woman had to pay 85 rubles in rent. In his facility, according to the director, everything was available, from a Komsomol unit to theater, literary, and sport facilities and even an amateur orchestra band. Szyndler was shown some photographs: the women were nicely dressed and smiling.

It is not difficult to guess that the reality the director fabricated — the smiling former prostitutes who wanted to start a new life — did not convince the Polish guest. When Szyndler saw the facility itself, his impressions were different. The medical facilities were very small, with primitive implements, plaster falling off the walls, and no waiting room. The lodgings were small, with four or eight beds each and badly worn-out bedding. Each room was equipped with nothing more than small tables and hangers on the wall. The dining hall was decrepit; the entire hospital was filled with the stench of a stuffy, dirty room. Szyndler saw fifty women, none of them working despite the fact that the visit took place during working hours. A policewoman guarded the women outside. She stood

---

[12] Ibid., d. 59, l. 38.

next to the door of the building where the foreign delegation was lodged. "Typical," the Polish observer commented.

The women did not look as happy as in the photographs the director had presented. They were sad and dressed in dirty and worn-out clothing. Citing one of the members of the delegation, a French journalist, as an example, Szyndler reflected on how easily and uncritically the Western media sometimes accepted the propaganda served up by the Bolsheviks. This journalist did not understand Russian, and the director's message was translated for him. The journalist took meticulous notes on everything the director said, but he did not bother to make any additional observations. "One can expect an enthusiastic press article to appear in France announcing that prostitution has been eradicated in Russia, since he clearly paid no attention to the real state of affairs," the Polish observer of this Bolshevik-organized farce soberly concluded.

Szyndler wrote that prostitution did exist in Russia, but its scale was small: "there are not too many of them, but they can be seen on the main streets."[13] Stanisław Suchecki, who worked in the consular department in Moscow before he came to Kharkiv, remarked that, compared to Moscow, people did not talk much about prostitution in Kharkiv: "I had no personal contact with this [phenomenon]. One hears that prostitution is a rarity here." According to Suchecki, the scale of prostitution was greater in Moscow than it was a year before. "One can see sex workers on the streets of Moscow at night. I experienced this myself three times. One prostitute I met showed me her factory pass and said that she earned 110 rubles per month, which forced her to earn extra money this way because otherwise she would not be able to cope financially."[14]

Sometimes the Bolshevik agitators went so far with their sermons on how horrible everything was in the capitalist world that their stories were downright absurd. The deputy director of the Polish Border Protection Corps, Major Jan Gurbski, sent a report on February 23, 1937, to Major Stanisław Szaliński (head of Department II-b, counterintelligence) and Jerzy Niezbrzycki (head of the East Section in the *Dwójka*) covering the radio interception of conversations between Moscow and Soviet officials abroad. He described a conversation that took place in January 1937 between Erasimovich, a Soviet foreign correspondent in London, and his superiors. The correspondent received an order to write an article on

---

[13] CAW, Oddz. II SG, sygn. I.303.4.3159, k. 248–49.
[14] RGVA, f. 308 k, op. 19, d. 63, l. 263.

England's depopulation. He was advised to include statistical data sent from Moscow in his article. Erasimovich refused to write this text because, if he quoted the data he received from Moscow, the conclusion that would logically follow would be that in forty years there would only be the elderly left in England, which was absurd. Despite his objections, Erasimovich was again ordered to write the article exactly as he was told.[15]

The Soviet press did occasionally write about problems in domestic living conditions or certain "excesses." Frequently these were explained as the alleged harmful activity of the enemy, various saboteurs, Trotskyites, Bukharin followers, spies, and so on. If one reads the Soviet press attentively, especially beyond the first few pages, much valuable information about Soviet reality can be uncovered. For example, information was published about cases of inappropriate treatment of Soviet citizens by officials in power at all levels (including the Party and state apparat), as were also cases of shortages of water, electricity, and basic goods, such as food, clothes, shoes, children's accessories, and even nails.

Several times Polish observers emphasized the dual nature of Soviet reality—the one fabricated in the media and the one they witnessed in the streets on a few occasions. During the November 15 to 20, 1935 business trip of Stanisław Sośnicki, Jan Łagoda, and Ludwik Michałowski in the Donbas, the following incident took place in the Stalin Machine Tools Factory in Kramatorsk. When the Polish group visited the dining hall, the deputy director, Zamiel, who was their guide in the factory, pointed to a worker, who was eating bread and an apple, and said: "Could one even imagine a worker eating fruit before the war?" Consul Sośnicki commented on this remark in a report to the ambassador: "If this is supposed to be evidence proving the material well-being of the working class, then Stalin is certainly right when he says that the Stakhanovite movement was born out of the 'affluent life' [*zazhitochnaya zhizn'*] of the workers." The dining hall itself, Sośnicki wrote, was used mostly by workers who were bachelors, because a worker who had a family could not afford to eat there. The modest meal consisting of soup, a tiny portion of meat, and a fruit drink, cost 1.5 to 2 rubles. Hence most workers ate at home, and they alleviated their impoverished condition with vegetables from their small garden plots.[16]

---

[15] ASG, Dowództwo KOP, sygn. 541/566, k. 50–50 v.
[16] RGVA, f. 308 k, op. 19, d. 59, l. 37.

From September 22 to 30, 1936, Sośnicki and Michałowski were on a business trip to Kharkiv, Mariupol, Berdiansk, and Kerch. The consul witnessed a comic event that highlighted both the extent of Soviet duplicity and the people's attitude toward the propaganda of well-being that they were being fed. While they were visiting a state farm, Michałowski spoke with its director about some statistics of the recent grape harvest. Overhearing their conversation, two workers laughed at the figures the director mentioned and one said to the other, "Ouch, what a horrible lie" (*Oi, kak breshet uzhasno*).[17]

Jerzy Matusiński noted the parallel nature of Soviet reality when he wrote about the enormous lines that formed in front of stores in Kyiv. Particularly comical in this context were the propaganda posters and slogans on the storefronts. They painted a wonderful, wealthy picture of Soviet society: "Organizational chaos in retail trade, shortages, and the poor quality of Soviet products all contrast both sadly and comically with this small-scale bluff with which Soviet propaganda tries to cover reality. The same subterfuge is applied on a larger scale to other areas of life. In stores, where people are suffocating in long lines, one can read that produce in all quantities can also be ordered on the phone. It will be delivered to one's place of residence. We heard a good joke on this subject at the circus: 'Comrade, says a customer, turning to a salesperson in a state-run shoe store—I won't even make it home in these [poor-quality] shoes.' 'You are absolutely right, comrade,' the salesperson replies, 'but we have predicted this already. We have just received an order to deliver shoes on demand to your homes.' The audience went wild with laughter and merriment."[18]

6.1.1. Sovietization of the Polish National Minority

The observations of the Polish diplomatic and consular corps about Soviet nationalities policy are also worthy of attention, especially with respect to the propagandistic support the Polish national minority received, at least on paper. As is well known, the Soviet authorities had established the ethnic Polish Marchlewski Raion. A Polish Institute for Proletarian Culture had been opened, and Polish newspapers and books were published as part of the policy of *korenizatsiia* aimed at Sovietizing national minorities in the USSR. Representatives of the Second Polish

---

[17] CAW, Oddz. II SG, sygn. I.303.4.1867, k. 122.
[18] AAN, MSZ, sygn. 6830, k. 30.

Republic were aware of those aims from the very beginning. They were also aware of the fact that the alleged flourishing of the Polish national minority under "the sun of socialism" was largely a propagandistic fabrication. On January 28 and 29, 1934, Consul Stanisław Sośnicki visited Marchlewski Raion to verify the press statements about "the raion's achievements." He was skeptical because he had already met many inhabitants of Marchlewski Raion who had come to the consulate asking for help. There was no bread in the villages, and the people, left without any possibility of earning money, could not purchase it in the nearby cities.

After his visit to the raion, Consul Sośnicki confirmed his earlier opinion. After he had familiarized himself with the statistical data and the situation on the ground, he concluded: "Marchlewski Raion, compared with previous years, can certainly boast a certain amount of progress in some areas of its very modest and primitive life, but it is certainly not in such a wonderful position as was so loudly proclaimed recently in the Polish-[language] Soviet press."[19]

The "certain amount of progress" the consul had in mind was the construction of a factory and the expansion of education. For the latter purpose, 55 percent of the raion's budget had been dedicated. There were eighty-two schools in the raion. The news about growing incomes, similar to other fantastic data the Soviet press served up, was a fairy tale. Based on his own observations, Consul Sośnicki concluded that the community, on average, earned incomes similar to everyone else's in Soviet Ukraine — that is, one to two kilos of grain for one *trudoden'*. However, to get paid for one *trudoden'*, one often had to work two days.

All official signs on public buildings (schools, pharmacies, hospitals, the workers' club, the bank, the trade-union house, the court, the raion's executive committee) were posted in both Polish and Ukrainian. In practice, use of Polish was rare. According to the consul, Ukrainian was the main language spoken at sessions of the village soviet. Moreover, the consul witnessed an event that, to some extent, reflected the artificial nature of how the Polish language was used in Marchlewski Raion. A crowd gathered in front of the raion's Party committee in Marchlewsk right next to where the consul's car was parked. A policeman tried to

---

[19] RGVA, f. 308 k, op. 3, d. 314, l. 52.

disperse it. He did so speaking exclusively in Russian. Only after he saw Consul Sośnicki did he try (with little success) to speak some Polish.[20]

A year and a half after Sośnicki's visit, Jan Karszo-Siedlewski decided to visit Marchlewski Raion during one of his trips around the consular district without informing the Soviet side about his travel plans, to make sure they did not make any special preparations. He arrived there on July 5, 1935. Only after his arrival did he visit the raion's executive committee. It turned out that the head of the committee was a Russian, and his deputy, a Jew. Both were new to the region. They barely understood Polish and did not speak it. The only person in the committee of Polish ethnicity was the secretary, whose parents had been forced to evacuate from Warsaw to Ukraine during the First World War. According to Karszo-Siedlewski's research, Polish people made up only 50 to 51 percent of the raion's population rather than the official figure of 63 percent. The number of Polish signs had decreased since Sośnicki's visit in January 1934. Aside from the few signs in Polish on public buildings in Marchlewsk, signs in Ukrainian and Russian were present everywhere—road signs, on the main store (*univermah*), and the local kindergarten, where all the children's books were in Ukrainian—and even the childcare supervisor could not speak Polish.[21]

According to the Soviet authorities, Polish culture flourished in the USSR. Consul Sośnicki was able to experience its "flourishing" personally. In the second half of July 1935, a Polish theater troupe came to Kharkiv from Kyiv. The performances took place in the local opera house. They were not very popular. Only 350 persons attended the first one, in a space that could seat 2,000. As a result, the Party administration ordered the theater to be filled to its full capacity to show support to "the theater of a national minority." The Ludwik Waryński Polish Club distributed tickets free of charge (250 of them were distributed on July 21). They were also sent to Party committees and factories.

On July 23, 1935, Sośnicki was present at a performance of Valentin Kataev's *Flower Road*. The audience was 95 percent Russian and Jewish. Almost no Polish could be heard. The performers, most of whom were Jewish, Sośnicki wrote, "were no better than a weak provincial theater. The actors could not speak Polish, the performance was horrible, the entire show, compared with what the local Russian groups did, looked very bad.

[20] Ibid., l. 43, 51–53.
[21] Ibid., op. 19, d. 57, l. 78–79.

In the eyes of the audience, this kind of performance by a "Polish group" must have made the worst kind of impression. It highlighted the gap in artistic quality between the Russian-language and the pseudo-Polish theater. This must have led to a feeling of superiority and pity for the Polish national minority represented, unfortunately, in this case, by Jews."[22] The group performed ten times, and all its performances most likely elicited similar reactions from the audience.

6.1.2. The Civil War in Spain

As the Spanish Civil War raged, Soviet propaganda not only dedicated considerable space to condemning the enemies of "the people's Spain" and highlighting the "dangers of fascism," but also promoted the idea of collecting aid in the USSR to help the victims of that war, women and children in particular. Originally the idea was for Soviet women and children to help Spanish women and children. After a week, the campaign was limited to women, and then it was expanded to include men. On the initiative of the Stalin car factory in Moscow, a resolution was passed that male workers should also join the aid drive. The workers declared at a meeting that they were going to donate 2 rubles each (a quarter of their daily income). Workers from other factories followed their example. Moreover, large pro-republican demonstrations in Moscow, Leningrad, and Kharkiv (100,000 participants) took place. During the demonstrations, charity donations were collected and a reenactment of the Spanish conflict took place.[23]

Between September 12 and 20, 1936, 7 million rubles were collected — 1,220,000 in Soviet Ukraine, 1,150,000 in Moscow oblast, and 910,000 in Leningrad oblast. The money was used to purchase food supplies: 30,000 poods of butter, 95,500 poods of sugar, and 17,000 poods of canned food. All this was dispatched to Alicante, Spain, on September 18, 1936, on the ship *Neva*.[24] Tadeusz Jankowski reviewed these figures and noted, in a letter to Foreign Minister Beck (dated September 28, 1936), that this offered some relief to the provisioning commissariat, because they were able to empty the depots where sugar products were stored (12,000 poods): these reserves could not be purchased by the Soviet people because they were unaffordable.[25]

---

[22] Ibid., l. 94–95.
[23] AAN, SG, sygn. IV/8, dok. 133, b.p.
[24] Ibid.
[25] Ibid.

Ambassador Grzybowski noted, in a report to the MFA, that by October 2, 1936, 14 million rubles had been collected in the USSR to help Spanish women. Soviet Ukraine was the leader in this charity drive, with 2,141,000 rubles collected, followed by Moscow and Leningrad oblasts. The *Neva*, and then the *Kuban'* were dispatched from the port of Odesa with food on board. The *Kuban'* delivered 30 thousand poods of flour, 27 thousand poods of butter, 61 thousand poods of sugar, 11 thousand poods of smoked fish, 250 thousand of canned foods, and one thousand crates of eggs. On October 4, another ship, the *Zhirianin*, was sent from Odesa, also carrying food for Republican Spain.[26]

Jan Karszo-Siedlewski commented that this charity campaign was another manifestation of Bolshevik hypocrisy. A society that was extremely impoverished had, on its own (alleged) initiative, to help the Spaniards. The diplomat had kept an eye on the situation in Soviet Ukraine and said that a difficult winter awaited its people and that "one could already see the signs of penury among the lowest-paid groups of society, who could not afford to buy a coat, clothes, or shoes and were undernourished." The forced charity campaign was ridiculous in this context. Spain was to to be supplied by people who were certainly in no better condition. The Bolsheviks wanted to turn their own society's attention away from its own poverty.[27]

6.2. The Soviet Press as a Source of Information about the Country

An examination of the Soviet press also provided many useful sources that helped to get closer to the truth about Soviet reality. Jan Karszo-Siedlewski wrote in January 1936 that, in order to resist Bolshevik propaganda, which was making more and more inroads in the West, one had to rely on one's own data obtained from official publications or speeches: "One should not forget that the Bolsheviks are masters of propaganda, something they will never renounce in international relations, even with respect to the most friendly nations, and in order to fight it effectively, only facts obtained from one's very own sources should be used."[28]

Unable to find a single critical article in the Polish press about the Soviet situation, the diplomat sent some excerpts from the Soviet press to

---

[26] Ibid., MSZ, sygn. 6650, k. 183.
[27] CAW, Oddz. II SG, sygn. I.303.4.1867, k. 416–17.
[28] Ibid., k. 373.

the MFA so that they could be used by the Polish press.[29] Karszo-Siedlewski also suggested some drafts of articles himself. He examined the contents of the Soviet press and compared it with Soviet everyday life. He drafted an article titled "Wesołe Życie w Sowietach" (Merry Life in the USSR) for publication in Poland. Karszo-Siedlewski sent it to Ambassador Juliusz Łukaszewicz in April 1936. Given its interesting content, the article is worth quoting in its entirety:

> The Soviet press, recently, in association with the annual celebration of the proletarian May First holiday, wrote extensively about the unemployment, poverty, and hunger present in Poland and juxtaposed it all with life in the "Soviet paradise," where, as they say, "life has become better, life has become merrier." Let us see how this more comfortable, merrier life looks in practice. This beautifully sounding claim that there is no unemployment in the Soviet Union is true on paper, but in practice looks less attractive. It is very easy to liquidate unemployment when you send everyone who cannot be paid for their work to do forced labor at canal and highway construction sites, to work in the forest in the Far North or in Siberia, in gold mines, etc. All this work has to be done for little food in the swamps and in extreme cold, with conditions so bad that our barracks for the homeless look like palaces in comparison. Not surprisingly, hundreds, thousands of people perish quietly alone, because no one dares to say a word about them in the Soviet press. This reality is far detached from everything that the tourists and foreign workers' delegations see when they come to visit; for them, everything is prepared and fabricated in advance, with no one allowed to look and learn on their own.
>
> What does the better and merrier life of an average Soviet worker look like? About 50 percent of the workers earn 100–150 rubles per month; more is earned by fewer than 10 percent. All the rest do not even have 100 rubles per month; some receive 50 rubles per month. What is the ruble worth? Its nominal worth is 3 francs, but in reality not that much perhaps, if one kilogram of plain bread costs 90 kopecks, i.e., roughly one zloty. In such conditions, most of the working families starve. They can afford neither butter nor meat. It is even worse when it comes to clothing, underwear, shoes. There is simply not enough to go around for most Soviet citizens. At the same time, there is a small group of privileged persons among the 10 percent mentioned above, who earn up to a few thousand rubles per

---

[29] RGVA, f. 308 k, op. 19, d. 58, l. 276.

month; they have a comfortable, multiroom apartment, while an average worker's or clerk's family has to live in a room with a few [other] persons. This is what social equality looks like in the fatherland of the proletariat, the leaders and guardians of which (from the GPU [NKVD]) reside in palaces and build bathrooms of marble stolen from cemeteries, and they do not drive cars from their own factories, of which they are so very proud, but drive exclusively Lincolns, Buicks, and other luxury limousines.

This is what can be done by means of skillful propaganda, bluff, and shamelessness. We witness this combination when we read comparative descriptions of life in capitalist countries and in the USSR in the Soviet press. This principle applies to all areas of life. A few examples can be cited to demonstrate how it works. Nearly every day we read about some amazing Soviet achievements like the recent journey to the stratosphere, flights over the Northern Pole, the Chelyuskin adventures, but we do not learn how much more difficult it is for a Soviet citizen to reach another city by train or taxi or a tram that is so packed with people that it resembles a bunch of grapes. We learn from the press that television-telegraphic communication has been established between Kyiv and Moscow, but how can an ordinary citizen benefit from it if he must wait an entire day for an ordinary phone connection between Kyiv and Moscow, only to learn that the connection has broken down? At best case, he will have to put his throat at risk if he wants to be heard at the other end. There are countless numbers of examples of plane connections that exist only on paper, which an ordinary traveler has no way of getting. An example of such a connection was reported in the newspaper *Izvestiia* on April 5, 1936, in an article titled "Jokers." It is unclear whether a Soviet citizen's life is indeed better and merrier thanks to jokes like that.[30]

A month later, Karszo-Siedlewski wrote and sent (confidentially) another draft of an article (for the Polish press), titled "Life in Soviet Ukraine." He wrote it based on information gleaned from the Soviet press. The diplomat quoted Moscow's *Izvestiia* from May 10, 1936, which wrote about a man who was given a doctor's prescription and took it to pharmacy no. 48 in Stalino. He received the response "Please keep this prescription as a souvenir." He was informed that the stomach medicine he was requesting had not been seen in three months.

---

[30] CAW, Oddz. II SG, sygn. I.303.4.1867, k. 438–40.

The diplomat then quoted another *Izvestiia* article, from May 9, 1936, which was about the most luxurious hotel in Kharkiv, on Dzerzhinsky Square. The hotel boasted 500 furnished rooms with bathtubs, showers, and all kinds of amenities. "But it was enough to enter that hotel to learn that that these luxuries were no longer all present. It is unbelievable how quickly this hotel, opened a year ago, could become so thoroughly dilapidated. Without exception, all the showers have broken down. The showerheads have been removed by guests. Even the wardrobes did not escape demolition: there is not a single nail left in them, not a single hanger left upon which to hang one's clothes. Most of the night lamps are broken, their plugs torn off. The plaster is falling off the walls, [and] the broken locks make it impossible to secure the door."

Summing up these two stories, Karszo-Siedlewski wrote: "The two vignettes presented above accurately depict the condition of cultural life in Soviet Ukraine, about the residents of which Ukraine's dictator Postyshev recently said that they stood several cultural levels above a Westerner. The Soviet press tirelessly emphasizes how bad conditions are elsewhere, particularly in Poland, in comparison with the paradise on Earth named the Soviet Union. This paradise exists, of course, only on paper. It was meticulously fabricated by the anything-but-independent media, which dutifully report both to the authorities and to the people that the plan has been completely fulfilled. These kinds of lies are exposed occasionally, particularly when they are extreme. A lot of noise is made in response to cover them up, a frequent phenomenon in the Soviet press."[31]

6.3. The Constitution and Parliamentary Elections

In the second half of the 1930s, a few other propaganda campaigns were organized to demonstrate, for both domestic and (in particular) foreign audiences, that the USSR was "the most democratic country in the world." The most important moment in this respect was the introduction of the new constitution in 1936, followed by, on December 12, 1937, the organization of elections to the Supreme Soviet of the USSR, and then, in June 1938, to the Supreme Soviets of the individual republics (these took place on June 26, 1938 in Ukraine). The Stalin Constitution formally, for the first time, guaranteed equal rights to all citizens, e.g., universal, equal, secret, and direct voting rights and freedom of conscience, speech, publishing, and assembly. This was all fine, in theory.

---

[31] Ibid., sygn. I.303.4.1985, n.p., dok. 18 (1936).

The parliamentary elections, both on the union and republic levels, were a sham. Officially the attendance rate in the USSR election was 96.8 percent (91,113,153 persons voted out of the 94,138,159 who were eligible). In all the voting districts, the Communist Party and the non-aligned ("partyless") won. Only they could have won, since no other voting lists were available. The Communists and the non-aligned candidates received 89,844,271 votes in the entire USSR—98.6 percent. Of these, 636,808 votes were invalid. In Soviet Ukraine, candidates from the Communist and non-aligned list received 17,156,278 votes, or 97.8 percent.[32]

A similar trend held for the republican Supreme Soviet elections. Officially, the participation rate in Soviet Ukraine reached 99.62 percent, with 99.55 percent of the votes going to the Communist and non-aligned candidates.[33]

The members of the Polish diplomatic and consular corps who witnessed these elections had no doubt that it was all a giant caricature of democracy. Jan Karszo-Siedlewski had no illusions. In a report on June 25, 1936, even before the Stalin Constitution was adopted in 1936, he informed the *Dwójka* that what the Bolsheviks were interested in was the public-relations effect abroad.[34] The *Dwójka*'s main office shared his opinion. In a letter to him, they complained about the fact that even in Poland there was a great deal of misunderstanding about the real nature of the Stalin Constitution: "Our press is unfortunately so infinitely stupid that they completely misunderstand what it is all about, and they bother our citizens with very deep and philosophical [but purely speculative] reflections."[35]

In the MFA's informational bulletin *Polska i Zagranica*, the authors of a summary of the "Soviet democratic experiment" correctly pointed out that the passing of the new constitution did not lead to any changes to political, social, or economic life in the USSR. The only change was the introduction of elections that, according to the new rules, were supposed to be universal, equal, and secret. They took place in one-mandate electoral districts. "This promising experiment ended in the usual

---

[32] "Soobshchenie Tsentralnoi izbiratrelnoi komissii ob obshchikh itogakh vyborov v Verkhovnyi Sovet SSSR," *Pravda*, December 17, 1937.
[33] See *Pravda*, June 29, 1938.
[34] CAW, Oddz. II SG, sygn. I.303.4.1985, dok. 28.
[35] Ibid., dok. 29 (1936), n.p.

[undemocratic] way," they concluded. Apart from two exceptions (in the provinces), each district had only one candidate on the list.[36]

The vice-consul in Kyiv, Adam Koch, aptly characterized the electoral campaign in Kyiv. On October 30, 1937, in a report to Ambassador Grzybowski, he noted: "The real, genuine mood of the people of Ukraine is never revealed because they are silenced by the official voices fabricated on the occasion of the election. The pre-election propaganda intensity is extremely high. One has to admit that its quality is quite good. It highlights, very cleverly, all the real and fabricated achievements, particularly in the economic sphere, of the past two decades. The pressure for the elections to end with a desirable outcome is great. Any kind of shortcoming in the preparatory work is immediately condemned, which means that all the necessary business goes ahead as planned, i.e., most of the candidates have already been eliminated. Then the remaining candidates are elected "enthusiastically," [and] no opportunity is missed to glorify, in an Asiatic manner, Comrade Stalin, who is greeted at the meetings as the first candidate, 'the leader of nations, genius of mankind, father of our victories, friend and teacher, who has sacrificed his entire life, his entire wisdom, for the happiness of his people.'"[37]

Koch also emphasized that "the fact that the electoral campaign was managed by the current, virtually exclusive dictator of Ukraine, Leplevsky, guaranteed that the election would proceed 100 percent according to the plan of the Party and government."[38]

6.4. People's Opinions of the Propaganda Campaigns

The Polish reports also dealt with people's attitudes toward the various mass meetings that the Bolsheviks organized, for example, on revolutionary holidays. They tried to present the entire spectrum of opinions about propaganda as a whole. It should be emphasized that most ordinary citizens, regardless of what Soviet propaganda, Party functionaries, and state officials declared, always perceived the regime as alien and hostile to the people. Polish diplomats often stressed that most ordinary Soviet citizens always used the word "they" when referring to the Party and the government.

---

[36] AAN, MSZ, sygn. 119, k. 70.
[37] CAW, Oddz. II SG, sygn. I.303.4.1867, k. 678.
[38] Ibid., k. 679.

People learned quite quickly to filter the propagandistic pulp the Bolsheviks served them. They were not really interested in the struggle with the Trotskyites,[39] or in the reforms that were being introduced (e.g., the new constitution),[40] correctly assuming that these would not have any positive influence on their lives. In fact, they simply hoped that things would not get worse. Stanisław Suchecki reported on a few representative responses that emerged during the debate over the Stalin Constitution. In August 1936, he talked to a Polish citizen, Jan Laszczkowski, a coppersmith from a brick factory in Sloviansk and a former soldier in the Habsburg army. Laszczkowski said that the workers were not interested in the constitution project because they did not believe their conditions would improve. They did not believe it was possible for the NKVD to lose their unfettered power.[41]

After the Polish intelligence officer in the Kharkiv area had numerous other conversations, his opinions were confirmed. He again discovered that Soviet society was not generally interested in the constitution. The exception to this rule was the intelligentsia, who were naively hoping that the constitution would make life in the Soviet Union better. Overall, most people did not believe that their scope of liberty would be expanded. Their Polish interlocutor pointed out to the Soviet citizens that the new constitution gave them new rights of assembly, organization, and speech. What he heard in response was that he was not familiar with Soviet conditions, so he could not have known that there was never any liberty under Russia, and there never would be any—at least, not until some foreigners came and made it happen.[42]

The mass meetings that the Bolsheviks forced people to attend were met with indifference. They were seen as "their" events, which had to be attended. The largest assemblies were organized to commemorate the Bolshevik rise to power (November 7) and May Day. After the official segment, made up of parades and speeches, was over, there were festivities with live music and dancing.[43] But most people approached the forced entertainment part with resignation. They participated because

---

[39] See chapter 4, section 4.
[40] The sections that had to do with freedom of religion were the exception; see chapter 5, section 4.
[41] RGVA, f. 308 k, op. 19, d. 63, l. 149.
[42] Ibid., l. 188.
[43] See, e.g., "Narodnye gulania," *Pravda*, November 6, 1938.

they were afraid of the consequences of not doing so: one had to participate to stay out of trouble.

The acting head of the Kharkiv consulate, Tadeusz Błaszkiewicz, who observed the October Revolution anniversary in 1936 in Kharkiv, noticed no enthusiasm in the assembled crowd. It showed no reaction to the slogans uttered during the speeches, e.g., those associated with supporting the republican cause in Spain: "From among the dignitaries [in the parade stands], to the best of our knowledge, one heard critical comments about the meager attendance rate of officials and workers in the parade. One could see that, while the first rows included the eight persons who were supposed to be there according to plan, the rows farther back were manned by six persons. From one of the branches of the Hammer and Sickle factory, only eighteen people participated instead of the planned three hundred. Furthermore, the low level of enthusiasm of the crowd was also noticeable. In particular, its acclamatory response to a speaker praising the cause of Republican Spain was weak. It should be noted that on November 4 (perhaps plus or minus a few days), a Party council of directors and secretaries of local city committees was held, at which the participants were advised to influence the employees of the institutions and factories in their area to make sure the attendance was as close to 100 percent as possible. Despite this, the parade was smaller than the year before."[44]

Vice-Consul Adam Koch, who observed the October Revolution anniversary celebrations in Kyiv, wrote to the ambassador to inform him that on November 8, 1937 a scheduled big folk festival took place, accompanied by dancing in the streets: "It is hard to assess whether the people who participate in them have fun. Apart from the few young couples who danced for real, everyone else in the crowd wandered around aimlessly with sad expressions, which reflected the true attitude of the people."[45]

After the official observances were over, people took the opportunity to get drunk,[46] a phenomenon that, of course, never existed officially because it would throw negative light on the "new Soviet man." Stanisław

---

[44] AAN, SG, sygn. IV/8, dok. 50, n.p.

[45] CAW, Oddz. II SG, sygn. I.303.4.1867, k. 654.

[46] See K. Petrone, *Life Has Become More Joyous, Comrades: Celebrations in the Time of Stalin* (Bloomington: Indiana University Press, 2000); and D. Hoffmann, *Stalinist Values: The Cultural Norms of Soviet Modernity (1917–1941)* (Ithaca and London: Cornell University Press, 2003), 131.

Sośnicki witnessed those scenes. After the May Day parade in Kharkiv in 1936, people stayed in the streets until the wee hours, resulting in a high number of intoxicated people. A similar incident took place the next day. In connection with the May Day celebrations and the official joy about "better and happier life," fourteen or fifteen train cars at the Kharkiv railway station were filled with ragged homeless people every few days. They were sent off to the Far East or to Siberia. A large number of young boys and girls were among them. Railway workers were told, under threat of severe punishment, not to tell anyone about those transports of the homeless.[47]

Earlier, on August 20, 1935, Consul Sośnicki noted: "the slogans uttered in the press and at public gatherings had no affect on most people. The worker laughed when he was told that he worked for himself; he said that the "spa hotel was for the leadership" and the house of rest for him, the worker, but there was nothing to eat there. Exploitation by the current state was worse than by the tsarist one, because one did not starve, the way one does currently, while earning the money he received at the factory owned by a capitalist."[48]

Most adults were immune to this kind of propaganda, but children usually were not. They had no experience of any other reality, and the one they knew was supposedly ideal. A refugee from the USSR, a peasant from Volhynia who reached Poland in the spring of 1934, reported on the indoctrination of children in Soviet schools and the reaction of their parents. In all school books, children read that "in olden days there were lords and slaves, but there are no lords and slaves anymore." Children were told something else at home. "His mother tries to correct what he learned in school, teaching him to say that, back in the day, everyone ate well, [but] today there is nothing to eat. The child does not say it, because he is afraid, but he thinks and considers. The Komsomol activists and Pioneers usually hang up portraits of [Taras] Shevchenko, [while] older people tear them to pieces and throw them away."[49]

The permanent indoctrination, especially among children, who knew no other reality, did have some results. Jan Łagoda, who visited the Donbas in November 1935, was able to talk a bit to the children he met there. The children did not suspect that they were speaking with a foreigner. An eleven-year-old in the third grade of a primary school told

---

[47] CAW, Oddz. II SG, sygn. I.303.4.1867, k. 203.
[48] RGVA, f. 308 k, op. 6, d. 21, l. 289.
[49] Ibid., op. 19, d. 58, l. 123.

him that he knew Lenin and Stalin, his acolyte, well. He was taught what one had to do to make the life of workers better and how to self-organize, and after one was organized one could go "and beat the bourgeoisie around the world [*poidem bit' burzhuev na tselom mire*]. Another student, in a similar tone, declared that he knew all about Japan, Germany, and Poland. The USSR did not like these countries because Japan wanted to annex Siberia, and Germany wanted Ukraine. Poland conspired with Germany to invade the USSR. Another boy, a ten-year-old wondered out loud in a store, at the high prices for candy, 35 rubles per kilogram. Łagoda reminded him that some items were meant to be purchased by the wealthy, who have a lot of money. The boy replied: "They have been annihilated—they are no more."

Conclusion

Poland's foreign service and military intelligence had, in general, a fairly accurate picture of the developments taking place in the USSR and in Soviet Ukraine in the 1930s. Officials who worked at the Polish consulates in Kyiv and Kharkiv not only produced descriptions of events that they witnessed, but also tried to generate deeper analyses of the processes unfolding both in Soviet Ukraine and in the entire USSR. The conditions in which they had to work were very difficult, often prison-like. In the second half of the 1930s, the USSR resembled one giant concentration camp. All the residents of the "Soviet paradise," even the most devoted functionaries, were constantly under threat of suddenly finding themselves in a Gulag camp and labeled "an enemy of the people." The permanent terror, spy hysteria, surveillance, and denunciations— including by one's closest family members—were accompanied by material deprivation. This combination was the basis for Stalin's power and its maintenance.

In contrast to some fellow Western consular officials or foreign guests (journalists), Polish observers were never duped by the show tours of collective farms, dining halls, health-care facilities, and factories that the Bolsheviks organized, which were supposed to be proof of the enormous, constant progress in the "country of workers and peasants."

Polish diplomats and consular officials not only described and analyzed events, but they also tried to assist persecuted individuals. Their actions were meant to help not only Polish citizens (current and former) who found themselves in the USSR, but also ethnic Poles who were Soviet citizens. Head of the consulate general in Kyiv Jan Karszo-Siedlewski often intervened with the Soviet Ukrainian authorities on behalf of the persecuted, deported, and missing Poles. He was able to meet with the head of the Soviet Ukrainian NKVD, Vsevolod Balytsky. A meeting with a top official from within the terror apparat was a rare feat for a member of a foreign diplomatic corps. Karszo-Siedlewski often brought the persecuted Polish community in Soviet Ukraine to the attention of the Polish ambassadors in Moscow—Juliusz Łukasiewicz and then Wacław Grzybowski—and urged them to intercede. His efforts were doomed to failure. Even if the ambassadors had intervened (they did not), they would not have been of much help to the Poles who lived in the USSR. What was needed was for the Polish state to take systematic and determined measures. But such measures did not take place. Warsaw stuck firmly to the principle of equilibrium between Germany and the Soviet Union and tried to avoid anything that might irritate the latter. The only exception occurred in mid-July 1938, when the impossible conditions Polish diplomatic and consular officials had to endure in the USSR led Warsaw to initiate a retaliatory campaign against the corresponding Soviet posts in Poland. The campaign lasted for a month and led to negotiations and then an agreement with the Soviet side. The working conditions for the Polish diplomats in the USSR, including surveillance, improved somewhat for a time, but eventually they returned to the old norm.

Examination of the records of the Polish MFA and the *Dwójka* allows for the conclusion that, beyond any doubt, the most knowledgeable person in the field of Soviet affairs was the counselor to the embassy and the head of the consulate general in Kharkiv and later in Kyiv—Jan Karszo-Siedlewski. He had no illusions about the repressive campaigns initiated against the peasantry, national minorities, or other mythical enemies of the Soviet state. Let me quote, again, his words from March 1935 that he uttered to the ambassador in Moscow: "What we are dealing with in [Soviet] Ukraine is an enemy who still wears a mask, but who [we should harbor no doubts] really hates us and tries, wherever he can, to destroy the remnants of Polishness on his territory—[we are dealing with] an uncouth brute who recognizes only sheer force [as a factor in politics]." For the Polish dimplomat, the only correct policy was to apply countermeasures similar to those the Bolsheviks applied, because "the only language they understood was brute force."

Two years before the Second World War, Karszo-Siedlewski predicted that the Soviet system—after having invaded all spheres of social life, after having formed the new Soviet man, and after having mastered the mass application of terror—would become a great threat to Western civilization, but especially for its direct neighbors, Poland in particular. As early as during the Holodomor, the diplomat asked the MFA to inform Polish communities, at least those living in the eastern part of Poland, of the threat that was looming in the east. Ultimately the threat became visible in its full manifestation on September 17, 1939, and after. The MFA did not respond to Karszo-Siedlewski's appeals. Ambassador Grzybowski did not share his evaluation. He wrote to Warsaw in November 1937 that a "serious military conflict was probably beyond Russia's [the USSR's] present capabilities."

Furthermore, the counselor sent excerpts from the Soviet press to the Polish press. He even drafted some articles himself. Those drafts were based on official Soviet data. The Bolshevik press, despite its enormous bias, still produced much useful information, for example, on material living conditions, the condition of the highways, shortages, problems meeting coal output quotas in the Donbas, and so on.

Of course, the Polish observers could not be correct in all of their analyses. They did not know what exactly had happened to persons arrested during the years of the Great Terror. Difficult to understand were the causes of the Great Terror. Some aspects were diagnosed correctly — such as the internal Party struggle and economic problems (blaming "the enemies of the people" — the Trotskyites most of all — for the constant problems with shortages of the most basic goods). What the Polish observers (apart from Jan Karszo-Siedlewski) did not see was that the Soviet Union would become a very serious threat in the near future. They did not realize that by eliminating those whom Stalin viewed as "the fifth column" (all the "uncertain" people, such as national minorities, immigrants, and former opposition members), he was readying the country for war. Poland was the first target. The persecution of national minorities in the USSR, including their deportation and execution, was a peculiar kind of training ground for similar operations that unfolded after the September 1939 invasion of Poland. The main difference was that the 1934–38 persecutions were directed mostly at ordinary people, whereas after September 17, 1939, they were directed first against the elite of Polish society and then against anyone who did not agree with the new order established in Moscow.

Bibliography

Archival sources

Archiwum Akt Nowych w Warszawie (AAN)
- Ambasada RP w Moskwie
- Ministerstwo Spraw Zagranicznych
- Sztab Główny

Archiwum Instytutu Pamięci Narodowej w Warszawie
- Ministerstwo Bezpieczeństwa Publicznego w Warszawie

Archiwum Straży Granicznej w Szczecinie
- Dowództwo Korpusu Ochrony Pogranicza, 1924–1939

Arkhiv upravlinnia Sluzhby bezpeky Ukrainy v Mykolaïvs'kii oblasti
- fond 26

Centralne Archiwum Wojskowe w Warszawie (CAW)
- Akta personalne oficerów
- Grupa zespołów akt Samodzielnych Referatów Informacyjnych DOK oraz Samodzielnego Referatu Informacyjnego Dowództwa Floty z lat 1919–1939. Samodzielny Referat Informacyjny DOK nr IX Brześć nad Bugiem
- Kolekcja Akt Rosyjskich
- Oddział II Sztabu Głównego (Generalnego) Wojska Polskiego z lat 1921–1939

Gosudarstvennyi arkhiv Rossiiskoi Federatsii v Moskve
- fond R–9479 s: 4–i Spetsotdel MVD SSSR, 1930–1958

Haluzevyi derzhavnyi arkhiv Sluzhby bezpeky Ukraïny u Kyievi
- fond 42 – Operatyvno-statystychna zvitnist'

Józef Piłsudski Institute of America in New York (JPIA)
- Archiwum Ryszarda Wragi (Antoniego Jerzego Niezbrzyckiego)

Narodowe Archiwum Cyfrowe w Warszawie (NAC)
- Koncern Ilustrowany Kurier Codzienny – Archiwum Ilustracji

Rossiiskii gosudarstvennyi arkhiv noveishei istorii v Moskve
- fond 89: Kollektsiia kopii dokumentov, rassekrechenykh pri vypolnenii tematicheskikh zaprosov v protsesse nauchno-isledovatel'skoi raboty

Rossiiskii gosudarstvennyi arkhiv sotsialno-politicheskoi istorii v Moskve
- fond 81: Kaganovich, Lazar Moiseevich (1893–1991)
- fond 558: Stalin, Iosif Vissarionovich (1878–1953)
- fond 671: Yezhov, Nikolai Nikolaevich (1895–1940)

Rossiiskii gosudarstvennyi voennyi arkhiv v Moskve (RGVA)
- fond 308k: Vtoroi otdel General'nogo shtaba Pol'shi, g. Varshava
- fond 453k: Dokumentalnye materialy o deiatel'nosti razvedki burzhuaznoi Pol'shi protiv SSSR (kollektsiia)
- fond 462k: Ekspozitura nomer 5 otdela General'nogo shtaba, g. Lvov
- fond 464k: Biuro inspektsii pri General'nom inspektore Vooruzhennykh sil Pol'shi, g. Varshava

Tsentralnyi derzhvanyi arkhiv hromads'kyh obiednan' Ukraïny u Kyievi
- fond 1: Tsentralnyi komitet Kompartiï Ukraïny, 1917–1991
- fond 39: Instytut istoriï partiï pry TsK Kompartiï Ukraïny

Library sources
Biblioteka Narodowa w Warszawie
Rosja Sowiecka: Wykład wygłoszony w dn. 3 marca 1936 r. na Kursie Naukowym dla urzędników służby zagranicznej przez p. Stanisława Zabiełłę, kierownika referatu w MSZ. N.p., n.d.

Author's personal sources
- Correspondence with Larysa Krushel'nyts'ka, 2012.

Published sources
Basiński, E., T. Cieślak, and W. Gostyńska et al., eds. Dokumenty i materiały do historii stosunków polsko-radzieckich. Vol. 6. 1933–1938. Warsaw: Książka i Wiedza, 1967.
Bednarek, J., P. Kułakowski, S. Kokin et al., eds. Polska i Ukraina w latach trzydziestych-czterdziestych XX wieku: Nieznane dokumenty z archiwów służb specjalnych. Vol. 8. Wielki Terror: Operacja polska, 1937–1938. Parts 1 and 2. Warsaw and Kyiv: Instytut Pamięci Narodowej, 2010.
Bondarenko, A., et al., eds. God krizisa, 1938–1939: Dokumenty i materialy. Vol. 1. 29 sentiabria 1938 g.–31 maia 1939 g. Moscow: Politizdat, 1990.
Bruski, J. J., ed. Hołodomor 1932–1933: Wielki Głód na Ukrainie w dokumentacji polskiej dyplomacji i wywiadu. Warsaw: PISM, 2008.
Danilov, V., R. Manning, and L. Viola et al., eds. Tragediia sovetskoi derevni: Kollektivizatsiia i raskulachivanie. Dokumenty i materialy v 5 tomakh, 1927–1939. Vol. 4. 1934–1936. Moscow: ROSPEN, 2002.

Danilov, V., and R. Manning, eds. *Tragediia sovetskoi derevni: Kollektivizatsiia i raskulachivanie. Dokumenty i materialy v 5 tomakh, 1927–1939*. Vol. 5. *1937–1939*. Book 1 (1937). Moscow: ROSSPEN, 2004.

———. *Tragediia sovetskoi derevni: Kollektivizatsiia i raskulachivanie. Dokumenty i materialy v 5 tomakh, 1927–1939*. Vol. 5. *1937–1939*. Book 2 (1938–1939). ROSSPEN, Moscow: 2006.

Grzywacz, A., ed. "Oddział II Sztabu Głównego: Raport ppłk. Józefa Englichta." *Arcana*, 1999, no. 2.

Holodomor: The Great Famine in Ukraine, 1932–1933. Warsaw and Kyiv: Institute of National Remembrance, 2009.

Iakovlev, A., ed. *Deti GULAGa, 1918–1956*. Moscow: Mezhdunarodnyi fond "Demokratiia," 2002.

———, et al., eds. *Lubianka: Stalin i Glavnoe upravlenie gosbezopasnosti NKVD, 1937–1938*. Moscow: Materik, 2004.

Iakovleva, L., B. Chyrko, and S. Pyshko, eds. *Nimtsi v Ukraïni, 20–30-ti rr. XX st.: Zbirnyk dokumentiv z derzhavnykh arkhiviv Ukraïny*. Kyiv: Instytut istorii Ukrainy, 1994.

Kokin, S. A., and M. Junge, eds. *Velykyi teror w Ukraïni: "Kurkul's'ka operatsiia" 1937–1938 rr.* 2 vols. Kyiv: Vydavnychyi dim "Kyievo-Mohylians'ka akademiia," 2010.

Kornat, M., ed. *Polskie Dokumenty Dyplomatyczne: 1938*. Warsaw: PISM, 2007.

Kostiushko, I., ed. *Materialy "Osoboi papki" Politbiuro TsK RKP(b)-VKP(b) po voprosu sovetsko-pol'skikh otnoshenii 1923–1944 gg.: Sbornik dokumentov*. Moscow: Institut slavianovedeniia i balkanistiki RAN, 1997.

Kuśnierz R., "Głód na Ukrainie w latach 1932–1933 w świetle zbiorów Archiwum Akt Nowych oraz Centralnego Archiwum Wojskowego w Warszawie." *Dzieje Najnowsze*, 2007, no. 2.

———, ed. *Pomór w "raju bolszewickim": Głód na Ukrainie w latach 1932–1933 w świetle polskich dokumentów dyplomatycznych i dokumentów wywiadu*. Toruń: Wydawnictwo Adam Marszałek, 2008.

Kwiecień, M., and G. Mazur. "Wykłady pułkownika Stefana Mayera o wywiadzie polskim w okresie II RP." *Zeszyty Historyczne* 142 (2002).

Official Documents Concerning Polish-German and Polish-Soviet Relations, 1933–1939. London and Melbourne: Ministerstwo Spraw Zagranicznych, 1940.

Patek S., *Raporty i korespondencja z Moskwy (1927–1932)*. Edited by M. Gmurczyk-Wrońska. Warsaw: Neriton and Instytut Historii PAN, 2010.

Polish–Soviet Relations, 1918–1943: Documents. New York: Polish Government Information Center, 1943.

Stępień, S., ed. *Polacy na Ukrainie: Zbiór dokumentów*. Part 1, *1917–1939*. Vol. 1. Przemyśl: Południowo-Wschodni Instytut Naukowy, 1998.

———. *Polacy na Ukrainie: Zbiór dokumentów*. Part 1, *1917–1939*. Vol. 2. Przemyśl: Instytut Południowo-Wschodni, 1999.

— — —. *Polacy na Ukrainie: Zbiór dokumentów*. Part 1, *1917–1939*. Vol. 3. Przemyśl: Instytut Południowo-Wschodni, 2001.

— — —, and O. Rubl'ov, eds. *Polacy na Ukrainie: Zbiór dokumentów*. Part 1, *1917– 1939*. Vol. 5. Przemyśl: Instytut Południowo-Wschodni, 2005.

"Represovana UAPTs: Politychni represiï proty sviashchennykiv Ukraïns'koï Avtokefal'noï Pravoslavnoï Tserkvy (1919–1938); Za dokumentamy Haluzevoho derzhavnoho arkhivu Sluzhby bezpeky Ukraïny." *Z arkhiviv VUChK-GPU-NKVD-KGB*, 2005, no. 1/2 (24/25); 2006, no. 1/2 (26/27).

Rubl'ov, O., and N. Rubl'ova, eds. *Ukraïna-Pol'shcha 1920–1939 rr.: Z istoriï dyplomatychnykh vidnosyn USSR z Druhoiu Richchiu Pospolytoiu. Dokumenty i materialy.* Kyiv: Dukh i litera, 2012.

Sommer, T., ed. *Rozstrzelać Polaków: Ludobójstwo Polaków w Związku Sowieckim w latach 1937–1938. Dokumenty z centrali.* Warsaw: Biblioteka Wolności, 2010.

"Sviashchennyky Ukraïns'koi Avtokefal'noï Pravoslavnoï Tserkvy pid represyvnym tyskom totalitarnoho rezhymu." *Z arkhiviv VUChK-GPU-NKVD-KGB*, 2007, no. 1 (28).

United States Department of State. *Foreign Relations of the United States: Diplomatic Papers. The Soviet Union, 1933–1939.* Edited by E. R. Perkins. Washington, DC: Government Printing Office, 1952.

"Vlada i kostel v Radians'kii Ukraïni, 1919–1937 rr.: Rymo-katolyts'ka Tserkva pid represyvnym tyskom totalitaryzmu." *Z arkhiviv VUChK-GPU-NKVD-KGB*, 2003, no 2 (21).

Memoirs

Biesiedowskij, G. Z. *Pamiętniki dyplomaty sowieckiego.* Katowice: Polski Instytut Wydawniczy, 1985.

Drymmer, W. T. "Wspomnienia." *Zeszyty Historyczne* 127–31 (1974).

— — —. *W służbie Polsce.* Warsaw: Warszawska Oficyna Wydawnicza "Gryf," 1998.

Dzwonkowski, R., SAC, ed. *Głód i represje wobec ludności polskiej na Ukrainie, 1932– 1947. Relacje.* Lublin: Towarzystwo Naukowe KUL, 2005.

Herwarth, H. Von. *Między Hitlerem a Stalinem: Wspomnienia dyplomaty i oficera niemieckiego, 1931–1945.* Warsaw: Bellona, 1992.

Krushel'nyts'ka, L. *Rubaly lis—Spohady hahychanky.* Lviv and New York: Vydavnytstvo M. P. Kots', 2001.

Łoziński, M. *Operacja polska: Stalinowska zbrodnia na Polakach w latach 1937–1938.* Kłodawa: Drukarnia Braci Wielińskich, 2008.

"Memuary Nikity Sergeievicha Khrushcheva." *Voprosy istorii*, 1990, nos. 4–6.

Michniewicz, W. *Wielki bluff sowiecki.* Chicago: Publishing Wici, 1991.

Skalski, T. *Terror i cierpienie: Kościół katolicki na Ukrainie, 1900–1932. Wspomnienia.* Lublin, Rome, and Lviv: Norbertinum, 1995.

Słowikowski, M. *W tajnej służbie: Jak polski wywiad dał aliantom zwycięstwo w Afryce Północnej.* Poznań: Dom Wydawniczy REBIS, 2011.

Stpiczyński, A. *Wbrew wyrokowi losu.* Warsaw: Pax, 1981.

Szembek, J.. *Diariusz i teki Jana Szembeka (1935–1945)*. Vol. 3 (1937). Edited by T. Komarnicki. London: Polish Research Center, 1969.

———. *Diariusz i teki Jana Szembeka (1935–1945)*. Vol. 4 (1938–1939). Edited by J. Zarański. London: Polish Research Center, 1972.

Trocki [Trotsky], L. *Zbrodnie Stalina*. Warsaw: Biblioteka Polska, 1937.

———. *Zdradzona rewolucja: Czym jest ZSRR i dokąd zmierza?* Wrocław: ZW ZSMP, 1988; Warsaw: Oficyna WIBET, 1991.

Scholarly publications

Bazhan, O. "Represiï sered dukhovenstva ta viruiuchykh v URSR v chasy 'velykoho teroru'. Statystychnyi aspekt." *Z arkhiviv VUChK-GPU-NKVD-KGB*, 2007, no. 2 (29).

Belkovets, L. *"Bolshoi terror" i sud'by nemetskoi derevni v Sibiri (konets 1920-kh–1930-e gody)*. Moscow: IVKD, 1995.

———, and S. Belkovets. "Konsulskie otnosheniia Germanii i Sibiri w 1920–1930-e g." In V. Molodin, N. Pokrovskii, E. Romodanowskaia et al., *Nemetskii etnos w Sibiri*. Novosibirsk: Izdatelstvo Novosibirskogo universiteta, 1999.

Bolabolchenko, A. *SVU: Sud nad perekonanniamy*. Kyiv: Kobza, 1994.

Bruski, J. J. "Bolshoi golod na Ukraine v svete dokumentov polskoi diplomatii i razvedki." *Evropa*, 2006, no. 6.

———. *Między prometeizmem a Realpolitik: II Rzeczpospolita wobec Ukrainy Sowieckiej, 1921–1926*. Kraków: Historia Iagiellonica, 2010.

———. "Między ukrainizacją a rusyfikacją: Sowiecka polityka narodowościowa na Ukrainie w ocenach dyplomacji i wywiadu II RP." *Prace Komisji Środkowoeuropejskiej PAU* 17 (2009).

———. "Nieznane polskie dokumenty na temat Hołodomoru: Efekty rekonesansu archiwalnego w Moskwie." *Nowa Ukraina*, 2008, no. 1–2.

———. "Polska wobec Wielkiego Głodu n Ukrainie, 1932–1933." In *Polska–Ukraina-Osadczuk: Księga jubileuszowa ofiarowana Profesorowi Bohdanowi Osadczukowi w 85. rocznicę urodzin*. Lublin: Wydawnictwo UMCS, 2007.

———. "Sowieckie przygotowania wojenne w 1930 r. w ocenie attaché wojskowego RP w Moskwie." *Arcana*, 2006, no. 2 (68).

Bugai, N. *Narody Ukrainy w "Osoboi papke Stalina."* Moscow: Nauka, 2006.

Chojnowski, A. *Ukraina*. Warsaw: Trio, 1997.

Conquest, R. *The Great Terror: A Reassessment*. Oxford: Oxford University Press, 2008.

———. *Stalin and the Kirov Murder*. Oxford: Oxford University Press, 1989.

———. *Zhnyva skorbot: Radians'ka kolektyvizatsiia i holodomor*. Kyiv: Lybid', 1993. Trans. of *The Harvest of Sorrow: Soviet Collectivization and the Terror-Famine*. New York: Oxford University Press, 1986.

Daniel, A., L. Ieromina, E. Zhemkowa et al., eds. *Repressii protiv rossiiskikh nemtsev. Nakazannyi narod: Po materialam konferentsii "Repressii protiv rossiiskikh nemtsev v Sovetskom Soiuze v kontekste sovetskoi natsionalnoi politiki," provedennoi Nemetskim kul'turnym tsentrom im. Gete v Moskve sovmestno s Obshchestvom "Memorial", 18–20 noiabria 1998 goda*. Moscow: Zvenia, 1999.

Debicki, R. *Foreign Policy of Poland, 1919–39: From the Rebirth of the Polish Republic to World War II*. New York: Praeger, 1962.

Dullin, S. *Stalin i ego diplomaty: Sovetskii Soiuz i Evropa, 1930–1939 gg*. Moscow: ROSSPEN, 2009.

Dzwonkowski, R., SAC. *Kościół katolicki w ZSSR, 1917–1939: Zarys historii*. Lublin: TN KUL, 1997.

— — —. *Losy duchowieństwa katolickiego w ZSSR, 1917–1939: Martyrologium*. Lublin: TN KUL, 1998.

— — —. "Represje wobec duchowieństwa katolickiego w ZSRR, 1918–1939." In *Skazani jako "szpiedzy Watykanu": Z historii Kościoła katolickiego w ZSRR, 1918–1956*. Edited by R. Dzwonkowski, SAC. Ząbki: Apostolicum, 1998.

— — —. "Sowieckie państwo wyznaniowe." *Roczniki Nauk Społecznych* 25, no. 1 (1997).

— — —. "Stan badań nad historią Kościoła i życiem religijnym katolików obrządku łacińskiego w ZSRR (1917–1990)." In *Mniejszości polskie i polonia w ZSRR*. Edited by H. Kubiak et al. Wrocław, Warsaw, and Kraków: Zakład Narodowy im. Ossolińskich, 1992.

— — —. "Władze II RP a Kościół katolicki w ZSRR." *Więź*, 1996, no. 5.

Eberhardt, P. "Klęski głodu na Ukrainie w pierwszej połowie XX wieku na podstawie literatury ukraińskiej." *Studia z Dziejów Rosji i Europy Środkowo-Wschodniej* 40 (2005).

Figes, O. *Szepty: Życie w stalinowskiej Rosji*. Warsaw: Magnum, 2008.

Gajownik, T. "Pierwsze lata kariery Stefana Antoniego Mayera jako oficera polskiego wywiadu: Przyczynek do biografii." *Echa Przeszłości*, 2009, no. 10.

Geller M., *Maszyna i śrubki: Jak hartował się człowiek sowiecki*. Paris: Instytut Literacki, 1988.

Genis, V. "Grigorii Zinovevich Besedovskii." *Voprosy istorii*, 2006, no. 7.

Gershberg, S. R. *Stakhanov i stakhanovtsy*. Moscow: Izdatelstvo politliteratury, 1981.

Getty, J. A., and O. Naumov. *The Road to Terror: Stalin and the Self-Destruction of the Bolsheviks, 1932–1939*. New Haven: Yale University Press, 1999.

Głuszek, Z. *Polscy Olimpijczycy, 1924–1984*. Warsaw: Sport i Turystyka, 1988.

Gmurczyk-Wrońska, M. "Negocjacje polsko-sowieckie o pakt o nieagresji w roku 1927 i w latach 1931–1932." *Dzieje Najnowsze*, 2012, no. 3.

Goldman, W. Z. *Terror and Democracy in the Age of Stalin: The Social Dynamics of Repression*. Cambridge and New York: Cambridge University Press, 2007.

Grajżul, T. "Poselstwo i Konsulat Rzeczypospolitej Polskiej w Charkowie w latach 1921–1937." In *Polska dyplomacja na Wschodzie w XX–początkach XXI wieku*, edited by H. Stroński and G. Seroczyński. Olsztyn and Kharkiv: LITTERA, 2010.

Gregorowicz, S. "Koncepcja paktu wschodniego na tle stosunków polsko-sowieckich." In *Międzymorze: Polska i kraje Europy Środkowo-Wschodniej, XIX–*

XX wiek. Studia ofiarowane Piotrowi Łossowskiemu w siedemdziesiątą rocznicę urodzin. Edited by A. Ajnenkiel, W. Balcerak, H. Bułhak, et al. Warsaw: Instytut Historii PAN, 1995.

Gregorowicz, S., and M. J. Zacharias. *Polska-Związek Sowiecki: Stosunki polityczne, 1925–1939.* Warsaw: Instytut Historii PAN, 1995.

Hoffmann, D. *Stalinist Values: The Cultural Norms of Soviet Modernity (1917–1941).* Ithaca and London: Cornell University Press, 2003.

Ieremenko, T. *Pols'ka natsionalna menshyna v Ukraïni v 20-30-ti roky XX stolittia.* Kyiv: Instytut istoriï Ukraïny NAN Ukraïny, 1994.

Iwanow, M. "Kościół katolicki w ZSRR wobec radzieckiej polityki wyznaniowej, 1921–1938." In *Chrześcijaństwo w ZSRR w dobie pierestrojki i głasnosti: Materiały z sesji Eklezjologiczno-Mitologicznej, Pieniężno 28–30 IX 1989*, edited by W. Grzeszczak, SVD, and E. Śliwka, SVD. Warsaw and Pieniężno: Verbinum, 1992.

— — —. "Kościół najbardziej prześladowany." *Więź*, 1990, no. 2–3.

— — —. *Pierwszy naród ukarany: Stalinizm wobec polskiej ludności kresowej (1921–1938.* Warsaw: PWN, 1991.

— — —. *Polacy w Związku Radzieckim w latach 1921–1939.* Wrocław: Wydawnictwo Uniwersytetu Wrocławskiego, 1990.

Jabłonowski, M., and J. Prochwicz. *Wywiad Korpusu Ochrony Pogranicza, 1924–1939.* Warsaw: Aspra-Jr, 2004.

Jankowski, T. *Studium ZSRR: Dzieje wewnętrzne. Ustrój. Polityka zagraniczna.* London: Szkoła Nauk Politycznych Społecznych, 1953.

Junge, M., G. Bordiugov, and R. Binner. *Vertikal' Bolshogo terrora: Istoriia operatsii po prikazu NKVD no 00447.* Moscow: Novyi khronograf, 2008.

Khlevniuk, O. *1937-i: Stalin, NKVD i sovetskoe obshchestvo.* Moscow: Respublika, 1992.

— — —. *Udarniki pervoi piatiletki.* Moscow: Znanie, 1989.

Kmiecik, T. *Sztab Generalny (Główny) Wojska Polskiego w latach 1918–1939.* Słupsk: Wydawnictwo Pomorskiej Akademii Pedagogicznej, 2005.

Kołakowski, P. *Czas próby: Polski wywiad wojskowy wobec groźby wybuchu wojny w 1939 r.* Warsaw: Demart, 2012.

— — —. *Między Warszawą a Pragą: Polsko-czechosłowackie stosunki wojskowo-polityczne, 1918–1939.* Warsaw: Bellona, 2009.

— — —. *Pretorianie Stalina: Sowieckie służby bezpieczeństwa i wywiadu na ziemiach polskich, 1939–1945.* Warsaw: Bellona, 2010.

Kornat, M. "Ambasador Wacław Grzybowski i jego misja w Związku Sowieckim (1936–1939)." *Zeszyty Historyczne* 142 (2002).

— — —. *Polska 1939 roku wobec paktu Ribbentrop-Mołotow: Problem zbliżenia niemiecko-sowieckiego w polityce zagranicznej II Rzeczypospolitej.* Warsaw: PISM, 2002.

— — —. "Posłowie i ambasadorzy Polscy w Związku Sowieckim (1921–1939 i 1941–1943)." *Polski Przegląd Dyplomatyczny*, 2004, no. 5.

Kruszyński, M. *Ambasada RP w Moskwie, 1921–1939.* Warsaw: Instytut Pamięci Narodowej, 2010.

———. "Inwigilacja polskich placówek dyplomatycznych w ZSRR w okresie międzywojennym." In *Między I a IV Rzeczpospolitą: Z dziejów lustracji na ziemiach polskich w XIX i XX wieku*, edited by M. Korybut–Marciniak and P. Majer. Olsztyn: WUWM, 2009.

———. "O współpracy konsula Jana Karszo-Siedlewskiego z Oddziałem II w latach 1932–1936: Przyczynek do badań nad powiązaniami wywiadu ze służbą dyplomatyczną," *Przegląd Historyczno-Wojskowy*, 2009, no. 4.

———. "Z działalności konsulatu polskiego w Charkowie do początku lat 30. XX wieku." In *Stosunki polsko-ukraińskie: Historia i pamięć*, edited by J. Marszałek-Kawa and Z. Karpus. Toruń: Wydawnictwo Adam Marszałek, 2008.

Krzak, A. *Czerwoni Azefowie: Afera "MOCR-TRUST," 1922–1927*. Warsaw: WCEO, 2010.

———. "Kapitan Jerzy Antoni Niezbrzycki." *Rocznik Archiwalno-Historyczny Centralnego Archiwum Wojskowego*, 2009, no. 2/31.

———. *Kontrwywiad wojskowy II Rzeczypospolitej przeciwko radzieckim służbom specjalnym, 1921–1939*. Toruń: Wydawnictwo Adam Marszałek, 2007.

Książek, J. "Historia Konsulatu Generalnego RP w Charkowie: Fakty, refleksje, skojarzenia." In *Polska dyplomacja na Wschodzie w XX–początkach XXI wieku*, edited by H. Stroński and G. Seroczyński. Olsztyn and Kharkiv: LITTERA, 2010.

———. "Powstanie i działalność Poselstwa i Konsulatu Generalnego RP w Charkowie w okresie międzywojennym." *Polski Przegląd Dyplomatyczny*, 2006, no. 2 (30).

Kul'chyts'kyi, S. "Ukrains'ke selo pisla Holodomoru." *Problemy istoriï Ukraïny: Fakty, sudzhennia, poshuky* 19, no. 2 (2010).

Kulczycki, S. *Hołodomor: Wielki Głód na Ukrainie w latach 1932–1933 jako ludobójstwo. Problem świadomości*. Wrocław: Kolegium Europy Wschodniej im. Jana Nowaka-Jeziorańskiego, 2008.

Kupczak, J. *Polacy na Ukrainie w latach 1921–1939*. Wrocław: Wydawnictwo Uniwersytetu Wrocławskiego, 1994.

Kuromiya, H. *Głosy straconych*. Warsaw: Amber, 2008.

———. "Stalin's Great Terror and International Espionage." *The Journal of Slavic Military Studies* 24, no. 2 (2011).

———. "Stalin, Poles, and Ukrainians." In *Ofiary imperium: Imperia jako ofiary. 44 spojrzenia / Imperial Victims: Empires as Victims. 44 Views*, edited by A. Nowak. Warsaw: IPN–KŚZpNP and Instytut Historii PAN, 2010.

——— and A. Pepłoński. *Między Warszawą a Tokio: Polsko-japońska współpraca wywiadowcza, 1904–1944*. Toruń: Wydawnictwo Adam Marszałek, 2009.

Kuśnierz, R. "Afera Rana: Wpadka polskiego wywiadu w ZSRS w 1936 r." *Studia z Dziejów Rosji i Europy Środkowo-Wschodniej* 46 (2011).

———. "Bolszewicki 'spektakl' w Charkowie, czyli proces Związku Wyzwolenia Ukrainy." *Wrocławskie Studia Wschodnie* 10 (2006).

———. "Dokumenty pol's'koï dyplomatiï pro holodomor." *Ukraïns'kyi istorychnyi zhurnal*, 2008, no. 6.

———. "Dokumenty pol's'koi dypłomatiï ta rozvidky pro holodomor." In *Holod 1932–1933 rokiv v Ukraïni: Prychyny, demohrafichni naslidky, pravova otsinka. Materialy naukovoi konferentsiï, Kyïv 25–26 veresnia 2008 roku*, edited by I. Iukhnovs'kyi. Kyiv: Vydavnychyi dim "Kyievo–Mohylians'ka akademiia," 2009.

———. "Funkcjonowanie polskich placówek dyplomatycznych w ZSRS w warunkach Wielkiego Terroru (1937–1938)." In *Polska dyplomacja na Wschodzie w XX–początkach XXI wieku*, edited by H. Stroński and G. Seroczyński. Olsztyn and Kharkiv: LITTERA, 2010.

———. "Głód na Ukrainie w roku 1933 na łamach prasy." *Res Historica* 21 (2005).

———. "Holod v Ukraïni 1932–1933 rr. (za dokumentamy pol's'kykh dyplomativ)." *Arkhivy Ukraïny*, 2008, nos. 3–4.

———. " 'Kolektywna konsumpcja' w okresie pierwszej radzieckiej pięciolatki: Propaganda a rzeczywistość (Mało znany absurd bolszewicki)." *Dzieje Najnowsze*, 2008, no. 2.

———. "Komunistyczna zbrodnia Wielkiego Głodu w życiu społeczno-politycznym Ukrainy." In *Dziedzictwo komunizmu w Europie Środkowo-Wschodniej*, edited by J. Sadowska. Białystok: Wydawnictwo Uniwersytetu w Białymstoku, 2008.

———. "Kwestia Wielkiego Głodu w prezydenturze Wiktora Juszczenki." *Rocznik Instytutu Europy Środkowo-Wschodniej* 5 (2007).

———. "Obchody rocznic Wielkiego Głodu w niepodległej Ukrainie." In *Historia, mentalność, tożsamość: Miejsce i rola historii oraz historyków w życiu narodu polskiego i ukraińskiego w XIX i XX wieku*, edited by J. Pisulińska, P. Sierżęga, and L. Zaszkilniak. Rzeszów: Wydawnictwo Uniwersytetu Rzeszowskiego, 2008.

———. "Obraz głodującej wsi ukraińskiej w latach trzydziestych XX w. w dokumentach polskich przedstawicielstw dyplomatycznych w ZSRR i polskiego wywiadu." *Polska i Jej Wschodni Sąsiedzi*, 2009.

———. "Pogłodowa wieś ukraińska w polskich raportach wywiadowczych i konsularnych (1934–1937)." In *Studia nad wywiadem i kontrwywiadem Polski w XX wieku*, vol. 1, edited by W. Skóra and P. Skubisz. Szczecin: Wydawnictwo IPN, 2012.

———. "Próba kościelnej niezależności: Ukraińska Autokefaliczna Cerkiew Prawosławna (1919–1936)." *Więź*, 2006, no. 6.

———. "Problematyka głodu w 'raju bolszewickim' na łamach lwowskiego 'Diła.'" In *Ukraińcy w najnowszych dziejach Polski 1918–1989*, vol. 3, edited by R. Drozd. Słupsk: Wydawnictwo Akademii Pomorskiej, 2007.

———. "Próby interwencji dyplomacji polskiej w obronie prześladowanej Polonii na Ukrainie Sowieckiej w latach trzydziestych XX wieku." *Studia Polonijne* 32 (2011).

———. "Próby skompromitowania oraz werbunku przez sowieckie służby specjalne pracowników polskich placówek dyplomatycznych w ZSRS w latach 30. XX w." In *Służby specjalne w systemie bezpieczeństwa państwa: Przeszłość –*

Teraźniejszość – Przyszłość. Materiały i Studia, vol. 1, edited by A. Krzak and D. Gibas-Krzak. Szczecin and Warsaw: Wojskowe Centrum Edukacji Obywatelskiej, 2012.

———. "Propaganda radziecka w okresie Wielkiego Głodu na Ukrainie (1932–1933)." *Dzieje Najnowsze*, 2004, no. 4.

———. "Przemoc systemu komunistycznego wobec chłopów w latach 1929–1939 (na przykładzie Sowieckiej Ukrainy)." In *Ofiary imperium: Imperia jako ofiary. 44 spojrzenia / Imperial Victims: Empires as Victims. 44 Views*, edited by A. Nowak. Warsaw: IPN-KŚZpNP and Instytut Historii PAN, 2010.

———. "The Question of the Holodomor in Ukraine of 1932–1933 in the Polish Diplomatic and Intelligence Reports." *Holodomor Studies* 1, no. 1 (Winter-Spring 2009).

———. "Represje wobec Polaków na Ukrainie podczas Wielkiej Czystki: Wiedza i reakcja polskiej dyplomacji." In *Polska–Ukraina: Dziedzictwo i współczesność*, edited by R. Drozd and T. Sucharski. Słupsk: Wydawnictwo Akademii Pomorskiej, 2012.

———. "Sowieckie ustawodawstwo wobec kułaków." In *Społeczeństwo a władza: Ustrój, prawo, idee*, edited by J. Przygodzki and M. J. Ptak. Wrocław: Kolonia Limited, 2010.

———. "Unknown Polish Photographs of the Holodomor." *Holodomor Studies*, no. 2 (Summer–Autumn 2010).

———. *Ukraina w latach kolektywizacji i Wielkiego Głodu (1929–1933)*. Toruń: Wydawnictwo Adam Marszałek, 2005.

———. "Walka z religią na Ukrainie w latach trzydziestych." *Więź*, 2004, no. 6.

Ławrynowicz, M. "Jerzy Antoni Niezbrzycki (1901–1968): Przyczynek do działalności dyplomatycznej, wywiadowczej i publicystycznej." In *Polska dyplomacja na Wschodzie w XX–początkach XXI wieku*, edited by H. Stroński and G. Seroczyński. Olsztyn and Kharkiv: LITTERA, 2010.

Leinwand, A. *Sztuka w służbie utopii: O funkcjach politycznych i propagandowych sztuk plastycznych w Rosji Radzieckiej lat 1917–1922*. Warsaw: Instytut Historii PAN and Mazowiecka Wyższa Szkoła Humanistyczno-Pedagogiczna, 1998.

Libanova, E. "Otsinka demohrafichnykh vtrat Ukraïny vnaslidok holodomoru 1932–1933 rokiv." In *Holod 1932–1933 rokiv v Ukraïni: Prychyny, demohrafichni naslidky, pravova otsinka. Materialy naukovoï konferentsiï, Kyïv 25–25 veresnia 2008 roku*, edited by I. Iukhnovs'kyi. Kyiv: Vydavnychyi dim "Kyievo–Mohylians'ka akademiia," 2009.

Litzenberger, O. *Evangelichesko-liuteranskaia tserkov' i sovetskoe gosudarstvo (1917–1938)*. Moscow: Gotika, 1999.

Lizak, W. *Rozstrzelana Polonia: Polacy w ZSRR, 1917–1939*. Szczecin: Prywatny Instytut Analiz Społecznych, 1990.

Majzner R., *Attachaty wojskowe Drugiej Rzeczypospolitej, 1919–1945: Strukturalno-organizacyjne aspekty funkcjonowania*. Częstochowa: Wydawnictwo Akademii im. Jana Długosza, 2011.

— — —. "Wpływ stosunków polsko-radzieckich na organizacje i funkcjonowanie Attachatu Wojskowego przy Poselstwie/Ambasadzie RP w Moskwie (1921– 1939): Zarys problematyki." In *Stosunki polityczne, wojskowe i gospodarcze Rzeczypospolitej Polskiej i Związku Radzieckiego w okresie międzywojennym*, edited by J. Gmitruk and W. Włodarkiewicz. Warsaw: Muzeum Historii Polskiego Ruchu Ludowego and Siedlce: Uniwersytet Przyrodniczo-Humanistyczny, 2012.

Martin, T. "The Origins of Soviet Ethnic Cleansing." *The Journal of Modern History* 70, no. 4 (1998).

Materski, W. "Polska i ZSRR na przełomie lat dwudziestych i trzydziestych XX wieku." In *Białe plamy — czarne plamy: Spawy trudne w polsko-rosyjskich stosunkach 1918–2008*, edited by A. D. Rotfeld and A. Torkunow. Warsaw: PISM, 2010.

— — —. "Polsko-radziecka konwencja konsularna z 18 lipca 1924 roku." *Dzieje Najnowsze*, 1973, no. 4.

— — —. *Tarcza Europy: Stosunki polsko-sowieckie, 1918–1939*. Warsaw: Książka i Wiedza, 1994.

Matthews, M. *Privilege in the Soviet Union: A Study of Elite Life-Styles under Communism*. London and Boston: George Allen & Unwin, 1978.

Michalski, A. "Z działalności wywiadowczej konsulatu RP w Charkowie w latach dwudziestych i trzydziestych XX w. In *Polska dyplomacja na Wschodzie w XX– początkach XXI wieku*, edited by H. Stroński and G. Seroczyński. Olsztyn and Kharkiv: LITTERA, 2010.

Miedwiediew, R. *Pod osąd historii. Geneza i następstwa stalinizmu*. Vol. 1. Warsaw: Bellona, 1990.

Meierovich, M., E. Konysheva, and D. Khmelnitskii. *Kladbishche sotsgorodov: Gradostroitelnaia politika v SSSR, 1928–1932 gg*. Moscow: ROSSPEN, 2011.

Miłoszewski, Z. *Kolektywizacji wsi sowieckiej*. Printed by author. Jerusalem, 1947.

Misiuk, A. *Służby specjalne II Rzeczypospolitej*. Warsaw: Bellona, 1998.

Movchan, O. "Hromads'ke kharchuvannia robitnykiv URSR u 1930-ti roky." *Problemy istorii̇ Ukraïny: Fakty, sudzhennia, poshuky* 20 (2011).

Musiał, B. "Geneza paktu Hitler Stalin." In *Geneza paktu Hitler-Stalin: Fakty i propaganda*, edited by B. Musiał and J. Szumski. Warsaw: Instytut Pamięci Narodowej, 2011.

— — —. *Na Zachód po trupie Polski*. Warsaw: Prószyński i S-ka, 2009.

Nikol's'kyi, V. "Represiï za 'limitami' (1937–1938 rr.)." *Ukraïns'kyi istorychnyi zhurnal*, 2006, no. 3.

Nowinowski, S. M. "Specyfika funkcjonowania polskich placówek dyplomatycznych i konsularnych w Związku Sowieckim (1936–1939)." In *Z dziejów polskiej służby dyplomatycznej i konsularnej: Książka upamiętniająca życie i dzieło Jana Nowaka– Jeziorańskiego (1914–2005)*, edited by J. Faryś and M. Szczerbiński. Gorzów Wielkopolski: Sonar, 2005.

— — —. "Zakończenie działalności ambasady i konsulatów RP w Związku Sowieckim jesienią 1939 r." *Zeszyty Historyczne* 164 (2008).

Osokina, E "Sovetskaia zhizn': Obidennost' ispytaniia (po primere istorii Torgsina i OGPU)." *Otechestvennaia istoriia*, 2004, no. 2.

— — —. *Za fasadom "stalinskogo izobiliia": Raspredilenie i rynok v snabzhenii naseleniia v gody industrializatsii, 1927–1941.* Moscow: ROSSPEN, 2008.

— — —. "Za zerkal'noi dveriu torgsina." *Otechestvennaia istoriia*, 1995, no. 2.

— — —. *Zoloto dla industrializatsii: Torgsin.* Moscow: ROSSPEN, 2009.

Paduszek, K. "Meandry kariery Wiktora Tomira Drymmera w wywiadzie II Rzeczypospolitej." *Przegląd Historyczno-Wojskowy*, 2008, no. 4.

Pepłoński, A. *Organizacja i działalność Referatu "Wschód" Oddziału II Sztabu Głównego WP.* Warsaw: Urząd Ochrony Państwa, 1994.

— — —. *Wywiad a dyplomacja II Rzeczypospolitej.* Toruń: Wydawnictwo Adam Marszałek, 2005.

— — —. *Wywiad polski na ZSRR: 1921–1939.* Warsaw: Bellona, 1996.

Petrone, K. *Life Has Become More Joyous, Comrades: Celebrations in the Time of Stalin.* Bloomington: Indiana University Press, 2000.

Petrov, N., and M. Jansen. *"Stalinskii pitomets" — Nikolai Ezhov.* Moscow: ROSSPEN, 2008.

— — — and A. Roginskii. "The 'Polish Operation' of the NKVD, 1937–38. In *Stalin's Terror: High Politics and Mass Repression in the Soviet Union*, edited by B. McLoughlin and K. McDermott. Houndmills and New York: Palgrave Macmillan, 2003.

Pietrow, N. "Polska operacja NKWD." *Karta*, 1993, no. 11.

— — —. *Psy Stalina.* Warsaw: Demart, 2012.

Pirog, R. "Kak pogib predsedatel' Sovnarkoma Ukrainskoi SSR P. P. Liubchenko." *Izvestiia TsK KPSS*, 1990, no. 10.

Prelovs'ka, I. "Peresliduvannia ta likvidatsiia UAPTs (UPTs) (1921–1938 rr.): Ohliad arkhivno-kriminal'nykh sprav HDA SB Ukraïny ta TsDAHO Ukraïny." *Z arkhiviv VUChK-GPU-NKVD-KGB*, 2009, no. 1 (32).

Prystaiko, V., and Iu. Shapoval. *Mykhailo Hrushevs'kyi i HPU-NKVD: Trahichne desiatylittia: 1924–1934.* Kyiv: Ukraïna, 1996.

— — —. *Sprava Spilky vyzvolennia Ukraïny.* Kyiv: INTEL, 1995.

Rajca, C. *Głód na Ukrainie.* Lublin: Werset and Toronto: Polski Fundusz Wydawniczy w Kanadzie, 2005.

Rezmer, W. "Polsko-radziecki pakt o nieagresji z 1932 roku: Aspekty polityczne i militarne." In *Stosunki polityczne, wojskowe i gospodarcze Rzeczypospolitej Polskiej i Związku Radzieckiego w okresie międzywojennym*, edited by J. Gmitruk and W. Włodarkiewicz. Warsaw: Muzeum Historii Polskiego Ruchu Ludowego and Siedlce: Uniwersitet Przyrodniczo-Humanistyczny, 2012.

Romanek, J. *Totalitaryzm sowiecki w ocenie polskiej prasy wojskowej lat 1921–1939.* Toruń: Wydawnictwo Adam Marszałek, 2009.

Rosowski, W. "Polska dyplomacja w obronie Kościoła rzymskokatolickiego na Ukrainie Radzieckiej w latach 1921–1939." In *Polska dyplomacja na Wschodzie w*

XX–początkach XXI wieku, edited by H. Stroński and G. Seroczyński. Olsztyn and Kharkiv: LITTERA, 2010.

Rubl'ov, O. *Zakhidnoukraïns'ka intelihentsiia u zahal'nopolitychnykh ta kul'turnykh protsesakh (1914–1939)*. Kyiv: Instytut istoriï Ukraïny NAN Ukraïny, 2004.

———, and I. Cherchenko. *Stalinshchyna i dolia zakhidnoukraïns'koï intelihentsiï, 20–50-ti roky XX st.* Kyiv: Naukova dumka, 1994.

———, and V. Repryntsev. "Represiï proty poliakiv v Ukraïni u 1930-ti roky." *Z arkhiviv VUChK-GPU-NKVD-KGB*, 1995, no. 1–2.

Rybliuk, O. "Demokratyzatsia suspil'noho zhyttia iak faktor natsional'no-relihiinoho vidrodzhennia." In *Istoriia relihiï v Ukraïni: Tezy povidomlen' Mizhnarodnoho kruhloho stolu (L'viv, 3-5 travnia 1995)*, edited by V. Haiuk et al. Part 4. Kyiv and Lviv: [s.n.], 1995.

Rzemieniuk, F. "Obraz diecezji kamienieckiej w latach 1918–1939." *Przegląd Wschodni*, 2002, vol. 29.

Schlegel', K. *Terror i mechta: Moskva 1937*. Moscow: ROSSPEN, 2011.

Serczyk, W. A. *Historia Ukrainy*. Wrocław: Zakład Narodowy im. Ossolińskich, 2009.

Shapoval, Iu. "Peredden' i apohei Velykoho teroru." In V. Lytvyn and V. A. Smolii, *Politychnyi teror i teroryzm v Ukraïni XIX–XX st.: Istorychni narysy*. Kyiv: Naukova dumka, 2002.

———. *Ukraïna 20–50-kh rokiv: Storinky nenapysanoï istoriï*. Kyiv: Naukova dumka, 1993.

——— and V. Zolotariov. *Vsevolod Balyts'kyi: Osoba, chas, otochenia*. Kyiv: Stylos, 2002.

Shemshushenko, I., ed. *Zhertvy repressii*. Kyiv: IUrinform, 1993.

Siegelbaum, L. H. *Stakhanovism and the Politics of Productivity in the USSR, 1935–1941*. Cambridge: Cambridge University Press, 1988.

Skóra, W. "Organizacja i działalność służby konsularnej II Rzeczypospolitej na terenach Rosji, Ukrainy i ZSRR w dwudziestoleciu międzywojennym (1918–1939)." In *Stosunki polityczne, wojskowe i gospodarcze Rzeczypospolitej Polskiej i Związku Radzieckiego w okresie międzywojennym*, edited by J. Gmitruk and W. Włodarkiewicz. Warsaw: Muzeum Historii Polskiego Ruchu Ludowego and Siedlce: Uniwersytet Przyrodniczo-Humanistyczny, 2012.

———. "Porwanie kierownika polskiej placówki konsularnej w Kijowie Jerzego Matusińskiego przez władze radzieckie w 1939 r." In *Polska dyplomacja na Wschodzie w XX–początkach XXI wieku*, edited by H. Stroński and G. Seroczyński. Olsztyn and Kharkiv: LITTERA, 2010.

———. *Służba konsularna II Rzeczypospolitej: Organizacja, kadry i działalność*. Toruń: Wydawnictwo Adam Marszałek, 2006.

Smoliński, A. "Oddział II Sztabu Głównego Naczelnego Dowództwa Wojska Polskiego." *Wschodni Rocznik Humanistyczny* 3 (2006).

———. "Robotniczo-Chłopska Armia Czerwona jako obiekt rozpoznania polskiego wywiadu wojskowego: Próba oceny efektywności." In *Stosunki polityczne, wojskowe i gospodarcze Rzeczypospolitej Polskiej i Związku Radzieckiego w okresie międzywojennym*, edited by J. Gmitruk and W. Włodarkiewicz. Warsaw:

Muzeum Historii Polskiego Ruchu Ludowego and Siedlce: Uniwersytet Przyrodniczo-Humanistyczny, 2012.

— — —. "Sytuacja wojskowa, ekonomiczna i społeczna na Sowieckiej Ukrainie w latach 1921–1939 w ocenach Oddziału II polskiego Sztabu Głównego." *Pivdennyi arkhiv: Istorychni nauky*, 2004, no. 16.

Snyder, T. *Skrwawione ziemie: Europa pomiędzy Hitlerem a Stalinem*. Warsaw: Świat Książki, 2011.

Stroński, H. "Losy ludności polskiej na Ukrainie Sowieckiej a dyplomacja II RP w latach 1921–1939." In *Polska dyplomacja na Wschodzie w XX–początkach XXI wieku*, edited by H. Stroński and G. Seroczyński. Olsztyn and Kharkiv: LITTERA, 2010.

— — —. *Represje stalinizmu wobec ludności polskiej na Ukrainie w latach 1929–1939*. Warsaw: Stowarzyszenie Wspólnota Polska, 1998.

— — —. "Skazany na milczenie. Kościół rzymsko-katolicki na Ukrainie Radzieckiej w latach 1920–1930." *Więź*, 1996, no. 10.

Suvenirov, O. *Tragediia RKKA, 1937–1938*. Moscow: Terra, 1998.

Thurston, R. "The Stakhanovite Movement: Background to the Great Terror in the Factories, 1935–1938." In *Stalinist Terror: New Perspectives*, edited by J. A. Getty and R. T. Manning. Cambridge: Cambridge University Press, 1993.

Tokarz, T. "Architekt terroru: Józef Stalin w oczach prasy polskiej w okresie Wielkiej Czystki (1936–1939)." *Glaukopis*, 2007, no. 7-8.

— — —. "Interpretacje genezy 'Wielkiej Czystki' w ZSRR w prasie polskiej (1936–1938)." *Dzieje Najnowsze*, 2004, no. 4.

Tryhub, O. "Rozkol iak forma borot'by DPU USRR iz pravoslavnoiu tserkvoiu v Ukraïni (1922–1927 rr.)." *Z arkhiviv VUChK-GPU-NKVD-KGB*, 2009, no. 1 (32).

Urbańska, I. "Ambasada Rzeczypospolitej Polskiej w Moskwie w latach 1936–1939: Warunki pracy w rzeczywistości stalinowskiej." *Dzieje Najnowsze*, 2006, no. 4.

Vaughan, P. *Zbigniew Brzeziński*. Warsaw: Świat Książki, 2010.

Vasyliev, V. "Vplyv 'velykoho teroru' 1937–1938 rr. na ekonomichni protsesy v URSR." *Z arkhiviv VUChK-GPU-NKVD-KGB*, 2004, no. 1/2 (22/23).

Vlasovs'kyi, I. *Narys istoriï Ukraïns'koi Pravoslavnoï Tserkvy*. Vol. 4, part 1, *Ukraïns'ka pravoslavna tserkva Kyïvs'koho Patriiarkhatu*. Kyiv: Lybid', 1998.

Vrons'ka, T. "Stalins'ka henderna polityka u dobu 'Velykoho teroru' (1937–1938 rr.)." *Z Arkhiviv VUChK-GPU-NKVD-KGB*, 2009, no. 1 (32).

— — —. *Zaruchnyky totalitarnoho rezhymu: Represiï proty rodyn "vorohiv narodu" v Ukraïni (1917–1953 rr.)*. Kyiv: Instytut istoriï Ukraïny NAN Ukraïny, 2009.

Vynnychenko, I. *Ukraïna 1920–1980-kh: Deportatsiï, zaslannia, vyslannia*. Kyiv: Rada, 1994.

Wasilewski, A. "Gry dyplomatyczne." *Nowa Europa Wschodnia*, 2009, no. 5.

— — —. *Polskie Konsulaty na Wschodzie, 1918–1939*. Warsaw: MSZ, 2010.

Wieczorkiewicz, P. P. *Łańcuch śmierci: Czystka w Armii Czerwonej, 1937–1939*. Warsaw: Rytm, 2001.

— — —. *Sprawa Tuchaczewskiego*. Warsaw: Gryf, 1994.

Wilk, H. *Kto wyrąbie więcej ode mnie? Współzawodnictwo pracy robotników w Polsce w latach 1947–1955.* Warsaw: Trio, 2011.

Włodarkiewicz, W. *Przed 17 września 1939 roku: Radzieckie zagrożenie Rzeczypospolitej w ocenach polskich naczelnych władz wojskowych, 1921–1939.* Warsaw: Neriton, 2002.

Wolsza, T. *Za żelazną kurtyną: Europa Środkowo-Wschodnia, Związek Sowiecki i Józef Stalin w opiniach polskiej emigracji politycznej w Wielkiej Brytanii, 1944/1945–1953.* Warsaw: Instytut Historii PAN, 2005.

Wraga, R. " 'Trust.' " *Kultura,* 1949, no 4/21–5/22.

Wróbel, J. "Likwidacja: Polityka ZSRR wobec kościołów i religii w latach dwudziestych." *Przegląd Powszechny,* 1990, no. 3.

— — —. "Polityka ZSRR wobec kościoła katolickiego w latach 1917–1939." In *Polacy w kościele katolickim w ZSRR,* edited by E. Walewander. Lublin: Wydawnictwo KUL, 1989.

Wysocki, R. "Postawa społeczności ukraińskiej w Drugiej Rzeczypospolitej wobec 'wielkiego głodu' na Ukrainie w latach 1932–1933." *Annales Universitas Mariae Curie-Skłodowska,* Sectio F, 60 (2005).

Zacharias, M. J. *Polska wobec zmian w układzie sił politycznych w Europie w latach 1932–1936.* Wrocław: Zakład Narodowy im. Ossolińskich, 1981.

Zelenin, I. " 'Zakon o piati koloskakh': Razrabotka i osushchestvlenie." *Voprosy istorii,* 1998, no. 1.

Ziółkowska, A. *Kanada, Kanada . . .* Warsaw: Wydawnictwo Polonia, 1986.

Zolotar'ov, V. *Oleksandr Uspens'kyi: Osoba, chas, otochennia.* Kharkiv: Folio, 2004.

Zhukov, I. "Sledstvie i sudebnye protsesy po delu ob ubiistve Kirova." *Voprosy istorii,* 2000, no. 2.

Periodicals

Gazeta Polska (Warsaw), 1935

Ilustrowany Kuryer Codzienny (Kraków), 1935

Izvestiia (Moscow), 1935

L'vivs'ka hazeta, 2006

Pravda (Moscow), 1929, 1932, 1934–38

Visti (Kyiv), 1936

Wprost (Warsaw), 2007

Bibliographic publications

Burian, L., and I. Rykun, eds. *Holodomor v Ukraïni 1932–1933 rokiv: Bibliohrafichnyi pokazhchyk.* Odesa and Lviv: Vydavnytstvo M. P. Kots', 2001.

Historical questionnaire

"Pamięć wielkiej zbrodni: 75 rocznica 'operacji polskiej' NKWD. Ankieta historyczna (Nikita Pietrow, Hiroaki Kuromiya, Krzysztof Jasiewicz, Marek Jan

Chodkiewicz, Bogdan Musiał, Tomasz Sommer, Jerzy Bednarek, Jan Jacek Bruski, Marek Kornat, Henryk Głębocki)." *Arcana*, 2012, no. 4–5.

Prose

Shmerling, V. *Mariia Demchenko*. Moscow: Molodaia gvardiia, 1936.

Online sources

Amons, A. "Represovani heneral'ni prokurory URSR." Ukrains'ka asotsiatsiia prokuroriv. http://www.uap.org.ua/ua/journal/1_8.html?_m=publications&_t=rec&id=15343.

Belkovets, L., "Iz istorii konsul'skogo prava: Likvidatsiia inostrannykh konsul'skikh predstavitelstv v SSSR w kontse 1930-kh godov." http://justicemaker.ru/viewarticle.php?id=11&art=680.

Bilokin', S. "Holod (urywok iz statti)." http://zdibrova.narod.ru/base/annousements/bkgpdf.pdf .

"The German Ambassador in the Soviet Union (Schulenburg) to the German Foreign Ministry": 'Subject: The closing of Foreign Consulates in the Soviet Union and the Abolition of Soviet Consulates'." http://avalon.law.yale.edu/20th_century/nsa615.asp.

Hai-Nyzhnyk, Pavlo. http://hai-nyzhnyk.in.ua/doc2/1937%2802-06%29.spysok_pidsudnyh.php.

"Kerivnyky uriadiv Ukraïns'koi Radians'koï Sotsialistychnoï Respubliky, Bondarenko Mykhailo Illich." www.kmu.gov.ua/control/uk/publish/article?art_id=1261349&cat_id=66125.

"Kerivnyky uriadiv Ukraïns'koi Radians'koï Sotsialistychnoï Respubliky, Liubchenko Panas Petrovych." http://www.kmu.gov.ua/control/uk/publish/article?art_id=1261316.

Muzei Kirova. *Gibel Kirova: Fakty i versii*. kirovmuseum.ru/node/17.

Petrov, N., and K. Skorkin. *Kto rukovodil NKVD, 1934–1941: Spravochnik*. Moscow: Zvenia, 1999. Quoted from www.memo.ru/history /NKVD/kto/index.htm.

Shelekhes, Il'ia Savel'evych. http://www.mke.su/doc/ShELEKhES%20IS.html. http://www.turkey.mid.ru/20-30gg.html.

Vasyliev, V. "Kudriavtsev Serhii Oleksandrovych." Instytut istoriï Ukraïny Natsionalnoï akademiï nauk Ukraïny. www.history.org.ua/index.php?encyclop&termin=Kudryavtsev_S.

http://www.centrasia.ru/person2.php?&st=1255467340.

http://www.centrasia.ru/person2.php?&st=1173735940.

http://www.kmu.gov.ua/control/uk/publish/article?art_id=1261349&cat_id=66125.

http://www.turkey.mid.ru/20-30gg.html.

Appendix

The Polish-Soviet border crossing at Stoŭptsy (Polish:Stołpce)-Nieharelaie. The photograph was taken during the last exchange of prisoners between Poland and the USSR, which took place on September 15, 1932. *Photo:* NAC.

The Polish consulate in Kyiv, 1926. *Photo:* NAC.

Stanisław Zabiełło (left) and Captain Władysław Harland (right) during their journey in Soviet Ukraine in August 1933. *Photo:* CAW.

Captain Władysław Harland (left) and Stanisław Zabiełło (right) during their trip in Soviet Ukraine in August 1933. *Photo:* CAW.

Passengers on a ship sailing from Dnipropetrovsk to Zaporizhia during Stanisław Zabiełło and Captain Władysław Harland's journey to southern Ukraine in August 1933. *Photo:* CAW.

Photo of a grain depot on the banks of the Dnipro River, taken on the trip that Stanisław Zabiełło, Władysław Harland, and Zdzisław Miłoszewski made to southern Ukraine in August 1933. This picture demonstrates that the famine that ravaged Soviet Ukraine in 1933 was artificially caused. Grain lay in depots while the inhabitants were starving. On the reverse of the photograph Miłoszewski wrote: "One of the grain depots by the Dnipro River next to a port for vessels. It should be said that all depots (off-loading spots) looked the same. I took a picture of one of them as an example." *Photo:* CAW.

Jan Karszo-Siedlewski (left), counselor to the embassy in Moscow and head of the Polish consulate in Kharkiv and, later, in Kyiv. June 15, 1935. *Photo:* NAC.

Konsulat Rz. P.
w Kijowie

11/2/34
odpływu z U.S.R.R.
białoruskich emigrantów.

//sierpnia   4

20

ROZDZIELNIK:

Pan Ambasador R.P. w Moskwie.
M.S.Z. Pan Naczelnik Wydziału P.III.
M.S.Z. Wydział Prasowy.
Sztab Główny Oddział II.
Konsulat R.P. w Charkowie.

W okresie, poprzedzającym rozpoczęcie żniw, Konsulat
otrzymał szereg wiadomości o masowym odpływie z Ukrainy sowieckiej ludności, która w roku ubiegłym przybyła na tutejszy
teren z Białorusi oraz Rosji. Jak to urząd tutejszy w swoim
czasie komunikował, "przesiedleńcy" korzystali na Ukrainie
sowieckiej z dość znacznych ulg, otrzymywali ponadto niez-
będny inwentarz i byli osadzani w rejonach, jakie najbardziej
wyludniły się podczas głodu w r. 1933. Ludność miejscowa na-
ogół odniosła się do przybyszów bardzo niechętnie, starając
się wszelkiemi sposobami utrudnić im egzystencję. Przybyli
przydzielani byli do najsłabszych liczebnie kołchozów, korzystali z domów pozostałych po zmarłych lub "rozkułaczonych"
miejscowych gospodarzach i wobec perspektywy wysokich urodza-
jów, a co zatem idzie - również wysokich wypłat za "trudodnie",
cierpliwie znosili czynione wstręty. W r.b., gdy perspektywy
"wzbogacenia się" okazały się bardzo wątpliwemi, rozpoczęła
się masowa wędrówka powrotna.

Powyższe wiadomości potwierdza zamieszczona w moskiewskiej
"Prawdzie" /6.VIII.r.b./ korespondencja z obwodu Odeskiego,
w której masowy wyjazd białorusinów tłomaczy się jako jeden
z przejawów wypaczenia polityki narodowościowej oraz jako
dowód szkodliwej działalności miejscowych ukraińskich nacjona-
listów. Korespondencja podaje, iż z szeregu rejonów obwodu
Odeskiego wyjechało już ponad 25% "przesiedleńców". Ciekawem

- 2 -   KI

jest również tłumaczenie się oficjalnych władz miejscowych,
które, broniąc niejako miejscową ludność usiłują całą od-
powiedzialność złożyć na karb złego doboru ludzi przez od-
nośną organizację białoruską.

/Ref. P. Kurnicki/.

Kierownik Konsulatu Generalnego

Jan-Karszo-Siedlewski
Radca Ambasady.

Jan Karszo-Siedlewski's report about Belarusian settlers leaving Soviet Ukraine. *Source:* AAN.

3310/33/N.   Dnia 10.czerwca 1933 r.

Po dokładnem zaznajomieniu się
z treścią - bezwzględnie spalić!

Ogólna instrukcja organizacyjna.

I. Z dniem otrzymania niniejszego obejmuje Pan Kierow-
nictwo nad ośrodkami "N" i "O" w składzie następującym:
a/. Ośrodek "N"
    1/ Placówka "Ku" - p.P.K./pseudonim Napoleon NNalewajko/
    2/   "   "L.11"- p.L.G./pseudonim Norbert Neuman/
    3/   "   "Z.14"- p.M.P./pseudonim Nina Nowicka/
W ośrodku "N" jaknajściślejszą współpracę przyobiecał
również kierownik urzędu p.Sosn. /pseudonim Norman Nagel/
z którym ustawi Pan sobie kontakt służbowy w/g uznania.
b/. Ośrodek "O"
    1/ placówka "M.13" - p.Z.M./pseudonim Oleg Ostrowski/
        Placówka ta posiada w osobie żony Z.M.placówkę pomoc-
        niczą "H.23" /pseudonim Olga Oberman/.
    2/ placówka "X.22" - p.J.P./pseudonim Ola Osmólska/
Zarówno kierownika urzędu "O", jak też i jego dotychczasowe-
go zastępcę proszę do swojej roboty nie wciągać: Łączność
organizacyjną z ośrodkiem "O" proszę nawiązać osobiście do-
ręczając zainteresowanym osobom załączone koperty i jedno-
cześnie omówić jaknajszczegółowiej zakres zainteresowań

                                                            ./.

- 2 -

Pana i wykorzystanie poszczególnych osób.

II. Zadania informacyjne na oba ośrodki otrzymuje wyłącznie Pan; rozdziela je Pan w/g uznania. Ze swej strony zastrzegam sobie prawo korespondowania z poszczególnemi osobami w sprawach osobistych, a z ośrodkiem "O" w sprawie lliteratury i pism, które też będą stamtąd nadsyłane wprost do Centrali.

III. Budżety poszczególnych placówek przedstawiają się następująco:

"B.18"	100 dol.à 8.90	–	890 zł.	
"Ku "	30 " à 8.90	–	267 "	
"L.11"	25 " à 8.90	–	222.50 "	
"Z.14"	15 " à 8.90	9	133.50 "	
"M.13" i "H.23"	35.dol. oraz złotych.450	à 8.90–	311.50 "	

               które są przekazywane na miejscu, w/g
               życzenia zainteresowanych.

"X.22"	10 dol.à 8.90	–	89 zł.	

Budżety dla placówek z ośrodka "N" będą kierowane przez Pana. Pan otrzymywać będzie również i wysyłać do nas koperty zwrotne.

Budżet dla placówek z ośrodka "O" kierujemy bezpośrednio.

IV. W wypadku Pańskiej dłuższej nieobecności w m.p.Pana zastępcą dla spraw bieżących jest "ku" – Nalewajko, któremu Pan przekazuje tylko te sprawy, które uważa Pan za stosowne.

Organizational instructions for intelligence post B.18. *Source:* CAW.

B.18   W-80/1-28

3314/33/N.   Dnia 10.czerwca 1933 r.

Instrukcja łączności.
----

obowiązuje z dniem otrzymania.

1/. Korespondencja Centrali z Panem, jako kierownikiem ośrodka "N" i "O" oraz placówką "B.18" prowadzona jest stale przez jedną osobę, występującą w imieniu całej firmy i załatwiającej absolutnie wszystkie sprawy służbowe Pana i pańskich organów pomocniczych. Osoba ta bez względu na jej tożsamość podpisuje korespondencję, jako " Nel Niemirowicz". W korespondencji bezpośredniej do placówek Panu podległych taż sama osoba występuje jako "Nora Nikiels".

2/. Pana korespondencja winna być zawsze podpisywana pseudonimem "Nazar Niewiernyj". W stosunku do podległych sobie placówek występuje Pan, jako "Nepomucyn Niewiarowski".

3/. Przesyła Pan do nas całą pocztę wspólnie w jednym pokiecie, bez względu na to, czy są to materjały Pana, czy też podległych Panu placówek.

Forma Pana zapisek, notatek, meldunków, opracowań jest najzupełniej obojętna, byle były czytelne. Korespondencję ogólną i organizacyjną proszę pisać na specjalnie załączonych blokach.

4/. Poniżej podaję kryptonimy do zastosowania na przyszłość w korespondencji z nami:

Konsul Sons.   - Dante wzgl.pseudonim służbowy,
Vicekons.Kurnicki   - Piotrkowski, wzgl. jak pseudonim,
Giżycki   - Dowgal, wzgl.jak pseudonim,
Połońska   - Serafinowicz, wzgl.jak pseudonim,
Karszo-Siedlewski   - Przeszczepiński,
Miłoszewski   - Witoldowski,
Weze   - Mitrofan,
Konsul niem.w Kijowie   - Raube,
Baum   - Wincenty,
Konsulat R.P.w Kijowie-   Szkatułka,
     "   "   w Charkowie   - skarbiec,
     "   "   w Mińsku   - sekretera,
     "   "   w Tyflisie   - szafa,
     "   "   w Leningrodzie-skarbonka,
     "   "   w Moskwie   - sejf,
Ekspozytura nasza we Lwowie - składnica. ./.

Poselstwo R.P. w Moskwie   - uroczysko,
Poseł Łukasiewicz   - emir,
Attache wojskowy w Moskwie   - sułtan,
M.SZ.Centrala   - łaźnia,
Drymmer   - Wernyhora,
Nacz.Wydz.Osob.M.S.Zagr.   - Siemiątkowski,
Schätzel   - bonza,
Furgalski   - mag
Mayer   - derwisz,
Ciastoń   - Pluszkin,
Gen.Insp.Sił Zbr.   - Olimp,
Oddz.II.Szt.Gł.   - Parnas,
Sztab Główny   - Cyrk.

5/. Poczta służbowa do nas winna być opieczętowana
w jednym pakiecie specjalną pieczątką i lakiem, które załą-
czam do niniejszego.

Pakiet ten nie może zawierać listów na nazwiska konk-
retne i pism oficjalnych tamt.urzędu. Tego rodzaju listy i
pisma muszą być przesyłane w oddzielnym pakiecie, w którym
wówczas nie może być żadnych notatek ani listów specjalnych
z kryptonimami wzgl.pseudonimami, jak również informacyj
o charakterze wojskowym wzgl. wywiadowczym.

6/. Pakiet zaopatrzony winien być w adres:"JWielmożny
Pan Nal Niemirowicz do rąk własnych". Koperta zewnętrzna
"JWP.R-ca Zygmunt Mostowski Wydz.Wschodni M.S.Z.".

7/. Poczta nasza będzie wysyłana w 3-ch kopertach:

a/. zewnętrzna: adres Urzędu,
b/ środkowa: nazwisko kierownika urzędu lub "Ku", lub "L.11"
c/ wewnętrzna: na nazwisko "Nepomucyn Niewiarowski".

Pieczątka na tej ostatniej kopercie jak ta, którą pie-
czętujemy pocztę niniejszą.

8/. Sposób łączności.placówek z ośrodka- "O" z Panem
ustalam specjalnem pismem, odpis którego za-łączam. Odwrotną
łączność ustali Pan osobiście w/g uznania.

                              Nora Nikiels.

Communications instructions for intelligence post B.18. *Source:* CAW.

B.18

3907/33/N.   Dnia 26.sierpnia 1933r.   60

      W uzupełnieniu ogólnej instrukcji organizacyjnej
/Nr.3310/33/N./, instrukcji łączności/Nr.3314/33/N./ podpo-
rządkowuję Pan-u p.Z.K., jako czwartą placówkę pomocniczą
- "Z.12" /pseudonim "Nela Narbut/.
      Jednocześnie załączam odpis pisma do "Z.12"/L.3905/
      W wypadku przydzielenia do Pana ośrodka p.Zal.,usta-
wiam go jako pana upełnomocnionego zastępcę, którego proszę
wprowadzić w całokształt prac, zapoznać z organizacją i
aktami. Ustawiam go, jako placówkę "B-41" /pseudonim -
"Nal Niger"/.

                                        Nal Niemirowicz.

Addendum to organizational instructions for intelligence post B.18.
Source: CAW.

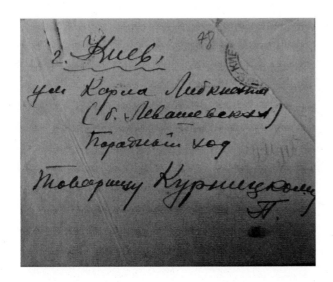

Envelope addressed to the vice-consul in Kyiv, Piotr Kurnicki. *Source:* CAW.

The Polish consulate in Kharkiv. *Photo:* NAC.

Pavel Postyshev (center) and Stanislav Kosior (right).

A 1937 *Pravda* article on misery and hunger in Poland.

Polish military intelligence photograph of Kinetspil, south of Pervomaisk near Odesa, in 1935. *Photo:* CAW.

Polish military intelligence photograph of Kryve Ozero, south of Pervomaisk near Odesa, in 1935. *Photo:* CAW.

Polish military intelligence photograph of Velyki Kumary, west of Pervomaisk near Odesa, in 1935. *Photo*: CAW.

Lieutenant Stefan Kasperski (aka Albert Ran). *Photo*: CAW.

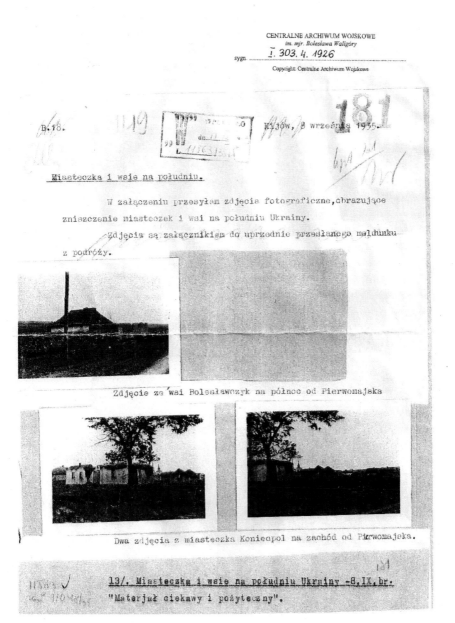

First page of an intelligence report from post B.18 with photos of post-famine Soviet Ukrainian villages and towns in 1935. *Source:* CAW.

List ot rukingstyjane
_____

Kochany ojcze duchowny
Ja witam Was i całuje
w biały rencski i zgore
serdecznie i zdrowia Kochany
ojcze donosze Wam ze
mnie przedano moja
rodzina na to ze ja byłem
rukingstyjanem i chodziłem
rozpytkamy mnie u miłości
poniedzieli ze ja chodziłem
i A gieteliołem czego nigdy
nie było i ja nie agieteliat
Kochany ojcze duchowny
donosze Wam gdzie ja znaj-
dujesie my mieszkamy u
koszaruch nad biało morsk
kunanto mnie bardzo cietno
ze tutej dlatego ze
mnie udoma wszystko za
brali krowo zbozo
parekis i ja ta przyje
chałem tylko u jednych
kryznierckach i zjednym
starym fasneru i wcencej
niemam zednego ubrania
i ja niemam ratunku nie
od kogo A tylko od da Boga
wopiebie łaske i prosze
Boga oratunek my mieszka
na pustyni ogromna pusza
Bardzo mnie zal zeta
niema koszcioła i niewiem
kiedy zobacze

A letter from the deported sacristy assistant Jan Tetera to the parson of his parish. *Source*: CAW.

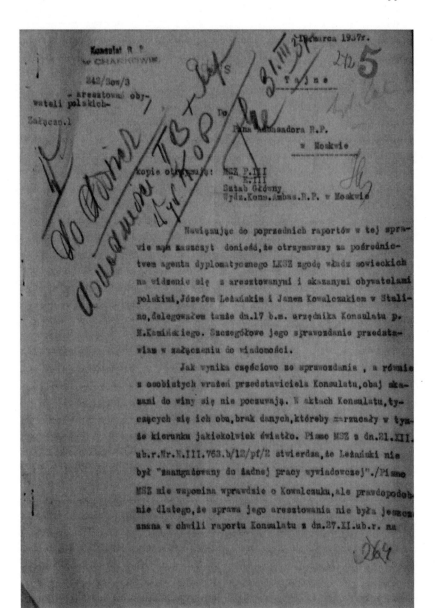

na który to raport wspomniane pismo Ministerstwa było od-
powiedzią/. Z aktów Konsulatu wynika natomiast,że tak Le-
dański, jak Kowalczuk przybyli na teren sowiecki z Kana-
dy w r.1931, na zasadzie kontraktu, po którego upływie
już od 2.lat nosili się z myślą wyjazdu z Z.S.R.R.

Być może,że będąc robotnikami kwalifikowanymi
i o pewnym poziomie inteligencji o tym i owym wypowiada-
li swe zdanie. To oraz niechęć do wypuszczenia zagranicę
tego typu robotników po kilkuletniej ich pracy w ważnych
działach przemysłu sowieckiego, mogło wystarczyć, aby
przy swoistych metodach przewodu sądowego przypisać im
kontrrewolucyjne nastawienie i szpiegostwo.

W tym stanie rzeczy proszę o rozważenie możli-
wości interwencji w sprawie Ledańskiego i Kowalczuka na
gruncie moskiewskim.

W sprawie pomocy oddziałowej dla Ledańskiego proszę równocześnie Wydział Konsularny Ambasady o porozumie-
nie się z Czerw.Krzyżem.

Konsul Generalny

Dr.T.Brzeziński

A report from Consul Tadeusz Brzeziński about the arrests of Polish citizens in Soviet Ukraine in 1937. *Source*: CAW.

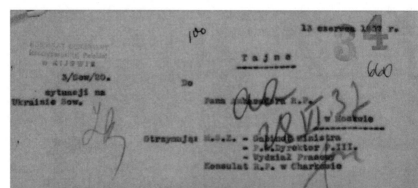

100   13 czerwca 1937 r.

                                                                                    34

KONSULAT GENERALNY
Rzeczypospolitej Polskiej
w KIJOWIE   T a j n e   660

3/Sow/20.
sytuacji na   Do
Ukrainie Sow.
                                     Pana Ambasadora R.P.
                                                                          w Moskwie

                        Otrzymują: M.S.Z. - Gabinet Ministra
                                          - P.N.Dyrektor P.III.
                                          - Wydział Praaowy
                                    Konsulat R.P. w Charkowie

W ślad za informacją podaną w sprawie aresztowania gen.Jaki-
ra i Komisarza Balickiego, Konsulat Generalny R.P. w Kijowie do-
nosi, że w nocy z 10 na 11 i z 11 na 12 przeprowadzono,według
otrzymanych informacyj, w Kijowie masowe aresztowania wśród wyższych wojskowych z komendantem miasta Gołubkowym, na czele.

Aresztowanych oficerów wyprowadzano a rodziny ich i meble
usuwano natychmiast w nocy z zajmowanych mieszkań. Wszystkim ro-
dzinom zaaresztowanych oficerów zabroniono osiedlenia się w centrum Kijowa a zezwolono jedynie na zamieszkanie przedmieść wzglę-
nie okolic Kijowa. Jedynym wyjątkiem w tym wypadku jest żona
byłego komendanta miasta, której zezwolono zamieszkać w centrum
Kijowa.- Należy przyznać, że tak drakońskie sposoby eksmisji
i to w dodatku w odniesieniu do większej ilości rodzin wyższych
oficerów stanowi dość charakterystyczny w obecnie panujących
stosunkach.

Ponadto - jak z otrzymanych informacyj wynika - przeprowadzono przed kilku dniami aresztowania wyższych oficerów również
w garnizonach Berdyczowa i Żytomierza.

Należy spodziewać się, że w dniach najbliższych będzie moż-
uzyskać informacje jakie rozmiary przybrały te aresztowania w Kijowie i na Ukrainie.

Charakterystyczną rzeczą jest milczenie ulicy na zarówno fakt
rozstrzelania Tuchaczewskiego, Jakira i innych generałów, jak

                                                                   693 c/s

i ma wiadome już w mieście aresztowania w Kijowie wyższych oficerów.

Otóż nie można było zaobserwować w czasie ostatniego "przed-
wychodnoj" i "wychodnoj" najmniejszego przygnębienia czy zaintere-
sowania ulicy bieżącymi wypadkami. Wydaje się, jak gdyby ludność
żyła swym życiem a bieżące wypadki odbywały się zgoła poza sferą
jej jakichkolwiek zainteresowań. Uderzał jedynie wyjątkowy - jak
na dzień świąteczny-brak na ulicach oficerów oraz żołnierzy ma-
wet w uwzględnieniu, że garnizon znajduje się poza miastem w let-
nim obozie.

w/z Kierownik Konsulatu Generalnego:

Dr.Adam Koch
Wicekonsul

A report from Vice-consul Adam Koch on the situation in Soviet
Ukraine after the trial of Mikhail Tukhachevsky in 1937. *Source:* CAW.

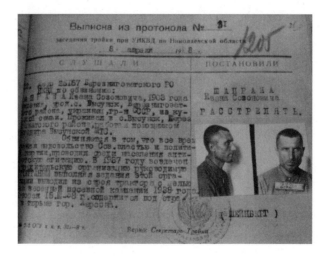

A typical report from an NKVD troika in Mykolaiv oblast in 1938, about the death sentence of Ivan Sharpan, who was sentenced for anti-Soviet agitation and alleged participation in a wrecker's organization that damaged tractors. *Source:* AUSBUMO.

Larysa Krushelnytska, Lviv, 1933. *Credit:* Reproduced from L. Krushel'nyts'ka, *Rubaly lis—Spohady halychanky* (Lviv and New York: Vydavnytsvo M. P. Kots', 2001), by permission of the author as are all the other photographs of Larysa Krushelnytska.

Larysa Krushelnytska
with her mother, Olena,
before leaving for Soviet
Ukraine, 1934.

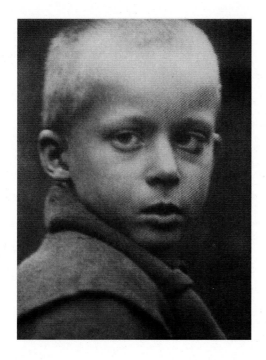

Larysa Krushelnytska
after she returned to
Poland from the USSR,
1936.

The persecuted Krushelnytsky family. Standing, from left: Ostap, Olena, Ivan, Nataliia, and Bohdan; sitting, from left: Volodymyra, Taras, Mariia, Larysa, and Antin.

Stefaniia Krushelnytska with her daughter, Kursk, 1935.

Contemporary photograph of the Lubianka, the Moscow headquarters of the former NKVD and subsequently the KGB and FSB. *Photo:* R. Kuśnierz.

Index